The International Criminal Court in Its Third Decad

# Nijhoff Law Specials

VOLUME 109

The titles published in this series are listed at *brill.com/nlsp*

# The International Criminal Court in Its Third Decade

*Reflecting on Law and Practices*

*Edited by*

Carsten Stahn

*Assistant Editor*

Rafael Braga da Silva

BRILL | NIJHOFF

LEIDEN | BOSTON

Cover illustration: Reproduced with the kind permission of contemporary visual artist Alexis Portilla. It is entitled *Three Worlds*, Oil on linen, New York, 2016.

Library of Congress Cataloging-in-Publication Data

Names: Stahn, Carsten, 1971- editor. | Silva, Rafael Braga da, assistant editor.
Title: The International Criminal Court in its third decade : reflecting on law and practices / edited by Carsten Stahn ; assistant editor, Rafael Braga da Silva.
Description: Leiden ; Boston : Brill/Nijhoff, 2024. | Series: Nijhoff law specials, 0924-4549 ; vol.109 | Includes index.
Identifiers: LCCN 2023032029 (print) | LCCN 2023032030 (ebook) | ISBN 9789004529922 (paperback) | ISBN 9789004529939 (ebook)
Subjects: LCSH: International Criminal Court–History.
Classification: LCC KZ7312 .I5794 2024 (print) | LCC KZ7312 (ebook) | DDC 341.5/5–dc23/eng/20230919
LC record available at https://lccn.loc.gov/2023032029
LC ebook record available at https://lccn.loc.gov/2023032030

Typeface for the Latin, Greek, and Cyrillic scripts: "Brill". See and download: brill.com/brill-typeface.

ISSN 0924-4549
ISBN 978-90-04-52992-2 (paperback)
ISBN 978-90-04-52993-9 (e-book)
DOI 10.1163/9789004529939



This book is printed on acid-free paper and produced in a sustainable manner.

# Contents

## PART 3
## *New Frontiers in Investigations and Prosecutions*



## PART 4
## *Revisiting Trials and Procedures*

## PART 5
## *Cooperation and Complementarity*



## PART 6
## *Confronting Institutional Challenges*

## PART 7
## *Looking to the Future*

# Foreword

This publication has its origins in a conference titled "International Criminal Court at 20: Reflections on the Past, Present and the Future", which took place in The Hague on 1 July 2022, exactly twenty years after the entry into force of the Rome Statute, the founding treaty of the International Criminal Court (ICC, Court). It was the main event by the ICC to commemorate the institution's 20th anniversary, organised with the support by the European Commission, the Municipality of The Hague and the Embassy of France.

When I was contemplating at the end of 2021 how that momentous milestone should be marked, one of the first things I decided was that the affair should not be a purely ceremonial event or one that simply serves to shower praise on the Court. Rather, I felt that the best way to celebrate the ICC's 20 years in the fight against impunity was to foster open, professional exchange of views about the Court's concrete operations, with a view to generating ideas as to how to best equip the Court for its third decade.

As important as the cooperation and support of States is for the ICC, I did not want diplomats to dominate the stage on this occasion. Instead, my colleagues and I decided to invite leading scholars, practitioners and civil society leaders to provide their insights and frank observations on key aspects of the ICC's work. Because, as we reflect on the past and the present, we must be prepared to learn lessons for the future – and to learn lessons, we must have an open mind to hearing diverse views.

In the same vein, I was keen to ensure that the valuable reflections provided by the speakers would not evaporate in the air at the closure of the event – and that is where the idea of a conference publication emerged. A publication that would preserve in written form the numerous expert interventions prepared for the conference, with considerable effort.

As the ICC does not have the capacity or the expertise required for editing and issuing a publication of this kind, we set out to look for a partner – and we were fortunate that an international criminal law scholar of Prof. Carsten Stahn's calibre agreed to take on that role. Beside the sizeable task of editing this volume, he assisted us in the lead-up to the conference with the fine-tuning of the concept and served as rapporteur on the day itself.

Prof. Stahn also identified a number of additional contributors in addition to those who spoke at the conference held on 1 July 2022, so as to further enrich the contents of the publication. Obviously, all chapters in the book – including those by current or former ICC officials – consist of the personal views of the authors alone and do not represent the official position of the Court.

Looking at the final contents, I am delighted to state that this volume provides a unique, in-depth reflection on the International Criminal Court, rich in its diversity of topics and viewpoints. There is a strong emphasis on future perspectives, which I find especially important. While the ICC has in its first two decades managed to firmly establish its place in the international judicial and legal architecture, at 20 years old it is still a young permanent institution. And – regrettably – there is no shortage of work for the ICC in sight. Ending impunity is still far beyond the horizon. Thus, it is pivotal that we keep on improving the Court's operations in every way possible. This has been my top priority as ICC President all along – enhancing the Court's delivery of justice, in order to reduce the gap of impunity and to strengthen the prevention of future crimes.

Indeed, much has been achieved in strengthening the ICC in recent years in terms of the Court's judicial operations as well as institutional practices. Examples of the former are the adoption of time limits on the issuance of judgments and key decisions and the continuous development of the Chambers Practice Manual, including with guidelines on judgment structure and drafting. On the institutional front, key successes include the appointment of an Ombudsperson, the creation of a Focal Point on Gender Equality, the adoption of the Court's first Strategy on Gender Equality and Workplace Culture, and introducing an enhanced and coordinated approach to the Court's strategic planning, budget process and risk management.

With this emphasis on continuously strengthening the ICC's work, I find the combination of contributions from practitioners, scholars and civil society leaders in the present volume particularly valuable. The Court is independent, but it cannot perform its work in a vacuum. We must engage in professional and intellectual dialogue with the society at large that surrounds us.

Many of the chapters in this book are written by people who have long been directly involved in the ICC in one role or another – sometimes several roles over a long stretch of time. I find it crucial that those with first-hand experience share their views on challenges faced, good practices identified and lessons learnt, as they see them. In order to improve, we must drill in to the details of the Court's operations – and that is best done by those who live that reality on a daily basis.

The relationship between the ICC and the academic world is of special significance. As a long-time judge and university professor myself, I know personally how valuable the connection between the judiciary and the academia is. The Court's practice and jurisprudence is at all times accompanied by a rich scholarly debate. This an important aspect of the free exchange of ideas in a democratic society, and it is pivotal for the quality of the Court's work in the long term. As such, we must embrace academic conversation, even when we may disagree with some of the views expressed.

Global civil society played a key role in the ICC's creation and non-governmental organisations continue to provide an indispensable, independent voice to policy discussions surrounding the Court, particularly in the context of the Assembly of States Parties to the Rome Statute. Civil society organisations, gathered under the Coalition for the International Criminal Court, act as an important link to communities affected by the crimes under the Court's jurisdiction as well as global public opinion, and they are not afraid to provide their honest opinion about the work of the Court or the actions of States in the Rome Statute framework. Including that independent voice in the conference and this publication was an easy decision.

I am thrilled by the high calibre of contributors to this volume – the authors of the chapters between these covers are truly top experts in their respective fields. Yet one of them deserves special mention above others – that is Mr. Philippe Kirsch, who honoured the Court's 20th anniversary conference as its keynote speaker.

As the first President of the ICC, from 2003 to 2009, Mr. Kirsch played a pivotal role in the institution-building of the ICC. Yet, his part in the ICC's genesis goes far beyond that. He chaired the Committee of the Whole of the Rome Conference of 1998, where the ICC's Statute was famously adopted on the very last night of the five-week negotiations, and he subsequently chaired the Preparatory Commission for the ICC until the Statute's entry into force.

It hardly requires stating that Mr. Kirsch was uniquely placed to cast light on the ICC's birth and early development, as the backdrop of the Court's further path. His keynote address, which opens this volume, provides fascinating insights of great value to anyone wishing to have a deep understanding of the Rome Statute system.

Finally, let me offer a few personal reflections on the 20th anniversary of the ICC. The Court has come incredibly far. Year after year, we have witnessed how high the demand on the ICC's mandate is. In response, the Court has opened investigations in 17 situations, concerning conflicts and alleged crimes on four different continents. The Court's three courtrooms are in full use and an ever-increasing number of cases moves through the legal process from pre-trial to trial and appeals, and where applicable, the reparation of victims and the enforcement of sentences. Accused persons have been convicted and others acquitted, following meticulously fair trials.

The ICC has ushered in a victim-centred concept of international criminal justice. More than 21,000 individual victims have formally participated in ICC proceedings so far. Around 3,000 victims have received court-ordered reparations, and this number is rising all the time as implementation progresses. Another hundred thousand individuals have directly benefitted from projects of the Trust Fund for Victims under its assistance mandate.

The ICC's jurisprudence has broken new ground on matters such as the participation of victims in proceedings, crimes against children, destruction of cultural heritage, sexual and gender based crimes, including reproductive violence. The Court has demonstrated that it can interpret, apply and enforce key principles of international law in a credible manner.

Global awareness about the ICC is higher than ever, and the Court has beyond any doubt become one of the pillars of the international legal system. Majority of the world's states has joined the system and numerous countries have criminalised atrocity crimes using the Rome Statute as a model for national legislation. With 123 States Parties, the Rome Statute system is a global network of countries committed to pursuing individual accountability for the gravest infractions under international law.

It is humbling to serve an institution which embodies so much hope on behalf of those who have suffered immensely. An institution that for a long time was not more than a distant dream. An institution that whole generations of activists, diplomats and lawyers spent building.

By holding perpetrators accountable, we show that heinous actions have consequences, and we help to deter future crimes. By holding meticulously fair trials that uphold the rights of the defence, we underline that justice must always be impartial to be credible. By putting victims at the centre of the ICC's work, we show that justice is not only about retribution; it is also about repairing the harm caused by the crimes.

As the ICC embarks on its third decade, we should cherish the fact that the world now has a permanent, independent international court, which is dedicated to the fight against impunity for genocide, crimes against humanity, war crimes, and the crime of aggression.

We cannot afford to take the International Criminal Court for granted; we must all do what we can to strengthen it——whether through judicial cooperation, political support, advocacy, professionalism, or scholarship. This publication is one contribution to that end.

*Piotr Hofmański*
President of the International Criminal Court

# Preface

The Rome Statute and the jurisprudence of the International Criminal Court (ICC) differ significantly from the law and practice of other international criminal tribunals. After two decades of operation, many operational aspects of the ICC have come under critique and review. The Independent Expert Review has offered a wealth of recommendations to improve practices. The war in Ukraine marks both, an opportunity and a test case for the ICC. It has renewed engagement and support for the institution, but also caused new tensions in relation to double standards of the West. With the emergence of new accountability mechanisms, changing evidentiary landscapes, and the transformation of geopolitics, the Court is under considerable pressure to adjust its strategies, working methods, and practices.

This volume reflects on the ICC's law and practices, ranging from preliminary examination to the afterlife of cases. It investigates some of the main areas, in which we witness change and transformation: New frontiers in investigations and prosecutions, the mapping of trials and procedures, the intersections between complementarity and cooperative approaches, major institutional challenges, as well as some of the gaps and blind-spots in the ICC regime. It looks back to lessons learned from the institutional set-up of the Court, and proposes ways to address shortcomings and critiques and re-imagine the ICC.

The cover painting by contemporary artist Alexis Portilla reflects this spirit. It is entitled 'Three Worlds'. It captures, in a figurative sense, the interconnected nature of the ICC's three decades through circles. The main three circles are related to a larger past. They share synergies and mutual spaces, but also evolve in configuration and colour – as the Court itself. The red cloud bears synergies with the changing context, challenges and turmoil that the institution is facing over time. The image as a whole conveys not only evolution, rupture and transformation, but also some degree of optimism, which is symptomatic of the current *status quo*.

The book as a whole is a truly collective effort. It has its origins in a conference marking the 20th anniversary of the operations of the Court. It was organized by the ICC in the World Forum in The Hague on 1 July 2022. In the follow-up process, contributors transformed their interventions into academic contributions. Additional voices were invited to cover additional themes, which have not been treated at the original conference.

The idea of the project was very warmly supported by ICC President Piotr Hofmański. He encouraged the idea of an independent academic volume since its inception and kindly provided the preface. Matias Hellman and Hirad

Abtahi from the ICC Presidency deserve special credit for their role behind the scenes. They were instrumental in mapping themes, preparing the Conference, and shaping the concept of the volume.

The book would not been possible without the time and energy by our contributors, whose invaluable perspectives invite us to re-think law and practices, and the exemplary work by the wonderful Assistant Editor, Rafael Braga da Silva. He took a fresh look at the interrelation of chapters, shaped the final composition, transformed the individual pieces into a broader whole, and composed the annex, in addition to contributing a chapter.

Warmest thanks are due to Paola Dolfato, who provided essential editorial assistance to the volume, while completing her LL.M. Advanced degree in Public International Law at Leiden, and Valentina Kobler, who assisted with editing during her internship at the ICC. Special thanks also to our editors: Lindy Melman, whose passion, enthusiasm and personal touch to publishing made this project special, and Bea Timmer, who brought it to successful fruition.

The volume is dedicated to the memory of Benjamin Ferencz (1920–1923), whose life-long work, courage, and optimism provides hope and incentives to re-think international criminal justice beyond its existing imperfections.

*Carsten Stahn*
The Hague, May 2023

# Figure and Tables

## Figure



## Tables

## Notes on Contributors

*Philipp Ambach*
is Chief of the Victims Participation and Reparations Section at the International Criminal Court (ICC). He previously served as the ICC President's Special Assistant for over six years. Before that, he worked at the UN ad hoc tribunals ICTY and ICTR as a legal adviser to the Judges of the Appeals Chamber. Prior to that, he worked as an associate legal officer in the ICTY Registry. Mr. Ambach holds a Ph.D. in international criminal law from Free University of Berlin and has been admitted as prosecutor in the Public Prosecutor's Office of Cologne, Germany. He obtained his Masters degree in law in 2004 from Humboldt-University of Berlin, Germany.

*Olympia Bekou*
is a Professor of Public International Law and Head of School, School of Law, University of Nottingham, UK.

*Rafael Braga da Silva*
is an Associate Appeals Counsel at the International Residual Mechanism for Criminal Tribunals (IRMCT). He holds a LL.M. from University for Peace and United Nations Interregional Criminal and Justice Research Institute (UNICRI). He also holds a LL.M. Adv. Studies in Public International Law *cum laude*, from the Grotius Centre for International Legal Studies, Leiden University.

*David Donat Cattin*
has been the Secretary-General of Parliamentarians for Global Action ('PGA') from 2014 to March 2023. He holds a post-doctorate diploma from the Centre for Studies and Research of The Hague Academy of International Law (2002), a Ph.D. in Public International Law (2000) from the Faculty of Law of the University of Teramo (Italy) and a Law Degree from LUISS-Guido Carli University at Rome. He is Adjunct Professor of International Law at New York University (NYU) Center for Global Affairs since 2012, and Adjunct Professor of the Law of International Organizations at University of Verona, Faculty of Law since 2023.

*Chile Eboe-Osuji*
is the Former President and Appeals Judge, International Criminal Court; Distinguished International Jurist, Lincoln Alexander School of Law, Toronto Metropolitan University; Paul Martin Senior Professor of Political Science,

International Relations and Law, University of Windsor; Visiting Professor, University of Los Angeles, School of Law; formerly Herman Phleger Visiting Professor, Stanford Law School (2021–2022); formerly Senior Fellow, Carr Center, Harvard Kennedy School.

*Mohamed M. El Zeidy*
is the Senior Legal Adviser to the President, Kosovo Specialist Chambers (2019-present); Legal Officer, Pre-Trial Division, International Criminal Court (2007–2021); Chancellor, State Lawsuits Authority, Egyptian Ministry of Justice (2022-present); Judge and Senior Public Prosecutor, Egyptian Ministry of Justice (1997–2007); Ph.D. and LL.M. (Ireland); LL.M. (Cairo); Licence en droit & Bachelor of Police Sciences (Cairo).

*Elizabeth Evenson*
is the International Justice Director, Human Rights Watch. This contribution was prepared during the time the author served as the director of the Coalition for the International Criminal Court Secretariat (January–July 2022).

*Silvia Fernandez de Gurmendi*
is President of the Assembly of States Parties to the Rome Statute and former President of the International Criminal Court.

*Carla Ferstman*
is a Professor at the School of Law and Human Rights Centre, University of Essex, former Director of REDRESS (2004–2018).

*Olivia Flasch*
is a Legal Consultant in Public International Law, London.

*Stuart Ford*
is a Professor of Law at the University of Illinois Chicago (UIC) School of Law. International Justice Director, Human Rights Watch. This contribution was prepared during the time the author served as the director of the Coalition for the International Criminal Court Secretariat (January–July 2022).

*Lindsay Freeman*
is the Director of Technology, Law, and Policy at the Human Rights Center, UC Berkeley School of Law.

*Priya Gopalan*
is a Malaysian lawyer specialising in international criminal law, human rights law and gender. She was a prosecutor and appeals counsel at the UN International Criminal Tribunal for the former Yugoslavia. She served as the first Legal Advisor for sexual and gender-based crimes at the International, Impartial and Independent Mechanism for Syria (the IIIM Syria). She was Gender Advisor for the UN Investigation on Sri Lanka and Senior Advisor to the Truth, Reconciliation and Reparations Commission of The Gambia. In 2021, Priya was appointed by the UN Human Rights Council to the Working Group on Arbitrary Detention, as the member from the Asia-Pacific region. She holds a LL.M in Public International Law (Distinction) from the London School of Economics and Political Science and a B.A. Jurisprudence (Hons) from the University of Oxford, where she was a UK Commonwealth Chevening Scholar from Malaysia.

*Piotr Hofmański*
is President of the International Criminal Court. He holds a Ph.D. from the Nicolaus Copernicus University in Toruń. Prior to joining the Court, he has been Professor of the Jagiellonian University in Krakow, where he holds a Chair in Criminal Procedure Law. He has also served as judge of the Criminal Chamber of the Polish Supreme Court.

*Dov Jacobs*
is Co-Counsel at the International Criminal Court, co-founder of Strategic International Legal Consulting (SILC) and former Vice-President of the International Criminal Court Bar Association (ICCBA).

*Karim Khan*
is Prosecutor of the International Criminal Court. He is a barrister and King's Counsel with more than 30 years of professional experience as an international criminal law and human rights lawyer. He served inter alia as first Special Adviser and Head of the United Nations Investigative Team to promote accountability for crimes committed by Da'esh/ISIL in Iraq (UNITAD) between 2018 to 2021 and as President of the ICC Bar Association.

*Philippe Kirsch*
is the former President and Judge of the ICC (2003–2009); Chair of the Committee of the Whole of the United Nations Diplomatic Conference of

Plenipotentiaries on the Establishment of an International Criminal Court (1998); Chair of the Preparatory Commission for the International Criminal Court (1999–2002). Mr Kirsch joined the Foreign Service of Canada in 1972, where he served, *inter alia,* as Ambassador to Sweden, Assistant Deputy Minister for Legal, Consular, and Passport Affairs, Deputy Permanent Representative to the United Nations, and legal advisor with the Department of External Affairs.

*Alexa Koenig*
holds a Ph.D. and JD. She is Co-Executive Director and Co-Faculty Director of the Human Rights Center and a lecturer at UC Berkeley School of Law, where she teaches classes on human rights and international criminal law.

*Peter Lewis*
was elected Registrar of the International Criminal Court (ICC) on 28 March 2018 for a period of five years and was sworn in on 17 April 2018. Before joining the Court, Mr Lewis was Chief Executive of the Crown Prosecution Service (CPS) in England and Wales between 2007 and 2016. Mr Lewis was a UK delegate to the United Nations Preparatory Commission for the Rules of Procedure and Evidence of the ICC in 1999–2000 and a member of the expert working group on the draft regulations of the ICC Office of the Prosecutor. Mr Lewis was made a companion of the Order of the Bath in the Queen's birthday honours list in 2012.

*Fiona McKay*
is an international justice consultant, former Senior Managing Legal Officer at the Open Society Justice Initiative and former Chief of the Victim Participation and Reparations Section at the ICC.

*Angela Mudukuti*
is a Zimbabwean human rights lawyer, specialised in international criminal law. She has worked for a number of organisations including the International Criminal Court (ICC), Open Society Foundations, Human Rights Watch, the Southern Africa Litigation Centre (SALC).

*Jennifer Naouri*
is Lead Counsel at the international criminal court and co-founder of Strategic International Legal Consulting (SILC) and former President of the International Criminal Court Bar Association (ICCBA).

*Phoebe Okowa*
is a Professor of Public International Law, Queen Mary University of London; Member, United Nations International Law Commission.

*Raul C. Pangalangan*
is a Professor of Law and former Law Dean, University of the Philippines; former Judge, International Criminal Court.

*Priya Pillai*
heads the Asia Justice Coalition Secretariat, a network of organizations focused on justice and accountability in Asia. She holds a Ph.D. in international law and transitional justice from the Graduate Institute of International and Development Studies in Geneva, an LL.M from New York University, and a B.A., LL.B. (Hons.) degree from the National Law School of India University, Bangalore.

*Astrid Reisinger Coracini*
is a Postdoctoral Lecturer and Researcher at the Department of European, International and Comparative Law at the University of Vienna.

*Darryl Robinson*
is a Professor at Queen's University, Faculty of Law (Canada).

*Leila Nadya Sadat*
is the James Carr Professor of International Criminal Law, Washington University School of Law; Visiting Fellow, Orville Schell Center for Human Rights, Yale Law School; Special Adviser on Crimes Against Humanity, International Criminal Court Prosecutor.

*Lorraine Smith-van Lin*
is an International justice consultant and specialist on victim matters. She is also the Founder and Executive Director of Tallawah Justice for Women.

*Carsten Stahn*
is Professor of International Criminal Law and Global Justice at the Leiden Law School and Queen's University Belfast. He holds a Ph.D. and habilitation from Humboldt University Berlin.

*Minerva Tavárez Mirabal*
is the Chair of the Board of Directors of the Trust Fund for Victims.

*Muriel Ubeda-Saillard*
is a Professor at Lille University (France), Co-Director of the graduate course on International Criminal Justice.

# PART 1

## *Setting the Scene*

CHAPTER 1

# The ICC in Its Third Decade: Setting the Scene

*Carsten Stahn*

## 1 On ICC Birthdays

The ICC has entered its third decade. Is it a moment of jubilation, stagnation or re-engagement? In international practice, it has become a tradition to commemorate birthdays of international courts and tribunals. They have ritual features.[1] They are moments in which the international community comes together to reaffirm its values to itself and to others. They have certain integrative (*Durkheim*)[2] or performative features, but also mark a moment to transcend the routine of daily operations and reflect on the macro picture.[3]

At the ICC, there are many birthdays. It is easy to get confused. There is the yearly celebration of the entry into force of the Statute on International Justice Day. The Rome Statute had its 25th anniversary in 2023.[4] Then, we have the start of operations of the Court. It saw its 20th anniversary in July 2022. One never knows whether one should be happy or sad at these occasions. One can look at it with a laughing eye, and with a crying eye. The sheer existence of the Court continues to mobilize hope and resistance to international crimes. It challenges state-centric conceptions of international law, the dictates of *Realpolitik* or the marginalization of victims. But each case is also a symbol of the challenges of international institutions, states and civil society to prevent atrocities or investigate and prosecute crimes nationally or regionally. The ICC carries with it the weight of histories, memories and expectations. Birthdays are thus also a sobering moment, communicating loss, mourning or imperfections. They carry a certain sense of *déjà-vu* or nostalgia, and a longing for

---

1 See H Charlesworth, 'Rituals and Ritualism in the International Human Rights System' in N Bhuta (ed.) et al., *The Struggle for Human Rights: Essays in honour of Philip Alston* (Oxford: Oxford University Press, 2021).

2 E Durkheim, *The Division of Labour in Society* (Basingstoke: Palgrave Macmillan, 2013).

3 For an analysis of the sociological aspects of birthdays, including some of their critiques (e.g., elitism, entrenching power), see M J Christensen, 'Celebrating international criminal justice: A sociology of the twentieth anniversary of the International Criminal Court' (2021) 9 *London Review of International Law* 351, 355.

4 There are contributions on the 'ICC at 25', see 'The International Criminal Court at 25, Reassessing Processes and Outcomes', *Journal of Human Rights*, Vol. 22 (2023). On the ICC

 | DOI:10.1163/9789004529939_002

a better future. This spectrum of perspectives is captured in this volume. It is part of the living history of the ICC. It is not a tribute to the Court, but a reflexive volume, engaging with merits, challenges and critiques of ICC practices.

## 2 The Journey towards the Third Decade

The establishment of the ICC came as a surprise.[5] It marked in many ways a compromise between different ideals: A more consensual vision, and the idea of a court with compulsory jurisdiction.[6] This tension has never fully gone way.

The Court has gone through different phases. First, a process of emancipation. It was shaped by the ambition to develop the Court as an independent entity, but relied significantly on consensual methods to minimize opposition or confrontation with states. We have witnessed the making of the Court's Regulations,[7] its operational and judicial set-up,[8] the first referrals, trials and reparations, the development of an independent institutional and legal culture, different from the *ad hoc* tribunals, and the important development of the aggression definition at Kampala in 2010.[9] This phase was marked by construction and experimentation (e.g., disclosure, victim participation),[10] as well as attempts to build confidence in the work of the Court. The OTP sought to win trust by states through the encouragement of self-referrals and positive complementarity policies.[11] The Assembly of States Parties (ASP) developed its working structures. The relationship towards non-States parties was marked by pragmatism. The Court showed that it can stand on its own feet, even without membership of major powers, such as the US, China, Russia or India. The

at 20, see C Kress, 'Der Internationale Strafgerichtshof nach 20 Jahren', in P Donath et al. (eds.), *Der Schutz des Individuums durch das Recht* (Heidelberg: Springer, 2023) 103–113, who traces the journey of the Court by way of the following metaphors: 'difficult birth', 'magic of the beginning', 'thunderclouds', 'storm', 'weather lightning', 'brightening' and 'signs on the horizon'.

5 See the chapter by Kirsch in this volume.

6 L E Gissel, 'Nomos and Narrative in International Criminal Justice' (2022) 20 JICJ 117. For a discussion of African positions, see id., 'A different kind of court: Africa's support for the International Criminal Court, 1993–2003' (2018) 29 EJIL 725.

7 Regulations of the Court, adopted by the Judges of the Court on 26 May 2004.

8 On narratives of progress in institutional set-up (e.g., from 'inefficient bureaucracy to efficient and well-managed organization'), see R Clements, 'From bureaucracy to management: The International Criminal Court's internal progress narrative' (2019) 32 LJIL 149.

9 C Kreß and L von Holtzendorff, 'The Kampala Compromise on the Crime of Aggression' (2010) 8 JICJ 1179.

10 M J Christensen and N M Orina, 'The International Criminal Court as a Law Laboratory' (2022) 20 JICJ 699.

11 C Stahn, 'Complementarity: A Tale of Two Notions' (2008) 19 *Criminal Law Forum* 87.

fact that the situation in Darfur was referred to the ICC by the Security Council demonstrated that the Court's existence was accepted even by the three P5 members which did not become party to the ICC.[12]

The formative years were followed by years of consolidation and contestation. The docket of the ICC grew, but with it also risks of stalemate, confrontation and inequality. Drawing on Hannah Arendt, William Schabas criticized the 'banality of international justice'.[13] The Security Council referrals did not garner the political support for the ICC that many had hoped for. Fatou Bensouda stressed the need to 'speak truth to power'. Her turn towards a 'without fear or favour' approach[14] made the Court relevant to some of the most protracted political conflicts in the world and extended its focus beyond Africa. However, it also caused clashes and resistance. The 'honeymoon with the Court' was over, as David Luban put it.[15] The Court encountered pushback from states in the Global South in light of its selectivity and action against heads of state and government.[16] It encountered increased pressure from Western powers over its decision to open investigations in relation to Palestine or Afghanistan. In September 2020, the Trump administration imposed unprecedented sanctions against court officials and staff.[17] The *Kenyatta*, *Gbabgo* or *Bemba* cases showed the fragility of the court: Weaknesses in investigative methods, risks of witness

12 SC Resolution 1593 (2005) was adopted with eleven votes in favour, and four abstentions (Algeria, Brazil, China, United States of America). Russia supported the referral as 'an effective solution in the fight against impunity in Darfur'. See SC, 5158th meeting, 31 March 2005 S/PV.5158, 10. The US stated: 'We decided not to oppose the resolution because of the need for the international community to work together in order to end the climate of impunity in the Sudan and because the resolution provides protection from investigation or prosecution for United States nationals and members of the armed forces of non-State parties'. Ibid., 3. China noted it 'cannot accept any exercise of the ICC's jurisdiction against the will of non-State parties', and would 'find it difficult to endorse any Security Council authorization of such an exercise of jurisdiction by the ICC'. Ibid. 4.

13 See W Schabas, 'The Banality of International Justice' (2013) 11 JICJ 545.

14 Fatou Bensouda, "Without Fear or Favour": Reflections on my term as Prosecutor of the International Criminal Court, 15 June 2021, 3 at https://www.icc-cpi.int/sites/default/files/itemsDocuments/20210615-prosecutor-fatou-bensouda-end-of-term-farewell-statement.pdf.

15 D Luban, 'After the Honeymoon: Reflections on the Current State of International Criminal Justice' (2013) 11 JICJ 505.

16 See O Ba 'Constructing an international legal order under the shadow of colonial domination' (2023) 22 *Journal of Human Rights* 4; D Tladi, 'The African Union and the International Criminal Court: The battle for the soul of international law' (2009) 34 *South African Yearbook of International Law* 57.

17 S Lamony, 'ICC Sanctions Symposium: Implications of Trump Administration's Sanctions on International Criminal Court Officials' *Opinio Juris*, 22 April 2021, at http://opiniojuris.org/2021/04/22/icc-sanctions-symposium-implications-of-trump-administrations-sanctions-on-international-criminal-court-officials/.

tampering, the limited means of the Court to build cases against acting political leaders, weaknesses in judicial culture or a lack of coherence in jurisprudence.[18] Some problems were grounded in policies and practices of the ICC (e.g., flaws in investigative methodology, divergent interpretive approaches by chambers on key issues, deficits in internal management). Others are related to lack of support by states (e.g. arrests, witness and victim protection, zero growth budget). These difficulties overshadowed the record of other complex, but far less discussed trials, such as the *Ntaganda* judgment, with dealt with 18 counts, including rape and sexual slavery.[19] A symptomatic moment of the turn is the open statement by the UK at the 17th ASP:

> [W]e cannot ... pretend everything is fine when it isn't ... it is undeniable that the Rome project still falls short of the expectations of the participants at that ground-breaking conference in Rome. The time has come for States to take a fundamental look at how the Court is operating.[20]

In its third decade, the Court remains at a rock and hard place.[21] The Court is not only a legal, but also a social actor. It is embedded in a hierarchical and relational order, in which different actors struggle over power. It's treaty-based foundation, its roots in civil society and its symbolic value, count among its greatest strengths.[22] The mere existence of the Court, and its imagined role,[23]

18 See E Evenson, 'Too Few Trials, Too Many Tribulations: The ICC's Terrible Year and Where to Go from Here' (2020) 52 *Case Western Reserve Journal of International Law* 433.

19 Trial Chamber VI, Judgment, ICC-01/04-02/06-2359, 8 July 2019.

20 Statement by Andrew Murdoch, Legal Director to the International Criminal Court Assembly of States Parties, at its 17th session in The Hague, 5 December 2018, at https://www.gov.uk/government/speeches/uk-statement-to-icc-assembly-of-states-parties-17th-session. See also D Guilfoyle, 'This is not fine: The International Criminal Court in Trouble' EJIL Talk, 21 May 2019, at https://www.ejiltalk.org/part-i-this-is-not-fine-the-international-criminal-court-in-trouble/.

21 M De Hoon, 'The Future of the International Criminal Court' (2017) 17 *International Criminal Law Review* 591; T Buchwald, 'The Path Forward for the International Criminal Court: Questions Searching for Answers' (2020) 52 *Case Western Reserve Journal of International Law* 417; D Guilfoyle, 'Lacking Conviction: Is the International Criminal Court Broken? An Organisational Failure Analysis' (2019) 20 *Melbourne Journal of International Law* 401; J Fraser and McGonigle Leyh (eds.), *Intersections of Law and Culture at the International Criminal Court* (Cheltenham: Edward Elgar 2020).

22 S Muhammad, B Holá, A Dirkzwager. 'Reimagining the ICC: Exploring Practitioners' Perspectives on the Effectiveness of the International Criminal Court' (2021) 21 *International Criminal Law Review* 126, 149.

23 M Aksenova, 'Symbolism as a Constraint on International Criminal Law' (2017) 30 LJIL 475.

strengthen the commitment of domestic societies to prevent and prosecute international crimes, sometimes in unexpected ways, or keeps atrocity situations on the radar.[24] Ironically, the backlash from major powers, such as the US, and the Ukraine situation have re-connected the Court more closely to some its friendly critics. However, there is also a deeper sense of critical self-reflection and course correction, partly encouraged by the Independent Expert Review process.[25]

The in-built tensions of the Court's mandate, and its weaknesses,[26] remain very visible. The concept of individual criminal responsibility is still revolutionary in politics. The Court continues to face critiques, misrepresentation or politicization from very different strands of the political spectrum. It has been criticized by activists and NGOs, who want to see the Court actively involved in as many atrocity contexts as possible, sometimes based on very narrow jurisdictional basis. It is under constant scrutiny by states, who are eager to keep tight control over budget, seek to limit its docket, or confront it through political rhetoric or even disinformation.[27]

The Palestine situation is a showcase of inevitable tensions. The Court faced critiques in light of its adoption of a functional concept of statehood under the Statute. However, backlash and allegations of double standards (e,g., a two-tier system of State Parties) would be even harsher, had it found that it lacked jurisdiction. As Stefan Talmon has argued, the train had left the station when the Assembly decided to admit Palestine as state party to the Rome Statute.[28]

In some areas, such as aggression, environmental crime, corporate responsibility or new technologies, gaps or double standards in the Court's architecture become more apparent. The Rome is still modern, but with growing age, it also gains wrinkles. The gender definition under Art 7 (3) under the ICC Statute, which refers to the two sexes, male and female, within the context of society, is

24 G Dancy, 'The hidden impacts of the ICC: An innovative assessment using Google data' (2021) 34 LJIL 729.

25 ICC, Independent Expert Review of the International Criminal Court and the Rome Statute System, Final Report, 30 September 2020.

26 On weakness as a structural feature of the ICC, see S Dezalay, 'Weakness as Routine in the Operations of the Intentional Criminal Court' (2017) 17 *International Criminal Law Review* 281.

27 G Dancy, Y Dutton, T Alleblas and E Aloyo, 'What Determines Perceptions of Bias toward the International Criminal Court? Evidence from Kenya' (2020) 64 *Journal of Conflict Resolution* 1443.

28 S Talmon, 'Germany publicly objects to the International Criminal Court's ruling on jurisdiction in Palestine', *German Practice in International Law*, 11 February 2021, DOI: 10.17176/20220627-173023-0.

being re-read.[29] For instance, in its Crimes against humanity project,[30] which draws heavily on the Rome Statute, the ILC removed the gender definition, since it does not reflect current realities.[31]

New accountability mechanisms have emerged in contexts where the Court cannot exercise jurisdiction (e.g., Syria) or in ongoing ICC situations (e.g. Central African Republic). It is essential to develop new ways to make the Court less 'distant'[32] and more resilient to pressure, to critically review ICC structures and polices, and to develop or re-imagine its relationship to other justice mechanisms.

## 3 Achievements and Challenges

What are some of the Court's main achievements and challenges? In its over two decades of operation, the Court can look back to certain successes. It has brought certain macro changes, The Court has contributed to the idea of system of justice. It produces effects, even when it does not act.[33] Its actual or imagined presence shapes accountability discourses or empowers the voice of those, who struggle for justice in domestic contexts. Its effectiveness cannot be measured solely by the quantity of cases or the length of proceedings[34] – it is also linked to the quality of jurisprudence, the development of procedures and new approaches, and potential lessons for domestic and other international proceedings.[35]

The idea of an independent international Prosecutor, which was still an utopian vision throughout much of the 20th century, has become a core element

29 The OTP Policy Paper on Gender interprets gender as a social construct in light of Art. 21 (3), see OTP, Policy on the Crime of Gender Persecution, December 2022, 3.

30 ILC, Prevention and punishment of crimes against humanity, A/CN.4/L.935, 15 May 2019.

31 See MADRE, 'Gendering the Crimes Against Humanity Treaty', at https://www.madre.org/genderingCAH ('A text that does not properly account for current understanding of gender could sideline women, lesbian, gay, bisexual, transgender, intersex, and queer (LGBTIQ) persons and other marginalized and vulnerable victims').

32 P Clark, *Distant Justice: The Impact of the International Criminal Court on African Politics* (Cambridge: Cambridge University Press, 2018); .

33 The Statute sets express or implicit normative benchmark for behavior for investigations and prosecutions by states, UN entities or other courts, even if it is not always applied verbatim.

34 B Gumpert and Y Nuzban, 'What can be done about the length of proceedings at the ICC?' EJIL Talk, 15 November 2019, at https://www.ejiltalk.org/part-i-what-can-be-done-about-the-length-of-proceedings-at-the-icc/.

35 See C Stahn, *Justice as Message* (Oxford: Oxford University Press, 2020).

of international criminal justice. It reflects to a certain extent 'a global conscience'.[36] The Court remains dependent on states, but it has also shown the ability to act, even without a Security Council or state referral. This independence is particularly critical at a time where multilateralism is under fire.

The idea of complementarity has evolved. Complementarity is not merely a legal concept to solve problems of concurrent jurisdiction or admissibility disputes before the Court, but an organizing principle for the interaction of domestic, international, or hybrid justice institutions or universal jurisdiction. From a governance perspective, it reflects the 'Court's desire to govern the atrocity space by being both near to it while also retaining a separation to justify further intervention'.[37] It not a one-way, but a two way street between the Court and states. Ideally, it reflects a shared endeavor to promote investigations and prosecutions, rather than race or fight over jurisdiction. The movement towards more specialized crimes divisions in domestic jurisdiction or regional organizations, and the current turn towards strengthening universal jurisdiction,[38] is one of the most important effects of complementarity. It is not a threat to the Court, but an indication of its success. However, individual elements of OTP practice or ICC jurisprudence (e.g., ICC centricity, detachment from social context) have encountered critique.[39]

In its third decade, the OTP is developing news ways to encourage domestic investigations and prosecutions through complementarity agreements.[40] This form of 'contracted complementarity' builds on earlier policies on 'positive complementarity'.[41] It is grounded prosecutorial discretion over the timing of ICC investigations and prosecution. It uses domestic consent as leverage to enhance accountability. It has been used in different ways. In Colombia, it provided a completion strategy from a more than a decade long preliminary

---

36 On the relevance of Durkheim to international criminal justice, see I Tallgren, 'The Durkheimian Spell of International Criminal Law?' (2013) 71 *Revue interdisciplinaire d'études juridiques* 137.

37 R Clements, 'Near, Far, Wherever You Are: Distance and Proximity in International Criminal Law' (2021) 32 EJIL 327, 348.

38 Report of the Secretary-General, 'The scope and application of the principle of universal jurisdiction', A/77/186, 18 July 2022.

39 C De Vos, *Complementarity, Catalysts, Compliance: The International Criminal Court in Uganda, Kenya and the Democratic Republic of Congo* (Cambridge: Cambridge University Press, 2020); P Labuda, *International Criminal Tribunals and Domestic Accountability* (Oxford: Oxford University Press, 2023).

40 See the chapter by Pillai in this volume.

41 OTP, 'Policy Paper on Preliminary Examinations', November 2013, 23–24.

examination.[42] In Guinea or Venezuela, it served as a window of opportunity for domestic proceedings. Complementarity agreements offer creative ways to shape accountability and make best use of limited resources of the Court. However, they require at the same time vigilance against abuse by domestic politics and monitoring structures. The absence of a complementarity agreement in relation to US conduct in the Afghanistan situation, and the de-prioritization of investigations may easily create the perception of double standards in relation complementarity approaches.

The operation of the Court has contributed towards a thicker vision of justice. International criminal trials are not only about defendants as agents, as the classical liberal trial models suggests, but increasingly also about victims and survivors. Fairness, Defence rights and role of victims are not a trade-off.[43] The role of victims does not necessarily come at a price of lesser fairness towards the Defence or greater conviction bias.[44] In some cases, criminal proceedings can potentially affirm the personhood and dignity of both, perpetrators and victims and survivors.

The ICC performs law inside and outside of the Courtroom.[45] Jurisprudence of the Court has made important contributions to the reading and clarification of substantive criminal law, including the understanding of the policy requirement of crimes against humanity,[46] sexual and gender crimes against women and men,[47] intra-party offences against children,[48] destruction of cultural

42 In 2021, the OTP adopted a policy on situation completion, see OTP, Policy on Situation Completion, 15 June 2021.

43 See the chapter by Ambach in this volume.

44 On this tension, see S Zappalà, 'The Rights of Victims v. the Rights of the Accused' (2010) 8 JICJ 237.

45 J Meierhenrich, 'The practice of international law' (2014) 76 *Law and Contemporary Problems* 1.

46 PTC II, Situation in Republic of Kenya, Public Decision Pursuant to Article 15 of the Rome Statute on the Authorization of an Investigation into the Situation in the Republic of Kenya, ICC-01/09-19-Corr, 31 March 2010.

47 Ongwen was convicted for crimes of rape, sexual slavery, forced pregnancy, and forced marriage as other inhumane acts. In the *Al Hassan* case (*Prosecutor v. Al Hassan*, ICC-01/12-01/18), charges included persecution on gender ground.

48 In *Ntaganda*, the ICC broke novel ground, by extending the war crimes of rape and sexual slavery to victims from the same armed forces as the offender. See ICC, *Prosecutor v. Ntaganda*, Judgment on the Appeal of Mr Ntaganda Against the "Second Decision on the Defence's Challenge to the Jurisdiction of the Court in Respect of Counts 6 and 9" ICC-01/04-02/06 OA5, 15 June 2017. For a discussion, see C Kenny & Y McDermott, 'The Expanding Protection of Members of a Party's Own Armed Forces Under International Criminal Law' (2019) 68 ICLQ 943; M Longobardo, 'The Criminalisation of Intra-Party Offences in Light of Some Recent ICC Decisions on Children in Armed Conflict' (2019) 19 *International Criminal Law Review* 600.

property,[49] reproductive rights,[50] and the re-conceptionalization of modes of liability beyond the jurisprudence of the *ad hoc* tribunals.[51] Some judgments, such as the ICC decision on immunity in the *Jordan Referral re Al-Bashir* appeal have departed from the more state-centric jurisprudence of the ICJ.[52] In the Myanmar situation, the Pre-Trial Chamber drew on the ICJ's reasoning in *Reparation for Injuries*[53] to argue that the 'more than 120 States, representing the vast majority of the members of the international community', endowed the ICC with 'objective international personality, and not merely personality recognized by them alone'.[54]

In terms of procedure, the divide between adversarial and inquisitorial traditions[55] remains visible in certain practices, such as disclosure, admission of evidence[56] or 'proofing' of witnesses.[57] Classical ideal types are in flux. New institutional cultures are being framed. Court practices develop new

49 In *Al Mahdi*, the ICC clarified that 'international humanitarian law protects cultural objects as such from crimes committed both in battle and out of it'. See TC VIII, *Prosecutor v. Al Mahdi*, Judgment and Sentence, ICC-01/12-01/15, 27 September 2016, para. 15.

50 In *Ongwen*, the Trial Chamber recognized that the crime of forced pregnancy crime of forced pregnancy is 'grounded in the woman's right to personal and reproductive autonomy and the right to family protects the value of reproductive autonomy'. ICC, TC, *Prosecutor v. Ongwen*, Public Redacted Trial Judgment ICC-02/04-01/15-1762-Red, 4 February 2021, para 2717. See R Grey, 'The ICC's First 'Forced Pregnancy' Case in Historical Perspective' (2017) 15 JICJ 905, C Laverty and D de Vos, 'Reproductive Violence as a Category of Analysis: Disentangling the Relationship between "the Sexual" and "the Reproductive" in Transitional Justice' (2021) 15 *International Journal of Transitional Justice* 616.

51 See the chapter by Sadat in this volume. See generally J de Hemptinne, R Roth and E van Sliedregt (eds.), *Modes of Liability in International Criminal Law* (Cambridge: Cambridge University Press, 2019).

52 See Appeals Chamber, Judgment in the Jordan Referral re Al-Bashir Appeal, ICC-02/05-01/09-397, 6 May 2019. For a discussion, see the chapter by Chile Eboe-Osuji.

53 ICJ, *Reparation for Injuries Suffered in the Service of the United Nations*, Advisory Opinion, [1949] ICJ Rep. 174, p. 185.

54 PTC I, 'Decision on the "Prosecution's Request for a Ruling on Jurisdiction under Article 19(3) of the Statute"', 6 September 2018, ICC-RoC46(3)-01/18, para. 48.

55 See the chapter by Pangalangan in this volume.

56 F Guariglia, 'Admission v. Submission of Evidence at the International Criminal Court: Lost in Translation?' (2018) 18 JICJ 315.

57 It has been allowed in some cases, see TC V, *Prosecutor v. Ruto et al.*, Decision on Witness Preparation, ICC-01/09-01/11-524, 2 January 2013, para 35, where the Chamber found that 'properly conducted, witness preparation is also likely to enhance the efficiency, fairness and expeditiousness of the present trial'. It stated that risks could be curtailed by vise-recording. See para. 47. Other decisions have not allowed it. See TC IX, *Prosecutor v. Ongwen*, 'Decision on Protocols to be Adopted at Trial' ICC-02/04-01/15-504, 22 July 2016, para. 10 ('Witness preparation has an inherent risk of approaching a rehearsal of the witness's testimony').

approaches which are best suited to address the complex goals and challenges of atrocity crime litigation.[58] Judges have made proposals to amend rules. In some areas, such as sexual and gender-based violence,[59] victim participation[60] or reparative practices for victims and survivors,[61] emerging ICC practices are often at the forefront or ahead of developments domestically, despite their imperfections.[62]

However, a birthday is not only an occasion to cheer, clap and offer songs of praise. It is moment to reflect, engage and look ahead. The permanent nature of the Court should not be a reason for complacency.[63] Some challenges go beyond occasional fix and repair and require innovation, imagination and re-invention.

Ukraine is a critical test for the ICC.[64] What impact does the Court have on the ongoing conflict? How can we deal with 'information warfare'[65] and the magnitude of evidence? Unlike in previous decades, the problem is not to get evidence, but to process and deal with the large amount of evidence, and to ensure better coordination.[66] This requires both, new partnerships and

58 J Jackson, 'Finding the Best Epistemic Fit for International Criminal Tribunals: Beyond the Adversarial–Inquisitorial Dichotomy' (2007) 7 JICJ 17.

59 See generally R Grey, *Prosecuting Sexual and Gender-Based Crimes at the International Criminal Court* (Cambridge: Cambridge University Press, 2019).

60 B.N. McGonigle Leyh, *Procedural Justice? Victim Participation in International Criminal Proceedings* (Cambridge, Antwerp, Portland: Intersentia, 2011); See S. Vasiliev, 'Victim Participation Revisited: What the ICC Is Learning About Itself', in C. Stahn (ed.), *The Law and Practice of the International Criminal Court* (Oxford University Press, 2015) 1133.

61 L Moffett, 'Reparations for victims at the International Criminal Court: a new way forward?' (2017) 21 *International Journal of Human Rights* 1204.

62 For a critique, see C Van den Wyngaert, 'Victims before International Criminal Courts: Some Views and Concerns of an ICC Trial Judge' (2011) *44 Case Western Reserve Journal of International Law* 475; S. Kendall and S. Nouwen, 'Representational Practices at the International Criminal Court: The Gap between Juridified and Abstract Victimhood' (2013) 76 *Law and Contemporary Problems* 235.

63 See also Evenson (n 18) 445.

64 S Vasiliev, 'Watershed Moment or Same Old? Ukraine and the Future of International Criminal Justice' (2022) 20 JICJ 893; K Ambos, 'Ukraine and the Double Standards of the West' (2022) 20 JICJ 875; K J Heller, 'Russia's War on Ukraine Options for Prosecuting Russian Aggression Against Ukraine: A Critical Analysis' (2022) *Journal of Genocide Research*, https://doi.org/10.1080/14623528.2022.2095094; O Ba 'Constructing an international legal order under the shadow of colonial domination' (2023) 22 *Journal of Human Rights* 4.

65 S Masol, 'Ukraine and the International Criminal Court: Between Realpolitik and Post-truth Politics' (2022) 20 JICJ 167.

66 Y Tan and S Yang, 'The Joint Investigation Team in Ukraine: An Opportunity for the International Criminal Court?' (2023) 22 *Chinese Journal of International Law*, https://doi.org/10.1093/chinesejil/jmad005.

structures of cooperation, and the development of a new scientific community around novel technologies.[67] There is a need to investigate more thoroughly how digital evidence affects fairness and dynamics in the courtroom, and to what extent the digital age creates new dependencies on large tech corporations.

The Statute is built on the idea of a mosaic and a plurality of legal traditions. But in everyday practice, international criminal justice often remains self-centered. We hardly engage with legal systems or traditions that are more difficult to access, such as Islamic law or non-Western systems.[68] It is convenient to stay within the realm of the known and accepted. Making international justice more universal requires more intellectual curiosity and inclusivity. This goes beyond language or membership. It requires efforts to make the law itself more accessible, inclusive and pluralist. The ways in which proceedings present women's or gendered experiences of atrocities, the identities of actors in conflict ('rebels')[69] or images of victimhood[70] deserve greater attention.

The drafters have mapped out some of the central structure of adjudication – yet the peripheries of cases are critically underdeveloped. This starts with preliminary examinations and investigations. The existing experiences have shown that the nexus between investigations and charges is essential for trial. Novel institutions, such as the pre-trial confirmation procedure,[71] or the no case to answer motions[72] have caused posed challenges. Court practice has shown

67 See the chapters by Khan and Koenig and Freeman in this volume.

68 In 2022, the 2,300-page online Commentary on the Statute of the International Criminal Court was made available in Arabic, at https://cilrap-lexsitus.org/ar. On pluralism, see E van Sliedregt and S Vasiliev, *Pluralism in International Criminal Law* (Oxford: Oxford University Press, 2014). The issue became relevant in the *Al Hassan* Case, which dealt with the imposition of new rules on the Timbuktu population by the armed group *Ansar Dine*. Prosecutor Khan appointed Professor Intisar Rabb as special adviser on Islamic Law. See J Fraser, 'Exploring legal compatibilities and pursuing cultural legitimacy: Islamic law and the ICC' in J Fraser and B McGonigle Leyh (eds.), *Intersections of Law and Culture at the International Criminal Court* (Cheltenham: Elgar, 2020) 378–396

69 R Gaskins, *The Congo Trials in the International Criminal Court* (Cambridge: Cambridge University Press, 2020).

70 C Schwöbel-Patel, 'The "Ideal" Victim of International Criminal Law' (2018) 29 EJIL 703.

71 V Nerlich, 'The Confirmation of Charges Procedure at the International Criminal Court: Advance or Failure?' (2012) 10 JICJ 1339.

72 A. T. Cayley and A. Orenstein, 'Motion for Judgment of Acquittal in the Ad Hoc and Hybrid Tribunals' (2010) 8 JICJ 581. It was enshrined in Rule 98bis of the ICTY Rules of Procedure and Evidence, but has not been expressly regulated in the ICC context, since there is a confirmation of charges procedure. The majority of the Appeals Chamber accepted the motion in *Prosecutor v. Gbagbo and Blé Goudé*, 'Judgment in the appeal of the Prosecutor against Trial Chamber I's decision on the no case to answer motions', ICC-02/11-01/15 A, 31 March 2021. For a critique, see Dissenting Opinion of Judge Luz del Carmen Ibáñez Carranza, 31 March 2021, 02/11-01/15-1400-Anx4, 36 et seq.

that it is in the interest of all parties and participants to have case trial-ready at pre-trial, in order to streamline disclosure and avoid unnecessary litigation. Early release practice continues to pose difficulties. The *Bemba* case has illustrated the problems of the management of frozen assets. Bemba's post-acquittal claim for compensation and damages, including the lack of maintenance of his Boeing 727–100 plane at the airport in Faro, has highlighted the need for better asset management at the ICC. As Daley J. Birkett has argued, 'the ICC could play a more prominent role in supervising how frozen assets are managed after the responsible authorities of the requested state(s) have taken enforcement action pursuant to the procedures available under their respective national laws'.[73]

As the institution matures, it is important to look behind the scenes and address some visible facets of operation. Judicial and institutional culture have come under critical scrutiny.[74] Both, collegiality, and the culture of deliberation, are in need of improvement, in order to enhance decision-making practices and the quality of reasoning. Courtroom advocacy and interaction might benefit from virtues which legal feminism has brought to the forefront, such as sensitivity, attention to tone, leadership by professional acting and doing, rather than posture or loud voice. Courtroom gestures, such as respect to litigants and victims, reading out names of victims in a judgment, such as in *Ongwen*, may do a lot to improve working relations or communicative bonds.

The hierarchies, dependencies, inequalities and risks of abuse arising from workplace culture need to be confronted in more effective and transparent ways. The number of ILO proceedings, which the Court faced as a result of staff complaints,[75] shows that the rights of individuals inside the institution may gain less attention than the global image of the Court as moral and legal beacon of humanity. Pay-gaps and equal treatment of Defence staff remain sensitive issues.[76]

73 D Birkett, 'Managing Frozen Assets at the International Criminal Court' (2020) 18 JICJ 767, 784–85.

74 The IER report has highlighted problems arising from the lack of coherence of practices across Chambers, the absence of prior notification and/or motivation in case of departure from leading decisions, and the resulting uncertainties. See also the closing chapter in this volume.

75 On the problems caused by reorganization of the Registry, see S. Maupas, 'ICC Under Fire for Internal Mismanagement', *JusticeInfo.net*, 26 February 2018, R Clements, 'ReVisiting the ICC Registry's ReVision Project' (2019) 17 JICJ 259.

76 Defence teams have complained that the Legal Aid Policy of the ICC creates a 'situation of fundamental inequality within the Court system' since it does not 'not afford Defence Support Staff any form of paid parental leave, annual leave, or sick leave, or a right to enjoy Court holidays as non-working days'. See *Prosecutor v. Yekatom and Ngaïssona*, 'Corrected version of "Urgent Joint Defence Motion for an Adjournment and for a Suspension of Deadlines"', ICC-01/14-01/18, 1 December 2022, para. 4.

## 4 The Ukraine Warrants – a Game Changer?

The situation in Ukraine is undoubtedly a defining moment in the ICC's third decade. With the issuance of the Ukraine warrants against Vladimir Vladimirovich Putin and Maria Alekseyevna Lvova-Belova,[77] the ICC has opened a new chapter in its institutional history.[78] Although the OTP has examined a number of situations involving alleged criminal responsibility of nationals of permanent members of the Security Council (Iraq: UK; Afghanistan: US; Georgia: Russia), few would have thought that the Court would ever issue warrants of arrest against an acting head of state or senior state officials of the P5. Prosecutor Khan rightly stressed that this historic juncture is not a triumphant moment for international criminal justice, but 'a very sad occasion and a very sombre occasion'.[79]

Legally, the ICC has a solid jurisdictional basis to try genocide, crimes against humanity or war crimes rests, based on the Court's jurisprudence on *ad hoc* declarations accepting the court's jurisdiction.[80] Through its open-ended temporal clause, the 2015 Ukrainian declaration of acceptance recognized ICC jurisdiction over crimes committed in the current conflict, although it was initially launched in response to events in Crimea and Eastern Ukraine in 2014.[81] The territorial scope covers not only Crimea and Eastern Ukraine, but the 'territory of Ukraine' more broadly. However, it is somewhat ironic that a situation involving two non-state-parties becomes a defining event for ICC's third decade.[82] Historically, the idea that the government of a non-state party could

---

77 ICC, Press Release, 'Situation in Ukraine: ICC judges issue arrest warrants against Vladimir Vladimirovich Putin and Maria Alekseyevna Lvova-Belova' 17 March 2023.

78 J Fernandez, 'Mandat d'arrêt contre Vladimir Poutine: la Cour pénale internationale a-t-elle franchi le Rubicon?' *Le Rubicon*, 20 March 2023, at https://lerubicon.org/publication/mandat-darret-contre-vladimir-poutine-la-cour-penale-internationale-a-t-elle-franchi-le-rubicon/; R Hamilton, 'The ICC Goes Straight to the Top: Arrest Warrant Issued for Putin', *Just Security*, 17 March 2023, at https://www.justsecurity.org/85529/the-icc-goes-straight-to-the-top-arrest-warrant-issued-for-putin/.

79 Reuters, 'ICC's Khan says Putin arrest warrant a "sombre occasion"', 20 March 2023, at https://www.reuters.com/world/justice-ministers-meet-london-build-support-icc-after-putin-warrant-2023-03-20/#:~:text=%22It%20is%20really%20a%20very,Security%20Council.%22.

80 C Stahn, M El Zeidy, H Olásolo, 'The International Criminal Court's Ad Hoc Jurisdiction Revisited' (2005) 99 AJIL 421.

81 The second declaration, filed by the government of Ukraine on 8 September 2014, extended jurisdiction to crimes committed 'in the territory of Ukraine since 20 February 2014'. See OTP, 'ICC Prosecutor extends preliminary examination of the situation in Ukraine following second article 12(3) declaration', ICC-OTP-20150929-PR1156, 29 September 2015.

82 Ukraine has not become a State Party to the ICC, based on fears that its own nationals might be investigated or prosecuted. See I Marchuk and A Wanigasuriya, 'The ICC concludes its

grant the ICC jurisdiction over crimes committed by nationals of another non-state-party was one of the biggest objections by the US to the ICC.[83]

In its current set-up the Court lacks jurisdiction over aggression. This means that it cannot investigate and prosecute individuals for the waging of the war of aggression or their participation in it, as such, although it marks the foundation of killings and destruction, or the 'accumulated evil of the whole',[84] as the Nuremberg trial put it. This is a result of the narrow framing of the Kampala compromise in 2010,[85] which turned the crime of aggression more than other crimes under the Statute into an expressivist norm with limited jurisdiction, also based on strong pressure by some members of the P5. Formally, the three existing core crimes might provide a sufficient basis to hold perpetrators criminally accountable. But the criminality of aggression can only be reflected indirectly in charges or convictions, namely as part of the contextual elements of crimes, the common plan or purpose element, or as an aggravating factor in sentencing. This creates significant gaps in relation to the adjudication of many acts or violations that may be lawful under the laws or war, but are commited as part of aggressive warfare. The war in Ukraine as such is a painful reminder of the need to amend the ICC regime of aggression and bring it closer in line with the other three crimes, as persuasively argued by Claus Kress in his 2023 Nuremberg Academy Lecture on 'The Ukraine War and the Crime of Aggression' and suggested in the Nuremberg Declaration on the Crime of Aggression, dated 8 May 2023.[86]

The issuance of the warrants for unlawful deportation and transfer of Ukrainian children marked a historic moment.[87] It moved the Court a step away from the critiques that is mainly targeting 'Black criminality'. It sent a message

preliminary examination in Crimea and Donbas: What's next for the situation in Ukraine?' EJIL Talk, 16 December 2020, at https://www.ejiltalk.org/the-icc-concludes-its-preliminary-examination-in-crimea-and-donbas-whats-next-for-the-situation-in-ukraine/.

83 See R Wedgwood, 'The International Criminal Court: An American View' (1999) 10 EJIL 93, 102; J Ralph, *Defending the Society of States* (Oxford: Oxford University Press, 2007) 130.

84 International Military Tribunal (Nuremberg), *Judgment and Sentences*, (1947) 41 AJIL 172, 186.

85 ASP, Review Conference, Resolution RC/Res.6 (Crime of aggression), 11 June 2010.

86 Nuremberg Declaration on the Crime of Aggression, Nuremberg, 8 May 2023, at https://www.nurembergacademy.org/news/detail/b75fc3207d3463bbf20b452732f6bb0e/nuremberg-declaration-on-the-crime-of-aggression-680/#:~:text=On%208%20May%202023%2C%20the,order%20to%20prevent%20future%20wars. See also Claus Kress, Nuremberg Academy Lecture, 'The Ukraine War and the Crime of Aggression', 4 May 2023, at https://www.nurembergacademy.org/fileadmin/user_upload/Lecture_Prof_Kress_-_The_Ukraine_War_and_the_Crime_of_Aggression_-_Nuremberg_Academy_Lecture_on_4_May_2023.pdf.

87 S Vasilev, 'The International Criminal Court goes all-in: What now?', EJIL Talk, 20 March 2023, at https://www.ejiltalk.org/the-international-criminal-court-goes-all-in-what-now/.

that even the most powerful leaders are answerable before the law. It expressed the intergenerational impact of crimes. It showed the relevance of the Court, and shifted some of attention away from the debate over an additional special or hybrid court, and the tension over resource allocation, connected to it. Historically, it is a tipping point, which can develop in different ways. It might present a 'Nicaragua' moment for the ICC.[88] It may create some buy-in from those who have been skeptical towards the lack of accountability of individuals from major powers, including the P5. However, the fact that the ICC went directly to the top, in an ongoing conflict, also poses significant challenges, including unknowns and uncertainties.

As Mark Kersten has argued, one of the most immediate consequences is the risk that 'for the foreseeable future, perhaps even decades, there will be no Security Council referrals of situations to the ICC'.[89] The warrant against Vladimir Putin is a test case for the still fragile *Al Bashir* jurisprudence on the lack of personal immunity in relations towards the ICC. The decision enables states parties to the ICC to disregard immunities of heads of states of non-state parties in the execution of an ICC request for arrest and surrender. It has received some support,[90] but also mixed reactions in academia and capitals. It stands in tension with a voluntarist reading of the jurisprudence of the ICJ in the *Arrest warrant* case.[91] The Putin scenario differs from the *Al Bashir* case. In the latter case, the obligation of states parties to arrest *Al Bashir* as head of state could be derived from the impact of the Security Council referral. The new warrant is a test case for the acceptance of the jurisprudence of the Appeals Chamber, which argued that immunities are not applicable under customary international law in relation to international courts, such as the ICC, irrespective of a Chapter VII resolution of the Council.[92] States challenging the ICC's interpretation of customary law may seek to invoke Art. 98 of the ICC Statute to justify non-compliance with ICC requests, based on need to respect immunities in relation towards Russia.

88 On the implications of Nicaragua judgment of the ICJ, see T M. Lieverman, 'Law and Power: Some Reflections on Nicaragua, the United States, and the World Court' (1986) 10 *Maryland Journal of International Law* 29.

89 M Kersten, 'Straight to the top: The International Criminal Court issues an arrest warrant for Russia's Vladimir Putin', 17 March 2023, https://justiceinconflict.org/2023/03/17/straight-to-the-top-the-international-criminal-court-issues-an-arrest-warrant-for-russias-vladimir-putin/.

90 See chapter by Chile Eboe-Osuji in this volume. See also C Kress, *Preliminary Observations on the ICC Appeals Chamber's Judgment of 6 May 2019 in the Jordan Referral re Al-Bashir Appeal* (Brussels: Torkel Opsahl Academic EPublisher, 2019).

91 ICJ, *Arrest Warrant of 11 April 2000 (Democratic Republic of the Congo v. Belgium)*, Judgment, 14 February 2002, 25–26, para. 61.

92 ICC, *Prosecutor v. Al Bashir*, Judgment in the Jordan Referral re Al-Bashir Appeal, ICC-02/05-01/09-397, 6 May 2019, para. 1 and 2.

As Alonso Gurmendi has shown, initial reactions by states have been mixed. The warrants enjoyed most support from Western or 'Western-aligned states'.[93] Many states in the Global South have been less enthusiastic. They are critical of the aggressive war, and have condemned it in the General Assembly, but do not necessarily wish to be seen as siding with Western countries on accountability, since it may complicate cooperation within BRICS partners or upset relations with Russia. Few of them 'want to be put in a position where they must choose between rival great powers squaring off in a war that is thousands of miles away'.[94] In April 2023, the South African government has expressed its intention to 'domesticate' article 98 of the Statute and consider 'potential withdrawal from the ICC' as an option of 'last resort', to deal with dilemmas of arrest caused by the ICC warrants.[95]

Although ICC requests for arrest and surrender create binding obligations towards states parties, they are only part of the factors that play a role in domestic decision-making processes. Existing experiences show that cooperation and support with the ICC may enhance the broader reputation of a state in the international arena, but also cause frictions in domestic power relations, conflict with economic or military interests, or raise even more fundamental challenges to well-being and security.[96] For some states, the risks of being seen as non-compliant with ICC warrants is simply a lesser evil than the ripple effects that arrest may create. The ICC may confirm charges *in absentia*, in order to put pressure on states to arrest, present the depth of evidence, and enable witnesses and survivors to provide their accounts.[97] However, afterwards, accountability depends on political will of states, since the Court cannot hold trials *in absentia*.

---

93 A Gurmendi, 'Tracking State Reactions to the ICC's Arrest Warrant against Vladimir Putin', *Opinio Juris*, 29 March 2023, at https://opiniojuris.org/2023/03/29/tracking-state-reactions-to-the-iccs-arrest-warrant-against-vladimir-putin/.

94 International Crisis Group, 'A New Court to Prosecute Russia's Illegal War?', 29 March 2023, at https://www.crisisgroup.org/global-ukraine/new-court-prosecute-russias-illegal-war.

95 Presidency of South Africa, Press statement, 'South Africa remains a participant in the International Criminal Court', 25 April 2023, at https://www.thepresidency.gov.za/press-statements/south-africa-remains-participant-international-criminal-court.

96 T Henningsen and L Gissel, 'Non-cooperation with the International Criminal Court in gatekeeper states: Regime security in Deby's Chad' (2022) 35 *Cambridge Review of International Affairs* 826.

97 The Prosecution has requested this in the case of Joseph Kony, also as part of a completion strategy for the situation. See OTP, 'Statement of the Prosecutor of the International Criminal Court, Karim A.A. Khan KC: Request to hold hearing on confirmation of charges against Joseph Kony in his absence', 24 November 2022.

The decision of the OTP to go immediately to the top raises delicate peace and justice dilemmas. This is where charging strategy meets politics. In the context of peace and security, criminal accountability is only one among many competing prerogatives. Critics fear that the warrants may lead to lesser cooperation in the UN in relation to other pressing peace and security concerns, such as access to humanitarian assistance or peacekeeping. The fact that the ICC targets the most senior Russian officials has raised concerns about the prospects of peace negotiations. For instance, Serbian President Aleksandar Vucic, has criticized ICC action for creating 'great reluctance to talk about peace (and) about truce'.[98]

The warrants create a certain point of no return. They signal that there can be no sustainable peace without leadership responsibility. Politically, they may be interpreted as an effort to promote regime change in Russia. This orientation may have counterproductive effects. It may create a 'lock in' and prolong hostilities or intensify conflict. It communicates to the Russian government 'that its options are to win or to lose power and face prosecution'.[99] Under such circumstance, the continuation of the war may become 'existential'.[100]

Russian officials may be reluctant to engage in peace negotiations, while facing the threat of prosecution in their aftermath. Once issued by a Chamber, warrants cannot simply be withdrawn by Prosecution. The power of the Security Council to defer investigations and prosecutions under Art. 16 of the ICC Statute is only temporary. The OTP has adopted a narrow reading of the interests of justice clause, which implies that considerations of peace and security do not *per se* bar accountability.[101] Dealing with the ICC warrants may thus require creative strategies, or even a re-calibration of existing 'no peace without justice' formulas. In contexts, such as Uganda[102] or Colombia, the issue of accountability for serious crimes was addressed in the course of peace negotiations between governments and non-state actors. It is unclear whether there is sufficient leverage to push for a similar approach in the context of peace negotiations with Russia.

The Ukraine warrants mark undoubtedly a turning point for the Court. They are more than symbolic acts. They have produced a number of immediate

98 M Corder, 'War-crimes warrant for Putin could complicate Ukraine peace', AP News, 2 April 2023.

99 International Crisis Group (n 94).

100 Ibid.

101 OTP, Policy Paper on the Interests of Justice, September 2007, 8.

102 In the Juba peace talks, the LRA demanded the removal of ICC arrest warrants. Their existence did not block peace talks, but Kony ultimately failed to sign the agreement.

effects. They contributed to the stigmatization of crimes, restricted potential travel options, and highlighted the global relevance of the Court in the ongoing conflict. They have prompted new discussions on cooperation between the ICC and the US. However, they also carry risks. They reveal political divisions among states parties. They make the ICC vulnerable to lawfare. In case of lack of compliance, the Court will be perceived as a toothless tiger. Those who are critical of the Court's strong focus in Ukraine, and risks of double standards, will likely use the Ukraine as a precedent to assess the decisiveness and effectiveness of response in other ongoing or future ICC situations.

## 5 Reflections on Practices

This volume is an attempt to set these developments into perspective. It started with a symposium marking the 20th anniversary of the Court's operation in the World Forum in The Hague. Conversations and content were refined with the elaboration of chapters and the integration of additional authors and novel developments. The work as a whole reflects on the ICC's law and practices, ranging from preliminary examination to the afterlife of cases. It engages with both, some of the merits and successes of the Court, as well as its ongoing challenges and critiques. It encompasses voices from inside the Court, and from outside. It integrates perspectives from negotiators, Court principals, different agents in proceedings (Judges, Prosecution, Defence, victims), legal practitioners, civil society and academia. It discusses not only macro issues (universality, selectivity, complementarity, fairness, role of victims, reparations) and recurring challenges in the life cycle of cases (legal culture, evidence), but also some lesser discussed institutional aspects, such as gender and geographical imbalance, funding and governance issues, 'intersectional' approaches towards crimes or gaps in the ICC system.

### 5.1 *General Reflections*

The contributions in the first part contain general reflections on the first two decades. Philippe Kirsch, Chair of the Rome Conference and first President of the Court, looks back at the Rome negotiations and the ICC's first practice. He shows the success of the Statute as a treaty regime, but also admits that it was never meant to be a 'rose garden'. He admits that the drafters at Rome might have underestimated the complexity of the challenges that the Court faces in current times. He argues that despite its inherent tensions, the Court still responds to a need that is 'more present than ever'.

Silvia Fernandez de Gurmendi, Chair of the Working Group drafting the Rules of Procedure and Evidence, former President of the Court and President of the ASP, analyses key aspects of the global nature and legitimacy of the Court. According to Fernandez, the drafters understood that the universality of the Court could only be achieved through a hybrid legal system. She shows how understandings of complementarity have changed beyond the initial vision at Rome. Through Court practices, complementarity began to be seen as opportunity for cooperation and strengthening domestic jurisdiction, rather than a mechanism protecting domestic against ICC intervention. She argues that there is no 'magic formula' to make the Court more universal. In her view, the effectiveness and legitimacy of the Court depend on investment in the quality of justice, principles of inclusion and respect for diversity.

Minerva Tavárez Mirabal, Chair of the Board of Directors of the Trust Fund for Victims, provides an overview of the ICC's reparation practice. She argues that the ICC's mandate in relation to reparation is grounded in an optimistic 'stubbornness' regarding human rights. She shows that the Trust Fund assistance mandate and activities have laid important foundations for the Court-ordered reparations programmes. According her, consultation and building trust with victims and survivors are key to the success of reparations. She highlights at the same time the 'funding gap' of the Trust Fund, namely the discrepancy between the value of orders for reparations, which have been extended to indigent defendants,[103] and the limited assets of the Trust Fund.

Elizabeth Evenson, International Justice Director at Human Rights Watch, examines they key role of civil society in the creation of the ICC and its practice. She shows the diversity of civil society contributions to the Court's operations. She argues that civil society organizations have a dual role. They provide critical expertise on violations, build trusted relationships with victims and in affected communities,[104] and bridge the Court's physical or cultural distance to situations. At the same time, they serve as a critical watchdog, which is needed to press Court officials and states parties to improve the effectiveness, independence and fairness of the Court.

The contribution by David Donat Cattin, former Secretary-General of Parliamentarians for Global Action, looks back to the historical significance

103 ICC, *Prosecutor v. Lubanga Dyilo*, Decision establishing the principles and procedures to be applied to reparations, ICC-01/04-01/06-2904, 7 August 2012. For a discussion, see C Stahn, 'Reparative Justice after the Lubanga Appeal Judgment: New Prospects for Expressivism and Participatory Justice or 'Juridified Victimhood' by Other Means?' (2015) 13 JICJ 801.

104 E Evenson, 'ICC Preliminary Examinations and National Justice: Opportunities and Challenges for Catalysing Domestic Prosecutions', in M Bergsmo and C Stahn (eds.), *Quality Control in Preliminary Examination: Volume 2* (Brussels: Torkel Opsahl Academic EPublisher, 2018) 711.

of the Statute and lessons learned from two decades of practice. The chapter argues that the adoption of the Statute marks the incarnation of an 'international culture of legality', which challenges power-based relationships. It then identifies certain flaws in the Court's practice, such overly focused investigations and prosecutions resulting 'in too few and narrow cases, a false expectation in complementarity policies that States would exercise their primary responsibility to investigate and prosecute, the neglect of cases in the situation in Afghanistan, based on an 'inferiority complex vis-à-vis counterterrorism', insufficient application of witness and victim protection in the Kenya cases. It makes the important point that the principle of complementarity should be used more actively to ensure the realization of victims' rights at the domestic level.

### 5.2 *New Frontiers in Investigations and Prosecutions*

The next part of the volume is devoted to investigative and prosecutorial strategies, an area, in which the Court has faced challenges and critiques. The OTP has faced evidence problems, based on heavy reliance on material protected by provider's confidentiality (Art. 54 3 (e) of the Statute), use of intermediaries, external interference with witnesses or the vulnerability of witness testimony.[105] It has inter alia been criticized for its lengthy preliminary examinations, rushed investigations, its sometimes narrow case selection and charging strategy, and a poor record of convictions.[106] The *Gbabgo* and *Bemba* acquittals have been at the center of calls for review of OTP strategies. They have demonstrated the impartiality and fairness of ICC proceedings,[107] but have also called in question prosecutorial choices and working methods. The chapters assembled here examine new ways and methods of investigation, including opportunities and risks of new technologies, new frames of collaboration and coordination, as well as approaches to address selectivity and choice in situation and case selection.

The chapter by Prosecutor Karim Khan argues that the ICC is facing a 'new evidential landscape' to which Court strategies need to be adapted in a responsible manner. It shows how the OTP seeks to embrace the advances of technological advancement, while curtailing corresponding risks. It claims that

105 De Vos C M De Vos, 'Investigating from Afar: The ICC's Evidence Problem' (2013) 26 LJIL 1009, N Combs, 'Testimonial Deficiencies and Evidentiary Uncertainties in International Criminal Trials' (2009) 14 *UCLA Journal of International Law and Foreign Affairs* 235.

106 Evenson (n 18).

107 R Goldstone, 'Acquittals by the International Criminal Court' *EJIL Talk*, 18 January 2019, at https://www.ejiltalk.org/acquittals-by-the-international-criminal-court/.

new technologies offer a valuable means to go beyond witness testimony and overcome the temporal and/or geographical distance between the Courtroom and alleged crimes. The contribution shows how recent Court cases have broken new ice, by introducing new ways of presenting evidence and material through geo-location or digital platforms (*Al-Mahdi*, *Al-Hassan*) or reliance on social media (*Al-Werfalli*). Khan explains new OTP strategies, which may innovate existing Court practices, such as reliance on new cognitive services for the analysis of large volumes of digital or digitized data, refined methodologies for identification and disclosure, as well as a new e-Discovery platform which will also facilitate more efficient sharing of information with national authorities. The chapter discusses plans to leverage public-private partnerships and the need address certain risks, such as the 'hypervisibility' of certain crimes through new technologies, potential access or selection bias, use of 'deep fake' images or challenges to the fairness of proceedings. It argues that the role of victims, and the hearing of their testimony, will remain central in criminal proceedings at the ICC, but that the law is equipped to accommodate the challenge of technological advancement.

Rafael Braga da Silva discusses the role intermediaries in ICC investigations and the broader impact of third-party investigations on evidence collection. He shows how the growing involvement of NGOs in gathering material and evidence transforms the ethics and practices of investigation.[108] The chapter argues that the increased role of society has changed OTP practices. It demonstrates how the broadening of the investigative landscape has prompted a more communicative and engaging relationship with civil society organizations, which goes beyond one-sided sharing of material and evidence with the Court. It traces how the Court used self-regulatory instruments, such as the Guidelines on Intermediaries or the new OTP/Eurojust Guidelines on the documentation crimes and human rights violations for accountability purposes,[109] to mitigate dilemmas, such as lack of transparency or accountability in investigations or risks of over-documentation, which have become evident in the context of Ukraine. Braga da Silva analyzes the new OTP/Eurojust guidelines for civil society organisations, which set out principles, such as 'Do no harm', 'informed consent', 'objectivity, impartiality and independence', as well as do's and don'ts' on interviews, witness statements or methods of documenting

108 R Braga da Silva, 'Sherlock at the ICC? Regulating Third-Party Investigations of International Crimes in the Rome Statute Legal Framework' (2020) 18 JICJ 59.

109 OTP/Eurojust, Documenting international crimes and human rights violations for accountability purposes: Guidelines for civil society organisations, 21 September 2022, at https://www.eurojust.europa.eu/sites/default/files/assets/eurojust-icc-csos-guidelines.pdf.

crimes. He argues they are not only a means for the OTP to claim space or signal international standards, but part of a policy of sharing lessons learned and best practices with others.

In the following chapter, Priya Gopalan demonstrates how intersectionality may broaden and improve approaches towards investigation and prosecution of international crimes, including sexual and gender-based crimes. The concept of intersectionality has its origin in Black feminist literature and critical race theory (*Kimberlé Crenshaw*).[110] It is used as an analytical frame in the social sciences to understand how harm, abuse, discrimination, inequality or disadvantage are produced through the interconnection of different categories of social identity, such as race, gender, sexual orientation, socio-economic disadvantage or disability. Drawing on the work of Patricia Sellers[111] and Alexandra Lily Kather,[112] Gopalan argues that intersectionality offers not only a means to better understand individual identity traits, harms or inequalities, which are produced in atrocity contexts, but also the systems of power, privileges, or forms oppression which drive the commission of crimes.[113] At the ICC, intersectionality may serve both, as a frame to inform the interpretation and application of internationally recognized human rights standards (Art. 21 (3) of the Statute), and as a useful lens to guide operative practices, such as identification of contextual elements of crimes, investigative methods, protection of witnesses or victims or reparative policies.[114] The chapter shows how intersectionality underpins some of the existing OTP policies, including sexual and gender-based crimes, children, and in particular, gender persecution,[115] and emerging Court practices, such as the confirmation of charges in

110 K Crenshaw, 'Demarginalizing the Intersection of Race and Sex: A Black Feminist Critique of Antidiscrimination Doctrine, Feminist Theory and Antiracist Politics' (1989) 8 *University of Chicago Legal Forum* 139.

111 P V Sellers and L C Nwoye, 'Conflict-related male sexual violence and the international criminal jurisprudence' in M Zalewski, P Drumond, E Prugl and M Stern (eds.), *Sexual Violence Against Men in Global Politics* (London: Routledge, 2018) 211.

112 A Lily Kather, 'What do intersectionality, feminist leadership and feminist foreign policy have to do with justice?, 28 October 2022, at https://www.boell.de/en/2022/10/21/justice-sexual-and-gender-based-crimes-conflict-what-does-intersectionality-feminist.

113 P Gopalan, 'Rejecting Notions of "Honor" to Mitigate Stigma' (London: LSE Centre for Women, Peace & Security, 2021).

114 Kather (n 112), G Maučec, 'The International Criminal Court and the Issue of Intersectionality – A Conceptual and Legal Framework for Analysis' (2021) 21 *International Criminal Law Review* 1. On OCTY practice, see M Isaac and O Jurasz, 'Towards an Intersectional Understanding of Conflict-Related Sexual Violence: Gender, Sexuality, and Ethnicity at the ICTY' (2018) 18 *International Criminal Law Review* 853.

115 See OTP, Policy on the Crime of Gender Persecution, 7 December 2022, para. 55. See also G Maučec, 'On Implementation of Intersectionality in Prosecuting and Adjudicating

*Al-Hassan.*[116] It demonstrates the limitations and risks that flow from a characterization of 'sexual violence as a weapon of war. It argues that intersectional approaches can bring out how crimes are embedded and facilitated through unequal power structures, relations and dynamics, such as patriarchal structures and gender hierarchies. The argument is supported by three historical examples: (i) the case of the Comfort women in Korea, where sexualized enslavement coincided with colonial power structures, ageism, patriarchy, militarism, and categories of class, (ii) the 'Srebrenica Syndrome' of Bosnian Muslim women, whose lived experience of crimes was not only shaped by ethnicity, but by religion and their stature in a patriarchal society focused on marital status, and (iii) and sexual violence against ethnic Tamil men and boys in Sri Lanka, which was driven by nationalist narratives of the ruling class, as well as cultural and ethnic hegemonies.

The last chapter in this part by Darryl Robinson takes a fresh look on dilemmas of selectivity in the selection of situation and cases. It argues that the mandate of the Court, and its links to politics, places the ICC at the center of conflicting expectations and critiques. The dilemma is that many of the relevant shortcomings or critiques have some degree of merit, and cannot be easily reconciled through a balancing of concerns and objections. Building on the idea of dyads,[117] Robinson illustrates the conflicts and tensions through five different problems in situation or case selection: (i) reaching too high v. remaining too low, (ii) being to imperious v. being too deferential, (iii) opting for safe approaches v. pursuing overly ambitious goals, (iv) charging 'too broad' or 'too narrow', and (v) the virtues of acting slow v. acting fast. In each of these cases, recording concerns and reversing policies in one-way will not solve the complexity of the underlying problem. As a way out, the chapter proposes a more 'holistic' and 'multi-dimensional' analysis of no win scenarios. It argues that state officials, judges, external observers or critics should move way from one-dimensional problem analysis and consider that the approach taken in the respective context might be one of several reasonable, but contestable choices.

---

Mass Atrocities by the International Criminal Court' (2021) 21 *International Criminal Law Review* 534.

116 *Prosecutor v. Al Hassan*, Confirmation of Charges, ICC-01/12-01/18, para. 702 ('violence against women could also have been motivated by considerations linked to skin color, since women with dark skin were more affected by this violence than others; the same goes for dark-skinned men who, according to some witnesses, were [more] persecuted than those with light skin').

117 D Robinson, 'Inescapable Dyads: Why the International Criminal Court Cannot Win' (2015) 28 LJIL 323.

Under this logic, balancing conflicting prerogative might require acceptance of options which are the 'least bad in an all-things-considered assessment'.

### 5.3 *Re-visiting Trials and Procedures*

The subsequent chapters move on to a discussion of fundamental aspects of trials and proceedings. The ICC Statute is in many respects a *sui generis* regime, which introduced procedural innovations and dilemmas. Both, the interplay between the role of the Prosecutor as master of proceedings and the powers of the Pre-Trial Chamber, and the interplay between pre-trial and trial more generally, have caused tensions, which needed to be addressed in practice. The confirmation procedure has been criticized for turning into a 'mini-trial'.[118] It has been disputed whether pre-trial should mainly serve as filter for trial, or also assume an additional preparatory function for trial proceedings. The Court had to navigate conflicts between inquisitorial and accusatorial features in a predominantly adversarial trial structure, confront constructive ambiguities or deal with idiosyncrasies and novelties, which have no clear-cut precedent in domestic or international criminal procedure.[119] Jurisprudence has been affected by differences between legal cultures, and divergent conceptions of the role of judges, the powers of parties and participants in proceedings, or the overall goal of the trial. This is visible in areas, such as the no case of answer motion, the treatment of witnesses, the admissibility of evidence, or the role of judges in the modification of the legal characterization of facts. Given the ambiguities of the Statute (e.g. the umbrella clause under Art. 68 (3)), judges needed to define at each stage of the process, how victims could enjoy a meaningful role in proceedings, without compromising the rights of the Defence.[120] The chapters by El Zeidy, Pangalangan, Naouri and Jacobs, and Ambach, examine these problems from different perspectives: Judges and the judiciary, the Defence, and victims.

Mohamed El Zeidy's chapter addresses the delicate interplay between prosecutorial discretion in the investigation and prosecution of crimes and powers of judicial review. Art. 53 of the Statute is a hallmark of ambiguity and compromise. It seeks to make prosecutorial action transparent and answerable

118 PTC II, *Prosecutor v Said Abdel Kani*, 'Decision on the confirmation of charges against Mahamat Said Abdel Kani', ICC-01/14-01/21, 9 December 2021, para 42 ('the confirmation hearing is not, nor should be seen or become, a "mini-trial" or "a trial before the trial"').

119 See K Ambos, 'International criminal procedure: "adversarial", "inquisitorial" or mixed?' (2003) 3 *International Criminal Law Review* 18.

120 See generally Y McDermott, *Fairness in International Criminal Trials* (Oxford: Oxford University Press, 2016), A Clooney and P Webb, *The Right to a Fair Trial in International Law* (Oxford: Oxford University Press, 2021).

through notification and judicial review, but fails to specify what types of prosecutorial inaction (e.g. decisions not to investigate entire situations, particular groups of persons within a situation, or individual cases) are subject to judicial review, and to what extent review powers apply to *proprio motu* proceedings under Art. 15, i.e. decisions of the OTP not to seek authorization to open an investigation.[121] In the first phase of the Court, this relationship was marked by mutual mistrust. Chambers were eager to get information on the progress of investigations and to keep a tight grip of prosecutorial activities, whilst the OTP was keen to preserve utmost prosecutorial discretion. El Zeidy analyzes how this relationship developed over time. He shows that the practice of Chambers remains inconsistent and marked by different philosophies regarding judicial review. He argues that jurisprudence has navigated between four different approaches: judicial interventionism, deference, jurisprudential revolution, and a balancing of interests.

Former ICC judge Raul Pangalangan provides a fresh perspective on the inquisitorial/adversarial divide. He has argued that the Court derives 'its legitimacy from its adherence to the rules, the soundness of its juridical reasoning, and the fairness of its procedure'.[122] In this chapter, he shows that the debate between both traditions has been visible at the Court – not in the form of a contest between legal systems, but rather in the spirit of finding the methodology that offers the best fit in the context of the Statute. He identifies the different positions underlying the role and interpretation of four practices, which have been at the core of doctrinal debate: the 'No Case to Answer' motion, witness preparation, guilty plea, and Regulation 55.[123] He argues, that ultimately, ICC practice has not simply imported or copied domestic approaches, but adopted an autonomous interpretation of legal concepts, which is anchored in the history and unique context of the legal framework of the ICC.

---

121 See Art. 15 (6) of the Statute and Rule 48 of the ICC Rules of Procedure and Evidence. The Appeals Chamber left wide leeway to the OTP in the Afghanistan decision, arguing that 'it would be contrary to the very [nature of the power accorded to the Prosecutor under article 15] to suggest that a duty to investigate could be imposed by the pre-trial chamber in the absence of a request for authorisation of investigation by the Prosecutor'. See ICC, 'Judgment on the appeal against the decision on the authorisation of an investigation into the situation in the Islamic Republic of Afghanistan', ICC-02/17 OA4, 5 March 2020, para. 31.

122 R Pangalangan, 'The International Criminal Court and the Burdens of Non-Traditional Expectations' (2020) 55 *Gonzaga Journal of International Law* 237, 247.

123 On the history, see C Stahn, 'Modification of the Legal Characterization of Facts in the ICC System: A Portrayal of Regulation 55' (2005) 16 *Criminal Law Forum* 1.

In the following contribution, Jennifer Naouri and Dov Jacobs examine the status of the rights of the Defence at the ICC. They inquire whether ICC practice provides the Defence with the necessary space and means to fulfill its role as agent of justice in ICC proceedings. Despite calls for reform,[124] the Defence is not a separate organ of the Court, as for instance the Defence Office at the Special Tribunal for Lebanon.[125] This institutional separation reflects the independence of the Defence, but has also raised structural problems in relation to equality of arms, Defence investigations,[126] access to resources, legal aid and working conditions. Naouri and Jacobs argue that the Defence is comparable to the magic mirror of the Queen in the Snow White tale. It requires international criminal justice to look itself into the mirror: Mirror, mirror on the wall, who's the fairest of them all? Is the ICC really 'the fairest of them all'? The chapter shows some of the existing deficiencies. It argues the right of the accused to an expeditious trial should not be turned against the defendant. It makes the point that the use of video-links in lieu of live testimony in Court and overuse of bar table motions may compromise the right to challenge evidence. It shows that excessive use of in-court protective measures and discussion of evidence and testimony in private session may conflict with the publicity and transparency of trials and compromise the didactic functions of proceedings. The authors also highlight institutional problems, which challenge the principle of equality of arms and create gaps between the legal teams of the Defence and the Prosecution in daily operations. They insist on the need to reform the Court's legal assistance system, ensure equal working conditions between the Defence and the Prosecution, and highlight the importance of the rights of the Defence in ICC communication policy and public discourse.

Philipp Ambach revisits the regime of victim participation. It presents a 'major departure from the essentially retributive model of international criminal justice'[127] The recognition of the agency, dignity and harm of victims

124 X-J Keïta, 'Evolution or Revolution: The Defence Offices in International Criminal Law', ICTR Legacy Symposium, November 2014, at https://unictr.irmct.org/sites/unictr.org/files/publications/compendium-documents/iii-evolution-or-revolution-icl-keita.pdf.

125 In the context of the STL, the Defence Office was branded as an institution which 'has evolved in the practice of United Nations-based tribunals as part of the need to ensure equality of arms'. See UN Security Council, Report of the Secretary-General on the Establishment of a Special Tribunal for Lebanon, U.N. Doc., S/2006/893, 15 November 2006, para. 30.

126 C Buisman and D Hooper, 'Defense Investigations and the Collection of Evidence' in C Rohan and G Zyberi (eds.), *Defense Perspectives on International Criminal Justice* (Cambridge: Cambridge University Press, 2017) 519.

127 Independent Expert Review (n 25), para. 834.

constitutes one of the innovative features of ICC procedures. The position of victims is unique. They are neither a 'second prosecutor', as feared by some, nor a mere object of proceedings. The application of victims' rights has caused significant debate from different perspectives. It reflects the dyads dilemma identified by Robinson. The drafters sought to make victim participation meaningful, but not to the detriment of Defence rights, or at the price of longer or more costly proceedings. For some, it is not meaningful enough. For others, it is too labor-and resource-intense, overly complex and not effective enough from a cost-benefit perspective. Drawing on both, ICC practice, and the Independent Expert Review, Ambach traces developments in relation to access of victims to proceedings and their modalities of participation. He argues that there are advances which provide ground for optimism. He shows changes in the development of the victim application process. Through trial and error, Chambers and the Registry gradually transformed a long and user-unfriendly process, which caused significant backlogs of applications, into a more effective and realistic process. He also demonstrates how the Court managed to accommodate larger number of applications through the introduction of the 'ABC' system, which distinguishes more clearly between those victims 'who clearly qualify as victims (Group A)', 'those who clearly do not qualify as victims (Group B)' and 'those for whom the Registry could not make a clear determination (Group C)'. Based on examples, he challenges the stereotype that victim participation causes significant delay in proceedings. At the same time, standardization of procedures and progress in management of applications and representations do not solve some of the fundamental socio-legal dilemmas underpinning victim participation, such as discrepancies in the treatment of victims of the situation and case-related victims, risks of hierarchization of claimants, commodification of harms, or secondary conflicts between or within communities of victims.[128]

### 5.4 *Intersecting Complementarity and Cooperation*

The next part of the volume deals with cooperation and complementarity. They form the backbone of the operation of the Court. In the Statute, they are formally treated in different parts. However, in practice the interconnections between two concepts have come out.[129] The OTP has included considerations

128 See Kendall and Nouwen (n 62), Schwöbel-Patel (n 70), L Fletcher, 'Refracted justice: The imagined victim and the International Criminal Court' in C De Vos, S Kendall and C Stahn (eds.), *Contested Justice* (Cambridge: Cambridge University Press, 2015) 302.

129 HP Kaul and C Kress, 'Jurisdiction and Cooperation in the Statute of the International Criminal Court: Principles and Compromises' (1999) 2 *Yearbook of International Humanitarian Law* 143.

of cooperation in its prosecutorial strategy, in particular in the context of the turn to 'positive complementarity'. At the same time, state cooperation, and implementation of the Rome Statute, are influenced by complementarity. The contributions in this part examine challenges and innovations arising from the interplay between cooperation and complementarity. They show that complementarity is much more than a 'one-way, top-down process' through which the ICC sets the 'gold standard' for local justice processes.

Former Registrar Peter Lewis takes a look at some lesser visible facets of proceedings, namely the role of the Registry in relation to arrest, protection of witnesses, and victim participation and reparation. He shows that the role of the Registry goes beyond mere technical or administrative tasks. It requires not only coordination and interaction with the OTP and Chambers, but diplomatic follow-up on non-execution of arrest warrants, engagements with states to mobilize support for witness protection, or measures enabling victims to make claims for participation or reparation. He argues that lack of political will is one of the main challenges of Registry practice. He suggests that the work of the Court will be 'more geographically spread across the world' and require 'new cooperation partnerships' in the future.

During his tenure, Prosecutor Khan has placed renewed emphasis on burden-sharing and collaboration. Priya Pillai takes a look at developments and changes in complementarity approaches. She examines in particular, to what extent the link between complementarity, cooperation and compliance in complementarity agreements provides a new avenue to address some of dilemmas and critiques of the ICC practices, such as ICC centricity, lack of cooperation, and open-ended preliminary examinations. She argues that the Court has adopted a narrow approach towards admissibility through the combination of the mirror test[130] and the requirement of 'tangible, concrete and progressive investigative steps'. She shows that this test exposed the ICC to critiques in domestic settings, such as the Philippines, where the Court's approach was associated with fears of passing judgment over domestic jurisprudence or reducing domestic justice to 'second class' justice. Pillai then examines complementarity agreements as a new approach to mitigate conflicts. She contrasts the agreement on cooperation and complementarity with the Colombian government with the Memorandum of Understanding regarding Venezuela and the agreement with Guinea. She argues that such agreements may have three beneficial effects: They may clarify state obligations and make commitments

130 See C Stahn, 'Admissibility Challenges before the ICC: From Quasi-Primacy to Qualified Deference?' in Stahn, *The Law and Practice of the International Criminal Court* (n 60) 228.

more tangible, provide space to show greater deference to transitional justice mechanisms, and attenuate the perception of neo-coloniality[131] through cooperative arrangements and assistance and support from the Court to domestic jurisdictions. She pleads at the same time for greater consistency in application, in order to avoid selectivity.

Lorraine Smith-van Lin and Fiona McKay argue for greater space for victims in the context of the ICC's state-centric complementarity regime.[132] They make a case that victims should enjoy greater participatory rights in the review of deferral requests of states under Art. 18 of the Statute. In the context of the Afghanistan situation, the Pre-Trial Chamber held that victims have no procedural standing at this early stage.[133] The authors support a more inclusive victim-friendly interpretation of Art. 18. They suggest that the Chamber should read the provision in light of Article 68(3) and Article 21(3), or use their inherent powers to give a victims a greater voice in this context. Smith-van Lin and McKay suggest that the ICC may gain more legitimacy, by embracing as a more holistic, 'circular' approach to complementarity', which offers all organs of the Court an opportunity to support domestic investigations and prosecutions and promotes continuous communication and knowledge-sharing between the OTP, victims and affected communities. They propose a number of creative ways to strengthen the role of victims based on this model. They argue that the OTP should use future complementarity agreements more actively to support rights and interests of victims and survivors, by insisting on adequate protection of victims and witnesses, victim participation in domestic proceedings and reparations, or sufficient legal aid for representation of victims, which lacked in proceedings before the Uganda International Crimes Division. Building on the Independent Expert Review, they suggest that the Court should promote 'reparative complementarity' policies, by ordering reparations that 'feed into and reinforce national reparative justice and reparations efforts'.[134] Finally, states should pay greater attention to victims' rights in domestic implementing legislation.

131 N Sekhon, 'Complementarity and Post-Coloniality' (2013) 27 *Emory International Law Review* 799.

132 Traditionally, complementarity is a way of organizing concurrent jurisdiction. Victims have enumerated participation rights.

133 PTC II, Situation in the Islamic Republic of Afghanistan, 'Decision regarding applications related to the Prosecution's "Notification on status of the Islamic Republic of Afghanistan's article 18(2) deferral request"', ICC-02/17-156, 3 September 2021, paras 23 and 25.

134 Independent Expert Review (n 25), Recommendation 353.

The subsequent chapter by Olympia Bekou sheds closer light on the status of ICC implementing legislation. It shows that implementation of crimes under the Statute is not *per se* legally required, but a critical precondition for complementarity and cooperation. It then analyses trends in domestic jurisdiction.[135] Bekou demonstrates that only half of all State Parties have adopted domestic implementing legislation for the four core crimes. Domestic practice varies in terms of the modalities. Some states include express references to the Rome Statute or replicate crimes.[136] Others reformulate or rephrase ICC crimes, sometimes using more restrictive or broader definitions. The chapter concedes that domestic investigations and prosecutions do not have to follow an 'ICC-style trial'. However, it offers a few recommendations to guide practices. It argues that prosecuting conduct under an ordinary crime label may not reflect the nature, gravity and scale of core international crimes fully. Ordinary criminal law provisions may contain gaps in relation to modes of liability or superior responsibility. Domestic sentencing frameworks may not always reflect the seriousness of core international crimes. Bekou draws attention to the need to capture the irrelevance of official capacity or the non-applicability of statutes of limitations in domestic legislation and to ratify the Agreement on Privileges and Immunities. She concludes that the ASP should play a more active role in facilitating discussions between States to accelerate the pace of national implementation processes.

### 5.5 *Confronting Institutional Challenges*

The following contributions cover some of the less frequently studied institutional challenges of the Court: Issues of representation and internal organization, budgetary issues, the Court-wide relevance of new technologies, and the question how the Court can do better to provide meaningful justice. They identify some of the weaknesses and vulnerabilities of the Court, but also recommendations to improve practices.

Angela Mudukuti offers a sobering, and much needed account of gender and geographical imbalance at the ICC. The Court is a complex organization with an 'amalgam of management cultures'.[137] The GQUAL Campaign has highlighted the chronic under-representation of women across international courts and tribunals. The Independent Expert Review stressed the need to 'improve

135 For a survey, see also J B Terracino, 'National Implementation of ICC Crimes: Impact on National Jurisdictions and the ICC' (2007) 5 JICJ 421.

136 This method has advantage of offering clarity and predictability.

137 Independent Expert Review (n 25), para. 205.

ethics'[138] and promote greater gender and geographical balance.[139] The chapter demonstrates shortcomings in geographical and gender representation. It argues that the limited geographical diversity in leadership positions affects the legitimacy of the Court and makes it vulnerable to arguments of 'white supremacy'. It shows that it is related to deeper structural causes, such as the link between geographical representation and the financial contribution of states, which is borrowed from the UN system and may reinforce the impression that the ICC is a tool of wealthy states. The contribution also highlights that existing imbalances may have negative impacts on investigation and prosecution, or adjudication more broadly, due to a lack of understanding of the social and cultural norms relevant to the situation or the lived experience of different women. Mudukuti points to certain advances, such as the introduction of Gender Focal points, the ICC Strategy on Gender Equality and Workplace Culture, or the contemplation of term limits for leadership positions at D or P-5 level, but pleads for more determinative structural change.

Stuart Ford examines the budgetary challenges of the Court.[140] Funding politics are a constant battle. Some states parties appear to be guided by a taxpayers' attitude, expecting the Court to 'deliver full value for the funding' in terms of 'reducing the incidence of the crimes set out in the Rome Statute, through convictions and deterrence'.[141] This argument tends to overlook the complexity of international criminal justice. It is at odds with the insight that the justice of ICC procedures extends beyond cases or convictions. Within the Court, there is a perception that 'States Parties seem to be more interested in reducing the budget than in providing the resources needed for the Court to function fully'.[142] Ford shows that there is light and shadow. The ICC's budget has increased over time, but not in a linear fashion. The Ukraine situation has triggered an additional influx, which offers opportunities and risks. The OTP has resisted earmarking and pledged to use funds to support some of the under-resources investigations beyond Ukraine, in order to counter the impression that Western states can use their budgetary power to realize their policy objectives. However, the comparative increase of resources for OTP

138 Ibid., para. 207.
139 Ibid., para. 214.
140 See also E Wiebelhaus-Brahm and K Ainley, 'The evolution of funding for the International Criminal Court: Budgets, donors and gender justice' (2023) 22 *Journal of Human Rights* 31; S Ford, 'How Much Money Does the ICC Need?' in Stahn, *The Law and Practice of the International Criminal Court* (n 60) 90.
141 Independent Expert Review (n 25), para. 949.
142 Ibid. para. 948.

investigations may fail to reflect the need for broader Court-wide resources. Arrears of states remain a structural problem. At the same time, the ASP has broken new ground, by recognizing that the 'quality of justice' also depends on the effectiveness and independence of the Defence, and expressing concern about the lack of burden-sharing in relation to the costs of Security Council referrals.

Alexa Koenig and Lindsay Freeman examine prospects, limitations and institutional challenges arising from the turn to digital technologies. They argue that this development is neither 'good' or 'bad', nor 'neutral', since it creates immediate and potentially unexpected effects for the Court. The chapter concurs with the argument made in the chapter by Khan that digital technology is an area in which the ICC can serve as example for other institutions or domestic justice system and share lessons learned. But it also shows that the pace of developments creates a 'preparing for the future' problem. Budgetary constraints, complex procurement procedures, and long hiring processes make it difficult to secure adequate resources, infrastructure, and personnel to keep up with technological change. The authors further emphasize that the OTP needs to strengthen its cyber investigative capacity and ability process relevant digital evidence, in order to address changing methods of warfare, such as use of unmanned vehicles, autonomous systems and artificial intelligence, or cyber operations, including those in the war in Ukraine.

Carla Ferstman returns to the problem of expectations and impact. She argues that the role of victims is an important counter-movement to the increased professionalization and standardization of the field. She pleads against a bureaucratic vision and commodification of the voices of victims, which has become an important critique of the ICC.[143] In her view, victims should not be treated as a mere 'echo chamber'. She suggests a role reversal: It is the 'we' that needs to change in order to encompass victims. The Court should not strive to 'manage' expectations, but seek to meet them. The chapter concedes that is impossible to provide 'full justice' to victims through ICC proceedings. But it argues that the ICC should be more open and prepared to give space to unfiltered voices of victims and to be transformed by these experiences. This might require greater inclusiveness in relation to application processes, protective measures, rights of audience, or reparations. Ferstman concludes with a few concrete measures to make the role of victims more meaningful, namely providing a 'modicum of legal representation for victims' during the early phases of proceedings, enabling victims to 'e-meet' with legal representatives or

143 See n 128.

court officials in safe spaces or address judges 'through mobile phone or video technology', and increasing the agency of victims in reparation proceedings.

### 5.6 *Looking to the Future*

The final part is devoted to 'big picture' issues and reflections on the future. It engages with the space of the Court within geopolitics and the shifting international institutional landscape. It addresses some of the most pressing discussions relating to future amendments of the ICC regime, such as environmental damage and the future regime of the crime of aggression. It also identifies avenues to re-imagine the Court in a multi-polar world.

Muriel Ubeda-Saillard situates the role of the ICC in a broader context of the evolving system of international criminal justice. She shows that the current justice architecture is marked by a certain 're-nationalization', which is reflected in the quiet renaissance and strengthening of the exercise of domestic jurisdiction,[144] and a trend towards hybridization, exemplified by the turn to new (quasi-judicial) investigative mechanisms and hybrid courts. She argues that the effectiveness of the ICC may be improved through investment in means for arrest and surrender, as contemplated by new instruments (e.g. ILC Draft articles on Prevention and Punishment of Crimes Against Humanity,[145] Convention on International Cooperation in the Investigation and Prosecution of the Crime of Genocide, Crimes against Humanity, War Crimes, and other International Crimes),[146] consideration of the legal responsibility of corporations, a stocktaking of the benefits and downsides of *in absentia* trials and a clear methodology for the assessment of damages in the context of reparations. She cautions at the same time against the risk of over-criminalizing human rights violations, arguing that criminal law is a measure of last resort.

---

144 M Langer and M Eason, 'The Quiet Expansion of Universal Jurisdiction' (2019) 30 EJIL 779.

145 ILC, Draft articles on Prevention and Punishment of Crimes Against Humanity, adopted by the International Law Commission at its seventy-first session, in 2019, at https://legal.un.org/ilc/texts/instruments/english/draft_articles/7_7_2019.pdf. See L Sadat (ed.), *Forging a Convention for Crimes against Humanity* (Cambridge: Cambridge University Press, 2011). See also G Mettraux, *International Crimes: Law and Practice, Volume II: Crimes Against Humanity* (Oxford: Oxford University Press, 2020).

146 See Draft Convention on International Cooperation in the Investigation and Prosecution of the Crime of Genocide, Crimes against Humanity, War Crimes, and other International Crimes, 30 November 2022, at file:///C:/Users/StahnC/Downloads/MLA%20Draft%20Convention%20-%20ENG%20CLEAN.pdf.

Leila Sadat reflects on the future of the ICC, drawing on a previous essay by the late ICC Judge Kaul.[147] She first traces the complex geo-political environment which the ICC faces. She argues that there is a 'sea change in US attitudes' about the ICC as a result of both, sustained advocacy within the US and the convergence of interests in the conflict with Ukraine. She shows that the Court is at the same time affected by the power configuration in the Security Council and institutional pushbacks, reflected in the fragmented jurisdiction over aggression under the Kampala compromise or the immunity provisions in the Malabo Protocol. Some assumptions have worked less well than anticipated. For instance, all three referral mechanisms have generated problems. The interpretation of the modes of liability under article 25 of the Statute, with the turn to control of the crime theory has generated significant controversy.[148] On the other hand, the Court has also seen unexpected successes. The ICC has given greater attention to peacetime enforcement of international criminal law, with consideration of post-election violence in Kenya, allegations of extrajudicial killings in the Philippines, or the allegations against the government in the Venezuela situation. The jurisprudence has provided important clarifications on the definition of armed conflict, protection of child soldiers, the treatment of sexual slavery, forced marriage and forced pregnancy or the shaping of reparations. Sadat notes that the ICC did not yet have a '*Tadić* moment', i.e. a context in which it set out the Court's jurisdiction in a comprehensive way. She makes a case for the idea of conferred, rather than delegated jurisdiction. She argues that it would helpful to denationalize the way in which Court's jurisdiction is critiqued, expand domestic implementation of mutual legal assistance and cooperation obligations or domestic laws on new crimes, and develop a more robust public outreach and media presence of the ICC to present its own side of the story. She concludes that 'we can, and should, expect the unexpected' in the next two decades.

Phoebe Okowa and Olivia Flasch address the contemporary debate about the inclusion of environmental crimes in the jurisdictional regime of the ICC.[149] They show that the idea of penalizing environmental harms has a

147 HP Kaul, 'The ICC of the Future', in Proceedings of the Sixth International Humanitarian Law Dialogs, 26–28 August 2012, Chautauqua Institution, Washington, 2013, at https://www.legal-tools.org/doc/4f7c26/pdf.

148 E van Sliedregt, 'The ICC Ntaganda Appeals Judgment: The End of Indirect Coperpetration?' *Just Security*, 14 May 2021, at https://www.justsecurity.org/76136/the-icc-ntaganda-appeals-judgment-the-end-of-indirect-co-perpetration/, J Stewart, 'The End of "Modes of Liability" for International Crimes' (2012) 25 LJIL165.

149 See M Gillett, *Prosecuting Environmental Harm before the International Criminal Court* (Cambridge: Cambridge University Press, 2022).

conflicted history. Domestic courts have largely shied away from investigating and prosecuting environmental crimes under international law. The ILC considered proposals to include willful and severe damage to the environment as a crime against the peace and security of humankind. But the idea was dropped in light of disagreement about gravity and the threshold of criminalization. In the ICC negotiations, environmental crimes were mainly treated under the umbrella of war. The chapter argues that the proposal to include ecocide as a separate category of crime into the jurisdiction would have some merits. It would allow criminalization in cases of serious and persistent environmental damage in peacetime, have a strong expressive value, and take into account the contemporary threat of environmental change and its potential source of conflict. However, ultimately the authors remain skeptical towards the feasibility of amending the Statute. They argue that the definition of ecocide, adopted by the Independent Expert Panel, might entrench and exacerbate the existing environmental and economic inequalities, since it fails to take into account the historical responsibility for existing damages. The Court's current anthropocentric focus would need to be re-oriented towards an eco-centric concept of victimhood. Additional obstacles arise in relation to the principle of legality and the application of complementarity, due to the absence of international crime prohibitions at the domestic level. On balance, Okowa and Flasch conclude that the imposition of emission targets and other standards by authorities, as well as the strengthening of existing principles and institutions for compliance, including advocacy and litigation, may offer more effective ways to address egregious environmental harm.

Former ICC President Chile Eboe-Osuji discusses a particular angle of aggression against Ukraine, namely the applicability of immunity in relation to the crime of aggression. He concedes that scholarly opinion remains divided on the subject, but defends the view that functional immunity does not bar exercise of jurisdiction over international crimes, including the crime of aggression immunity. The chapter explains the historical context and legal position developed by the ICC Appeals in the Judgment in the *Jordan Referral re Al-Bashir Appeal* which held that 'neither State practice nor opinio juris that would support the existence of Head of State immunity under customary international law vis-à-vis an international court'.[150] It argues that the ICC jurisprudence, which found that the 'absence of a rule of customary international law recognising Head of State immunity vis-à-vis international courts' also applies 'in the horizontal relationship between States',[151] is consistent with

150 See ICC, *Jordan Referral re Al-Bashir Appeal*, n 51, para. 1.
151 Ibid. para. 2.

the observations of the International Court of Justice in paragraph 61 of the *Arrest Warrant* case, according to which that 'an incumbent or former Minister for Foreign Affairs may be subject to criminal proceedings before certain international criminal courts, where they have jurisdiction'.[152] Eboe-Osuji supports the proposition that customary international law recognizes no immunity for state officials when prosecuted in foreign national courts for international crimes. He shows that the *Jordan Referral re Al-Bashir* ruling does not only have relevance for ICC proceedings in the context of Ukraine, but would also serve other international criminal tribunals, including a proposed international tribunal for the crime of aggression in Ukraine.

Astrid Reisinger Coracini examines the complex regime governing the amendment of the ICC Kampala compromise on aggression which is subject to mandatory review in 2025.[153] This issue has gained significant relevance in light of concerns regarding the selectivity and double standards of the establishment of an international or hybrid tribunal for aggression against Ukraine.[154] Treating Ukraine as an isolated case, without corresponding review of the limited ICC regime, out of fear that it might set a precedent for other cases, reinforces perceptions of hypocrisy. The chapter identifies three potential pathways to adjust the conditions for the exercise of jurisdiction over the crime of aggression. A first option is the elimination of all jurisdictional exceptions from the Court's exercise of jurisdiction over the crime of aggression. It would ensure an unrestricted application of Art 12 (2) of the Statute to the crime of aggression. The second option is a removal of exceptions linked to the non-party status of a State. It has been discussed in relation to future Ukraine scenarios,[155] but might create imbalances between non-state parties and States parties that have not accepted/ratified the Kampala amendments. The third option is the alignment of the status of a non-State party to that

152 See ICJ, *Arrest Warrant of 11 April 2000* (Democratic Republic of the Congo v Belgium) (Judgment) [2002] ICJ Rep 3, para. 61.

153 F Abken and P Rob, 'Amending the Amendment: In Search of an Adequate Procedure for a Revision of the Jurisdictional Regime for the Crime of Aggression in the Rome Statute', EJIL Talk, 13 January 2023, at https://www.ejiltalk.org/amending-the-amendment-in-search-of-an-adequate-procedure-for-a-revision-of-the-jurisdictional-regime-for-the-crime-of-aggression-in-the-rome-statute/.

154 Jennifer Trahan, 'Don't be Fooled By U.S. Smoke and Mirrors on the Crime of Aggression', *Just Security*, 14 April 2023, at https://www.justsecurity.org/85986/dont-be-fooled-by-u-s-smoke-and-mirrors-on-the-crime-of-aggression/.

155 Luis Moreno Ocampo, 'A Pragmatic Legal Approach to End Russia's Aggression', *Just Security*, 23 February 2023, https://www.justsecurity.org/85218/a-pragmatic-legal-approach-to-end-russias-aggression/.

of a Statute party that has not accepted the Kampala amendments. It would bring non-States parties within the default jurisdiction under Art 12 (2) of the Statute, while leaving them the option to opt-out. Reisinger Coracini discusses the complex problems regarding the amendment procedure in relation to the three options. She concludes that necessary support for amendments may not be realistic in the immediate future, but that it is essential to start this conversation as soon possible.

The closing chapter offers propositions to re-imagine the ICC beyond the recommendations made in the Independent Expert Review. They relate inter alia to (i) a polycentric vision of international criminal justice, (ii) a focus on structures of criminality, rather than symptoms, (iii) better engagement with existing hegemonies[156] and claims to universality, (iv) the improvement of resilience and conflict resolution strategies, and (v) greater attention to coherence, fairness and the peripheries of cases, including conceptions of punishment, release and enforcement of sentences.

## 6 To Be Continued

Where does this lead us? Many of the paradoxes that underpin the ICC will continue to persist in the future. The legitimacy of the Court is based on its distance to politics, but it will remain fundamentally dependent on states. The complex identity of the Court, and the tensions underlying it, are likely to endure. The Court not a single court, but multiple courts in one. It is first and foremost a criminal court, but also a forum to settle claims, for instance, in relation to reparation, and a governance mechanism. It will not provide 'Alice in Wonderland accountability'. Whatever the Court does will be criticized, by one or the other side ('Damned if you do, and damned if you don't'). This is not necessarily a reason for despair, but an integral part of the justice process.

However, the third decade also marks an urgent occasion for re-engagement. In an era, marked by misinformation, disinformation and parallel truths,[157] the judicial or procedural truths brought out through ICC proceedings are likely to gain even greater importance. The Court itself is a cognitive entity. It should 'put in place internal learning mechanisms and be open to considering

156 F Jessberger, L Steinl and K Mehta, *International Criminal Law – A Counter-Hegemonic Project?* (The Hague: TMC Asser Press, 2022).

157 B Kotecha and D J Birkett, 'International Criminal Justice in an "Age of Misinformation": Introduction' (2022) 20 JICJ 1.

institutional (re-)designs'.[158] A key element for the future is the continuing willingness to learn and listen and the openness to unlearn. It is essential to adopt a persuasive methodology to address the underlying tensions of the Statute in line with the goals of the Court, and to explain choices and reasons for choices in a more transparent and coherent way. In this way, even difficult choices may gain greater acceptance.

At the same time, it remains important to 'guard the guardian'. Overall, this volume is an attempt to contribute to this process. It seeks to facilitate dialogue and critical engagement, which ought to be continued.

158 See M Glasius, 'Do International Criminal Courts Require Democratic Legitimacy?' (2012) 23 EJIL 43, 65.

# PART 2

## *The ICC in Context: General Reflections*

CHAPTER 2

# Reflections on the 20th Anniversary of the International Criminal Court

*Philippe Kirsch*

## 1 Introduction*

For anything major to happen in international law—new institutions, new mechanisms, new rules—you need a special set of circumstances. One factor is the recognition by States of a need which often is brought to light by a major crisis. Another is an element of pressure which comes from States, Media and Civil Society. Yet another is a degree of harmony in interstate relations that is necessary to avoid blockage.

The creation of the ICC was no exception. The 1998 Rome Conference[1] took place in an environment where the need to repress major crimes was recognized. The tragic events that took place in the former Yugoslavia and Rwanda were on everyone's mind.

The spread of information about those crimes was unprecedented. It was also recognised that more was needed than an ever-expanding series of ad hoc tribunals.[2]

Also, at the time, a period of fruitful interstate cooperation had started, including powerful states. That did not last long but it existed for a few years. I have vivid memories of the achievements that period of collaboration made

---

* This article reproduces, with minimal edits, the keynote speech given by Philippe Kirsch at the Conference 'International Criminal Court at 20: Reflections on the Past, Present and the Future' held in The Hague on 1 July 2022.

1 United Nations Diplomatic Conference of Plenipotentiaries on the Establishment of an International Criminal Court, held in Rome from 15 June to 17 July 1998 pursuant to United Nations General Assembly Resolution A/RES/52/160 of 15 December 1997 ('Rome Conference') All States were invited to participate and a large majority of them—160 in total—did. In the evening of the last day of the Conference, the Rome Statute of the International Criminal Court was adopted with 120 States voting in favour, 7 against and 21 abstaining.

2 The United Nations International Criminal Tribunal for the former Yugoslavia (ICTY) and the United Nations International Criminal Tribunal for Rwanda (ICTR) were established by the United Nations Security Council in 1993 and 1994, respectively, through resolutions adopted under Chapter VII of the UN Charter.

 | DOI:10.1163/9789004529939_003

possible, well before the ICC, as a Canadian diplomat working in the UN environment. Long-standing international problems could finally be resolved.

An international criminal court of some kind had been contemplated long before. I will not go into that history you know well. The creation of a court was deferred time and again under legal pretexts that covered the real reason: it could not be established in a world that was subsumed in rival political blocs.

But in the 1990's, support for the creation of the Court became irresistible. Even states that, to say the least, lacked enthusiasm, knew that. Not being able to stop its creation, they rather turned to what they saw as a damage-limitation exercise.

Before turning to the Rome Conference, I would like to make a brief comment which underlies the rest of this contribution. As I mentioned, a fundamental reason for creating the ICC was to stop creating ad hoc tribunals 'a la pièce'. It would be much more practical and sensible to have one single institution able to deal with crimes committed in the future regardless of time and place.

But that sensible goal was also the major problem of the future court. The jurisdiction of the Nuremberg and Tokyo tribunals, the Security Council's ad hoc tribunals and others was strictly circumscribed. Within certain parameters, all knew and agreed who should be tried. By contrast, the ICC jurisdiction was unpredictable.

## 2 The Rome Conference and Aftermath

The Rome Conference never promised the ICC a rose garden. In fact, the Conference ensured that there would be no rose garden by multiplying what could be variably called safeguards or obstacles in the Court's operations. The Statute of the Tribunal for the Former Yugoslavia has 30 so articles, the ICC's about 130 including an exceptionally difficult amendment procedure.[3] Contrary to other tribunals where the rules of procedure were consistently left to the judges, States insisted on drafting the ICC rules themselves.[4]

3 The amendment procedure is set out in articles 121 and 122 of the Rome Statute of the International Criminal Court (signed 17 July 1998, entered into force 1 July 2002) 2187 UNTS 3 ('Rome Statute').

4 Article 51 of the Rome Statute; Resolution F, Annex I to the Final Act of the UN Diplomatic Conference of Plenipotentiaries on the Establishment of an International Criminal Court' (17 July 1998) UN Doc A/CONF.183/10, para. 5(a).

Why all that? Partly for sound reasons, to ensure fairness in proceedings. But also because States wanted to make sure that this Court's unpredictable exercise of its jurisdiction would be compensated by extraordinary predictability in its functioning.

I often asked myself if it would have been possible to design a system that would be lighter, less encumbered. In terms of adoption in Rome, it would not have been terribly difficult to achieve a different system, by calling to votes on specific issue. Majorities at the time were guaranteed for provisions ensuring considerable independence a Court enjoying.

But there would have been a high price to pay: a great court on paper without the necessary practical, balanced support from different types of states to ensure a successful future. That is why, faced with a negotiating process that was paralysed on some fundamental issues, a package eventually was presented that was deemed to represent an acceptable balance.

Yet, a vote could not be avoided in Rome. There were requests for further steps restricting the independence of the Court or tightening its jurisdiction. To give you an example, it was proposed to exempt some individuals from the Court's jurisdiction by virtue of their official position, exactly the opposite of what the creation of the Court was meant to achieve.[5] It was the view of those managing the conference that to accede to those requests would jeopardize the core of the system. Believe me, that was discussed until the last minute under tremendous pressure.

The Rome Conference then ended in relative division: enthusiasm for the majority of states, disagreement in other parts.

That is why the Preparatory Commission that took over made sustained efforts from 1999 to 2002 to attract as wide global support for the system as possible.[6] Indeed, consensus was achieved on almost everything, including

5 Ultimately, the Statute was adopted with the provision in article 27(2), according to which '[i]mmunities or special procedural rules which may attach to the official capacity of a person, whether under national or international law, shall not bar the Court from exercising its jurisdiction over such a person'.

6 The Preparatory Commission for the Establishment of an International Criminal Court was established by resolution F of the Rome Conference (Contained in Annex I of Final Act of the Rome Conference, n 4). The Preparatory Commission was tasked with developing the Court's legal subsidiary instruments—the Rules and Procedures and Evidence and the Elements of Crimes—which provide more detail to and supplement what was agreed in the Statute. Resolution F provided that the Preparatory Commission would be transitory in nature, ceasing to exist once the Assembly of States Parties completed its first meeting. More information on the work of the Preparatory Commission is available at <https://legal.un.org/icc/prepcomm/prepfra.htm> accessed 30 March 2023.

fundamental instruments such as the Rule of Procedure and Evidence of the Court[7] and the Elements of Crimes.[8]

The pace of ratifications exceeded expectations and the requisite number of 60 States joining the system was surprisingly fast, in less than four years.[9]

## 3 First Years of the Court

A few words now on the first years of the Court. Those were largely devoted to institution-building, the construction of a solid legal and administrative framework. There is no need to get into details but it was done as efficiently as possible, before investigations and judicial work picked up speed.

At the time, judicial work even at its peak did not of course compare to the massive workload the Court is managing today, but judges had a lot to learn and understand, including novel elements of the Statute. For example, for those first years, the participation of victims in proceedings, one of the major achievements of the Rome Statute, was the subject of about half the interlocutory appeals, the rest being largely devoted to admissibility of evidence.

Administration had its own challenges. Discussions in the Court's Coordination Council,[10] which consists of the Court's principals, were rather animated. The Court today, as I am told, lives in internal harmony. Well, it took a while in the first years to understand that to achieve the Court's mission, its organs needed to cooperate fully, that overlapping mandates inherent in

---

7 The finalised draft text of the Rules of Procedure and Evidence prepared by the Preparatory Commission, contained in document PCNICC/2000/1/Add.1, was adopted as such by the Assembly of States Parties at its first session, held 3–10 September 2002. Assembly of States Parties to the Rome Statute of the International Criminal Court, Official Records, ICC-ASP/1/3, 3–10 September 2002 (First Session of the ASP), para. 22 and Annex I, para. 6.

8 The finalised draft text of the Elements of Crimes prepared by the Preparatory Commission, contained in document PCNICC/2000/1/Add.2, was adopted as such by the Assembly of States Parties at its first session, held 3–10 September 2002. ICC-ASP/1/3 (n 7) para. 22 and Annex I, para. 7.

9 The deposit of the 60th ratification of the Rome Statute on 11 April 2002 triggered, in accordance with article 126(1), the treaty's entry into force on 1 July 2002.

10 Regulation 3 of the Regulations of the Court, adopted by the ICC's judges on 26 May 2004 and subsequently accepted by the Assembly, created the Coordination Council. Comprising the President on behalf of the Presidency, the Prosecutor and the Registrar, the Coordination Council is mandated to 'discuss and coordinate on, where necessary, the administrative activities of the organs of the Court'. It is the primary forum for coordination between the organs of the Court at the highest level.

the Rome system needed to be managed together without competing. I am tempted to give examples but I will not.

What I will say though is this: of course, the Rome Statute provides for some organs of the Court an independence that needs to be fully respected.[11] That is an essential part of the exercise of different judicial responsibilities. But that independence should not be synonymous with insufficient inter-organ communication. The Court is more than the sum of its parts. It cannot be fully functional if it is composed of silos living in splendid isolation.

Institution-building then in those years, yes, but not only. The Court had to find its place on the international plane and build support. That first took the form of formal agreements with the United Nations, the host state and a large number of other agreements that were necessary for its operations.[12]

That period also required extensive outreach to make the Court better known and above all better understood by states and international organisations. It is no secret that at the beginning of its existence the Court faced strong opposition. That was largely due to domestic political reasons but also to a stated apprehension that the Court might behave as a political organ. The duty of the Court was to respect its judicial mandate strictly. It did so, opposition softened and cooperation developed.

That said, it is fair to recognise that the difficulties experienced by the Court in its external relations at the time pale in comparison to those it faced later. An important reason for this is that the first situations were generated by referrals by states of their own situation, or by the Security Council.[13]

---

11 Article 40 of the Rome Statute establishes the independence of the ICC's judges. Article 42(1) of the Statute provides that the Office of the Prosecutor 'shall act independently as a separate organ of the Court'.

12 The Agreement between the International Criminal Court and the United Nations, resolution 58/318 of the United Nations General Assembly, which entered into force on 4 October 2004, provides a framework for the relationship between the two organisations, UNGA Res 58/318 (13 September 2004) UN Doc A/Res/58/318. The Headquarters Agreement between the International Criminal Court and the Host State, ICC-BD/04-01-8, entered into force on 1 March 2008. The International Criminal Court has also entered into cooperation agreements on other aspects with State Parties, such as witness relocation agreements, provided for by Rule 16(4) of the Rules of Procedure and Evidence, enforcement of sentences, which is comprehensively set out through Part X of the Rome Statute and Article 103 and Rule 200(1)(5) of the RPE, and the interim release of persons, provided for by Rule 185(1) of the Rules of Procedure and Evidence.

13 In accordance with Articles 13 of the Rome Statute, the Court's exercise of its jurisdiction can be triggered in one of three ways; a referral of a situation to the Prosecutor by a State Party; a referral of a situation to the Prosecutor by the UN Security Council; or the Prosecutor's decision to initiate an investigation *proprio motu*, out of his or her own initiative. In the latter case, the opening of the investigation must be authorised by a

Later, States that in principle supported the Court began to find flaws with it when they found themselves subject to investigations they had not initiated, or simply did not like the direction other investigations were taking. That is in the nature of the beast. The Court is bound to affect important political and economic interests. It will always generate tensions and criticisms that are not always terribly fair or accurate.

That is not to say that the ICC has made no mistakes. It does benefit from oversight and recommendations. Improvements can be made in the judicial, prosecutorial and administrative areas of the ICC's activities. I note for example that the Court is responding positively to the recent Independent Expert Review.[14] But those are reasoned recommendations aimed at achieving improvements, not attacks for political reasons.

## 4 Further Reflections

Until now, I have mainly discussed events which I witnessed myself. I would like in this final part to turn briefly to a couple of more current issues. But since I left the Court a long time ago, these are essentially reflexions for your appreciation.

A word on cooperation, the *sine qua non* of the ICC system. In the great majority of cases, States are willing to cooperate with the Court in good faith. However, a majority of cases is not sufficient. Lack of cooperation with respect

---

Pre-Trial Chamber in accordance with article 15. As of 1 September 2022, the ICC had seventeen situations under investigation. The first four investigations opened were either self-referred by the States where the alleged crimes took place or referred by the Security Council. A majority of the latter thirteen investigations were initiated *proprio motu* by the Prosecutor, or referred by a group of other States Parties than the territorial State.

14 The Assembly of States Parties, in its Resolution ICC-ASP/18/Res.7 of 6 December 2019 (Ninth Plenary Meeting of the ASP), titled 'Review of the International Criminal Court and the Rome Statute system', commissioned an Independent Expert Review 'with a view to making concrete, achievable and actionable recommendations aimed at enhancing the performance, efficiency and effectiveness of the Court and the Rome Statute system as a whole'. Nine experts were appointed to cover three clusters of issues: Governance, Judiciary, and Prosecution and Investigation. The experts submitted their final report, containing 384 recommendations, on 30 September 2020. The final report is contained in Independent Expert Review of the International Criminal Court and the Rome Statute System: Final Report—30 September 2020, ICC-ASP/19/16, 9 November 2020 (Nineteenth Session of the ASP).

to the arrest of suspects, or access to key evidence, has hampered the Court's effectiveness.[15]

That as such is not a surprise: opposition was to be expected. Many States liked the idea of a court that would target others, not thinking that their own nationals, let alone leaders, could come under scrutiny.

Disappointing, certainly, but what is more disappointing is what comes next, or rather does not. When the Court was created, it was expected that the States Parties would denounce those states that did not respect their obligations.

Institutionally at least, that has not happened. To date, the Assembly of States Parties,[16] which has a statutory obligation to consider any issue of non-cooperation, has been repeatedly prevented from providing a sufficiently strong response to cases of non-cooperation or political attacks on the Court.[17]

The concern to maintain harmonious relations between states, or to avoid turmoil in the Assembly, has trumped the objective of ensuring much needed cooperation. There are reasons for this, but it is not the way the system is supposed to work, and it certainly does not escape the attention of those who are thinking of not cooperating, or who contemplate going after the Court.

On a related point, the relative stagnation in the total number of States Parties is regrettable, as is indeed a couple of departures.[18] That reflects the current state of the rule of law on the international level, the test put on multilateralism, and other factors that are external to the Court.

---

15 Not having any enforcement powers of its own, the ICC is highly reliable on state cooperation for carrying out its activities. In accordance with Article 86 of the Rome Statute, States Parties have the general obligation to cooperate fully with the Court on matters related to its investigations and prosecutions. The legal framework underpinning the cooperation and assistance expected of the States Parties during the different phases of the Court's activities is further elaborated particularly in, although not limited to, parts 9 and 10 of the Statute.

16 Established by Article 112 of the Rome Statute, the Assembly of States Parties is the Court's management oversight and legislative body and is composed of representatives of all States Parties to the Rome Statute.

17 Pursuant to Article 112(2)(f) of the Rome Statute, the Assembly shall '[c]onsider pursuant to article 87, paragraphs 5 and 7, any question relating to non-cooperation'. A list of non-cooperation findings made by the Court can be found at <https://asp.icc-cpi.int/non-cooperation> accessed 30 March 2023.

18 The number of State Parties reached 120 on 1 February 2012. Since then, five States have ratified the Rome Statute, while two States have withdrawn from the treaty. In accordance with Article 127 (1) of the Rome Statute, the withdrawals of Burundi and the Philippines from the Rome Statute took effect on 27 October 2017 and 17 March 2019, respectively, one year after the deposit of their notices of withdrawal.

The second topic I would touch upon is the ICC's workload, and the related issue of complementarity.[19] At the Rome conference, the focus was on getting the treaty adopted and creating an institution based on sound principles. I do not think anyone understood at the time the immensity of the challenges the Court would face in the kind of situation it faces today, with 17 open situations, and investigations and cases on different continents with infinite variations.

There is evident tension between that growing workload and resources available to the Court. The ICC may prioritise between but that is no in-built pressure valve in the system that would resolve that tension.

That brings us back to the basics, the principle that international crimes must be dealt with in national courts, the ICC being a court of last resort. 20 years after the Court's creation, there remain gaps in national legislations even on key principles.[20] Another essential but highly volatile factor is political will and national commitment to law enforcement. Much like with cooperation, States' behaviour affects the actions of other States, positively and negatively.

## 5 Conclusions

Could the ICC be created today? Without a doubt, the Court is still responding to a need that is—sadly—more present than ever. Allegations of crimes under the Rome Statute are staggering, including in forms that we all believed or hoped belonged to the past. Contempt that is shown for the most basic rules of international humanitarian law, indeed for human life, is truly shocking. In this context, it is clear that certain national systems are quite unwilling or

---

19 Pursuant to the provisions of the Rome Statute, the ICC is complementary to national criminal jurisdictions, which have primacy. In accordance with Article 17 of the Statute, the Court shall determine that a case is inadmissible 'where it is being investigated or prosecuted by a State which has jurisdiction over it, unless the State is unwilling or unable genuinely to carry out the investigation or prosecution'.

20 The Preamble of the Rome Statute recalls that 'it is the duty of every State to exercise its criminal jurisdiction over those responsible for international crimes'. Taking furthermore into account the principle of complementarity discussed above, it is clear that the Statute is based on an expectation that the national jurisdictions of States should actively investigate, prosecute and adjudicate the crimes listed in the Statute. For national courts to be able to effectively fulfil that role, domestic legal provisions that incorporate the crimes in the national criminal code and implement key principles of international criminal law must be in place.

unable to ensure the repression of crimes, when they are not part themselves in their commission.

But the world has changed. Interstate relations are no longer what they used to be. The world today is more divided, more fragmented than it was in the 1990s. That is in fact an excellent reason, as 2022 marked the 20th anniversary of the entry into force of the Rome Statute, to celebrate the fact that the ICC was created when it was possible, and in a way that allowed the great majority of States to be brought into the system.

The ICC exists and will not disappear. It must continue to do its work despite resistance, with diligence and adjustments, and show that the system works. We will see where that take us in the next few years.

CHAPTER 3

# Looking Back and Looking Forward: How to Expand the Global Reach of the ICC?

*Silvia Fernández de Gurmendi*

## 1 Introduction

The International Criminal or 'ICC' was an idea seeking to become reality. The adoption of the Rome Statute on 17 July 1998 was a gigantic step forward in this direction.

Immediately after its adoption by the Rome Diplomatic Conference, a campaign was launched to promote the rapid entry into force of this founding treaty of the ICC, which was accomplished in only four years, on 1st July 2002. On that day, following the sixty required ratifications, the necessary process was put in place to set up the Court at its headquarters at The Hague, in the Netherlands.

During the two decades that followed, judges and prosecutors of the Court had the privilege and great responsibility of making operational an institution both supported and feared by different actors of the international community. In doing so, they had to face the huge expectations generated by its creation. Indeed, many states and civil society representatives expected the Court to bring about major changes to the international world order considering its powers to ensure accountability for any crime within its jurisdiction regardless of the rank or position of the perpetrators. By the time of the start of operations, the Court had become a beacon of hope and justice for all victims of atrocious crimes.

Almost inevitably, reality brought disillusion and two decades down the road, some have concluded that the Court has not lived up to its full potential.[1] Among other problems, one cannot but recognize that insufficient participation in the Rome Statute has seriously hampered the Court's ability to fulfil its main goal of promoting accountability for all serious crimes wherever

1 See Open Letter by Four Former Presidents of the ICC Assembly of States Parties, Al Hussein et al., 'The International Criminal Court needs fixing' (*Atlantic Council*, 24 April 2019) <https://www.atlanticcouncil.org/blogs/new-atlanticist/the-international-criminal-court-needs-fixing/> accessed 30 March 2023.

 | DOI:10.1163/9789004529939_004

and whomever committed. This, in turn, has left many victims behind. Indeed, despite global aspirations, the Court is not vested with universal jurisdiction and the Rome Statute, while joined by almost two-thirds of the States making up the United Nations, lacks universal participation.

Therefore, unless the Security Council refers a situation to the Prosecutor or the relevant non-states parties make an ad hoc declaration of acceptance of the Court's jurisdiction, entire situations of atrocity crimes may not be able to be addressed. This undermines not only the effectiveness of the Court but also affects its legitimacy. It is inevitable that justice rendered for some, but not for others, will be perceived as selective and will raise questions of 'double standards'. It is therefore crucial that more States join the system for the Court to be able to fulfil its ambitious mandate. Not surprisingly, enhancing the universality of the Rome Statute system is an absolute priority for the Assembly of States Parties.

How to convince others to join? While support for multilateralism and the rule of law appears to wane, accountability for atrocity crimes still attracts a great deal of support. However, this support may not necessarily translate into support for the ICC itself. For this to happen, it is necessary to be able to demonstrate the added value of the Court in advancing accountability. To do this and taking stock of the experience of the last twenty years of operations of the Court, it is important to strengthen key aspects of the Rome Statute system, in accordance with the drafters' vision.

## 2 Strengthening the Court's Architecture

### 2.1 *Stressing Complementarity*

To expand the global reach of the Court, it is never redundant to stress that the Court has not been established to compete with national systems but indeed created as an institution of last resort.

It is worth recalling that the International Tribunals for the former Yugoslavia and Rwanda established before the Court had primacy over the national jurisdictions, with the power to remove certain cases from the national sphere when they considered it to be in the interest of international justice.[2] Instead, the ICC was designed on the basis of the principle of complementarity, according to which it cannot address cases that are being or have been investigated

2 Article 9(2) of the Statute of the International Tribunal for the former Yugoslavia, UNSC Res 827 (25 May 1993) UN Doc S/RES/827, Annex; Article 8(2) of the Statute of the International Tribunal for Rwanda, UNSC Res 955 (8 November 1994) UN Doc S/RES/955, Annex.

or tried by the national justice system, unless it determines that the national action does not pursue the genuine goal of bringing those responsible to justice.[3] Thus, the Court was conceived as a 'back up' to national system, with the power to step in only in cases of inaction or non-genuine action on the part of the national systems.

The complementarity regime was the only important aspect on which agreement was reached during the preparatory negotiations for the Rome Statute, before the start of the Diplomatic Conference. During the negotiating process, the drafters defined the principle of complementarity, as well as the substantive and procedural provisions to make it operational. As said, the entire regime was substantially completed before the Rome Conference, not because it was easy but because it was indeed the central aspect of the architecture of the Court.[4] To bring the International Criminal Court project to fruition, it was essential to reconcile first two apparently contradictory goals, the goal of safeguarding national sovereignty with that of creating a strong and effective international judicial institution.

However, when the Court began its operations, the prevailing circumstances at the time showed that both objectives were not necessarily incompatible. Shortly after its establishment, the Court began its activities, not in opposition but upon the explicit request of the States concerned. In 2004, Uganda was the first State to refer situations of atrocities committed on its own territory to the Prosecutor, followed shortly after by the Democratic Republic of the Congo and the Central African Republic, and later by others. This early display of confidence by States in the Court's action surprised many as it contradicted the traditional assumption of tension between sovereignty and internationalism.

In parallel to these unforeseen events, a tendency to recognize the practical limits of internationalism had started to develop. In 2002, the Special Court for Sierra Leone was established by the government of Sierra Leone and the United Nations to prosecute not all perpetrators but only those persons bearing 'the greatest responsibility for serious violations of international humanitarian law and Sierra Leonean law' committed in the country's territory since 30 November 1996.[5] Shortly thereafter, the mandate of the International

3 Articles 1 and 17 of the Rome Statute of the International Criminal Court (signed 17 July 1998, entered into force 1 July 2002) 2187 UNTS 3 ('Rome Statute').

4 For the history of negotiations see for instance J Holmes, 'The Principle of Complementarity' in R S Lee (ed.), *The International Criminal Court: The Making of the Rome Statute* (Kluwer Law International 1999) 41.

5 Article 1(1) of the Statute of the Special Court for Sierra Leone, UNSC Res 1315 (14 August 2000) UN Doc S/RES/1315.

Tribunals for the former Yugoslavia and Rwanda was also reduced. Through amendments approved by the United Nations Security Council, completion dates were imposed for their work, in addition to the obligation to focus action on the most serious crimes, leaving the rest to national systems.[6] These changes led these Courts and Tribunals to design new strategies to promote and monitor national justice efforts, demonstrating that primacy and complementarity were not necessarily mutually exclusive concepts. In both cases, the division of labour between international and national jurisdictions was not only possible, but also desirable. In the same vein, in one of his initial documents on prosecutorial strategy, the ICC's first prosecutor also recognized that the Court, due to its global nature, could not deal with all situations or all crimes committed within the framework of a given situation and should limit its action to a few more serious cases.[7] Therefore, to reduce the impunity gap, it was necessary not only to respect but also to promote judicial action at the national level actively.[8] Progressively, complementarity ceased to be considered as a barrier to the Court's action and began to be appreciated instead as an opportunity to optimize the use of its resources and reduce impunity through joint national and international efforts. With this change in perspective, the concept of 'positive complementarity' was coined and a new debate was born—which continues to this day—on the advantages and risks of cooperating with national investigations and prosecutions, as well as on the role to be played by the Court in strengthening the capacity of States to investigate and prosecute.

As said, it is never redundant but indeed necessary to stress the complementary nature of the ICC in all cases. To attract more support, it is important to reassure States that the Court is not intended to replace the national systems or to compete with them, but rather to respect the exercise of jurisdiction by others and when necessary to contribute and cooperate with these efforts. This appears to be particularly important today as we witness a renewed interest in the exercise of national jurisdiction over international crimes, based on territorial or universal and other forms of jurisdiction. This is an important trend that must be encouraged and indeed supported by all, including by the ICC itself.

6 The three-phase plan was endorsed by the UN Security Council in UNSC Res 1503 (28 August 2003) UN Doc S/RES/1503 and UNSC Res 1534 (26 March 2004) UN Doc S/RES/1534. It envisioned completion of investigations by the end of 2004, completion of all first instance trials by the end of 2008, and completion of all work in 2010 (para. 7 of both resolutions).

7 Report on Prosecutorial Strategy, Office of the Prosecutor, 14 September 2006, para. 2(b) <https://www.icc-cpi.int/sites/default/files/ProsecutorialStrategy20060914_English.pdf> accessed 30 March 2023.

8 Ibid., para. 2(a).

### 2.2 *Delivering High Quality Justice*

When no genuine national action takes place and the Court steps in, the added value of the Court will be demonstrated first and foremost by the quality and speed of its own proceedings.

Considering growing criticism by internal and external observers regarding the length and quality of proceedings, much has been done to enhance the efficiency and effectiveness of investigations, prosecutions and the system of participation and reparations to victims, as well as to improve the overall governance of the institution.

In 2010, the Assembly of States Parties and the Court joined efforts in a so called 'lessons learned process', which aimed at harmonizing practices and speeding up procedures, through some specific amendments to the legal framework and other mechanisms to identify and consolidate best practices.[9]

Efforts to improve proceedings and enhance judicial cohesion have continued until present days. Among the most recent ones, it is worth highlighting the Chambers Practice Manual issued by the Judges to promote the uniformity of practices in key procedural areas. This constitutes a non-binding evolutionary document that reflects the agreements reached by all Judges on certain matters. Initially issued in 2015 to address the confirmation of charges and other preliminary matters, new chapters on other phases or aspects of the procedure were gradually added to the Manual, as additional agreements were reached through collective discussions.[10]

In addition to other past and current efforts, the Assembly and the Court have now embarked on a welcomed holistic review, which aims at strengthening the Court and the Rome Statute system. This review process, which was established by the Assembly during its 18th session in December 2019,[11] mandated a group of independent experts to make 'concrete, achievable and

9 The Assembly emphasized that enhancing the efficiency and effectiveness of the Court is of a 'common interest both for the Assembly [...] and the Court'. See Establishment of a study group on governance, Resolution ICC-ASP/9/Res.2, 10 December 2010 (Fifth Plenary Meeting of the ASP). In 2012 the Working Group on Lessons Learnt was established by the Court to determine whether amendments to the Rules of Procedure and Evidence were required. See Study Group on Governance: Lessons learnt: First report of the Court to the Assembly of States Parties, ICC-ASP/11/31/Add.1, 23 October 2012 (Eleventh Session of the ASP), para. 13.

10 The fifth edition of the Chambers Practice Manual of the judges of the International Criminal Court was issued on 25 March 2022 <https://www.icc-cpi.int/sites/default/files/2022-06/20220323-chambers-practice-manual-fifth-edition-eng_2.pdf> accessed 30 March 2023.

11 Review of the International Criminal Court and the Rome Statute System, ICC-ASP/18/Res.7, 6 December 2019 (Ninth Plenary Meeting of the ASP).

actionable recommendations aimed at enhancing the performance, efficiency and effectiveness of the Court and the Rome Statute system as a whole, [...] and submit those to the Assembly and the Court for consideration'.[12]

On 30 September 2020, the independent experts issued a comprehensive final report (the 'IER' Report) containing an extensive analysis of the work and functioning of the Court, which included 384 short and long-term recommendations addressed to the Court and States Parties.[13] On 18 December 2020, during its 19th session, the Assembly adopted the Resolution on the Review of the International Criminal Court and the Rome Statute system,[14] which established a 'Review Mechanism' mandated to follow up on the IER Report. Currently the Mechanism is coordinating the assessment and implementation process of the IER recommendations together with States Parties, the Court and civil society.

These efforts undertaken over the past decade are indeed essential to improve the system and, ultimately, to promote universal recognition of the important role of the Court in the global fight against impunity.

### 2.3 *Enhancing the Victim's Participation and Reparations Regime*

The victim participation and reparation system are, without a doubt, one of the most innovative elements of the Rome Statute. This system incorporated for the first time in the field of international criminal justice elements of reparative justice by which victims are given access to participate in the procedure to formulate their observations and concerns, and to request reparation for the damage suffered. These elements, inspired by civil law, and highly controversial during the negotiations of the Statute, are today an integral part of international criminal justice. There is growing recognition of the crucial importance of a victim-centred approach to justice, to provide victims with a comprehensive remedy for the harm suffered, maximize the impact of criminal justice within the communities directly affected by atrocities, and ensure greater contribution of justice to peace and reconciliation. After their introduction for the ICC, the legal systems of the Extraordinary Chambers of the Courts of Cambodia, the Special Tribunal for Lebanon and the Specialized

12 Ibid., para. 6.

13 Independent Expert Review of the International Criminal Court and the Rome Statute System: Final Report—30 September 2020, ICC-ASP/19/16, 9 November 2020 (Nineteenth Session of the ASP).

14 Review of the International Criminal Court and the Rome Statute System, ICC-ASP/19/Res.7, 18 December 2020 (Fifth Plenary Meeting of the ASP).

Chambers of Kosovo also recognized a new dimension for the victims of the crimes committed.

In practice, victims' access to international justice entails multiple legal and operational challenges, due to the massive nature of international crimes and the fact that proceedings generally take place thousands of kilometres away from the communities directly affected. To deal with them adequately, the Court needed to find suitable mechanisms to provide the victims sufficient information about the proceedings in progress; to process thousands of requests to participate; and to ensure genuine representation systems for participating victims. Likewise, it needed to decide on modalities of participation compatible with the defendant's right to a fair and expeditious trial. Given the difficulties, the significant progress made by the Court in the effective implementation of the system throughout twenty years of operations should be appreciated. Such progress was achieved thanks to various initiatives, including by designing more effective communication strategies to reach the largest possible number of victims and putting in place tools to simplify the administration of victims' requests to participate. The Judges also contributed to such progress by clarifying aspects related to the legal representation of victims and modalities of participation in the various phases of the procedure, all of which are very important aspects for the credibility and legitimacy of the system.

After issuing the first final judgements, the Court also had to find satisfactory solutions to ensure effective reparations. In contrast to other issues, in these matters the drafters of the Statute delegated to the Court itself the task of establishing the applicable principles, as well as the power to directly issue a reparation decision against a convicted person or to order, when appropriate, that it be paid through the Trust Fund for the benefit of victims provided by the Statute.[15] The Fund, which functions as an autonomous subsidiary body of the Assembly of States Parties, is funded by voluntary contributions and other assets and sums received from the Court as fines or confiscations. After twenty years of operations in fulfilment of its mandate, the Fund has acquired crucial importance in providing effective reparations to victims, even beyond what was originally envisaged. Indeed, given the situation of indigence declared by those convicted by the Court, the Fund has become the main source of financing for Court ordered reparations as well as assistance projects, which increases the pressure on the Assembly of States Parties to increase their voluntary contributions to the Fund.

15 See Article 75 of the Rome Statute.

In fact, in this and other areas of the system, the first twenty years of the International Criminal Court have clearly demonstrated that the institution's future efficiency and effectiveness will increasingly require the joint efforts of the Court and States.

## 3 Strengthening Inclusiveness

The Court was created through an inclusive negotiating process that allowed and indeed encouraged the participation of all States and civil society organisations. States, during the negotiations, avoided the North-South divide and sought instead to find cross regional agreements on central issues and shared values.

At the time of the negotiations, like minded States worked in partnership with civil society to promote the creation of the Court and its current architecture, and this partnership continues until this day. There was then and continues today a persistent effort to design the applicable system based on broad agreements among all participants.

It is crucial to continue to reach broad agreements through inclusive and transparent dialogue among all stakeholders—the Court, States, and civil society—to strengthen, improve or amend such system. This is indeed the approach to the Review process that is currently underway.

As part of this quest for inclusiveness, it is worth recalling that the drafters emphasized the importance of diversity in the composition of the Court and the legal system itself.

### 3.1 *Respect for Diversity in the Composition of the Court*

The Rome Statute includes explicit obligations for States to consider in the election of Judges. These include the need to ensure adequate representation of the principal legal systems of the world, equitable geographic representation, and a fair representation of female and male judges.[16] This adequate representation within the Judiciary is essential but not sufficient. The appointment of other elected officials as well as the recruitment of staff must also ensure adequate representation of systems, regions, and gender.[17]

16 Article 36 8(a)(i), (ii), and (iii) of the Rome Statute.

17 The Assembly of States Parties emphasized 'the importance of equitable geographical representation and gender balance in the organs of the Court and, as appropriate, in the work of the Assembly and its subsidiary bodies' in Strengthening the International Criminal Court and the Assembly of States Parties, ICC-ASP/20/Res.5, 9 December 2021

While the Court makes efforts in this regard, States and civil society could also assist in the search for good candidates for elected and staff positions at the Court, for instance by disseminating all relevant information, including vacancy announcements, as much as possible, within the relevant agencies and sectors of their society. In 2023 there will be an important election of six new judges in which all States Parties and civil society have an important role to play to promote the best candidates for the position, considering the need to respect diversity in all fronts.

### 3.2 *The Rome Statute—a Hybrid Legal System*

Since the beginning of its operation and during the two subsequent decades, the Court has had to respond to numerous and varied questions raised in the application of its unprecedented legal regime. For two decades, the Judges have had the difficult task of interpreting innovative and sometimes ambiguous provisions to apply effectively this unique institutional framework.

The ICC system, different from the one applied by the International Tribunals for the former Yugoslavia and Rwanda, was specifically designed for the Court to avoid favouring any national system. To achieve this, states developed a hybrid regime that combines elements of the main legal traditions of the world. All states were invited to participate in the negotiations and many of them indeed contributed to the elaboration of this regime. As part of this quest for inclusiveness, negotiators had the underlying concern of ensuring sufficient representation of all legal systems. The drafters thought that, by definition, a universal system could not be attached to a particular legal system or set of values but represent them all in a hybrid system, which is the one governing the Court today.

Amendments to improve the legal framework may be needed and indeed some of the amendments already made to the Rules of Procedure and Evidence have had a tangible positive impact on the proceedings.[18] However, all those involved in new initiatives should seek to preserve the general balance of the system as conceived in the negotiations by the drafters. Preserving the balance

---

(Eighth Plenary Meeting), Preamble. The Assembly in the same resolution also 'welcome[d] the Court-wide, Office of the Prosecutor and Registry Strategic Plans for 2019–2021 and their three-year programme of action to improve the geographical representation and gender balance as one of the Court's priorities', para. 129.

18 See for example Amendments to the rules of procedure introduced by Resolution ICC-ASP/10/Res.1, 20 December 2011 (Seventh Plenary Meeting of the ASP), Resolution ICC-ASP/11/Res.2, 21 November 2012 (Eighth Plenary Meeting of the ASP), ICC-ASP/12/Res.7, 27 November 2013 (Twelfth Plenary Meeting of the ASP), and Resolution ICC-ASP/15/Res.4, 24 November 2016 (Tenth Plenary Meeting of the ASP).

between systems of the world continues to be key to advance the cause of universality.

## 4 Conclusion

Expanding the universality of the Court is vital to its effectiveness and legitimacy. Today the world needs justice more than ever. The tragic circumstances that currently surround us in various parts of the world demonstrate, once again, that no society is immune to violence and crime. The atrocities of the twentieth century, which led the international community to create the International Criminal Court and other international or mixed courts, have not subsided. In our century, the civilian population continues to be the main victim of the wars and conflicts that devastate several continents. We are also witnessing a growing disbelief in the ability of multilateral institutions to resolve conflicts, overcome fragmentation and help build cooperative relationships.

In this unfavourable context, there is, however, room for hope. Despite the current weakening of institutions and the rule of law, the international community has not only maintained, but has intensified its demand for justice and multiplied initiatives to carry it out. As evidenced by its first twenty years of activities, the International Criminal Court is making progress in fulfilling its mandate and redoubling its efforts to revitalize and improve its performance. At the same time, states more frequently assume their obligation to investigate and prosecute at the national level, based on territorial or universal jurisdiction. Likewise, while the work of other international or mixed courts continues, new mechanisms are created to ensure the collection and preservation of evidence—such as those created for Syria and Myanmar—to help the investigation and prosecution by competent national or international jurisdictions.

We are thus witnessing the emergence of a global system of justice, within which international and national courts have a role to play, sometimes a central role, sometimes a complementary or supporting role. As the twenty eminent jurists who participate in this publication demonstrate, the International Criminal Court, based on the system of complementarity, can effectively play each and every one of these roles. Given what has already been accomplished in its first two decades of its existence, it can be affirmed that the ICC has the potential to contribute significantly to the consolidation of this justice system in the decades to come.

There is no magic formula to attract more States to the system, only the need for hard work and persistent efforts—by the Court, the States, and civil society—to ensure that high quality justice is done, and that the principles of inclusion and respect for diversity are truly upheld and respected.

CHAPTER 4

# Reparations: a Critical Aspect of Justice at the ICC

*Minerva Tavárez Mirabal*

## 1 Introduction

My mother, two of my aunts, my father, and thousands of men and women of three generations were assassinated in the Dominican Republic under the orders of the dictator Rafael Trujillo and those who governed after him. These were crimes against humanity. This tragedy, which marked my life and my country, has committed me to work for future generations to ensure that the rule of law governs our lives as a civilisation.

I have sought to undertake my fight with 'stubborn optimism',[1] a term used very often by a dear friend, the late Felipe Michelini, former Chair of the Board of Directors of the Trust Fund for Victims (TFV) at the International Criminal Court (ICC). I use this term because it is a shared characteristic of many of the people I have met and worked with in the context of human rights.

In my country, which gave the Rome Statute of the International Criminal Court[2] (Rome Statute) its 99th ratification, as in many of the 123 where I witnessed, up close, the efforts for ratification, it was the stubborn optimism from victims and activists that drove discussions across party lines to define what we wanted the future of our countries, and the world as a whole, to look like. It is simple: a world governed by the rule of law, of never again. *NuncaJamás!*

It is, thus, important to recall that while diplomats and lawyers drafted the Rome Statute, the ink of their pens is made of the dreams and pain, optimism and stubbornness of victims.

For these reasons, it is an honour, and an obligation, to write these words with these victims in mind:

> The victims of the past, those whose optimistic stubbornness drove the international community to ensure the adoption of the Rome Statute. These include countless survivors of the Second World War and the

1 F Michelini, 'Why international justice is stubbornly optimistic', *Buenos Aires Times* (30 November 2017) <https://www.batimes.com.ar/news/opinion-and-analysis/why-international-justice-is-stubbornly-optimistic.phtml> accessed 4 October 2022.

2 Rome Statute of the International Criminal Court (signed 17 July 1998, entered into force 1 July 2002) 2187 UNTS 3 ('Rome Statute').

 | DOI:10.1163/9789004529939_005

Holocaust from Eastern and Western Europe, including Madame Simone Veil, the first Chairperson of the Board of Directors of the Trust Fund for Victims, and other victims from all regions of the world;

The victims of the not-so-distant past, those who have suffered even after the Rome Statute was ratified and adopted, in each and every country that is today an ICC situation country;

The victims in each and every country that should be a situation before the Court but that is not yet recognised as such;

The victims of the future, a certainly tragic one, as growing corners of our world turn increasingly armed, unequal and authoritarian.

When parliaments around the globe, those elected by the people, ratified the Rome Statute, they accepted, applauded, and welcomed every single, complex dimension of this founding document. They accepted the four core crimes, including the crime of aggression; they committed to support the independence of the Prosecutor and of the judges; they applauded victim participation, and they welcomed the establishment of the Trust Fund for Victims, which I am honoured to chair since December 2021.

It has always been, and remains, upon us, international bureaucrats, to make those defining features of the Rome Statute a reality. To set up the Court, many challenges and impossibilities have been overcome: securing cooperation, upholding the principle of no impunity, defining the crime of aggression, protecting witnesses. These issues are as politically, financially and operationally complex as the goals of victim participation and victims' reparations. This complexity is even greater considering that victims are hundreds of thousands and the convicted are indigent.

Therefore, there is no space for compromise or abandonment. Victim participation and victims' reparations are rights, and are essential features of the Rome Statute. They cannot be questioned, brushed over or neglected. It is our responsibility to see that the right to reparations is realised.

## 2 The Trust Fund for Victim's Reparative Mandate

The Trust Fund for Victims is a Rome Statute body, created by the Assembly of States Parties pursuant to Article 79.[3] Together with Article 75 and Rule 98 of the Rules of Procedure and Evidence, these provisions form the Trust Fund's

3 Rome Statute, Article 79(1).

legal basis within the ICC framework, and elucidate the Trust Fund's mandate to ensure that the financial means of the convicted person be made available to the victims of the convicted persons' crimes to repair their harm,[4] and that 'other resources' of the Trust Fund be made available for the benefit of victims within the jurisdiction of the Court.[5] Accordingly, the TFV has a reparative mandate, to design and fund transformative reparations for and with victims of Rome Statute crimes through TFV programmes in relation to Court cases and ICC situation countries.

The criteria for the management of the Trust Fund were created by the ASP through various resolutions pursuant to Article 79(3) of the Statute, and in particular by establishing the Regulations of the Trust Fund (TFV Regulations) adopted in 2005.[6] The TFV Regulations provide for two ways in which the 'other resources' can be utilised: (i) to 'complement' the payment of the award for reparations of the convicted person ordered by the Court against that person, pursuant to Article 75 of the Statute;[7] and, (ii) to provide physical or psychological rehabilitation or material support for the benefit of victims of crimes within the jurisdiction of the Court, and their families.[8]

## 3 Developments to Date

Since its first Order for Reparations in the *Lubanga* case, issued in 2012,[9] and amended on appeal in 2015,[10] the Court has awarded reparations to victims in each and every case resulting in conviction for Rome Statute crimes and confirmed on appeal. In all four cases, the ICC ordered reparations *through*

4 Rome Statute, Article 75; Rules of Procedure and Evidence of the International Criminal Court, PCNICC/2000/1/Add.1, adopted 9 September 2002 by the ASP, ICC-ASP/1/3, 3–10 September 2002 (First Session of the ASP), Rule 98 (1) and (4) ('Rules of Procedure and Evidence').

5 Rules of Procedure and Evidence, Rule 98 (5).

6 Regulations of the Trust Fund for Victims, Resolution ICC-ASP/4/Res.3, 3 December 2005 (Fourth Plenary Meeting of the ASP), Regulation 56 ('TFV Regulations').

7 TFV Regulations, Regulation 56.

8 TFV Regulations, Regulation 50(a).

9 Decision establishing the principles and procedures to be applied to reparations, *Lubanga, Situation in the Democratic Republic of the Congo*, ICC-01/04-01/06-2904, TC I, ICC, 7 August 2012.

10 Judgment on the appeals against the 'Decision establishing the principles and procedures to be applied to reparations' of 7 August 2012 with AMENDED order for reparations (Annex A) and public annexes 1 and 2, *Lubanga, Situation in the Democratic Republic of the Congo*, ICC-01/04-01/06-3129, AC, ICC, 3 March 2015.

the Trust Fund.[11] At the time of writing, a fifth—the *Ongwen* case—is in the judicial reparations phase of proceedings, shortly after the conviction and sentence were confirmed on appeal. In order of value, the convicted persons were respectively ordered to award reparations of USD 1 million (*Katanga*),[12] EUR 2.7 million (*Al Mahdi*),[13] USD 10 million (*Lubanga*),[14] and USD 30 million (*Ntaganda*).[15]

The implementation of reparations in the case of *Katanga* and the implementation of individual and symbolic awards in *Al Mahdi* are approaching a close, while the implementation of collective reparations in *Lubanga* and *Al Mahdi* started in 2021 on the basis of multi-annual programmes with constantly increasing numbers of victims receiving reparations.

Today, in mid-2022, there are around 900 beneficiaries in Ituri Province, Democratic Republic of the Congo (DRC) and around 800 beneficiaries in Mali who received compensation or rehabilitation measures either through seven of the Trust Fund's implementing partners or the Trust Fund itself.

In ICC situation countries, the Trust Fund implements programmes in Uganda and the DRC since 2008, and since 2020 in the Central African Republic and Côte d'Ivoire. In 2021 alone, TFV programmes have benefitted around 17,000 victims, including many survivors of conflict-related sexual violence. The Trust Fund's programmes outside of court-ordered reparations have laid the ground for Court-ordered reparations programmes and may achieve support among victims for the work of the ICC even in situations where accused persons were acquitted or arrests cannot easily be achieved.

## 4 Lessons Learnt

To implement transformative reparations, the TFV has built its competence in ensuring participatory, harm-based and victim-centred programmes for victims of Rome Statute crimes. Centring these approaches in reparations design,

11 Rules of Procedure and Evidence, Rule 98 (3).

12 Order for Reparations pursuant to Article 75 of the Statute, *Katanga, Situation in the Democratic Republic of the Congo*, ICC-01/04-01/07-3728-tENG, TC II, ICC, 24 March 2017.

13 Reparations Order, *Al Faqi Al Mahdi, Situation in the Republic of Mali*, ICC-01/12-01/15-236, TC VIII, ICC, 17 August 2017.

14 Corrected version of the 'Decision Setting the Size of the Reparations Award for which Thomas Lubanga Dyilo is Liable', *Lubanga, Situation in the Democratic Republic of the Congo*, ICC-01/04-01/06-3379-Red-Corr-tENG, TC II, ICC, 21 December 2017.

15 Reparations Order, *Ntaganda, Situation in the Democratic Republic of the Congo*, ICC-01/04-02/06-2659, TC VI, ICC, 8 March 2021, reversed on appeal in September 2022.

implementation and programming safeguards victims' agency in accessing reparations as well as their involvement in every stage of the process.

We have come to learn that it is of utmost importance to manage victims' expectations from very early on in the proceedings. This is especially important in the context of the Rome Statute framework, and it must not be forgotten that many applicants of reparations have been waiting many years for justice, amidst the instability of ongoing conflict, public health emergency, and climate collapse. The time that has elapsed since the commission of the crimes, compounded by the volatility of displacement, as well as repeat human rights violations, increases the likelihood that the reparations ultimately do not correspond with what individuals had hoped to access years ago.

It is, thus, more important than ever that the TFV is efficient to ensure that harm is redressed as far as possible. At the same time, other lessons that have been learnt over the years include the need to plan within sufficient time to bond with community members and build trust in the reparation process; detailed explanations of the methods and means by which victims can participate in the consultative process and the confines of the eligibility assessments to access programmes; and, working across multidisciplinary teams to harmonise methodologies in the design of reparation measures, all while remaining as efficient as is feasible.

## 5 So Much to Be Done

Evidently, there has been important progress, but it is certainly not enough. As per Regulation 56 of the TFV Regulations, the Board of Directors shall 'determine whether to complement the resources collected through awards for reparations with "other resources of the Trust Fund"' and 'make all reasonable endeavours to manage the Fund taking into consideration the need to provide adequate resources to complement payments for awards [...] taking particular account of ongoing legal proceedings that may give rise to such awards'.[16] The Board of Directors is seized and active in addressing the challenges, but requires support.

First, there is the issue of need. Orders for Reparations to date have a value of nearly EUR 38 million. Yet, at the time of writing, the Trust Fund has received only EUR 330,000 from fines, proceeds from forfeiture or reparation payments. Reparations are therefore funded through voluntary contributions by States

16 TFV Regulations, Regulation 56.

Parties. To date, thanks to these contributions, the Trust Fund has been able to fully complement the payments of reparations in the case of *Katanga* and will be able to complement it in the case of *Al Mahdi*, but there is still a funding gap.

The Trust Fund belongs to all States Parties, and all contribute to its staff and core operations through their assessed contributions to the Court, given the TFV Secretariat's budget is approved by the Assembly of States Parties. However, only an average of EUR 2.63 million per year in the past 15 years has been received through voluntary contributions from States, an amount close to the cost of running the Secretariat. This situation must be addressed with urgency, and the Board of Directors has taken it as central to its revitalisation strategy.

The priority for the Trust Fund is, and will remain, to raise considerably more funds. Private donors must be pursued, and will be pursued as a matter of priority for the Board. The Trust Fund will continue considering donations by States Parties. However, only 50 of 123 States Parties have contributed to the Trust Fund, and only 14 of them have contributed more than 10 times in 18 years. Contributions need to come from all States Parties, more regularly, and in higher amounts to match the needs, value and commitment of the Assembly and its States Parties to victims' rights.

One of the biggest criticisms of the Trust Fund has been the time it has taken to initiate its programmes. There are at least two reasons for this: one is the need to develop operational pathways for the Trust Fund to engage with victims, conduct procurement in light of due diligence requirements, administration and payments, evaluations, financial control, all required by the multiple donors. The other reason is the obvious learning curve in setting up an entity like the Trust Fund, with its uniquely reparative mandate, large and diverse beneficiary populations, and varied activities.

After twenty years, there is still so much to do.

The Trust Fund must enhance its participatory, community-based, victim-centred, and gender-responsive implementation of holistic reparative measures. The Trust Fund must also administratively deliver reparations as efficiently as possible, ensuring that most of every euro reaches the victims. Rehabilitation remains central but so too are other forms of reparation.

The Trust Fund needs to work conceptually, programmatically and operationally in a way which is as integrated with the Court as possible. The Court and the Trust Fund are both, after all, an integral part of the Rome Statute's reparative justice pillar, and the TFV is ultimately embedded in the Court's administrative structure. What does this mean? At the conceptual level, the reparative measures to be implemented should contribute and must be understood by victims to be delivered as part of an integral set of rights enshrined in the Rome Statute. In terms of operational synergies, there has been a lot of progress in this regard, thanks to the Registrar and the Registry. Continued work is ongoing to strengthen this collaboration.

Finally, the Trust Fund must do better in communicating progress and results, to allow further engagement and involvement of the States Parties and civil society to ask questions, and to compel us to results. The Report of the Independent Expert Review has made clear findings. The Board of Directors has committed to take specific actions to address the findings, and to enable the Trust Fund to be in a position to face the challenges ahead: additional ICC situations, with more cases and greater victim populations.

## 6 To Conclude

In 2017, Felipe Michelini offered a reflection that remains valid today:[17]

> Despite the progress made, there is still a lot to do. Strengthening preventative measures so that these serious acts that threaten the dignity of the victims do not occur is an ongoing concern. It is necessary that states take action in a timely manner when investigating and punishing crimes of great severity. Victims must also be provided with reparations that grant them dignity as individuals.
>
> Continuing to work on the three factors of the Rome Statute—prevention, punishment and reparation—is an ethical, legal and political imperative for the entire international community.

We made the Court a reality. Now, we will ensure, with stubborn optimism and with the help of the Court, its States Parties and Civil Society, to fully realise victims' right to reparations, as enshrined in the Rome Statute.

17 See Michelini (n 1).

CHAPTER 5

# The International Criminal Court at 20: the Role of Civil Society

*Elizabeth Evenson*

## 1 Civil Society in the Rome Statute System*

For 27 years, the Coalition for the International Criminal Court (the Coalition) has joined together non-governmental organizations from the grassroots to the global level to champion justice for victims of serious international crimes. The Coalition, supported by a secretariat, is the world's largest partnership advancing the cause of international justice.[1] With member organizations across the globe, the Coalition is leading the fight to end Rome Statute crimes through a commitment to the core values of human rights and justice. The Coalition works to promote a fair, effective, independent, and universal International Criminal Court (ICC) and accountability and redress for victims through the Rome Statute system.

Together, the Coalition campaigned first for an International Criminal Court. And then, fittingly, given that this commemoration marks 20 years since the Rome Statute's entry into force, for the ratifications that would make the court a reality. A universal court remains an absolutely key goal to extend the reach of justice, not only before this ICC, but also to ensure national authorities play their primary role in responding to the rights of victims and affected communities to access justice. Many of the Coalition's member organizations around the world continue their advocacy to this day for ratification and the implementation of the Rome Statute into national law. The success of those campaigns has depended on civil society determination and creativity, but also partnership with government actors, like parliamentarians, or other states that

---

* This contribution was prepared during the time the author served as the director of the Coalition for the International Criminal Court Secretariat (January–July 2022). The piece represents the views of the author and not those of the Coalition for the International Criminal Court or Human Rights Watch position.

1 For more information follow the Coalition on twitter @ngos4justice or online at <www.coalitionfortheicc.org> accessed 30 April 2023.

 | DOI:10.1163/9789004529939_006

can use their influence to encourage ratification and implementation.[2] In this the court's Assembly of States Parties, as well as the ICC presidency, remain key partners. The Assembly has continued to maintain a focus on universality through the annual appointment of facilitators, currently the governments of The Netherlands and the Republic of Korea.[3]

Indeed, that unique partnership—with states, but also with ICC officials—is a theme that runs across the myriad roles played by civil society in the Rome Statute system. Beyond campaigning for universality, there is a nearly endless list of roles played by civil society in the Rome Statute system. These roles are relevant to national accountability efforts and also the court's own work.

The Coalition's member organizations and other partners in civil society report on and document human rights violations, bringing them to the world's attention and the attention of the court to create the impetus for justice. They do this often in the most difficult circumstances imaginable and at personal risk.

Civil society organizations support victims directly to access their rights of participation and to reparation, and to make representations in article 15 proceedings regarding the authorization of proprio motu investigations. Civil society organizations monitor fair trial rights and the development of jurisprudence. They work to raise awareness and to make justice visible, at times in direct partnership with the court's outreach unit and country offices. Critically, NGOs lend a lived experience and policy expertise to the development of court practice.

Experience has demonstrated that the ICC's investigations must be conducted by the Office of the Prosecutor.[4] At the same time, strong relationships

---

2 'ICC 20th Anniversary with the Coalition for the International Criminal Court' (*Asymmetrical Haircuts* podcast, 30 June 2022) <www.asymmetricalhaircuts.com/episodes/icc-20th-anniversary-with-the-coalition-for-the-international-criminal-court/> accessed 22 October 2022.

3 See, for example, Report of the Bureau on the Plan of Action of the Assembly of States Parties for achieving universality and full implementation of the Rome Statute of the International Criminal Court, ICC-ASP/20/17, 30 November 2021 (Twentieth Session of the ASP).

4 See C De Vos, 'Prosecutor v. Lubanga "Someone who comes between one person and another": Lubanga, Local Cooperation, and the Right to a Fair Trial' (2011) 12(1) *Melbourne Journal of International Law* 217; Independent Expert Review of the International Criminal Court and the Rome Statute System: Final Report—30 September 2020, ICC-ASP/19/16, 9 November 2020 (Nineteenth Session of the ASP), paras 777–84; OTP, 'ICC OTP Kenya Cases: Review and Recommendations: Executive Summary of the Report of the External Independent Experts', Annex I Full Statement of the Prosecutor, Fatou Bensouda, on external expert review and lessons drawn from the Kenya situation (November 26, 2019), paras E17–E18. The Office of the Prosecutor, together with Eurojust and the EU Network for investigation and prosecution of genocide, crimes against humanity, and war crimes, released in 2022 a set of guidelines aimed at increasing the usability of human rights violations documentation

with civil society are needed to create conducive circumstances for those investigations to take place through promoting awareness of the court's role within affected communities, and advocating for full cooperation with the court and investigations, including those conducted by the defense. Globally, civil society campaigns to stimulate the political will to support the Court across its work and to defend it against threats to that work.

There is the what civil society does, but there is also a why.

One part of this is a practical dimension. The court is a single institution working at this writing across 17 situations under investigation, gradually extending to all regions of the world. It will often enter a situation in which civil society groups have been working for many years to address impunity. Civil society is there—with critical expertise on violations taking place, on the state of national judicial proceedings, and with trusted relationships among victims and in affected communities.

This expertise has a particular role to play during the period of the Office of the Prosecutor's preliminary examinations. Preliminary examinations are carried out by the Office to determine whether Rome Statute criteria to open a formal investigation are met. The Office's practice on preliminary examinations has evolved over the first 20 years of the court's existence, from a period in which there was little public information available about these examinations to increasingly detailed annual reporting across the examinations to what appears to be now a preference to revert to more limited annual reporting across the work of the Office as a whole.[5]

The increased transparency of the Office's preliminary examinations facilitated civil society engagement with these examinations, which are often the subject of article 15 communications. This transparency allows civil society organizations to get a sense of where the gaps may be in information available to the Office, and to then seek to fill those gaps through public reporting or additional article 15 communications. This can be relevant to the Office's

---

by non-governmental organizations in criminal proceedings, should organizations choose to find this falls within their independent mandates. The guidelines acknowledge, however, 'civil society organisations cannot replace or substitute the actions of competent investigative authorities mandated to enforce the law.' Office of the Prosecutor, International Criminal Court (ICC), Eurojust, and the EU Network for investigation and prosecution of genocide, crimes against humanity, and war crimes, *Documenting international crimes and human rights violations for accountability purposes: Guidelines for civil society organisations* (September 2022), 6.

5 Compare ICC OTP, 'Report on Preliminary Examination Activities 2020' (14 December 2020) with ICC OTP, 'Towards a more just world every day: Annual report of the Office of the Prosecutor' (1 December 2022).

assessment of whether to act to open the court's own investigations (or seek to act, where judicial authorization is required), but it is also relevant to what the Office, at least in the past, has also articulated a secondary, policy goal: using its engagement with national authorities during preliminary examinations to seek to catalyze national proceedings that may limit the need for the ICC to act as a court of last resort.[6] This policy goal has been applied in only a limited number of situations, and has been queried by states parties and the Assembly-commissioned Independent Expert Review.[7] To the extent the Office decides to continue to aim at this policy goal, information from civil society groups can provide critical information to complement that received from national authorities which may tell only a partial story as to the state of national proceedings.

Civil society has urged the court to come closer to affected communities—to have more robust presences in countries where it conducts preliminary examinations and investigations, and to develop its own expertise.[8] In fact, it is fair to say that civil society organizations have felt that too much is asked of them. In light of the court's limited resources, there can be a sense that civil society is expected to carry the work of the court. Those are issues that should be addressed by the court going forward, but the fact is that civil society is there, and will always be there, and will have lived experience to contribute to making the court's work truly meaningful in affected communities.

But beyond practicalities, there's also though an important principle at stake. How does the court establish its legitimacy? This is a question for any court in any system, but perhaps a particularly profound question for a criminal court operating as an international tribunal.[9] Legitimacy is a product of the legal framework, the ratification of governments, and the embedding of the statute into national law. But the ICC also needs to earn that legitimacy in the eyes of the people it serves, ultimately the heterogenous communities affected by the crimes tried before it. Civil society confidence in the court and

6 ICC OTP, 'Policy Paper on Preliminary Examinations' (November 2013), paras 100–103 ('Ending Impunity through Positive Complementarity').

7 See, Independent Expert Review of the International Criminal Court and the Rome Statute System, Final Report 30 September 2020 (n 4) paras.721–736. The Independent Expert Review is discussed further below.

8 See, for example, International Federation of Human Rights and Kenya Human Rights Commission, 'The victims' mandate of the International Criminal Court: disappointments, concerns and options for the way forward: Observations and recommendations for the Independent Expert Review' (June 2020), 23–26.

9 See M M deGuzman, 'Choosing to Prosecute: Expressive Selection at the International Criminal Court' (2012) 33(2) *Michigan Journal of International Law* 265.

in states parties to live up to their commitments is an important element of this legitimacy, and requires then robust civil space within court and states parties processes.

## 2 Pressing for an Effective, Independent, and Fair ICC: Looking Back and Looking Ahead

Civil society has an essential advocacy role to play to press court officials and states parties, including within the Assembly of States Parties's framework, toward the common aim of an effective, independent, and fair ICC.

The ICC's effectiveness depends equally on decisions made by court officials, on the one hand, and, on the other hand, on decisions made by states (often, although not exclusively, its states parties). This means civil society advocacy spans both court officials and representatives of states.

With ICC officials, these are officials of an independent judicial institution. Civil society actors recognize that there are clear boundaries to out-of-court advocacy. And when it comes to states parties, civil society actors are careful not to encourage them to overstep their boundaries in exercising management oversight of the administration of the ICC, a judicial, rather than political, institution. In fact, civil society often does just the opposite: pressing states to take political decisions that support and affirm that independence.

Sometimes it can be difficult to navigate these various boundaries, but it is important to do so. Results can be achieved that respect the various roles each actor—civil society, court officials, and states parties—have to play. Two examples from the past suggest the importance of equivalent work today.

When one looks back to the start of the ICC's outreach activities—that is, its efforts to provide public information to affected communities—that was really the product of states parties, on the back of NGO advocacy and drawing lessons learned from the ad hoc tribunals, and the International Criminal Tribunal for the former Yugoslavia, in particular, as well as the Special Court for Sierra Leone, taking a real interest in the importance of justice not only being done but being seen to be done. States parties then urged the court and, critically, agreed to provide funding for the court to start up its outreach unit.[10]

Looking to today, there is once again the need for a renewed partnership to ensure the court has the resources it needs across all of its work.

---

10 Human Rights Watch, 'Courting History: The Landmark International Criminal Court's First Years' (2008), 118–21.

In 2022, there was an enthusiastic response by many states parties to the prosecutor's call for voluntary contributions of both human and financial resources.[11] This response was a positive show of support for the court's mandate. At the same time, however, the resort to voluntary contributions confirms the chronic underfunding of the court. It has been clear for many years that the court does not have the resources it needs to meet the legitimate expectations placed upon it.[12] This has without a doubt affected victims' access to justice and served as an excuse for underperformance by the court.

While the need for resources is real, the prosecutor's call for voluntary contributions took place in the context of unprecedented attention to the role of the ICC in connection with the expansion of the conflict in Ukraine. Although the court's financial regulations do not permit earmarking voluntary contributions or seconded personnel to specific investigations, this did not prevent many states from calling attention to their contributions and connecting those contributions to support for the ICC's investigation in Ukraine. This has risked perceptions of selectivity and politicization in the work of the Court. The former concern has raised alarm bells among Coalition membership across the globe, where member organizations have asked whether justice for some victims should be prioritized over others, based on availability of resources.[13]

Voluntary contributions also raise significant risks when it comes to the sustainability of funding, as more resources for one organ do not address the resource needs of other organs and offices. In addition, there are policy considerations in the use of gratis personnel, including perceptions that seconded personnel may have divided loyalties.

Given its mandate, the court will always operate in politically charged circumstances. The best protection for its global mandate and prosecutorial and judicial independence is to be found in ensuring it has an adequate annual budget funded through assessed contributions. Momentum and focus on the court's critical role should really drive states parties and the court towards a fundamental reconsideration of the resources needed in the regular budget to execute its mandate, without arbitrary limitations that may have a political effect or damage perceptions of the court's legitimacy and independence.

---

11 Report of the Committee on Budget and Finance on the work of its thirty-ninth session, ICC-ASP/21/15, 15 October 2022 (Twenty-first Session of the ASP), paras. 237–254.

12 See, for example, F Bensouda, '"Without Fear or Favour": Reflections on my term as Prosecutor of the International Criminal Court' (Farewell end of term statement, 15 June 2021), 8.

13 'Victims could lose out with states' double-standard on International Criminal Court resources' (*Coalition for the International Criminal Court*, 30 March 2022).

A second example, and a second current need.

In 2019, the Assembly commissioned an Independent Expert Review (IER). The review was tasked with assessing the work of the court to make 'concrete, achievable, actionable recommendations aimed at enhancing the performance, efficiency and effectiveness of the Court and the Rome Statute system as a whole.' The review or a review-like process was requested by the court's leadership, but also pressed by civil society. Following a number of disappointing setbacks in cases, it was evident that change processes were needed. At the same time, however, civil society was alert to the fact that the IER or anything like it, could be easily captured by interests that were not aimed at strengthening the court, but rather on narrowing and revisiting the role of the court, particularly given contested discussions around its relationship to national jurisdictions.[14]

Given this risk, in calling for the review, and civil society organizations also called for (1) respect for the judicial and prosecutorial independence of the court; (2) genuine dialogue among all stakeholders; and (3) transparency.[15] By partnering with states that could recognize these challenges as well, civil society helped to ensure that negotiations around the set-up and follow-up to the review have respected these parameters.

Looking to the future, the court and the Assembly will need to make more of the Independent Expert Review's extensive and comprehensive report. In advance of the Assembly's assessment of the expert recommendations, the Coalition for the International Criminal Court Review Team issued an

14 See Human Rights Watch, 'Briefing Note for the Eighteenth Session of the International Criminal Court Assembly of States Parties' (November 2019), 1–8; 'Statement by Andrew Murdoch, Legal Director to the International Criminal Court Assembly of States Parties, at its 17th session in The Hague' (December 5, 2018) ('But as a State that supports the Court, it is important that we also speak plainly about the concerns we have. A founding principle of the Court is complementarity. The Court is not there to second guess, still less to review, the decisions of competent, functioning national systems of justice. Justice should in principle be done at the state level. The Court should step in only where States are genuinely unable or unwilling to do so themselves. We believe the Court must reaffirm and apply the principle of complementarity in all it does. And similarly, the Court has no mandate, and no jurisdiction, nor will it ever have nearly enough capacity, to act as a human rights monitoring organisation for the whole world. It must focus on its core and essential task, set out under the Statute.')

15 See, for example, Coalition for the International Criminal Court Review Team, 'Recommendations for the proposal of an action plan for the assessment of the Independent Expert Review recommendations' (June 9, 2020), 9–10 (restating principles that had been the subject of civil society advocacy throughout the process).

extensive position paper outlining several areas of IER recommendations of particular importance to civil society in the following areas:
- putting victims and affected communities at the centre of the Court's work;
- ensuring effectiveness of victims' rights, including participation;
- guaranteeing the highest standards of fair trial rights;
- improving the Office of the Prosecutor's methodologies;
- addressing issues of gender equality and workplace conduct;
- ensuring the court has adequate resources to carry out its mandate;
- improving cooperation and strengthening political support; and
- ensure merit-based elections of highly qualified Court officials. for an extensive discussion of the IER recommendations.[16]

In the first-half of 2022, several representatives of civil society presented their views during a meeting of the Review Mechanism regarding the report's recommendations on its relationship with the court, as well as that of media, and the court's communications strategies more generally (IER Recommendations R153-R162, R162-R166).[17]

While many recommendations have already been assessed, implementation will be an ongoing project. A concern for excellence in the court's delivery of justice will never have an expiration date. The court, in particular, should do more to consult directly with civil society organizations as part of their assessment and eventual implementation. This is particularly true in areas that are closely intertwined with the lived experience of non-governmental organizations working in countries where the ICC has ongoing investigations. These include victims' rights, the principle of complementarity and positive complementarity, outreach and public information, and strategies to ensure the court's eventual closure of certain investigations contributes to a tangible legacy for the rule-of-law.

For consultative processes to have meaning, however, the court (and, as relevant, the Assembly of States Parties) should increasingly take into account that translation and wide dissemination of materials in different languages and different countries, as well as sufficient time within a consultation process, are necessary.

These are just come examples of the unique partnership between civil society, court actors, and the Assembly of States Parties. This partnership will be necessary to continue to strengthen the court, particularly in the face of politicized opposition by those adverse to accountability.

16 Ibid.

17 See Report of the Review Mechanism on the overall progress of its work (30 June 2022), para. 19.

To play its role effectively, civil society needs ICC states parties and the court to guard civil society space and respond to threats to non-governmental organizations. This can be done in several ways, including making use of existing frameworks at national, regional, and international levels on the protection of human rights defenders. Visibility itself is often part of a strategy of protection. The inclusion of civil society representatives in high-level events not only allows such events to benefit from expertise of those working closely with affected communities, but also contribute to protection strategies that protect the ability of groups to continue to work.

The relationship between civil society, on the one hand, and states parties and court actors, on the other hand, will at times look like partnership, and it will at times be more adversarial. But it will be driven on the side of civil society with the common goal in mind of a more just, more peaceful, more secure world. This is what motivated our Coalition to come together in 1995, and is still with us today, as the court turns twenty.

CHAPTER 6

# The ICC at 20 from the Rome Statute's Entry into Force: Looking Backwards and Forward, or Learning from Mistakes and Building on Achievements

*David Donat Cattin*

## 1 17 July 1998: the Rome Statute's Adoption

The first anniversary concerning the only permanent system of integrated international and domestic justice for the most serious crimes of international concerns is 17 July, as on 17 July 1998 an historic United Nations' Conference of Plenipotentiaries that met for five weeks in Rome adopted the Rome Statute of the International Criminal Court (ICC). Only 7 States voted against its adoption on the basis of a purely jurisdictional objection raised by the United States of America on Article 12 prescribing the preconditions for the exercise of the Court's jurisdiction. The US was rejecting the principle of territoriality as one of the foundations for the Court's exercise of jurisdiction, which—according to the US position—should have depended exclusively on the consent of the State of nationality of the perpetrator (principle of active personality) as only criteria for jurisdiction that would have not derived from a referral of a situation contained in a UN Security Council's resolution under Chapter VII of the UN Charter. The US position was defeated as it was supported only by another permanent member of the Security Council, the People's Republic of China, as well as by Iraq, Israel, Qatar, Syria and another State that did not declare, explain or otherwise reveal its unrecorded vote. This meant that all the 160 States that attended the Rome Conference had agreed on the definitions of crimes and the general principles of International Law, which reflected a minimum common denominator that was universally acceptable by these States.[1]

1 In so far as the definition of international crimes was concerned, at the Rome Conference there was general agreement on Article 10, which contains a non-prejudice clause vis-à-vis any progressive development and subsequent codification of International Criminal Law. Article 10, the only one without heading in the Statute, reads as follows: 'Nothing in this Part [2] shall be interpreted as limiting or prejudicing in any way existing or developing rules of

 | DOI:10.1163/9789004529939_007

Similarly, the other UN Member States that failed to attend this open-ended conference implicitly concurred with the conclusions of the Rome negotiations given that they did not make any official statement negating the codification of International (Criminal) Law that had taken place in the Eternal City.[2]

The existence of the Rome Statute of the ICC, in and of itself, triggered a number of consequences that are still visible today, considering that a significant number of States started to reform their national laws and aligned their domestic legislation to the definitions and general principles of law contained in the Statute. Some States adjusted their military training manuals and their rules of engagement in situations of armed conflict to the definition of Article 8 (war crimes) of the Rome Statute, even if they did not express an intention to ratify it. Within States, certain institutions took decisions that were partially justified by the realization that, after 17 July 1998, there was a global consensus on the international customary law nature of the definitions of international crimes, an understanding that encouraged Spanish Judge Baltazar Garzon and his team to issue an arrest warrant and a request for extradition against former Chilean President Pinochet while he was visiting the United Kingdom in

international law for purposes other than this Statute'. Part 3 of the Rome Statute did not necessitate to include a norm similar to Article 10 as the rubric of the Part 3, namely 'General Principles of [International] Criminal Law', indicated without ambiguities that the norms reflected in this Part corresponded to general (customary) international law. In the following years, certain States started to express critical positions in selected international fora (e.g. the Assembly of the African Union or the VI Committee of the United Nations' General Assembly) on the purported non general acceptance of the principles and norms contained in the Rome Statute: however, it can observed that these States appear to have developed their positions as a reaction to investigations and prosecutions, preliminary examinations or simply allegations that their Heads of State or Government were implicated, either directly or indirectly, in the alleged perpetration of crimes defined in the Rome Statute. Therefore, it is not obvious that their statements shall be assessed as reflecting an objection to the general international law nature of the norms contained in Part 2 and 3 of the Rome Statute as their positions appear to be generated by the defense-strategies of accused persons, suspects or potential suspects rather than a revision of previous policy-decisions that informed the negotiation and adoption, as well as the ratification and—at times—domestic implementation of the Rome Statute, or to their positive vote on the UN Security Council's resolutions establishing the Court's jurisdiction over two States' situations (Sudan/Darfur and Libya) that would have fallen outside of the territorial competence of the Court.

2 The consent of all UN Member States to the norms of substantive criminal law contained in the Rome Statute were reaffirmed when States unanimously adopted the ancillary instrument of the Elements of Crimes in the final session of the Preparatory Commission for the ICC on 30 June 2000. See C K Hall, 'The First Five Sessions of the UN Preparatory Commission for the International Criminal Court' (2000) 94(4) *American Journal of International Law* 773.

September 1998.[3] Even the United States' initiatives aimed at slowing down the States' ratification-wave and then trying to erode the jurisdiction of the nascent Court throughout the negotiation of bilateral non-surrender agreements to bar the potential transfer to the ICC of US nationals and the *ultra vires* UN Security Council Resolutions 1422 (2002) and 1487 (2003)—which were adopted under Chapter VII of the UN Charter in the absence of a threat to the peace, breach to the peace or act of aggression (hence, without legal basis)[4]—indirectly proved that the Rome Statute was not setting-up another weak 'paper-tiger' institution within the International Community: the Statute represented (and continues to represent) an effective milestone for the universal effort to fight impunity for international crimes in line with the Nuremberg precedent of 1945, because it erected a tribunal on permanent and modern foundations eliminating ad hoc jurisdictional limitations and the outdated model of 'victors' justice'. There is no doubt that the adoption of the Rome Statute of the ICC was the most important manifestation of the United Nations' decade of International Law, the 1990s.

## 2 1 July 2002: the Rome Statute's Entry into Force

As 66 States had deposited their instrument of ratification with the United Nations' Secretary-General by the month of April 2002, the Rome Statute

3 The author of this chapter had a conversation with the Spanish Judge a few years after the Pinochet case in the UK, and Judge Garzon stated that he decided to issue and serve the arrest warrant and extradition-request against General Pinochet in the UK when, after 17 July 1998, he learned that the Rome Statute of the ICC had been adopted by an overwhelming majority of States, hence reflecting a new stage of the practice of International Criminal Law. As of mid-1998, Judge Garzon had been investigating and collecting evidence on General Pinochet for several years. See also J G White, 'Nowhere to Run, Nowhere to Hide: Augusto Pinochet, Universal Jurisdiction, the ICC, and a Wake-Up Call for Former Heads of State' (1999) 50 *Case Western Reserve Law Review* 127.

4 F Lattanzi, 'La Corte penale internazionale: una sfida per le giurisdizioni degli Stati' (2002) III *Diritto Pubblico Comparato ed Europeo* 1365, 1372–1374. Amnesty International commented this doctrinal contribution as follows: '*Necessity for an Article 39 determination*. A recent study by a distinguished Italian international lawyer of every single Security Council resolution adopted under Chapter VII since 1946 has demonstrated that in each case the Council made a determination that there was a threat to or breach of international peace and security. She concluded that "[t]he absence of such a finding is unprecedented in the 57 years of practice of the Security Council itself!". Amnesty International, 'International Criminal Court: The unlawful attempt by the Security Council to give US citizens permanent impunity from international justice', AI Index: IOR 40/006/2003 (May 2002), 63 and fn 182 <www.amnesty.org/en/wp-content/uploads/2021/06/ior400062003en.pdf> accessed 30 April 2023.

entered into force on 1 July of the same year. The ICC started to exist and became operational in the following months, especially after that the first session of the Assembly of States Parties (ASP) met in New York in September 2002[5] to adopt the Rules of Procedure and Evidence and the Elements of Crimes and the procedures for nominating and electing the first 18 Judges and the Prosecutor of the Court. The consequent decision-making processes of the first ASP ended only on 21 April 2003 with the unanimous decision by 78 States Parties to elect the first Prosecutor.[6] Thereafter, the Rome Statute system started to function, given the central role played by the Prosecutor as its international 'engine'. The ratification-wave progressively slowed down in the following years, with the exception of a relatively positive counter-trend in the year 2011 as a consequence of the successful holding of the first Review Conference of the Rome Statute in May-June 2010 at Kampala. As of 1 July 2022, the Rome Statute counts on the participation of 123 Member States, including 122 UN Member State and a State in free-association with New Zealand (the Cook Islands).[7]

---

5 As of 20 November 2022, the documentation of the first Assembly of States Parties (ASP) is not available in the ASP site, but it can be found in the following UN webpage: <https://legal.un.org/icc/asp/first.htm> accessed 30 April 2023.

6 'World court elects first prosecutor', *BBC News* (21 April 2003) <http://news.bbc.co.uk/2/hi/americas/2965147.stm> accessed 30 April 2023.

7 The ratification process of the Cook Islands was triggered by this author's address, on behalf of Parliamentarians for Global Action (PGA), in the plenary session of the Africa-Caribbean-Pacific—European Union Joint Parliamentary Assembly (ACP-EU JPA) held in Ljubljana, Slovenia, in March 2008. In response to the call for universal ratification by all ACP-EU States contained in this author's address, the Co-President of the JPA, Mr. Wilkie Rasmussen MP (Speaker of the Cook Islands), stated that his sovereign country should have promptly acceded to the Rome Statute and requested the assistance of PGA by becoming one of its members. The Cook Islands completed its accession process on 18 July 1998, 10 years after the ceremony held in the 'Campidoglio', the City Hall of Rome, when the Rome Statute was opened for signature and ratification. Like Mr. Rasmussen, PGA Members directly contributed to, and at times led, the national ratification processes in 78 out of the 125 States that ratified or acceded to the Rome Statute of the ICC, including Burundi and The Philippines, which withdrew from the Statute in 2016 and 2018 as a reaction to the opening of investigations that might have brought about the incrimination of their respective Heads of States. The withdrawal of Burundi was authorized by Parliament, whereby the one by The Philippines was the result of a unilateral decision of the President of the Republic without concurrence by the Senate, which had voted pro-ratification with a two-thirds majority in 2011. Two other States notified the UN depository of the treaty that they were exiting from the Rome Statute system, namely South Africa and The Gambia in 2016, but these States withdrew their withdrawals before that these entered into force 12 months after notification. All data concerning ratifications and accessions, as well as notifications of withdrawals and other treaty-related actions, are available at <https://treaties.un.org/pages/ViewDetails.aspx?src=TREATY&mtdsg_no=XVIII-10&chapter=18#2>

In 1998, the ICC was hailed as '*a gift of hope for future generations*' by Kofi Annan, UN Secretary-General. Two decades later, in reference to situations where international crimes are attributable to the individual responsibility of the highest authorities of a given State bound by the Statute, the ICC has been described as follows: '*the ICC is the only hope for the countless victims crying out for justice*'.[8] As of today, the most important feature of the ICC continues to be inherent to its very existence and can be subsumed in the object and purpose of the Rome Statute, which is 'to put an end to impunity for the perpetrators of [...] the most serious crimes of concern to the International Community as a whole'.[9] Such crimes are the reflection of four norms of *jus cogens*, or peremptory norms under International Law, namely, the non-derogable prohibitions of (the crime of) aggression, genocide, crimes against humanity and (large-scale) war crimes.[10] As such, the Rome Statute of the ICC is *de facto* a

accessed 30 April 2023, with the exception of Malaysia, which acceded the Statute in 2019, but withdrew its instrument of ratification before that the Statute entered into force for Malaysia itself. The relevant notification of withdrawal can be found at <https://treaties.un.org/doc/Publication/CN/2019/CN.185.2019-Eng.pdf> accessed 30 April 2023.

8 Athaliah Molokomme, Attorney General of Botswana, Statement at the Fifteenth Session of the ASP (2016) <www.facebook.com/BotswanaGovernment/photos/a.336021353147196/1141012299314760/?type=3> accessed 30 April 2023.

9 Combined language from *considerando* 6 and 5 of the Preamble, Rome Statute of the International Criminal Court (signed 17 July 1998, entered into force 1 July 2002) 2187 UNTS 3.

10 For the international practice on the *jus cogens* pertaining to the prohibition of the 'core crimes' until 2017, reference is made to D. Donat Cattin, 'Intervention of Humanity or the Use of Force to Halt Mass Atrocities, the Peremptory Prohibition of Aggression and the Interplay between Jus ad Bellum, Jus in Bello and Individual Criminal Responsibility on the Crime of Aggression' in P Acconci, D Donat Cattin, A Marchesi, A Palmisano, V Santori (eds), *International Law and the Protection of Humanity* (Boston/Leiden: Brill Nijhoff 2017) 353, 385–391. In the most recent ILC Report containing conclusions on the norms of *jus cogens*, Special Rapporteur Dire Tladi included a 'non-exhaustive list' under Conclusion 23, which reads as follows: "Without prejudice to the existence or subsequent emergence of other peremptory norms of general international law (jus cogens), a non-exhaustive list of norms that the International Law Commission has previously referred to as having that status is to be found in the annex to the present draft conclusions. Annex: (a) The prohibition of aggression; (b) The prohibition of genocide; (c) The prohibition of crimes against humanity; (d) The basic rules of international humanitarian law; (e) The prohibition of racial discrimination and apartheid; (f) The prohibition of slavery; (g) The prohibition of torture; (h) The right of self-determination." In the 2022 inconclusive debate at the Sixth Committee of the United Nations' General Assembly, some States voiced their objection to the inclusion in this list of the right of self-determination while not disputing the customary international law rank of the principle of self-determination. In the humble of opinion of this author, the only uncontested norms of *jus cogens* regard the absolute prohibition of the (four) core crimes under International Law. In fact,

'super-treaty', or a treaty of constitutional relevance for the international legal order, as it is built upon underlying norms forming part of universally accepted customary law of the highest rank. Therefore, the Rome Statute of the ICC is a benchmark for the realization of an international culture of legality, to be opposed to a culture of power-based relationships and lawlessness, which is rather pervasive in international affairs.[11] The Rome Statute system provides a permanent reminder to all actors at global level that there cannot be any sustainable concept of international Rule of Law if there would be impunity for the gravest violations of International Law that are triggering the application of the principle of individual criminal responsibility, which occurs only as an *extrema ratio* within the framework of the traditionally State-centered fabric of Public International Law.

## 3 20 Years of ICC Operations: Selective Reflections on a Few Lessons Learned or to Be Learned

Two decades after that the ICC became progressively operational and its States Parties increased from 66 to 123, there is one essential question that deserves to be addressed: has the Rome Statute of the ICC system performed in accordance with the object and purpose of the Statute itself? The answer is positive in principle and, at the same time, it is still suspended in practice.

In a broad sense, the ICC has been able to become a recognized international entity, in association with its seat in the City of The Hague, whereby "go-to-The-Hague" with respect to certain dictatorial leaders of States and "war-lords" (Non-State Actors) has been assuming the meaning of being

---

norm (d) above encompasses the prohibition of war crimes. The prohibition of apartheid (e) falls under the prohibition of crimes against humanity, given that apartheid, as such, may not be perpetrated outside a framework of systematic or widespread pattern of conduct directed against any civilian population. Point (e) in respect of racial discrimination and points (f) and (g) may be only partially subsumed under the corresponding crimes against humanity (namely, persecution, enslavement and torture) as the Special Rapporteur identifies the *jus cogens* nature of their prohibition regardless of their systematic or widespread dimension. Cf. ILC, 'Peremptory norms of general international law (jus cogens): Texts of the draft conclusions and Annex adopted by the Drafting Committee on second reading', UN Doc A/CN.4/L.967 (11 May 2022).

11 See, for example, the cynical views expressed by Henry Kissinger in *Foreign Affairs* as early as in 2001, which were promptly rebutted by former Nuremberg Prosecutor Benjamin Ferencz in the *Brown Journal of World Affairs* also in 2001. H A Kissinger, 'The Pitfalls of Universal Jurisdiction' (*Foreign Affairs*, 1 July 2001) <www.foreignaffairs.com/world/pitfalls-universal-jurisdiction> accessed 30 April 2023; B B Ferencz, 'A Nuremberg Prosecutor's Response to Henry Kissinger' (2001) 8(1) *The Brown Journal of World Affairs* 177.

wanted by, and eventually brought before, the Court. In terms of public perceptions, the ICC has also been able to inherit the legacy of the Hague-based ad hoc International Criminal Tribunal for the former Yugoslavia (ICTY) and, also, of the impactful trial of former Liberian Head of State Charles Taylor, who was adjudicated in an ICC Court-room that was hosting the Special Court for Sierra Leone (SCSL), an ad hoc Tribunal established by agreement between the UN and the territorial State just a few months before the Rome Statute's entry into force.

However, the ICC has been criticized for having been able to initiate and, above all, complete a rather limited number of cases in its first 19 years of effective practice:[12] this case-load is surprisingly sparse when compared with the impressive number of situations regarding which the Office of the Prosecutor has been conducting preliminary examinations and investigations. While the ICC had to confront itself with the policies of the largest States Parties targeting austerity and budget reductions during most of the life-span of the Court, most notably since the global financial crisis of 2008, this limited ability of the ICC in bringing about cases can be also attributed to a number of non-budgetary factors, which would deserve a dedicated study, but nonetheless can be enumerated here in this non-exhaustive list:

### 3.1 *Focused Investigations and Extremely Limited and Sparse Cases*

The policy of the first two Prosecutors has been to conduct 'focused investigations' (few, representative cases in larger situations of mass-atrocities) and alert the general public that the ICC would have been able to handle only very few cases per situation-country. This dramatically weakened almost all the ICC interventions in specific situations. Since International Criminal Law deals with situations characterized by mass-atrocities, including aggressive wars that are planned and launched through the perpetration of the crime of aggression, it is inevitable that relevant investigations and prosecutions should bring about the realization of complex trials, which must necessarily cover a large scope of crimes and mass victimization (i.e., widespread or systematic attacks

12 According to the ICC website's page entitled '[a]bout the Court—Facts and Figures' <https://www.icc-cpi.int/about/the-court> (accessed 30 April 2023): "There have thus far been 31 cases before the Court, with some cases having more than one suspect. ICC judges have issued 38 arrest warrants. Thanks to cooperation from States, 21 people have been detained in the ICC detention centre and have appeared before the Court. 14 people remain at large. Charges have been dropped against 5 people due to their deaths. ICC judges have also issued 9 summonses to appear. The judges have issued 10 convictions and 4 acquittals". However, only 4 convictions are for perpetrators of Rome Statute crimes.

against civilians within the framework of trials on crimes against humanity, which, by definition, are featuring this high gravity-threshold that differentiate them from other human rights' violations). The most significant change introduced by the third Prosecutor of the ICC in 2021–22 has been the commitment to broaden the scope of prosecutions before the ICC, as evidenced in the recent report to the UN Security Council on Libya[13] and on strategies regarding the atrocities committed in the context of the aggressive war *in and against* Ukraine.

### 3.2 *The Misunderstanding on the Real Meaning of Complementarity*

The misinterpretation of the principle of complementarity, which was *conceived* as a negative principle, reflected in negative notions, i.e., the *unwillingness* or *inability* of States to genuinely investigate and prosecute international crimes, but was promoted by the Office of the Prosecutor and other actors as a positive principle, namely, 'positive complementarity'. This has been understood as giving a pro-active mandate to the ICC to incentivize States to fight impunity, whereby the Rome Statute simply reaffirms pre-existing obligations of States to prosecute the most serious crimes of international concern.[14] The

13 Due to its profound significance, the relevant report must be read in its entirety to understand the essential role that the Prosecutor is playing in a prolonged situation of conflict as the one of Libya: See Statement of ICC Prosecutor, Karim A. A. Khan KC, to the United Nations Security Council on the Situation in Libya, pursuant to Resolution 1970 (2011) (11 November 2022) <www.icc-cpi.int/news/statement-icc-prosecutor-karim-khan-kc-united-nations-security-council-situation-libya> accessed 30 April 2023. The most enlightening language that reveals a new approach to prosecutions in terms of scope and also number of cases is the following part of Prosecutor Karim Khan's statement before the Council in video-link from Libya: 'I can today announce that further applications for warrants of arrest are being submitted to the independent judges of the ICC. But those are confidentially submitted, it is for the judges of the ICC to determine. So, I can't speak in more terms and give any greater details. But there will be further applications that we will make, because the victims want to see action and the evidence is available and it's our challenge to make sure we have the resources, we prioritize the Libya situation, to make sure we can vindicate the promise of the Security Council in Resolution 1970. And this approach represents, in my respectful view, a new paradigm for action by my Office'.

14 Art. 1, Convention on the Prevention and Punishment of the Crime of Genocide (signed 9 December 1948, entered into force 12 January 1951) 78 UNTS 277; Art. 1, (common to the) Geneva Conventions (1949): Geneva Convention (I) for the Amelioration of the Condition of Wounded, Sick and Shipwrecked Members of Armed Forces in the Field (adopted 12 August 1949, entered into force 21 October 1951) 75 UNTS 31; Geneva Convention (II) for the Amelioration of the Condition of Wounded, Sick and Ship-wrecked Members of Armed Forces at Sea (adopted 12 August 1949, entered into force 21 October 1950) 75 UNTS 85; Geneva Convention (III) relative to the Treatment of Prisoners of War (adopted 12 August 1949, entered into force 21 October 1950) 75 UNTS 135; Geneva Convention (IV) relative

OTP and representatives of (the Assembly of) States Parties, at times supported by NGOs, insisted on the concept of "positive complementarity", but they omitted to consider that the principle of complementarity was essentially defined by the drafters of the Rome Statute (see Article 17) as a negative criteria to be met by the ICC before it would start prosecutorial and judicial action (i.e. States must be [subjectively] unwilling or [objectively] unable to genuinely investigate *and* prosecute international crimes, otherwise the Court may not proceed with its own investigations and prosecutions). States retain primary jurisdiction over international crimes, but the ICC has residual jurisdiction that complements the one of States and there is no requirement in the Statute that would refer to the condition of "previous exhaustion of domestic remedies", which normally applies in respect of regional Human Rights Courts. In Colombia and Guinea, the steps undertaken by Prosecutor of the ICC effectively incentivized the realization of a certain measure of justice and accountability at domestic level, albeit with limitations that generated controversies. But in most of the other situations falling under the Court's jurisdiction, this phenomenon did not take place. In conclusion, there has been a false expectation that States would have exercised their primary responsibility to fight impunity vis-à-vis the ICC as Court of last resort. Only in very few situations, States were able to step up their efforts and genuinely investigate *and* prosecute Rome Statute crimes. In particular, there has not been a single circumstance in which States Parties' domestic jurisdictions were able to put an end to the impunity of major State-actors/Government officials. The misleading concept of positive complementarity has also been used by certain States to keep the budget of the ICC and, in particular, of the OTP within a rather limited size. 20 years after the entry into force of the Rome Statute, it is time to rectify perceptions on the rhetorical paradox of a 'Court of last resort' *in abstracto*,

---

to the Protection of Civilian Persons in Time of War (adopted 12 August 1949, entered into force 21 October 1950) 75 UNTS 287; Art. 3, ILC, 'Draft Articles on Prevention and Punishment of Crimes against Humanity' (2019), adopted by the ILC at its 71st session (A/74/10), available at <https://legal.un.org/ilc/texts/instruments/english/draft_articles/7_7_2019.pdf> accessed 30 April 2023; the latter norm reflects an obligation that exists under customary international law, which applies to all States, not only the States Parties to the Rome Statute. In fact, the 6th *considerando* of the Preamble, Rome Statute, contains the following reaffirmation of general International Law: 'Recalling that it is *the duty of every State* to exercise its criminal jurisdiction over those responsible for international crimes'. In the context of a legally-binding instrument in the field of International Criminal Law, the ordinary meaning of the term 'duty' coincides with obligation (legal duty), not moral duty. This general obligation extends also to the crime of aggression and regards *all* States, not only the States Parties to the Rome Statute.

which, as matter of fact and as a matter of law, can be 'the only available Court' *in concreto* (depending on the concrete circumstances and situations).

### 3.3 *The Negative Influence of the 'War on Terror' on the Fight against International Crimes: Decades of Stalemate on Afghanistan, the Only Non-African Situation of Atrocity-Crimes under the Court's Jurisdiction Since 2003*

One year before the entry into force of the Statute, in the aftermath of 11 September 2001, State actors decided to change their hierarchy of 'threats' in global affairs and tragically placed 'terrorism' as their highest priority, to the inevitable detriment of genocide, crimes against humanity, war crimes and the crime of aggression.[15] The reluctance to qualify as crimes against humanity the extremely serious breaches of International Law allegedly perpetrated by Substitute al-Qaeda leaders,[16] who were aided and abetted by the Taliban

15 On 12 September 2001, the UN Security Council took action in response to the 11 September attacks against the United States perpetrated through the use of civilian aircrafts: in 'Resolution 1368 (2001) [...] [t]he Security Council, [r]eaffirming the principles and purposes of the Charter of the United Nations, [d]etermined to combat by all means threats to international peace and security caused by terrorist acts, [r]ecognizing the inherent right of individual or collective self-defence in accordance with the Charter, 1. Unequivocally condemns in the strongest terms the horrifying terrorist attacks which took place on 11 September 2001 in New York, Washington, D.C. and Pennsylvania and *regards such acts, like any act of international terrorism,* as *a threat to international peace and security*'. (emphasis added). UNSC Res 1368 (12 September 2001) UN Doc S/RES/1368(2001). In expanding its determination to other international terrorism's attacks as threats to international peace and security, the Security Council went beyond its mandate under the UN Charter as it extended an *ad hoc* situation under Article 39 of the Charter to an unspecified and generalized type of situations. In order to secure unanimous approval of Res. 1368, Member States had agreed to a diplomatic *demarche* of the Russian Federation, which was aimed at justifying its repressive policies in Chechnya and other Caucasian territories in the name of self-styled 'counterterrorism'. UN principle organs' appeasement to the Russian Federation's abusive policies ended only with the UN General Assembly Resolution A/RES/ES-11/1, which was adopted with the vote of 141 UN Member States. UNGA, 'Aggression against Ukraine' UN Doc A/RES/ES-11/1 (18 March 2022); the relevant voting record and text are available at<https://digitallibrary.un.org/record/3959039?ln=en> accessed 30 April 2023.

16 As it has been recently written in one of the most authoritative International Law blogs housed in a US academic institution, New York University, 'it is deeply problematic that the United States has still failed to try the 9/11 defendants after twenty years': J Hafetz, 'The Last, Best Chance for Accountability at Guantanamo? A Negotiated Plea for the 9/11 Defendants' (*JustSecurity*, 15 November 2022) <www.justsecurity.org/84108/the-last-best-chance-for-accountability-at-guantanamo-a-negotiated-plea-for-the-9-11-defendants/> accessed 30 April 2023.

regime of Afghanistan, reflected two decades of policies and strategies in which the notion of justice was replaced by a prevailing logic of violent retaliation and revenge under the labels of 'war on terror' or 'counter-terrorism', and the suspected 'terrorists' were often the object of military actions or 'targeted killings' rather than public trials. This serious problem might have, at a minimum, influenced the treatment by the OTP and Pre-Trial Chamber of the situation of Afghanistan, which remained in the interim stage of 'preliminary examinations' for approximately 11 years and has been subsequently at the epicenter of extremely controversial judicial decisions. In February 2003, the Executive of transitional Afghanistan, under the leadership of President Karzai, ratified the Rome Statute of the ICC with the precise policy-objective to ensure that justice and accountability would apply internationally to elements of the new regime (warlords of the Northern Alliance) and of the former (Taliban) regime who otherwise would have enjoyed impunity. But such impunity continued to be 'enjoyed', also as a consequence of the protracted inaction by the ICC competent organs. In the humble opinion of this author, the ICC as international organization (consisting of an independent judiciary, an independent prosecutorial organ, and a legislative and executive collegiate body of States) did not engage adequately with Afghanistan as a State Party and was unable to perform any prosecutorial or judicial function on its most serious scenario of alleged atrocities falling under the Court's territorial jurisdiction outside the African continent from May 2003 to, at least, 2011.[17] In fact, as of today, no single case has been opened against any individual who may have committed Rome

17 In the last 20 years, the practice of the OTP has been consistently based on the principle of territorial jurisdiction, and not on the one of active personality (nationality of the perpetrator). As of today, all situations in which the Prosecutor has opened cases have been based either on the ratification of the territorial State (often followed by the referral of one's own territorial situation to the Prosecutor), the *ad hoc* acceptance of jurisdiction by the territorial State, and the referral of a situation defined in territorial terms (e.g., Darfur/Sudan and Libya) by the UN Security Council through a Chapter VII resolution. States' referrals and *proprio motu* decisions concerning investigations and prosecutions have always been based on the ability of the Prosecutor to extend her/his investigations on an entire territorial situation, and not on a few members of the organization(s) implicated in the commission of Rome Statute crimes. For example, while Members of Parliaments from the Middle East and North Africa (MENA) region requested the Secretariat of Parliamentarians for Global Action (PGA) to alert the ICC Prosecutor that some suspected leaders of ISIS/ISIL/IS were nationals of States Parties to the Rome Statute (e.g., Tunisia, Jordan, Belgium, UK, France, Maldives etc.) and that she could have exercised jurisdiction on the basis of the nationality principle, the Prosecutor explained to this author that she would have not requested to the Pre-Trial Chamber an authorization to open relevant investigations on account of the forecasted inability to extend OTP's investigations and prosecutions on the most responsible persons for ISIS' alleged atrocities, regardless of their nationality.

Statute crimes in Afghanistan. Can this be explained by the pressures exercised by States (Parties and Non-Parties to the Rome Statute) on the Office of the Prosecutor and other organs of the Court to block and impede any investigation in respect of the unspeakable atrocities that victimized Afghani civilians? A satisfactory answer must be given to this question, which is the most serious one that may affect, in the long term, the legacy of the ICC as an ensemble of organs devoted to the object and purpose of putting an end to impunity for the most serious crimes of international concern. On 15 August 2021 some of the individuals whose impunity could have been partially ended (at least through the issuance of an international arrest warrant) have tragically returned to power, and are now capacitated to implement widespread and systematic policies to persecute and even enslave Afghani civilians who are not freely adhering to the totalitarian ideology of the Taliban regime, including children who are enslaved and brainwashed into the fundamentalist doctrine of violent extremism.

### 3.4 *Shortcomings in Applying the 'Proper Law' of the ICC: the Negative Consequences of the Summons to Voluntary Appear for the Accused Persons in the Kenya Situation*

Since the 20th anniversary of the adoption of the Rome Statute, an Independent Expert Review (IER) process has been implemented to strengthen, and, when possible, bring about reforms to, the Rome Statute system. This brief chapter does not address this extremely important exercise. Suffice it to say, looking backwards and moving forward, that many of the findings of the IER Panel of Experts chaired by Justice Richard Goldstone stemmed from shortcomings of the Court's individual organs (e.g., the Judges or the Prosecutor) in applying the law. In the humble opinion of this author, the clearest example of the shortcomings by the Court organs in applying the 'proper law' (or internal law) of the ICC was represented by the omissions of the Pre-Trial Chamber and the Prosecutor concerning Rome Statute's Article 58 and Article 68, paragraph 1: these norms should have been applied to the persons who were summoned to voluntarily appear before the ICC in the Kenyan situation when it became factually clear that extremely powerful accused persons (Mr. Ruto was a Member of Parliament at the time of the opening of the case, became Vice-President of Kenya during the proceedings, and then became President of Kenya after the halting of the proceedings; Mr. Kenyatta was Deputy Prime Minister of Kenya at the time of the opening of the case against him, and was elected President of the Republic during the ICC proceedings) were interfering with the integrity of the proceedings and unduly influencing witnesses and survivors of the Kenyan post-electoral violence of 2007–08. Even if the Prosecutor had made an agreement with the defense of these prominent suspects regarding their voluntary cooperation and participation at ICC hearings, it became apparent in the course of the proceedings that—as provided in Article 58—'the arrest of the person appears[ed] necessary: [...] (ii) To ensure that the person does not obstruct or endanger the investigation or the court'. However, nothing was done, the accused persons travelled back to Kenya and multiple sources indicated that they exercised enormous influence on the behavior of witnesses and victims. As an alleged result, no witness or victim was available to the organs of justice of the Court to provide the necessary evidence in support of the charges on crimes against humanity brought by the Prosecutor and initially confirmed by Pre-Trial Judges on the basis of the standard of proof applicable at that stage. Hence, all cases against Kenyan suspects had to be halted or dismissed before adjudication in the merits due to insufficient evidence. Under Article 68, paragraph 1, all the organs of the Court shall take any necessary measure to protect the safety, security, privacy and well-being of victims and witnesses. This norm was not applied to the Kenyan cases in so far as the most effective measure of protection was concerned: to impede that an accused person return from The Hague to his/her country of nationality during the proceedings against him/her.[18]

## 4 Learning Lessons: Trying to Improve the Rome Statute System

Twenty years after the Rome Statute's entry into force and its functioning as "jurisdictional system" centered on two pillars, (i) the principle of complementarity and (ii) the obligation to cooperate, can all the subjects (i.e., States, the ICC as international organization and its individual organs) and actors within the Rome Statute system build upon its achievements and learn from its shortcomings? The answer is a forceful 'yes', provided that there is genuine political will to act accordingly, and all relevant institutional organs (within and outside the Court) and stakeholders that form part of the system are ready to play their respective role and fulfil their mandate: from States' delegations to NGOs' representatives, from independent academic experts to practitioners who litigate matters before the Court or domestic jurisdictions, to other relevant international organizations and entities that identified the existence of the ICC and the operationalization of the Rome Statute as a '*conditio sine qua non*' for the

18 See, for all, H Corell, 'Challenges for the International Criminal Court', *International Judicial Monitor* (Winter 2014 Issue) <www.judicialmonitor.org/archive_winter2014/specialreport1.html> accessed 30 April 2023.

creation of a Rules Based International Order and the setting up of an international Rule of Law.

The main impact of the Rome Statute is, indeed, inherent to its very existence: this is proved by the fact that its adoption and subsequent entry into force triggered the biggest wave of domestic implementing legislations in the history of International Criminal Law. As States have to effectively prove their ability, capacity and willingness to bring to justice perpetrators of international crimes in order to complement the ICC and avoid its interventions, this has meant that approximately 70 States reformed or modernized their criminal laws and incorporated the substantive norms and principles of Parts II and III of the Rome Statute in their internal legal orders. A comparably dynamic process did not take place after the adoption of other pivotal treaties (e.g., the Geneva Conventions of 1949, the penal provisions of which remained largely unapplied until the *ad hoc* tribunals and ICC were established). Looking forward, the efforts to domesticate the Statute and all relevant standards of International Criminal Law, International Humanitarian Law and Human Rights Law must continue and intensify to ensure that the principle of complementarity and the duty of cooperation are effectively fulfilled by all States that are bound to the Statute. This process of domestic implementation continues to offer a unique opportunity to incorporate principles of law that are not reflected in the Statute, but are instrumental to its object and purpose, such as the principle of universal jurisdiction and the retrospective application of Rome Statute crimes before national jurisdictions to the time in which such crimes were deemed as part of customary international law.[19]

The Rome Statute had also a uniquely important normative mandate to accomplish, namely, it gave effect to Article VI of the Genocide Convention of 1948. But the normative impact of the Statute is also forward-looking,

19 While the text of the Rome Statute contains twice the principle of non-retroactivity, States are bound by their pre-existing obligations if they have ratified the International Covenant of Civil and Political Rights or the European Convention on Human Rights, which define the principle of legality not only in relation to domestic criminalization, but also in relation to international criminalization, respectively at Articles 15, paragraph 2 ('Nothing in this article shall prejudice the trial and punishment of any person for any act or omission which, at the time when it was committed, was criminal according to the general principles of law recognized by the community of nations') and Article 7, paragraph 2 ('This Article shall not prejudice the trial and punishment of any person for any act or omission which, at the time when it was committed, was criminal according to the general principles of law recognised by civilised nations'). The same principle of customary law is reflected in the coherent jurisprudence of the Inter-American Court of Human Rights on access to justice for victims of international crimes and 'no-impunity'.

given that the ILC draft articles (for a convention) on crimes against humanity essentially reflect the norms and standards contained in the Statute, especially in its Article 7. Additionally, there is a standard-setting potential that the Rome Statute has still to unleash in respect of the fourth international crime, the crime of aggression, the definition of which was adopted by the Kampala Review Conference in 2010 and entered into force on 17 July 2018, even though for a rather limited number of enlightened States Parties, while others probably had too much trust in future UN Security Council referrals to the ICC jurisdiction under Article 13(b) of the Statute, which will cover all the four core crimes under International Law since 17 July 2018. As demonstrated by the full-scale war of aggression and annexation launched by the Russian Federation *in and against* Ukraine on 24 February 2022 and the policy of vetoes blocking the Security Council, the crime of aggression cannot be seen anymore as an obsolete remnant of the past or a matter that can satisfactorily be addressed through Security Council referrals. States were right in including the crime of aggression in Article 5 of the Rome Statute in 1998 and in agreeing on its definition in Article 8bis at Kampala in 2010. However, this normative job is not yet concluded, given that the preconditions for the exercise of the Court's jurisdiction on this crime agreed in Kampala are characterized by the insertion in Article 15 bis of the Statute of two clauses that are running counter to the object and purpose of the Statute, which is to put an end to impunity of the perpetrators of the (4) core crimes that shock humankind (on the basis of the jurisdictional principles of territoriality or active personality in the absence of a UN Security Council referral ex Chapter VII of the UN Charter). In fact, paragraph 5 of Art. 15 bis is exempting nationals of States Non Parties to the Statute from the jurisdiction on this crime, even when aggression would be committed *in and against* the territories and the peoples of a State that has accepted the Court's jurisdiction on aggression. Additionally, eleven words contained in paragraph 4 of Art. 15 bis require that an individual would be punishable for the crime of aggression *only if* he or she, as leader, would be using the military forces of a State that has ratified the Rome Statute and the Kampala amendments.[20]

20 Article 15 bis '*Exercise of jurisdiction over the crime of aggression (State referral, proprio motu)*' of the Rome Statute provides in its paragraphs 4 and 5: 4. The Court may, in accordance with article 12, exercise jurisdiction over a crime of aggression, *arising from an act of aggression committed by a State Party*, unless that State Party has previously declared that it does not accept such jurisdiction by lodging a declaration with the Registrar. The withdrawal of such a declaration may be effected at any time and shall be considered by the State Party within three years. 5. *In respect of a State that is not a party to this Statute, the Court shall not exercise its jurisdiction over the crime of aggression when committed by that State's nationals or on its territory.* (Emphasis added). According to a proposal presented

These jurisdictional provisions have been unintendedly benefitting the leader(s) of the Russian Federation, a State that can veto any Security Council binding referral and can protect itself from the ICC's limited jurisdiction on the crime of aggression by remaining a Non State Party. The origins of these provisions that are de facto impeding the exercise of the ICC 'automatic jurisdiction' on one the four core crimes of concern to the International Community as a whole can be found in the United States' advocacy at the Kampala Review Conference. As Senator John Kerry wrote in the enlightening report that the Foreign Relations Committee of the US Senate published on 2 September 2010:

> As this report highlights, the Kampala Conference adopted a complicated decision that envisions the future addition of a crime of aggression to the ICC's jurisdiction. The proposed aggression regime is flawed in several respects, but nonetheless contains important protections for U.S. interests. Most significantly, U.S. persons, including U.S. officials and military members, could not be investigated or prosecuted for aggression by the ICC without the consent of the United States. The proposed regime will not enter into force for at least seven years, and will do so only after a further decision by the ICC's parties to bring it into force. U.S. participation at the Kampala Conference played an important role in securing these protections.[21]

If the 'protections' of Article 15bis, paragraphs 4 and 5, for nationals or armed forces of States Non Parties will continue to be part of the Rome Statute normative framework, this regrettable status quo may preclude the international community to apply the most basic principle for any credible legal system, the principle of equality of all (individuals) before the law, to the crime of

---

by Parliamentarians for Global Action (PGA) since March 2022 to a group of interested States, including EU Member States, the above language *in italics* shall be urgently deleted from Article 15 bis by the Assembly of States Parties through an amendment-process to be informed by entry into force under Article 121, paragraph 5, of the Statute, in continuity with the Kampala process. The PGA proposal has been cited by a prominent academic: C Kress, *The Ukraine War and the Prohibition of the Use of Force in International Law* (Brussels: Torkel Opsahl Academic EPublisher 2022), fn 101.

21 'ICC Review Conference, Kampala, Uganda, May 31–June 11, 2010: A Joint Committee Staff Trip Report prepared for the use of the Committee on Foreign Relations, US Senate, 111th Congress, Second Session, September 2, 2010', Letter of Transmittal by Sen. John Kerry (2010) <www.foreign.senate.gov/imo/media/doc/International%20Criminal%20Court%20Review%20Conference%20Kampala%20Uganda%2009022010.pdf> accessed 30 April 2023.

aggression before the ICC. In the face of the Russian Federation's alleged act of aggression against Ukraine, which is supposedly arising from the planning and ordering of a full-scale aggressive war to be allegedly attributable to the individual criminal responsibility of the Russian Federation's leader(s) —hence, it is the act of State of aggression that derives from, and is consequential to, the crime of aggression, and not *vice-versa*, as illogically stated in the above-cited controversial sentence of paragraph 4 of Article 15bis—, States Parties to the Rome Statute have the political and moral responsibility to re-align, at least partially, the jurisdictional regime on the crime of aggression to the one that applies to genocide, crimes against humanity and war crimes. The fight against impunity for the most serious crimes of international concern entails that the four core crimes must be treated equally by the ICC. In fact, as a matter of law, all the Rome Statute crimes can be punished with a maximum penalty of a term of thirty years of imprisonment or, alternatively, 'life imprisonment when justified by the extreme gravity of the crime and the individual circumstances of the convicted person'. This norm on penalties of Article 77 applies to *all* core crimes contained in the Statute, without distinctions. Therefore, there is no hierarchy of gravity or importance amongst the four core crimes contained in the Rome Statute.[22]

All the above normative reforms must be undertaken by the Assembly of States Parties to the Rome Statute of the ICC, and must be viewed in parallel with the efforts that the ICC organs and the jurisdictional and prosecutorial organs of States should be undertaking to ensure that the shortcomings of the first twenty years of the Rome Statute system will not be repeated. Notwithstanding the challenges that are affecting this system, which this chapter has tried to describe with selected examples ([i] excessively focused investigations and prosecutions resulting in too few and narrow cases; [ii] misleading reliance on a supposedly 'positive' dimension of complementarity; [iii] inferiority complex *vis-à-vis* counterterrorism and appeasement to States' pressures not to open cases in situations of overlap between terrorists' offences and crimes against humanity; [iv] insufficient application of provisions of the Statute on witness and victim protection), there is one unprecedented milestone for international justice that the ICC has achieved, namely, the participation of victims in ICC

22 This view certainly applies to genocide, crimes against humanity and the crimes of aggression. In respect of war crimes, the provisions of Article 124 (the deletion of which did not yet enter into force under Article 121, paragraph 4), Article 33 (paragraph 2) and Article 8 (paragraph 1) of the Rome Statute might be systematically interpreted as entailing lesser gravity of (certain) war crimes *vis-à-vis* the other three core crimes. But there is no jurisprudence to support this interpretation.

proceedings and the affirmation of their access to justice, truth and reparation. Victims' rights are central to any credible strategy and action aimed at reducing the accountability-gap for international crimes: over these two decades, more than 40,000 individual victims applied to participate in ICC proceedings and/or requested that a measure of reparative justice would at least partially remedy the immense suffering and harm that stemmed from their victimization. Participation and protection of victims, coupled with reparations for victims and their families, have marked a radical change in the development of international criminal law, with the ICC being able to deliver not only punishment directed to the perpetrators (when found 'guilty beyond reasonable doubt' (Article 66, paragraph 3) after a trial in which the rights of the accused are thoroughly respected), but also reparations for the benefit of victims. In each of the first four judgements ending with convictions for Rome Statute crimes, the relevant Trial Chamber decided not only to 'establish principles relating to reparations to, or in respect of, victims, including restitution, compensation and rehabilitation' (Article 75, paragraph 1), but also to 'make an order directly against a convicted person specifying appropriate reparations to, or in respect of, victims, including restitution, compensation and rehabilitation [...] through the Trust Fund provided for in article 79' (Article 75, paragraph 2).[23] The Trust Fund for Victims started to play an increasingly important role in the Rome Statute system, highlighting the concept that the fight against impunity for the gravest violations of International Law cannot limit itself to stop and sanction the perpetrators, but must engage with, and be centered on, the rights of the victims, who are directly suffering the tragic consequences of inhumane acts. Therefore, the jurisprudence of the ICC has been able to consistently translate the abstract notion of 'the most serious crimes [...] that deeply shock the conscience of humanity' (Preamble) into the concrete notion of victimization and harm suffered by individuals whose humanity has been directly violated by the criminal conduct for which perpetrators have been found guilty. In this respect, it is time for all subjects and actors in the Rome Statute system to recognize that the principle of complementarity operates also towards the realization of victims' rights,[24] and States shall ensure that, at a minimum, all the international standards protecting victims (including survivors) be applicable,

23 For an interpretation of the mandatory provision of paragraph 1 *vis-à-vis* the permissive provision of paragraph 2 of Article 75, reference is made to: D Donat Cattin, 'Article 75—Reparations to Victims' in K Ambos (ed.), *The Rome Statute of the International Criminal Court: A Commentary* (CH Beck/Hart/Nomos 2021) 2240–2275.

24 See D Donat Cattin, 'Victims' Rights in the International Criminal Court' in M Natarajan (ed.), *International and Transnational Crime and Justice* (Cambridge University Press 2019) 421–426.

*mutatis mutandis*, to victims of international crimes at the domestic level. This is absolutely necessary to fulfil the rights of victims of crimes that will not be adjudicated before the ICC and, also, may not be adjudicated before national jurisdictions, given that the 'impunity rates' in national systems are, at times, extremely high. Therefore, victims shall be given access to reparations even in cases in which access to justice and truth may not be possible. This is the consequence of the correct interpretation of the definition of victims and their rights as unanimously adopted in the 'Declaration of Basic Principles of Justice for Victims of Crimes and Abuse of Power' annexed to United Nations General Assembly Resolution 40/34 of 29 December 1985, also included in ECOSOC Resolution 1996/14, which reads:

> 1. 'Victims' means persons who, individually or collectively, have suffered harm, including physical or mental injury, emotional suffering, economic loss or substantial impairment of their fundamental rights, through acts or omissions that are in violation of criminal laws operative within Member States, including those laws proscribing criminal abuse of power.
> 2. A person may be considered a victim, under this Declaration, *regardless of whether the perpetrator is identified, apprehended, prosecuted or convicted* and regardless of the familial relationship between the perpetrator and the victim. The term "victim" also includes, where appropriate, the immediate family or dependants of the direct victim and persons who have suffered harm in intervening to assist victims in distress or to prevent victimization. [Emphasis added.]

While this definition was incorporated in a UN General Assembly Resolution, which, as such, is not a legally-binding instrument ('soft law'), the Assembly of States Parties' decision to incorporate its essential features in the binding Rules of Procedure and Evidence of the ICC at Rule 85 transformed this definition into 'hard law', as part of the applicable law of the ICC in accordance with Article 21 of the Statute.[25] This is yet another achievement upon which to

25 Paragraph 2(c) of Article 21 of the Rome Statute prohibits the application of 'general principles of law derived from national laws of legal system of the world' when such principles would be 'inconsistent with [the] Statute and with international law and internationally recognized norms and *standards*' (emphasis added). The last term clearly refers to 'soft-law' instruments like the above-cited UN Declaration on Basic Principles of Justice for Victims (1985). For a systematic reconstruction of the innovations brought about by Article 21 on applicable law, reference is made to this author's contribution to the Italian commentary on the Statute: D Donat Cattin, 'Il Diritto Applicabile' in G Lattanzi

strengthen international cooperation for the fulfillment of victims' rights and yet another demonstration of the normative importance of the Rome Statute system for the progressive development and codification of International Law.

---

and G Monetti (eds), *La Corte Penale Internazionale: Organi-Competenza-Reati-Processo* (Milano: Giuffrè 2006) 269–312.

# PART 3

## *New Frontiers in Investigations and Prosecutions*

CHAPTER 7

# Innovation and Technology in Building Modern Investigations and Prosecutions at the ICC

*Karim Khan*

## 1 The ICC at 20: the Journey of International Justice

A review, however brief, of the interrelationship between international justice and technology, is one that requires a horizon that extends beyond the first 20 years of the International Criminal Court. Technological advances in society have naturally had ripple effects in the court room. The historic courtroom 600 at Nuremburg was in fact redesigned to facilitate simultaneous translation for the trials in 1945, which also marked the first time video recordings were used as evidence in trials. Technology is not, of course, an end in itself. But, criminal trials must harness technology to better develop and present cases. Prosecutors and investigators, and in fact all courtroom users, must also understand technology to be alive to where information may be stored and available for retrieval, analysis or use. Criminal justice processes, domestic or international, must be able to grapple with technology from this evidential perspective. This is because the now omnipresent devices from computers and tablets to phones and watches, all create, send and retrieve information, that may become relevant to criminal proceedings. Relatedly, the ubiquitous use around the planet of social media platforms like Facebook, Tik Tok, YouTube and a myriad of search engines constitute perhaps obvious examples of advances in technology that may have evidential relevance depending upon what is recorded and the facts in issue that need to be proved. Indeed, some of these platforms may be used not only to store and record content, but may be vehicles for incitement of crimes such as hate crimes. The Islamic State's exploitation of social media in the recent past, producing over 90,000 tweets and other posts per day at peak, recorded and directed its crusades of violence, recruited members, spread propaganda and even created virtual 'slave markets' to facilitate its crimes against the Yazidis.

Whilst the technological advances increase at almost exponential rates, and we see massive data sets being produced that could not have been anticipated even a few years ago, we also know that international criminal justice has

 | DOI:10.1163/9789004529939_008

always sought to embrace technology to enhance the investigation, preparation and presentation of it cases.

For example, the Nuremberg and Tokyo Trials not only saw the enrichment of cases with documentary evidence left behind by 'methodical record-keepers',[1] materials provided by war correspondents, and footage shot by American and Soviet liberators, but also the revolutionising of courtroom interpretation. Partnership between Col. Leon Dostert and a friend at IBM resulted in the testing and successful implementation of a system allowing for simultaneous translation in the courtroom—and thus substantially contributing to trials that were fair and more expeditious.[2] Symbiotically, the needs for justice prompted a technological transformation, even as the technology helped make international justice more of a reality.

The establishment of the International Criminal Tribunals for the Former Yugoslavia and Rwanda fifty years later likewise coincided with technological advancements in the fields of forensic science (for example, DNA profiling) and remote sensing (for example, satellite imagery), that led to the use of new types of evidence being presented in the courtroom and new kinds of expert witnesses being called to place such evidence in its proper context.

Cases at the Special Tribunal for Lebanon and the ICC have likewise illustrated the significance of cellular phones, the popularisation of the internet, and social media. Today, international crimes often leave behind new footprints (such as on-site video recordings, or contemporaneous interviews and (social) media campaigns or material product by armed groups). The increasingly ubiquity of digital technology also now means that countless citizens stand ready to capture crucial evidence and have the ability to transmit it at the blink of an eye. Indeed, relevant evidence may be captured without knowing or intending to do so.

Today, due to the transformation in the production and analysis of digital media over the last decade, conflicts and international crises generate such material on a truly massive scale. Actors cannot take law to the frontlines, where conflict wages and civilians all too frequently suffer, without modern equipment and without understanding and embracing technology.

1 L Freeman, 'Digital Evidence and War Crimes Prosecutions: The Impact of Digital Technologies on International Criminal Investigations and Trials' (2018) 41 *Fordham International Law Journal* 283, 285.

2 N Porzucki, 'How the Nuremberg Trials Changed Interpretation Forever' (*The World*, 29 September 2014) <https://alanguages.com/how-the-nuremberg-trials-changed-interpretation-forever/> accessed 19 September 2022.

New technologies bring not only opportunities to gather and analyse more data and evidence—they also bring risks and challenges which may range from the need to authenticate digital materials (addressing so-called 'shallow' or 'deep fakes', for example) to addressing potential imperfections in our understanding of evidence. These may arise from the manner in which we seek and identify information (selection bias) and also from the nature of information that may be more readily available to us (access bias). Reflecting these challenges, we need a profound shift in the way the Office of the Prosecutor of the ICC (OTP) harnesses technology and digital tools.

This chapter will first briefly consider the changed (and ever evolving) reality in which international justice now operates (Section 2). It will then outline several steps taken by the OTP to revolutionise and enhance its efficiency and effectiveness through the use of modern technology (Section 3). In addition, it will consider how to capitalise on opportunities (such as fully exploiting available evidence) and how to mitigate risks related to the use of technology (Section 4). While by no means a comprehensive overview, this chapter will seek to demonstrate the necessity of further embracing technological advancement—while duly managing risks—to enable the Court to comply with its mandate and further honour and vindicate the rights of survivors and affected communities.

## 2 The Playing Field of Technological Advancement

The *ad hoc* tribunals contributed significantly to setting the agenda for contemporary international criminal law. The advances showcased by the ICTY and ICTR in harnessing evidence derived from technology and deploying it as either primary, or evidence corroborating other evidence, such as witnesses,[3] is noteworthy. For example, the ICTR case *Prosecutor vs Nahimana et al.* recognized and crystalised the real power of broadcast messaging in the commission of crimes, admitting into evidence radio recordings made available years after the broadcast. Hundreds of these RTLM recordings[4] provided relevant

3 See e.g., Judgment and Sentence, *Al Mahdi, Situation in the Republic of Mali*, ICC-01/12-01/15, TC VIII, ICC, 27 September 2016, e.g., para. 38, relying, among others, on video evidence, as establishing the attacks and Al Mahdi's responsibility. See also generally *Bemba et al* Judgement (relying, inter alia, on telephone communication logs); Judgment pursuant to Article 74 of the Statute, *Bemba, Situation in the Central African Republic*, ICC-01/05-01/08-3343, TC III, ICC, 21 March 2016.

4 Radio Télévision Libre des Milles Collines.

and probative evidence that was admitted before the Trial Chamber and which helped lead to the conviction of three individuals for crimes including direct and public incitement to commit genocide. In this case, known as the 'media trial', the very tool used for the commission of this crime helped establish not only the constituent physical acts of the offence—but also the *mens rea* of Ferdinand Nahimana.[5] It was an apt outcome as Mr. Nahimana had himself stated on a radio broadcast presented to the judges of the ICTR that 'today's wars are not fought using bullets only, it is also a war of media, words, newspapers and radio stations'.[6]

Likewise, at the ICTY case of *Prosecutor v. Tolimir*,[7] the Prosecution made use of aerial images provided by the United States government.[8] The Trial Chamber accepted the relevance, probative value and authenticity of these images, after hearing defence challenges, as they were often corroborated by the testimony of fact and expert witnesses.

5 Judgment and Sentence, *Nahimana et al.*, ICTR-99-52-T, TC I, ICTR, 3 December 2003,, e.g., para. 1017 (finding that the "[e]ntirety of the RTLM broadcasting from July 1993 through July 1994, the alleged impact of which culminated in the events that took place in 1994, falls within the temporal jurisdiction of the Tribunal *to the extent that the broadcasts are deemed to constitute direct and public incitement to genocide*". Emphasis added); see also paras. 1031–1032; and paras. 1033 (finding that Nahimana acted with genocidal intent, considering that he was responsible for RTLM programming); para. 966 (finding that, Nahimana as the mastermind of the RTLM, he "set in motion the communication weaponry that fought the "war of the media, words, newspapers and radio stations" he described in his Radio Rwanda broadcast of 25 April as the complement to bullets. Nahimana also expressed his intent through RTLM, where the words broadcast were intended to kill on the basis of ethnicity, and that is what they did"). e.g., para. 1017 (finding that the '[e]ntirety of the RTLM broadcasting from July 1993 through July 1994, the alleged impact of which culminated in the events that took place in 1994, falls within the temporal jurisdiction of the Tribunal *to the extent that the broadcasts are deemed to constitute direct and public incitement to genocide*'. Emphasis added); see also paras 1031–1032; and para. 1033 (finding that Nahimana acted with genocidal intent, considering that he was responsible for RTLM programming); para. 966 (finding that, Nahimana as the mastermind of the RTLM, he 'set in motion the communication weaponry that fought the "war of the media, words, newspapers and radio stations" he described in his Radio Rwanda broadcast of 25 April as the complement to bullets. Nahimana also expressed his intent through RTLM, where the words broadcast were intended to kill on the basis of ethnicity, and that is what they did').

6 Ibid., 184.

7 Trial Judgment, *Tolimir*, IT-05-88/2-T, TC II, ICTY, 12 December 2012 67–70, 564.

8 Ex. P00214, p. 1. Rule 70(C) provides that 'the Trial Chamber [...] may not order either party to produce additional evidence received from the person or entity providing the initial information, nor may the Trial Chamber for the purpose of obtaining such additional evidence itself summon that person or a representative of that entity as a witness or order their attendance'. Trial Judgment, *Tolimir*, IT-05-88/2-T, TC II, ICTY, 12 December 2012, para. 68.

In its early cases, the ICC faced some criticism for its over-reliance on witnesses and under-reliance on physical or forensic evidence. The potential vulnerabilities of that approach were acknowledged in the ICC's very first trial judgment when Trial Chamber I recalled that witness testimony may sometimes be flawed or unreliable, especially when based on experiences of witnesses testifying in relation to Rome Statute crimes that often involves extremely traumatic events.[9] For similar reasons, especially in the early years of the ICC, local documentary sources were very often scant or unreliable.

While efforts were made subsequently to diversify evidentiary sources, the ICC's first trial involving significant reliance on technology and digital evidence was *Bemba et al.*, in which Trial Chamber VII accepted the authenticity and reliability of telephone communications logs and Western Union records.[10] The adjusted approach and use of more diversified and digital evidence shows the OTP's increasing awareness of the need to supplement its reliance on witness evidence.

This realisation found form in the OTP strategic plans for the periods 2012–2015, 2016–2018, and 2019–2021. In 2013, the Office noted that it:

> is also facing an explosive growth in its access to digital data, whether it is coming from (smart)phones and tablets, servers or from the possibilities offered by the internet. The increased access to such evidence in combination with its high degree of reliability is causing the Office to focus on expanding its capabilities to collect different forms of scientific evidence.[11]

The OTP added that investigation plans would from then on include 'a systematic review of the options for obtaining evidence alternative to witness statements' from the start of the investigation.[12] In 2015, the OTP similarly noted that new technologies 'offer new ways of presenting cases in Court through the use of, for instance, 3-D scanning, 360 degree photography, and facial recognition'.[13]

9 Judgment pursuant to Article 74 of the Statute, *Lubanga, Situation in the Democratic Republic of the Congo*, ICC-01/04-01/06-2842, TC I, ICC, 14 March 2012, paras 102–104.

10 Judgment pursuant to Article 74 of the Statute, *Bemba, Situation in the Central African Republic*, ICC-01/05-01/13-1989-Red, ICC, TC VII, 19 October 2016.

11 ICC OTP, 'Strategic plan June 2012–2015' (11 October 2013), 44 <https://www.icc-cpi.int/sites/default/files/iccdocs/otp/OTP-Strategic-Plan-2013.pdf> accessed 19 September 2022.

12 Ibid.

13 ICC OTP, 'Strategic plan 2016–2018' (16 July 2015), 21.

The OTP took initial steps to bring this strategy to fruition in the *Al-Mahdi*, *Al-Hassan*, and *Al-Werfalli* cases. In the case of *Al-Mahdi*, which concerned the war crime of attacks intentionally directed against buildings dedicated to religion and historical cultural monuments, including nine mausoleums and a mosque in Timbuktu, Mali, the Prosecution collected a wealth of digital evidence. Indeed, based upon his own words so recorded, the Trial Chamber found that Mr. Al Mahdi, 'had overall responsibility for the execution phase of the attack, [...] justifying the attack to the broader world through media interviews'.[14] In addition, Mr Al-Mahdi had allowed journalists to video record the destruction of the cultural heritage which was central to the charges against him.[15] In preparing its case, the OTP had created 360 degree images which were compiled by SITU Research—together with other digital evidence—into an innovative platform that showed six of the key sites in question before, during, and after the destruction of protected objects.[16] While Mr Al-Mahdi's admission of guilt meant that the evidence was not challenged, the platform ensured that the evidence was organised and accessible and helped the judges, parties and public alike more keenly understand what was alleged and established by the evidence. Presenting the evidence through this digital reconstruction tool allowed the judges to get a grasp of the scene and to bridge, to some extent, the geographical and temporal gap between the events and Hague-based proceedings. Indeed, it may be that the authentic and reliable nature of the evidence disclosed to the defence helped lead to the admission of guilt by the accused. The case was eventually closed with only three context and expert witnesses.[17] The hearing of the evidence was completed in three days, and Mr Al-Mahdi received his verdict a little over a month after the proceedings begun.

In the case against *Al-Hassan*, where a broader set of crimes also committed in Timbuktu were alleged, the OTP subsequently introduced a more elaborate digital platform to help present its case.[18] This platform compiled different pieces of evidence to present a reconstruction of Timbuktu, including different locations, objects, and (audio-visual) materials related to alleged crimes.

14 Judgment and Sentence, *Al Mahdi, Situation in the Republic of Mali*, ICC-01/12-01/15-171, TC VIII, ICC, 27 September 2016, para. 53.

15 Ibid., para. 38.

16 SITU Research compiled the platform *pro bono*. See: SITU Research, 'ICC Digital Platform: Timbuktu, Mali' (2016) <https://situ.nyc/research/projects/icc-digital-platform-timbuktu-mali> accessed 20 September 2022.

17 Trial Chamber VIII Transcript, *Al Mahdi, Situation in the Republic of Mali*, ICC-01/12-01/15-T-4-Red-ENG, ICC, TC VIII, 22 August 2016.

18 Trial Chamber X Transcript, *Al Hassan, Situation in the Republic of Mali*, ICC-01/12-01/18-T-018-Red-ENG, ICC, TC X, 15 July 2020, 18.

The potential advantages of this way of presenting such evidence are manifold and may include: avoiding the necessity of certain potentially dangerous site visits for the judges; presenting evidence to the judges in a user-friendly and accessible manner; and enabling witnesses in the courtroom to discuss relevant evidence in a more comprehensive way. Trial Chamber X's acceptance of the platform shows that the law and procedure of the ICC is ready to accommodate forward-thinking approaches to the presentation of evidence. Notably, counsel representing Mr Al-Hassan did not challenge the use of the platform themselves, provided that all evidence presented therein would be admitted into evidence separately. Indeed, the defence sought full access to the virtual platform, and required (and were provided) training and guidance on its use, so that they could also deploy it as needed. As noted by Trial Chamber X, the parties reached mutual agreement with regard to the defence's access to the platform.[19]

In the case of *Al-Werfalli*, the OTP relied on technology to prove its allegations in an even more direct way. Thus, the Prosecutor successfully relied on social media posts to present Pre-Trial Chamber I with sufficient evidence to justify the issuance of a warrant of arrest against Mr Al-Werfalli.[20] These 'posts depicted several incidents in relation to which the Pre-Trial Chamber I noted that 'the posting on social media of the videos depicting the executions, and the frequency and particular cruelty with which they are carried out satisfy the Chamber that Mr Al-Werfalli is unlikely to cooperate with a summons to appear [...]. Thus, the issuance of a warrant of arrest is necessary'.[21]

The significant increase in user-generated evidence shows that *Al-Werfalli*, known to some as the 'social media case',[22] is clearly a trend that is only increasing. In its 2019–2021 Strategic plan, the OTP noted that:

---

19 Public redacted version of Third Decision on the introduction of prior recorded testimonies pursuant to Rule 68(2)(b) of the Rules, *Al Hassan, Situation in the Republic of Mali*, ICC-01/12-01/18-1402-Red2, TC X, ICC, 14 April 2021.

20 Warrant of Arrest, *Al-Werfalli, Situation in Libya*, ICC-01/11-01/17-2, PTC I, ICC, 15 August 2017. The Pre-Trial Chamber shall issue a warrant of arrest if, among other considerations, it is satisfied that there are reasonable grounds to believe that the relevant person has committed a crime within the jurisdiction of the Court: Art. 58, Rome Statute. Proceedings in this case were subsequently terminated in light of the death of Mr Al-Werfalli: Decision terminating proceedings against Mr Mahmoud Mustafa Busayf Al-Werfalli, *Al-Werfalli, Situation in Libya*, ICC-01/11-01/17-24, PTC I, ICC, 15 June 2022.

21 Warrant of Arrest, *Al-Werfalli, Situation in Libya*, ICC-01/11-01/17-2, PTC I, ICC, 15 August 2017, para. 29.

22 L Freeman, 'Digital Evidence and War Crimes Prosecutions: The Impact of Digital Technologies on International Criminal Investigations and Trials' (2018) 41(2) *Fordham International Law Journal* 283, 332.

> Science and technology remain very important aspects to the work of the Office. Both the Al Mahdi and the Al-Werfalli cases have shown how online investigations combined with the right forensic approach can help to prove cases. Team requests for support by the Office's forensic team have increased considerably. The world of science and forensics covers, however, such a vast terrain, and evolves at such a high pace that the Office cannot master this on its own. In the 2016–2018 period, the Office has intensified its network, which could support it in being aware of the many opportunities and challenges that science and technology bring, and in knowing how to tackle them. To date, different partners have expressed and demonstrated their willingness to assist the Office: the Scientific Advisory Board, the Technology Advisory Board, the University of California Berkeley Human Rights Centre, the Carnegie Mellon University Centre for Human Rights Science, Europol, and Interpol, to name but a few. The Office will continue its present strategy with these partners so that it can develop a good understanding of how technology will influence its work and how to adapt itself to this new reality.[23]

The emergence of vast quantities of user-generated and other digital data and the need to secure this type of evidence has been recognised as an important focus for new mechanisms created in recent years to collect, collate, analyse and preserve evidence of international crimes. These include the UN investigative mechanisms for crimes committed by Da'esh/ISIL (UNITAD), for the situation in Myanmar since 2011 (IIMM), and for the situation in the Syrian Arab Republic since 2011 (IIIM).[24] For instance, UNITAD's evidentiary repositories are reported to be populated with terabytes of open-source data chronicling ISIL activities and propaganda,[25] battlefield evidence from a significant volume of seized ISIL hard drives and mobile phones,[26] numerous 3D models and

23 OTP ICC, 'Strategic Plan 2019–2021' (17 July 2019).

24 See: UNGA Res 71/248 (21 December 2016) UN Doc A/RES/71/248 (IIIM); UNSC Res 2379 (21 September 2017) UN Doc S/RES/2379 (UNITAD); and UN HRC Res 39/2 (27 September 2018) UN Doc A/HRC/RES/39/2 (IIMM).

25 UNSC, Letter dated 7 November 2022 from the Special Adviser and Head of the United Nations Investigative Team to Promote Accountability for Crimes Committed by Da'esh/ Islamic State in Iraq and the Levant addressed to the President of the Security Council (8 November 2022) UN Doc S/2022/836.

26 UNSC, Letter dated 24 November 2021 from the Special Adviser and Head of the United Nations Investigative Team to Promote Accountability for Crimes Committed by Da'esh/ Islamic State in Iraq and the Levant addressed to the President of the Security Council (24 November 2021) UN Doc S/2021/974.

maps through terrestrial scans,[27] and over 175000 facial profiles extracted from tens of thousands of image and video holdings,[28] among other digital or digitized data. The Investigative Team is noted to be leveraging advanced methodologies to efficiently exploit this data and address the challenges of increasing volumes of digital evidence, including employing technology assisted-review and predictive-coding technologies. Similarly, the IIIM notes exploitation of internet sources as well as multimedia analysis as a key focus in its reporting, highlighting efforts in relation to the collection of large volumes of digital data.[29]

National investigations have similarly increased their reliance on social media evidence and other user-generated data, such as in the investigation conducted jointly by the Dutch and other authorities concerning the d owning of Malaysian Airlines Flight MH17 over eastern Ukraine. In addition, digital applications have been created to capture the required metadata to facilitate reliance on user-generated information in the courtroom.

The successful use of technology in *Al-Mahdi*, *Al-Hassan* and *Al-Werfalli* shows its potential to have a positive impact on the OTP's work, including by strengthening the cases presented in court. Technology that helps to overcome the temporal and/or geographical distance between the courtroom and the alleged crimes will help meet one of the ICC's key challenges—limited access to, and understanding of, the context in which crimes allegedly took place. In addition, greater acceptance of user-generated evidence (meeting suitable standards) has the potential to democratise international criminal investigations and may help transform them into a bottom-up process. This may provide at least a partial response to the well-known critique of 'Hague-based investigators flying into African countries to take evidence from the local population and then flying out again'.[30] But while there has been discernible progress in

27 UNSC, Letter dated 7 November 2022 from the Special Adviser and Head of the United Nations Investigative Team to Promote Accountability for Crimes Committed by Da'esh/Islamic State in Iraq and the Levant addressed to the President of the Security Council (n 25).

28 UNSC, Letter dated 1 May 2021 from the Special Adviser and Head of the United Nations Investigative Team to Promote Accountability for Crimes Committed by Da'esh/Islamic State in Iraq and the Levant addressed to the President of the Security Council (3 May 2021) UN Doc S/2021/419.

29 UNGA, International, Impartial and Independent Mechanism to Assist in the Investigation and Prosecution of Persons Responsible for the Most Serious Crimes under International Law Committed in the Syrian Arab Republic since March 2011 (16 February 2023) UN Doc A/77/751.

30 R J Hamilton, 'New Technologies in International Criminal Investigations' (2018) 112(4) *American Society of International Law Proceedings* 131, 132.

how cases are being presented in the court room, there is about to be a revolution as to the quantities of evidence collected, ingested and analysed and the means deployed to achieve this.

## 3 Steps to Revolutionise and Enhance Efficiency and Effectiveness Through the Use of Modern Technology

As is clear from the sections above, audio-visual, electronic, log based, and documentary records generated by participants, survivors and bystanders and stored across cloud and application based systems—constitute a significant part of contemporary investigations of international crimes. The need to grapple with these new complex data sets and underlying metadata, alongside continued focus on more traditional activities such as the collection of testimonial evidence constitutes the new normal for the OTP, now and most likely for years to come.

The new evidential landscape that confronts the OTP requires it to significantly adapt its processes and indeed create new ones—and to acquire and apply new tools, to more effectively handle the massive data sets that are frequently—and increasingly—the hallmark of situations within the Court's jurisdiction. In fact, it is fair to say that an objective assessment has made it clear that a fundamentally new approach is required to the collection, storage and analysis of material to ensure that the Prosecutor's Article 54 obligations to investigating incriminating and exonerating evidence equally are implemented in practice.

Harnessing technology more effectively is essential in almost every area of the work of the Office. These include in order to collect, filter and analyse video and audio materials; identify and plot potential key crime scene locations, suspected perpetrators, and other evidential reference points; and to deploy it so as to better protect staff from the risk of secondary trauma (by preventing or reducing repeated exposure to graphic and disturbing video content relevant to investigations).

In March 2022, the OTP created a Trust Fund for Advanced Technology and Specialised Capacity, inviting States Parties to contribute through voluntary financial contributions and with the secondment of qualified staff. 50% of this Trust Fund ('TF') has been used to acquire and implement advanced new technological tools and equipment, and thus enhance the collection, analysis, and language-processing of evidence. This should accelerate the OTP's work and will represent a quantum leap in the tools available to discharge its statutory responsibilities. Specifically, with the TF, the OTP has initiated a comprehensive information systems project aimed at three key elements: big data analysis services, software, and human resources.

### 3.1 *Cognitive Services*

The OTP is currently working with Microsoft, Accenture Avanade, and other partners to develop cutting-edge solutions and cognitive services for the analysis of large volumes of digital or digitized data—often composed of heterogeneous file types, much of it photographs, videos, and scans of hand-written material—collected through its investigative activities.

The OTP will leverage artificial intelligence and machine learning tools to effectively analyse these large volumes without compromise to functionality. In relation to audio-visual data, these tools will automate the identification of spoken languages including several local languages relevant to its investigations, to transcribe and translate spoken word into searchable formats. This would also apply to documentary and other textual material which would not only be made searchable in a language of choice but also navigable in native formats (tweets, messages, emails, forms) for a more contextual document review. Building on this technology will ensure more expeditious investigations: analysts and investigators will be able to interact more directly and easily with source material through targeted searches, reserving the assistance of language assistants or translators for official translations.

In addition, the responsible use of artificial intelligence will increase the OTP's capacity to search for and detect individuals, objects, and locations, across copious amounts of visual media, allowing for its inquiries to be directed more precisely, as well as facilitating the swift review of relevant material by analysts, investigators and lawyers. The OTP intends to adhere to best practices on the ethical use of artificial intelligence.

### 3.2 *Software*

The OTP will develop its software to ensure that enriched evidentiary data can be efficiently drawn on by investigators and analysts. In addition, the development of a customized evidence lifecycle management system will centralise knowledge and critical information for the OTP.[31]

---

31 ELMS manages evidence through its entire lifecycle and assures that all relevant evidence is collected and stored in a manner consistent with international standards. This begins at the source, tracking all source development, investigation, forensics, e-discovery and analysis tasks. ELMS captures evidence intake and registration, including by investigators in the field with its companion mobile application. In keeping with the highest international standards, ELMS reliably documents chain-of-custody in an auditable format and

The move to cloud-based technology will also improve the OTP's data security, as it will be able to benefit from the collective security systems of a market-leaders such as Microsoft, in addition to its existing array of data security measures. Moving to the cloud is clearly a necessary step given many platforms and tools are cloud based and given the imperative of working more consistently in the field. Cloud based solutions allows evidence and information to be uploaded from different locations and also accessed securely from various locations by OTP staff requiring access.

### 3.3 *Consultation and Collaboration*

A critical aspect in advancing the OTP's vision to leverage modern technology and address the evolving evidentiary landscape, is recognizing that a cohesive approach is central to fully exploit the potential of such technology. Naturally, in taking these software developments further the OTP will engage with numerous stakeholders and organs including the Chambers, Registry, and the International Criminal Court Bar Association (ICCBA) which represents legal representatives of the victims and Defence. Such engagement will be of a multi-faceted and continuous nature, during the preliminary roll-out of new systems as well as on a case-by-case basis.

As a part of this engagement, the OTP will propose refined methodologies for identification and disclosure of relevant evidence and invite dialogue to better ensure the upholding of international best practices in relation to the rights of the accused and inspection of material. A key aim of modernizing systems remains to simplify and accelerate disclosure to better serve these rights. Revised modalities would thus be firmly grounded in the Prosecutor's duty to extend the investigation to cover all facts and evidence relevant to an assessment of criminal responsibility, including investigating exonerating circumstances and disclosing exculpatory evidence.

Equally, this modality would give effect to the right of the defence to inspect material relevant to the preparation of the defence, and seek to provide such inspection in an accessible format. While the OTP's methodology will involve employment of comprehensive search and review strategies, it will also allow

---

records the location of physical and digital evidence. This careful tracking and activity logging continues through electronic discovery and the management of incoming and outgoing information requests. Using QR-code labelling and scanning, with plans to implement radio-frequency identification technology, evidence is tracked when moved into or out of a controlled and secured with biometric locks and CCTV cameras evidence room. The system also manages forensics and evidence-analysis tasks, and includes dashboards, visualisations and reporting features.

Defence to contemplate new search parameters and inspect relevant material within parts of the new technologically empowered environment.

In parallel, the OTP intends to provide training in relation to relevant capabilities within these platforms, and provide backstopping technical support, and if agreed and after consultations, Court-wide seminars and workshops to not only familiarize with but advance the discourse of use of technology, are also envisaged. In this way, it is hoped evidence can be rendered more useful and accessible, and modern technology prove advantages to all parties. The trust that may hopefully be fostered by this new dialogue may also lead to more focused trials with ever greater focus on the facts in dispute.

### 3.4 *Human Resources*

The OTP will invest in data processors and cybersecurity specialists to assist in getting the maximum benefit from the new tools available. In particular, the OTP will need to invest in diversifying the skillsets available among its staff. This is not so much a matter of developing a new generation of investigators and analysts but rather complementing the OTP's present strengths in its human resources with new insights, experiences and approaches. Ensuring that the new technology is actually *usable*—and is used—is crucial to ensuring that the OTP's objective of its ground-breaking collaboration with Microsoft and other partners comes to fruition. Specifically, this means that the type and quantity of evidence gathered for use in court is increased, and that investigators and analysts can act ever more promptly, removing some of the sources of friction may act to delay investigations and proceedings. If these tools live up to their potential, they may not only support and sustain more rapid decision making but also more harmonious workflow within the OTP. For example, translators enriching the continuous decision making of analysts and investigators, contributing to stronger cases presented in court by the OTP's trial lawyers.It is anticipated that harnessing technology will, therefore, not only minimise unnecessary operational lag, but also enrich the scope of available evidence, increase the efficiency and effectiveness of the OTP, and improve working conditions for staff members faced with making sense of multiple terabytes of relevant information.

Beyond its own staff, the OTP is also actively leveraging public-private partnerships to increase its digital transformation capacity. For years the Office has built relationships with NGO's and some universities and advisory groups. This needs to be deepened and expanded to include relevant private and state-actors who may contribute to the cause of justice with financial and in-kind donations in the form of hardware, software, time, knowledge and expertise. The current drive to improve the Office is also being augmented with the secondments and funds provided through the TF—thereby further setting the stage for the OTP to present the most reliable evidence available, to be tested by the parties and ultimately scrutinised and assessed by the independent judges of the Court. More reliable evidence and access to a wider range of evidence will make for ever better decisions by the Office and by the Court and so to help to build confidence in the ICC as whole. It must be noted that the primary responsibility to provide resources for a sustainable model of justice lays with those states that make up the Assembly of States Parties. Additional resources are obviously needed and the case to provide them is comeppling from any vantage point.

Finally, with the roll out of the new e-Discovery platform in autumn 2022, the OTP is building an information hub that will facilitate the more efficient sharing of the information it collects with national authorities for them both to use and to assess—and hence to further narrow what is far too frequently an impunity gap at domestic levels. In this way, the Rome Statute system can better live up to its potential—foreshadowed by the principle of complementary and as also provided for in Article 93(10) if the Stature—to serve as a two-way street, in which the OTP works as a hub in the centre of international criminal justice, rather than a detached apex. Using the new technologies available, the OTP looks to revolutionise its performance in managing information compared to the first 20 years of its existence—for example, in addressing incoming requests for assistance, the OTP hopes that it will be able to shorten response time from an estimated 180 days to less than 30 days by end of 2023 or early 2024.

In particular, the overhaul of the OTP's technological architecture will facilitate receiving and processing larger data sets, setting the OTP up to leverage the unprecedented level of (digital) information as a key advantage in its work. The use of an evidence life-cycle management system, digital forensics, crime scene tools, and various eDiscovery tools will facilitate efficient evidence analysis in the OTP. Crucially, a detailed overview of available evidence will put the OTP in a unique position to provide evidence and analytical products in support of national proceedings, and to efficiently and effectively respond to States Parties that request assistance. In these ways, the OTP can show that it provides tangible value to national investigators and prosecutors. Receiving prompt, valuable, and regular assistance from the OTP will ensure that accountability for Rome Statute Crimes becomes a reality in both national and international contexts.

Re-visualising the OTP as a hub for international justice also complements other key relationships, including with civil society and national authorities, in order to maximise the impact in areas of mutual interest, and to manage the inflow of evidence generated by modern conflict. For example, in September 2022, the OTP and Eurojust (including through its Genocide Network) published guidelines for civil society organisations on documenting international crimes and human rights violations for accountability purposes[32]—including advice and checklists on a range of relevant activities such as the conduct of online investigations and the taking of videos and photographs.

## 4 Harnessing Technology: a Critical Decision Making to Capitalise on Opportunities and Mitigate Risks

Over the course of its 20-year existence, the OTP has been nearing a crossroad. Today, it has undoubtedly reached the point where the influx of digital information is such that it is no longer possible for its staff to review and act on it properly *without* more effectively harnessing technology. Perhaps all on going situations where alleged crimes are being committed, in which large quantities of data exist, underline the critical importance of enhancing the OTP's capacity to gather; review the growing variety of evidence. These frequently amount to multiple terabytes of relevant information, hundreds of thousands of video and audio files, and millions of document files in various languages and dialects. Without adjusting to the changed technological landscape, the OTP would be left behind, its investigations and prosecutions would slow down, and pressure on resources (both material and human)[33] would increase yet further– an unsustainable model that would negatively affect the functioning of the Court, its impact, and the credibility of the Rome Statute system as a whole. Put another way, the risks of *not* engaging with technological advancement are clear, significant, and highly likely to materialise. In such a context, while it certainly cannot be said that there are no risks arising from the use of new technologies, what is important is whether those risks can be identified and mitigated—and whether in the final analysis those risks weigh less than those associated with a failure to change.

32 OTP, Eurojust, Network for investigation and prosecution of genocide, crimes against humanity and war crimes, *Documenting international crimes and human rights violations for accountability purposes: Guidelines for civil society organisations* (2022), <https://www.eurojust.europa.eu/sites/default/files/assets/eurojust-icc-csos-guidelines.pdf> accessed 28 April 2023.

33 In 2020 the Independent Experts commented on work pressures, noting that it is a point of attention for all Principles of the Court. 'Independent Expert Review of the International Criminal Court and the Rome Statute System: Final Report—30 September 2020, ICC-ASP/19/16, 9 November 2020 (Nineteenth Session of the ASP).

In 2015, the UN Special Rapporteur on extrajudicial, summary or arbitrary executions, Mr Christof Heyns, noted that:

> increasing digital capacity is greatly enhancing the ability of ordinary people to participate in human rights monitoring. Digital ICTs create opportunities for pluralism that can democratize the process of human rights fact-finding [...] [s]ocial media have created a wealth of opportunities for civilians to highlight human rights violations that they have witnessed, often unmediated by formal intergovernmental or non-governmental structures.[34]

Yet this bold aspiration is undeniably matched by risk, and we can immediately identify several examples. First, the pluralism of fact-finding and information-sharing is relative. Not everyone has access to the tools that allow sharing of user-generated data. Indeed, factors such as gender, income, age, internet penetration, and government interference (for example through orchestrated black-outs)[35] influence an individual's access.[36] In addition, there is a risk that certain crimes will be easier or more often recorded, risking hypervisibility, 'drawing attention to those crimes like shiny objects, while detracting from other online information, such as that related to sexual violence, which may not as easily be captured by machines'.[37] Nor are sexual and gender-based crimes necessarily unusual in that respect—crimes against children and the crime of starvation may, for example, also be less visible.

Second, while user-generated data can provide investigators access to invaluable insights, it may transfer some or all of the protection risks involved from

34 HRC, Report of the Special Rapporteur on extrajudicial, summary or arbitrary executions, Christof Heyns (254 April 2015) UN Doc A/HRC/29/37.

35 For example, in September 2019 the government of Bangladesh banned 3G and 4G internet and the use of SIM cards by Rohingya refugees in Cox's Bazar due to security concerns. Internet access was restored a little shy of a year later in August 2020. See: F D'Alessandra and K Sutherland, 'The Promise and Challenges of New Actors and New Technologies in International Justice' (2021) 19(1) *Journal of International Criminal Justice* 9, 22.

36 Y McDermott, D Murray, A Koenig, 'Digital Accountability Symposium: Whose Stories Get Told, and by Whom? Representativeness in Open Source Human Rights Investigations'(*Opinio Juris*, 19 December 2019) <http://opiniojuris.org/2019/12/19/digital-accountability-symposium-whose-stories-get-told-and-by-whom-representativeness-in-open-source-human-rights-investigations/> accessed 21 September 2022.

37 Koenig and Egan in Y McDermott, A Koenig, and D Murray, 'Open Source Information's Blind Spot Human and Machine Bias in International Criminal Investigations' (2021) 19(1) *Journal of International Criminal Justice* 85, 92–93.

a professional investigator on a mission to a lay witness with a hand-held device uploading information. While there are initiatives to provide free training and resources to inform individuals on how to safely document crimes of international concern—take, for example, the WITNESS initiative[38] which provides assistance with regard to the use of video and technology to protect and defend human rights—these cannot eliminate the risks entirely.

Third, there are risks associated with the collection of digital materials online, even by professional investigators. While reliance on digital evidence may help to limit some vulnerabilities such as selection bias in selecting witness interviews, this does not mean that bias is limited overall. Other relevant biases may arise, including access bias, selection bias caused by hypervisibility, and the 'availability heuristic'[39]—all of which may serve to drown out information relating to events that are, for whatever reason, under-reported.[40]

Fourth, the use of presentation technology may also have the potential to bias the user, as the way information is presented can have a profound impact on an individuals' conclusion. Since, as Zarmsky notes, 'digital reconstructions can be so easily believed to be true even if there is a significant possibility for human bias or error, this technology needs to be approached with caution through a critical lens when used in international criminal courtrooms in order for justice to be progressed and not hindered'.[41] Further to this critical outlook in dealing with presentation technology, it is also important to consider the effect that widely-shared photographs or videos may have on witnesses' accounts: such materials may, without care, (un)consciously influence

38 WITNESS See it Film it Change it, <https://www.witness.org/our-work/> accessed 21 September 2022.

39 Access bias: 'the bias around who has access to the technologies and tools needed for documenting events'. Selection bias: 'When particular groups or individuals are over-or under-represented in a study population, leading to a systematic error in extrapolating results to a broader population'. Availability heuristic: 'The tendency to base decisions or conclusions on information that can be easily accessed or brought to mind'. See McDermott, Koenig, and Murray, 'Open Source Information's Blind Spot Human and Machine Bias in International Criminal Investigations' (2021) 19(1) *Journal of International Criminal Justice* 85, 85, 89–90.

40 Alexa Koenig, and Daragh Murray, 'Open Source Information's Blind Spot Human and Machine Bias in International Criminal Investigations' (n 37) 96. See also the chapter by Koenig and Freeman in this volume.

41 S Zarmsky, 'Why Seeing Should Not Always Be Believing: Considerations Regarding the Use of Digital Reconstruction Technology in International Law'(2021) 19(1) *Journal of International Criminal Justice* 213, 221.

a witness, for example through the belief that the shared incident is the (only) one investigators wish to talk about or that merits investigation.[42]

In other words, while user-generated evidence is beneficial in that it may provide victims and affected communities easy access to investigators and prosecutors to share what they witnessed, that same facility of communication may also mean that certain presumptions or expectations are shared no less easily.

Fifth, while new technologies offer the potential of new forms of collecting or authenticating relevant evidence, they also offer new opportunities to falsify or forge evidence. For example, so-called 'deep fake' images or imagery—which are doctored, staged, or otherwise misleading, sometimes produced with considerable technical sophistication—may be perceived as confirming the guilt of a suspect in the eyes of affected communities even before such material is scrutinized or its authenticity confirmed in a courtroom. Alternatively, they may seek to exculpate those responsible by blaming innocent people. So called 'false flag' operations may be used to construct false narratives or justify conduct that is subject to an investigation. In the worst case, there may even be fears whether falsified materials can even be identified as such by experts.

In any event, it is uncontested that investigators increasingly have to deal with both mis-and disinformation. State-engendered disinformation is a concern. So too may be grassroot counterfactual narratives which, through their decentralisation, may be especially pervasive and resilient.[43] (Ironically, such disinformation may nonetheless become *genuine* evidence in certain circumstances—for example, disinformation used to incite violence may be genuine evidence of the incitement, if not of the truth of the underlying claims.)

Sixth, digital evidence may in some circumstances be at greater risk of destruction, degradation, or loss. For example, certain criminal acts committed through the use of social media (such as incitement to violence) will often be against user regulations, causing platforms to remove the relevant content swiftly, even though it is evidence of a crime. Correctly preserving this evidence will be key to ensuring the evidence can be authenticated and admitted, as will questions of 'forward compatibility' as technological systems continue to change.

---

42 McDermott, Murray, Koenig, 'Digital Accountability Symposium: Whose Stories Get Told, and by Whom? Representativeness in Open Source Human Rights Investigations' (n 36).

43 G Fiorella, C Godart, N Waters, 'Digital Integrity: Exploring Digital Evidence Vulnerabilities and Mitigation Strategies for Open Source Researchers' (2021) 19(1) *Journal of International Criminal Justice* 147, 156.

Seventh, there may be a risk that new kinds of evidence are seen—even if incorrectly—as devaluing 'old' kinds of evidence. As McDermott et al. note:

> humans have a cognitive tendency to process visual content as being more convincing or credible than written or oral evidence. [...] Where in the past, the testimony of a credible eyewitness (especially if corroborated by another piece of evidence or testimony) was seen as the gold standard, investigators tell us that there is a growing feeling that 'just' testimony, no matter how powerful, will not be enough.[44]

Considering the ICC's unique role—including in enabling victims to play an active role in proceedings—this is a disconcerting development to which we must pay attention. Yet it cannot mean that it is wrong to use digital evidence where appropriate in a case, and in particular where it may minimise protection and other risks to human witnesses, as in *Al-Mahdi*. Rather, digital and other forms of evidence—including the testimonial evidence of witnesses—should be seen as mutually reinforcing, with each possessing particular strengths and weaknesses. The focus must therefore be on the circumstances of each individual case, and the professionalism of the prosecutors marked by their ability to identify and present the particular 'blend' of evidence apt for that case.

Eighth, and finally, it is essential that the right to fair and expeditious trial is safeguarded and not adversely affected by the use of technology. For example, in cases such as *Al-Hassan* where use was made of a digital platform to present evidence, it was appropriate to organise training sessions to ensure that the Defence and all parties had a solid understanding of the tools in questions, and were not disadvantaged.

While by no means an exhaustive list, this section has discussed a number of the risks and challenges that may arise from the use of new technologies in and outside the courtroom, or the use of new types of evidence. Our awareness of such risks and challenges may itself go some way to mitigating them, but of course it cannot be sufficient to deal with them all entirely. Yet, viewing the balance of risks as a whole, and taking account of the factors that international criminal justice mechanisms cannot control—such as the increasingly 'digital' nature of the world at large—it seems incontrovertible that the OTP must embrace the new paradigm, even while being conscious of its imperfections. In order to remain effective, the OTP must be as pragmatic and as principled in

44 McDermott, Murray, Koenig, 'Digital Accountability Symposium: Whose Stories Get Told, and by Whom? Representativeness in Open Source Human Rights Investigations' (n 36).

its approach to these and other risks, taking remedy where possible, yet continuing to strive to reap the new opportunities which are also made available. Likewise, in the final report of the independent expert panel commissioned by the ICC Assembly of States Parties, it was observed that 'the Court should also be vigilant to take advantage of any currently available technological facilities that can be deployed, and that may be readily adapted, to further enhance the efficiency of the Court'.[45]

Of course, this does not mean that we cannot take steps already to meet some of the anticipated challenges. For example, evidence review sessions can be used not only to test the strength of the evidence in any given case, but also to actively scrutinise any unconscious bias that might have informed an investigation. Technology can also play its part. For example, eDiscovery platforms allow advanced and detailed data analytics and searching, assisting with the prevention or detection of unconscious bias which impacts the work of investigators and analysts. The use of an evidence life-cycle management system in conjunction with an eDiscovery platform may provide a macro-level overview of the sources, geographical distribution, and language distribution of available evidence. Such tools will allow analysts and investigators both to refine their searches as well as harness against access bias.

Similarly, while mis-and disinformation cannot be stopped, investing in resources (both technical and human) to swiftly identify fakes and accredit legitimate materials is essential in ensuring a functional OTP. These challenges are not new, and some capacity already exists. Yet the surge in availability of digital material may mean that reprioritisation in this respect is needed. It is also notable in this context that access to material posted and then removed from (social) media platforms such as Facebook (Meta), Twitter, or TikTok requires collaboration with the platforms themselves. Undoubtedly, investing in relations with private sector entities will strengthen prosecution services, even if appropriate measures are taken to safeguard their independence, similarly to their relationships with States or other actors.

Finally, it is worth noting that technology can also remove or assuage risks which were previously inherent to the investigation of the most serious crimes of international concern, or at least ensure that developments in the quantity of relevant evidence does not lead to corresponding growth in the deleterious effects of that evidence on those who may be required to review it. In particular, as the nature of the evidence in cases falling under the jurisdiction of the

45 Independent Expert Review of the International Criminal Court and the Rome Statute System Final Report (n 33) 189.

ICC is often disturbing or graphic, it is key to minimise exposure of those working on cases to potentially traumatic evidence. Gearing technology to filter out duplicate content and flag graphic images and videos may be a significant step in helping to protect the mental health of those reviewing sensitive materials. UNITAD's 'ZETEO' platform is an example of such a tool,[46] and the OTP may also soon be able to avail itself of similar or even greater functionality.

## 5 Technology at Work: a New Chapter for International Criminal Justice

In conclusion, while the amount of digital and user-generated evidence now available to the OTP is perhaps unprecedented, the significant impact of new technologies on international justice is not. The two have history, each challenging the other to become more efficient, more effective, and to generate more impact. Looking back on the first 20 years of the ICC, it is undeniable that the digital landscape in which it operates has changed unrecognisably—a process that has been evident since the Nuremberg and Tokyo Trials. This has affected the cases brought to court, as well as the way in which they are presented. While not an exhaustive overview of all the opportunities, challenges, and risk associated with harnessing new technologies in the work of international criminal investigators and lawyers, this chapter has shown that we cannot take law to the frontline of today without modern equipment.

Without a doubt the technological landscape will continue to develop and change. Yet the law is equipped to accommodate the technological advancement of today and tomorrow. It is up to us to introduce it in the courtroom to further the cause of international justice. The OTP's experiences in various cases show that the Court is ready to build on the opportunities technology offers. Mindful of the challenges and opportunities associated with harnessing technology and guided by the law, the OTP recognises the important of assessing the use of technology in its work against existing practices, rules and regulations, and *vice versa*. Awareness of how the law aligns with the use of tools, technological or otherwise, is key in the successful discharge of the OTP's mandate and delivering results in the courtroom.

It is clear that the role of victims, and the hearing of their testimony, will continue to be central in criminal proceedings at the ICC. At the same time,

46 UNITAD, 'Harnessing Advanced Technology in International Criminal Investigations' (2021).

since the ICC's creation, the OTP has increasingly strived to place technology at the centre of its strategic planning, and taken notable steps in this regard in cases such as *Al-Hassan, Al-Mahdi, Al-Werfalli,* and *Bemba et al.* Faced with the reality that processing all digital information shared with the OTP is not possible by human means alone, the OTP has taken rapid steps to adopt new technologies that will assist in the more efficient and effective discharge of its mandate. Adapting to this new landscape in a responsible manner requires awareness of the associated risks, and deliberate action to minimise them, while pursuing with vigour the prospect of their positive impact on the cause of justice. This includes (re)prioritising investment in resources and skills related to accreditation of legitimate as opposed to fake materials, security, and the use of acquired hard-and software. The expertise and goodwill of private tech companies are essential in successfully ensuring the ICC's relevance in the future—as is carefully ensuring the OTP's independence when forging new partnerships.

In short, through its new Trust Fund and the support provided by States Parties, partners, and victims and affected communities, the OTP is getting ready for a future that started yesterday. Not only by ensuring efficient, fair, and expeditious proceedings, but also by becoming a hub that supports the (international) justice community at large in pioneering new ways. A lesson we must take from the first two decades of the ICC's operations is that it is not a panacea and there is not one solution for accountability. We must go forward on the strength of enhanced information sharing, and innovative ways of working together in support of domestic and regional accountability efforts. The effective delivery of international criminal justice can take many forms and requires support of all those invested in ending impunity for atrocities and contributing to their prevention. Embracing technology means we get one step closer.

CHAPTER 8

# Collaboration between the Office of the Prosecutor and Third-Party Investigators

*Rafael Braga da Silva*

## 1 Introduction*

Since the idea of creating an international criminal tribunal came into discussion, it was known that there would be a significant demand of resources to sustain a court whose jurisdiction that has almost global reach in terms of territory. Twenty years after the International Criminal Court ('the Court' or 'the ICC') started operating and the Rome Statute entered into force, the Court, has had its work deeply affected by the lack of resources. The Office of the Prosecutor ('OTP') has been particularly transparent about how its activities have been limited by the resources available throughout its existence.[1] Particularly during the Review Process, the OTP "has repeatedly referred to the lack of resources, especially in terms of staff, as one of the reasons for its inability to perform at the levels expected of it by the States Parties and other stakeholders".[2]

Perhaps one of the most visible effects of the lack of resources granted to the OTP is its so-called 'evidence problem'.[3] Limited investigative resources

---

* The views expressed in this chapter are those of the author alone and do not necessarily reflect the views of the International Residual Mechanism for Criminal Tribunals or the United Nations in general. The author would like to thank Felicina Hawa for her assistance on the article.

1 See, e.g., ICC OTP, 'Annual Report of the Office of the Prosecutor-2022' (1 December 2022) (stating the need to optimize the 'Office's finite resources'); ICC OTP, 'Report on the Implementation of the OTP Strategic Plan | 2016–2018' (23 August 2019) (where the Prosecutor states that other investigations have not advanced as quickly as desired 'in large part due to limited resources').

2 ICC ASP, 'Independent Expert Review Report of the International Criminal Court and the Rome Statute System: Final Report 30 September 2020' (9 November 2020) ICC Doc No ICC-ASP/19/16, para. 176a.

3 See, eg, C M De Vos, 'Investigating from Afar: The ICC's Evidence Problem' (2013) 26(4) Leiden Journal of International Law 1009, 1009. See also P L Labuda, 'The ICC's "Evidence Problem"' (*Volkerrechtsblog*, 18 January 2019) available online at <https://voelkerrechtsblog.org/the-iccs-evidence-problem/> accessed 9 March 2023; D Guilfoyle, 'Part 1—This Is Not Fine: The International Criminal Court In Trouble' (*EJIL:Talk! Blog of the European Journal of*

 | DOI:10.1163/9789004529939_009

have translated into the OTP, which is the organ mandated to investigate and prosecute international crimes, seeing its investigative work challenged by an 'apparent lack of situation country knowledge (...) and the lack of OTP field presence during investigations'.[4]

Enter non-governmental organizations ('NGOs') and intergovernmental institutions. Apart from the important role they play in representing victims in bringing their views before the Court and lobbying their positions in policy forums such as the Assembly of State Parties, NGOs and intergovernmental institutions have played an increasingly important role in gathering information that would be processed and used as evidence by the OTP. Therefore, the OTP has, in addition to the work of its own professional investigators, also benefitted from what I called somewhere else 'third-party investigators',[5] a term which encompasses investigators and factfinders from all kinds of entities that are not affiliated to either Prosecution or Defence and are not acting upon request of the Court.[6]

In this chapter I address the cooperation between civil society and the ICC OTP through the lenses of third-party investigations. I examine what are the considerations that come into play when analysing the evidentiary value of materials collected and conclusions drawn by third-party investigators. In order to do so, I will first provide an overview of the available avenues that the OTP and third parties can publicly collaborate in order to address the issue of accountability to international crimes (Section 1). I will then turn to the specific issue of how the evidence gathered by third-party investigators has been treated by case law throughout the existence of the ICC (Section 2). Lastly, I will discuss how the OTP has responded to issues raised in relation to third-party investigations (Section 3).

---

*International Law* (hereafter 'EJIL: Talk!'), 21 March 2019) available online at <https://www.ejiltalk.org/part-i-this-is-not-fine-the-international-criminal-court-in-trouble/> accessed 9 March 2023; D Groome, 'No Witness, No Case: An Assessment of the Conduct and Quality of ICC Investigations' (2014) 3 *Penn State Journal of Law & International Affairs* 19.

4 ICC ASP (n 2) para. 743.

5 Also called private investigators (A Heinze, 'Private International Criminal Investigations' (2019) 14(2) *Zeitschrift für Internationale Strafrechtsdogmatik* 169) and, for a specific subset, Non-Governmental Investigatory Bodies (A C U Nwadikwa-Jonathan and N E Ortiz, *The Past, Present and Future of Integrity in International Justice the International Criminal Court* (Torkel Opsahl Academic EPublisher 2021)).

6 See R Braga da Silva, 'Sherlock at the ICC? Regulating Third-Party Investigations and International Crimes in the Rome Statute Legal Framework' (2020) 18 *Journal of International Criminal Justice* 59, 64.

## 2 The Office of the Prosecutor and The Role of Third-Parties in the ICC

The responsibility of building a system of international criminal justice as an accountability tool is held by many stakeholders. Starting from the developments of World War II, the 20th century was the period when many countries, NGOs, international organizations and institutions pushed for ways of delivering accountability for international crimes.[7] NGOs and other intergovernmental institutions have been at the center of the discussions regarding having a permanent international criminal tribunal.[8] For instance, together with the momentum created by the establishment of the ICTY and ICTR, the Coalition for an International Criminal Court, then a group of 25 human rights organizations, started campaigning in 1995 for states to establish a permanent international criminal court.[9]

Picking up on the motto of having a 'joint goal for justice', the CICC focused on 'the circulation and promotion of new research and expert documents prepared by its member organizations'.[10] The objective was to the centralized Secretariat of the CICC to trickle down information about new developments to the associated NGOs, as well as organize their efforts in getting traction of states to understand, support and ultimately sign the treaty establishing the Rome Statute.[11] One aspect of this, for example, was the strategies and actions of the CICC to get an independent Prosecutor, which was noted as 'the most important point on which the NGOs booked success'.[12]

---

7 UNGA, Letter dated 21 August 1989 from the Permanent Representative of Trinidad and Tobago to the United Nations addressed to the Secretary General (21 August 1989) UN doc A/44/195; International criminal responsibility of individuals and entities engaged in illicit trafficking in narcotic drugs across national frontiers and other transnational criminal activities: establishment of an international criminal court with jurisdiction over such crimes (4 December 1989) UN doc A/RES/44/39.

8 See K Lohne, 'NGOS for International Justice, Criminal or Victim's Justice?' in A Føllesdal & G Ulfstein (eds), *The Judicialization of International Law: A Mixed Blessing?* (Oxford University Press 2018).

9 For more on this subject, see the chapter on the CICC in this volume. See also W Pace, 'Reflecting on 25 Years of the CICC', (*Coalition for the International Criminal Court*, 20 July 2020), available at <https://www.coalitionfortheicc.org/news/20200720/reflecting-25-years-cicc> accessed 9 March 2023.

10 W R Pace, Globalizing justice: NGOs and the need for an international criminal court' (1998) 20(2) *Harvard International Review* 26.

11 See M Glasius, 'How activities Shaped the Court', (*Crimes of war*, December 2003), available at <http://www.crimesofwar.org/icc_magazine/icc-glasius.html> accessed 9 March 2023.

12 Ibid.

That goal was ultimately carried out through advocacy in and out the formal settings of negotiation of the Rome Statute. Throughout the Preparatory Committee on the Establishment of an International Criminal Court, convened by the UN General Assembly, NGOs were invited to participate in the Conferences, with the exception of taking part in the drafting group of the Rome Statute.[13] When the treaty was adopted, NGOs still had an important policy role in participating in the work of the Preparatory Commission, mandated to put in place the now agreed on Statute of the International Criminal Court. In its second convening, the Assembly of State Parties recognized the importance of non-governmental organizations, in special the CICC, in creating and establishing the ICC.[14] Moreover, one key aspect that was highlighted was the role that the CICC had in coordinating and facilitating interactions between other NGOs and the broader community invested in the project of an International Criminal Court. After the push to establish the ICC, came July 2002 and with it the possibility of NGOs to turn to a tool for judicial accountability of international crimes.

Although policy-based advocacy continued throughout these twenty years of functioning of the ICC, I will now focus on the role that NGOs and other third parties have in cooperating with the mandate of the OTP, in special the investigation of international crimes. The OTP can benefit from several sources of information coming from, *inter alia,* individuals NGOs, and UN agencies. Either through Article 15 Communications, or later requests for assistance to acquire documents with other organizations, the recourse scarcity and practical difficulties while investigating demand that the OTP rely on stakeholders that are familiar with the situation on the ground.[15] Moreover, the OTP—and the Court—heavily rely on practical knowledge that other institutions already have of the situation on the ground, allowing for strategic approaches to supporting victims and delivering aid, gathering evidence and discharging its mandate more widely.

In the first investigation that the ICC Prosecutor came to tackle, the Situation in the DRC,[16] even before the referral, several NGOs and individuals had been already communicating with the OTP through Article 15 Communications

---

13 UNGA Res 52/160 (28 January 1998) UN Doc A/RES/52/160.

14 Recognition of the coordinating and facilitating role of the NGO Coalition for the International Criminal Court ICC-ASP/2/Res.8, 11 September 2003 (4th Plenary Meeting of the ASP).

15 See Braga da Silva (n 6) 68.

16 See Democratic Republic of the Congo, Situation in the Democratic Republic of the Congo, ICC-01/04, available online at <https://www.icc-cpi.int/drc> accessed 9 March 2023.

about the situation in the DRC.[17] However, difficulties resulting from the lack of presence of OTP investigators hampered the ability of actually investigating what those communications were about. As explained by staff members that identified during the *Lubanga* trial, difficulties ranged from the ongoing conflict and safety concerns when engaging witnesses and gathering evidence.[18] These difficulties could then be overcome by engaging with local actors or international stakeholders with presence in the affected region.

Local and transnational NGOs are usually the 'first responders' to situations where atrocities are occurring, being able to document and establish what happened, securing eyewitnesses' testimonies and other relevant information that assist in the investigation,[19] as well as contact victims and support them. Having a presence in the local of atrocities therefore present NGOs with information and several tools that the OTP do not have at a first moment and to which this ICC organ—and the institution as a whole—rely on heavily if there comes to be a situation where they are involved in it. The reliance can be twofold: one related to investigators engaging with individuals in the local scene and one related to the OTP relying on fact-finding reports conducted by NGOs and intergovernmental organizations.

In relation to the first set of individuals, they are known as 'intermediaries', providing and facilitating contact between organs of the ICC and victims, witnesses or beneficiaries of reparations.[20] Their initial appearance in ICC proceedings showed that they played an important yet controversial role in the first case brought in the Situation in DRC, *Lubanga*.[21] The relationship between intermediaries and the International Criminal Court (ICC) came under scrutiny because of the wide range of roles that they were playing throughout proceedings, which could be seen as overstepping their bounds. These roles included providing assistance to victims, offering psychosocial services,

17 See 'Prosecutor receives referral of the situation in the Democratic Republic of Congo', ICC Press Release (19 April 2004) <https://www.icc-cpi.int/news/icc-prosecutor-receives-referral-situation-democratic-republic-congo> accessed 28 April 2023.

18 See Judgment pursuant to Article 74 of the Statute, *Lubanga, Situation in the Democratic Republic of the Congo*, ICC-01/04-01/06-2842, TC I, ICC, 14 March 2012, paras 135, 139–40, 142, 151–52, 16; Lavigne Deposition, ICC-01/04-01/06-Rule68Deposition-Red2-ENG, 4, 72.

19 S SaCouto, 'Improving NGO and IGO Capacity to Gather Evidence' in R H Steinberg (ed), *The International Criminal Court: Contemporary Challenges and Reform Proposals* (Brill Nijhoff 2020), 22–36.

20 Section 1 ICC, Guidelines Governing the Relationsbetween the Court and Intermediaries for the Organs and Units of the Court and Counsel working with Intermediaries (March 2014).

21 See Lubanga Judgment, ICC-01/04-01/06-2842 (n 18) paras 482–483.

conducting outreach, and gathering evidence. However, concerns were also raised about how intermediaries were engaging with potential witnesses on behalf of the Office of the Prosecutor (OTP) and the possibility that they were manipulating witnesses and their testimonies.[22]

In the first judgement ever issued by the ICC, the Trial Chamber in the Lubanga case identified issues with intermediaries possibly having manipulated witnesses and their testimonies.[23] One alarming issue at trial was when the first alleged child soldier witness recanted and told judges that an intermediary instructed him to lie, with several other witnesses following suit.[24] Similar problems also arose in subsequent cases, such as Katanga, where witnesses told the Court that intermediaries asked them to change their accounts of the facts.[25] After such issues were raised, the ICC took stock and made a Court-wide effort to issue guidelines governing the relations between the Court and intermediaries.[26] These guidelines are an important effort towards avoiding issues such as the ones encountered in earlier cases.

In cases such as *Ntaganda* and *Gbagbo and Blé Goudé*, the issue of intermediaries was not at the forefront of the evidentiary analysis of the cases. More recently, the Defence in *Ongwen* objected to the involvement to the witness P-0078, a Major who assisted the Prosecutor's selection of witnesses and collection of evidence with the assistance of an intermediary that closely participated in the conflict between the LRA and the Government of Uganda.[27] The Defence alleged that the Trial Chamber failed to assess the objections regarding the involvement of P-0078 in the conflict and the allegation that he acted contrary to the Statute and the Code of Conduct of the Office of the Prosecutor.[28]

22 Redacted Decision on Intermediaries, *Lubanga, Situation in the Democratic Republic of the Congo*, ICC-01/04-01/06-2434-Red2, TC I, ICC, 31 May 2010, paras 136, 138, 140. See also C Buisman, 'Delegating Investigations: Lessons to be Learned from the Lubanga Judgment', (2013) 11 *Northwestern Journal of International Human Rights* 33.

23 Lubanga Judgment, ICC-01/04-01/06-2842 (n 18) paras 63–220.

24 Ibid., para. 375 (mentioning several witnesses who had given evidence with regard to possible manipulation by intermediary P-321).

25 Judgment on the Appeal of Mr. Germain Katanga against the Oral Decision of Trial Chamber II of 12 June 2009 on the Admissibility of the Case, *Katanga, Situation in the Democratic Republic of the Congo*, ICC-01/04-01/07-1497, AC, ICC, 25 September 2009, paras 124, 256.

26 ICC, Guidelines Governing the Relations between the Court and Intermediaries for the Organs and Units of the Court and Counsel working with Intermediaries (March 2014).

27 Judgment on the appeal of Mr Ongwen against the decision of Trial Chamber IX of 4 February 2021 entitled 'Trial Judgment', *Ongwen, Situation in Uganda*, ICC-02/04-01/15-2022-Red, AC, ICC, 15 December 2022, paras 409–411.

28 Ibid., para 413.

For the first objection, the Appeals Chamber, however, recalled that the Trial Chamber's assessment that the involvement of P-0078 in facilitating the Prosecution's investigation, absent any specific allegation and proof, does not mean that the Prosecution failed to carry out an impartial investigation.[29] In relation to the second objection, the Appeals Chamber noted that the alleged misuse of funds and resources provided by the Prosecutor, as well as the allegation of a purported pressure on other witnesses, were duly investigated and that this purported misconduct did not affect the collection by the Prosecutor and the reliability of that evidence.[30]

From filings available in the public domain, intermediaries have been exercising functions of contacting victims and building—and maintaining—relationship with Victims' Representatives and Registry[31] with victims and witnesses. This could be a result of a decrease on the reliance of the OTP on intermediaries for other factors, such as the Situation in Uganda and the accessibility of witnesses,[32] but that shows that intermediaries having a prominent role in gathering evidence might be a role that the OTP is not willing to widely delegate anymore.

Apart from individuals that facilitate the gathering of evidence and connection with people affected by international crimes, the OTP often relies on the fact-finding already conducted by NGOs and other intergovernmental institutions in order to build their cases. The shared objective with the OTP of bringing those responsible for international crimes into account make the work of those institutions an important starting point of cooperation between them.[33] The systematic documentation of human rights violations and international conducted by those institutions, which often relying on established protocols and practices, is a necessary tool for the OTP to identify incidents, leads, and individuals in order to deploy its resources more efficiently. The network of

29 Ibid., paras 414–416.

30 Ibid., paras 418–419.

31 See, e.g. Sixth Periodic Report on the Victims Admitted to Participate in the Proceedings, *Yekatom and Ngaïssona, Situation in the Central African Republic II*, ICC-01/14-01/18-1695, TC V, ICC, 12 December 2022, para. 3.

32 See OTP Investigator interview in T B Bouwknegt, 'Cross-examining the past: Transitional justice, mass atrocity trials and history in Africa' (2017) [Thesis, externally prepared, Universiteit van Amsterdam], available at <https://pure.uva.nl/ws/files/17790046/6.pdf> accessed 28 April 2023.

33 M Bergsmo and W Wiley, 'Human Rights Professionals and the Criminal Investigation and Prosecution of Core International Crimes' in S Skåre, I Burkey, & H Mørk (eds), *Manual on Human Rights Monitoring: an Introduction for Human Rights Field Officers* (University of Oslo 2008), 2.

sources, contact points, and material gathered by professionals working with human rights' organizations is key for deploying OTP investigators—which are always 'a day late and a dollar short' when compared to other investigators—with enough information so they can work around the resource scarcity that challenges the work of the OTP.[34]

However, there must be a differentiation between gathering lead evidence underlying reports published by NGOs and international institutions and relying on those reports for the matters of evidence. In the first situation, reports are used by the OTP to conduct its own investigation, serving only as a starting point for their own queries—which would have to comply with the Rome Statute framework related to OTP investigations. However, in relation to the second situation, the direct reliance on human rights as evidence has been seen with suspicion by Judges. In *Mbarushimana,* from the outset, Pre-Trial Chamber I noted that NGO reports, in general, would be given low probative value.[35] Moreover, the Pre-Trial Chamber was not satisfied by on the reliance of the Prosecution on information contained on UN Reports or NGOs reports where sources of the information were anonymous[36] or there was not enough detail about incidents.[37] As explained later by another Pre-Trial Chamber, in *Gbagbo and Blé Goudé*: '[e]ven though NGO reports and press articles may be a useful introduction to the historical context of a conflict situation, they do not usually constitute a valid substitute for the type of evidence that is required to meet the evidentiary threshold for the confirmation of charges'.[38] Later, when the No Case to Answer decision was issued by Trial Chamber I in *Gbagbo and Blé Goudé*, the majority decision, lead by Judge Henderson, noted that such evidence should be categorised as anonymous hearsay or 'low probative value'.[39] Judge Tarfusser noted in his appended reasons that evidence of journalists or staff of international organizations or NGOs is problematic, being not 'suitable to constitute the basis for, or otherwise contribute to, the fundamental determinations as to the innocence or guilt of the accused'.[40] Ultimately, the Trial

34 ICC OTP, 'Policy Paper on Case Selection and Prioritisation' (15 September 2016), para. 12.

35 Decision on the Confirmation of Charges, *Mbarushimana, Situation in the Democratic Republic of the Congo*, ICC-01/-04-01/10-465-Red, PTC I, ICC, 16 December 2011, para.78.

36 Ibid., para. 117.

37 Ibid., para.118.

38 Decision adjourning the hearing on the confirmation of charges pursuant to article 61(7)(c)(i) of the Rome Statute, *Gbagbo, Situation in the Republic of Côte d'Ivoire* (ICC-02/11-01/11-432), PTC I, ICC, 3 June 2013, para. 35.

39 Public Redacted Version of Reasons of Judge Geoffrey Henderson, *Gbagbo and Blé Goudé, Situation in the Republic of Côte d'Ivoire*, ICC-02/11-01/15-1263-AnxB-Red, TC I, ICC, 16 July 2019, paras 1151, 1372.

40 Ibid., paras 23–24.

Chamber I's decision was upheld by the Appeals Chamber, albeit without specifically mentioning the issue of reliance on NGO and UN reports.[41]

One reason on why such NGO and UN reports are being considered as low probative value may be two-folded. One, as already identified by the jurisprudence analysed above, is the fact that most of the statements brought by UN and NGO reports are anonymous, in order to protect their providers. The Rome Statute provides for the possibility of the collection of evidence in a confidential manner, as posed by Article 54(3)(e) of the Rome Statute and Rule 82(5) of the Rules of Procedure and Evidence—however, solely for the purpose of generating new evidence, unless the provider of the information consents. The privilege of non-disclosure of confidential information is an important feature on human rights' reporting for security and in order to maintain an effective dialogue with parties involved, and for that reason is recognized in Article 54(3)(e) and specifically for certain institutions as the ICRC.[42] It would be thus acceptable to respect the confidentiality of the sources to NGO and UN reports and use them as evidence.

Another issue, as discussed by the Appeals Chambers in in *Lubanga*[43] and in *Katanga and Ngdujolo*,[44] is the tension between collecting information from the UN and NGOs under the—sometimes necessary—veil of confidentiality and the duty to disclose potentially exculpatory evidence to the Defence. Ultimately, the Appeals Chamber in *Lubanga* seems to remain the law on the matter: confidentiality agreements should be used in exceptional situations—gathering leads—and that those agreements may be scrutinized by judges in the case of disclosable evidence.[45]

---

41 Judgment in the appeal of the Prosecutor against Trial Chamber I's decision on the no case to answer motions, *Gbagbo and Blé Goudé, Situation in the Republic of Côte d'Ivoire*, ICC-02/11-01/15-1400, AC, ICC, 31 March 2021.

42 Rule 73 (4)-(6).

43 Judgment on the Appeal of the Prosecutor against the decision of Trial Chamber I, 'Decision on the consequences of non-disclosure of exculpatory materials covered by Article 54(3)(e) agreements and the application to stay the prosecution of the accused, together with certain other issues raised at the Status Conference on 10 June 2008', *Lubanga, Situation in the Democratic Republic of the Congo*, ICC-01/04-01/06-1486, AC, ICC, 21 October 2008, para. 43.

44 Decision on Art. 54(3)(e) Documents Identified as Potentially Exculpatory or Otherwise Material to the Defence's Preparation for the Confirmation Hearing, *Katanga, Situation in the Democratic Republic of the Congo*, ICC-01/04-01/07-621, PTC I, ICC, 20 June 2008, para. 46.

45 Judgment on the Appeal of the Prosecutor against the decision of Trial Chamber I (n 43) para. 46.

Notwithstanding the challenges that their contributions face inside the courtroom, international and intergovernmental institutions, as well as NGOs, are central stakeholders to the international criminal justice project. Together with their advocacy supporting the role of the ICC from its inception, the support provided on the ground for victims and witnesses, as well as the documentation of human rights violations are of the uttermost relevance for the OTP to discharge its statutory functions. However, the use of investigatory work product from those third parties to the Rome Statute has been discussed in the jurisprudence, often highlighting difficulties in the efficient collaboration between the OTP and its many partners.

## 3 Challenges of Third-Party Investigators in Collecting Evidence to Be Used by the OTP

The collection of evidence by third-parties investigators has been lauded as an important tool for international criminal justice for some time now. The advantages and difficulties as discussed in the jurisprudence are multifaceted. With the appearance of new models of NGOs, such as the CIJA, Bellingcat, and international institutions investigating international crimes, such as the investigative mechanisms for Syria and Myanmar—which can be dubbed as a 'criminalization turn' of human rights' reporting—recent scholarship has identified and classified the shortcomings of having NGOs, international agencies and individuals collecting evidence of international crimes.[46] As discussed in the introduction, I use the terminology of third-parties investigators[47] to identify those stakeholders, since they can be classified as third parties when considering the legal framework of the Rome Statute. Third-parties investigators are not bound by the legal framework of the ICC.[48] They are not investigators from the Prosecution or the Defense, as well as not Court-mandated investigators. Although what they collect will likely be used as evidence, the manner in which they collect the information, having many standards to do so (1), as well as integrity standards which they operate in (2) can cause issues when the information gathered is submitted as evidence (3).

46 See, e.g., Heinze, 'Private International Criminal Investigations' (n 5).

47 See C M De Vos, 'Investigating from Afar: The ICC' Evidence Problem', (2013) 26 *Leiden Journal of International Law* 1009; N A Combs, 'Investigative Delegations: Predictable Predicaments' (2019) 113 American Journal of International Law Unbound 267. See also R Braga da Silva (n 6).

48 Braga da Silva (n 6).

Having a multitude of investigative standards in documenting atrocities in the context of international criminal law can create several issues. One of the main challenges is the lack of consistency and comparability between different investigative standards, which can make it difficult to compare and evaluate the evidence collected by different investigators. For instance, the ICC has received investigative reports from several different institutions which are not usually geared towards criminal investigations. This can hinder the ability to build a strong and consistent case against the perpetrators of atrocities.

Another issue is the potential for conflicting or contradictory findings, as different investigators may use different standards or approaches to gather and analyze evidence. This can create confusion and uncertainty, and may undermine the credibility and reliability of the investigation as a whole. Additionally, the use of multiple investigative standards can also create difficulties in sharing and coordinating information between different investigators and stakeholders. This can make it more difficult to build a comprehensive and accurate picture of the atrocities that have been committed, and can hinder the ability of investigators to identify and pursue the perpetrators. Overall, the use of multiple investigative standards in documenting atrocities can create challenges and complications in the pursuit of justice in international criminal cases.

Closely related to the problem of having a multitude of investigative and reporting standards is the issue of over-documenting atrocities. The fact that the scale of human rights violations in any situation where international crimes have been allegedly committed means that 'no actor can effectively document the situation alone'.[49] However, the fact that several actors are on the ground on a well-intentioned 'frenzy of documentation' may cause an 'overconcentration of these efforts on a small percentage of the affected community'.[50] This documenting frenzy of statements from victims and witnesses can cause secondary traumatization, and also generate multiple accounts over the same facts, which in turn may bring questions to the accuracy of the information gathered. To avoid this situation, it is important for actors involved in documenting human rights violations to prioritize coordination and adhere

49 See E Buzo, 'Capturing a Crisis: What lessons can we learn from the "overdocumentation" of the Rohingya crisis?' (*Justice in Conflict*, 20 May 2020) available at <https://justiceinconflict.org/2020/05/20/capturing-a-crisis-what-lessons-can-we-learn-from-the-overdocumentation-of-the-rohingya-crisis/> accessed 9 March 2023.

50 See, E Buzo, 'The Legacy of the Rohingya Overdocumentation Myth: Lessons for Ukraine' (*Opinio Juris*, July 15 2022) available at <http://opiniojuris.org/2022/07/25/the-legacy-of-the-rohingya-overdocumentation-myth-lessons-for-ukraine/> accessed 9 March 2023.

to the 'do no harm' principle.[51] This means avoiding re-contacting witnesses and victims who have already given their statements to other documenters. By working together and avoiding unnecessary duplication of efforts, investigators and reporters can ensure that their documentation is accurate and avoids causing harm to those affected by the violations.

Third-party investigators, differently from their institutional counterparts, are not bound by any rules stemming from the ICC. As they are not employed or procured by the Court, these investigators have distinct conceptions of professionalism and professional standards,[52] which may impact on the usability of the evidence collected by them in court. These differences in governing rules of their work can cause what has been deemed as 'ethical dilemmas'.[53] Apart from the most apparent one related to conflict of interests and funding,[54] I would like to focus on an issue that directly impacts the work of the OTP: the collection of information and evidence. The distinct frameworks that these third-party investigators operate create a difficulty in the OTP's duty to investigate both inculpatory and exculpatory evidence.[55] The collection of evidence is done in challenging environments and the lack of a clear standard on what to gather may hamper the OTP's duty to use the evidence gathered by third-parties. As noted by Judge Henderson in *Gbgabo and Blé Goudé*, narratives presented by those actors often are an 'one-sided portrait'[56] of the situation being investigated by them. This is especially complicated when these third-party investigators justifiably enter into confidentiality agreements—a

51 See, B McGoningle Leyh, Ukraine Symposium – Documentation and Investigation Responses to Serious International Crimes, Lieber Institute West Point (July 13 2022), available at <https://lieber.westpoint.edu/documentation-investigation-responses-serious-international-crimes/> accessed 9 March 2023.

52 A Heinze, 'Private Investigators Helped Germany Arrest Two Former Syrian Secret Service Officers' (*EJIL:Talk!*, 26 February 2019) <https://www.ejiltalk.org/private-investigators-helped-germany-arrest-two-former-syrian-secret-service-officers/> accessed 9 March 2023. Also Braga da Silva (n 6) 73.

53 Heinze, ibid. Also Braga da Silva, ibid.

54 Ibid. Also, M Bergsmo and V Dittrich, *Integrity in International* Justice (Torkel Opsahl Academic EPublisher 2020) 640.

55 N Combs, 'Investigative Delegations: Predictable Predicaments' (2019) 113 *American Journal International Law Unbound* 267, 269.

56 Reasons of Judge Henderson, *Gbagbo and Blé Goudé* (n 39) para. 78. See also D Guilfoyle, 'A Tale of Two Cases: Lessons for the Prosecutor of the International Criminal Court? (Part 1)' (*EJIL: Talk*!, 28 August 2019) available online at <https://www.ejiltalk.org/a-tale-of-two-cases-lessons-for-the-prosecutor-of-the-international-criminal-court/> accessed 9 March 2023.

tool also available for the OTP[57]—with its sources as disclosing that 'would breach express or implied promises of confidentiality or endanger informants'.[58] However, when turning their investigative product to the OTP, third-party investigators have to be conscious that these confidentiality agreements may hamper the full use of the evidence in court. Nevertheless, even if these stakeholders investigate using the same standards of the OTP, collecting both inculpatory and exculpatory evidence, they are not obligated to disclose exculpatory evidence, as noted by the Appeals Chamber in *Katanga and Ngdujolo*.[59]

The act itself of collecting of evidence by third-parties can also pose problems. Investigators acting under the authority of the ICC enjoy the institutional protection of the Court when doing their work.[60] They also have a clear Code of Conduct that they are bound to,[61] being liable if they commit any illicit conduct while collecting evidence. As discussed above, acting in different frameworks, third-party investigators do not enjoy the same protections, as well as they do not have a clear disciplinary framework, being liable directly in the country they are conducting investigations. As this may be argued as freedom form bureaucratic restraints stemming from the ICC framework,[62] it also bring, on the other hand, concrete dangers to the individuals gathering evidence and their sources, such as imprisonment[63]

57 Rome Statute of the ICC (signed 17 July 1998, entered into force 1 July 2002) 2187 UNTS 3, Article 54(3)(e).

58 A Heinze, 'Private Investigators Helped Germany Arrest Two Former Syrian Secret Service Officers' (n 52).

59 Judgment on the Appeal of Mr Katanga Against the Decision of Trial Chamber II of 22 January 2010 Entitled 'Decision on the Modalities of Victim Participation at Trial', *Katanga, Situation in the Democratic Republic of the Congo*, ICC-01/04-01/07-2288, AC, ICC, 16 July 2010, paras 43–48, 87.

60 Agreement on the Privileges and Immunities of the International Criminal Court (APIC), ICC-ASP/1/3, 3–10 September 2022 (First Session of the ASP) (entered into force 22 July 2004), Art. 16.

61 ICC, Code of Conduct for Investigators, ICC/AI/2008/005, 10 September 2008.

62 W H Wiley, 'Private Partnerships for Effective Investigation of Core International Crimes: Beyond Bureaucratic Domination' (Florence, 28 October 2017) available online at <https://www.cilrap.org/cilrap-film/171028-wiley/> accessed 9 March 2023. See also M Rankin, 'The Future of International Criminal Evidence in New Wars? The Evolution of the Commission for International Justice and Accountability (CIJA)' (2018) 20 *Journal of Genocide Research* 392.

63 See, the case of four ICC staff members imprisoned by Libyan authorities, later released, and the discussion of waiving immunities and privileges by domestic authorities in Human Rights Watch, 'Libya: ICC Staff Detentions Raise Justice Concerns', 3 July 2012, available online at <https://www.hrw.org/news/2012/07/03/libya-icc-staff-detentions-raise-justice-concerns> accessed 9 March 2023; M Kersten, 'Tinker, Tailor, Lawyer: ICC

in the country where conduct is being investigated or, ultimately, death.[64]

Additionally to the challenges of the act of gathering the evidence, third-party investigators face the challenge regarding the (il)legality of the evidence collected. Article 69(7) of the Rome Statute, which provides the framework for the exclusionary rule in the ICC's jurisdiction, does not focus on who collected the evidence in order to lay its two-pronged test: first, the Chamber must determine whether the evidence in question was obtained through the violation of the Statute or internationally recognized human rights; Having met the conditions in the chapeau of the article, the Chamber must also examine whether the violation casts substantial doubt on the reliability of the evidence or if the admission of the evidence would be antithetical and would seriously damage the integrity of the proceedings.

The drafting history of such provision suggests, however, that such Article 69(7) was intended to focus only on evidence collected by the Prosecutor, the accused, national authorities or when requested by the Court itself. Therefore, evidence collected by third-party investigators are left out of such framework, remaining to be analysed by a Chamber. I argue that, if the route of analysing evidence illegally gathered by third-party investigators through the framework of Article 69(7) is not available, the illegality of the evidence collected by third-parties could be ultimately analysed under Article 69(4) when conducting the assessment on whether the admissibility and probative value of evidence would present a prejudice to a fair trial. Notwithstanding the rather flexible framework of such provision,[65] and the fact that domestic laws are not to be considered in evidentiary analyses, according to Article 69(8), illegally obtained evidence by third-party investigators 'questions the moral authority of the verdict and its legitimacy'.[66] While there is limited-to-none guidance in case law about this issue, in case the OTP uses an illegally obtained evidence

Staff Arrested in Libya for "Spying"' (*Justice in Conflict*, 10 July 2023) <https://justiceinconflict.org/2012/06/10/tinker-tailor-lawyer-icc-staff-arrested-in-libya-for-spying/> accessed 9 March 2023.

64 J Borger, 'Smuggled Syrian Documents Enough To Indict Bashar Al-Assad, Say Investigators', *The Guardian* (12 May 2015), <https://www.theguardian.com/world/2015/may/12/smuggled-syrian-documents-indict-assad-investigators> accessed 9 March 2023.

65 See, e.g., Corrigendum to Decision on the admissibility of four documents, *Lubanga, Situation in the Democratic Republic of the Congo*, ICC-01/04-01/06-1399-Corr, TC I, ICC, 20 January 2011, para 24.

66 Heinze, 'Private International Criminal Investigators' (n 5) 252.

collected by a third-party investigator, such an issue could be resolved by not admitting the evidence due to the prejudice to a fair trial.

The need for coordination between OTP and NGOs during the investigations is something foreshadowed since the inception of the ICC. However, the collision of different worlds—the criminal investigations one with human rights reporting—shows that differences between standards, ethical frameworks and, more specifically, goals of these different stakeholders can be problematic. The OTP's challenges of gathering evidence of international crimes by itself will always be part and parcel of the work of the Office. However, collaborating with third-parties investigators may be one of the solutions to such problem, allowing the OTP to assemble disperse efforts in bringing into account perpetrators of international crimes, coordinating and honing the evidence collection process.

## 4 ICC and OTP and Initiatives to Address Evidence Shortcomings: Guidelines

In 2020, the Independent Expert Review recognized the important relationship between the OTP and CSOs, especially 'in the context of fact-finding during Preliminary Examinations and investigations'.[67] The OTP's unique position at the receiving end of the material collected by third-parties investigators could be a pathway to address the issues of third parties gathering evidence discussed above, provided the Office engage with the material critically and proactively. As put by the Independent Expert Review, 'civil society can only complement or facilitate the work of the OTP if a clear and mutually reinforcing relationship is in place'.[68] However, as recognized, at that point in time there are no guidelines for CSOs to ensure that their work is complementary to that of the OTP.[69]

Such situation changed after 'several years of calls from civil society for clearer guidance on elements and materials to submit to the OTP',[70] academic

67 See Independent Expert Review of the International Criminal Court and the Rome Statute System: Final Report—30 September 2020, ICC-ASP/19/16, 9 November 2020 (Nineteenth Session of the ASP), para 382.

68 See, ibid., para 382.

69 See, ibid., para 382.

70 See, 'FIDH Recommendations to the 21st Session of the Assembly of States Parties to the Rome Statute of the International Criminal Court The Hague, 5–10 December 2022' (November 2022/N 800a) 9.

commentary on that regard[71] and lessons learned from previous situations provided the starting point to change such situation. Starting February 2022, this issue of collaboration between third-party investigators and the OTP arose again with the start of hostilities between Ukraine and Russia. The 'first responders', several NGOs, intergovernmental institutions and other organizations stepped up and deployed its resources to be physically present in the battlefield or gathering digital evidence of international crimes, starting collecting evidence as soon as the conflict broke.[72] In March of the same year, Eurojust and the Genocide Network assisted Lithuania, Poland and Ukraine with the setting up of a Joint Investigation Team (JIT) into core international crimes allegedly committed in Ukraine.[73] The need for coordinate their efforts in order to have 'a coherent and effective approach'[74] towards accountability was something stressed by states joining the JIT, as well as Eurojust. Usually an international cooperation tool dealing with transnational crimes occurring across borders, the Ukraine JIT support efforts of gathering evidence and exchange between EU states and third states. In April, the OTP announced that it had joined the JIT, a first for the ICC organ,[75] deploying its team of investigators to Ukraine in the context of the JIT in May 2022.[76]

Nevertheless the cooperation between EU states, Eurojust participants and the ICC, there is still a need to coordinate with civil society's efforts in

71 Braga da Silva (n 6), Heinze, 'Private International Criminal Investigations' (n 5).

72 See, R Hamilton and L Freeman, 'The Int'l Criminal Court's Ukraine Investigation: A Test Case for User-Generated Evidence' (*Just Security*, 2 March 2022) available at <https://www.justsecurity.org/80404/the-intl-criminal-courts-ukraine-investigation-a-test-case-for-user-generated-evidence/> accessed 9 March 2023.

73 See, 'Eurojust supports joint investigation team into alleged core international crimes in Ukraine', European Union Agency for Criminal Justice Cooperation', Eurojust Press Release (28 March 2022), available at <https://www.eurojust.europa.eu/news/eurojust-supports-joint-investigation-team-alleged-core-international-crimes-ukraine> accessed 9 March 2023.

74 See, Government of the Netherlands 'The Netherlands to co-host international accountability conference for Ukraine', News Item (13 June 2022), available at <https://www.government.nl/latest/news/2022/06/13/the-netherlands-to-co-host-international-accountability-conference-for-ukraine> 9 March 2023.

75 See, 'Statement by ICC Prosecutor, Karim A.A. Khan QC: Office of the Prosecutor joins national authorities in Joint Investigation Team on international crimes committed in Ukraine', ICC.

76 See, Ukrainian Government, 'Офіс прокурора МКС приєднався до спільної слідчої групи України, Литви та Польщі щодо розслідування злочинів РФ' (25 April 2022) available at <https://www.gp.gov.ua/ua/posts/ofis-prokurora-mks-prijednavsya-do-spilnoyi-slidcoyi-grupi-ukrayini-litvi-ta-polshhi-shhodo-rozsliduvannya-zlociniv-rf> accessed 9 March 2023.

gathering evidence in Ukraine. The stakeholders in the JIT issued guidelines for 'Documenting international crimes and human rights violations for accountability purposes'[77] ('Guidelines'). Such document, as posited by the Prosecutor in its launch event, 'represent a response to many different requests we have received from many different organisations for clarity, for clearer guidance, as to what approaches to documentation can be most supportive to action before national and international courts'.[78] These Guidelines 'build upon similar products' previously developed by civil society, showing that their drafters were concerned with consolidating and enhancing existing efforts in relation to established international standards.[79] As a joint effort between civil society, national prosecutors and international partners, certainly the Guidelines represent a direct response to the recommendation made by the Independent Expert Review when it asked for clarification and formalization of the relationship between the OTP and civil society,[80] as well as the need for communication and sharing of the OTP's expertise and what is considered to be the best practices in evidence collection.[81]

The main purpose of the Guidelines is to 'consolidate and enhance existing efforts already undertaken by civil society organizations to ensure their work is carried out effectively and in accordance with international standards'.[82] As a reminder, the Guidelines define itself as a living tool, inviting civil society organizations 'to share their experiences and provide further input' in relation to them. This purpose can be traced back to the issue of positive complementarity and the role that the OTP arrogated to itself: sharing 'lessons learned and best practices available for use, and to contributing participants, where possible and within its means, to the expert-level meetings, trainings and seminars organised by others'.[83] The issuance of the joint Guidelines with Eurojust shows that there is a will in continuing with such goal.

With the intention of assisting the collection and preservation of information that can ultimately become admissible evidence in both national and

77 See, 'Documenting international crimes and human rights violations for accountability purposes: Guidelines for civil society organisations', Eurojust, ICC (2022).

78 See, 'Civil society organisations briefed on guidelines for documenting core international crimes', Eurojust News (7 October 2022) 00:01:12–00:01:24 in the video available at <https://www.eurojust.europa.eu/news/civil-society-organisations-briefed-guidelines-documenting-core-international-crimes> accessed 9 March 2023.

79 See, Eurojust, ICC (n 77) 6.

80 See, Final Report (n 67) para. 382. See Recommendation 158 and Recommendation 160.

81 Seee ibid., para. 383.

82 See, Eurojust, ICC (n 77) 6.

83 ICC OTP, 'Strategic Plan 2019–2021' (17 July 2019), para 51.

international courts, the Guidelines provide key principles to ensure that documentation preserves the integrity of information and evidence and increases the ability of accountability actors to draw on the work done by CSOs.[84] This amalgamation of NGOs' work products could be an institutional answer to the issue of having a multitude of investigative standards when collecting information of atrocities. With centralized Guidelines, the OTP and Eurojust may be signalling to stakeholders what they consider the international standards to be followed—whether they are already being followed or not, the Guidelines make it clear that stakeholders 'are encouraged to reflect [them] in their standard practices'.[85] At the same time, following such standards may 'be supportive of action before national and international courts'.[86]

Apart from providing a coordinated, international standard for documenting atrocities, the Guidelines also seem to address another issue related to third-party investigators discussed in the previous section of this chapter. One of them is the issue of over-documentation. In specific to the conflict in Ukraine, the ICC Prosecutor[87] and Deputy Prosecutors have been warning stakeholders about over-documentation, especially having in mind the lessons learned from the investigation into the Cox's Bazar in Bangladesh.[88] The Guidelines are geared towards tackling that issue, aiming to standardize the collection of evidence in order to avoid the risk of over-documentation.[89] The risk of multiple civil society organizations and stakeholders collecting evidence is acknowledged, pointing to the detrimental effect that 'repeated comprehensive interviewing of the same individual' can have to the

84 See, Eurojust, ICC (n 77) 4.

85 See, ibid., 6.

86 See, 'Eurojust and ICC Prosecutor launch practical guidelines for documenting and preserving information on international crimes: Joint press release of Eurojust and the Office of the Prosecutor at the International Criminal Court, European Union Agency for Criminal Justice Cooperation', Eurojust Press Release (21 September 2022), available at <https://www.eurojust.europa.eu/news/eurojust-and-icc-prosecutor-launch-practical-guidelines-documenting-and-preserving-information> accessed 9 March 2023.

87 See, 'Pursuing Justice for Mass Atrocities: A Conversation with ICC Prosecutor Karim Khan' (United States Institute of Peace, 26 April 2022), available at <https://www.usip.org/events/pursuing-justice-mass-atrocities-conversation-icc-prosecutor-karim-khan> accessed 9 March 2023. 'At this event, the ICC Prosecutor warned about the danger of over-documentation'. See also, P Shankar, 'Going after war crime perpetrators' (*Made for Minds* 14 July 2022) available at <https://www.dw.com/en/icc-chief-calls-for-overarching-strategy-to-probe-war-crimes-in-ukraine/a-62476910> accessed 9 March 2023.

88 See, 27th IAP Annual Conference and General Meeting (Tbilisi, Georgia)—Special Session: Effective Responses to War Crimes, ICC (27 September 2022) 8.

89 See, Eurojust, ICC (n 77) 6.

person themselves and, ultimately, the evidence that is being provided. The Guidelines highlight the need for coordination in relation to 'multiple overlapping forms of documentation' and the necessity of building 'relationships with these other individuals and organisations and coordinate activities with them'.[90]

What is, however, the legal nature of such Guidelines? Can civil society expect any legal effect—such as admissibility of evidence that they have collected following those Guidelines—should they abide by them? Differently from the ICC-wide Guidelines for Intermediaries, nowhere in the document is there an express disclaimer that they are not legally binding but only represent standards to be followed at the NGO's own risk.[91] Moreover, when specifically considering guidelines issued by the OTP—notably, the Guidelines for Agreements Regarding Admission of Guilt[92]—the Prosecutor has stated that their purpose was to 'set forth the ICC Prosecutor's policy with respect to agreements regarding admission of guilt', regulating when and in what terms such agreements can be entered.[93]

The drafters of Guidelines assert them as being 'a series of proposed "do's and don'ts" from the perspective and advice of national investigative and prosecuting authorities and the Office of the Prosecutor of the ICC'.[94] Therefore, the Guidelines are presented by the OTP and Eurojust as 'advice on key areas',[95] and not as a document that produces any legal effects towards those that follow them. In that regard, the Guidelines would not be legally binding, following the idea of the Guidelines for Intermediaries as only standards for the collection of evidence. I have argued elsewhere that guidelines that are issued by the Court as a whole would not be binding on the OTP, Defence or Chambers but would nevertheless 'provide some transparency and certainty as to what the Court expects from third-party investigators'.[96]

---

90 Ibid., 10.

91 See, ICC, Guidelines Governing the Relations between the Court and Intermediaries for the Organs and Units of the Court and Counsel working with Intermediaries (March 2014) 3: 'The Guidelines are based first and foremost on the legal structure of the Court, and take into consideration the relevant jurisprudence of the Court. It is recognized that the Guidelines do not in any way bind or limit the Chambers' exercise of their powers'.

92 ICC, Guidelines for Admission of Guilt (October 2022) hereinafter 'Guidelines for Admission of Guilt'.

93 Guidelines for Admission of Guilt, 1–2.

94 See, Eurojust, ICC (n 77) 5.

95 See, Eurojust and ICC Joint Press Release (n 86).

96 Braga da Silva (n 6) 85.

At the same time, however, the Guidelines also appear to set forth the OTP's policy in relation to the role of civil society in the work of the OTP, in special the collection of evidence of international crimes. Such appearance seems part of the OTP policy of developing 'making its standards, lessons learned and best practices available for use',[97] a role that flows from the Statute and draws from the cooperation framework it establishes.[98] In that regard, being an instrument of OTP's policy, it could be argued that such Guidelines are issued under the Prosecutor's power to issue self-regulatory acts under the principle of legality.[99] As such, the OTP would be bound by the Guidelines in the sense that it would have to act in a consistent and coherent manner in relation to the Guidelines.

The discussion on the legal nature of such Guidelines is not settled and may never be. It may even be artificial to find what legal consequences such Guidelines bring to the OTP when taking into account the ultimate goal of bringing those responsible for international crimes into account. Considering that Article 69(4) of the Rome Statute gives the Chamber the power to take into account a multitude of elements with a wide degree of discretion, the OTP could argue—without binding itself—that evidence collected following its joint Guidelines with Eurojust have enough probative value and reliability, especially when considering that the OTP would be the one submitting the evidence having done its review.

As with many of the developments in the OTP, time will tell how these new Guidelines will apply and whether they will serve the purpose for which they were created—facilitate the cooperation between the OTP and NGOs investigating international crimes.

## 5 Conclusions

In 20 years since its functioning, the collaboration of civil society to the ICC continued to grow and evolve together with the developments of the Court. Starting from their support to the creation of the Court, and continuing to

---

97 See, ICC OTP, 'Strategic Plan 2019–2021' (17 July 2019), para. 51.

98 See, ibid., para. 51.

99 R Braga da Silva and P Baldini Miranda da Cruz, 'The Hole in the Doughnut – The OTP Strategic Plans and Self-Regulatory Actions in International Criminal Law' (*EJIL:Talk!*, 10 April 2019), available at <https://www.ejiltalk.org/the-hole-in-the-doughnut-the-otp-strategic-plans-and-self-regulatory-actions-in-international-criminal-law/> accessed 9 March 2023.

advocates of its mandate, civil society organizations and other third parties have created a strong relationship with the OTP since its inception. Looking to the past, such relationship is key to many of the successes of the OTP in its investigative work, as well as in its advocacy.

As a new development of the roles of NGOs in the field of international criminal justice, and particularly the ICC, the last two decades have seen a crescendo in the involvement of NGOs specialized in criminal investigations gathering information and evidence that can be used in trials at international criminal tribunals. Without any specific framework to work in or special relationship with the ICC, and more specifically the OTP, these NGOs have conducted their work in parallel with ICC investigators. These 'third-parties' investigators have many advantages when compared with investigators from the OTP, as they are purportedly working without bureaucratic constraints. However, many disadvantages are also present, which is best summarized in the open question on whether pieces of evidence collected by third-parties investigators can be accepted in court as reliable and credible.

One way to tackle the issue is doing precisely what the OTP has done with the Guidelines. In providing NGOs and other stakeholders with guidelines on the collection of evidence, the Prosecutor has signaled what his Office believes are best practices in collecting evidence. While there is a question in the usefulness of these Guidelines in terms of reliability and credibility of evidence collected by NGOs in court, it can be said the Guidelines shift the OTP's stance from only receiving evidence to a more communicative and engaging relationship with NGOs that are investigating international crimes. Setting the standards, while being open to critique and development of the standards themselves by NGOs, is the best way forward to advance and deepen the relationship between these two actors that have the 'joint goal for justice'.

CHAPTER 9

# Intersectional Approaches to Investigating and Prosecuting International Crimes: Sexual and Gender-Based Crimes

*Priya Gopalan*

## 1 Introduction*

Intersectionality—variously described as a concept, methodology, praxis, critical social theory, and tool for critical analysis—is gaining greater visibility and purchase in the practice of international criminal law. This chapter seeks to examine the relevance, significance, utility, as well as the challenges associated with incorporating intersectionality into the practice of international criminal law. In doing so, I address two questions. First, what is intersectionality? Second, why does intersectionality matter in the investigation and prosecution of sexual and gender-based crimes?

Within these overarching questions, and drawing on the seminal work of Kimberlé Crenshaw, I trace the origins of intersectionality within domestic anti-discrimination legislation in the United States of America, its entrenchment into the framework of international human rights law and its manifestations within international criminal law. In seeking to illustrate why intersectionality matters when investigating and prosecuting international crimes, including sexual and gender-based crimes, I explore three diverse case studies: the enslavement of Korean 'Comfort Women' during the Second World War, Bosnian Muslim women survivors of the Srebrenica genocide diagnosed with the 'Srebrenica Syndrome', and conflict-related sexual violence perpetrated against Tamil men and boys by Sinhalese state actors.

I then consider the limits and criticisms of intersectionality as a methodology within international criminal law, highlighting some areas of disjuncture

* This chapter is based on my speech delivered *at 'The International Criminal Court at 20: Reflections on the Past, Present and the Future', Conference marking the 20th anniversary of the entry into force of the Rome Statute of the International Criminal Court, The Hague, 1 July 2022*. I thank Alexandra Lily Kather, co-founder of the Emergent Justice Collective for our discussions and their comments on this chapter. I am also indebted to Kirsten Campbell, Ulic Egan, Carla Ferstman, Solange Mouthaan and Patricia Sellers for their reviews of earlier drafts and to Gianpaolo Mascaro for his research assistance.

 | DOI:10.1163/9789004529939_010

and tensions. In considering these challenges, I turn to lessons offered by gender analysis—another tool of critical analysis in the practice of international criminal law—which serves as a forerunner to intersectionality. I argue that intersectionality can break down binaries and essentialist narratives which have resulted from a narrow application of gender analysis. In advocating for greater intentionality in avoiding these rigidities and presumptions, I discuss the significance of positionality.

An intersectional approach demands that practitioners create the necessary conditions to surface victims'/survivors' intersecting perspectives, experiences, and harms. Equally, intersectionality seeks to surface colliding and compounding forms of systemic dominance and discriminations that fuel and shape international crimes. Thus, intersectionality is a potent tool to further a fundamental precept of the international criminal law project—better and fuller justice processes and outcomes for victims/survivors.

## 2 What Is Intersectionality?

In examining the relevance, significance, utility, as well as the challenges associated with incorporating intersectionality into the practice of international criminal law, it is necessary to understand its origins in domestic anti-discrimination legislation and its subsequent transposition into international human rights law.

Kimberlé Crenshaw, an African American legal scholar and lawyer coined the term 'intersectionality' in 1989 to describe the simultaneous and intersecting bind of racial and gender discrimination faced by Black women in the employment context in the United States of America.[1] Crenshaw's focus on the intersections of race and gender highlighted 'the need to account for multiple grounds of identity when considering how the social world is constructed'.[2] It

1 K Crenshaw, 'Demarginalizing the Intersection of Race and Sex: A Black Feminist Critique of Antidiscrimination Doctrine, Feminist Theory and Antiracist Politics' (1989) 1(8) *University of Chicago Legal Forum* 139–167; also Columbia Law School website: 'Kimberlé W Crenshaw is a pioneering scholar and writer on civil rights, critical race theory, Black feminist legal theory, and race, racism, and the law. In addition to her position at Columbia Law School, she is a Distinguished Professor of Law at the University of California, Los Angeles. Crenshaw's work has been foundational in critical race theory'. <www.law.columbia.edu/faculty/kimberle-w-crenshaw> accessed 1 February 2023.

2 K Crenshaw, 'Mapping the Margins: Intersectionality, Identity Politics, and Violence against Women of Color' (1991) 43(6) *Stanford Law Review* 1241–1299, 1245. While intersectionality originated within the legal framework, it has flourished in social justice and grassroot

was a response to anti-racism and anti-sexism legislation that was anchored on the protection of Black men and White women, respectively. This left Black women 'theoretically erased',[3] because the feminist and antiracist policies that gave rise to these laws were predicated on the discrete experiences of these two groups (Black men and White women), and failed to properly capture the interactions of race, gender and class as experienced by Black women.[4]

Crenshaw turned to the courtroom to illustrate this lacuna, analysing three cases that concerned employment discrimination claims brought by Black women in the late 1970s and early 1980s.[5] The legal outcomes in all three cases highlight 'the conceptual limitations of the single-issue analyses that intersectionality challenges'.[6] As Aisha Nicole Davis writes, '[b]ecause the courts interpreted laws banning sex and race discrimination as mutually exclusive, the interaction between both forms of discrimination in the lives of Black women fell into the negative space'.[7]

According to Crenshaw:

> A single-axis framework erases Black women in the conceptualization, identification and remediation of race and sex discrimination by limiting inquiry to the experiences of otherwise-privileged members of the group. In other words, in race discrimination cases, discrimination tends to be viewed in terms of sex-or class-privileged Blacks; in sex discrimination cases, the focus is on race and class-privileged women.[8]

Crenshaw's intersectionality is configured through employment discrimination experienced by Black women, as mediated through the intersections of facets of their identity (sex and race) to shape the multiple dimensions of their discrimination.[9] Patricia Hill Collins, an African American legal scholar, approaches intersectionality thorough her concept of the 'matrix of

---

movements, and also in sociological feminist theory, behavioural science, labour and employment, as well as in Marxist-feminist critical theory. See A N Davis, 'Intersectionality, and International Law: Recognising Complex Identities on the Global Stage' (2015) 28 *Harvard Human Rights Journal* 205–241, 212, internal citations omitted.

3 Crenshaw, 'Demarginalizing the Intersection of Race and Sex' (n 1) 139.

4 Ibid., 140.

5 *DeGraffenreid v General Motors* (E D Mo 1976) 413 F Supp 142; *Moore v Hughes Helicopter* (9th Cir 1983) 708 F2d 475; *Payne v Travenol* (5th Cir 1982) 673 F2d 798.

6 Crenshaw, 'Demarginalizing the Intersection of Race and Sex' (n 1) 149.

7 Nicole Davis, 'Intersectionality and International Law' (n 2) 211.

8 Crenshaw, 'Demarginalizing the Intersection of Race and Sex' (n 1) 140.

9 Ibid., 139–167.

domination', which centralises structures of oppressions.[10] Collins' matrix of domination looks at the overall organization of power in society within which intersecting oppressions originate, develop, and are contained.[11] She argues that 'heteropatriarchy, neo-colonialism, capitalism, racism and imperialism constitute forms of oppression that characterise global politics, take different forms across different nation states and catalyse social inequality. Intersectionality's emphasis on intersecting systems of power suggests distinctive forms of oppression will each have their own power grid, a distinctive "matrix" of intersecting power dynamics'.[12] In the United States of America, intersectionality thus provided a much-needed multi-dimensional framework for domestic discrimination law to surface the distinct violations experienced by Black women due to their race, sex, and class.

At its very core, an intersectional analysis reveals the unique and compounded forms of discrimination that result from intersecting structures of oppression. Simply put, an intersectional analysis demonstrates that the sum (of discrimination) is greater than its parts. Intersectionality thus permits the articulation and recognition of the combined effects or accumulation of different forms of discrimination that coalescence, multiply and emerge as different and distinct prejudicial outcomes. As such, intersectional discriminations result in specific harms that are distinct to those that arise when discriminations are assessed separately; persons affected by intersectional discriminations suffer consequences that are different from those suffered by persons subjected to only one form of discrimination.[13]

## 3 Intersectionality and International Human Rights Law[14]

From its roots in domestic anti-discrimination legislation and litigation, intersectionality branched outwards into the field of international human rights

10 P Hill Collins, *Black Feminist Thought: Knowledge, Consciousness, and the Politics of Empowerment* (New York: Routledge 2000).

11 Ibid., 227.

12 Ibid., 274–276 cited in P Hill Collins, *Intersectionality as Critical Social Theory* (London: Duke University Press 2019) 239.

13 See e.g. *Case of Gonzales Lluy et al v Ecuador*, Judgement (Preliminary objections, merits, reparations, and costs) Inter-American Court of Human Rights, IACHR Series C No 298 (1 September 2015), para. 290; Concurrent opinion of Judge Eduardo Ferrer Mac-Gregor Poisot, paras 11–12.

14 For a detailed discussion on the origins and development of the concept of intersectionality within human rights law, see A Martin Beringola, 'Intersectionality: A Tool for the Gender Analysis of Sexual Violence at the ICC', (2017) 9(2) *Amsterdam Law Forum* 84, 86–89.

law. As the principle of equality and non-discrimination is a foundational tenet of human rights law, it is unsurprising that intersectionality has found deep roots within this framework.

In 2000, the Committee on the Elimination of Racial Discrimination (CERD) led the charge in developing intersectionality as a methodology and analytical tool within the framework of human rights law. In its General Recommendation No 25, on the gender-related dimension of racial discrimination, it makes explicit the way in which race and gender 'collide' (to paraphrase Crenshaw) to produce compounded violations.[15]

In 2006, the Convention on the Rights of Persons with Disabilities (CRPD) followed suit as the first human rights treaty to recognize multiple and intersecting forms of discrimination. Its General Comment No 6 on Equality and Non-Discrimination elaborates that:

> Discrimination can be based on a single characteristic, such as disability or gender, or on multiple and/or intersecting characteristics. 'Intersectional discrimination' occurs when a person with a disability or associated to disability suffers discrimination of any form on the basis of disability, combined with, colour, sex, language, religion, ethnic, gender or other status. Intersectional discrimination can appear as direct or indirect discrimination, denial of reasonable accommodation or harassment. For example, while the denial of access to general health-related information due to inaccessible format affects all persons on the basis of disability, the denial to a blind woman of access to family planning services restricts her rights based on the intersection of her gender and disability.[16]

15 UN Committee on the Elimination of Racial Discrimination (CERD), General Recommendation No 25 on Gender Related Dimensions of Racial Discrimination (20 March 2000) in UNGA, Report of the Committee on the Elimination of Racial Discrimination, UN Doc A/55/18, Annex V, para. 2: 'Certain forms of racial discrimination may be directed towards women specifically because of their gender, such as sexual violence committed against women members of particular racial or ethnic groups in detention or during armed conflict; the coerced sterilization of indigenous women; abuse of women workers in the informal sector or domestic workers employed abroad by their employers. Racial discrimination may have consequences that affect primarily or only women, such as pregnancy resulting from racial bias-motivated rape; in some societies women victims of such rape may also be ostracized. Women may also be further hindered by a lack of access to remedies and complaint mechanisms for racial discrimination because of gender-related impediments, such as gender bias in the legal system and discrimination against women in private spheres of life'.

16 CRPD, General comment No 6 on equality and non-discrimination (26 April 2018) UN Doc CRPD/C/GC/6, para. 19. See also CRDP General comment No 3 on women and girls with disabilities (25 November 2016) CRPD/C/GC/3, paras 4 (c) and 16.

In 2010, in its General Recommendation No 28, the Committee on the Elimination of Discrimination against Women (CEDAW) highlighted that gender and sex-based discrimination against women cannot be analysed in isolation because it is 'inextricably linked' or in other words intersects with multiple aspects of women's identities, both fixed and transient:

> Intersectionality is a basic concept for understanding the scope of the general obligations of States parties contained in article 2 [of the Convention on the Elimination of All Forms of Discrimination against Women]. The discrimination of women based on sex and gender is 'inextricably linked' with other factors that affect women, such as race, ethnicity, religion or belief, health, status, age, class, caste, and sexual orientation and gender identity. Discrimination on the basis of sex or gender may affect women belonging to such groups to a different degree or in different ways than men.[17]

Subsequent general recommendations and case law from CEDAW have served as building blocks to this foundation and explore a myriad of factors that intersect with gender.[18]

Intersectionality is also utilised as an analytical tool to dissect various categories of human rights violations in other parts of the UN system, such as within the UN Special Procedures. The Special Rapporteur on the Right to Health, Tlaleng Mofokeng, has made explicit an intersectional approach to her work, proposing an intersectional, non-discriminatory and gender (non-binary) approach to understanding gender-based violence.[19] Similarly, the

17 CEDAW, General Recommendation No 28 on the Core Obligations of States Parties under Article 2 of the Convention on the Elimination of All Forms of Discrimination against Women (19 October 2010) UN Doc CEDAW/C/2010/47/GC.2, para. 18. See also para. 26.

18 CEDAW, General Recommendation No 26 on Women Migrant Workers (5 December 2006) UN Doc CEDAW/C/2009/WP.1/R; General Recommendation No 24 on Women and Health (1999) in UNGA, Report of the Committee on the Eliminationof Discrimination against Women, UN Doc A/54/38 (Part 1); and General Recommendation No 19 on Violence Against Women (1993) in UNGA, Report of the Committee onthe Elimination of Discrimination against Women, UN Doc A/47/38. A number of cases which address the issue of intersectionality have also been referred to the CEDAW Committee via the Optional Protocol procedure that deals with individual complaints. See e.g., Communication no 17/2008, *da Silva Pimentel v Brazil*, Views adopted on 25 July 2011 in UN Doc CEDAW/C/49/D/17; Communication No 32/2011, *Isatou Jallow v Bulgaria*, Views adopted on 23 July 2012 in UN Doc CEDAW/C/52/D/32/2011; Communication No 19/2008, *Kell v Canada*, Views adopted on 28 February 2012 in UN Doc CEDAW/C/51/D/19/2008.

19 Violence, and its impact on the right to health: Report of the Special Rapporteur on the right of everyone to the enjoyment of the highest attainable standard of physical and mental health, Tlaleng Mofokeng, Human Rights Council, Fiftieth session, UN Doc A/HRC/50/28 (2022).

Independent Expert on Protection against Violence and Discrimination based on Sexual Orientation and Gender (SOGI), Victor Madrigal-Borloz, in emphasizing that the prevention of grave harms encompass States' due diligence obligations, explains that grave harms 'must be addressed through an intersectional lens that recognizes how factors such as race, class, gender, age, and disability compound SOGI discrimination in shaping health outcomes and inequalities'.[20] In examining the climate crisis, E. Tendayi Achiume—the Special Rapporteur on contemporary forms of racism, racial discrimination, xenophobia, and related intolerance- exposes the racially discriminatory and unjust roots and consequences of environmental degradation, including climate change. She writes that:

> Environmental racism and climate injustice interact with other forms of social exclusion, such as discrimination on the grounds of gender, age, and disability. Intersectional analyses of environmental and climate-related human rights violations should recognize that women, older persons, persons with disabilities, and gender and sexually diverse persons who are members of racially marginalized peoples face distinct human rights violations.[21]

Pivoting away from the international stage, regional human rights bodies such as the African Commission on Human and Peoples' Rights[22] and

---

20 The right to the enjoyment of the highest attainable standard of physical and mental health of persons, communities and populations affected by discrimination and violence based on sexual orientation and gender identity in relation to the Sustainable Development Goals: Report of the Independent Expert on protection against violence and discrimination based on sexual orientation and gender identity, Human Rights Council, Fiftieth session, UN Doc A/HRC/50/27 (2022), para. 19. See also Promotion and protection of the human rights and fundamental freedoms of Africans and of people of African descent against excessive use of force and other human rights violations by law enforcement officers: Report of the International Independent Expert Mechanism to Advance Racial Justice and Equality in Law Enforcement, Human Rights Council, Fifty-first session, UN Doc A/HRC/51/55 (2022), which contains numerous references to intersectionality.

21 Report of the Special Rapporteur on contemporary forms of racism, racial discrimination, xenophobia and related intolerance on ecological crisis, climate justice and racial justice, E. Tendayi Achiume, in UNGA Contemporary forms of racism, racial discrimination, xenophobia and related intolerance, UN Doc A/77/549 (2022), para. 47.

22 See e.g. *Egyptian Initiative for Personal Rights and INTERIGHTS v Egypt*, Decision, Communication No. 323/2006, (African Commission on Human and People's Rights (ACmHPR) Dec. 2011).

Inter-American Court of Human Rights[23] have also followed an intersectional approach in analysing discrimination. In 2015, the Inter-American Court of Human Rights expressly used the concept of intersectionality to surface the intersecting discrimination faced by a female minor with HIV who lived in poverty. The court found that 'the discrimination experienced was caused not only by numerous factors, but also arose from a specific form of discrimination that resulted from the intersection of those factors; in other words, if one of those factors had not existed, the discrimination would have been different'.[24]

Thus, within the framework of international human rights law, intersectionality is relied upon as a well-established analytical tool to surface the distinct and compounded causes and effects of discrimination and violations experienced by individuals as a result of their individual characteristics and memberships in certain group(s) or collectivities. As highlighted by the CPRD, intersectional discrimination acknowledges 'that individuals do not experience discrimination as members of a homogenous group but rather, as individuals with multidimensional layers of identities, statuses, and life circumstances'.[25]

## 4 Intersectionality and International Criminal Law

In contrast to international human rights law, intersectionality is less explicit in its manifestation and application within international criminal law. It is found embedded in the contours that frame international crimes.

As Patricia Visseur Sellers writes:

> All core international crimes protect certain collectivities in their respective provisions. For example, war crimes protect civilians, the wounded and sick, prisoners of war, the shipwrecked during an international armed conflict. In the context of a non-international armed conflict, war

---

23 See e.g. IACtHR, *Case of Gonzales Lluy et al v Ecuador* (n 13) para. 290.

24 Ibid.

25 CRDP, General Comment no 3 on women and girls with disabilities (n 16), para. 16. While intersectionality is well-rooted within the framework of human rights, its place and presence in this field, nonetheless, remains open to inquiry. Shreya Atrey and Peter Dunne query the interplay between human rights and intersectionality, and specifically whether 'the human rights discourse, based on its universal and common values, has tools, methods, or theories to capture and respond to the difference in people's lived experience of rights'. See S Atrey and P Dunne (eds), *Intersectionality and Human Rights Law* (Oxford: Hart Publishing, 2020).

> crimes protect civilians and those who have laid down their arms. Crimes against humanity protects civilians in war or in peace time. Genocide protects racial, religious, ethnic, and national groups. It is the task of investigators, prosecutors and ultimately judges to 'determine whether victims and survivors are members of such collective groups'. As such, international criminal law endeavours to prevent harm to these collectivities. In other words, 'collective protection is the doctrinal spinal cord of international criminal law'.[26]

Sellers thus advocates for a historical understanding of the legal genesis of international crimes to understand intersectionality's function in prompting these prohibitions.[27] Intersectionality, characterised as honing-in on individual traits and membership within certain protected groups, is thus embedded in international crimes, although explicit emphasis or engagement with it as an analytical tool has been limited.

Within the legal framework of the ICC, an intersectional approach is embedded in Article 21(3) of the Rome Statute. This Article requires that the application and interpretation of law pursuant to this Article must be consistent with internationally recognized human rights and be without any adverse distinction founded on grounds such as gender, as defined in Article 7(3),[28] age, race, colour, language, religion or belief, political or other opinion, national, ethnic or social origin, wealth, birth or other status. Article 21(3) thus serves as a bridge between international criminal law and international human rights law (in which intersectionality finds deeper roots, as discussed above). This lays the important substantive and procedural groundwork to link an

26 P Visseur Sellers, 'Gendered Intersections of Human Rights and International Criminal Law, International Course on Human Rights Investigation, Fact-Finding, Documenting, Monitoring, Online Module, Buenos Aires, Argentina' <www.facebook.com/watch/live/?v=802737697228445&ref=watch_permalink 14> accessed 1 February 2023.

27 P Visseur Sellers, 'Intersectional Approaches to International Criminal Law and Practice: What Can Intersectionality Mean for International Justice?' (Webinar series, 6 December 2021) <www.youtube.com/watch?v=wXc5mEsA290> accessed 1 February 2023. See also K Campbell, *The Justice of Humans: Subject, Society, and Sexual Violence in International Criminal Justice* (Cambridge: Cambridge University Press, 2022), 83–85.

28 Under Article 7(3) of the Rome Statute ('Statute'), 'gender' is understood as the two sexes, male and female, within the context of society. Gender refers to sex characteristics and social constructs, and to criteria used to define maleness and femaleness, including roles, behaviours, activities and attributes. As a social construct, gender varies within societies and from society to society and can change over time. This understanding of gender is in accordance with Article 21 of the Statute. See ICC OTP, 'Policy on the Crime of Gender Persecution' (7 December 2022).

intersectional analysis to the application and interpretation of the law under the Rome Statute.

The ICC Policy Paper on Sexual and Gender-Based Crimes recognises that 'multiple' factors of discrimination may underlie sexual and gender-based crimes, that that these crimes may be motivated by underlying inequalities, as well as a 'multiplicity' of other factors, *inter alia,* religious, political, ethnic, national, and economic reasons.[29] As such, the policy highlights underlying structural inequalities and systemic oppression within a particular social context—which are foundational to an intersectional framework. In a similar vein, the ICC Policy on Children highlights the significance of attributes like age and birth, and the degree to which they may give rise to multiple forms of discrimination and social inequalities, either alone or as they intersect with other factors: race, ability, or disability; religion or belief; political or other opinion; national, ethnic, or social origin; gender, sex, sexual orientation; or other status or identity.[30]

The recently released ICC Policy on the Crime of Gender Persecution continues and enhances the ICC's engagement with intersectionality.[31] It explores the application of intersectionality with regard to specific violations, for example those pertaining to sexual and gender-based crimes, children or cultural heritage.[32] On the issue of gender persecution in particular, the policy states that '[g]ender persecution may, and frequently does, intersect with and constitute multiple forms of persecution based on political, racial, national, ethnic, cultural, religious or other grounds that are universally recognised as impermissible under international law'.[33] The policy sets out that, 'in accordance with article 54(1)(b) of the Statute and as reflected in the Policies on Sexual

29 ICC OTP, 'Policy Paper on Sexual and Gender-Based Crimes' (June 2014), para. 19.

30 ICC OTP, 'Policy on Children' (November 2016), para. 37. See also para. 51.

31 ICC OTP, Policy on the Crime of Gender Persecution (n 28).

32 Ibid., see e.g. paras 8, 29 and 33.

33 Ibid., para. 55. The *Al Hassan* Pre-Trial Chamber commented on the intersectionality between forms of gender and racial discrimination, noting that 'violence against women could also have been motivated by considerations linked to skin color, since women with dark skin were more affected by this violence than others; the same goes for dark-skinned men who, according to some witnesses, were [more] persecuted than those with light skin'. Decision on the Confirmation of Charges, *Al Hassan, Situation in the Republic of Mali,* ICC-01/12-01/18-461-Corr-Red, PTC I, ICC, 13 November 2019, para. 702. Gender persecution was also charged along with intersecting ethnic, political and/or religious discriminatory grounds in the Said and Al Rahman cases. Decision on the Confirmation of Charges, *Al Rahman, Situation in Darfur, Sudan,* CC-02/05-01/20-433, PTC II, ICC, 9 July 2021; and Decision on the Confirmation of Charges, *Said, Situation in the Central African Republic II,* ICC-01/14-01/21-218-Red, PTC II, ICC, 9 December 2021.

and Gender-Based Crimes and Cultural Heritage, the Office will take a holistic approach to investigating gender persecution in understanding its intersection with culture and other persecutory grounds'.[34]

These legal and policy frameworks that engage with intersectionality provide the substantive and procedural foundation to explore the application of intersectionality in the practice of international criminal law. According to Alexandra Lily Kather:

> Intersectionality, [...] necessitates us to ask questions about systems of power and oppression at play: in the context in which the crimes are being committed where those involved and impacted are situated and among individuals, organizations, institutions, and bodies tasked with international (criminal) justice work—where evidence is being gathered, analysed and where the law is being interpreted and applied. For example, there are structural reasons that influence and predetermine people's perception of what violence is (for example, sexual violence = rape), what an international crime looks like (mass killing of cis-male bodies). White supremacist, colonial and heteropatriarchal thought patterns are determining factors that result in the creation of hierarchy of crimes, of certain crimes being perceived to be more easily prosecutable than others, or of underlying acts of international crimes. [...] As a consequence of a repeated concentration on certain crimes committed against certain groups, other subgroups or members are being excluded.[35]

The historical impunity for sexual and gender-based crimes is an example of such exclusion. The pursuit of accountability for these crimes has been hamstrung by many myths, including the misconception that these violations are less serious than other conflict-related crimes.[36] For example, during the early days at the International Criminal Tribunal for the Former Yugoslavia,

34 ICC OTP, 'Policy on the Crime of Gender Persecution' (n 28) para. 28, citing ICC OTP, 'Policy Paper on Sexual and Gender-Based Crimes' (n 29) para. 20; ICC OTP, 'Policy on Cultural Heritage' (June 2021), paras 3 and 16. See also paras 67 and 81.

35 A L Kather, 'What do intersectionality, feminist leadership and feminist foreign policy have to do with justice?' (*Heinrich Böll Foundation, Global Unit for Feminism and Gender Democracy*, 28 October 2022) <www.boell.de/en/2022/10/21/justice-sexual-and-gender-based-crimes-conflict-what-does-intersectionality-feminist> accessed 1 February 2022.

36 M Jarvis and K Vigneswaran, 'Challenges to Successful Outcomes in Sexual Violence Cases', in S Brammertz and M Jarvis (eds), *Prosecuting Conflict-related Sexual Violence at the ICTY* (Oxford: Oxford University Press 2016) 33–72.

'some staff within the OTP held the perception that working on sexual violence cases was a "soft" or less prestigious assignment, reflecting hierarchies imported from domestic criminal law offices'.[37] Certain lawyers had a strong preference for working on murder cases, while others sought to avoid sexual violence investigations.[38] 'There were comments made by investigators, who were admittedly overworked at the time, saying things like, "I've got ten dead bodies, how do I have time for rape? That's not as important", or "So a bunch of guys got riled up after a day of war, what's the big deal?"'.[39]

Amongst other reasons, such attitudes amongst practitioners laid bare the need to properly account for and fight impunity for sexual and gender-based crimes. From a starting point of invisibility,[40] strides have been made in achieving accountability for sexual and gender-based crimes as international crimes.[41] Violence against women reflects underlying unequal power structures, relations and dynamics that are embedded in patriarchal structures and gender hierarchies which exist in so-called times of peace and which are exacerbated in conflict. Gender analysis has achieved much to surface crimes

---

37 Ibid., 37.

38 P Kuo, 'Prosecuting Crimes of Sexual Violence in an International Tribunal' (2002) 34(3) *Case W Res JIL* 305, 310–311 <https://scholarlycommons.law.case.edu/cgi/viewcontent.cgi?article=1467&context=jil> accessed 1 February 2023. See also X A Aranburu, 'Beyond Dogma and Taboo: Criteria for the Effective Investigation of Sexual Violence' in M Bergsmo, A Butenschøn Skre and E Wood (eds), *Understanding and Proving International Sex Crimes* (Beijing: Torkel Opsahl Academic EPublisher 2012) 269, para. 37 (recounting comments made by lawyers within the OTP that they sought to avoid sexual violence because it was 'very annoying and difficult to prove'); in M Jarvis and K Vigneswaran, 'Challenges to Successful Outcomes in Sexual Violence Cases' (n 36) 37.

39 Kuo, 'Prosecuting Crimes of Sexual Violence' (n 38) 305, 310–311.

40 Ibid., 305–309. The military sexual enslavement of women and girls by the Japanese discussed in the next section, while a notorious example, is only one of many instances of the historical disregard for women's suffering, as manifested by the marginalisation of and impunity for sexual and gender-based crimes.

41 See e.g. the definition of rape in Trial Judgment, *Furundzija*, IT-95-17/1-T, TC II, ICTY, 10 December 1998, para. 185; sexual slavery in Trial Judgment, *Kunarac et al.*, IT-96-23-T & IT-96-23/1-T, TC II, ICTY, 22 February 2001, para. 543; rape as genocide in Trial Judgment, *Akayesu*, ICTR-96-4-T, TC I, ICTR, 2 September 1998, paras 507–508; forced marriages before the SCSL, *Brima et al.*, SCSL-2004-16-A, AC, SCSL, 22 February 2008, paras 195–196; forced marriages before the ECCC in Trial Judgment, *Chea and Samphan*, 002/19-09-2007/ECCC/TC, TC, ECCC, 16 November 2018, paras 3686–3687 and forced pregnancy and forced marriage before the International Criminal Court in Appeals Judgment, *Ongwen, Situation in Uganda*, ICC-02/04-01/15-2023, AC, ICC, 15 December 2022. See also Trial Judgment, *Đorđević*, IT-05-87/1-T, TC II, ICTY, 23 February 2011, para. 887 (crimes of sexual violence 'must not be treated differently from other violent acts simply because of their sexual component').

against women as well as these underlying unequal power structures that drive violence in conflict.[42]

Yet, as I have argued elsewhere, gender—while a significant aspect of a person's identity—is an insufficient framework to surface the breadth and depth of harms experienced by survivors. There is a need to recognise and account for factors beyond gender. Gender, together with other factors like gender identity and sexual orientation, as well as age, ethnicity, race, indigenous or minority status, disability, socio-economic status and religion or belief, marital and/or maternal status, displacement, education level, migrant, HIV/AIDS, *inter alia*, are other relevant aspects of an individual's identity - factors that are crucial to take into account when considering the impacts of crimes.[43] These factors create and reinforce inequalities and privileges, not only *between* genders but also *among* genders, as well as between victims/survivors and perpetrators. Such distinctions matter in understanding sexual and gender-based crimes, which are often tethered to power inequalities, which not only manifest in conflicts, but also drive and exacerbate them.[44]

Unravelling intersecting individual traits which occur within and flow from structural inequalities allows for a more comprehensive and accurate assessment of the gamut of harms suffered by victims/survivors and lays the foundation for pursuing accountability for violations. The three case studies below demonstrate why intersectionality matters in the field of international criminal law when investigating and prosecuting sexual and gender-based crimes.

---

42 ICC OTP, 'Policy Paper on Sexual and Gender-Based Crimes' (n 29). '"Gender analysis" examines the underlying differences and inequalities between women and men, and girls and boys, and the power relationships and other dynamics which determine and shape gender roles in a society and give rise to assumptions and stereotypes. In the context of the work of the Office, this involves a consideration of whether, and in what ways, crimes, including sexual and gender-based crimes, are related to gender norms and inequalities', 4. '[G]ender analysis looks at the roles of females and males; the different patterns of involvement, behaviour, and activities that they have in economic, social, and legal systems; the constraints they face relative to one another; and available opportunities. The significance of this is that the lives and experiences of females and males, including their experience of the legal system, occur within complex sets of differing social and cultural expectations'., para. 20.

43 World Food Programme, 'Gender Equality Policy 2015–2020', para. 12 <https://documents.wfp.org/stellent/groups/public/documents/communications/wfp276754.pdf> accessed 6 February 2023.

44 P Gopalan, 'Breaking Binaries and Honing-in on Harms: Inclusive Approaches Towards Sexual and Gender-Based Crimes', in T B K Sendze, A Adeboyejo, H Morrison, S Ugwu (eds), *Contemporary International Criminal Law Issues: Contributions in Pursuit of Accountability for Africa and in the World*, (The Hague: Asser Press 2023).

### 4.1 *The Sexualised Enslavement of Women and Girls by the Japanese Military during the Second World War: 'Comfort Women'*

The sexualised enslavement of women and girls by the Japanese military during the second world war is a seminal case of conflict-related sexual violence. Estimates indicate that up to 200,000 women and girls were captured, forced, or tricked into sexual slavery.[45] They were drawn from China and various countries in Southeast Asia and the Pacific, but mainly from Korea, which was then a colony of Japan. What can an intersectional analysis bring to the crime of sexualized enslavement ?

Pyong Gap Min writes that in the case of the women and girls from Korea, Japan's colonisation of Korea was a critical factor in their enslavement: a state-supported patriarchal system in Japan facilitated the establishment of military brothels, while patriarchal customs in Korea perpetuated further victimisation on their return home. Being drawn largely from impoverished families, Korean victims/survivors were enslaved due to their economic and social status.[46] Consequently, even when eventually freed from slavery, their future prospects were constrained, forcing some to work as sex workers for economic survival.[47]

An intersectional analysis reveals that for these Korean women and girls, gender—along with colonialism, ageism, patriarchy, militarism, and class—coalesced to produce unique violations that, for some, continued to permeate lives well beyond the specific acts and temporal duration of the enslavement. An intersectional approach widens the horizon to unpack the various and diverse drivers and consequences of the violations experienced.

### 4.2 *Bosnian Muslim Woman: the Srebrenica Syndrome*

The systematic killing of 8,000 Bosnian Muslim men and the removal of Bosnian women, children, and elderly from the Srebrenica enclave in July 1995—27 years ago at the time of writing—provides the factual backdrop to the 'Srebrenica Syndrome'.[48] Expert testimony in the *Kristić* case before the ICTY

---

45 G Hicks, *The Comfort Women: Japan's Brutal Regime of Enforced Prostitution in the Second World War* (New York: WW Norton, 1995) xxi, cited in K Askin, 'Comfort Women—Shifting shame and stigma from victims to victimizers' (2001) 1(5) *International Criminal Law Review* 5, 25.

46 Pyong Gap Min, 'Korean "Comfort Women": The Intersection of Colonial Power, Gender, and Class' (2003) 17(6) *Gender and Society* 938, 939–940.

47 G Hicks, 'The Comfort Women' (n 45) 25.

48 Trial Judgment, *Krstić*, IT-98-33-T, TC I, ICTY, 02 August 2001, para. 1. 'Within a few days, approximately 25,000 Bosnian Muslims, most of them women, children and elderly people who were living in the area, were uprooted and, in an atmosphere of terror, loaded onto overcrowded buses by the Bosnian Serb forces and transported across the confrontation

identified the 'Srebrenica Syndrome' as a specific impediment to female survivors' recovery. One of the primary factors giving rise to the syndrome is that, with few exceptions, the majority of the men of Srebrenica were listed as missing and their fate unknown. For Bosnian Muslim women, having a clear marital status was of paramount significance within their community.[49] A woman whose husband was missing lacked this clarity of status, and many consequences flowed from this uncertainty.[50] This included psychological impacts, as their ability to recover from their loss and trauma was hampered by not knowing with certainty the fate of their men. This in turn meant that they were unable to bury and grieve for loved ones lost.[51]

An intersectional approach demonstrates that this syndrome was a specific response to the lived experiences of the women—the social and cultural context that permeated the violations—such as their religion as Bosnian Muslims and their stature in a patriarchal society, where marital status mattered immensely. The individual harms experienced by each woman were also woven into the fabric of inter-community and inter-generational harms. Referring to her own family, a former Srebrenica resident explained: 'With the fall of Srebrenica [...] from the face of the earth were wiped off three generations of men in the cruellest way possible'.[52] As the Trial Chamber stated, 'In little over one week, thousands of lives were extinguished, irreparably rent or simply wiped from the pages of history'.[53] These findings were met with the approval of the Appeals Chamber which held:

> The Trial Chamber was also entitled to consider the long-term impact that the elimination of seven to eight thousand men from Srebrenica would have on the survival of that community. In examining these consequences [...] [it] focused on the likelihood of the community's physical survival [...] The massacred men amounted to about one fifth of the overall Srebrenica community. Given the patriarchal character of the Bosnian Muslim society in Srebrenica, the destruction of such a sizeable number of men would 'inevitably result in the physical disappearance of the Bosnian Muslim

lines into Bosnian Muslim-held territory. The military-aged Bosnian Muslim men of Srebrenica, however, were consigned to a separate fate. As thousands attempted to flee the area, they were taken prisoner, detained in horrific conditions, and then executed. More than 7,000 people were never seen again'.

49 Ibid., paras 91–93.

50 Ibid.

51 Ibid.

52 Ibid., para. 90; Ms. Mirsada Malagić, T. 1983–84.

53 Ibid., para. 2.

> population at Srebrenica'. […] With the majority of the men killed officially listed as missing, their spouses are unable to remarry and, consequently, to have new children. The physical destruction of the men therefore had severe procreative implications for the Srebrenica Muslim community, potentially consigning the community to extinction.[54]

Analysing this context through an intersectional lens demonstrates the full contours and complexities of the harms experienced by Bosnian Muslim women arising from their 'disappeared' husbands and following the fall of Srebrenica. Intersectionality matters here, as it uncovers overlapping violations, taking into account an understanding of the past, present and future realities of victims/survivors as the multi-dimensional and complex human beings we all are.

### 4.3 *Sri Lanka: Sexual Violence against Men and Boys*

Another example of why intersectionality matters in international criminal law relates to conflict-related sexual violence in Sri Lanka perpetrated by Sinhalese state actors against ethnic Tamil men and boys.[55] Sinhalese perpetrators employed ethnic slurs and referred to them as 'slaves' or 'gay'. Many of these men and boys felt degraded by the use of this abusive language (ethnic and gendered slurs) that underscored the perpetrators' sense of superiority. The victims/survivors articulated feelings of shame and 'emasculation' associated with sexual violence.[56] Here, gender intersected with nationalist narratives on

54 Appeals Judgment, *Krstić*, IT-98-33-A, AC, ICTY, 19 April 2004, para. 28. As P Visseur Sellers highlights, the remaining females also experienced a reduction in their procreation capacity. See P V Sellers, 'Genocide Gendered: the Srebrenica Cases' (Fifth Annual Katherine B Fite Lecture, Proceedings of the Ninth International Humanitarian Law Dialogs, 30 August–1 September 2015).

55 P Gopalan, 'The Long Journey to Justice for Sri Lanka's Victims (Part 1)' (*IntLawGrrls*, 29 September 2015) <https://ilg2.org/2015/09/29/the-long-journey-to-justice-for-sri-lankas-victims/> accessed 22 October 2022. The post-independence government policies that favoured the Sinhalese majority disadvantaged by colonialism ostensibly offered redress, but effectively marginalised and radicalised segments of the Tamil community. Tamil separatists' calls for a separate state began in the 1970s. In 1983, after the LTTE killed government soldiers, the communal violence of 'Black July' set the country firmly on the warpath, though hostilities waxed and waned thereafter. In 2006, at least 520,000 Sri Lankans were displaced by the conflict—one of the largest displacement crises in Asia. The LTTE's crushing defeat by government forces officially ended the conflict in May 2009.

56 Schulz highlights that the term 'emasculation' is problematic as it links socio-culturally constructed masculinities with biologically male sex and reinforces the gendered notions which value masculinity over femininity. However, as the term is commonly used in the literature, and as more appropriate language gains purchase, it is used in quotation marks

the dominance of the Sinhalese ruling class, and the cultural and ethnic hierarchies that not only fed this dominance but also fuelled the sexual violence perpetrated against Tamil men and boys. These were juxtaposed against the legacies of colonialism and their minority status of being Tamil in Sri Lanka.[57]

## 5 Why Does Intersectionality Matter?

In Crenshaw's words, 'Intersectionality is a lens through which you can see where power comes and collides, where it interlocks and intersects. It's not simply that there's a race problem here, a gender problem here, and a class or LBGTQ problem there'.[58] Within international criminal law, intersectionality can serve as an analytical framework that enables the surfacing of systems of power, privilege, and oppression (for example, patriarchy, colonialism, racism) that not only manifest in the identities of victims/survivors and perpetrators, but also drive and form the backdrop to international crimes.

As Kirsten Campbell and Gorana Mlinarević write, this includes gendered systems of power and domination, including patriarchal structures that are integral to the organisation and systemic criminality of conflict. The construction of militarised masculinities and ideologies of ethno-nationalism fuels conflicts. Perpetrators use sexual violence to assert their identity within the hegemonic masculinity of the highly militarised group they identify with. In order to understand the cause and effects of mass violence on individuals, communities and states, the relationship between patriarchal heteronormative structures (such as the military or police), economic organisation and

in this chapter. P Schulz (2015), '"I Felt Useless and Not Man Enough": Deconstructing the Impact of Conflict-Related Sexual Violence on Male Survivors' Masculinities'. Paper presented at the 58th Annual Convention of the International Studies Association (ISA), Baltimore, MD in M Zalewski et al. (eds), *Sexual Violence Against Men in Global Politics* (Abingdon: Routledge 2018) 88.

57 A report by the International Truth and Justice Project Sri Lanka, an NGO that documents conflict-related sexual violence and torture in Sri Lanka, focuses on sexual violence against mostly Tamil men and boys. It contains a narrative analysis of the experiences of more than 100 male victims of sexual violence by the state security forces in Sri Lanka 2014–2018. Most were detained and abused multiple times. H Touquet, 'Unsilenced: Male Survivors Speak of Conflict-Related Sexual Violence in Sri Lanka' (*International Truth and Justice Project*, 2018), 31–34 <http://www.itjpsl.com/assets/ITJP_unsilenced_report-final.pdf> accessed 10 April 2022.

58 K Crenshaw, Isidor and Seville Sulzbacher Professor of Law, Columbia Law School, <www.law.columbia.edu/faculty/kimberle-w-crenshaw> accessed 1 February 2023.

social stratification (gender, sexuality, class, race, age, ethnicity)[59] requires unpacking.

The case studies above illustrate how, alongside gender, other factors relating to identity such as class, social and economic status, age, culture, ethnicity, religion, and the contextual and structural settings within which these identities intersect, compound and combine to produce specific and nuanced violations and harms. As demonstrated by these case studies, identities are not fixed in time, and violations and harms can occur at an individual and community level, while straddling the past, present and the future. Thus, intersectionality can make visible other pertinent factors and structural inequalities, alongside gender, that are often disregarded, overlooked, or accorded insufficient attention. A single axis analysis cannot do justice to the experiences of victims/survivors in this way.

Feminist scholars have highlighted that the framing of conflict-related sexual violence within the narrative of an ethnic conflict illustrates the inadequacy of single axis analysis. Doris Buss wrote that 'the tribunals see rape only as an added layer to ethnic conflict, and that an overdetermination of ethnicity constrains the types of sexual violence—and victims—that tribunals are able to see'.[60] According to Chiseche Mibenge, this approach focuses on a 'single axis construction of discrimination', which is ethnicity.[61] In discussing the crime of genocide, Mibenge argues that the 'narrative of ethnic genocide, by privileging ethnicity as the requisite condition of sexual victimisation, denies gender-based discrimination [and] suggests that sexual violence [...] is a type of ethnic violence rather than gender-based violence'.[62] 'Accordingly, it does not provide an adequate conceptualisation of sexual violence in genocide, nor of the structuring of ethnic based harms through other axes of discrimination beside ethnicity, such as gender, age, or class'.[63] Given these issues,

---

59 K Campbell and G Mlinarević, 'A Feminist Critique of Approaches to International Criminal Justice in the Age of Identity Politics. A case study of Conflict-Related Sexual Violence Prosecutions before the International Criminal Tribunal for the Former Yugoslavia' in I Rosenthal, V Oosterveld, and S SáCouto (eds), *Gender and International Criminal Law* (Oxford: Oxford University Press 2022) 90–96.

60 D Buss, 'Sexual Violence, Ethnicity, and Intersectionality in International Criminal Law' in E Grabham, D Cooper et al (eds), *Intersectionality and Beyond* (London and New York: Routledge-Cavendish 2008), 118 cited in Campbell, 'Justice for Humans' (n 27) 91.

61 C Mibenge, *Sex and International Tribunals* (Pennsylvania: University of Pennsylvania Press, 2013), 86, cited in Campbell, 'Justice for Humans' (n 27) 91.

62 Ibid., 62.

63 Ibid., 75–76.

Kirsten Campbell rightly points out that international criminal law does not provide a legal conceptualisation of sexual violence as a form of collective victimisation.[64]

Against this backdrop, an intersectional approach provides another tool in the armoury to deepen our contextual understandings of affected individuals, communities and groups of individuals/collectives, and the privileges and disadvantages that define them. Intersectionality thus deepens and enhances the contextualisation of crimes at an individual and structural level to surface the power dynamics that create and fuel conflict. Such insights are invaluable in transitional justice processes. Understanding the root causes and drivers of violence can be powerful tools for prevention and serve as early warnings for mass atrocities.

Intersectional analysis allows us to broaden our gaze beyond factors relating to gender and to better recognise and articulate the implications of other aspects of identity. In addition, intersectionality surfaces intertwined structural drivers of mass violence resulting from historical and contemporary supremacies in a given context. According to Collins, 'because intersectional analysis of violence reframes violence not as a matter of human nature or circumstance, but as fundamental to power as domination, conceptualizing violence as a saturated site of intersecting power relations provides a potentially important perspective on political domination'.[65]

Developments in investigating and prosecuting sexual and gender-based crimes highlight the significance of context—not just the context or circumstances in which the crimes occurred—but their linkages to other violations, and their relationship with structural inequalities which served as triggers and contributed to conflict-related violations.[66] By building on this analytical framework, intersectionality deepens our contextual understanding, enabling a more precise and thorough articulation of the nature of violations, harms, and their impacts, thus providing a fuller picture of affected individuals.

64 Campbell, 'Justice for Humans' (n 27) 93–94.

65 P Hill Collins, *Intersectionality as Critical Social Theory* (Duke University Press 2019) 239.

66 See e.g. A Martin Beringola, 'Intersectionality: Explaining SGBV Interlinked with Terrorism and Other International Crimes' (2020) 1(2) *Journal of Human Trafficking, Enslavement and Conflict-Related Sexual Violence* 135–161.

## 6 Applying Intersectionality—Its Critics and Limits

From being labelled a tool of victor's justice after the Tokyo and Nuremberg War Crimes Tribunals that followed the Second World War, international criminal prosecutions have sought to shed accusations of partiality, while better incorporating victims'/survivors' voices and lived experiences into the judicial process. Through the application of the concepts of do-no-harm, informed consent and gender analysis, the practice of international criminal law has sought to uphold victim/survivor agency and participation in justice processes. Recent commitments to victim/survivor-centred approaches further illustrate this trajectory.[67] Against this canvas of best practices, intersectionality enters the fray as a relative newcomer. Questions as to how it might be best applied thus require exploration.

Critically, intersectionality can make visible what is excluded and unseen at first glance. It seeks to draw out what has fallen through gaping holes, cracks and interstitial spaces in the justice chain–elements which are relevant both to understanding victims'/survivors' experiences and informing the justice they demand. How can we unearth what is buried and seemingly invisible or inconsequential? As Kather writes, 'an intersectional understanding of violence and its causal link to existing systems of oppression constitutes a gap in both expertise and practice within international(ised) justice processes around the world'.[68] How do we remedy this?

---

67 See e.g. S Ferro Ribeiro and D van der Straten Ponthoz on behalf of the UK Foreign & Commonwealth Office, 'Second edition of the International Protocol on the Documentation and Investigation of Sexual Violence in Conflict', March 2017 <https://www.gov.uk/government/publications/international-protocol-on-the-documentation-and-investigation-of-sexual-violence-in-conflict>, and Kinshasa Declaration on Reparations for Conflict-Related Sexual and Gender-based Violence, 22–24 November 2021 <https://static1.squarespace.com/static/5ff7d9f4dd4cdc650b24f9a4/t/61e0651201a3d2067d8a513e/1642095892194/2021+12+20++Kinshasa+Principles_Survivors+Hearing_EN.pdf> and the Murad Code <www.muradcode.com/> all accessed 4 February 2023. The Murad Code's full title is the 'Global Code of Conduct for Gathering and Using Information about Systematic and Conflict-Related Sexual Violence'. The Code is named after the Nobel Peace Prize laureate, Nadia Murad, which reflects its objective to place survivors' rights and well-being at its heart. It is a global, voluntary code of conduct for those collecting information from survivors of systematic and conflict-related sexual violence. See also, 'Response to the Draft of the "Global Code of Conduct for Investigating and Documenting Conflict-Related Sexual Violence"' (January 2021) <https://responsetodraftmuradcode.wordpress.com/> accessed 10 February 2023.

68 A L Kather, '"Within the context of society": Building Intersectional Models and Strategies for International Criminal Law and Practice', Hertie School Fundamental Rights Research Colloquium, 19 May 2021 (notes on file with author).

## 7 Lessons Learned from Gender Analysis

The arduous journey in pursuing accountability for sexual and gender-based crimes and incorporating gender analysis into the practice of international criminal law offers some lessons. Gender analysis has laid the groundwork for international criminal law practitioners to engage with personal traits (albeit a single trait) as relevant to the risk and experiences of international crimes.

Having historically focussed on remedying the marginalisation of crimes against women in conflict, a narrow understanding of gender analysis has led to 'gender' being seen as synonymous with 'women'. As gender is seen as a 'women's issue', there is a scarcity of gender analysis relating to certain male experiences of conflict such as sexual violence against men and boys. Notably, this conflation of 'women' and 'gender' restricts 'gender' to a binary approach of male vs female. Such a constrained understanding of the notion of 'gender' ignores sexual orientation, non-binary gender identities, expressions, or sexual orientation of victims/survivors, thus perpetuating the lack of recognition and redress under international criminal law for certain categories of victims/survivors such as Lesbian, Gay, Bisexual, Transgender, Queer, and Intersex identified ('LGBTQI+') persons.[69]

When it comes to women, the focus has been on sexual violence as the predominant conflict-related violation against women, leading to limited analysis of gendered impacts on non-sexual violations. A thread that unites these challenges is a tendency to take a binary approach: whether male vs female vs LGBTQI+ persons and those with non-binary gender and sexual identities, or rape vs other forms of sexual violence.[70] As will be discussed below, intersectionality, as an approach that eschews rigidity, can offer a framework to break down these binaries.

However, an intersectional approach does raise some points of disjuncture with existing processes and practices in the field of international criminal law. First, how can an intersectional approach be reconciled with investigative and prosecutorial approaches that categorise crimes by types of harms—e.g. as sexual and gender-based crimes? Conflict-related sexual violence does not occur in isolation but within a continuum of conflict-related crimes (e.g.

69 ICC OTP, 'Policy on the Crime of Gender Persecution' (n 31) 3: 'The plus sign represents people who identify with the broader LGBTQI communities but use other terms for self-identification. While the acronym LGBTQI+ is inclusive of a broad range of persons, it is not exhaustive, nor is it the universally standard acronym'.

70 For detailed explorations of these issues see Gopalan 'Breaking Binaries and Honing-In on Harms' (n 44).

detention, deportation, killings, torture). As a consequence of the focus on sexual and gender-based crimes as a specific category, are survivors reduced to a monolithic identity based on a single violation?

Second, a blinkered focus on sexual violence, in particular rape, has created a hierarchy of crimes and victimhood. Crenshaw has made a comparable argument, noting that while 'Black women's experiences are much broader than the general categories that discrimination discourse provides [...] the continued insistence that Black Women's demands and needs be filtered through certain categorical analyses that completely obscure their experiences guarantees that their needs are seldom addressed'.[71]

Can parallels be drawn within the practice of international criminal law, where donors and governments stipulate the crimes that they would like to support? For example, international efforts and reparations processes that focus on sexual violence.[72] Consequently, victims'/survivors' ability to access support is predicated on an articulation and prioritisation of their harms that conforms with these frameworks. As Dubravka Žarkov writes, 'according to successive Security Council Resolutions, the rape of a local woman by a local man during a war is a threat to international security. But demolishing a woman's home, destroying her water source, stealing her land, and expelling her from her ancestral territory are not'.[73] Thus, pursuing accountability for sexual and gender-based crimes to remedy the widespread impunity for these crimes has inadvertently led to another hierarchy that can truncate the full expression of harms experienced by victims/survivors.

Moreover, hierarchies, tropes, and gender stereotypes have plagued efforts to make visible sexual and gender-based crimes and to place them on an equal footing with other conflict related crimes.[74] These are, therefore issues to guard against when applying intersectionality. Žarkov highlights that during the conflict in the former Yugoslavia, a nexus of male sexual bestiality towards women and essentialised ethnic identities produced clear-cut victims and villains. The age-old trope of the male sexual violator and female victim was assigned local ethnic identities: in the former Yugoslavia, the Serb male rapist and Muslim

71 Crenshaw, 'Demarginalizing the Intersection of Race and Sex' (n 1) 149–150.

72 See e.g. the Global Survivors Fund's global study on reparations for survivors of conflict-related sexual violence <www.globalsurvivorsfund.org/guide> and the UK Government's 'Preventing Sexual Violence in Conflict Initiative' <www.gov.uk/government/organisations/preventing-sexual-violence-in-conflict-initiative> both accessed 20 January 2022.

73 D Žarkov, 'From Women and War to Gender and Conflict, Feminist Trajectories' in F Ní Aoláin, N Cahn, D Francesca Haynes, N Valji (eds), *Oxford Handbook of Gender and Conflict* (Oxford: Oxford University Press 2018) 28.

74 See Gopalan, 'Breaking Binaries and Honing-In on Harms' (n 44).

female victim still stand as a symbol of conflict.[75] These tropes and stereotypes are reproduced in other conflicts—whether the male Hutu rapist and female Tutsi victim, or the male Singhalese rapist and Tamil victim of any gender. Simply adding ethnicity, race, or religion to gender, while ostensibly intersectional, may in effect solidify divisions, as discussed below.

## 8 Sequencing—Take Gender and Add Intersectionality?

Moving away from a single axis analysis that relies solely on a gender lens, questions remain as to how to apply an intersectional analysis of the discriminatory grounds relevant to international criminal law.[76] While Crenshaw has grounded her analysis on the intersections of race and sex in the United States, the concept of intersectionality does not mandate the inclusion of race or sex as the starting point of an intersectional analysis for the purposes of international criminal law.[77]

Is gender analysis a prerequisite to an intersectional analysis, or is gender one of many factors to be considered in the mix of an intersectional analysis? An intersectional feminist approach 'foregrounds women's and girls' experiences in order to demonstrate systematic discrimination against them and advance their struggle for equality', with the application of an intersectional lens to reflect 'overlapping systems of oppression and their interaction such as their connection between discrimination and violence based on gender, race, class, sexuality, religion and disability'.[78]

If gender is taken as the starting point of intersectional analysis, does that mean that gender is prioritised as the dominant quality? If so, is that advisable? While gender must be addressed as a relevant factor in an intersectional analysis, does it acquire dominance as the overriding characteristic of the individual instead of other attributes—for example disability, being displaced or minority status? How do we answer these questions in a field where

---

75 Žarkov, 'From Women and War to Gender and Conflict' (n 73) 27.

76 See Campbell, 'Justice for Humans' (n 27) 93.

77 Crenshaw acknowledges other critical factors such as class and sexuality in shaping the experience of women of colour. Her focus on the intersections of race and gender only highlights the need to account for multiple grounds of identity when considering how the social world is constructed. See Crenshaw, 'Mapping the Margins' (n 2) 1245.

78 UNFPA (Whole of Syria Gender-Based Violence Area of Responsibility), 'Voices from Syria: Assessment Findings of the Humanitarian Needs Overview', 2021, 18 <www.humanitarianresponse.info/sites/www.humanitarianresponse.info/files/documents/files/voices_2021_-_final_180521_eng.pdf> accessed 1 February 2023.

many questions remain as to what justice is and who decides this, as raised by Carla Ferstman[79]? While not insurmountable, there is work to be done on the relationship between intersectional analysis and gender analysis, and more broadly on the sequencing and interactions between factors of discriminations and systems of domination within the framework of international criminal law.

Aside from questions relating to the application of intersectionality, detractors also raise broader issues as to its viability as an analytical tool deployed within a legal framework. Jane Conaghan questions the use of law as a basis for intersectionality because the law seeks to categorise and compartmentalise, whereas intersectionality inherently eschews generalisations and seeks instead to drill down to the granular.[80] The judicial process requires that evidence be gathered, analysed, distilled, and categorised into legal qualifications. As I have argued elsewhere, international criminal prosecutions which import many characteristics of the Anglo-Saxon adversarial systems, including an emphasis on securing a verdict, entail the winnowing out of evidence deemed less critical to the case strategy.[81] As such, the judicial process, through the use of legal concepts and categorisation, is channelled towards specific outcomes. This is at odds with intersectionality which, *prima facie*, seeks to unpick the composite of an individual into different constituent components.

How does one apply a concept (intersectionality) within a framework (the judicial process) when ostensibly the concept and framework seem to have divergent goals and approaches? How can the intended finality of the justice process be reconciled with intersectional approaches that apparently seek to parse, distil, and unravel? Another critic of intersectionality, Richard Delgado, has argued that if applied without constraint, intersectionality can result in the creation of subcategories *ad infinitum*.[82]

---

79 See the chapter by Ferstman in this volume.

80 J Conaghan, 'Intersectionality, and the Feminist Project in Law', in E Grabham *et al.* (eds), *Intersectionality and Beyond: Law, Power and the Politics of Location*' (London: Routledge Cavendish 2008) 41: 'If we are truly to get to grips with the issues intersectionality raises, we need a theoretical framework which is genuinely *multidimensional*, possessing breadth, depth and, most importantly, mobility. We must not allow our conception of the problems—and solutions—to become caught within a narrow legal aesthetic'. Cited in Davis, *Intersectionality and International Law* (n 2) 213.

81 P Gopalan, 'Conflict-Related Sexual Violence in Kosovo: Gendering Justice Through Transformative Reparations' in S Mouthaan and O Jurasz (eds), *Gender and War in International and Transitional Justice Perspectives* (Cambridge: Intersentia 2019), 293.

82 R Delgado, 'Rodrigo's Reconsideration: Intersectionality and the Future of Critical Race Theory', (2011) 96 *Iowa Law Review* 1247, 1263–1266, citing to A P Harris, 'Race and Essentialism in Feminist Legal Theory' (1990) 24(3) *Stanford Law Review* 581, 588. Cited

Moreover, legal accountability for violations of international criminal law is bound by the principle of individual criminal responsibility. Campbell and Mlinarević, in looking at the ICTY's prosecutions of sexual violence, argue that this principle, as conceptualised in some ICTY cases, disconnects individual acts of conflict-related sexual violence from the wider gendered patterns and effects of these crimes, and therefore conceals the wider structures that enable gender-based crimes. In order to account for the collective dimensions of mass atrocity, the ICTY used ideas of identity to stand in for organisational or systemic criminality and the social and political structures that enable them.[83]

Ideas of identity inhabit the core of intersectionality. Who decides on questions of identity or identities? Is it the victims'/survivors' self-identification, or the perpetrators' perceptions?[84] Moreover, identities are not immutable.[85] Campbell and Mlinarević shed light on the significance of identity using ICTY case law. They argue that 'because the ICTY understood the conflict in terms of warring ethnic identities, it privileges ethnicity as the primary dimension of identity', thus, 'ignoring other relevant axes of social differentiation and subordination, such as gender, class, sexuality, and disability, that structure

in Davis, *Intersectionality and International Law* (n 2) 214. This chimes with more general critiques surrounding identity politics. See e.g. P Corfield 'Being Assessed as a Whole Person: A Critique of Identity Politics' (2021) *Academia Letters*, Article 101 <www.academia.edu/44975382/Being_Assessed_as_a_Whole_Person_A_Critique_of_Identity_Politics> accessed 27 January 2023.

83 Campbell and Mlinarević, 'A Feminist Critique of Approaches to International Criminal Justice' (n 59) 86–94.

84 See P Gopalan (2021) 'Rejecting Notions of "Honour" to Mitigate Stigma: Prosecutions for Sexual Violence before the Bangladeshi International Criminal Tribunals' (2021) *Centre for Women, Peace and Security Working Paper Series* (LSE Centre for Women Peace and Security) <www.lse.ac.uk/women-peace-security/assets/documents/2021/WPS27Gopalan.pdf> accessed 21 December 2022, where I argue that the characterisation of crimes of sexual violence as offences against chastity and honour endorses the perpetrators' constructions of sexual violence and their intent on perpetrating this crime to instil notions of the destruction of the enemy community's honour, by destroying/ harming women's sexual purity. See also J Mertus, 'Shouting from the Bottom of the Well: The Impact of International Trials for Wartime Rape on Women's Agency' (2004) 6 (1) *International Feminist Journal of Politics*, 110–128. One of the criticisms made of the first case before the International Criminal Tribunal for the Former Yugoslavia that prosecuted only sexual violence was that the examination of the survivors in the courtroom took the perpetrator's perspective in eliciting the details of the crime, with little room for the survivors to narrate the crime as experienced and leaving them disempowered by the process.

85 Visseur Sellers, 'Intersectional Approaches to International Criminal Law and Practice: What Can Intersectionality Mean for International Justice?' (n 27).

victimisation or frames them within dominant ethnic discourses'.[86] This led to the ICTY seeing women through the identity that the perpetrator assigned them, irrespective of the women's self-image or their agency in deciding this. Crimes such as rape are framed through ideas of ethnic heteronormativity, with perpetrators' statements of intent to impregnate the women being relied upon as evidence of discriminatory intent.[87]

When an intersectional analysis is skewered towards identity, and in particular a single aspect of identity (for example, gender or ethnicity), the results are unsatisfactory, as described above. When fully fleshed out, intersectionality reveals individual characteristics and their interplay with the matrix of domination as causal factors that inform and shape an individual's intersecting identities. The granularity of individual identities and the macro systems of structural inequalities intersect and coalesce in a feedback loop that is mutually reinforcing. Intersecting aspects of individual identity occur within particular contexts of intersecting structural oppressions.

Intersectionality offers a pathway to look beyond individual identity traits and ask questions that also unearth the systems of oppression inherent in a given matrix of domination. Why did one ethnicity become identified as the predominant perpetrator group and why was the other consigned to victimhood? What were the root causes of the violence that led to this ethnicity-based binary of victim and perpetrator? What intersecting forms of structural discrimination inhabit the matrix of domination? For example, how does colonialism and its ongoing effects (coloniality)[88] drive ethnic and religious hierarchies that underlie the victim-perpetrator binary solidified along these divisions. This is seen in many conflicts, including those in Sri Lanka and the former Yugoslavia discussed above.

## 9 Embracing Positionality and Intentionality

Intersectionality seeks to recognise and grapple with systems of domination whether patriarchy, colonialism, homophobia, heteronormativity, or militarised masculinities within which notions of identity are expressed. As discussed above, structural discrimination based on ethnicity, or religion, informs the structures and systems that perpetrators operate within, and the

86 Campbell and Mlinarević, 'A Feminist Critique of Approaches to International Criminal Justice' (n 59) 87.
87 Ibid., 91–92.
88 See e.g. S Tamale, *Decolonization and Afro-Feminism* (Canada: Daja Press, 2022).

crimes that they commit. Nevertheless, concepts of systemic discrimination relating to systems of power and privilege do not generally feature in the daily lexicon of international criminal law practitioners. Aside from a lack of familiarity and likely lack of comfort with these issues, substantively, these are challenging issues to address in the workplace. Personal attitudes, and bias, even and especially when unconscious, require careful navigation, as these issues closely correlate with personal beliefs, and a sense of self. Moreover, discussions about gender, race, or sexuality do not exist and occur in a neutral space. On the contrary, these issues are subject to contesting narratives that ebb and flow within current social, cultural, and political discourse (hence the term 'identity politics').[89]

How can we be better prepared for resistant or even hostile responses that are likely to follow when self-reflection and concerted efforts to change assumptions, behaviours, and practices are required? Again, efforts made to incorporate gender analysis and develop a gender-competent cadre of human rights and judicial practitioners offer some useful insights on potential stumbling blocks. In 2011, the UN Secretary General made an express commitment to ensure that all commissions of inquiry and UN investigative bodies had dedicated gender expertise and access to specific sexual violence investigative capacity.[90] Despite this leadership demonstrated at the highest levels, gender experts who were deployed as part of this commitment have faced hostility, or what is called 'gender backlash', within the teams they were sent to support. While not intractable, these experiences highlight the sensitivity of these issues, thus underscoring the need for prudent engagement.

In this regard, an awareness of positionality can be useful. Positionality refers to the ways in which individual identities—including factors such as race, gender, sexuality, class, and ability status—situate individuals as having relatively more or less power within social, cultural, economic, political, and legal contexts. Positionality relates to 'how our identities, and the privileges and dis-privileges that flow from them, influence our perspectives and ways of

89 In this regard, it is noted that the first webinar in the Emergent Justice Collective webinar series 'Intersectional Approaches to International Criminal Law and Practice: What Can Intersectionality Mean for International Justice?' 6 December 2021 was trolled by violent and racist remarks in the chat function. <www.youtube.com/results?search_query=What+Can+Intersectionality+Mean+for+International+Justice%3F+6+December+2021> accessed 1 February 2023.

90 Report of the Secretary-General on women and peace and security, UN Doc S/2011/598, para. 69.

being in the world'.[91] Positionality would encompass reflection on our individual privileges and biases, as well as those of the team, on power dynamics and relationships, biases, and hierarchies both implicit and explicit, and the gaps in knowledge and understanding relating to the work undertaken.[92]

Koenig and Egan write, 'To investigate is to exercise power—to determine which crimes are worthy of the time, money and other resources needed to determine the facts underlying those crimes, and whose voices, experiences and perspectives should be prioritized'.[93] Those investigating thus have the power to make invisible certain categories of victims/survivors. In light of this power dynamics embedded in the investigative process, issues related to ethics, power, privilege, and positionality including the identity of the victims/survivors and investigators, require careful navigation.[94] For example, when investigating international crimes, there may be perceptions of power differentials which may influence or limit survivors' choices. In certain cultures, saying 'no' can be seen as being impolite or rude.[95] This is only exacerbated by any real or perceived power differential between the investigator and victim/survivor. Bearing in mind that the psychological trauma associated with sexual violence may have destructive effects on self-esteem, any sense of hierarchy between the investigator and victim/survivor is only heightened. In these situations, what steps are needed to ensure informed consent? What impact might such power dynamics have in terms of how victims/survivors engage? How might this be mitigated?[96]

Related to an awareness of positionality is the practice of intentionality. Being intentional can provide a disciplined approach that prevents us

---

91 G Ajele and J McGill, Intersectionality in Law and Legal Contexts, Women's Legal Education and Action Fund (LEAF) 2020 <www.leaf.ca/wp-content/uploads/2020/10/Full-Report-Intersectionality-in-Law-and-Legal-Contexts.pdf> 6 accessed 1 February 2023.

92 A Lily Kather, 'Within the context of society' (n 68).

93 A Koenig and U Egan, 'Power and Privilege: Investigating Sexual Violence with Digital Open Source Information' (2021) 19(1) *Journal of International Criminal Justice* 55, 62.

94 Ibid.

95 This observation is based on my experiences in investigating and prosecuting international crimes. Another example is the importance of eye contact. Certain cultures might view the failure to make eye contact as demonstrating shiftiness or untrustworthiness, but in other cultures making direct eye contact might be perceived as being disrespectful, confrontational or aggressive..

96 The Murad Code (n 67). The Murad Code recommends that practitioners 'proactively mitigate factors that can pressure survivors to share information. Such factors include real or perceived imbalances in power, status, gender or age, and social etiquette, politicisation, or family and community influences (also recognising that concerns for their community can be positive motivators for survivors)', para. 2.6.

assuming that victims/survivors of sexual and gender-based crimes are a monolithic group, who are only able to testify about these crimes—when we know that sexual and gender-based crimes do not occur in isolation, but within a continuum of conflict-related violence, against a backdrop of systemic inequalities. Intentionality is acknowledging that each victim/survivor is a unique individual, that they do not have identical interests and needs, nor do they speak with one voice. Intentionality is being mindful of who is being excluded in these processes—are there men and boys and LGBTQI+ individuals who also experienced sexual and gender-based crimes alongside women and girls? What happened to the children in the conflict? Intentionality is seeking to confront the silences, presumptions and dogmas that might undergird these questions, by opening a space for less encumbered engagements with victims/survivors.[97]

Considering the obstacles faced by victims/survivors when sharing their experiences is critical. Providing space for victims to share the breadth and depth of their experiences is one way. Language is a common barrier in the practice of international criminal law. It is of course easier to consult, investigate and prosecute when there is a common language. Depending on the language one speaks best, it could be more convenient to engage with victims/survivors who speak English or another lingua franca, or to engage with well-established/known international NGOs, who report in that language. However, in many conflicts, this decision could privilege victim/survivors who had the opportunity to learn this language and international NGOs, to the exclusion of grassroot organisations that operate in their local languages.

As such, when making the decision to undertake victim/survivor consultations, roundtables, or workshops, equally critical is the scoping and mapping exercise to determine who gets a seat at the table. How do we capture a representative spectrum of voices? Instead of following the path of least effort, a willingness to take extra steps to ensure a diversity of sources and voices

97 In Gopalan 'Breaking Binaries and Honing-In on Harms' (n 44), I have argued that avoiding rigidity can also mean greater intentionality in drawing from other disciplines to inform and nourish an intersectional approach in international criminal law. As discussed above, the field of human rights, with its proximity to international criminal law, offers fertile ground for exploration. Further afield, Denov and Drumbl rely on an interdisciplinary framework that merges elements of law and social science, drawing on ethnographic fieldwork to reframe the crime of forced marriage to enhance accountability. See M S Denov and M A Drumbl, 'The Many Harms of Forced Marriage: Insights for Law from Ethnography in Northern Uganda' (2020) 18(2) *Journal of International Criminal Justice* 349.

is an example of intentionality in practice.[98] While exclusion is multi-layered and permeates the justice chain, a seat at the table is a critical aspect of inclusion. Who gets to speak—whether for themselves or on behalf of others? Who decides? Lived experiences matter. It is no coincidence that Crenshaw, a legal scholar who is a Black woman, coined the term 'intersectionality' to describe the experiences of a subset of Black women.

## 10 Conclusion

Intersectionality offers a pathway to ensure that the practice of international criminal law does not, to paraphrase Crenshaw, reflect 'an uncritical and disturbing acceptance of dominant ways about thinking about discrimination'.[99] It demands that practitioners reject rigid assumptions that straitjacket victims/survivors. It is a call to action demanding that practitioners 'look beneath the prevailing conceptions of discrimination and to challenge the complacency that accompanies the belief in the effectiveness of this framework'.[100] The practice of intersectionality requires curiosity and humility.

Intersectionality is a prism that disentangles multiple, systemic, and interconnected forms of discrimination which are not only personal to the victims/survivors and perpetrators but are also simultaneously embedded in the fabric of their communities and in the systems of power they inhabit. Intersectionality has the power to set us on a trajectory towards more victim/survivor-centred justice processes and outcomes. Can the practice of international criminal law rise to this challenge?

98 On the issue of the diversity of voices, one of the criticisms of intersectionality relates to its apparent disregard for interventions from the Global South: 'What I find revealing in debates on intersectionality, even among its critics, is the total lack of engagement with literature outside the Euro—North American (at most Australia)', N Menon, 'Is Feminism about "women"? A critical view on intersectionality from India' (*International Viewpoint – online socialist magazine*, 18 May 2015) <https://internationalviewpoint.org/spip.php?article4038> accessed 7 February 2023, 11. See also, N Dhawan and M do Mar Castro Varela, '"What Difference Does Difference make?": Diversity, Intersectionality and Transnational Feminist Politics' (2016) 16 *Wagadu: A Journal of Transnational Women's and Gender Studies* 11.

99 Crenshaw, 'Demarginalizing the Intersection of Race and Sex' (n 1) 150.

100 Ibid., 167.

CHAPTER 10

# 'No-Win Scenarios' in Situation and Case Selection: a Call for a Holistic Conversation

*Darryl Robinson*

## 1 Introduction*

This chapter differs from most publications on the selection of situations and cases in international criminal law. Most works on this topic invoke some specific desiderata and lament that current practices fall short in advancing those particular desiderata. This chapter, by contrast, aims to draw attention to recurring patterns and shortcomings in the discourse, rendering it more superficial and less productive than it could be. The aim is to pave the way ing for deeper, more thoughtful arguments and conversations.

If one peruses the literature and commentary of the last twenty years, one will read that the International Criminal Court ('Court', 'ICC') has been constantly getting everything wrong at every turn, particularly when it comes to situation and case selection. For every decision, perfectly credible arguments point to some clearly important value that the Court has inexplicably failed to satisfy. These seemingly-baffling failures by the Court are routinely ascribed to two main causes: 'politics' or incompetence.[1] This chapter adds an alternative, widely-overlooked possibility, by pointing out that the Court sits at the centre of a web of literally contradictory expectations and requirements. Importantly, there is no 'just right' balance: every possible stance can be credibly condemned as flawed according to some plausibly-applicable value. On issue after issue, these threads of irreconcilable desiderata entangle the Court in a series of 'no-win scenarios'. The deep conundrum is that most of the arguments pointing out problems with every given approach are *correct*.

As a result, the discourse on case and situation selection at the ICC is a kaleidoscope of contradictory criticisms and recommendations. While there appears to be broad agreement on the urgent need for reforms, on more

* This research was supported by funding from the Social Sciences and Humanities Research Council of Canada.

1 See below, Section 2.

 | DOI:10.1163/9789004529939_011

studious inspection one can discern that the prescriptions actually pull in countless *opposing* directions. Some tensions are direct and obvious[2] and others are indirect and subtle.[3] I suggest that this pattern—a panoramic circle of irreconcilable requirements—still goes inadequately noticed, impoverishing the conversation. I point out this broad pattern to show the need for more subtle, holistic analyses.

First, a key message of this chapter is that, currently, many evaluations are *'one-dimensional' analyses of multi-dimensional problems*. By 'one-dimensional', I mean that they consider only a limited set of the desiderata.[4] Accordingly, they identify problems with reference to those limited desiderata and advance 'simple' solutions to remedy those problems. The shortcoming of one-dimensional analyses is that they do not consider the conflicting desiderata and how every solution to one problem aggravates a different perceived problem. As a result, their prescriptions are not based in a holistic assessment.

Second, I highlight and problematize the commonplace thinking—in ICC discourse and elsewhere—that to identify a *problem* is to identify an *error* in need of reform. In other words, the common thinking is that if there is a sound criticism of something, then we should change it. However, given the web of contradictory requirements, *every possible position is problematic*. Thus, the commonplace thinking is too simplistic: identifying a problem is valuable, but it is only the *first step* of an argument. Given that every option is flawed, it is not enough to point out flaws: we need a holistic assessment to try to identify the all-things-considered 'least bad' option. The alternating barrages of one-dimensional analyses, and the implicit idea that ICC's approaches should not have 'problems', have led to a debate that is often more shallow, repetitive, and sensationalized than it could be.

Third, a holistic conversation recognizes that multi-dimensional issues require *multi-dimensional analysis*. On a multi-dimension analysis, we carefully consider all of the conflicting desiderata, not just one. We look for the *normative* tensions: that for each value that one observer credibly invokes, another

2 Some tensions are direct and ideological, such as the tension between those who urge the Court to put more emphasis on pursuing powerful states versus those who urge the Court to build support from powerful states.

3 Some desiderata are not conceptually opposed but come into conflict in *practice*; for example tensions between desiderata of speed, comprehensiveness, and quality, or between reflecting the patterns of criminality in a situation versus budgetary efficiency.

4 Those desiderata sometimes conflict; for example, building support of states or building support of various populations, appropriate deference to other interests (harm avoidance, peace) or exclusive focus on one's mandate.

observer credibly invokes an opposing value.[5] We also look for the *practical* tensions: i.e. in a world of finite resources, reducing one set of concerns inescapably aggravates a different set of concerns (eg speed *v.* quality *v.* comprehensiveness *v.* fiscal restraint). Then we have the real debate, a much more subtle debate: about *which problems to embrace* and to which extent.

There will still be intense disagreements, because different thinkers will prioritize different desiderata. But once we realize that we are discussing trade-offs between different plausible desiderata and different viable viewpoints, the debate would hopefully be less absolutist and strident. The debate is not about right-versus-wrong, nor is it about 'simple solutions'. It is a much more humble, open-minded, difficult debate about which flawed positions to adopt.

This chapter generally assumes a level of familiarity with the legal issues and the main debates, but I should explain 'case selection' and 'situation selection' at the International Criminal Court (ICC), for relative newcomers. *Case selection* is one of the most important, sensitive, and controversial functions of an international prosecutor, and of the judges who have varying degrees of review over those decisions.[6] Case selection is governed by Statute criteria,[7] but (*i*) the criteria are rudimentary and require considerable interpretation, and (*ii*) given that the number of potential cases meeting the criteria so vastly outstrips capacity, considerable prosecutorial discretion must be exercised to select the few cases that will proceed. The ICC also has to engage in *situation selection*.[8] Whereas previous international tribunals were created by states to address particular identified situations, the ICC is permanent, with a much broader jurisdictional reach.[9] Thus the ICC must select which 'situations' to investigate.[10] The process of evaluating referrals and communications in order to select situations is called '*preliminary examination*'.[11] Once a preliminary examination is concluded and a situation is selected,[12] the ICC can begin an

5 See Section 2.

6 Article 53(2) and 58 of the Rome Statute of the International Criminal Court (signed 17 July 1998, entered into force 1 July 2002) 2187 UNTS 3 ('ICC Statute').

7 Article 53 of the ICC Statute lists the relevant requirements: jurisdiction, admissibility (complementarity), admissibility (gravity), as well as consideration of the interests of justice.

8 ICC Statute, Article 13, 15, 17, 53.

9 ICC Statute, Articles 1, 11, 12, and 13.

10 ICC Statute, Article 53.

11 ICC Statute, Article 15(6); and see also ICC Statute, Articles 13, 14, 15, 53; Rules of Procedure and Evidence, Rules 46–50.

12 ICC Statute, Articles 15 and 53. In the absence of a referral by a State Party or the Security Council, the Prosecutor needs approval of the Pre-Trial Chamber to proceed with an investigation: Article 15.

'investigation' into that situation; in the course of the investigation, specific 'cases' (charging particular accused persons with particular crimes) will be identified and selected.

## 2 'Inescapable Dyads'

I have previously written about *'inescapable dyads'*,[13] surveying some of the continuously recurring pairs of opposing criticisms of the ICC: that it reaches to too high/too low; it selects cases that are too hard/too easy; it arrives too soon/too late, it is too close/too far from States, and so on. Viewed in isolation, each argument is powerful, because it relies on a value that can be credibly regarded as a value properly underlying international criminal justice. However, it is only when one views them all together that one sees the panorama of contradictory demands and values. I have presented the 'dyads' to many audiences, and there is always a stir of surprise and recognition, because people had heard the different types of arguments, but had never juxtaposed them to notice the full repetitive pattern of the discourse. It is striking to realize that, regardless of what choices are made, the Court can be criticized with completely plausible concerns. Indeed, many criticisms are not merely 'plausible' but 'correct', in terms of their own limited desiderata. Thus, the Court is forever getting everything 'wrong', according to some plausible standard. Carsten Stahn has aptly described the pattern as 'damned if you do, damned if you don't', and he has pointed out several additional dyads of contradictory demands.[14]

Many dyadic tensions reflect the fault-lines masterfully explored by Martti Koskenniemi in his illuminating dissection of international legal arguments.[15] Koskenniemi demonstrated that any possible legal argument is vulnerable to either an 'apology' or 'utopia' critique (or both). The 'apology' critique is that one is too *close* to the policies and interests of states, and thus one is merely reflecting the edicts of powerful actors, which is normatively uninspiring. The 'utopia' critique is that one is too *divorced* from the policies and interests of states, and thus one is lacking the legal or political legitimation that comes

---

13 D Robinson, 'Inescapable Dyads: Why the International Criminal Court Cannot Win' (2015) 28 *Leiden Journal of International Law* 323.

14 C Stahn, 'Damned If You Do, Damned If You Don't: Challenges and Critiques of Preliminary Examinations at the ICC' (2017) 15 *Journal of International Criminal Justice* 413.

15 M Koskenniemi, *From Apology to Utopia: The Structure of International Legal Argument* (Cambridge: Cambridge University Press 2006).

from grounding in social authority; one is *imposing* one's personal vision or ambitious interpretation, exceeding the consent of authority-granting bodies. The 'apology-utopia' dilemma permeates law itself, because law aims to be grounded in social authority and yet also normatively compelling.[16] However, these tensions are even more raw and exposed in the embryonic and uncertain project of introducing and solidifying criminal law on the international plane.[17]

One might fancy that the solution to such tensions is that the Court must simply find the 'just right' balance (the 'Goldilocks principle').[18] Indeed, a great many works recognize the underlying tensions, but they decry that the Court failed to reach the 'right' balance.[19] Crucially, however, there is no 'just right' balance: every possible position on the spectrum can be criticized for falling short of the values of at least one end of the dyad, and in most cases, from *both* ends. Hence, the search for the 'best' balance, or rather, the '*least bad*' balance, will require us to articulate underlying assumptions with more care than we currently typically do. It will clarify matters if I provide some examples of these dyads.

### 2.1 *Too High/Too Low*

An excellent example is the 'too high/too low' dyad. The ICC Prosecutor is continuously and simultaneously criticized for reaching too high *and* too low in case selection. The '*too low*' critique is that the Prosecutor is not going after 'big fish', that the Prosecutor is steering away from powerful actors because he or she is over-cautious about challenging power.[20] It is an

---

16 Ibid., 16–20, 58, and 65–7.

17 Robinson, 'Inescapable Dyads' (n 13) 326. International law employs a fairly horizontal and cooperative model, whereas criminal law employs a fairly vertical and coercive model. Of course, the ICC is empowered to issue orders to states, but in the current system, instant obedience cannot be assumed—even within national systems with the rule of law, it took centuries for the highest courts to build up a habit of obedience from other branches. People today may take compliance with national court orders as some kind of 'given', but historically that habit had to be built up. US President Andrew Jackson is reported to have responded to US Supreme Court decision with 'let them enforce it'. See e.g. C Bassiouni, 'The Future of International Criminal Justice' (1999) 11 *Pace International Law Review* 309.

18 Robinson, 'Inescapable Dyads' (n 13) 325.

19 See discussion in Robinson, 'Inescapable Dyads' (n 13) 326, 341, 343–45. Such arguments are not 'one-dimensional' in the manner I described in the introduction above, since they consider the opposing desiderata. But intuitions about the 'right' balance generally go unarticulated.

20 W Schabas, 'The Banality of International Justice' (2013) 11 *Journal of International Criminal Justice* 545; R Murphy, 'Gravity Issues and the International Criminal Court'

'apology' critique. The *'too high'* critique is that the ICC Prosecutor is *over*-focused on big fish, and thus is indulging in grandstanding and pointless gestures rather than manageable cases, and jeopardizing peace and other interests for no tangible benefit.[21] It is a 'utopia' critique. Both types of arguments have continued and evolved over the decades.[22] Most recently, in March 2023, the ICC issued an arrest warrant for President Vladimir Putin of Russia for alleged unlawful deportation of children,[23] a rather ambitious move,[24]

---

(2006) 17 *Criminal Law Forum* 281; A Branch, 'Uganda's Civil War and the Politics of ICC Intervention' (2007) 21 *Ethics and International Affairs* 179; M Drexler, 'Whither Justice? Uganda and Five Years of the International Criminal Court' (2010) 5 *Interdisciplinary Journal of Human Rights Law* 97; Schabas, *supra* note 21 at 32–33; Human Rights Watch, *Unfinished Business: Closing Gaps in the Selection of ICC Cases* (2011) 16.

21 D Davenport, 'Happy Birthday, International Criminal Court', *Forbes* (1 July 2012) ('The new prosecutor should spend less time on highly visible and politicized cases and bring some cases of war crimes and crimes against humanity she can actually try and win'); D Kaye, 'Who's Afraid of the International Court?' (2011) 90 *Foreign Affairs* 118, 126 ('having chosen to pursue the big fish and failed to catch many, now [the Prosecutor] does not have much to show for his efforts'.); D Saunders, 'Ocampo's Crusades Tainted the Idea of International Justice', *Globe & Mail* (10 September 2012) ('Mr. Ocampo's desire to be seen threatening leaders with trials runs the risk of keeping those leaders in power longer'); J Flint and A de Waal, 'To Put Justice Before Peace Spells Disaster for Sudan', *The Guardian* (6 March 2009); O McDoom, 'Justice Clashes with Peace on Darfur Bashir Warrant', *Reuters* (14 July 2008); T Murithi, 'The African Union and the International Criminal Court: An Embattled Relationship?', *Institute For Justice and Reconciliation Policy Brief* (8 March 2013), 3–4; A Mackie, 'Perceptions, Politics, and Peace: The Limits of Globalization in Legitimizing the International Criminal Court', (2012) 30 *Macalester International* 132, 135.

22 See, relatively recently, W Ferdinandusse and A Whiting, 'Prosecute Little Fish at the ICC' (2021) 19(4) *Journal of International Criminal Justice* 759. Significantly, that article engages with the strengths and weaknesses of the different approaches and thus would match what I would call a 'holistic' and 'multi-dimensional' approach, as opposed to assuming a limited set of desiderata and criticizing the departure from those desiderata.

23 'Situation in Ukraine: ICC judges issue arrest warrants against Vladimir Vladimirovich Putin and Maria Alekseyevna Lvova-Belova', ICC Press Release (17 March 2023) <www.icc-cpi.int/news/situation-ukraine-icc-judges-issue-arrest-warrants-against-vladimir-vladimirovich-putin-and> accessed 23 March 2023.

24 S Pomper, 'How will the ICC's Arrest Warrant for Putin Play out in Practice' (*Just Security*, 20 March 2023) <https://www.justsecurity.org/85597/how-will-icc-arrest-warrant-for-putin-play-out/> accessed 23 March 2023; A Orakhelashvili, 'Putin in the dockyard? Or whatever international lawyers ought to (have) reflect(ed) on' (*Birmingham Blogs*, 20 March 2023) <https://blog.bham.ac.uk/lawresearch/2023/03/putin-in-the-dockyard-or-whatever-international-lawyers-ought-to-have-reflected-on/> accessed 23 March 2023. Both posts, perfectly reasonably, discuss possible negative effects, such as causing the leader to dig in, complicating peace efforts, undermining the Court's stature if it fails.

understandably triggering the latest re-iterations of 'too high' and 'too low'[25] arguments.

The 'too high/too low' dyad also applies on a larger scale, in situation selection. The ICC is vigorously criticized for unfairly pursuing cases that implicate weak countries *and* for unfairly pursuing cases that implicate powerful countries. In other words, the ICC is simultaneously criticized as (a) a neo-colonial tool of great powers to target and harass the weak[26] and (b) as a tool of lawfare of NGOs and small states to target and harass and powerful.[27] The ICC has suffered severe fallout from the opposite criticisms from the African Union and the United States.[28] My aim here is not to unpack the merits of the arguments (the African concern is at least supported by the fact that, at one

---

25 See eg. C A Odinkalu and S Nakandha, 'Putin Arrest Warrant: International Law and Perceptions of Double Standards' (*Opinio Juris*, 27 March 2023) <http://opiniojuris.org/2023/03/27/putin-arrest-warrant-international-law-and-perceptions-of-double-standards/> accessed 27 March 2023, arguing, plausibly, that even this step is still not challenging enough to international interests.

26 K M Clarke, *Affective Justice, The International Criminal Court and the Pan-Africanist Pushback* (Duke University Press 2019); M Mamdani, *Saviors and Survivors: Darfur, Politics, and the War on Terror* (Pantheon, 2019); I Eberechi, 'Rounding Up the Usual Suspects: Exclusion, Selectivity, and Impunity in the Enforcement of International Criminal Justice and the African Union's Emerging Resistance' (2011) 4 *African Journal of Legal Studies* 51; and see discussion in L Schneider, 'The International Criminal Court (ICC)—A Postcolonial Tool for Western States to Control Africa?' (2020) 1(1) *Journal of International Criminal Law* 90.

27 R Rose, 'The ICC Ruling on Israel: Ongoing Lawfare with Real-World Consequences' (*B'nai B'rith International*, 15 March 2021) <https://www.bnaibrith.org/the-icc-ruling-on-israel-ongoing-lawfare-with-real-world-consequences-html/> accessed 23 March 2023; A Derri, 'The ICC's Prosecutor in the service of Palestinian Lawfare' (2021) 27 *Israel Affairs* 105; A Tiemessen, 'The International Criminal Court and the Lawfare of Judicial Intervention' (2016) 30 *International Relations* 409.

28 Some states withdrew or threatened to withdraw from the Statute, because of the Court's heavy focus on African continent, while the USA imposed *personal* punitive sanctions on Prosecutor Fatou Bensouda and staff member Phakiso Mochochoko because the OTP dared to examine alleged war crimes by US forces in Afghanistan, an ICC State Party. See M Ssenyonjo, 'State Withdrawals from the Rome Statute of the International Criminal Court: South Africa, Burundi, and The Gambia' in C Chernor Jalloh, I Bantekas (eds), *The International Criminal Court and Africa* (Oxford Univeristy Press, 2017) and S Lamony, 'ICC Sanctions Symposium: Implications of Trump Administration's Sanctions on International Criminal Court Officials' (*Opinio Juris*, 22 April 2021) <http://opiniojuris.org/2021/04/22/icc-sanctions-symposium-implications-of-trump-administrations-sanctions-on-international-criminal-court-officials/> accessed 23 March 2023. The fact that ICC officials endured sanctions is interesting. Many people make a despairing 'apology' critique that the ICC will never challenge power and should be abolished; they seem not to consider that the ICC has gone further in defence of principles than almost any state, so abolishing it would *worsen* the situation in term of their stated desiderata.

point, a staggering 10 out of 11 situations were in Africa—a severe imbalance that was eventually alleviated as 6 of the subsequent 7 situations are in other continents—whereas the US objection relies on a risible and self-serving claim that jurisdiction over nationals of non-parties is unwarranted, even when they commit atrocities on foreign territory).[29] My point for now is simply that, regardless of what choice is made, credible accusations can be marshalled. The Court is criticized for over-focusing on Africa (neocolonial), but if it doesn't move quickly to take an additional situation in Africa, then it is criticized for being neglectful of African lives.[30] If it takes a situation implicating a powerful country, then it is self-aggrandizingly and dangerously reaching 'too high'; if it does not, then it is cowardly in reaching 'too low'.[31]

Seeing this pattern helps one to realize the inexorable inevitability of accusations of 'politicization', regardless of what decision is made, and that it is impossible to rebut such accusations. The Palestine situation offers a vivid illustration. When the Palestine Authority submitted an Article 12(3) declaration, submitting itself to the Court's jurisdiction, this raised the question of whether Palestine was at that time a 'State', as required by the Statute. The Prosecutor's legal determination, following the practice of the UN Secretary General, the depositary for the Rome Statute, was to show institutional deference to the UN General Assembly; thus, Palestine did not qualify, since it was only an 'observer entity' within the UN.[32]

That legal determination was met with accusations of bias and politicization: 'the pandering to the Security Council is clear'; 'politics of compromise trump the rights of Palestinians'; 'demonstrated an explicit political bias in favour of the status quo and the desires of the European and North American

---

29 M Morris, 'High Crimes and Misconceptions: The ICC and Non Party States' (2000) 64 *Law and Contemporary Problems* 131; see in response, M Scharf, 'The ICC's Jurisdiction over the Nationals of Non-Party States: A Critique of the US Position' (2001) 64 *Law and Contemporary Problems* 98; F Mégret, 'Epilogue to an Endless Debate: The International Criminal Court's Third Party Jurisdiction and the Looming Revolution of International Law' (2001) 12 *European Journal of International Law* 241; D Akande, 'The Jurisdiction of the International Criminal Court over Nationals of Non-Parties: Legal Basis and Limits' (2003) 1 *Journal of International Criminal Justice* 618.

30 See, as one example among many, Odinkalu and Nakandha (n 25).

31 See e.g. the Israel/Palestine example in the following paragraphs.

32 ICC Office of the Prosecutor, 'Situation in Palestine', 3 April 2012, https://www.icc-cpi.int/sites/default/files/NR/rdonlyres/C6162BBF-FEB9-4FAF-AFA9-836106D2694A/284387/SituationinPalestine030412ENG.pdf> accessed 23 March 2023.

powers—and thus against the Palestinians';[33] 'this dangerous decision opens the ICC to accusations of political bias and is inconsistent with the independence of the ICC'.[34] These are 'apology' critiques. At the same time, the Prosecutor also received the opposite (utopia) accusations of politicization for even *considering* the matter: 'the vexatious brief should never have even got this far and ought to have been thrown out after the first glance';[35] 'precisely the kind of politicization and overreaching that was feared from an independent prosecutor'.[36]

When Palestine secured recognition in the General Assembly as an 'Observer State' and acceded to the Rome Statute, the Prosecutor and Pre-Trial Chamber—consistently with the previous legal determination and UN practice—accepted Palestine's ability to confer jurisdiction.[37] This finding was greeted with more accusations of bias and politicization, now with the completely opposite valence of the initial condemnations: 'undiluted anti-Semitism and the height of hypocrisy',[38] 'lawfare', 'politicized', 'speaks volumes about the political agenda and anti-Israel bias of the court',[39] 'politicized', 'the ICC's efficacy and credibility are suffering from lawfare',[40] 'quasi-messianic'.[41] These are classic 'utopia' criticisms. For any possible decision, disappointed observers can (and do) ascribe inappropriate 'political' motivations, such as craven cowardice or reckless grandstanding. There is nothing a Prosecutor can do to rebut such allegations, because such motives can be ascribed, without evidence, to any possible decision. Any effort to point to the legal criteria can

33 See e.g. M Kearney and J Reynolds, 'Palestine, and the Politics of International Criminal Justice' in W A Schabas et al. (eds), *The Ashgate Research Companion to International Criminal Law: Critical Perspectives* (Aldershot: Ashgate 2012) 407, 408 and 426.

34 Amnesty International, 'ICC Prosecutor statement: Fears over justice for Gaza victims' (4 April 2012) (link no longer available). And see J Dugard, 'Palestine and the International Criminal Court: Institutional Failure or Bias' (2013) 11 *Journal of International Criminal Justice* 563. The title offers two options: institutional failure or bias.

35 A Ostrovsky, 'Victory: ICC Rules that Palestine is Still Not a State', *Huffington Post* (4 March 2012).

36 D Davenport, 'Happy Birthday, International Criminal Court', *Forbes* (1 July 2012).

37 Decision on the 'Prosecution request pursuant to article 19(3) for a ruling on the Court's territorial jurisdiction in Palestine', *Situation in the State of Palestine*, ICC-01/18–143, PTC I, ICC, 5 February 2021.

38 Israeli Prime Minister Benjamin Netanyahu, quoted in Coalition for the ICC, 'ICC Prosecutor initiates an investigation of the Situation in Palestine' (9 March 2021) <www.coalitionfortheicc.org/news/20210309/icc-prosecutor-initiates-investigation-situation-palestine> accessed 23 March 2023.

39 Rose (n 27).

40 Tiemessen (n 27).

41 J Bracha, 'A False Messiah? The ICC in Israel/Palestine and the Limits of International Criminal Justice' (2021) 54 *Vanderbilt Journal of Transnational Law* 283, 283.

be (and routinely is) easily dismissed as 'unconvincing pretext'. The 'too high'/ 'too low' critiques are inescapable.

### 2.2 *Too Imperious/Too Deferential*

A second 'no-win scenario' is the following: In selecting situations or cases, should the Prosecutor consider possible repercussions or harmful consequences? For example, should the Prosecutor bear in mind possible impacts on a peace process, risks of resumed fighting and criminality, or risks of humanitarian aid workers getting expelled? Any conceivable answer will be vehemently and plausibly condemned. If you *don't* take into account the consequences, then you are too imperious: you are disruptive and disrespectful of other actors and interests.[42] This is a utopia critique: you are a grandstanding, arrogant spoiler, narrowly focused on your own mandate, and ignoring the 'political' consequences of your decisions and the disruptions to other legitimate aims of the international community. But if you *do* consider consequences, you are too deferential: for many, it is inappropriate for a Prosecutor to even think of such things.[43] For formalists, the principled maxim is *fiat justitia ruat caelum*—'let justice be done though the heavens may fall', or in other translations, 'though the world may perish'.

You might think (as do I) that the right answer is some kind of 'balance', in which external consequences may be given at least some limited consideration. (After all, causing the world to perish in the pursuit of one's mandate might be considered irresponsible.) Importantly, however, there is no 'just right' balance that will not raise perfectly legitimate concerns and objections. For penal formalists, *any* prosecutorial consideration other than criminal justice is inappropriate and 'political'; whereas for people who see the ICC as an organ of international society, any disregard of other legitimate aims of the

42 See e.g. J Moody, 'Does the ICC Obstruct Peace?' (*Foreign Policy*, 22 October 2021) <foreignpolicy.com/2021/10/22/icc-peace-reconciliation-laurent-gbagbo-ivory-coast/> accessed 23 March 2023 ('the court's blind pursuit of justice undermined reconciliation efforts'); L Vinjamuri, 'The ICC and Conflict Zones' (*Open Canada*, 7 May 2012) <opencanada.org/leslie-vinjamuri/> accessed 23 March 2023; Branch (n 20) 182–86; B Schiff, 'The ICC's Potential for Doing Bad When Pursuing Good' (2012) 26 *Ethics & International Affairs* 73; Kaye (n 21); Flint and de Waal (n 21); P Clark, 'Law, Politics and Pragmatism: The ICC and Case Selection the Democratic Republic of Congo and Uganda' in N Waddell and P Clark (eds), *Courting Conflict? Justice, Peace and the ICC in Africa* (Royal African Society 2008).

43 See e.g. Amnesty International, 'Open letter to the Chief Prosecutor of the International Criminal Court: Comments on the concept of the interests of justice' (17 June 2005) available <www.amnesty.org/en/documents/ior40/023/2005/en/> accessed 23 March 2023; Human Rights Watch, 'The Meaning of "The Interests of Justice" in Article 53 of the Rome Statute' (1 June 2005) <http://www.hrw.org/node/83018> accessed 23 March 2023.

international community is inappropriate and 'political'. Notice again how the *same terms* get invoked for *opposite meanings*: you are 'political' if you consider non-criminal law implications, and you are 'political' if you do not (arrogantly pursuing your mandate to the detriment of all else).[44]

### 2.3 *Too Cautious/Too Ambitious*

Should the *feasibility* of successful investigation and arrest be a consideration in selection? This is a perennial question. Every possible answer is problematic. One possible answer is, 'Yes, feasibility matters, because we don't want to be wasting time and resources, raising hopes of victims, putting witnesses at risk, and diverting efforts from feasible cases, to pursue cases that will never actually materialize'. It is also often argued that pursuing unsuccessful cases will undermine the Court and reveal it to be a paper tiger.

On the other hand, if feasibility matters, then one ends up giving a 'free pass' to the the powerful, because they are in a position to make your investigations non-feasible.[45] Many commentators rightly emphasized this latter point in reaction to a a Pre-Trial Chamber decision that would have declined authorization in the Afghanistan situation on the grounds of feasibility.[46]

Both of these diametrically-opposed criticisms are perfectly *correct.* That is the conundrum. To require feasibility rightly draws an 'apology' critique, on the grounds that one is privileging the powerful and departing from equal application of the law; whereas failing to consider feasibility rightly draws a 'utopia' critique, on the grounds that one is spending resources on gestures rather than

44 See examples in n 42.

45 ICC OTP, 'Policy Paper on Preliminary Examinations' (November 2013), para. 70: 'Weighing feasibility as a separate self-standing factor, moreover, could prejudice the consistent application of the Statute and might encourage obstructionism to dissuade ICC intervention'.

46 L Moreno Ocampo, 'Deconstructing the Int'l Criminal Court's Decision on Afghanistan' (*Just Security*, 24 April 2019) <https://www.justsecurity.org/63746/deconstructing-the-intl-criminal-courts-decision-on-afghanistan/> accessed 23 March 2023; K J Heller, 'One Word for the PTC on the Interests of Justice: Taliban', (*Opinio Juris*, 13 April 2019) <http://opiniojuris.org/2019/04/13/one-word-for-the-ptc-on-the-interests-of-justice-taliban/> accessed 23 March 2023; C DeVos, 'No ICC Investigation in Afghanistan: A Bad Decision with Big Implications' (*International Justice Monitor*, 15 Aril 2019) <https://www.ijmonitor.org/2019/04/no-icc-investigation-in-afghanistan-a-bad-decision-with-big-implications/> accessed 23 March 2023; D Jacobs, 'ICC Pre-Trial Chamber rejects OTP request to open an investigation in Afghanistan: some preliminary thoughts on an ultra vires decision' (*Spreading the Jam*, 12 April 2019) <https://dovjacobs.com/2019/04/12/icc-pre-trial-chamber-rejects-otp-request-to-open-an-investigation-in-afghanistan-some-preliminary-thoughts-on-an-ultra-vires-decision/> accessed 23 March 2023.

effective cases. One argument focuses on efficiency, fiscal responsibility, and achieving concrete results, the other focuses on fearless equal application of the law, demonstrating impartiality, and the expressive function of criminal law.

Again, the soundest policies might fall somewhere in the middle between the two extremes—perhaps feasibility is a mere 'factor' in case prioritization, among cases with similar profiles. Or perhaps the case load should include some mix of 'safe' and 'ambitious' cases. Of course, any 'in-between' solution raises, to a lesser degree, *both* sets of problems (to the extent feasibility matters, one may be privileging powerful and uncooperative actors, to the extent it does not, one is diverting resources from cases likely to produce arrests). In-between solutions are also more messy and unclear than the absolute answers at each extreme. In any case, a holistic analysis would at least acknowledge the contradictory considerations, indicate how feasibility will be weighted (and why), and acknowledge that the approach is imperfect and flawed, like all possible approaches.

### 2.4 *Too Broad/Too Narrow*

Some dyads are not based on the apology-utopia fault-line, but involve instead *practical* tensions between two legitimate desiderata. One example is that the scope of charges will be 'too broad' and 'too narrow'. 'Too broad' means that one is charging too many crimes or incidents, creating excessive complexity, delay, and risk. 'Too narrow' means that one has failed to properly reflect the suffering of victims. The ICTY was criticized for bringing 'too broad' charges; thus its Prosecutor was criticized for bringing an overly elaborate case against Slobodan Milosevic, who died before the entire case could be presented.[47] Accordingly, an independent expert group recommended that the ICC Prosecutor should bring narrow cases based on the strongest evidence.[48] The ICC Prosecutor brought a narrow case in *Lubanga*, and was widely criticized for that narrowness. Of course, there is a lot of space between the narrow *Lubanga* case and the broad *Milošević* case. But any cases of intermediate scope can be criticized *both* for not including particular victims or forms of victimization (expressive function, vindication of victim's rights), and also for being too large and thus

47 Human Rights Watch, 'Lessons from the Slobodan Milosevic Trial' (13 December 2006) <https://www.hrw.org/reports/2006/milosevic1206/5.htm> accessed 23 March 2023.

48 ICC OTP, 'Informal expert paper: Measures available to the International Criminal Court to reduce the length of proceedings' (2003) <https://asp.icc-cpi.int/sites/asp/files/asp_docs/library/organs/otp/length_of_proceedings.pdf> accessed 23 March 2023.

taking too long to present (efficiency, risks to witnesses, diverting resources from other cases).

Many of the recommendations of the 2020 Independent Expert Review (IER) panel[49] reflect the impossible dyadic conflicts of the demands on the Court. The report echoes criticisms of the *Lubanga* investigation for bringing 'charges which insufficiently represent the underlying crime pattern',[50] but then it also criticizes the attempt to 'represent as much as possible the true extent of the criminality which has occurred in a given situation', because of the 'challenges in proving complicated cases with representative charges of victimisation'.[51] Accordingly, the IER recommended narrow charges and more focused cases.[52]

At times, the Office of the Prosecutor has adopted this philosophy of focusing where the evidence is strongest, for example, in its preliminary examination in Venezuela, thus focusing on detention cases.[53] In doing so, the Office of the Prosecutor was condemned by the Organization of American States, for neglecting the broader crime pattern.[54]

The conundrum is that both sets of opposing criticisms are *correct*, even though they are jointly inescapable. Broad charges *do* lead to slow, ponderous cases involving large numbers of witnesses, taking resources that might go to other cases. Narrow charges *do* fail to reflect the patterns of criminality and victimization. If one seeks an intermediate position ('medium'-sized charges?), then the result will be criticized from both perspectives, because the case will still exclude some victims and crimes, and will still be complex. Viewed in isolation, each criticism is correct and convincing. It is only when one puts the criticisms side by side that one sees the intractable, inescapable

49 The IER was created by the Assembly of States Parties to make recommendations to enhance the performance and effectiveness of the ICC. See IER Panel, Independent Expert Review of the International Criminal Court and the Rome Statute System: Final Report—30 September 2020, ICC-ASP/19/16, 9 November 2020 (Nineteenth Session of the ASP) <https://www.legal-tools.org/doc/cv19d5/> accessed 23 March 2023 ('IER Report').

50 Ibid., para. 658.

51 Ibid., para. 673.

52 Ibid., para. 674.

53 ICC OTP, 'Report on Preliminary Examination Activities 2020' (14 December 2020) <www.icc-cpi.int/sites/default/files/itemsDocuments/2020-PE/2020-pe-report-eng.pdf> accessed 23 March 2023, paras 203–204.

54 OAS Secretary General L Almagro and J Genser, *Fostering Impunity: The Impact of the Failure of the Prosecutor of the International Criminal Court to Open an Investigation into the Possible Commission of Crimes Against Humanity in Venezuela* (Organization of American States, 2 December 2020) <www.oas.org/documents/eng/press/Crimes-Against-Humanity-in-Venezuela-II-ENG.pdf> accessed 23 March 2023, 41–43.

difficulty. Thus, we must have a more nuanced conversation about which 'mistake' to make, or which balance of the two mistakes.

### 2.5 *Too Slow/Too Fast*

A very strong and understandable current of criticism is that preliminary examinations often continue too long, and thus should have time limits.[55] There are many good reasons for this view: obviously, preliminary examinations should not be dilatory; persons sending communications have a right to a response that should not be unduly frustrated; and preliminary examinations extended for no reason lead to a loss of evidence. In circumstances where all necessary facts to reach a determination are available, some benchmarks are in order.

However, for a multi-dimensional analysis, we must reflect on the less-obvious ways that time limits may be detrimental to other important desiderata. First, if a situation is dynamic and hovering just under the gravity threshold, it seems undesirable to close the preliminary examination because of a deadline, only to have to immediately reopen it as more crimes occur.[56] This would lead to confusion in public messaging as the preliminary examination is opened, closed, and reopened (a 'revolving door' problem), and it would also lead to a loss of any salutary effects from monitoring (eg. pressure on the government to genuinely investigate). A second consideration is 'queueing'. The ICC has a significant budget, but it is still not remotely sufficient for the demand on the Court, and thus situations often warrant investigation but no investigation team is yet available. Early opening of an 'investigation' with no resources merely converts the problem of a 'slow' preliminary examination into a different problem of a slow investigation. Given the higher profile of investigations, the latter problem is arguably worse.

A third scenario where time limits may be undesirable is where national proceedings are underway. The Prosecutor has a statutory duty to monitor proceedings until he or she is able to conclude that there is or is not a reasonable basis to find them non-genuine.[57] Under the Statute, that duty is ongoing: the

---

55 See discussed in IER Report (n 49) paras 714–717, including statements by Pre-Trial Chambers that examinations must be conducted in a reasonable time; A Murdoch, 'UK statement to ICC Assembly of States Parties 17th session' (5 December 2018) <https://www.gov.uk/government/speeches/uk-statement-to-icc-assembly-of-states-parties-17th-session> accessed 23 March 2023; A Pues, 'Towards the "Golden Hour": A Critical Exploration of the Length of Preliminary Examinations' (2017) 15 *Journal of International Criminal Justice* 440.

56 D Bosco, 'Putting the Prosecutor on a Clock? Responding to Variance in the Length of Preliminary Examinations' (2018) 112 *American Journal of International Law Unbound* 158.

57 ICC Statute, Article 17.

Prosecutor is obliged to consider new information and to reconsider decisions based on new information.[58] Even in the most stable and well-resourced countries, complex cases (investigation, trial, appeal) can take a decade; over that time, the intentions of state actors can shift and change. Thus, it may not make sense to impose a two-year time limit[59] to monitor a ten-year process. Being obliged to stop assessing after only two years seems incompatible with the duty to assess something that continues for years and that may change in character. Monitoring may help prompt state officials to run proceedings diligently; announcing that one is no longer looking removes that incentive.

These are merely quick illustrations of how even the seemingly simplest and most obvious prescription can have unforeseen detriments (in this case, potentially undermining the duty to assess proceedings, removing an incentive for genuine national proceedings, and generating new public confusion with 'revolving door' preliminary examinations and 'unfunded investigations'). A multi-dimensional, holistic assessment has to consider all the conflicting desiderata and weigh them globally to find the soundest reforms.

Here is another dilemma. If a state is rebuilding and developing its own justice response to mass atrocities, but needs time, should you give them a chance? If you do not give them a chance (as the IER proposed),[60] then you will be plausibly condemned for trampling over states and the spirit of complementarity. If you do give them a chance, then you will be plausibly condemned because your preliminary examinations are taking too long. The preliminary examination of Colombia continued for a very long 17 years, as Colombia went through the complex steps to establish a novel system for peace and justice. Thus, that preliminary examination was repeatedly cited as the most egregious illustration of a preliminary examination continuing too long.[61] The IER, responding to the criticisms of long preliminary examinations, made recommendations intended to shorten them.[62] If the only issue were short examinations, then one might imagine that when Prosecutor Karim Kham closed the Colombia preliminary examination, the decision would greeted with rejoicing.

58 ICC Statute, Article 15(2), 15(6), 53(4).

59 The IER report (n 49) rejects firm time limits, inter alia because they could be misused by governments (para. 717), but suggests a soft limit of two years (Recommendation 256).

60 Ibid., paras 723–24, 729–733, Recommendation 262.

61 See e.g. Pues (n 55).

62 IER Report (n 49) paras 706–19, 727, Recommendation 262 and 264. Many of the IER recommendations come at the cost, however, of opening 'investigations' that are 'unfunded'. This solution to one problem arguably creates new and bigger problems, including public confusion over a new third category (investigations that are not really investigations), and does nothing to solve the initially-identified problems, such as evidence growing stale.

But instead, of course, the decision was widely condemned: it was decried as as 'premature', 'not yet ripe', and 'counterproductive',[63] and 'baffling'.[64] The lesson is: there are no 'simple' solutions. When we hear a plausible concern, we still have to look for the non-obvious contradictory connections to other desiderata. It is not sufficient to collect all the criticisms and simply recommend doing the opposite, because doing the opposite will *also* cause problems and draw plausible criticisms. Holistic recommendations need to carefully consider and weigh the conflicting desiderata, and recognize that every possible approach will be flawed on some legitimate metric.

## 3 Implications: a Call for Multi-dimensional Analyses

The foregoing offered only a very cursory survey of a few of the 'no-win' dilemmas. I have surveyed a few others elsewhere: for example, the ICC is too close to states (corrupted) or too far from states (ineffective); it intervenes too soon (disruptive) or too late (neglectful); and all three possible trigger mechanisms (state referrals, Security Council referrals, proprio motu initiation) have all been plausibly singled out as especially problematic.[65] Carsten Stahn has helpfully surveyed several additional dilemmas relevant to preliminary examination and selection:[66] these include 'breadth versus depth' (perhaps the ICC should take fewer situations, doing 'deeper' investigations in each and gaining economies of scale, but in doing so the Court will be condemned for neglecting victims in other situations); transparency versus confidentiality; judicial review versus prosecutorial discretion; and so on.[67]

I have pointed out these patterns in the hopes of facilitating a more thoughtful and fruitful conversation. Of course, we will all continue to advance our criticisms and arguments about how the Court should operate.[68] In my view,

63 J M Vivanco and E Evenson, 'Colombia: Letter to the Prosecutor of the International Criminal Court' (*Human Rights Watch*, 30 September 2021) <www.hrw.org/news/2021/10/14/colombia-letter-prosecutor-international-criminal-court> accessed 23 March 2023.

64 'Colombia: ICC Prosecutor's baffling choice to close preliminary examination must be reversed', International Federation for Human Rights Press Relese (27 April 2022) <https://www.fidh.org/en/region/americas/colombia/colombia-international-criminal-court-no-investigate-grave-crimes> accessed 23 March 2023.

65 Robinson (n 13).

66 Stahn (n 14).

67 Ibid.

68 Or, for those who completely oppose international criminal justice, *not* operate.

the foregoing observations support the following suggestions for a 'holistical' and 'multi-dimensional' analysis.

(1) We would proceed with awareness of these 'inescapable dyads'—these clusters of no-win scenarios, arising from the many contradictory values and goals invoked in international criminal justice, with the result that any possible ICC policy or decision in these areas can be credibly criticized as a failure in terms of one of those values.
(2) As a corollary, we would move beyond the popular mindset that identifying a 'problem' is a sufficient analysis (i.e. that a 'problem', in terms of one value or criterion, means that reform is needed).[69] The implicit assumption is that the ICC should stop having 'problems', but it will not and cannot stop. Given the many threads of contradicting demands, all possible positions are problematic. Thus, the only available choice is which sets of problems to accept.
(3) Where one identifies a problem (in terms of some desiderata), one would not leap quite so quickly to the two main explanations commonly ascribed in the discourse: politics or incompetence. One would also consider another explanation: the threads of irreconcilable requirements. One would recall that the all possible choices are problematic points on a spectrum. Even if one disagrees with the balance struck, one might humbly and open-mindedly consider—at least consider—that the approach could be one of the reasonable but contestable choices on how to balance the conflicting desiderata. With each Prosecutor that the ASP elects, we must surely be granting then at least some leeway to make their differing professional judgements, even if they are not identical to our own.

69 While I think that the Independent Expert Review panel did a wonderful job under difficult circumstance, I think that at times it fell into the trap of one-dimensional analyses. The IER listened to the many concerns and criticisms of the Court's operations, and as a result generated 384 Recommendations. Some of those recommendations are being set aside because they would seem to cause worse problems than those they sought to remedy. That is my message here: to simply collect concerns and reverse policies that raise problems is too simplistic, because for *any* approach there will be concerns. I suggest that, on a holistic, multi-dimensional analysis, one might make fewer, much more carefully reasoned recommendations, after careful all-things-considered assessments, including carefully inspecting the detriments of a proposed solution on a different set of desiderata.

(4) We would not immediately assume that 'smoke' implies 'fire'. Some accusations of politicization by partisans in a case may be performative—they are public advocacy efforts seeking to motivate the Court by attacking it where it is most vulnerable—its legitimacy.[70] Furthermore, we would carefully disentangle that some powerful terms—'politicized', 'credibility', 'legitimacy'—are routinely used for different and opposite meanings. (For example, arguments are often made that the Prosecutor is 'political' because he or she considers consequences, or does not, or because he or she challenges power, or does not). What sounds like a monolithic shared concern will often, on inspection, dissolve into multiple contradictory allegations and preferences. Careful, sincere scholars and commentators, rather than citing and believing the most sensational claim, will look more carefully at the evidence when advancing arguments for what should change.

(5) Most importantly, when forming views and advancing arguments for change, those who agree with the foregoing would attempt a multi-dimensional analysis, rather than seizing on a single consideration. This means searching for the contradicting desiderata. Some of the tensions may be normative—different observers and audiences have different preoccupations, and one can at least be humble and open-minded in considering and potentially accommodating other perspectives.[71] Other tensions are practical: for example, tensions between speed, quality, comprehensiveness, and economic restraint. At that point we can embark on the real conversation, the hard conversation: which options are the least bad in an all-things-considered assessment.

It is my hope that observers, academics, activists, state officials, OTP staff and judges might shift away from the alternating barrages of one-dimensional analyses. Currently, the debate is somewhat limited and circular, because of its implicit assumption that there is a 'problem-free' approach. A more mature debate sees that the menu only contains imperfect, criticizeable options in setting the procedures and criteria for the Court. We only get to decide which mixture of problems to have, and in what proportion. There are many different visions of the procedures, criteria and priorities, which are all plausibly

70 See e.g. the opposing strident criticisms in notes 30–38.

71 See e.g. above, Section 2.1.

compatible with the Rome Statute, and thus there are many interesting choices yet to be made in articulating the system. If we recognize that we are debating trade-offs between a range of plausible and irreconcilable values, I hope the conversation might be less strident, less accusatory, more humble, and more open-minded.

# PART 4

## *Revisiting Trials and Procedures*

CHAPTER 11

# Judicial Control of Investigations: Some Synopsis of Past and Present Approaches

*Mohamed M. El Zeidy*

## 1 Introduction*

This chapter addresses the concept of judicial control in the practice of the International Criminal Court (ICC). The topic requires an understanding of relationship between the role of the prosecuting authority and the judiciary. This is always a delicate relation. It requires maintaining a proper balance that preserves the independence of the Prosecutor without compromising the judicial scrutiny needed to ensure the fairness of the judicial process.

Historically, prosecutor's decisions were not subject to judicial review due to the existence of the constitutional doctrine of separation of powers. However, overtime some form of judicial control emerged in national systems. The nature and extent of judicial control over prosecutorial activities depends on the domestic model and the powers provided to the prosecuting authority within the institutional framework in a given country.[1]

When it comes to the ICC, the Prosecutor remains the *dominus litis* – the master of his situations/cases. Yet, the concept of judicial control under the Rome Statute is broadly reflected and thus, it should be understood within the context it operates. As such, it has no counterpart in domestic systems. The founding fathers of the Rome Statute envisaged the concept of judicial control and reflected it in different provisions, which regulate various stages of the judicial process. In doing so, the drafters relied heavily on the idea of checks and balances.

Some of the provisions or areas, which found their way in the Rome Statute remained surrounded with what is known as 'constructive ambiguity' – a term credited to Henry Kissinger, the Former US Secretary of State, who endorsed

* The views expressed in this chapter are those of the author and do not necessarily reflect the views of the International Criminal Court.

1 For a comprehensive overview, see C Stahn, 'Judicial Review of Prosecutorial Discretion: Five Years On', in C Stahn and G Sluiter (eds), *The Emerging Practice of the International Criminal Court* (Leiden. Boston: Martinus Nijhoff Publishers 2009) 247.

 | DOI:10.1163/9789004529939_012

this tactic when negotiating sensitive topics.[2] As Stahn and Van den Herik correctly noted "[s]ometimes provisions [within the Rome Statute] were kept deliberately 'ambiguous' in order to facilitate political compromise and leave interpretation open to judicial practice".[3]

One such sensitive topic, for example, concerned the powers provided to the Prosecutor, particularly when acting *proprio motu*, and how to counterbalance such supranational powers without compromising prosecutorial discretion and independence. I will develop on this important point later in this chapter. Still the concept of judicial control as mentioned earlier is found in other provisions of the Statute and the degree of judicial oversight varies depending on the stage of the judicial process.

This chapter does not intend to discuss judicial control and prosecutorial discretion from a comparative perspective.[4] Rather, the aim is to look at the development of judicial control over prosecutorial activities within the context of the Rome Statute through the lens of judicial practice, which is predominantly apparent at the pre-trial phase. The chapter provides a glimpse of how different pre-trial chambers approached and developed judicial control over the past two decades, and how the Appeals Chamber played an active role in either clarifying or narrowing the scope of chamber's judicial oversight or even carrying out this role itself. In doing so, this chapter will only provide examples of key decisions from different pre-trial chambers and the Appeals Chamber, which reveal chambers' different perspectives *vis-à-vis* the concept of judicial control. The chapter concludes that judicial control over Prosecutorial activities went through at least four main phases or approaches that may be described as "interventionist", "deferential", "revolutionary" and "balanced".

2 L Roberto, 'Legal Aspects of the Kosovo Crisis and its Outcome: An Overview', (2000) 53 *Revue Hellenique de Droit International* 501, 519 n.47(noting Henry Kissiger's saying "about ambiguity being the stuff of diplomacy"); D Birju, 'Populism and the International Law of Self-Determination: Charting the Emergence of Populist Legal Movements from South Africa to Palestine', (2015) 18 *Palestinian Yearbook of International Law* 92, 104 n.65.

3 C Stahn and L van der Herik, 'Fragmentation', Diversification and '3D' Legal Pluralism: International Criminal Law as the Jack-in-the-Box?, in L van den Herik and C Stahn (eds.), *The Diversification and Fragmentation of International Criminal Law*, (Leiden.Boston: Martinus Nijhoff Publishers 2012) 21–89, 72 [hereinafter 'Fragmentation', Diversification and '3D'] .

4 For a comparative account of prosecutorial discretion and judicial review, see, A Perrodet, The Public Prosecutor, in M D-Martyand J.R. Spencer (eds.), *European Criminal Procedures*, (Cambridge: Cambridge University Press 2002) 415–458, at 443–448.

## 2 Judicial Control: Pre-investigative and Investigative Activities

Judicial control within the Rome Statute is predominantly apparent at the pre-trial stage, where the Prosecutor is responsible for many different activities. In this context, there are different modalities of judicial control depending on the nature of the matter under consideration. Due to the limited scope of this chapter, I will only focus on the key provisions where judicial control is directly connected to the Prosecutor's pre-investigative and investigative activities.

Starting with preliminary examinations, there is a noteworthy example in the early days of the Court's operation, which triggered judicial control even at the stage of preliminary examination namely, prior to the opening of an investigation. In December 2004, the Government of the Central African Republic (CAR) referred its own situation to the Court. The Prosecutor spent almost two years conducting his preliminary examination in order to decide whether or not to initiate an investiogation. In September 2006, the Government of the CAR complained to the Pre-Trial Chamber about the lengthy duration of the preliminary examination and requested, *inter alia*, information on the "alleged failure to decide, within a reasonable time, whether or not to initiate an investigation pursuant to [Article 53(1) of the Statute and] rules 105(1) and 105(4) of the Rules of Procedure and Evidence".[5]

Although Article 53 of the Rome Statute (Statute)[6] and Rule 105(1) of the Rules of Procedure and Evidence (RPE)[7] that govern this stage do not explicitly speak of judicial control in relation to the duration for conducting preliminary examinations, the then judges of Pre-Trial Chamber III felt the urge to request detailed information from the Prosecutor – thus, exercising judicial control through a sort of judicial creativity[8] or activism[9] inherent to their

5 Decision Requesting Information on the Status of the Preliminary Examination of the Situation in the Central African Republic, *Situation in the Central African Republic*, ICC-01/05-6, PTCIII, ICC, 30 November 2006, p. 3.

6 Art. 53 of the Rome Statute of the International Criminal Court (signed 17 July 1998, entered into force 1 July 2002) 2187 UNTS 3 ('ICC Statute').

7 Rules 105(1) of the Rules of Procedure and Evidence, Official Records of the Assembly of States Parties to the Rome Statute of the International Criminal Court, First Session, New York, 3–10 September 2002 (ICC-ASP/1/3 and Corr.1), part II.A. Notably, the references to the amendments of some of the Rules are reflected in the footnotes affiliated with the relevant Rule.

8 On judicial creativity, see C Stahn and L van der Herik, 'Fragmentation', Diversification and '3D', n.3, 71–74.

9 For a critical discussion on judicial activism within the context of the practices of international criminal tribunals, see W. A Schabas, 'Prosecutorial Discretion v. Judicial Activism at the International Criminal Court', (2008) 6 *Journal of International Criminal Justice* 731, 755–758.

duties in order to ensure fairness and transparency of the judicial process from the outset.

The judges' approach followed in this precedent reminds us of an early famous English case from the 1940s *Seaford Court Estates Ltd. vs Asher*, where Lord Denning said the following regarding interpretation of acts and judicial creativity:

> Whenever a statute comes up for consideration it must be remembered that it is not within human powers to foresee the manifold sets of facts which may arise, and, even if it were, it is not possible to provide for them in terms free from all ambiguity. English Knowledge is not an instrument of mathematical precision ... It would certainly save the judges from the trouble if the acts [...] were drafted with divine precision and perfect clarity. In the absence of it, when a defect appears, a judge cannot simply fold hand and blame the draftsman. ... He must set to work on the constructive task of finding the intention[behind it], and he must do this not only from the language of the statute, but also from a consideration of the social conditions which gave rise to it, and of the mischief which it was passed to remedy, and then he must *supplement the written word so as to give "force and life" to the intention of the legislature* (emphasis added).[10]

This quote portrays what the judges of this chamber tried to do. They simply refrained from folding their hands and blaming the drafters of the Statute for leaving the text surrounded by some sort of "ambiguity". Instead, they thought of giving force to Article 53 of the Statute and the RPE related thereto by way of opting for judicial creativity or activism. They requested the Prosecutor "to provide the Chamber and the Government of the Central African Republic [...] with a report containing information on the current status of the preliminary examination of the CAR situation, including an estimate of when the preliminary examination of the CAR situation will be concluded and when a decision pursuant to article 53 (1) of the Statute will be taken".[11] Thus, judges acted in the absence of a clear language in the relevant provisions to that effect.

This was a unique example during the early practice of the Court, which was not very well received by the Office of the Prosecutor (OTP)[12] for obvious

10 *Seaford Court Estates Ltd v Asher* [1949] 2 KB 481.

11 Decision Requesting Information on the Status of the Preliminary Examination of the Situation in the Central African Republic, *Situation in the Central African Republic*, ICC-01/05-6, PTCIII, ICC, 30 November 2006, p. 5.

12 Prosecution's Report Pursuant to the Pre-Trial Chamber III's 30 November 2006 Decision Requesting Information on the Status of the Preliminary Examination of the Situation

reasons. Even though the Prosecutor complied with the Chambers request, it disagreed with the basis on which the Pre-Trial Chamber based its decision. In this context, the Prosecutor argued that:

> The Pre-Trial Chamber's supervisory role, under Article 53 (3), only applies to the review of a decision under Article 53 (1) and (2) by the Prosecutor not to proceed with an investigation or a prosecution. The OTP submits that to date no decision under Article 53 (1) has been made, and that accordingly there is no exercise of prosecutorial discretion susceptible to judicial review by the Chamber. [...] The OTP notes that under the terms of the Statute, the referring State only has a right to make a request to the Pre-Trial Chamber to review a prosecutorial decision not to proceed with an investigation or a prosecution. The OTP's duty, pursuant to Rule 105 (1), is confined to promptly informing in writing the referring State of a decision not to initiate an investigation under Article 53 (1). [...] the OTP stresses that to date no decision has been made under Article 53 (1), and that accordingly the duty enshrined in Rule 105, and referred to by this Chamber in its 30 November 2006 Decision, has not arisen.[13]

Despite the OTP's vigorous opposition, arguably the Pre-Trial Chamber's decision was a turning point in introducing the possibility of judicial control at the very early stages of the judicial process without compromising the Prosecutor's independence in taking his final decision whether or not there was a reasonable basis to proceed with an investigation. More importantly this decision contributed to shape the OTP's future policy towards preliminary examinations. It paved the way for the practice of issuing policy papers explaining the legal test governing preliminary examinations in view of the jurisprudence of the Court and annual reports covering all situations pending before the Court, thus, ensuring full transparency of the internal process.

Indeed, in the 2013 policy paper, for instance, the OTP stated: "[i]n order to promote transparency of the preliminary examination process, the Office will provide reasoned decisions either to proceed or not to proceed with investigations, and will issue regular reports on its activities".[14] This became the practice of the OTP for many years until present.

---

in the Central African Republic, *Situation in the Central African Republic*, ICC-01/05-7, PTCIII, ICC, 15 December 2006.

13 ibid., paras 1, 11.

14 See,*inter alia*, ICC OTP, 'Report on Preliminary Examination Activities (2013)' (25 November 2013), para. 13. See also more recent reports echoing the same approach,

If we look at the practice of the Court after almost 16 years from this initiative, we will observe that judicial control over preliminary examinations is very limited. When Pre-Trial Chambers subsequently faced a request for judicial control, the preference was in favor of a much more reserved approach.

For instance, in the recent situation of the Bolivarian Republic of Venezuela I, the Government argued that "in the course of the Preliminary Examination, legal controversies and questions have arisen with the Prosecution which require a ruling by the Chamber".[15] It complained that the "Prosecution[sic] has not responded to any of its initiatives, reports and requests for information or guidance contrary to the principle of complementarity" and thus, it questioned, *inter alia*, "whether the Prosecution has sufficiently engaged in a 'constructive dialogue' with Venezuela at the Preliminary Examination phase, pursuant to the principle of complementarity".[16] Accordingly, the Government requested the Pre-Trial Chamber to exercise judicial control, and the Chamber, in turn not without good reasons, rejected this request *in limine*.[17]

This request was substantially different than the one concerning the CAR, as it was not confined to a mere request of information rather it required engagement with substantial questions premised on misleading legal basis. In this respect, the Chamber noted that: "[n]othing in these legal instruments [referred to by the Government] provides the Chamber the power to exercise Judicial Control over the Prosecution's preliminary examination in the manner sought by Venezuela".[18] Here, the last phrase "in the manner sought by Venezuela" begs the question whether the Chamber would have reacted differently if the request was formulated in a different "manner" or the question of judicial control during preliminary examinations was ruled out altogether as a matter of principle.

Without delving into further details, suffice to mention that the Chamber's overall line of reasoning suggests that it was not willing to read the unwritten text in favor of judicial control during preliminary examinations, and thus, it

---

'Report on Preliminary Examination Activities 2020' (14 December 2020), para. 14; 'Report on Preliminary Examination Activities (2019)' (5 December 2019), para. 14.

15 Public Redacted Version of 'Decision on the "Request for judicial control submitted to the Pre-Trial Chamber I of the International Criminal Court by the Bolivarian Republic of Venezuela pursuant to Articles 15 and 21.3 of the Statute and Rule 46.2 of the rules of the regulations of the Court"', *Situation in the Bolivarian Republic of Venezuela I*, ICC-02/18-9-Red, PTCI, ICC, 2 March 2022, paras 4,6. The original version was issued on 14 June 2021.

16 ibid., para. 4 (a).

17 ibid., para. 6.

18 ibid., para. 11.

preferred to take a more pragmatic approach at this early stage. In fact, this was not an unreasonable approach.

As the Prosecutor reaches the end of his preliminary examinations, an important stage of judicial control comes into play when the Prosecutor decides the existence of reasonable basis to proceed with an investigation of genocide, crimes against humanity and war crimes allegedly committed within the context of a specific situation. Here the Prosecutor acts *proprio motu* or *ex officio* due to the lack of a referral from either a State Party or the Security Council, and his activity requires judicial authorization. The *ratio* is quite clear. It is to counterbalance such power in order to prevent the Court's politicization.[19]

As mentioned earlier, this is one of the sensitive areas, where the drafters of the Statute and the RPE designed a detailed regime for its application.[20]

Judicial control at this stage serves as a safety net and has a direct impact on the scope of an investigation and the nature of cases that follows. The Court's jurisprudence over the last decade also reveals varying degree of judicial scrutiny starting from the first ever authorization decision issued in the context of the situation of Kenya by Pre-Trial Chamber II on 31 March 2010,[21] passing through the situations of Côte d'Ivoire;[22]

---

19 See, *inter alia*, Decision Pursuant to Article 15 of the Rome Statute on the Authorization of an Investigation into the Situation in the Republic of Kenya, *Situation in the Republic of Kenya*, ICC-01/09-19-Corr, PTCII, ICC, 31 March 2010, para. 18.

20 See, Arts 15 and 53(1) ICC Statute and Rules 48, 50 104 and 105 RPE and Regulation 49 of the regulations of the Court, Adopted by the judges of the Court on 26 May 2004 and as amended, Official documents of the International Criminal Court (ICC-BD/01-05-16). The most recent amendment entered into force on 24 November 2022.

21 Decision Pursuant to Article 15 of the Rome Statute on the Authorization of an Investigation into the Situation in the Republic of Kenya, *Situation in the Republic of Kenya*, ICC-01/09-19-Corr, PTCII, ICC, 31 March 2010. See also, Dissenting Opinion of Judge Hans-Peter Kaul, *Situation in the Republic of Kenya*, ICC-01/09-19-Corr, PTCII, ICC, 31 March 2010. Judge Kaul took a restrictive approach to the interpretation of the contextual elements for crimes against humanity, which shows the varying degree of judicial oversight within one and the same Chamber *vis-à-vis* the interpretation presented by the Office of the Prosecutor.

22 Corrigendum to "Decision Pursuant to Article 15 of the Rome Statute on the Authorisation of an Investigation into the Situation in the Republic of Côte d'Ivoire", *Situation in the Republic of Côte d'Ivoire*, ICC-02/11-14-Corr, PTCIII, ICC, 3 October 2011. See also, Corrigendum to "Judge Fernandez de Gurmendi's separate and partially dissenting opinion to the Decision Pursuant to Article 15 of the Rome Statute on the Authorisation of an Investigation into the Situation in the Republic of Côte d'Ivoire", *Situation in the Republic of Côte d'Ivoire*, ICC-02/11-15-Corr, PTCIII, ICC, 5 October 2011, paras 4–6. The dissenting opinion was notified on 6 October 2011. In this context, Judge Fernandez while agreeing with the majority to authorize the opening of an investigation into the situation, she

Georgia;[23] Burundi;[24] Afghanistan;[25] Myanmar;[26]and more recently Philippines.[27]

Starting with the impact of judicial control over the scope of investigations, the decisions authorizing the commencement of investigations into the situations of Burundi and Myanmar are good examples to prove such impact.

In *Burundi*, the Prosecutor requested the commencement of an investigation into the situation from 26 April 2015 until 26 October 2017, the effective date for Burundi's withdrawal from the Statute. Yet, upon review of the material submitted, the Chamber "underscored that some crimes, [...], were committed before 26 April 2015", and consequently, the Prosecutor was authorized to "extend her investigation over those crimes if the legal requirements of the contextual elements [were] fulfilled".[28]

The Chamber even went a step further by authorizing the Prosecutor to go beyond the end date specified, for those crimes that are of a continues nature.[29] The same hold true with respect to the material scope of the investigation, where the Prosecutor was "not restricted to the incidents and crimes

---

disagreed with the overall approach followed by the Majority in relation to the scope of the Chamber's supervisory function envisaged under Article 15 of the Rome Statute. This example also reveals the different degree of judicial scrutiny which results from the judges different understanding of the actual role of a pre-trial chamber.

23 Decision on the Prosecutor's request for authorization of an investigation, *Situation in Georgia*, ICC-01/15-12, PTCI, ICC, 27 January 2016.

24 Public Redacted Version of "Decision Pursuant to Article 15 of the Rome Statute on the Authorization of an Investigation into the Situation in the Republic of Burundi", ICC-01/17-X-9-US-Exp, 25 October 2017, *Situation in Burundi*, ICC-01/17-9-Red, PTCIII, ICC, 9 November 2017.

25 Decision Pursuant to Article 15 of the Rome Statute on the Authorisation of an Investigation into the Situation in the Islamic Republic of Afghanistan, *Situation in the Islamic Republic of Afghanistan*, ICC-02/17-33, PTCII, ICC, 12 April 2019. See also, Concurring and Separate Opinion of Judge Antoine Mindua, *Situation in the Islamic Republic of Afghanistan*, ICC-02/17-33-Anx-Corr, PTCII, ICC, 7 June 2019.

26 Decision Pursuant to Article 15 of the Rome Statute on the Authorisation of an Investigation into the Situation in the People's Republic of Bangladesh/Republic of the Union of Myanmar, *Situation in the People's Republic of Bangladesh/Republic of the Union of Myanmar*, ICC-01/19-27, PTCIII, ICC, 14 November 2019.

27 Decision on the Prosecutor's request for authorisation of an investigation pursuant to Article 15(3) of the Statute, *Situation in the Republic of the Philippines*, ICC-01/21-12, PTCI, ICC, 15 September 2021.

28 Public Redacted Version of "Decision Pursuant to Article 15 of the Rome Statute on the Authorization of an Investigation into the Situation in the Republic of Burundi", ICC-01/17-X-9-US-Exp, 25 October 2017, *Situation in Burundi*, ICC-01/17-9-Red, PTCIII, ICC, 9 November 2017, paras 191–192.

29 ibid., para. 192.

set out in the [...] decision but may, on the basis of the evidence, extend her investigation to other crimes against humanity or other article 5 crimes, i.e. war crimes and genocide, as long as they remain within the parameters of the authorized investigation".[30]

In *Myanmar*, Pre-Trial Chamber III followed a similar approach, where on the basis of the material available, it extended the scope of the investigation beyond the date requested by the Prosecutor, namely 9 October 2016, and instead it authorized investigation into crimes allegedly committed on or after 1 June 2010, the date of entry into force of the Statute for Bangladesh.[31] These are few recent examples that show the significance and impact of judicial control over the Prosecutor's investigations at the early stages of the proceedings.

With respect to the varying degree of judicial scrutiny, if we consider, for instance, the decisions authorizing the Prosecutor's investigation into the situation of Kenya, Côte d'Ivoire and Burundi on the one hand and Georgia on the other hand, it is apparent that there was a clear split in the approach of the Pre-Trial Chambers with respect to the level of detail in assessing the Prosecutor's information and material presented in these situations. This predominantly resulted from the judges different understanding of the role of a pre-trial chamber at this stage of the proceedings. These differences have been captured and explained in some detail in Judge Péter Kovács's separate opinion appended to the decision authorizing the Prosecutor to investigate into the situation in Georgia.[32]

Judge Kovács highlighted three areas of disagreement namely, the "scope and *ratio* underlying the Article 15 procedure and the envisaged role of the Pre-Trial Chamber";[33] the scope of assessment of jurisdiction [...] *ratione materiae*[34] as well as the scope of assessment of admissibility within the context of the situation.[35] Actually these are predominantly the main pillars for any authorization decision.[36]

---

30 Ibid., para. 193.

31 Decision Pursuant to Article 15 of the Rome Statute on the Authorisation of an Investigation into the Situation in the People's Republic of Bangladesh/Republic of the Union of Myanmar, *Situation in the People's Republic of Bangladesh/Republic of the Union of Myanmar*, ICC-01/19-27, PTCIII, ICC, 14 November 2019, para. 131.

32 Separate Opinion of Judge Péter Kovács, Decision on the Prosecutor's request for authorization of an investigation, *Situation in Georgia*, ICC-01/15-12, PTCI, ICC, 27 January 2016.

33 Ibid., para. 2.

34 Ibid.

35 Ibid.

36 As will be discussed later in the text, the Appeals Chamber in its recent judgment concerning the situation in Afghanistan considered that an admissibility assessment is not

Without delving into the details of each area, suffice to mention by way of example, that the disagreement mainly revolved around the nature of Article 15 procedure and the role a pre-trial chamber should play. The crux of the problem, as mentioned earlier, lies in the judges different understanding of the scope of "judicial control" at the pre-trial stage and how this should be carried out in practice. For the Majority, it is clear that Article 15 procedure "serves no other purpose than to prevent the abuse of power on the part of the Prosecutor".[37] The Majority believed that in carrying out such judicial oversight at this stage, "the Chamber's examination of the [Prosecutor's] Request and the supporting material [...] must be strictly limited".[38]

This approach contrasts the understanding of the minority judge who believed that it is irreconcilable with the idea of "judicial control", regardless of the stage of the proceedings.[39] According to the minority opinion, an understanding of "judicial control" and the effective application of Article 15(3) and (4) of the Statute read together with Rule 50(4) of the RPE, require "'an independent judicial inquiry' of the material presented as well as the findings of the Prosecutor that there is a reasonable basis to proceed with the opening of an investigation".[40] This also entails "a full and proper examination of the supporting material relied upon by the Prosecutor for the purpose of satisfying the elements of article 15(4) in conjunction with article 53(1)(a)-(c) of the Statute".[41] This principal split of opinions continued in a different situation/case and at a later stage of the proceedings namely, the confirmation of charges phase (Art. 61(7) of the Statute). In *Al Mahdi*, a similar disagreement arose between the judges of the Pre-Trial Chamber. However, this time the disagreement not only revolved around the role of a pre-trial chamber in exercising its judicial oversight, but also, *inter alia*, the lack of judicial reasoning to provide "a proper account of the events and evidence presented".[42] As such the Chamber showed a clear deference *vis-à-vis* the Prosecutor.

---

required for the purpose of authorizing the opening of an investigation pursuant to Article 15 of the Rome Statute. See, below n. 44.

37 Decision on the Prosecutor's request for authorization of an investigation, *Situation in Georgia*, ICC-01/15-12, PTCI, ICC, 27 January 2016, para. 3.

38 ibid., para. 3.

39 Separate Opinion of Judge Péter Kovács, Decision on the Prosecutor's request for authorization of an investigation, *Situation in Georgia*, ICC-01/15-12, PTCI, ICC, 27 January 2016, paras 3–12.

40 ibid., para. 6.

41 ibid.

42 Decision on the confirmation of charges against Ahmad Al Faqi Al Mahdi, *Prosecutor v. Ahmad Al Faqi Al Mahdi, Situation in the Republic of Mali*, ICC-01/12-01/15-84-Red, PTCI, ICC, 24 March 2016; Separate Opinion of Judge Péter Kovács, Decision on the

Although some authors believe that individual opinions have been predominantly neglected,[43] some of these opinions actually broaden the scope of the legal debate on some complex issues, which have been disregarded by the majority due to the split of opinions. The separate opinion of Judge Kovács in Georgia is one example on point. It was a useful judicial exercise, which brought to light a clear diversion between the judges regarding the nature and scope of the pre-trial phase.

The role of pre-trial chambers in exercising judicial control over the Prosecutor's investigation has experienced some further limitation after the issuance of the Appeals Chamber recent judgment concerning the request for authorization of an investigation into the situation in Afghanistan.

In its judgment of 5 March 2020, the Appeals Chamber apart from amending the decision of Pre-Trial Chamber II, which rejected the Prosecutor's request for authorization to open an investigation on the basis of the criterion of interest of justice,[44] it questioned the Pre-Trial Chamber's scope of judicial control over the Prosecutor's findings related to the admissibility of potential cases under Article 53(1)(b) of the Statute.[45] It actually removed the direct link between Articles 15(4) and 53(1) of the Statute thereby excluding the admissibility assessment from the scope of Article 15(4) of the Statute.[46] By doing so, the Appeals Chamber's finding *obiter dictum*, moved away from the Pre-Trial Chambers' steady jurisprudence on the subject, which has been out there for almost a decade.

Indeed, if we assess the recent decision authorizing the Prosecutor to investigate into the situation in Philippines, it becomes clear that the Pre-Trial Chamber refrained from exercising a full judicial control. Being guided by the

---

confirmation of charges against Ahmad Al Faqi Al Mahdi, *Prosecutor v. Ahmad Al Faqi Al Mahdi, Situation in the Republic of Mali*, ICC-01/12-01/15-84-Anx, PTCI, ICC, 9 May 2016, paras 1–6.

43 K Wigard, 'Matter of Opinion: Assessing the Role of Individual Judicial Opinions at the International Criminal Court', (2023) *International criminal Law Review* 1–29; see generally on the impact of separate opinions, N Combs, 'The Impact of Separate Opinions on international Criminal Law', (2021) 62 *Virginia Journal of International Law* 1.

44 For a critical analysis of the Pre-Trial Chamber's assessment and in particular with respect to the criterion of the interest of justice, see L P Rossetti, 'The Pre-Trial Chamber's Afghanistan Decision', (2019) 17 *Journal of International Criminal Justice* 585, 591–599; M Varaki, 'Afghanistan and the "interests of justice": An Unwise Exercise?', EJIL: Talk! Blog of the European Journal of International Law, 26 April 2019, available online at Afghanistan and the 'interests of justice'; an unwise exercise? – EJIL: Talk! (ejiltalk.org).

45 Judgment on the appeal against the decision on the authorisation of an investigation into the situation in the Islamic Republic of Afghanistan, *Situation in the Islamic Republic of Afghanistan*, ICC-02/17-138, AC, ICC, 5 March 2020, paras.

46 Ibid., paras 1, 25–37, 40.

Appeals Chamber's approach endorsed in the judgment referred to earlier, the Pre-Trial Chamber considered that judicial control over the Prosecutor should be exercised bearing in mind its 'limited mandate' under Article 15(4) of the Statute.[47] The Chamber also referred to the same judgment when it explicitly stated "that a decision under Article 15(4) does not involve determinations on admissibility and interests of justice".[48] And indeed the Chamber refrained from conducting an admissibility assessment as it had previously done.

The modality of judicial control within the context of Article 15 of the Statute is different when the request for authorization concerns the crime of aggression. In this situation, the authorization of the Pre-Trial Chamber is not sufficient. Rather what is required is an authorization by all judges assigned to the Pre-Trial Division.[49] Hitherto, the Court has not exercised any judicial control over the Prosecutor's assessment in relation to the crime of aggression. However, suffice to mention that exercising judicial control within the context of the crime of aggression poses more challenges for the Court, as securing a unanimous decision is more difficult to achieve in view of the political climate underlying the nature of this crime.

While the foregoing judicial oversight concerns the Prosecutor's investigations when acting *proprio motu*, the Court's legal framework regulates a different modality for judicial control when the decision to investigate is triggered by a State Party or Security Council referral. In this context, judicial oversight does not aim at authorizing the Prosecutor to start an investigation, rather it takes place only if the Prosecutor decided not to proceed with opening an investigation or pursuing a prosecution.[50]

In this context, it is worth mentioning that Pre-Trial Chamber I conducted three rounds of judicial review of the Prosecutor's decisions not to open an investigation in the situation on the vessels registered in the Union of the Comoros, the Hellenic Republic and the Kingdom of Cambodia, between January 2015 until September 2020.[51] The Second Review Decision

---

47 Decision on the Prosecutor's request for authorisation of an investigation pursuant to Article 15(3) of the Statute, *Situation in the Republic of the Philippines*, ICC-01/21-12, PTCI, ICC, 15 September 2021, paras 10–11.

48 ibid., para. 15.

49 See, Arts 15*bis*(8) and Regulations 45(3) and 46(4) RoC. See also, E Chaitidou, Eckelmans and B Roche, 'The Judicial Function of the Pre-Trial Division', in C Kress and S Barriga (eds.), *The Crime of Aggression: A Commentary*, Vol. 1, (Cambridge: Cambridge University Press 2017) 752, 752–815.

50 Art. 53(3)(a) ICC Statute.

51 Decision on the request of the Union of the Comoros to review the Prosecutor's decision not to initiate an investigation, *Situation on the vessels registered in the Union of the Comoros, the Hellenic Republic and the Kingdom of Cambodia*, ICC-01/13-34, PTCI,

is particularly worth mentioning as it explicitly pointed out the Prosecutor's failure to comply with the Chamber's findings set out in the First Decision, and accordingly, remanded the matter for reconsideration by the Prosecutor. This decision was upheld by the Appeals Chamber.[52]

Certainly, the Appeals Chamber's overall finding could be interpreted as giving force to the practice of judicial control over Prosecutorial activities, at least when it comes to preserving the integrity and legal validity of judicial decisions issued by the different chambers. In its key findings to the judgment of 2 September 2019, the Appeals Chamber stated:

> Neither article 53(3)(a) of the Statute nor rule 108(3) of the Rules preclude a pre-trial chamber from reviewing whether a decision of the Prosecutor that she considers to be 'final' actually amounts to a proper 'final decision'. The pre-trial chamber's power to review is derived from its statutory power to request reconsideration.[...] If a pre-trial chamber acting pursuant to article 53(3)(a) of the Statute requests the Prosecutor to reconsider her decision not to investigate on the basis of its interpretation of the applicable law, the Prosecutor is bound to follow this interpretation. Furthermore, the Prosecutor is bound to adhere to any directions of the pre-trial chamber to consider certain available information. In addition, when assessing gravity, the Prosecutor is obliged to follow any directions of the pre-trial chamber to take into account certain factors or information relating thereto.[53]

ICC, 16 July 2015 ("Frist Review Decision"). See also, Partly Dissenting Opinion of Judge Péter Kovács, Corrigendum of Annex to the Decision on the request of the Union of the Comoros to review the Prosecutor's decision not to initiate an investigation, *Situation on the vessels registered in the Union of the Comoros, the Hellenic Republic and the Kingdom of Cambodia*, ICC-01/13-34-Anx-Corr, PTCI, ICC, 16 July 2015; Decision on the "Application for Judicial Review by the Government of the Union of the Comoros", *Situation on the vessels registered in the Union of the Comoros, the Hellenic Republic and the Kingdom of Cambodia*, ICC-01/13-68, PTCI, ICC, 15 November 2018 ("Second Review Decision"). See also, Partly Dissenting Opinion of Judge Péter Kovács, Decision on the "Application for Judicial Review by the Government of the Union of the Comoros", ICC-01/13-68-Anx, PTCI, ICC, 15 November 2018; Decision on the 'Application for Judicial Review by the Government of the Comoros', *Situation on the vessels registered in the Union of the Comoros, the Hellenic Republic and the Kingdom of Cambodia*, ICC-01/13-111, PTCI, ICC, 16 September 2020 ("Third Review Decision").

52 Judgment on the appeal of the Prosecutor against Pre-Trial Chamber I's 'Decision on the "Application for Judicial Review by the Government of the Union of the Comoros"', *Situation on the vessels registered in the Union of the Comoros, the Hellenic Republic and the Kingdom of Cambodia*, ICC-01/13-98, AC, ICC, 2 September 2019.

53 ibid., paras 1–2.

While this entire exercise shows the important role to be played by a pre-trial chamber with respect to Prosecutor's decisions not to proceed with investigations, it also signals the lengthy period of litigation it took with respect to one aspect within one given situation.

Other significant areas requiring judicial control come into play after the opening of an investigation up until the confirmation of charges. This includes the Prosecutor's requests to the Pre-Trial Chambers to issue warrants of arrest and summons to appear,[54] conducting unique investigative opportunities,[55] review of pre-trial detention,[56] disclosure of evidence,[57] confirmation of charges and the possibility of amending one or more charges before the start of the trial.[58]

Monitoring the disclosure process and the quality of evidence is one of the key features of judicial control at the pre-trial stage. Chambers have always reminded the Prosecutor that he is expected to be "trial ready at anytime after applying for an arrest warrant".[59] One chamber even went a step further when it expected that the Prosecutor file "a request for the issuance of a warrant of arrest only when [...] ready to do so [in order to be prepared] [...] to honour [the] statutory disclosure obligations in a timely fashion on the basis of realistic estimates".[60] It is actually not the quantity of evidence, but the true relevance of evidence that is essential to the confirmation of charges decision, such as forensic evidence, audio/visual evidence, and testimony based on personal experience of witnesses, this Chamber added.[61]

---

54 Art. 58 ICC Statute.

55 ibid., Art. 56.

56 ibid., Art. 60.

57 ibid., Art. 61(3) and Rule 121(3) RPE.

58 ibid., Art. 61(9).

59 Second Order on disclosure and related matters, *Prosecutor v. Ali Muhammad Ali-Abd-Al-Rahman ('Ali Kushayb'), Situation in Darfur, Sudan*, ICC-02/05-01/20-169, PTCII, ICC, 2 October 2020, para. 14.

60 Decision on the 'Prosecution's Request to Postpone the Confirmation Hearing and all Related Disclosure Deadlines', *Prosecutor v. Alfred Yekatom and Patrice-Edouard Ngaïssona, Situation in the Central African Republic II*, ICC-01/14-01/18-199, PTCII, ICC, 15 May 2019, para. 32.

61 Second Order on disclosure and related matters, *Prosecutor v. Ali Muhammad Ali-Abd-Al-Rahman ('Ali Kushayb'), Situation in Darfur, Sudan*, ICC-02/05-01/20-169, PTCII, ICC, 2 October 2020, para. 21; See also, Decision on the Confirmation of Charges Pursuant to Article 61(7)(a) and (b) of the Rome Statute, *Prosecutor v. Francis Kirimi Muthaura, Uhuru Muigai Kenyatta and Mohammed Hussein Ali, Situation in the Republic of Kenya*, ICC-01/09-02/11-382-Red, PTCII, ICC, 23 January 2012, para. 82.

Also, in *Ali Kushayb*, Pre-Trial Chamber II, exercising strict judicial oversight over the Prosecutor's investigations, indicated that the start of the confirmation hearing "cannot be made conditional upon the completion of additional investigations, nor can the date of the confirmation hearing depend on wholly uncertain political developments that may have an impact on ongoing or planned investigations".[62]

Another notable example of judicial control during the stage of the confirmation of charges takes place when the Chamber decides to adjourn the hearing and request the Prosecutor to provide further evidence or conduct further investigations or amend a charges as the evidence presented establishes a different crime. I recall an example concerning the first ever adjournment decision issued by the Court in the case against Mr Jean Pierre Bemba, where Pre-Trial Chamber III explained the necessity of exercising its judicial oversight in order to overcome, *inter alia*, "deficiencies concerning the legal characterisation of the facts presented, which prevented the Chamber from issuing a final decision on the merits at this stage".[63] The Chamber considered that the evidence presented "appears to establish a different crime within the jurisdiction of the Court in accordance with article 61(7)(c)(ii) of the Statute", and accordingly, requested the Prosecutor to submit an amended document containing the charges addressing a different mode of liability.[64]

In *Gbagbo*, the issue of judicial control by way of adjourning the confirmation hearing also arose. But this time, the Pre-Trial Chamber I encountered a different problem namely, the quality of evidence presented. Exercising its judicial oversight, the Chamber noted that the evidence "cannot in any way be presented as the fruits of a full and proper investigation by the Prosecutor".[65] Accordingly, it requested the Prosecutor to "consider providing further evidence or conducting further investigation with respect to all charges".[66] This decision was upheld on appeal.[67]

---

62 Second Order on disclosure and related matters, *Prosecutor v. Ali Muhammad Ali-Abd-Al-Rahman ('Ali Kushayb'), Situation in Darfur, Sudan*, ICC-02/05-01/20-169, PTCII, ICC, 2 October 2020, para.19.

63 Decision Adjourning the Hearing pursuant to Article 61(7)(c)(ii) of the Rome Statute, *Prosecutor v. Jean-Pierre Bemba Gombo, Situation in the Central African Republic*, ICC-01/05-01/08-388, PTCIII, ICC, 3 March 2009, p. 7.

64 ibid., pp. 3, 19.

65 Decision adjourning the hearing on the confirmation of charges pursuant to article 61(7)(c)(i) of the Rome Statute, *Prosecutor v. Laurent Gbagbo, Situation in the Republic of Côte d'Ivoire*, ICC-02/11-01/11-432, PTCI, ICC, 3 June 2013, para. 35.

66 ibid., p. 22.

67 Judgment on the appeal of the Prosecutor against the decision of Pre-Trial Chamber I of 3 June 2013 entitled "Decision adjourning the hearing on the confirmation of charges

As to post-confirmation of charges, the nature and modality of judicial control is more focused on ensuring the fairness of the trial proceedings including every aspect related to the admission, relevance and assessment of evidence gathered by the Prosecutor. The level of judicial scrutiny required is higher, especially with respect to the assessment of evidence presented by the Prosecutor.

A form of judicial control at this stage lies in the power of the Trial Chamber to request submission of evidence that it deems necessary for the determination of the truth under Article 69(3) of the Statute.[68] Another example worth mentioning is the duty imposed on Trial Chambers to render inadmissible evidence obtained by means of a violation of the Statute or internationally recognized human rights pursuant to Article 69(7) of the Statute.[69] Moreover, the power of the Trial Chamber to recharacterize the facts pursuant to Regulation 55 of the Regulations of the Court is another illustration of judicial control within the context of charging.[70]

As to the Appeals Chamber, given its limited competence, the modality of judicial control over the Prosecutor's investigations is often indirect through the decisions issued either by the Pre-Trial or Trial Chambers. However, practice reveals that the Appeals Chamber may play an equally if not more important role in monitoring not only some of the Prosecutor's activities but also the scope of chambers' judicial oversight.

One notable example is the early Appeals Chamber's judgment of 13 October 2006 concerning the establishment of general principles restricting disclosure in the *Lubanga* case. Here the Appeals Chamber rejected the Pre-Trial Chamber's decision limiting the Prosecutor's right to investigate other alleged crimes of the suspect, and accordingly, it allowed the Prosecutor "to

---

pursuant to article 61(7)(c)(i) of the Rome Statute", *Prosecutor v. Laurent Gbagbo, Situation in the Republic of Côte d'Ivoire*, ICC-02/11-01/11-572, AC, ICC, 16 December 2013.

68 Art. 69(3) ICC Statute. See on Art. 69(3), Piragoff/Clarke, Evidence, in K. Ambos (ed.), *Rome Statute of the International Criminal Court: Article-by-Article Commentary*, Fourth Edition(C.H.Beck:Hart.Nomos. 2022) 2037–2088, at 2064–2065.

69 Art. 69(7) ICC Statute; Piragoff/Clarke, in Ambos (ed.), n. 68, at2082–2087.

70 Decision on the implementation of regulation 55 of the Regulations of the Court and severing the charges against the accused persons, *Prosecutor v. Germain Katanga and Mathieu Ngudjolo Chui, Situation in the Democratic Republic of the Congo*, ICC-01/04-01/07-3319-tENG/FRA, TCII, ICC, 21 November 2012; see also Judgment on the appeal of Mr Germain Katanga against the decision of Trial Chamber II of 21 November 2012 entitled "Decision on the implementation of regulation 55 of the Regulations of the Court and severing the charges against the accused persons", *Prosecutor v. Germain Katanga and Mathieu Ngudjolo Chui, Situation in the Democratic Republic of the Congo*, ICC-01/04-01/07-3363, AC, ICC, 27 March 2013.

continue his investigation in respect of crimes that are not covered by the document containing the charges" and "beyond the confirmation hearing, if this is necessary in order to establish the truth".[71]

Another example, which reveals the interplay between the Prosecutorial discretion and the Chambers' authority to exercise judicial oversight was explicitly spelled out by the Appeals Chamber in the *Gbagbo* case. In its judgment of 16 December 2013 concerning Pre-Trial Chamber's I decision to adjourn the confirmation hearing, the Appeals Chamber considered:

> [T]hat it is for the Prosecutor to plead the facts relevant to establishing the legal elements and for the Pre-Trial Chamber to determine whether those facts, if proven to the requisite threshold, establish the legal elements of attack. The question of how many of the incidents pleaded by the Prosecutor would suffice to prove an "attack" in the present case is a matter for the Pre-Trial Chamber to determine.[72]

The Appeals Chamber's approach suggests that it attempted to draw the fine line between prosecutorial discretion and independence and the extent of the chambers' judicial oversight. The Appeals Chamber divided the responsibilities between the two different organs in light of the particular circumstances of the case.

Finally, in a more recent development concerning the situation in Afghanistan, the Appeals Chamber also played a key role of critical judicial oversight when it found that Pre-Trial Chamber II erred in "deciding that 'an investigation into the situation in Afghanistan at this stage would not serve the interests of justice'".[73]

In this respect, the Appeals Chamber not only found an error of law on the part of the Pre-Trial Chamber when it assessed the criterion of the interest of

---

71 Judgment on the Prosecutor's appeal against the decision of Pre-Trial Chamber I entitled "Decision Establishing General Principles Governing Applications to Restrict Disclosure pursuant to Rule 81 (2) and (4) of the Rules of Procedure and Evidence", *Prosecutor v. Thomas Lubanga Dyilo, Situation in The Democratic Republic of the Congo*, ICC-01/04-01/06-568, AC, ICC, 13 October 2006, paras 51–52.

72 Judgment on the appeal of the Prosecutor against the decision of Pre-Trial Chamber I of 3 June 2013 entitled "Decision adjourning the hearing on the confirmation of charges pursuant to article 61(7)(c)(i) of the Rome Statute", *Prosecutor v. Laurent Gbagbo, Situation in the Republic of Côte d'Ivoire*, ICC-02/11-01/11-572, AC, ICC, 16 December 2013, para. 47.

73 Judgment on the appeal against the decision on the authorisation of an investigation into the situation in the Islamic Republic of Afghanistan, *Situation in the Islamic Republic of Afghanistan*, ICC-02/17-138, AC, ICC, 5 March 2020, para. 46.

justice under Article 53(1)(c) of the Rome Statute, but also it went a step further with its judicial oversight. Instead of reversing the impugned decision and remanding it to the Pre-Trial Chamber for a new decision on the Prosecutor's request, it chose to play a more active role in its judicial oversight functions.

The Appeals Chamber decided to amend the impugned decision and more importantly pass a judicial ruling on the scope of the requested investigation. The Appeals Chamber noted that the "Pre-Trial Chamber decided not to authorize the investigation [...][and] also made statements relating to the scope of any potential investigation".[74] According to the Appeals Chamber, the Pre-Trial Chamber's approach was "based on legal error and an incorrect understanding of its role under article 15(4) of the Statute [and thus] require[s] clarification".[75] In this context, the Appeals Chamber identified two main issues of concern, one of which is core to this discussion, namely "whether the authorization is limited to incidents mentioned in the [Prosecutor's Request] and those closely linked thereto".[76]

In responding to this enquiry, the Appeals Chamber stated:

> [T]hat restricting the authorised investigation to the factual information obtained during the preliminary examination would erroneously inhibit the Prosecutor's truth-seeking function. Such a restriction is also unnecessary to fulfil the purpose of article 15(4) of the Statute in ensuring that the Prosecutor does not embark on a frivolous or politically motivated investigation in that she remains restricted in her investigation to the contours of the situation authorised by the pre-trial chamber. Therefore, the Appeals Chamber considers that authorisation for an investigation should not be restricted to the incidents specifically mentioned in the Prosecutor's Request and incidents that are 'closely linked' to those incidents in the manner described by the Pre-Trial Chamber[...]. The Appeals Chamber considers that the alternative proposed by the Pre-Trial Chamber – that investigation of incidents not closely related to those authorised would be possible if they were the subject of a new request for authorisation under article 15 – is unworkable in practice in the context of an investigation into large-scale crimes of the type proposed by the Prosecutor.[77]

74 ibid., para. 56.
75 ibid.
76 ibid.
77 ibid., paras 61, 63.

More importantly, the Appeals Chamber also seems to have set the parameters for the permissible degree of judicial control to be conducted by a pre-trial chamber when it considered:

> [T]hat such continuous monitoring of the scope of the Prosecutor's investigation by the pre-trial chamber is contrary to the statutory scheme regulating the respective functions and powers of these two organs with respect to investigations. In this regard, the Appeals Chamber notes that article 42(1) recognises the independence of the Prosecutor and her responsibility for the conduct of investigations, while articles 56 and 57 of the Statute identify specific functions that may be exercised by the pre-trial chamber during the investigation.[78]

These passages and judicial findings demonstrate the degree of judicial control or scrutiny that the Appeals Chamber could occasionally decide to delve into. In the context of the Afghanistan judgment, the Appeals Chamber clearly decided to play a wider role of judicial oversight than in other appeals.

## 3 Conclusion

In conclusion, this chapter aimed at providing some examples, demonstrating that for more than a decade since the Court entered real operation, judicial control over the Prosecutor's investigations, which is predominant at the pre-trial stage, proved to be an integral and important aspect of the Rome Statute. The development of the jurisprudence of the Court on various aspects involving judicial control over the last 16 years is self-evident. Although, pre-trial chambers occasionally shared some common approaches, there remain to be clear discrepancies in exercising such control. This resulted from the judges different understanding of their role in conducting judicial review and the scope of such oversight.

By following the development of the Court's jurisprudence, one may observe that judicial control has gone through at least four main phases or approaches. The first phase may be defined as the "interventionist". It witnessed a pre-trial chamber's eagerness to exercise judicial control over the Prosecutor's passive activity during the preliminary examination in the situation of CAR. The second phase experienced a combination between a high degree of judicial control in

78 ibid.

some decisions and a contrary deferential approach *vis-à-vis* the Prosecutor in others. The former approach is reflected in the decisions authorizing the Prosecutor to open an investigation into the situations of Kenya, Côte d'Ivoire, and Burundi. Similarly, the Comoros Second Review Decision portrayed a powerful pre-trial chamber that is keen to preserve its judicial authority *vis-à-vis* the Office of the Prosecutor. The separate opinions of Judge Péter Kovács fall within this category.

The "deferential" phase or approach becomes apparent in the conservative approach followed by the Pre-Trial Chamber in responding to the request of the Government of the Bolivarian Republic of Venezuela I. Although this request was quite different than the one concerning the CAR, still the Chamber was not convinced that it possessed the authority to exercise judicial control over the Prosecutor at this early stage of the proceedings, and accordingly, was not willing to play a more creative or active role. The deferential approach could also be detected in the limited judicial oversight exercised by other pre-trial chambers in the context of Article 15 proceedings in situations such as Georgia and Philippines.

The third phase or approach featured what may be described as a "revolutionary". The Appeals Chamber developed this approach in the Afghanistan judgment of 5 March 2020. It weakened the scope of the Pre-Trial Chamber's supervisory role over the Prosecutor's determination under Article 15 of the Rome Statute to considerable extent, also by removing the admissibility assessment from the scope of judicial review, which was deemed one of the core requirements subject to the pre-trial chambers scrutiny for more than a decade. It explicitly questioned the competence of a pre-trial chamber to continuously monitor the Prosecutor's activities. The Appeals Chamber's findings not only narrowed the scope of judicial control by pre-trial chambers, but also gave force to the previous practice of limited judicial oversight within the context of Article 15 proceedings. The decision authorizing the Prosecutor to open an investigation in the situation in Philippines is a recent example on point.

The fourth phase or approach finds support in different periods of the Appeals Chamber's lifespan. Earlier jurisprudence reveals that the Appeals Chamber played a role in setting the contours of judicial control by the pre-trial chambers and drawing the balance of such control *vis-à-vis* the Prosecutor. I would thus define this stage as the "balanced" approach or phase, which can still be found in some of the Appeals Chamber's judgments.

In the *Lubanga* judgment of 13 October 2006, the Appeals Chamber played a role in defining the scope of the OTP's investigations, while in the *Gbagbo* judgment of 16 December 2013, it attempted to draw the line between the responsibility of Chambers and the Prosecutor, yet providing the former the final say in exercising its judicial oversight. It follows from the foregoing that there is still a need to find a delicate balance to be maintained between judicial oversight on the one hand and Prosecutorial discretion and independence on the other hand. This not only ensures harmony between the judiciary and prosecution, but also better quality of future cases.

CHAPTER 12

# The Inquisitorial/Adversarial Divide and Its Specific Context at the ICC

*Raul C. Pangalangan*

## 1 A Comparative Law Exercise at the Plane of Public International Law

The contrast and overlap between the inquisitorial and adversarial models of criminal justice are usually examined through the lens of comparative law that typically compares national legal systems. In the International Criminal Court, however, that discussion arises at the plane of public international law, namely, the interpretation of a treaty, the Rome Statute, and its underlying norms. Practices and principles identified with either model have been variously justified at the ICC, whether by tracing their roots in the system from which they originated, or by invoking the ICC's statutory instruments, its structure and procedure regardless of the system to which they originally belonged. The challenge lies in that even in case of the latter, these practices and principles often make sense mainly within the internal dynamic of either legal tradition, that is to say, within the context of the institutional forms (e.g., the respective roles of judge, prosecutor and defense counsel, or the vulnerabilities of lay juries vis-à-vis trained judges) from which they sprang and within they organically fit.

This chapter looks at this challenge and examines the reasoning used by the Court when faced with this challenge. It asks to what extent the Court situates the debate solely within the inquisitorial/adversarial divide or, on the other hand, 'whether concepts drawn from national law, once transposed to the international level, have acquired a new dimension, independent of their original meaning',[1] that is to say, when the Court looks at the question mainly in terms of its own norms (e.g., human rights, the fair trial rights of the accused, victims' claim to justice, etc.) and within its own institutional set-up (e.g., the powers of the prosecutor vis-à-vis the judicial chambers).

---

1 M Delmas-Marty, 'The Contribution of Comparative Law to a Pluralist Conception of International Criminal Law' (2003) 1(1) *Journal of International Criminal Justice* 13, 20; see also Appeals Judgment, *Erdemović*, IT-96-22-A, AC, ICTY, 7 October 1997, Separate and Dissenting Opinion of Judge Cassese.

 | DOI:10.1163/9789004529939_013

At the outset, some disclaimers. This chapter does not hold up any specific national jurisdiction to embody the quintessential model of either system. There are broad characteristics and institutional forms generally associated with the inquisitorial and adversarial models, and the typology is here used for mainly heuristic purposes. Finally, while the term 'inquisitorial', associated with the civil law tradition, is consistently used, its counterpart term 'adversarial', associated with the common law tradition, is sometimes substituted in some of the literature with the term 'accusatorial.'[2]

## 2 The Interface between Municipal and International Law

The Court's 'sources of law' draw from both *international* and *national* law. The Rome Statute states that the Court may apply international treaties and custom, and international standards like 'internationally recognized norms and standards',[3] 'internationally recognized human rights',[4] and the principle of non-discrimination.[5]

At the same time, the Court may also apply, in accordance with its hierarchy of sources, the 'general principles of law derived by the Court from national laws of legal systems of the world.'[6] These national laws embody elements of the inquisitorial or adversarial model in varying degrees. Moreover, when the Statute refers to national laws, it further specifies 'including, as appropriate, the national laws of States that would normally exercise jurisdiction over the crime.'[7] This must be read in conjunction with the principle of complementarity,[8] the foundational concept that the ICC is a court of last resort and acquires jurisdiction only when national authorities are 'unwilling or unable'

---

2 See e.g. J H Merryman and R Pérez-Perdomo, *The Civil Law Tradition: An Introduction to the Legal Systems of Europe and Latin America* 4th edn (Stanford University Press 2018); Delmas-Marty (n 1) 18.

3 Article 21(1)(c), Rome Statute of the International Criminal Court (signed 17 July 1998, entered into force 1 July 2002) 2187 UNTS 3 ('Rome Statute').

4 Ibid., Article 21(3) (see also Article 69(7), 'Evidence obtained by means of a violation of this Statute or internationally recognized human rights shall not be admissible if').

5 Ibid., Article 21(3) ('without any adverse distinction founded on grounds such as gender ..., age, race, colour, language, religion or belief, political or other opinion, national, ethnic or social origin, wealth, birth or other status').

6 Ibid., Article 21(1)(c).

7 Ibid., Article 21(1)(c).

8 Ibid., Preamble ('shall be complementary to national criminal jurisdictions'), Article 1 ('shall be complementary to national criminal jurisdictions'), and Article 17 ('Issues of admissibility').

genuinely to prosecute.[9] It has been proposed that this 'involves ... interaction rather than the absolute autonomy of each sphere of criminal justice, national and international, or a narrow subordination of one to the other.'[10]

Finally in this regard, the Rome Statute is not oblivious to the existence of these two legal traditions and expressly recognizes the 'need [for] representation of the principal legal systems of the world' in choosing the judges who will compose the Court. This chapter deals with only two of legal systems, the common law and the civil law. From among the 120 states that voted to adopt the Statute in the Rome Conference, there were certainly states that recognized other legal systems as well, say, Islamic law or customary law traditions as those in Asia. This contribution does not deal with whether these states actually proposed their own systems, or whether they advanced doctrines from the more familiar common or civil law systems, since former colonies typically continue to be influenced by the colonizer's law even after independence.

At the very least therefore national laws are relevant to the Court both as one of its 'sources of law' and as part of its complementarity determination.

It is entirely possible to see some of these national law concepts *qua* international law, since they may likewise constitute 'general principles of law recognized by civilized nations', one of the sources of international law under the Statute of the International Court of Justice.[11] However, this does not change the proposed analysis in this chapter. These 'general principles of law' become authoritative by virtue of their having been incubated within national law systems and their internal dynamic within those legal traditions and their legal forms.

Accordingly, there is sufficient textual basis and ample room within the Rome Statute for the Court to have recourse either to a comparative approach taking into account principles derived from national law, or a public international law approach taking into account norms affirmed in either treaty or custom law.

The discussion below draws from arguments made by the judges who confronted these competing approaches in their respective decisions.

9 Ibid., Article 17.

10 Delmas-Marty (n 1).

11 Statute of the International Court of Justice (signed 26 June 1945, entered into force 24 October 1945) Article 38(1)(c).

## 3 The Inquisitorial/Adversarial Divide: Situated in Actual Cases

### 3.1 *No Case to Answer: Transposed from the Adversarial Framework to the ICC*

The 'No Case to Answer' debate pertains to the Court's power to dismiss a case mid-stream, on the ground that the prosecution, having completed the presentation of its evidence, has failed to prove guilt beyond reasonable doubt and accordingly there is no need to hear the defence's case at all. This debate best captures the difficulty that this chapter seeks to explore.

This Court has granted No Case to Answer motions in two cases. The first was *Ruto and Sang* in which the Trial Chamber terminated the case without prejudice to future prosecution but did not acquit. The second was *Gbagbo and Blé Goudé* in which the Trial Chamber acquitted the accused and was affirmed by the Appeals Chamber. Until then, there was a question whether indeed ICC Trial Chambers had the power to grant No Case to Answer motions.

#### 3.1.1 On Whether ICC Trial Chambers Have the Power to Grant No Case to Answer Motions

Stated plainly, a No Case to Answer motion sits comfortably with the adversarial model of criminal justice, equivalent to the common law's 'demurrer to the evidence.' This was amply demonstrated in a separate opinion for the majority in *Gbagbo and Blé Goudé*, which emphasized the prosecution's burden to prove guilt beyond reasonable doubt.

> *In the context of a trial conducted within an adversarial framework*, a decision that there is 'no case' is made where a trial chamber concludes that the Prosecutor, having presented all her evidence, *has not discharged her evidential burden by submitting sufficient evidence capable of supporting a conviction* with respect to one or more of the charges. In essence, the issue to be decided is *whether the Prosecutor has discharged that burden.* [...] However, given that the onus is on the Prosecutor to prove the guilt of the accused, in deciding whether to give a statement or to submit evidence in his defence, an accused may ask the Trial Chamber to determine whether the Prosecutor has submitted sufficient evidence capable of supporting a conviction, and as such justifying the continuation of the trial.[12] (emphases added)

12 Reasons of Judge Geoffrey Henderson, *Gbagbo and Blé Goudé, Situation in the Republic of Côte d'Ivoire*, ICC-02/11-01/15-1263-AnxB-Red, TC I, ICC, 16 July 2019.

At the same time, the opinion likewise recognizes the logic of the inquisitorial model's resistance to the No Case to Answer acquittal, based on the possibility that incriminating evidence may yet come from sources other than the prosecution but it still concludes on the sheer absurdity that the court should prolong the trial on hope that the accused might unwittingly incriminate himself.

> It is possible for an accused to be convicted on the basis of evidence that was adduced by victims, by a co-accused, at the request of the Trial Chamber or even evidence that was submitted by the accused himself. [...] If at this stage, there is insufficient evidence capable of supporting a conviction on a charge or charges, it is incompatible with the presumption of innocence to continue the trial with the hope that the only incriminating evidence capable of supporting a conviction would be supplied by the accused.[13]

However, the Rome Statute contains no express clause specifically authorizing a judgment of acquittal before the trial is completed. Indeed, its clause on *Requirements for the Decision* states that the 'Trial Chamber's decision shall be based on its evaluation of the evidence and the *entire* proceedings'[14] (emphasis added). The 'entire proceedings' can very well be read to mean the full trial on the merits, where both the prosecution and defense present their evidence.

Yet as the separate opinion concludes, the Court's power to acquit on a No Case to Answer motion is actually grounded on the most important guarantees of fairness in the Rome Statute, namely, the principles of the presumption of innocence, the prosecution's burden to overcome that presumption, and that the evidentiary standard of proof beyond reasonable doubt.[15]

> The legal basis for the decision that the accused has no case to answer is thus article 66(2) of the Statute, which places the onus of proving the guilt of the accused squarely on the Prosecutor. This burden never shifts.[16]

By that reasoning, the Appeals Chamber affirmed the power of a Trial Chamber to grant a No Case to Answer motion on the basis of the Rome Statute itself, independent of its origins in the adversarial model.

---

13 Ibid.

14 Rome Statute, Article 74(2).

15 Rome Statute, Article 66.

16 *Gbagbo and Blé Goudé*, Reasons of Judge Geoffrey Henderson (n 12).

Moreover, in the very first No Case to Answer proceeding in the ICC in *Ruto and Sang*, responding to the argument that it has no statutory basis, a separate opinion reverses the argument and asks whether allowing the trial 'to drag on beyond the presentation of the case for the prosecution' despite insufficient evidence, is consistent with the Statute's requirement that the trial be 'efficient and expeditious.'[17]

> [T]here is no provision in the ICC basic documents that requires a Trial Chamber to continue with the presentation of evidence on behalf of the defence, where the evidentiary case for the prosecution was not [...] strong enough to warrant inviting the defence to present their case. Indeed, Article 64(2) [on "fair and expeditious" trials] of the Rome Statute must stand in the way of any proposition urged as involving any such requirement.[18]

### 3.1.2 The Applicable Test in No Case to Answer Motions

In *Ruto and Sang*, the two judges in the majority addressed the applicable test in a No Case to Answer motion. This Trial Chamber had earlier stated that, at this intermediate stage, the court must 'take the prosecution evidence "at its highest" and [...] "assume that the prosecution's evidence was entitled to c:redence unless incapable of belief" on any reasonable view.'[19] The test was:

> whether there is evidence on which a reasonable Trial Chamber *could* convict. ... The Chamber will not consider questions of reliability or credibility relating to the evidence, save where the evidence in question is incapable of belief by any reasonable Trial Chamber.[20] (emphasis in the original)

Based on that formulation by the Trial Chamber itself, two questions arise. *One*, does 'evidence on which a reasonable Trial Chamber *could* convict' require the *Ruto and Sang* Trial Chamber, even if it already found the prosecution's evidence insufficient, to proceed to full trial if some any other 'reasonable' Trial

---

17 Rome Statute, Article 64(2).

18 Decision on Defence Applications for Judgments of Acquittal, *Ruto and Sang, Situation in the Republic of Kenya*, ICC-01/09-01/11-2027-Red-Corr, TC V(A), ICC, 5 April 2016, Reasons of Judge Eboe-Osuji.

19 Decision No. 5 on the Conduct of Trial Proceedings (Principles and Procedure on 'No Case to Answer' Motions), *Ruto and Sang, Situation in the Republic of Kenya*, ICC-01/09-01/11-1334, TC V(A), ICC, 3 June 2014.

20 Ibid.

Chamber *could* convict? *Two*, is the *Ruto and Sang* Trial Chamber barred from weighing the prosecution's evidence?

One opinion in the majority says that since the Trial Chamber will eventually 'reach its own conclusions', it should not be forced to continue the proceedings if it has already found the evidence to fall below proof beyond reasonable doubt, and should thus have the power at that stage to look into the probative value of the prosecution's evidence.

> I wish to clarify here that in assessing *whether a reasonable Trial Chamber could convict*—in other words, could be satisfied beyond reasonable doubt of the guilt of the accused—the test [above] envisages a situation, whereby different reasonable triers of fact at the 'no case to answer' stage could come to different conclusions concerning the guilt or innocence of the accused concerned. However, this does not mean that the Trial Chamber actually conducting the 'no case to answer' assessment cannot reach its own final conclusions, and would be forced to continue the proceedings, even if it has concluded that, on the basis of the evidence before it, it would not be satisfied beyond reasonable doubt of the accused's guilt.[21] (emphasis in the original)

The other opinion in the majority looked at the institutional and structural 'differences between [ICC] trials and jury trials.'[22] It examined the relevant practice in some common law jurisdictions where lay juries are the triers of fact while the judge is allowed to direct the jury that there is no case to answer and to return a 'not guilty' verdict. In contrast, at the ICC, the same judges forming the Trial Chamber are at once triers of both fact and law.

> Given the *indivisibility of judicial functions in the same judges of the Trial Chamber*, as the tribunal of both fact and law, and the absolute absence of any question of usurpation of the credibility assessment functions of a jury, there is no essential obstacle to the Trial Chamber's freedom to engage in sensible evaluation of the credibility of Prosecution witnesses, for purposes of assessing whether the trial should be terminated at the close of the case for the Prosecution.[23] (emphasis added)

21 *Ruto and Sang* Decision on Defence Applications for Judgments of Acquittal (n 18), Reasons of Judge Fremr.

22 Ibid., Reasons of Judge Eboe-Osuji.

23 Ibid.

It further explains that this 'greater latitude [for the Trial Chamber] to make [the evidentiary] assessment at the conclusion of the prosecution case, in order to terminate a weak case' can be explained by the 'unique features of this Court, including the differences between its trials and jury trials.' He cites the International Criminal Tribunal for Yugoslavia which said that to thus confine the trial chamber's powers in No Case to Answer motions 'is certainly suited to a system in which cases are eventually sent to a jury or to a trier of fact other than the judge who evaluates the evidence at that stage.'[24]

> In such a system, if a judge finds that, while he himself cannot be satisfied of the guilt of the accused, a different trier of fact could come to a conclusion of guilt, he cannot stop the proceedings. Should he apply a higher standard of evaluation of the evidence, he would try the facts himself, instead of leaving the task of doing so to the jury.[25]

In contrast, at both the ICTY and the ICC, there was no jury, and the judges are the triers of fact. Significantly, by this analysis, international criminal tribunals like the ICTY and ICC are even more hospitable to a No Case to Answer motion.

In *Gbagbo and Blé Goudé,* a separate opinion echoed this interpretation and stated that to constrain the powers of the Trial Chamber is an 'artificial prohibition [that] sits uncomfortably in the ICC's procedural framework.'[26] If the Pre-Trial Chamber is empowered to weigh the probative value of evidence even at the preliminary stages of the case when the Prosecutor need not present its evidence in full, why prevent a Trial Chamber that has actually received the Prosecution's complete case? Moreover, the *Gbagbo and Blé Goudé* Chamber had not made contemporaneous admissibility rulings. Since there was no filter to sift the evidence that entered the record, the Chamber had to evaluate the evidence for both relevance and probative value. This 'sits uncomfortably with the traditional Adversarial/Common Law no-case to answer test, which instructs Chambers to consider the Prosecutor's evidence at its highest.'[27]

---

24 Appeals Judgment, *Jelisić*, IT-95-10, AC, ICTY, 5 July 2001, Partial Dissenting Opinion of Judge Pocar.

25 Ibid.

26 *Gbagbo and Blé Goudé*, Reasons of Judge Geoffrey Henderson (n 12).

27 Ibid.

Significantly, when the Appeals Chamber affirmed the acquittals in *Gbagbo and Blé Goudé*, it cited both international (e.g., other international criminal tribunals) and national (*inter alia*, cases from the United Kingdom) case-law.[28]

### 3.2 *Witness Preparation and the Truth-Seeking Process*

The inquisitorial/adversarial divide has also arisen in the recurring debate over witness preparation, a practice accepted in adversarial systems but rejected outright in inquisitorial systems. Witness preparation has been referred to as a 'fault line between two different procedural cultures', 'illustrat[ing a] polarization … that has caused considerable controversy in the international legal community.'[29] The issue remains unsettled in ICC case-law.

At the ICC, the initial view was that the preparation of witnesses by parties prior to trial is inimical to the truth-seeking process. In *Lubanga*,[30] the Trial Chamber rejected the Prosecution's request to allow 'witness proofing', saying there was no such thing as "witnesses of either party", only "witnesses of the Court."

> The Chamber had earlier allowed 'witness familiarization', namely, 'practice of familiarising witnesses with the courtroom and the procedures which they will encounter' including 'a visit to the courtroom and a "walk through"' of the experience of testifying. The Chamber recognized that witnesses may never have been to a courtroom, and some of them may be vulnerable, especially children. Significantly, the Chamber emphatically assigned the familiarization function to the Court's Victims and Witnesses Unit, quoting said Unit's statement that 'witnesses to a crime are the property neither of the Prosecution nor of the Defence and […] should therefore *not be considered as witnesses of either party, but as witnesses of the Court*'[31] (emphasis added).

On the other hand, the Chamber rejected the 'substantive preparation of witnesses for trial' as having no basis in the Rome Statute. Significantly for our analysis, the Chamber further found that it had insufficient basis either in national legal systems and, in particular, the civil law systems.

28 Judgment in the appeal of the Prosecutor against Trial Chamber I's decision on the no case to answer motions, *Gbagbo and Blé Goudé, Situation in the Republic of Côte d'Ivoire*, ICC-02/11-01/15-1400, AC, ICC, 31 March 2021.

29 J D Jackson and Y M Brunger, 'Witness Preparation in the ICC: An Opportunity for Principled Pragmatism' (2015) 13 *Journal of International Criminal Justice* 601.

30 Decision Regarding the Practices Used to Prepare and Familiarise Witnesses for Giving Testimony at Trial, *Lubanga, Situation in the Democratic Republic of the Congo*, ICC-01/04-01/06-1049, TC I, ICC, 30 November 2007.

31 Ibid.

> [T]he Trial Chamber does not consider that a general principle of law allowing the substantive preparation of witnesses prior to testimony can be derived from national legal systems worldwide, pursuant to Article 21(1)(c) of the Statute. Although this practice is accepted to an extent in two [national] legal systems, *both of which are founded upon common law traditions*, this *does not provide a sufficient basis for any conclusion that a general principle based on established practice of national legal systems exists*. The Trial Chamber notes that the prosecution's submissions with regard to national jurisprudence did not include any citations from the *Romano-Germanic legal system*.[32] (emphasis added)

The Chamber concluded that witness preparation may 'lead to a distortion of the truth and may come dangerously close to constituting a rehearsal of in-court testimony.'[33] Indeed the Chamber considered the 'spontaneity' of the witness as intrinsically bound up with the truth of what is said, as it were, the logic of *res gestae* writ large.

> [T]he Trial Chamber is of the opinion that the preparation of witness testimony by parties prior to trial may diminish what would otherwise be *helpful spontaneity* during the giving of evidence by a witness. The spontaneous nature of testimony can be of paramount importance to the Court's ability to find the truth, and the Trial Chamber is not willing *to lose such an important element* in the proceedings.[34] (emphasis added)

However, this principle was later rejected by another Trial Chamber in *Ruto and Sang*,[35] which held that while the Rome Statute is silent on 'witness preparation', it actually requires Trial Chambers to ensure the 'fair and expeditious conduct of the proceedings.'[36] Accordingly, the Chamber held that it had 'a significant degree of discretion' to allow measures like witness preparation to 'aid[] the process of human recollection [and] ensur[e] that the testimony of a witness is structured and clear' and 'elicit focused and structured testimony and to ensure that all probative evidence is presented.'[37]

---

32 Ibid.
33 Ibid.
34 Ibid.
35 Decision on witness preparation, *Ruto and Sang, Situation in the Republic of Kenya*, ICC-01/09-01/11-524, TC V, ICC, 2 January 2013.
36 Rome Statute, Article 64.
37 Ibid.

The Chamber expressly recognized reasons specific to the ICC. It cited the practice of other international criminal tribunals and national jurisdictions 'where the principle of the primacy of orality is followed and where trials heavily rely on the examination of live witnesses through questioning by the parties.' It noted that the crimes prosecuted at the ICC are 'complex, both as regards the factual circumstances and legal issues involved' and likewise recognized the time-gap between the events and the time when witnesses testify. Finally, the Chamber recognized that at the ICC, the witnesses 'come from places far from the seat of the Court and come from a variety of different cultural and linguistic backgrounds.'[38] A separate opinion explained that while the 'relative palliative effects' of witness preparation apply to the 'average Western society [with] witnesses native to that culture', the rationale applies with 'even greater force' to the ICC milieu which is 'wholly foreign' to the witness.[39]

The *Gbagbo and Blé Goudé* Trial Chamber rejected witness preparation outright. It recognized that witness preparation is 'common practice in common law jurisdictions' but stated that it is not provided expressly in the Court's statutory framework, nor can it be considered a 'general principle of law' under the Rome Statute's Article 21 sources of law.

The Chamber emphasized that the principles of 'orality and immediacy' require that 'evidence is brought before the Chamber in a genuine and undistorted manner, leaving it for the Judges to assess any inconsistencies or additional evidence which are, in any case, better tested in the courtroom before the Chamber.' The Chamber, in other words, considered witness preparation as anathema to a truth-seeking process based on what it calls the 'spontaneity' of the witness. The Chamber was also wary of the 'inherent risk of witness interference and the truth being distorted' and of impermissible practices like 'rehearsal, practice and coaching.'[40]

The dissenting opinion explained that witness preparation is needed in the ICC system which is, in this regard, more akin to an adversarial system where evidence is secured by the parties, not by the court.

> [T]he parties, not the judges, conduct investigations, which include both the interview of witnesses and taking of witness statements, as is done in an *adversarial* system. This is in contrast to the process in many

38 Ibid.

39 Ibid., Partly Dissenting Opinion of Judge Eboe-Osuji.

40 Decision on witness preparation and familiarization, *Gbagbo and Blé Goudé, Situation in the Republic of Côte d'Ivoire*, ICC-02/11-01/15-533, TC I, ICC, 2 December 2015.

> *inquisitorial* systems—including hybrid tribunals based primarily on an inquisitorial model (such as the Extraordinary Chambers in the Courts of Cambodia)—in which an impartial public authority or judge conducts all investigations. In accordance with the Court's framework and the Chamber's 'Directions on the Conduct of the Proceedings', *this trial will also be conducted on a basis that is more consistent with the practice and procedure of an adversarial trial than that of one conducted under the inquisitorial system*.[41] (emphasis added)

The ban on witness preparation 'overlooks the reality of the compromise system created by the drafters of the Rome Statute.' It is viable 'only in a purely inquisitorial system, where the judges bear primary responsibility for gathering and eliciting evidence.'[42]

The dissenting opinion acknowledges the risk of manipulation but points out ample safeguards in the Rome Statute[43] and in the ICC's ethical code for counsel,[44] both of which prohibit such conduct. It also points out reasons, already recognized in *Ruto and Sang*, for witness preparation that are unique to the ICC, namely, the multicultural challenges specific to international criminal trials and the vulnerability of witnesses specific to the nature of the crimes punishable by the ICC.[45]

Contrast *Gbagbo and Blé Goudé* to *Al Hassan*, which allowed witness preparation first, 'to assist the witness who will be giving evidence during the proceedings', and second, 'for the calling party to assess and clarify the witness's evidence in order to facilitate the focused, efficient and effective questioning of the witness during the proceedings.' In *Al Hassan*, the Chamber considered the lapse of time between the events and the trial, and the need to enable the witness to review their previous statements and understand on what matters they will be asked. It likewise recognized, as in *Ruto and Sang*,[46] the unfamiliarity of witnesses 'appearing for the first time in a foreign courtroom' and the

---

41 Partially Dissenting Opinion of Judge Henderson, *Gbagbo and Blé Goudé* Decision on witness preparation and familiarization (n 40), ICC-02/11-01/15-355-Anx1, 2 December 2015.

42 Ibid.

43 Rome Statute, Article 70. See Judgment on the appeal of Mr Jean-Pierre Bemba Gombo against Trial Chamber III's 'Judgment pursuant to Article 74 of the Statute', *Bemba, Situation in the Central African Republic*, ICC-01/05-01/08-3636-Red, AC, ICC, 18 June 2018.

44 Code of Professional Conduct for Counsel, ICC-ASP/4/Res.1, 2 December 2005 (Third Plenary Meeting of the Assembly of State Parties).

45 *Gbagbo and Blé Goudé* Decision on witness preparation, Partially Dissenting Opinion of Judge Henderson (n 41).

46 *Ruto and Sang*, Decision on witness preparation (n 35).

vulnerability of witnesses especially victims who are called upon to re-live traumatic experiences. Overall, witness preparation facilitates a 'more efficient and focused witness examination.' At the same time, responding to the risks of undue influence or interference with witnesses, it proposed that these perils were 'sufficiently mitigated by safeguards' contained in protocols issued by the Chamber.[47]

Significantly, the principle of orality was further tested in *Al Hassan* concerning the entry into evidence of a witness's prior recorded statement. The majority rejected it, stating that prior recorded statements were a 'deviation from the general principle of orality' under the Statute[48] and that introducing them into evidence without being tested under cross-examination was 'unduly prejudicial.'[49]

A partial dissent disagreed with the characterization of prior recorded statements as a deviation from the principle of orality, situating the debate in the inquisitorial/adversarial divide.[50]

> Article 69 ['Evidence'] in its entirety was drafted as a compromise between legal traditions and it is a cornerstone in establishing the hybrid nature of the Court's proceedings. In this context Article 69(2) of the Statute fully recognized that the requirement for in person testimony would be subject to variation as specified in the Rules of Procedure and Evidence. In that respect, I do not consider that introduction of prior recorded testimony in accordance with the Rules should be viewed as exceptional. To do so is to accord dominance to one legal tradition in contravention to the plain wording and intent of Article 69(2) of the Statute.

In that view, orality—and its antipathy to witness preparation and, in Al Hassan, to prior recorded statements—cannot be the default position, lest the deliberately 'hybrid nature' of ICC procedure be replaced by the 'dominance' of one tradition over the other.

---

47 Decision on witness preparation and familiarization, *Al Hassan, Situation in the Republic of Mali*, ICC-01/12-01/18-666, TC X, ICC, 17 March 2020.

48 Rome Statute, Article 69(2).

49 Public redacted version of Decision on the introduction into evidence of P-0130's prior recorded testimony pursuant to Rule 68(2)(b) of the Rules, *Al Hassan, Situation in the Republic of Mali*, ICC-01/12-01/18-2124-Red, TC X, ICC, 21 February 2022.

50 Partially Dissenting Opinion of Judge Kimberly Prost, *Al Hassan* Decision on the introduction into evidence of P-0130's prior recorded testimony (n 49), ICC-01/12-01/18-2124-Anx, 21 February 2022.

### 3.3 *The Common Law Notion of Plea of Guilt, within the ICC*

The Rome Statute provisions for *Proceedings on an admission of guilt*[51] are at variance with typical adversarial systems, where a guilty plea dispenses with the need for a trial. The admission of guilt is a plea, as it were, a statement by a party in its own pleadings; it is not merely evidentiary in character. Since the function of a trial is for the court to receive evidence to prove the pleas contained in the charges, if the accused enters a plea of guilt, there is no plea left to be proved. All that is left to be proved in the trial is the authenticity of the plea as free and knowing, that it was made voluntarily by the accused with full knowledge of its consequences.

In contrast, under the Rome Statute, the guilty plea does not dispense with the trial and the reception of the evidence-in-chief. In order for the Trial Chamber to be satisfied that the plea and its most important elements are established, the Chamber must 'consider the admission of guilt, together with any additional evidence presented.'[52] Indeed despite the guilty plea, the Chamber may require the Prosecution to 'present additional evidence, including the testimony of witnesses' for 'a more complete presentation of the facts.'[53]

This is consistent with notion in the civil law tradition that courts seek the material or *objective* truth, in contrast to the accused's admission which is merely his or her own *subjective* truth. Thus the guilty plea does not release the prosecution from its burden to present evidence to prove guilt beyond reasonable doubt.

Significantly, the Statute recognizes that the proceedings following a guilty plea are *sui generis*, as categorically distinct from what it calls 'the *ordinary trial procedures* provided by this Statute' which, if chosen by the Chamber, results in that the guilty plea is effectively vacated and deemed 'as not having made' (emphasis added).[54]

The ICC has had only one occasion to apply the procedure on admission of guilt. In *Al Mahdi*,[55] despite the plea of guilt entered by the accused, the Trial Chamber proceeded to conduct hearings, hear witnesses, and receive other evidence pursuant to Article 65(2) of the Rome Statute. Although *Al Mahdi* did not further discuss the *sui generis* character of Article 65(2) trials, it

51 Rome Statute, Article 65.
52 Ibid., Article 65(2).
53 Ibid., Article 65(4)(a).
54 Ibid., Article 65(4)(b).
55 Judgment and Sentence, *Al Mahdi, Situation in the Republic of Mali*, ICC-01/12-01/15, TC VIII, ICC, 27 September 2016. Author's Note: The author was President of Trial Chamber VIII which rendered the decision in *Al Mahdi*.

is useful in this context to recall the relevant discussion at the ICTY occasioned by a guilty plea in *Erdemović*.

Therein, the Presiding Judge, by way of dissent, inquired on 'The Notion of a Guilty Plea (Or: The extent to which an international criminal court can rely upon national law for the interpretation of international provisions).'[56]

He stated that a guilty plea must not be interpreted by reference to common law practice; instead it must be 'autonomously construed on the basis of the international provisions of the Statute.' He asked to what 'extent [...] an international criminal court may or should draw upon national law concepts and transpose these concepts into international criminal proceedings.' In reply, he proposed that 'legal constructs and terms of art upheld in national law should not be ... mechanically imported into international criminal proceedings.'[57]

> [E]ven in the case of international rules embodying national-law notions, an effort must be made to construe those notions in the light of the object and purpose of the international rules or of their general spirit.
>
> International criminal procedure results from the gradual decanting of national criminal concepts and rules into the international receptacle. However, international criminal procedure does not originate from a uniform body of law. It substantially results from *an amalgamation of two different legal systems, that obtaining in common-law countries and the system prevailing in countries of civil-law* (although for historical reasons, there currently exists at the international level a clear imbalance in favour of the common-law approach [referring to the *ad hoc* tribunals]).[58]

He noted that the notion of a guilty plea derives from the adversarial system.

> [The guilty plea] clearly drawn from the criminal procedure of common-law countries. This practice does not have a direct counterpart in the civil-law tradition, where an admission of guilt is simply part of the evidence to be considered and evaluated by the court. However, notwithstanding its origin in a particular national setting, the true import and scope of this notion may be grasped without necessarily referring to the legislation and case-law of common-law countries.[59]

---

56 Separate and Dissenting Opinion of Judge Cassese, *Erdemović* Appeal Judgment (n 1).
57 Ibid.
58 Ibid.
59 Ibid.

Yet the drafters of the ICTY Statute adopted the common-law concept of the guilty plea taking into account the specificities of international criminal proceedings: the difficulty of collecting evidence, the protection of victims and witnesses, the high cost of international proceedings (including translations and interpreters, and transport for victims and witnesses). Accordingly, the guilty plea promotes the public interest. It also benefits the accused as well in many ways: to atone for the crime, avoid the indignity of a trial, and get leniency from the court.

### 3.4 *Recharacterization of Charges: Institutional Roles of Prosecutors and Judges*

In the ICC statutory framework, the judicial phase begins with the filing of the 'document containing the charges on which the Prosecutor intends to bring the person to trial.'[60] The 'Document containing the charges' (or DCC) must contain *inter alia* the 'legal characterisation of the facts' pertaining to both the crime charged and the mode of attribution.[61] It is this document that is filed with the Pre-Trial Chamber which has the power to confirm the charges if it determines that there is 'sufficient evidence to establish substantial grounds to believe' that the accused committed the crime charged.[62] The Rome Statute also makes it clear that the Pre-Trial Chamber may confirm or decline to confirm,[63] but may not rewrite on its own the DCC. It will have to ask the prosecution to produce further evidence or 'amend the charge because the evidence submitted appears to establish a different crime.'[64] The only other way to revise the DCC is for the Prosecutor, before the trial begins, to seek leave of the Pre-Trial Chamber and with notice to the accused.[65]

In the adversarial model, the determination of what crimes to charge is the domain of the prosecution alone who assumes the burden of deciding what case he wishes to try, that is to say, that it lies within prosecutorial discretion to determine what charges and on which evidence he or she is prepared to litigate. In the ICC, however, that discretion is circumscribed. To start with, it is the Pre-Trial Chamber that approves the charges prepared by the prosecution. Next, under the Regulations of the Court, interestingly enough an instrument crafted and adopted by the judges,[66] the Trial Chamber has the power to

60 Rome Statute, Article 61(3)(a).
61 Regulations of the Court, ICC-BD/01-05-16, adopted 26 May 2004.
62 Rome Statute, Article 61(7)(a).
63 Rome Statute, Article 61(7)(a) and 61(7)(b).
64 Rome Statute, Article 61(7)(c).
65 Rome Statute, Article 67(9).
66 Rome Statute, Article 52.

'change the legal characterisation of facts ... without exceeding the facts and circumstances described in the charges.'[67]

Regulation 55 was first applied in the *Lubanga* case. The Pre-Trial Chamber had confirmed the charge of enlisting and conscripting child soldiers. However, during the trial, the victims asked to modify the legal characterization of the facts to include charges of sexual slavery and inhuman or cruel treatment.

The Appeals Chamber upheld the validity of Regulation 55. It noted that without the power to re-characterize, the Rome Statute 'bears the risk of acquittals that are merely the result of legal qualifications confirmed in the pre-trial phase that tum out to be incorrect, in particular based on the evidence presented at the trial.' For instance, the evidence may be insufficient to convict for the charged crimes but may yet suffice to prosecute for another crime. This would go against the 'principal purpose' of Regulation 55 'to close accountability gaps' in the effort to stop impunity.[68]

In the adversarial model, that is the prosecution's lookout and, in order to avoid technical acquittals, the prosecution files alternative or cumulative charges founded on the same facts and circumstances. In the ICC system, that dilemma was left deliberately to the judges to solve, 'in light of differences of views between common law countries and countries following the Romano-Germanic tradition',[69] and thus the issuance of Regulation 55.

However, the Appeals Chamber, while affirming the validity of Regulation 55, held that if the legal re-characterization is done during the trial, it 'may not be used to exceed the facts and circumstances described in the charges or any amendment thereto'[70] and it must be carried out without violating the fair trial rights of the accused. In other words, the same conditions that apply to legal re-characterization *after* completion of trial likewise apply if it is done *during* the trial.

In *Katanga*, the Trial Chamber exercised its Regulation 55 power and re-characterized the mode of liability. The accused had been charged as an indirect co-perpetrator but was convicted as an accessory.[71] The dissenting

67 Regulations of the Court (n 61), Regulation 55.

68 Judgment on the appeals of Mr Lubanga Dyilo and the Prosecutor against the Decision of Trial Chamber I of 14 July 2009 entitled 'Decision giving notice to the parties and participants that the legal characterisation of the facts may be subject to change in accordance with Regulation 55(2) of the Regulations of the Court', *Lubanga, Situation in the Democratic Republic of the Congo*, ICC-01/04-01/06-2205, AC, ICC, 8 December 2009.

69 Ibid., para. 70.

70 Ibid., para. 88.

71 Judgment pursuant to article 74 of the Statute, *Katanga, Situation in the Democratic Republic of the Congo*, ICC-01/04-01/07-3436-tENG, TC II, ICC, 7 March 2014.

opinion argued that it wasn't possible to re-characterize the mode of liability 'without substantially transforming the charges' and that re-characterization, if done too late in the day, violates the fair trial rights of the accused.[72]

The ICC framework is more akin to the inquisitorial system which entails greater judicial oversight over the prosecution in contrast to the prosecution's primacy over the filing of charges.

## 4 Conclusion

This chapter set out to examine the methodology used at the ICC to either adopt or reject concepts or practices identified with either the inquisitorial or the adversarial model of criminal justice. It asked to what extent these concepts or practices were explained on the basis of their internal dynamic within their original milieu in either model, or on the basis of the ICC's own norms and institutional forms. This inquiry situated itself in four key issues, the doctrinal battlegrounds of the debate to see how the different arguments and approaches play out in the context of actual court decisions.

*No Case to Answer: Validity under the Statute.* The most debated of these issues is the power of a Trial Chamber to dismiss a case mid-stream on the basis of a No Case to Answer motion, the ICC's equivalent of the common law's demurrer to the evidence. As recognized in *Gbagbo and Blé Goudé*, No Case to Answer sits comfortably within the logic of the adversarial model. The task of gathering evidence belongs to the parties, and if the prosecution fails to do its job, namely, discharge its evidentiary burden to present sufficient incriminating evidence, why expect the defense to do it for them?

On the other hand, No Case to Answer does not fit in the inquisitorial model, which assumes that incriminating evidence may yet come from evidence secured by the court, by the victims, the co-accused or even the accused himself, as acknowledged even by the *Gbagbo and Blé Goudé* majority. The inquisitorial model assumes the proactive judge who takes a direct hand in gathering the evidence, leading to the statement earlier cited that there is no such thing as 'witnesses of a party' since they are actually 'witnesses of the court.' Yet for a No Case to Answer motion, the *conditio sine qua non* is the notion of 'the prosecution's evidence'; that is certainly difficult to reconcile with an inquisitorial system where evidence is seen as 'evidence of the court', and not of the parties.

---

72 Minority Opinion of Judge Christine Van den Wyngaert, *Katanga* Judgment pursuant to article 74 of the Statute (n 71), ICC-01/04-01/07-3436-AnxI, 10 March 2014.

Yet when the Appeals Chamber validated the No Case to Answer procedure under the Rome Statute, it did not have to rely on this debate between the inquisitorial system's hands-on judge who actively seeks evidence and the adversarial system's 'accusatorial' prosecutor who alone bore the onus of proving guilt. In the end, though the Rome Statute does not expressly authorize No Case to Answer motions, it gave the Trial Chamber enough powers to 'ensure that a trial is fair and expeditious'[73] by taking measures that square with the presumption of innocence, the onus of the prosecution to prove guilt, and the proof beyond reasonable doubt evidentiary threshold.[74]

In this regard, ICC practice may hew more closely to the common law, with a judge less involved in the gathering of evidence which then falls upon the prosecutor, but the statutory basis of No Case to Answer lies squarely in norms and procedure grounded in the Rome Statute.

*No Case to Answer: Applicable Test.* The test for a No Case to Answer motion is whether a reasonable court 'could' convict, where the Trial Chamber is prohibited from weighing the 'reliability or credibility' of the evidence, and can look only at its quantity, not quality.

This is quite an exacting test—strangely enough adopted by the same Trial Chamber that now seeks to explain it away—and advocates of No Case to Answer actually have an easy way out: that is a debate is only for common law systems where a jury is the trier of law but it is the judge who is called upon to decide if there is No Case to Answer. It is not a problem within the ICC structure because there is no such division between jury and judge; the judges who decide if there is No Case to Answer will be the same judges who would decide the case if it were to go to full trial, or in the felicitous language of the court, the 'indivisibility of judicial functions in the same judges of the Trial Chamber.'[75] Moreover, the architecture of the ICC actually gives that power to weigh the evidence to the Pre-Trial Chamber. The proposed test for No Case to Answer would strangely deny that same power to the Trial Chamber, despite the express language of the Rome Statute which states that the Trial Chamber 'may exercise any function of the Pre-Trial Chamber that is relevant and capable of application in those proceedings [following confirmation of charges].'[76]

---

73 Rome Statute, Article 64(2).

74 Ibid., Article 66.

75 *Ruto and Sang* Decision on Defence Applications for Judgments of Acquittal (n 18), Reasons of Judge Eboe-Osuji.

76 Rome Statute, Article 61(11).

*Witness Preparation.* If the debate on No Case to Answer has been finally laid to rest, the fate of witness preparation has not been as conclusive. Various trial chambers continue to take different positions on this issue.

*Lubanga* and *Gbagbo and Blé Goudé* rejected witness preparation, saying that it has no basis in the Rome Statute, and that it risks distorting the truth by sliding into 'rehearsal, practice or coaching' of the witness. It destroys the 'spontaneity' of the witness, and undermines the 'orality' of testimony. Note too that, in the inquisitorial model, the goal of the trial is to establish the objective truth, not the preferred truth of either party, and that goal is paramount in the context of the ICC which is 'mindful [of] unimaginable atrocities that deeply shock the conscience of mankind'[77] and for which setting the historical record straight is important.

In contrast, *Ruto and Sang* traces the authority for witness preparation to the Rome Statute itself, namely, the Trial Chamber's duty to ensure that the trial is 'fair and expeditious'[78] which was earlier cited in support of No Case to Answer motions. Indeed, *Ruto and Sang* would actually dispute the *Lubanga* line, earlier mentioned as regards No Case to Answer, that there are no 'witnesses for the parties' and only 'witnesses for the court.' There is no such thing at the ICC, it is argued, because the evidence is secured by parties, not the judges, and it is the parties that call their witnesses. In this regard, the ICC system is more akin to the adversarial system.

Significantly, the arguments in support of witness preparation pertain to factors specific to the ICC, namely, the complexity of crimes and fact-situations, the lapse in time between the commission of the crimes and trial, the witnesses as strangers to the courtroom both culturally and linguistically, and the vulnerability of witnesses in atrocity crimes heard by the ICC. These factors are not rooted in the inquisitorial/adversarial divide but derive from the purposes and structure of the ICC.

In conclusion, witness preparation has been validated mainly on the basis of the Rome Statute in relation to factors specific to international criminal justice.

*Plea of Guilt.* The Rome Statute contains provisions on 'admission of guilt' which follow procedure that is more akin to the inquisitorial system. In adversarial jurisdictions, the admission of guilt goes into the pleas and dispenses with the need for a trial to receive evidence to prove the pleas. However, in inquisitorial jurisdictions, the admission is merely evidentiary. The admission

77 Ibid., Preamble.

78 Ibid., Article 64(2).

is also just the accused's subjective truth, and the court is duty-bound to seek the objective truth. That inquisitorial model is reflected in the Statute. In either model, it is indispensable that the admission be voluntary and informed. In the adversarial model, that alone would have sufficed, and all that needs to be proved is that the plea was made freely and knowingly. But at the ICC, the Statute requires, in addition, that the admission be 'supported by facts' contained in the charges and the evidence submitted by the prosecutor. It further states that the Trial Chamber will consider the admission of guilt 'together with any additional evidence' and 'additional evidence' that a pro-active Chamber may ask the prosecutor to submit.

Significantly, the Statute provides that if the Chamber finds the admission of guilt inadequate, it may order that 'trial be continued under the ordinary trial procedures',[79] thus implying the procedures for a guilty plea are *sui generis* and not 'ordinary trial procedures.'

*Legal re-characterization.* Should judges be allowed to tell the prosecutor how to litigate their cases? Can the Trial Chamber re-characterize the charges filed by the Prosecutor? In adversarial systems, the answer is a categorical "no." It falls within the prosecutor's discretion to draft the indictment telling the court what crime has been committed and how the crime is attributed to the accused. Conversely, the "Document containing the charges" is the document where the prosecution sets forth what it hopes to prove in the trial. That indictment is binding upon the court. In the classic common law scenario, the jury can only either convict or acquit, and may not ask the prosecution to revise those charges. The prosecution's case will rise and fall on the basis of the risks that it takes in that filing. In order to avoid the risk of dismissal, the prosecution will typically file cumulative or alternative charges, should the judges find his evidence inadequate for some charges but sufficient for the others. Stated plainly, in the adversarial model, it is unacceptable for a court to meddle into the prosecution's strategy by re-characterizing the charges that it files.

At the ICC, the judges have adopted the Regulations of the Court and, through Regulation 55, empowered the Trial Chamber to 'modify the legal characterization' of the 'facts and circumstances described in the charges.'[80] In doing so, it embraced the practice of inquisitorial jurisdictions which involve judicial oversight over the prosecution of cases.

To start with, that oversight is already built into the very structure of the ICC, with a Pre-Trial Chamber whose function precisely is to review the 'Document

79 Ibid., Article 65(4)(b).
80 Regulations of the Court (n 61). Regulation 55.

containing the charges' filed by the Prosecution and, if thus found adequate, to confirm those charges for trial. What Regulation 55 does is, in addition to that statutory set-up, to empower the Trial Chamber to recharacterize the facts to enable the court to convict the accused for a different crime from that charged by the prosecutor, or on the basis of a different mode of attribution. In other words, it avoids the 'accountability gap' that arises from technical dismissals, and aligns the procedure of the Trial Chamber with the ICC's purpose to 'put an end to impunity'[81] which lies at the normative core of the Rome Statute.

The re-characterization power of the Trial Chamber carries out the principle *jura novit curia* ('the court knows the law') that underpins the inquisitorial model. It also advances the Trial Chamber's duty to ensure a 'fair and expeditious trial' by obviating the need for the prosecutor to file cumulative and alternative charges. Accordingly, the prosecutor is free to build a more focused case and, if the Trial Chamber finds it inadequate, the Chamber may exercise its re-characterization powers and thus foster judicial economy.

*Concluding Points*. It was earlier remarked that legal notions borrowed from national jurisdictions should not be 'mechanically imported' into international criminal law but must be 'autonomously construed' on the basis of the normative framework of international law. This survey of four issues that fall on the inquisitorial/adversarial divide shows that, while ICC cases continue to cite national practices rooted in either model of criminal justice, the key arguments that have guided the Court's choices have been anchored on the foundational norms of the Rome Statute and on practical and historical factors specific to the ICC. The debate between the inquisitorial and adversarial models have surely continued, but no longer as a contest of which system is better than the other, but as a question of which practice or principle is more aligned to the ICC's structure and compatible with its foundational norms.

---

81 Rome Statute, Preamble.

CHAPTER 13

# Reflecting on the Rights of the Defense at the International Criminal Court: the Importance of Ensuring Fair Trials to Deliver Exemplary Justice

*Jennifer Naouri and Dov Jacobs*

## 1 Introduction*

The rights of the Defence represent one of the cornerstones of any democratic judicial system and are enshrined in regional[1] and international human rights instruments.[2] The way that a society treats those accused of even the most terrible crimes is arguably one of the surest symbolic signs of the maturity of that society. Indeed, when the popular pressure will push naturally towards convictions, the collective choice to uphold the presumption of innocence and its corollary, that is the obligation resting on the Prosecutor to prove the charges beyond reasonable doubt, is a recognition that there can be no judicial system that provides justice for all, fairly and legitimately, that does not include the role of the Defence and gives it all the procedural tools required to fulfill its mission. This is true of any domestic system respectful of due process and fairness, and should also be true at the supranational level, in the construction of an international justice system.

Indeed, ever since the Nuremberg trial, it has been claimed by the promoters of international justice that its legitimacy is premised on respect of the rights of the Accused. For Robert Jackson, the Chief Prosecutor in Nuremberg, respect for the rights of the Accused was all the more necessary in order to

* All views expressed here represent solely the views of the authors and not the institutions they work for.

1 Convention for the Protection of Human Rights and Fundamental Freedoms (European Convention on Human Rights, as amended) (signed 4 November 195, entered into force 2 September 1953) 213 UNTS 211, Article 6; American Convention on Human Rights, 'Pact of San José' (signed 22 November 1969, entered into force 18 July 1978) 1144 UNTS 123, Article 8; African Charter on Human and Peoples' Rights (signed 27 June 1981, entered into force 21 October 1986) 1520 UNTS 217, Article 7; Arab Charter on Human Rights (signed 22 May 2004, entered into force 15 March 2008), Article 16.

2 International Covenant on Civil and Political Rights (adopted 16 December 1966, entered into force 23 March 1976) 999 UNTS 171, Article 14.

 | DOI:10.1163/9789004529939_014

contrast with the practice during the Nazi regime itself: 'But they do have a fair opportunity to defend themselves-a favor which these men, when in power, rarely extended to their fellow countrymen'.[3] Indeed, denial of the principle of legality is a common feature of totalitarian regimes, and the Nazi regime was no exception, with the 1935 Penal Code providing for a person to be punished based on the fact that they would be 'deserving of punishment according to the fundamental idea of a penal law and the sound perception of the people'.[4]

Since Nuremberg, all other international tribunals have recognised, in principle, the importance of the respect for the rights of the Defence. The Statutes of these tribunals all formally recognise a series of rights for the Defence. As for the principle of legality, while it was not explicitly enshrined in their statutes, it was considered that it should be applied. For example, the UN Secretary General Report on the creation of the ICTY claimed without any ambiguity that 'the application of the principle *nullum crimen sine lege* requires that the international tribunal should apply rules of international humanitarian law which are beyond any doubt part of customary law'.[5] This pronouncement was followed by some recognition of the principle in the case law of the tribunal.[6] Similarly, the Appeals Chamber for the Special Tribunal for Lebanon noted that the principle of legality, which is in many ways the cornerstone for the protection of the rights of the Defence, was to be considered as a jus cogens norm of international law.[7] Finally, the Rome Statute for the International

3 Opening Statement before the International Military Tribunal, by Justice R H Jackson, Chief of Counsel for the United States (21 November 1945) <https://www.roberthjackson.org/speech-and-writing/opening-statement-before-the-international-military-tribunal/> accessed 30 April 2023.

4 'Whoever commits an action which the law declares to be punishable or which is deserving of punishment according to the fundamental idea of a penal law and the sound perception of the people, shall be punished. If no determinable penal law is directly applicable to the action, it shall be punished according to the law, the basic idea of which fits it best'. (Amendment to §2 of the German Penal Code, enacted by the National Socialist regime in 1935. Translation by Lawrence Preuss; L Preuss, 'Punishment by Analogy in National Socialist Penal Law' (1935–1936) 26 *Journal of the American Institute of Criminal Law and Criminology* 847, 847).

5 Report of the UN Secretary-General Pursuant to Paragraph 2 of Security Council Res 808 (1993), UN Doc S/25704 (3 May 1993), para. 34.

6 For an overview of the relevant case-law, see K S Gallant, *The Principle of Legality in International and Comparative Law* (Cambridge: Cambridge University Press 2009), 304–308. For examples of the, somewhat scant, specific reference to the strict construction of legal statutes, see W A Schabas, 'Interpreting the Statutes of the *ad hoc* tribunals' in LC Vorah et al. (eds), *Man's Inhumanity to Man: Essays on International Law in Honour of Antonio Cassese* (Kluwer Law International 2003) 847, 850.

7 Interlocutory Decision On The Applicable Law: Terrorism, Conspiracy, Homicide, Perpetration, Cumulative Charging, STL-11-01/I, AC, STL, 16 February 2011, para. 76.

Criminal Court formally includes the principle of legality, in a very clear manner: '1. A person shall not be criminally responsible under this Statute unless the conduct in question constitutes, at the time it takes place, a crime within the jurisdiction of the Court. 2. The definition of a crime shall be strictly construed and shall not be extended by analogy. In case of ambiguity, the definition shall be interpreted in favour of the person being investigated, prosecuted or convicted'.[8]

It would therefore appear that from Nuremberg to Rome and beyond, there has been an increased recognition of the principle of legality by international criminal jurisdictions, or, to put it in the words of the late Antonio Cassese, first President of the ICTY, and arguably one of the founding fathers of ICL, 'after the Second World War the doctrine of substantive justice [...] was gradually replaced by that of strict legality'.[9] More generally, respect for the rights of the Defense seems to be an accepted aspect of the work of international criminal tribunals.

It is in this context that, at the time of its creation, the International Criminal Court embodied a promise: to ensure fair and exemplary justice for all, in ways that would be recognized by all affected populations, Parties and participants involved in the proceedings. A model of justice that could inspire other criminal jurisdictions worldwide, allowing the Court's growing legitimacy to achieve universality. A model of justice, that could, through the principle of complementarity as enshrined in the preamble of the Rome Statute,[10] permit domestic jurisdictions to take ownership of justice process, in full respect of the rights of all involved, both Accused and participating victims.

More than twenty years after the entry into force of the Rome Statute, it is a perfect moment to reflect on the practice of the Court, and to ponder whether the International Criminal Court has delivered on its promise of delivering justice in full respect of the rights of the Defence. More precisely, are the proceedings before the International Criminal Court tangibly and inherently fair, and does the Court give the Defence the space it needs to serve its role?

8 Rome Statute of the International Criminal Court (signed 17 July 1998, entered into force 1 July 2002) 2187 UNTS 3 ('Rome Statute'), Article 22.

9 A Cassese, *International Criminal Law* 2nd edn (Oxford: Oxford University Press 2008) 40.

10 Preamble of the Rome Statute: 'Emphasizing that the International Criminal Court established under this Statute shall be complementary to national criminal jurisdictions'.

## 2 Taking a Look Back: the Rights of the Defence from Nuremberg to the ICTY

As the first international tribunal dealing with the prosecution of international crimes, the International Military Tribunal (IMT) was keenly faced with the question whether its Charter violated the principle of legality. The tribunal had jurisdiction over three crimes: crimes against peace,[11] war crimes[12] and crimes against humanity.[13] While the prosecution for war crimes could arguably be grounded in international law, given the decades-long history of the development of the laws of war, it is undeniably the case that both crimes against humanity and crimes against peace were new crimes the prosecution of which could be deemed to contradict the principle of legality. The defendants at Nuremberg did not fail to raise this challenge.[14]

In response to this challenge, the Tribunal attempted, particularly unconvincingly in the case of crimes against peace,[15] to ground these crimes in customary international law. Before doing so, however, it gave its own appraisal of the principle of legality:

> In the first place, it is to be observed that the maxim *nullum crimen sine lege* is not a limitation of sovereignty, but is in general a principle of justice. To assert that it is unjust to punish those who, in defiance of treaties

---

11 Article 6(a) Charter of the International Military Tribunal, Annex to the Agreement for the prosecution and punishment of the major war criminals of the European Axis (signed and entered into force 8 August 1945) 82 UNTS 279.

12 Ibid., Article 6(b).

13 Ibid., Article 6(c).

14 Cassese (n 9) 43. In relation to the possible criminal responsibility of individual members of criminal organisations, Eigon Kuruschok, the Counsel for the Reich Cabinet, linked the duty of the IMT to respect the principle of legality with its systematic violation by the Nazis: '[o]ne of the worst oppressions we in Germany suffered under the Nazi regime was the feeling of legal insecurity. [...] After the experience of the past we consider that the principle of justice in particular must be without compromise. One desires to live with the conviction that only he can lose his freedom whose criminal activity is established beyond question in a legal trial provided with all possible legal guarantees. That is why countless people look with eager expectation to the first tribunal which will help this principle to prevail, and be recognized by the world as an example-this principle which has been trampled under foot for years'. *Trial of the Major War Criminals before the International Military Tribunal, Nuremberg 14 November 1945 – 1 October 1946* (Nuremberg, IMT 1947), Proceedings 27 August 1946–1 October 1946, Vol XXII, 126.

15 On this issue, see T Weigend, '"In General a Principle of Justice": The Debate on the "Crime against Peace" in the Wake of the Nuremberg Judgment' (2012) 10 *Journal of International Criminal Justice* 41.

> and assurances, have attacked neighbouring states without warning is obviously untrue, for in such circumstances the attacker must know that he is doing wrong, and so far from it being unjust to punish him, it would be unjust if his wrong were allowed to go unpunished. Occupying the positions they did in the Government of Germany, the defendants, or at least some of them, must have known of the treaties signed by Germany, outlawing recourse to war for the settlement of international disputes; they must have known that they were acting in defiance of all international law when in complete deliberation they carried out their designs of invasion and aggression. On this view of the case alone, it would appear that the maxim has no application to the present facts.[16]

It is clear from this description[17] that the judges of the IMT were willing to ground convictions in the fact that the defendants should have known that their conduct was 'wrong', rather than just illegal, thus bringing in a moral evaluation of the conduct in addition to the legal one. In stating the principle in this way, the tribunal echoed the sentiment of Robert Jackson, the American Prosecutor in Nuremberg, who affirmed in his opening statement:

> When I say that we do not ask for convictions unless we prove crime, I do not mean mere technical or incidental transgression of international conventions. *We charge guilt on planned and intended conduct that involves moral as well as legal wrong*. And we do not mean conduct that is a natural and human, even if illegal, cutting of corners, such as many of us might well have committed had we been in the defendants' positions. It is not because they yielded to the normal frailties of human beings that we accuse them. It is their abnormal and inhuman conduct which brings them to this bar.[18]

The Nuremberg Trial was therefore very cleary designed as carrying a moral condemnation of the accused, not only as a symbolic consequence of a guilty

16 *Judgment of the Nuremberg International Military Tribunal 1946* (1947) 41 AJIL 172, para. 444.

17 On the ambiguities of the various versions of the judgment in French, English and Russian, see G Acquaviva, 'At the Origins of Crimes Against Humanity Clues to a Proper Understanding of the Nullum Crimen Principle in the Nuremberg Judgment' (2011) 9 *Journal of International Criminal Justice* 881.

18 *Trial of the Major War Criminals before the International Military Tribunal* (n 14) 102 (emphasis added).

verdict, which is in itself uncontroversial, as criminal trials necessarily carry this moral symbolic dimension, but *within* the actual working of the tribunal, which is certainly more problematic.

At the ICTY, despite the nominal attachement to the rights of the Defence and the principle of legality, the case law of the rapidlly confirmed the tendency to conflate moral and legal condemnation as a basis for determining the content of the prohibitions, in continued violation of a principled application of the requirements of legality.

In *Tadić*, the Appeals Chamber, when considering the application of prohibitions of certain means and methods of warfare to non-international armed conflicts, famously adopted the following reasoning: 'Indeed, elementary considerations of humanity and common sense make it preposterous that the use by States of weapons prohibited in armed conflicts between themselves be allowed when States try to put down rebellion by their own nationals on their own territory. What is inhumane, and consequently proscribed, in international wars, cannot but be inhumane and inadmissible in civil strife'.[19]

This claim, as a basis for prohibition, is hardly reconcilable with any of the requirements of the customary law process. In the following paragraphs the Appeals Chamber gave only a handful of examples of alleged *opinio juris*, which mostly related to the reaction of the European Union and the US to the use of chemicals weapons against the Kurds in Iraq and could not possibly be indicative of a general view of a sufficient number of States. The only example of State practice given is a 1972 Nigerian Supreme Court decision which related only to perfidy.[20] This is undoubtedly a weak demonstration of the existence of a customary norm, but even this minimal effort is sometimes completely absent. For example, in *Kupreskic*, the Trial Chamber, found that the Martens Clause[21] illustrated the fact that 'principles of humanitarian law may emerge through a customary process under the pressure of the demands

19 Decision on the Defence motion for interlocutory appeal on jurisdiction, *Tadić*, IT-94-1-A, AC, ICTY, 2 October 1995, para. 119.

20 Ibid., para. 125.

21 This clause was introduced in the 1899 Hague Convention on the Customs of War on Land and states that: 'Until a more complete code of the laws of war is issued, the High Contracting Parties think it right to declare that in cases not included in the Regulations adopted by them, populations and belligerents remain under the protection and empire of the principles of international law, as they result from the usages established between civilized nations, from the laws of humanity and the requirements of the public conscience'. 1899 Hague Convention II With Respect To The Laws And Customs Of War On Land and its annex: Regulations concerning the Laws and Customs of War on Land. The Hague, 29 July 1899 (signed 29 July 1899, entered into force 4 September 1900).

of humanity or the dictates of public conscience, even where State practice is scant or inconsistent'[22] and then applied it to the question of reprisals against civilians. It should be noted that the Trial Chamber earlier rejected the direct application of the Martens Clause as a source of ICL.[23] This practice of nominal adherence to traditional criteria of customary international law has been noted in the literature,[24] and, as pointed out by Robert Cryer, this illustrates the fact that international tribunals, while adopting a natural law perspective, usually veil it in a positivist reasoning.[25]

Another example: in the *Čelebići* Judgment, the Trial Chamber even went further, and one could even argue backwards to Nuremberg, when it found it justified that the principle of legality be applied differently at the international level than at the domestic level: 'It could be postulated, therefore, that the principles of legality in international criminal law are different from their related national legal systems with respect to their application and standards. They appear to be distinctive, in the obvious objective of maintaining a balance between the preservation of justice and fairness towards the accused and taking into account the preservation of world order'.[26] This statement was problematic in many ways.

From a theoretical point of view, one can challenge the idea that the societal role of criminal law in a domestic and international system is so different. Indeed, criminal law anywhere has a function of regulating socially unacceptable behaviour and restore public order.[27] Alleging a difference between the domestic and the international level to justify a more laxist approach to the principle of legality is a way for both the legislator and the judge to hide behind a falsely 'objective' reason for some decisions that might otherwise be difficult to justify and more importantly to deflect part of the responsibility for the consequences of adopting such decisions, by using the shield of the 'nature' of

22 Judgment, *Kupreškić et al.*, IT-95-16-T, TC II, ICTY, 14 January 2000, para. 527.

23 Ibid., para. 525.

24 See for example, L van den Herik, 'The Decline of Customary International Law as a Source of International Criminal Law' in C Bradley (ed), *Custom's Future: International Law in a Changing World* (Cambridge University Press, 2016) 230–252.

25 R Cryer, 'The Philosophy of International Criminal Law' in A Orakhelashvili (ed), *Research Handbook on the Theory and History of International Law* (Edward Elgar Publishing 2011) 232–267, 250.

26 Judgment, *Čelebići Case*, IT-96-21-T, TC, ICTY, 16 November 1998, para. 403–405.

27 On this, see D Jacobs, 'International Criminal Law' in J d'Aspremont and J Kammerhofer (eds), *International Legal Positivism in a Post-Modern World* (Cambridge: Cambridge University Press, 2014) 451–477.

the system to avoid having to accept putting forward personal (and subjective) moral reasons in the context of the decision making process.

From a practical point of view, such a statement puts the Defence in a difficult position: how can the rights of the Defence be any match to the "preservation of world order"? Moreover, this has a practical impact on the perception of the role of the Defence in the proceedings: if the rights of the defence are to be balanced with the 'preservation of world order', it follows that a Defendant (or his Counsel) advocating for a better respect of the rights of the Accused could automatically be perceived as going against world order.

## 3 Taking a Look Now: the Rights of the Defence at the ICC

### 3.1 *The Rights of the Defence within the Proceedings*

The primary purpose of the criminal trial is to determine, after an adversarial process, if the Prosecution has proven the guilt of the accused "beyond reasonable doubt", as provided for in in Article 66 of the Rome Statute. The fact that the burden of proof rests on the Prosecutor is a consequence of the presumption of innocence[28] and should the Prosecution not be in a capacity to meet that burden, this must naturally lead to an acquittal. In this sense, it is important to insist on the fact that the default setting throughout the trial is the innocence of the person that is being prosecuted, and this remains true until a final judgment. This means that any doubt must favor the Accused and lead to his or her acquittal, as required by the presumption of innocence.

Ensuring a fair process also entails that the Accused must benefit from adequate time and facilities[29] to review the evidence submitted by the Prosecution and the modalities for examining such evidence. In that regard, adversarial proceedings allow the evidence to be tested fairly and equitably.

To that end, the Defence must be able to use all existing procedural tools available to it. The Rome Statute provides for several of them, including the possibility for the Defence to conduct investigations, to hold confirmation of charge hearings to ensure that only cases in which there are substantial grounds to believe that the accused committed the crimes charged would be referred for trial, pre-trial review of the case presented by the Prosecution.

To safeguard the right to a fair trial, the Court must give the Defence the time to use those tools. One difficulty that needs to be highlighted in that

28 Rome Statue, Article 66.

29 Rome Statute, Article 67.

respect is that there is a continuous tension between allow the Defense sufficient time to prepare, which includes benefitting from sufficient time to analyse the evidence and investigate, and the increased pressure to accelerate the proceedings.

Can we say that this acceleration has been achieved at the expense of the rights of the accused, especially the right to address fundamental questions before the judges in an adversarial manner?

The answer is obviously nuanced: Indeed, the right to a fair trial includes the expeditious conduct of the proceedings, and one should not endorse non-streamlined and needlessly lengthy proceedings. However, we should not forget that the expeditious conduct of the proceedings is, first and foremost, a right of the accused and that one should not use it to the accused's detriment.

Indeed, it is unoriginal to say that international criminal trials are long and expensive. Each year, representatives of international courts must present solid arguments to donors to justify the budget of the institution. This financial pressure is a constant concern in the daily bureaucratic workings of international courts. As a consequence, while it is highly problematic it is no surprise that this concern finds its way in the judicial arena itself. This is done through a loose use of the concept of 'expeditiousness'. While this concept can be traditionally linked to the right of the Accused to be tried without undue delay, Judges have developed a notion of expeditiousness that goes beyond that in the context of the trial management function of the Chamber. As a result, expeditiousness, which is a right of the Accused, has often been used to limit other rights of the Accused.

Such a situation arose repeatedly in all international tribunals, be it at the ICTR,[30] the SCSL[31] or the ICC. In the *Katanga* case, Trial Chamber II considered that it was justified to limit the possibility for an Accused to present admissibility challenges in order to protect the interests of said Accused.[32] The *Gbagbo* trial at the ICC provides a perfect illustration of this tendency. In that trial, a number of practices have been justified by the Trial Chamber solely in order to expedite the proceedings: the use of video-links *in lieu* of live testimony in Court[33] which do not allow for the same interaction with

30 See Decision in the matter of proceedings under Rule 15*bis*(D), *Nyiramasuhuko et al.*, ICTR-98-42-T, TC II, ICTR, 15 July 2003.

31 Decision on Presentation of Witness Testimony on Moyamba Crime Base, *Norma*, SCSL-04-14-T, TC I, SCSL, 1 March 2005.

32 On this, see D Jacobs, 'The Importance of Being Earnest: The Timeliness of the Challenge to Admissibility in Katanga' (2010) 23 *Leiden Journal of International Law* 331, 340.

33 Version publique expurgée des 'observations de la Défense présentées à la suite de l'ordonnance de la Chambre "on the further conduct of the proceedings" du 9 février 2018

the witness; the admission of prior recorded testimony for about 40% of Prosecution witnesses—in some cases under Rule 68(2)(b) without the witness even being cross-examined by the Defence; the over-use of bar table motions—the Prosecutor in that case has asked that about 70% of his documentary evidence be introduced by bar table motions[34]—which means that the evidence will not have been tested in Court through a witness. These decisions have undoubtedly sped up the proceedings, but to the detriment of fundamental Defence rights, most notably the right of the Defence to challenge the evidence in Court.

More importantly, these developments have reduced the importance of the courtroom in the process, and by extension the publicity of debates. It is very difficult to follow a trial for an outside observer, if a large number of witnesses are in fact not called to testify in court and instead have their prior recorded testimony introduced and if most of the evidence is difficult in complicated and technical bar table litigation rather than being discussed in open court. To this must be added the fact that there is currently, at cases at the ICC, an extensive use of in-court protective measures, which often entail considerable use of private or closed sessions, which means that the live testimony will be equally difficult to follow.

Such opacity is not only a direct threat to the right of the Accused to get a public hearing, which is a fundamental right of the Accused,[35] but also undermines the broader pedagogic objective of international criminal courts towards those populations most affected by the proceedings in the situation countries. Indeed, the creation of the International Criminal Court is premised on the idea that conducting trials following periods of civil strife will contribute to establishing an accurate historical record of what happened in order to contribute to the overall transitional justice objective of reconciliation. To achieve this goal, the local population must be able to take ownership of the proceedings, which necessarily means that it be able to follow them. This is not possible if the evidence and testimony are discussed in private session or not even discussed in the courtroom at all.

---

(ICC-02/11-01/15-1124)' (ICC-02/11-01/15-1157-Conf), *Gbagbo and Blé Goudé, Situation in the Republic of Côte d'Ivoire*, ICC-02/11-01/15-1157-Red, Gbagbo Defence, ICC, 2 May 2018, para. 86.

34 Ibid., para. 91.

35 Rome Statute, Article 64; Judgment, *Gautrin and others v. France*, Applications No 21257/93, 21258/93, 21259/93, 21260/93, ECtHR, 20 May 1998, para. 42; Judgment, *Belashev v. Russia*, Application No 28617/03, ECtHR, 4 December 2008, para. 79.

### 3.2 *Respect for the Rights of the Defense within the Institution*

Historically, the Defence has had very little institutional recognition in international tribunals. In Nuremberg, the lack of consideration and institutional independence for the Defence was such that the Prosecutor did not see any problem in proposing to both nominate Defence Counsel and call witnesses for them, as recalled by Telford Taylor.[36] At the ad hoc tribunals, Defence issues were dealt with by a sub-office of the Registry that was also in charge of detention matters.[37] There was no mechanism by which the voice of the Defence could be heard within the institution. The ICTY famously provided a small room to share among Defence teams and it took years for the tribunal to gradually integrate the Defence in the various discussions. This only took place after Defence Counsel organised under an association, the ADC-ICTY ('Association of Defence Counsel practicing before the ICTY'), which allowed its voice to be heard.

At the ICC, the same path was followed. In the founding documents (Statute and Rules of Procedure and Evidence), there is no provision giving the Defence a specific voice within the institution. While the Statute recognises the Prosecution as an organ of the Court,[38] no such recognition is afforded to the Defence. The Rules merely provide that Defence matters are under the responsibility of the Registry.[39] It is only in the Regulations of the Registry that the creation of a Defence office was provided for.[40] The existence of this Defence office does not however change the fact that the Defence is not given the position that it would deserve in the institution.

In recent years, the creation of the International Criminal Court Bar Association (ICCBA) and its recognition by the Assembly of State Parties[41] as the representative body of Counsel (and their support staff) representing

36 T Taylor, *The Anatomy of the Nuremberg Trials: A Personal Memoir* (New York: Alphred A. Knopf, 1992), 144.

37 F Roux, *Justice internationale: La Parole est à la Défense* (Indigène Editions, 2016), 51.

38 Rome Statute, Article 34.

39 Rules of Procedure and Evidence of the International Criminal Court, PCNICC/2000/1/Add.1, adopted 9 September 2002 by the ASP, ICC-ASP/1/3, 3–10 September 2002 (First Session of the ASP), Rule 20.

40 On this, see X-J Keita, C Baugas, and G Danhoui, 'Les Droits de la Defense et L'Egalite Des Armes, Sous le Prisme D'Une Institution Nouvelle, le Bureau du Conseil Public Pour la Defense de la Cour Penale Internationale' (2006) 14 *African Yearbook of International Law* 145–169.

41 'ICCBA Officially Recognised by the ICC Assembly of States Parties', ICCBA Press Release (12 December 2019) <https://www.iccba-abcpi.org/post/iccba-officially-recognised-by-the-icc-assembly-of-states-parties> accessed 30 April 2023.

both Accused and Victims at the ICC has increased the visibility of the Defence within the institution, and that is a welcome development.

One last aspect of institutional recognition of the Defence needs to be addressed, that of the legal aid system. Twenty years after the Statute entered into force, the reform of the Court legal assistance system is still ongoing. It is now clear that the principle of equality of arms is in jeopardy.

As noted in the final report of the 'the Independent Expert Review of the International Criminal Court and the Rome Statute System', the legal aid system's goal and purpose is to ensure adequate representation of the Accused and respect for the principle of equality of arms, as a key component of the right to a fair trial.[42] Yet, today the means available to the Defence do not suffice anymore to ensure the equality of arms. The gap between the legal teams of the Defence and the Prosecution is hard to ignore, with basic compositions of Defence teams being inadequate to deal with the volume of evidence to be analysed and the amount of work to be done; and with members of the Defence team being paid half the same amount as members of the opposite team who have the same responsibilities. In the same vein, there is also the issue of equal working conditions between the Defence and the Prosecution, which is essential for realizing the equality of arms. Members of both legal teams must have identical working conditions. While Defense team members have the same responsibilities as their counterparts, they do not benefit from the same social protections (maternity leave, sick leave, official resting periods to prevent burnout, etc.). Such a reality hinders the realization of the principle of the equality of arms and a fair reform of the legal system should be a priority for all stakeholders.

In an era in which the Court is working on a strategy to improve its employees' working conditions and work culture,[43] as well as promoting gender equality,[44] it is crucial to involve the Defence in those debates.

---

42 Independent Expert Review of the International Criminal Court and the Rome Statute System: Final Report—30 September 2020, ICC-ASP/19/16, 9 November 2020 (Nineteenth Session of the ASP), Findings 812–816.

43 Report of the Court on Human Resources Management, ICC-ASP/18/4, 25 July 2019 (Eighteenth Session of the ASP), para. 12, *Engagement and Wellbeing Framework*: 'The well-being framework is not a project intended to be "finalized"; it is a value which the Court's leadership will continue to prioritize and develop and in which staff will continue to engage. With this framework, the aim is to ensure a culture of openness, support and development, in which the Court is committed to caring for its staff and staff members are equally committed to caring for their own well-being in the workplace'.

44 Ibid., para. 124.

Today, the case law provides that it is not for the judges to ensure that proceedings in a specific case allow members of the legal teams to get some resting periods, including during court recess. It is, therefore, necessary to find ways to offer working conditions that would foster genuine equality between the parties, with the aim of providing fair justice for all stakeholders.

### 3.3 *Respect for the Rights of the Defence in the General Public: the Responsibility of the Court*

Given the complex political nature of the situations which the International Criminal Court deals with, outside attention and more particularly media attention usually occurs well in advance of the court processes themselves. This necessarily taints any perception of the Accused, especially when they are high ranking military commanders or well-known political figures. Most international defendants will have been 'pre-judged' by the media and the general public, based on the role that people understand them to have had in the State apparatus. As a result, the expectation is that there will be a conviction, and the higher the position, the higher that expectation. Who would ever expect Muammar Ghadaffi, Saddam Hussein or tomorrow, Assad or Bashir to be acquitted? For such political figures, international trials are purely symbolic; a formal validation of what everybody thinks they already know about what they did. There is little room for concern about the rights of the Accused in such a context even though no fair, valid legal system can proceed without continued concern for such individual rights. In other words, there is often a presumption of culpability that displaces the presumption of innocence.

In this perspective, one can observe that the 'justice' of the international criminal trial is not generally measured by the fairness of the proceedings, but by the favourable outcome from the victims' perspective. Proof of that can be found in any reaction to convictions and acquittals. A conviction is often labelled by the advocates of international justice (such as NGOs and policy makers) as a 'victory for Justice',[45] whereas you will rarely hear such claim in the event of an acquittal (other than by Counsel for the acquitted person), despite the fact that an acquittal after a fair process should normally also be considered as a 'victory for Justice'.

In this context, international tribunals, and in particular the International Criminal Court, have a responsibility to systematically highlight the importance of the rights of the Defence in their public discourse.

---

45 See for example, in relation to the Taylor Judgment: D Jacobs, 'Taylor Judgment: "A Victory for Justice"', (*Spreading the Jam*, 26 September 2013) <https://dovjacobs.com/2013/09/26/taylor-judgment-a-victory-for-justice/> accessed 30 April 2016.

This has not always been the case. A symbolic example at the ICTY is a poster that everyone could see in the lobby of the tribunal, which shows two sets of handcuffs, one in a rudimentary fabric—used by some perpetrators against some victims of the conflict—and one in stainless steel—to be used on ICTY Defendants—, with the following text: 'bringing perpetrators to justice and justice to victims'. This illustrates perfectly the fact that justice for the Defendant means putting him in handcuffs, while the 'real' justice is for the victims. Moreover, beyond grand statements about the rights of the Defence, this poster vehiculates a simple 'eye for an eye' law of talion message. Needless to say that there is little room for the rights of the Defence in such a framework of analysis.

The ICC, as an institution, has shown considerable progress in that respect. Media campaigns on twitter regularly feature the Defence and the importance of guaranteeing fair trials rights.[46] Representatives of the Defence (in recent years the President of the ICCBA) are systematically invited to official events, be it the opening of the judicial year,[47] the swearing in of new judges,[48] or official celebrations, such as the one which led to the current publication.[49]

## 4 Conclusion: Taking a Look Forward

From the Defence's perspective, the ICC's legal framework provides several tools that the Defence can use to protect the right to a fair trial.

The practice of the last twenty years shows that if the Defence can use such tools, it ultimately helps the Court achieve its mission to provide justice for all in a fair manner.

46 From the ICC Twitter Account, 16 May 2020 <https://twitter.com/IntlCrimCourt/status/1261671020919996418?s=20>; 14 October 2018 <https://twitter.com/IntlCrimCourt/status/1051472817554944005?s=20>; 20 January 2022 <https://twitter.com/IntlCrimCourt/status/1484202072048381953?s=20>.

47 'International Criminal Court Marks Opening of the Judicial Year 2023', ICC Press Release (20 January 2023) <https://www.icc-cpi.int/news/international-criminal-court-marks-opening-judicial-year-2023>.

48 'Six new judges sworn in today at the seat of the International Criminal Court', ICC Press Release (10 March 2021) <https://www.icc-cpi.int/news/six-new-judges-sworn-today-seat-international-criminal-court-1>.

49 Conference marking the 20th anniversary of the entry into force of the Rome Statute of the International Criminal Court, 'International Criminal Court at 20: Reflections on the Past, Present and the Future' <https://www.icc-cpi.int/icc-20a-cpi>.

A legal proceeding is an evolving process that needs to adapt to different realities and cannot be generalized: each case before the Court has its own specificities. This is precisely the most valuable characteristic of the Court: Its capacity to adapt to different situations to provide justice for all parties involved.

The position of the Defense in the overall system is a difficult one, between centre an periphery. Indeed, as noted by one of the authors of this chapter: 'An effective Defence is a mirror that is put up to international justice's face and that shows it what is not working. Like the Queen in the Brothers Grimm *Snow White* fairy tale, international justice does not want to hear that she is not the fairest of them all. However, looking away from, ignoring or breaking the mirror will not change that fact. As long as international justice is content with basking in the illusion of its own fairness, it will never achieve any of its claimed ambitions, let alone respect the rights of the Defence'.[50]

The reality that must not be forgotten is that the Prosecutor, the Defence, Victims, and Judges all in the same boat, the boat of International Criminal Justice. Ensuring that all protagonists of the trial have the necessary means to guide the ship is ultimately for the benefit of a fair and legitimate justice, a justice that is acceptable for the international community and suits the needs of affected communities.

Therefore, we should not lose sight of those instruments, which have been enshrined in the Rome Statute for a reason. We must stay true to both the letter and the spirit of the Statute and correct some practices that currently undermine the rights of the Defence. This is how we can fulfill the promise made twenty years ago concerning the Defence: the promise of exemplary justice.

---

50 D Jacobs, 'Neither Here nor There: The Position of the Defence in International Criminal Tribunals' in Heller et al. (eds), *The Oxford Handbook of International Criminal Law* (Oxford University Press 2020), 87.

CHAPTER 14

# Victim Participation at the ICC—Putting the Concept in (Good) Practice

*Philipp Ambach*

## 1 Introduction

The victim participation regime at the ICC is hailed as one of the cornerstone achievements of the Rome Statute *vis-à-vis* its international criminal justice predecessors, most importantly the International Military Tribunals in Nuremberg and Tokyo in 1946 and 1947, respectively, as well as the two UN *ad hoc*-Tribunals ICTY and ICTR in the mid-nineties of the last century. The ICC is often characterised as a victim-centred court where the concepts of satisfaction, reconciliation and repair stand at equal footing with the traditional retributive prism of criminal justice. Yet, only a few provisions in the Rome Statute deal with victim participation across the entire life cycle of a situation before the ICC, from the (initiation of) investigation to potential reparations after the criminal process.[1] Even though these provisions have received concretisation in the ICC's legal texts such as the Rules of Procedure and Evidence and the Regulations of the Court (and the Registry), a lot has been left to those applying the law in order to transform the concept into practical implementation across the different procedural phases before the ICC.

This contribution attempts to highlight how two key pillars constituting the victim participation regime at the ICC have evolved in the more recent years of practical application. The first pillar pertains quite literally to victims' access to the ICC, i.e. when and how does the ICC connect victim communities across situation countries with the ICC as a justice concept, as an institution and as a courtroom. The second pillar constitutes victims' rights and possibilities in terms of interaction in courtroom proceedings, i.e. what can victims

1 Relevant provisions are: article 15(3) for victims' views and concerns on the Prosecutor's request to the Pre-Trial Chamber to initiate an investigation *proprio motu*; 19(3) for victims' observations to the Court on a question on jurisdiction or admissibility; 68(3) on victims' participation in (pre-trial, trial and appeal) proceedings; and 75(3) for victims' observations on reparations. Finally, although not strictly bestowing any participatory rights on victims, article 79 of the Statute stipulates the establishment of the Trust Fund for Victims (through the Assembly of States Parties).

 | DOI:10.1163/9789004529939_015

*do*—through their legal representative—once they have gained access to relevant court processes. Both pillars—access to the ICC and legal representation in the proceedings—have gone through a very dynamic process of calibration, standard-setting and fine tuning. So much that, as this contribution posits, we are today looking at a rather sophisticated and thoughtful transposition of the concept into practice, even if a number of key challenges remain—which shall also be briefly addressed.

## 2 Setting the Stage—How the Drafters Shaped the Concept in the Legal Framework

During the negotiations that led to the adoption of the Rome Statute of the International Criminal Court in July 1998, the issue of participation of victims in the proceedings was somewhat peculiar. On the one hand, there was support from human rights activists and the broader civil society landscape for the inclusion of victim participation into the criminal process at the ICC.[2] This was due to the growing consensus that its non-inclusion in the statutes of the two UN *ad hoc* Tribunals ICTY and ICTR had been a missed opportunity[3] (or, put more bluntly, a failure). On the other hand, there was a strong urge by many negotiators to focus on the 'core business' of the ICC, namely to process criminal trials. Negotiations on the very fundamental pillars of the latter were purported to be complex enough, and there was fear that if negotiations became to multi-facetted and complex, the whole project would fail.

In addition, and specifically on the issue of victims' participatory rights in the criminal process, different legal traditions led to diverse views on its scope and timing. While the continental-European national legal tradition pointed towards a rather powerful and inclusive participation regime, Anglo-Saxon criminal justice systems foresaw a much reduced role in the criminal process proper.[4]

2 See Amnesty International, 'The International Criminal Court: Making the right choices, Part II: Organizing the court and guaranteeing a fair trial', AI Index: IOR 40/11/97 (July 1997), at <https://www.amnesty.org/en/>; REDRESS, 'Promoting the Right to Reparation for the Survivors of Torture: What Role for a Permanent International Criminal Court?' (1997); Human Rights Watch, 'Commentary for the Preparatory Committee on the Establishment of an International Criminal Court' (August 1996); see also C Safferling, G Petrossian, *Victims Before the International Criminal Court: Definition, Participation, Reparation* (Springer, 2021), 98ff, 101.

3 C Jorda, J de Hemptienne, 'The Status and Role of the Victim' in A Cassese, P Gaeta, J R W D Jones, *The Rome Statute of the International Criminal Court: A Commentary* (Oxford University Press 2002), 1399ff.; *see also* D Donat Cattin, in: *Ambos* Commentary (Beck 2022), Art. 68 para. 3.

4 Safferling/Petrossian (n 1) 103.

A compilation of the preparatory works for the drafting of article 68 of the Rome Statute[5] shows how only in 1996 – two years into negotiations on the Rome Statute - a provision on "Rights of the victims" was tabled (by France) before the Preparatory Committee as a 'Working Paper'.[6] It stipulated that the Registrar is to collect victims' submissions and transfer them to the 'Preliminary Investigations Chamber'.[7] This, however, did not yet entail any mention of victims' active participation in any judicial proceedings. Similarly, the issue of potential compensation to victims—while already addressed in the earlier works in 1994—remained a topic of diverging views and limited appetite for in-depth discussion. Only in 1997, proper discussions on both victim participation and reparations commenced.[8] On victim participation, New Zealand tabled for the first time the wording of today's article 68(3),[9] which was then also picked up by the *Zutphen* draft in 1998[10] and finally found its way into the Statute. Of note, in the documentation that accompanied negotiations over the years, the issue of victim participation remained somewhat hidden between key provisions on (victim-)witness protection in-and outside the courtroom. Today's article 68 of the Statute displays quite palpably, representing by the way one of the single most fundamental provisions in the Rome Statute regarding victims before the ICC with a wide array of regulatory content: from the general protection of witnesses and victims who appear before the Court, to provisions on specific vulnerabilities (sexual and gender violence and violence against children), specific protective measures in-and outside the courtroom (through the Victims and Witnesses Unit) including the disclosure of evidence, to the protection of state agents and confidential or sensitive information. And, somewhere in the middle of this comprehensive provision, the participation of

---

5 Annex A to 'OPCV's analysis of the notions of "victims" and of "victims who appear before the court" with Annexes', *Lubanga, Situation in the Democratic Republic of the Congo*, ICC-01/04-01/06-1063-AnxA, Office of Public Counsel for Victims, 7 December 2007.

6 Draft statute of the International Criminal Court: working paper submitted by France, A/AC.249/L.3, UNGA Preparatory Committee on the Establishment of an International Criminal Court, 6 August 1996.

7 A/AC.249/L.3. 6 August 1996.

8 D Donat Cattin, 'Art. 68', para. 11, in O Triffterer and K Ambos (eds), *The Rome Statute of the International Criminal Court: A Commentary* 3rd edn (CH Beck/Hart/Nomos 2016); Safferling/Petrossian (n 1) 101ff (104–113 specifically on reparations).

9 Non-Paper/WG.4/No. 19, 13 August 1997 as well as the revised version Non-Paper/WG.4/No. 19/Rev.l, 13 August 1997, in ICC-01/04-01/06-1063-AnxA (n 4) 15; see also Donat Cattin (n 6) para. 5.

10 Report of the Intersessional Meeting, submitted in Zutphen, The Netherlands, A/AC.249/1998/L.13, UNGA Preparatory Committee on the Establishment of an International Criminal Court 4 February 1998 <https://digitallibrary.un.org/record/250636>.

victims. Also for reparations, discussions started with two proposals tabled in 1997, one from France and one from the United Kingdom.[11] As for victim participation, the 1998 the *Zutphen* draft was the first text to address 'Compensation to Victims' as such.[12]

The image of victim participation standing between other key concepts of criminal proceedings—and actually being influenced by them—is not just an impression after reading Article 68 of the Statute, but also delineates the framework in which discussions on the topic were held (just) before the adoption of the Rome Statute. One faction advocated for an inclusive victim participation regime, underlining the need that the victims' access to the ICC and the proceedings needs to be meaningful; many negotiators held against a too 'aggressive' victim participation regime the need for a fair trial from the defence perspective in terms of equality of arms; victim participation should not become a *de facto* second entity leading incriminating evidence into the proceedings ('prosecutor *bis*'). Also, under no circumstances should victim participation features slow down the proceedings (thus affecting the inherent defence right to expedited proceedings against the accused—particularly in case of his/her detention, which can be considered as the rule before international courts and tribunals). In addition, some delegations (not *only* from a common law background) were afraid that with a too inclusive catalogue of procedural rights (including at the earliest stages), victims could challenge the Prosecutor on his or her choices or methods. Finally, negotiators that disfavoured a strong victim role in the proceedings also posited that victim participation should not be too resource-intensive since the limited funds available to the ICC should be focused on what they perceived as its core business—carry out criminal trials to bring the worst perpetrators of international crimes behind bars. Victim participation—and reparations—would be secondary to the ICC's obligation to investigate, arrest and try alleged criminals.[13]

The issue of victim participation therefore found itself in a peculiar corner amongst negotiators: not having been considered a fundamental item at the

---

11 *See M Bachrach*, "The Permanent International Criminal Court: an Examination of the Statutory Debate, in: ILSA Journal of International & Comparative Law Vol. 5, No. 139, at: https://core.ac.uk/download/pdf/51091731.pdf, pp. 139, 164 ff.*; F Benedetti/K Bonneau/ J L Washburn*, "Major Results of the Negotiations and the Evolution of International Criminal Law", in: Negotiating the International Criminal Court, Brill 2014, pp. 145–168; on the topic generally the Human Rights Watch "Commentary for the March-April Preparatory Committee Meeting", 1997, Section H, at: https://www.hrw.org/legacy/campaigns/icc/docs/icc0398.htm.

12 *M Bachrach* (n. 11) pp. 139, 165.

13 See, on the concept of 'core business' of the ICC, J S A Fulford, 'The Reflections of a Trial Judge' (2011) 22 *Criminal Law Forum* 215–223, 216.

earlier stages of negotiations, discussions on the topic were held rather late at PrepComm level; still, there was overwhelming agreement that *some* measure of victim participation would have to be part and parcel of a modern international criminal justice mechanism like the ICC. Finally, the concept had to amalgamate multiple—each of them legitimate—postulates by the founders of the system. One could paraphrase it as: 'make it meaningful, but in line with defence rights and, importantly, not too expensive and without any slowing effects on the proceedings'.

To an extent, today's wording of Article 68(3) of the Statute seems to take heed of some of the key concerns in: (i) making victims' participation an non-derogable feature of the ICC process, as well as the Chamber's obligation to actually consider these views and concerns ('*shall* permit their views and concerns to be presented *and considered*'); while at the same time (ii) leaving the 'when' as well as the 'how' to the judges' discretion, whereby said discretion needs to pay particular heed to the rights of the defence and the need of a fair and impartial trial.[14]

A closer look at Article 68(3) reveals thus that the drafters managed to codify a wealth of regulatory content in just a few lines, making particularly the first sentence of the provision a powerful and well-crafted piece of legislation:

> Where the personal interests of the victims are affected, the Court shall permit their views and concerns to be presented and considered at stages of the proceedings determined to be appropriate by the Court and in a manner which is not prejudicial to or inconsistent with the rights of the accused and a fair and impartial trial.[15]

Still, the provision leaves ample space to subordinate laws and/or jurisprudence on key questions: (i) who is a victim?; (ii) what are 'personal interests'?;

---

14 The full wording of Article 68(3) of the Statute is as follows: 'Where the personal interests of the victims are affected, the Court shall permit their views and concerns to be presented and considered at stages of the proceedings determined to be appropriate by the Court and in a manner which is not prejudicial to or inconsistent with the rights of the accused and a fair and impartial trial. Such views and concerns may be presented by the legal representatives of the victims where the Court considers it appropriate, in accordance with the Rules of Procedure and Evidence'. Rome Statute of the International Criminal Court (signed 17 July 1998, entered into force 1 July 2002) 2187 UNTS 3 ('the Statute').

15 It should be noted that the provision was not an invention by the ICC drafters; the main text was in fact taken from para. 6 b) of the UN General Assembly's 1985 Declaration of Basic Principles of Justice for Victims of Crime and Abuse of Power, UNGA Res 40/34 of 29 November 1985.

(iii) what is encompassed by 'views and concerns'?; and (iv) what are appropriate stages of proceedings? Also, the provision stays silent on any and all operational aspects of victim participation apart from stipulating that '[s]uch views and concerns may be presented by the legal representatives of the victims where the Court considers it appropriate'[16]—thus clarifying that the channel of communication between victims and the judges and parties in the courtroom are legal counsel.[17] Relevant provisions of a more operational nature in the ICC's legal texts shed some more light on the drafters' initial ideas of how the system could work—but they also leave a broad margin of (constructive) ambiguity or indeed empty space to be filled by practice and jurisprudence.

In the following, this contribution highlights with a number of examples how, it is suggested, the 'blanks' have been filled with sensible practice and jurisprudence regarding victims' access to the ICC throughout the different stages of proceedings. Another key aspect closely related to the access is the legal representation in relevant proceedings, arguably making the access meaningful (or not). This item can be assessed from the angle of the procedural tools at counsel's disposition, as well as on the selection/choice of counsel itself. The present contribution will focus, however, on victims' access to the Court first and foremost, as this area has traditionally received little attention and evaluation by academia and civil society, as opposed to the topic of legal representation. Observations on the latter shall therefore be brief and point to remaining challenges without claiming to be exhaustive.

## 3 Victims' Access to the Court throughout the Different Stages

### 3.1 *Article 15(3) Victim Consultation*

A first instance where the Court's legal texts do foresee a role for victims but leave the operational details unregulated actually precedes even the initiation of an investigation: if and where the Prosecutor decides to open an investigation proprio motu (i.e. on her/his own accord). Article 15(3) of the Statute stipulates that where 'the Prosecutor concludes that there is a reasonable basis to proceed with an investigation, he or she shall submit to the Pre-Trial Chamber

16 Article 68(3), second sentence, of the Statute.

17 Van den Wyngaert mentions Article 68(3) of the Statute as an example of 'constructive ambiguity'. C Van den Wyngaert, 'Victims before International Criminal Courts: Some Views and Concerns of an ICC Trial Judge' (2011) 44(1) *Case Western Reserce Journal of International Law* 475–496, 478; on the term see also K Kress, 'The Procedural Law of the International Criminal Court in Outline: Anatomy of a Unique Compromise' (2003) 1(3) *Journal of International Criminal Justice* 603–617, 605ff.

a request for authorization of an investigation'. Importantly, the provision prescribes that 'Victims may make representations to the Pre-Trial Chamber, in accordance with the Rules of Procedure and Evidence'.

#### 3.1.1 Public Consultation Process as the Rule

The reference in article 15(3) to the Rules actually points to Rule 50 of the RPE, which reiterates the Prosecutor's *general* duty to inform victims, unless exceptional circumstances absolve him from this duty. This was for instance the case in the Burundi situation, where the Prosecutor requested, in September 2017, the initiation of an investigation *proprio motu* by way of a confidential *ex parte* communication to the Chamber (for war crimes and crimes against humanity allegedly committed since 2015).[18] Pre-Trial Chamber III ultimately authorised the investigation two months later.[19] Of note, the Chamber issued with its decision an important clarification regarding victims' rights at this stage of proceedings: the Prosecutor had posited that article 15 does not afford any participatory *rights* to victims as such, referring to rule 50 of the RPE, 'which expressly relieves the Prosecution of its duty to provide notice to victims', thus leaving it in the Prosecutor's free discretion whether or not to allow for victims' views to be collected.[20] The Chamber considered the OTP position as 'legally untenable' and held that

> Article 15(3) of the Statute grants victims an independent, direct avenue to make representations before a Pre-Trial Chamber seized of a request for authorization of an investigation. [...] Thus, the Prosecutor's interpretation that rule 50(1) of the Rules makes the victims' rights set forth in article 15(3) of the Statute subject to the Prosecutor's decision on giving notice must be rejected.[21]

The Chamber further underlined the exceptional nature of *ex parte* proceedings under article 15(3).[22] It held that only where, upon the Prosecutor's

18 Request for authorisation of an investigation pursuant to article 15, *Situation in the Republic of Burundi*, ICC-01/17-X-5-US-Exp, OTP, ICC, 5 September 2017 ('OTP Burundi Request'). A public redacted version was notified on 16 November 2017 (ICC-01/17-5-Red).

19 Public Redacted Version of 'Decision Pursuant to Article 15 of the Rome Statute on the Authorization of an Investigation into the Situation in the Republic of Burundi', ICC-01/17-X-9-US-Exp, 25 October 2017, *Situation in the Republic of Burundi*, ICC-01/17-9-Red, PTC III, ICC, 9 November 2017 ('PTC Burundi Art. 15 Decision').

20 OTP Burundi Request, para. 12, cited in PTC Burundi Art. 15 Decision, para. 7.

21 PTC Burundi Art. 15 Decision, para. 9.

22 PTC Burundi Art. 15 Decision, para. 21 ('this exceptional procedure is not to be seen as replacing the procedural right accorded to victims under article 15(3) of the Statute').

substantiated request, 'the Chamber considers that notifying victims would pose a danger to the integrity of the investigation or the life or well-being of victims and witnesses', it would authorise the exclusion of victims' views.[23]

Fortunately, the *Burundi* example has indeed remained an exception to the rule. Both beforehand[24] and afterwards, the Prosecutor filed relevant requests publicly—including relevant 'notifications' to victims pursuant to rule 50(1) of the RPE—and therefore provided victims with an important platform to communicate their views and concerns to relevant Chambers.

### 3.1.2 Content and Timing

Already during the first article 15(3) proceedings in the *Kenya* situation in 2009, the Pre-Trial Chamber clearly carved out the Registry's role in the proceedings as the key entity to collect, bundle and report victims' 'representations' to the Chamber as per Rule 50(3) of the RPE.[25] More specifically, Pre-Trial Chamber II requested the Registry's Victims Participation and Reparations Section ('VPRS') to (1) receive and register victims' representations submitted either by individuals or representatives of affected groups (collective representation); (2) make

23 PTC Burundi Art. 15 Decision, para. 11. In the following, the Chamber considered that the security threats and risks indeed warranted an under seal *ex parte* process in the present proceedings (paras 12ff).

24 The first ever Article 15(3) process ensued in the Kenya situation with the Prosecutor's request to commence an investigation to the Pre-Trial Chamber. A second request preceding the Burundi situation was filed in the Georgia situation on 13 October 2015. See Request for authorisation of an investigation pursuant to Article 15, *Situation in the Republic of Kenya*, ICC-01/09-3, OTP, ICC, 26 November 2009 ('Kenya request'); Request for authorisation of an investigation pursuant to Article 15, *Situation in the Republic of Côte d'Ivoire*, ICC-02/11-3, OTP, ICC, 23 June 2011 ('Côte d'Ivoire request'); Corrected Version of 'Request for authorisation of an investigation pursuant to article 15', *Situation in Georgia*, ICC-01/15-4-Corr, OTP, ICC, 16 October 2015 ('Georgia request').

25 The Chamber clarified at that juncture that the term 'victim' used inAarticle 15(3) of the Statute and Rule 50(3) of the RPE is defined in Rule 85, and that 'representations made in accordance with article 15(3) of the Statute and rule 50(3) of the Rules must be confined to those who qualify as "victims" within the meaning of [rule 85]'. Order to the Victims Participation and Reparations Section Concerning Victims' Representations Pursuant to Article 15(3) of the Statute, *Situation in the Republic of Kenya*, ICC-01/09-4, PTC II, ICC, 10 December 2009 ('Kenya Order'), para. 7. VPRS victim assessments to the present day have heeded this important finding of the Chamber as all victim assessments carried out by the Section are against the standard set by Rule 85 and relevant clarifying jurisprudence (see e.g. Judgment on the appeals of The Prosecutor and The Defence against Trial Chamber I's Decision on Victims' Participation of 18 January 2008, *Lubanga, Situation in the Democratic Republic of the Congo*, ICC-01/04-01/06-143, AC, ICC, 11 July 2008).

an initial *prima facie* assessment of victim status under rule 85 of the RPE[26] for each individual and/or group submitting a communication; and (3) produce a consolidated report setting out the characteristics and views of victims.[27]

This and the 2011 ruling by Pre-Trial Chamber III in the Côte d'Ivoire situation have since set the general tone for subsequent article 15 procedures for the definition of the term 'victim' in Article 15 of the Statute (i.e. following the standard of rule 85 of the RPE);[28] the applicable standard of assessment for victims' representations; and the lead entity to administer the victim consultation process: the VPRS of the Registry.[29]

Interestingly, neither the legal texts themselves nor jurisprudence have provided detailed guidance as to what the term 'representation' is to entail. Article 15(1) and (2) refers to any records, documents or other information relevant to the Prosecutor's investigation as 'information'; the use of the word 'representation' in Article 15(3) thus seems to suggest that victims' submissions under this provision are not just another vehicle to submit 'information' as they can do that already under Article 15(1) in submitting relevant records to the Prosecutor directly.[30] The rules and regulations stay silent on the specific content of

---

26 The Chamber set the relevant evidentiary standard to observe by the VPRS as follows: 'conditions set out in rule 85 of the Rules should be assessed on the basis of the intrinsic coherence of the information given by the victim(s)', Kenya Order, para. 8. In 2011, Pre-Trial Chamber III referred to a '*prima facie* standard', Côte d'Ivoire Order, para. 10. This standard has since been used in every Article 15—and more recently Article 18—proceeding before the Pre-Trial Chambers.

27 Kenya Order, para. 9. Of note, the Chamber clearly pointed towards the concept of 'collective representation' which has proven to be a very important means for the VPRS to collect the views of often many thousands of potentially affected victims in a representative fashion in the short time window provided for the article 15 process. In the Afghanistan situation, the Registry transmitted altogether 237 collective representation forms on behalf of thousands of individuals, see Decision Pursuant to Article 15 of the Rome Statute on the Authorisation of an Investigation into the Situation in the Islamic Republic of Afghanistan, *Situation in the Islamic Republic of Afghanistan*, ICC-02/17-33, PTC II, ICC, 12 April 2019, para. 9 and references to the altogether seven Registry reports on the Article 15(3) exercise in fn 10.

28 See in particular clarifications of Pre-Trial Chamber III in 2011 on the required information from victims in their representations as to their victimhood under the rule 85 standard: Côte d'Ivoire Order, para. 10.

29 It is noted that in the Côte d'Ivoire situation, the Pre-Trial Chamber was somewhat less permissive regarding Registry activities within the notice period in gathering victims' views (see Côte d'Ivoire Order, para. 8). Later decisions of Pre-Trial Chambers returned to a more permissive stance (Afghanistan Order, paras 15, 16).

30 See the Prosecutor's portal to receive article 15 information here: https://www.icc-cpi.int/about/otp/otp-contact.

'representations'.[31] Records from the negotiations leading to the wording of Article 15(3) in the Rome Statute do not provide much elucidation other than that it was the agreed wording amongst the French-and Spanish-speaking delegations that tabled the wording at the time, in the broad understanding that the provision should enable victims to make submissions that tie to their particular interests at that stage of proceedings (following the general logic of Article 68(3) of the Statute). In the *Kenya* situation, the Chamber gave brief yet powerful guidance: it defined the content of 'representations in the context of article 15(3) of the Statute [as] whether [victims] wish to express their position on a possible investigation or not'.[32]

The Registry has made good use of this guidance in the more recent processes: first, in order to render the collection process most efficient, the VPRS introduced a standard 'representation form' which it then helped victims and victim groups to fill in and submit to the Registry. The simple, three-page form was created based on lessons learned from Article 15 processes in Kenya and Georgia. It was first put to use in the Afghanistan victim representation process in 2017, and subsequently in the Myanmar/Bangladesh article 15 proceeding in 2019, followed by the process before the Pre-Trial Chamber in The Philippines.[33] The form collects all relevant information allowing the VPRS to make its *prima facie* rule 85 assessment, and asks the key questions of victims on content:

31 The use of the term 'representations' (by a State) in article 72(7)(a)(i) points towards a submission on the merits / subject-matter of the issue at hand; a similar interpretation lends itself to victims' 'representations' on reparations as per article 75(3) of the Statute – to be heard during a court hearing as per article 76(3).

32 Kenya Order, para. 10.

33 As the form is not a 'standard form' pursuant to Regulation 23(2) of the Regulations of the Court, the VPRS has submitted the form for approval by each respective Pre-Trial Chamber in the past three Article 15(3) processes; see e.g. the most recent approval decision in this regard in the Philippines article 15(3) process in 2021: Order to the Victims Participation and Reparation Section Concerning Victims' Representations, *Situation in the Republic of the Philippines*, ICC-02/17-6, PTC III, ICC, 9 November 2017, para. 9, following the VPRS' confidential submission of the form in the Registry's Request for Extension of Notice Period and Submissions on Aspects Related to the Article 15(3) Process, *Situation in the Islamic Republic of Afghanistan*, ICC-02/17-3-Conf, PTC III, ICC, 7 November 2017 with two confidential annexes. A public redacted version of the request is also available, ICC-02/17-3-Red.

Do the victim(s) want the ICC Prosecutor to investigate [the relevant crimes subject to the situation for which the investigation is sought[34]]?

If the answer is yes, what do the victim(s) think the investigation should include (time period, location, crimes)?

If the victim(s) do not want an investigation to proceed, what concerns with regard to this investigation do victim(s) have (i.e. explain the victim(s') reasons against such an investigation).

Do the victim(s) have any additional views or concerns that they want to share with the Court?[35]

Of note, the VPRS has provided explicit guidance to victims on how to explain their "position on a possible investigation or not".[36] It solicits not only victims' submissions why they consider an investigation important/opportune—or not—; it also provides a space for victims to provide their views on the scope of a potential investigation (temporal, geographic and subject matter); and finally, an open question on additional views or concerns yields a platform for diverse supplementary observations that victims want to make. Guidelines are issued alongside these forms helping victims to fully understand the context of the exercise as well as fundamental matters such as the ICC's jurisdiction in a given situation and the—limited[37]—scope of the article 15(3) exercise compared to the victim participation scheme applicable during judicial proceedings against an accused person.[38] Forms and guidelines are issued in all relevant languages per situation; forms exist in various electronic formats enabling

34 E.g. for Myanmar/Bangladesh: crimes against humanity of deportation, other inhumane acts and persecution allegedly committed against the civilian Rohingya population in Myanmar; see the link to the form in the following footnote (n 33).

35 See, for instance, the victim representation form in use at the time for the Myanmar/Bangladesh Article 15(3) process: <https://www.icc-cpi.int/sites/default/files/itemsDocuments/vprs-Representation-form-Myanmar-ENG.pdf>; or the Philippines process: <https://www.icc-cpi.int/sites/default/files/itemsDocuments/vprs/Philippines/2021VictimRepresentationForm-ENG-fillPDF.pdf> (questions 11–14), both accessed 30 April 2023.

36 Kenya Order, para. 10.

37 See Judgment on the appeal against the decision on the authorisation of an investigation into the situation in the Islamic Republic of Afghanistan, *Situation in the Islamic Republic of Afghanistan*, ICC-02/17-138, AC, ICC, 5 March 2020, para. 1; Decision Pursuant to Article 15 of the Rome Statute on the Authorisation of an Investigation into the Situation in the People's Republic of Bangladesh/Republic of the Union of Myanmar, *Situation in the People's Republic of Bangladesh/Republic of the Union of Myanmar*, ICC-01/19-27, PTC III, ICC, 14 November 2019, para. 12; and initially Decision Pursuant to Article 15 of the Rome Statute on the Authorization of an Investigation into the Situation in the Republic of Kenya, *Situation in the Republic of Kenya*, ICC-01/09-19-Corr, PTC II, ICC, 31 March 2010, para. 18.

38 See on that below.

physical filling-in as well as electronic filling-in and submission (including an online form on the ICC webpage).[39] In-depth engagement of the VPRS with victim interlocutors and representatives, civil society and other key actors during the (extended) Regulation 50 notice period flanks the above information collection framework.[40]

Already for the Article 15(3) processes in Kenya and Côte d'Ivoire in the earlier years, commentators noted that the VPRS reports on victims' representations were help-and meaningful; relevant Pre-Trial Chambers made ample references to the relevant Registry reports in their decisions authorising the investigation.[41] The increased and more diverse VPRS reporting of victims' views in the last years has significantly increased the impact of the victim representation process for all parties involved: (i) Chambers consider the Registry reports useful and at times even instrumental to corroborate the Prosecution's submissions;[42] (ii) the Prosecutor may find in the reports important leads on potential additional focus areas of future investigations; and, most importantly, (iii) victims are provided with a meaningful vehicle to submit, in an individualised or collective fashion (as they prefer), detailed views and considerations from their personal perspective on a potential ICC investigation. The Registry's emphasis that views are sought purely from a victim's perspective and *not* as a vehicle of potential evidence production provides additional emphasis to victims that they are considered a relevant participant to these proceedings. Of note, the VPRS reports do *not* contain detailed *legal* arguments and submissions (e.g. of victims' legal representative NGOs and/or associations). While some claim that this could further enrich the process, it remains open for debate what added value legal submissions could bring to a Pre-Trial Chamber (and on what) at this particular stage of proceedings.[43] The Registry

39 Relevant forms are as a rule only available on the ICC homepage for the duration of the relevant Article 15(3) exercise; again, this is due to the more limited scope compared to the victim participation regime in judicial proceedings against an accused—and the more comprehensive standard victim participation form used there (see <https://www.icc-cpi.int/about/victims> accessed 22 March 2023).

40 It is noted that the use of Registry forms is by no way obligatory: victims can submit their views by any other means, including audio and video files (which is actually a frequent occurrence).

41 M Bergsmo, D Zhu, 'Art. 15', para. 28, in K Ambos (ed.), *Rome Statute of the International Criminal Court: Article-by-Article Commentary* 4th edn (CH Beck/Hart/Nomos 2022).

42 PTC II, ICC-01/09-3, para. 196; more recently, see e.g. Decision on the Prosecutor's request for authorisation of an investigation pursuant to Article 15(3) of the Statute, *Situation in the Republic of the Philippines*, ICC-01/21-12, PTC I, ICC, 15 September 2021, paras 18–22 and throughout the decision.

43 This may indeed change where proceedings go to the appeal stage on specific legal questions.

submission of the victims' direct and personal voices to the Judges would thus appear to be an appropriate application in practice of the provision in Article 15(3) and Rule 50(3).[44]

On the timeline of the Article 15(3) process, Regulation 50(1) of the Regulations of the Court stipulates that victims may make representations within 30 days following the date of the Prosecutor's public notification that he seeks to open a *proprio motu* investigation. Already in the very first Article 15(3) process before the ICC, the Registry successfully pointed out to the Pre-Trial Chamber that 30 days are grossly insufficient to collect a representative sample of victims' views. ICC investigations at situation level usually comprise a prolonged time period, a vast geographic scope and, sadly, an often long list of potential crimes under the ICC's jurisdiction. The limited scope of the Myanmar/Bangladesh situation due to the ICC's lack of jurisdiction over crimes solely committed on Myanmar soil[45] is a notable exception to the rule. It is often very difficult to gain access to affected victim groups, particularly in situations where an (armed) conflict is still ongoing, where potentially powerful actors exert pressure on relevant victim communities and control media/communication; in addition, low infrastructure on the ground can pose a massive operational hindrance to reaching dispersed victim communities. This was particularly so for the Afghanistan Article 15(3) process in 2017. The VPRS assessed at the very outset of the process the vastness of the potential scope of the investigation in terms of time, geography and subject-matter, coupled with the size and diversity of victim communities and the relative inaccessibility of the country, low infrastructure and heavy security constraints. It was clear that within the regular 30-day timeline, the Section would be incapable of reaching out to any acceptable minimum sample of victims. Also with a view that this problem would likely be a common feature to future such processes, the VPRS established a standard practice followed since whereby its extension request of the deadline is made at the earliest possible stage of proceedings, i.e. at the time the Prosecutor informs the Presidency of his intention to file a public notice under Article 15(3) and Rule 50(1) of the RPE. As an effect, where the

44 This said, nothing prevents a Pre-Trial Chamber to *also* accept legal submissions, as it may find appropriate, by organisations/entities/persons legally representing victims, including the ICC in-house victim counsel of the Office of Public Counsel for Victims.

45 See Decision on the 'Prosecution's Request for a Ruling on Jurisdiction under Article 19(3) of the Statute', *Situation in the People's Republic of Bangladesh/Republic of the Union of Myanmar*, ICC-RoC46(3)-01/18-37, PTC I, ICC, 6 September 2018; and subsequently, Decision Pursuant to Article 15 of the Rome Statute on the Authorisation of an Investigation into the Situation in the People's Republic of Bangladesh/Republic of the Union of Myanmar, ICC-01/19-27, PTC I, ICC, 14 November 2019.

Chamber accepts such an extension of notice period for victims, the correct timeline will be communicated by the ICC to victims *from the outset of the process*, preventing confusion amongst victims on the correct timeline (e.g. where an original deadline is changed at some point in the notice period due to an extension, as was the case in Kenya).[46] VPRS requests for extended notice periods to victims in Afghanistan, Myanmar/Bangladesh and the Philippines highlighted situation-specific obstacles and argued that the general interest of an expeditious consideration of the Prosecutor's request should be balanced against the victims' interest to exercise their right to submit their views meaningfully.[47] In all situations, Pre-Trial Chambers accorded appropriate extensions by a number of weeks/months, enabling the VPRS to carry out a broad and comprehensive consultation process.[48] In order to already appraise the Judges of victims' views collected as of the earliest stages of the notice period, the VPRS established a practice of filing not just one final report on victims' representations, but multiple interim reports during the notice period. For example, in the Afghanistan situation, following the Chamber's decision granting an extension by almost two months for victims to make representations under Article 15(3) of the Statute,[49] the Registry provided altogether seven

46 Decision on Extension of Time Limit, *Situation in the Republic of Kenya*, ICC-01/09-7-Conf-Exp, PTC II, ICC, 23 December 2009, reclassified as 'Public' pursuant to Decision on Re-classification and on the 'Prosecutor's Application for Access to any VPRS Filing and any Decision by this Chamber', ICC-01/09-18, PTC II, ICC, 24 March 2010; in Côte d'Ivoire, only the *internal* deadline for the Registry to file its report to the Chamber was extended by a month, Decision on the VPRS request for an extension of time to report on victims' representations pursuant the Regulations of the Court, *Situation in the Republic of Côte d'Ivoire*, ICC-02/11-9, PTC III, ICC, 28 July 2011, para. 5.

47 See e.g. the Registry Request in Myanmar/Bangladesh. Public redacted version of 'Registry's Request for Extension of Notice Period and Submissions on the Article 15(3) Process', 26 June 2019, ICC-01/19-3, *Situation in the People's Republic of Bangladesh/ Republic of the Union of Myanmar*, ICC-01/19-3-Red, Regitrar, ICC, 26 June 2019.

48 The latest version of the Chambers Practice Manual acknowledges the need for expeditiousness of Article 15(3) proceedings in requiring that 'the written decision of the Pre-Trial Chamber under Article 15, paragraph 4 shall be delivered within 120 days from the date the Prosecutor's request for authorisation of an investigation is filed with the Court' (see version of 13 July 2023 <https://www.icc-cpi.int/about/judicial-divisions/chambers-practice-manual>), Section I, para. 2. Conveniently, provision is made for an 'exceptional' extension of this deadline in the last sentence of para. 2.

49 Order to the Victims Participation and Reparation Section Concerning Victims' Representations, *Situation in the Islamic Republic of Afghanistan*, ICC-02/17-6, PTC III, ICC, 9 November 2017.

reports to the Chamber,[50] with the final report on 20 February 2018.[51] Similarly, in the Myanmar/Bangladesh situation, following the Chamber's notice period extension by a similar margin,[52] the VPRS submitted reports on victims' representations on 30 August, 13 and 27 September, and 11 and its final report on 31 October 2019.[53] A similar process was followed in the Philippines process.[54] This enables Pre-Trial Chambers to issue their decisions pursuant to Article 15(4) of the Statute within the 120-day time limit suggested by the Chambers Practice Manual[55] while leaving a maximum of time to the Registry within that period to collect and report victim representations.

The by now established practice of extended Registry deadlines to collect and transmit victims' views alongside the comprehensive reporting scheme have further added to the meaningfulness of the victim representation process as such, while not negatively impacting on the general interest of expeditiousness of the process. Good practice has thus optimised a process that is governed somewhat inadequately by Regulation 50(1) of the Regulations of the Court.

### 3.1.3 Registry Facilitation

As a final point, the Chambers' decisions to task the Registry's VPRS with the collection and reporting of victims' views at the—incipient—article 15 stage

---

50 See reference to these reports in Decision Pursuant to Article 15 of the Rome Statute on the Authorisation of an Investigation into the Situation in the Islamic Republic of Afghanistan, ICC-02/17-33 (n 27) at fn 10.

51 Final Consolidated Registry Report on Victims' Representations Pursuant to the Pre-Trial Chamber's Order ICC-02/17-6 of 9 November 2017, *Situation in the Islamic Republic of Afghanistan*, ICC-02/17-29, PTC III, ICC, 10 February 2018.

52 Decision on the 'Registry's Request for Extension of Notice Period and Submissions on the Article 15(3) Process', *Situation in the People's Republic of Bangladesh/Republic of the Union of Myanmar*, ICC-01/19-6, PTC III, ICC, 28 June 2019.

53 ICC, Registrar, *Situation in the People's Republic of Bangladesh/Republic of the Union of Myanmar*, First Registry Report, ICC-01/19-10-Conf (a public redacted version was filed on 3 September 2019); Second Registry Report, ICC-01/19-11-Conf (a public redacted version was filed on the same day); Third Registry Report, ICC-01/19-12-Conf (a public redacted version was filed on 30 September 2019); Fourth Registry Report, ICC-01/19-15-Conf with Conf and Conf-Exp Annexes I and II (a public redacted version was filed on 17 October 2019).

54 See only Decision on the Prosecutor's request for authorisation of an investigation pursuant to Article 15(3) of the Statute (n 42) paras 7, 8 with relevant references.

55 Chambers Practice Manual (n 48) Section I, para. 2. See also Decision on the 'Registry Request for Extension of Notice Period and Submissions on the Article 15(3) Process', *Situation in the Republic of the Philippines*, ICC-01/21-9, PTC I, ICC, 17 June 2021, para. 8.

of ICC proceedings has turned out to be sensible. First, the Section's core mandate—and expertise—is to collect, throughout all phases of ICC processes, victim applications for participation in court proceedings and reparations in case of a conviction.[56] In other words, it is the section in most direct interaction with victim communities across all situations of the Court. This applies equally to the situation stage and subsequent judicial proceedings against accused persons.[57] Second, Chambers have made it clear that they seek the victims' immediate and personal views,[58] as opposed to specific legal arguments and submissions which could be solicited from entities and associations representing victims' legal interests. VPRS' reporting to Chambers strives to deliver on this requirement in reporting victims' views and considerations in the most direct fashion; relevant Registry reports contain a large number of 'soundbites', i.e. verbatim transpositions of victims' submissions (in anonymised fashion), so that relevant views are submitted to the Chambers in the victims' own words.[59] As submitted *supra*, the procedural stage of Article 15(3) would not seem to require extensive legal submissions *on behalf of* (not: *by*) victims, not least due to the limited scope and purpose[60] of the 15(3) procedure.[61]

That said, where an article 15 authorisation process enters the appeals stage—as was the case in the Afghanistan situation following the Pre-Trial

56 See Independent Expert Review of the International Criminal Court and the Rome Statute System Final Report 30 September 2020, paras 840 ff, 911 and Recommendations R336, 347. This has since been endorsed by the plenary of ICC Judges in spring of 2023.

57 Obviously, victims will also retain a privileged relationship to their (common) legal representative throughout judicial proceedings as of the moment of appointment at pre-trial.

58 Order to the Victims Participation and Reparation Section Concerning Victims' Representations (n 49) para. 15.

59 See e.g. in the Afghanistan article 15(3) process, Annex I-Red to the Final Consolidated Registry Report on Victims' Representations Pursuant to the Pre-Trial Chamber's Order ICC-02/17-6 of 9 November 2017, *Situation in the Islamic Republic of Afghanistan*, ICC-02/17-29-AnxI-Red, PTC III, ICC, 20 February 2018; for the Myanmar/Bangladesh process see Public Redacted version of Annex I to the Final Consolidated Registry Report on Victims' Representations Pursuant to the Pre-Trial Chamber's Decision ICC-01/19-6 of 28 June 2019, *Situation in the People's Republic of Bangladesh/Republic of the Union of Myanmar*, ICC-01/19-22-AnxI-Red, PTC III, ICC, 8 November 2019; and for the Philippines: Annex I to the Public Redacted Registry Report on Victims' Representations, ICC-01/21-11-AnxI-Red, PTC I, ICC, 27 August 2021.

60 Decision on the 'Registry Request for Extension of Notice Period and Submissions on the Article 15(3) Process' (n 55) para. 7 with further references.

61 The IER Report seems to contemplate the possibility of early involvement of legal representatives of victims. Independent Expert Review of the International Criminal Court and the Rome Statute System: Final Report—30 September 2020, ICC-ASP/19/16, 9 November 2020 (Nineteenth Session of the ASP) ('IER Report').

Chamber's initial denial of said authorisation—, it may be sensible to broaden the scope of admissible victim submissions to legal arguments, not least due to the nature of these appeal proceedings (e.g., in the Afghanistan appeal proceedings, around the scope and content of Article 15(4) of the Statute).[62] The Appeals Chamber's invitation at that stage to victims, including the ICC Registry's Office of Public Counsel for Victims, for their submissions[63] enriched the process.[64]

### 3.2 *Article 18(2) Victim Consultation*

As a more recent procedural phenomenon, the question had to be answered if victims have a role to play in proceedings under Article 18(2) of the Statute when the Prosecutor seeks the resumption of an investigation. This issue came up in the Afghanistan situation in 2021,[65] shortly thereafter in the Philippines situation,[66] and most recently in the Venezuela I situation before the ICC.[67]

Pre-Trial Chamber II, seized with the Prosecutor's Article 18(2) resumption request in the Afghanistan situation in September 2021,[68] was the first to address the issue of potential victim submissions. A number of organisations and persons in representation of potential victims had sought to submit observations on the Prosecutor's resumption request;[69] in reaction to this, the

62 Judgment on the appeal against the decision on the authorisation of an investigation into the situation in the Islamic Republic of Afghanistan (n 37).

63 Corrigendum of order scheduling a hearing before the Appeals Chamber and other related matters, *Situation in the Islamic Republic of Afghanistan*, ICC-02/17-72-Corr, AC, ICC, 27 September 2019, paras 3–6.

64 On the different question whether victims have a separate right to appeal a Pre-Trial Chamber's decision under article 15(4) of the Statute see Reasons for the Appeals Chamber's oral decision dismissing as inadmissible the victims' appeals against the decision rejecting the authorisation of an investigation into the situation in Afghanistan, *Situation in the Islamic Republic of Afghanistan*, ICC-02/17-137, AC, ICC, 4 March 2020 (by majority).

65 Request to authorise resumption of investigation under article 18(2) of the Statute, *Situation in the Islamic Republic of Afghanistan*, 27 September 2021, ICC-02/17-161, PTC III, ICC, 27 September 2021.

66 Prosecution's request to resume the investigation into the situation in the Philippines pursuant to article 18(2), *Situation in the Republic of the Philippines*, ICC-01/21-46, PTC I, ICC, 24 June 2022.

67 Prosecution request to resume the investigation into the situation in the Bolivarian Republic of Venezuela I pursuant to article 18(2), *Situation in the Bolivarian Republic of Venezuela I*, ICC-02/18-18, PTC I, ICC, 1 November 2022.

68 Request to authorise resumption of investigation under article 18(2) of the Statute, ICC-02/17-161 (n 65).

69 Transmission of 'Response to the Prosecution's "Request to authorise resumption of investigation under article 18(2) of the Statute"', *Situation in the Islamic Republic of Afghanistan*,

Chamber ruled at the outset 'that potential victims do not enjoy, as a matter of right, standing to participate in the proceedings pursuant to article 18(2) of the Statute without leave of the Chamber, or to seize and request the Chamber to take certain measures in their context'.[70] Consequently, it denied legal standing to the requestors and dismissed their submissions *in limine*.[71] However, it then recalled that Article 68(3) of the Statute provides Chamber with a certain margin of discretion 'in determining whether, and in what modalities, victims may appropriately be allowed to play a role at certain stages of the proceedings (including before or during the investigation stage), despite the absence of an explicit provision to this effect'.[72] Specific to the case at hand it found that 'the interests of potential victims may indeed be affected as a result of developments in these proceedings and that, accordingly, those potential victims may legitimately have and develop concerns worth being brought to the Chamber's attention'.[73] It however considered the 'disruptive potential of a system where any potential victim would enjoy permanent legal standing, namely be authorised to submit requests and observations before the Chamber at all times', potentially leading to an overload of submissions, particularly where many thousands of potential victims are affected.[74] To address this, the Chamber devised 'a mechanism allowing the views and concerns of those potential victims to reach the Chamber, whilst at the same time preserving the orderly conduct of the proceedings'.[75] In doing so, it considered the VPRS collection exercise of victims' views under Article 15(3) of the Statute as a suitable model

ICC-02/17-167, PTC II, ICC, 11 October 2021; Registry Transmission of 'Victims' Request for Leave to Submit Observations', *Situation in the Islamic Republic of Afghanistan*, ICC-02/17-168, PTC II, ICC, 13 October 2021.

70 Decision on submissions received and order to the Registry regarding the filing of documents in the proceedings pursuant to articles 18(2) and 68(3) of the Statute, *Situation in the Islamic Republic of Afghanistan*, ICC-02/17-171, PTC II, ICC, 8 November 2021 ('PTC Decision on Art. 18 Submissions'), para. 10; see also ibid., para. 9, where the Chamber refers to its previous decision on the issue of 8 October 2021 (Decision setting the procedure pursuant to rule 55(1) of the Rules of Procedure and Evidence following the Prosecutor's 'Request to authorise resumption of investigation under article 18(2) of the Statute', ICC-02/17-165) at para. 20 with reference to a French proposal at PrepComm for explicit reference to a victims' right to make submissions at the Article 18(2) stage which was however not retained in the Statute.

71 PTC Decision on Art. 18 Submissions, para. 10.

72 Ibid., citing ample ICC jurisprudence in fn. 15 on the issue of judges' discretion under art. 68(3) of the Statute.

73 Ibid., para. 12.

74 Ibid., para. 13.

75 Ibid., para. 14.

to be transposed to the Article 18(2) context—and ordered the VPRS to proceed accordingly.[76] In July of 2022, in the context of the deferral proceedings in the Philippines situation, Pre-Trial Chamber I followed this precedent and issued a similar order, tasking the VPRS to collect victims' 'views and concerns' on the Prosecutor's request to resume the investigation.[77] The Chamber followed this same process also in Article 18(2) proceedings in the Venezuela I situation most recently.[78] Of note, the Chambers' reference to the 'personal interests of victims' as stipulated in Article 68(3) of the Statute as well as their 'views and concerns' while at the same time adopting the Article 15(3) victim consultation process creates a logical coherence between all these processes under the normative umbrella of Article 68(3) of the Statute.

Following these rulings, the VPRS crafted and used victim consultation forms (as well as relevant guidelines on how to fill in such a form) that had been slightly modified for the purpose of Article 18(2) proceedings.[79] The VPRS victim consultation process followed the same logic and applied the same features as in the Article 15(3) context; this created a helpful standardisation of processes as well as synergies, leading to a sustainability of this type of exercise.

Of note, the question at the heart of the Article 18(2) consultation exercise obviously has a slightly different focus, asking: '[d]o you want the ICC Prosecutor to resume an investigation in the Situation [XY]', alongside the question on any additional views and concerns (including, in particular, where victims do *not* want an investigation to proceed). Particularly in the Philippines situation it transpired that particularly where the Article 15(3) and the 18(2) processes occur in close temporal proximity, victim submissions will by and large be similar, thus potentially providing only limited added value. Pre-Trial Chamber I recognised this explicitly and thus solicited the VPRS to focus on 'any additional or different views or concerns related to the Prosecutor's Request'.[80] In any event, the continued Registry engagement with relevant victim communities had an overall beneficial effect, if only to inform, manage expectations and provide a continuous channel for victims to communicate with the ICC.

76 Ibid.

77 Order inviting observations and victims' views and concerns, *Situation in the Republic of the Philippines*, ICC-01/21-47, PTC I, ICC, 14 July 2022, para. 14.

78 Order inviting observations and views and concerns of victims, *Situation in the Bolivarian Republic of Venezuela I*, ICC-02/18-21, PTC I, ICC, 18 November 2022, paras 10, 11.

79 In the Afghanistan process, the form went through an approval process by the Chamber: Decision on the 'Registry Submission Pursuant to Decision ICC-02/17-171 in Relation to Article 18(2) Proceedings', *Situation in the Islamic Republic of Afghanistan*, ICC-02/17-173, ptc II, ICC, 25 November 2021.

80 Order inviting observations and victims' views and concerns (n 77) para. 14.

For the most recent Article 18(2) proceedings in the Venezuela I situation however, the VPRS exercise is much more significant for victims as there has not been a previous Article 15(3) representation process (Venezuela I was referred to the ICC by a group of States pursuant to article 14 of the Statute—victims' views are not solicited during this process). The Judges' established practice to seek the victims' views and concerns in Article 18(2) proceedings is therefore all the more fortuitous and important for the victims' possibility to gain a level of ownership in ICC proceedings.

Lastly, in the Venezuela proceedings, the ICC Registry's Office of Public Counsel for Victims had requested the Chamber's leave to submit a filing, together with four Venezuelan lawyers, presenting the views and concerns of a number of victims, and in particular also legal submissions, on the Prosecutor's resumption request.[81] The Chamber denied this, holding that 'there is no reason to depart from [the VPRS-led] system of collection in the present case' as the latter 'will ensure that the views and concerns of any victims whose interests are not currently represented by the OPCV and/or the four named Venezuelan lawyers may also be collected and transmitted to the Chamber, and thus preserve the efficient and orderly conduct of the proceedings'.[82] In so ordering, the Chamber would seem to confirm, albeit not explicitly, that much like in the Article 15(3) scenario the Chamber is more interested in victims' layman's and personal views, concerns and observations than in legal submissions by anyone else than the statutory parties to these specific proceedings.

However, in ensuing appeal proceedings, the Appeals Chamber – as it had previously done in the Philippines situation[83] – granted the OPCV request to provide written observations on the appeal brief,[84] alongside a VPRS report on representations from any interested victims and victim groups. This generated a positive effect for victims in that at this stage of legal review, victims' voices were amplified by submissions of OPCV counsel on "the *general* interests of victims"[85], alongside the *specific* submissions of victims channeled through VPRS.

81 OPCV Request to Submit Observations on the Prosecutor's Request to Resume the Investigation under Article 18(2) of the Statute, ICC-02/18-19, PTC I, ICC, 3 November 2022, paras 3, 4.

82 Order inviting observations and views and concerns of victims, ICC-02/18-21 (n 78) para. 11.

83 Decision on requests for victims' involvement and access to filings, ICC-01/21-66, 21 March 2023 para. 2.

84 Decision on the OPCV's "Request to appear before the Appeals Chamber pursuant to regulation 81(4) of the Regulations of the Court", ICC-02/18-54, 21 July 2023 para. 7.

85 *Ibid* (*emphasis added*)*; see already in* Decision on requests for victims' involvement and access to filings, ICC-01/21-66, 21 March 2023 para. 2.

In conclusion, the very recent jurisprudential line of providing victims a forum also at the stage of a potential resumption of an investigation by the Prosecutor is a milestone for victim participation at the ICC as it adds their voice at an early yet crucial stage of proceedings. The transposition of the Article 15(3) process led by the Registry into the Article 18(2) context is sensible as it creates synergies and provides a powerful mandate to the Registry[86] as an intelligent enabler of victims' rights under Article 68(3) of the Statute while retaining its role of a neutral service provider.

### 3.3 *Victim Participation at the Situation Stage Absent Case Proceedings*

Article 68(3) of the Statute is silent as to the exact 'stage(s) of proceedings' when victim participation may commence, beyond leaving it to the discretion of the Judges ('determined to be appropriate by the Court', Article 68(3) of the Statute).[87] Rules 89 and following of the RPE as well as regulations 86 and following of the Regulations of the Court do not provide much more guidance; while a number of provisions specifically relate to judicial proceedings against one or more suspects/accused persons (or even the hearing of evidence at trial), others merely refer to 'proceedings'—which could be as early as an investigation (or even before that).[88] Particularly the victims' possibility to liaise with the Court at the situation stage and submit a victim application form pursuant to Regulation 86 of the Regulations of the Court is not prohibited—as long as the victim fulfils the requirements of Rule 85 of the RPE. This is so since the latter does not speak of the victim's harm as a result of a crime as charged *in a case* but rather 'the commission of any crime within the jurisdiction of the Court'.[89]

In the earlier years of ICC operations, Pre-Trial Chambers issued decisions in a number of situations ruling on the participatory status at the situation stage

86 This includes the OPCV in relevant appeal proceedings.

87 See on this point also the observations of the IER Repor, para. 839 with further references, noting that "Article 68(3) has been described as an example of 'constructive ambiguity' or 'obscurity'".

88 In the Palestine situation, Pre-Trial Chamber I issued its Decision on Information and Outreach for the Victims of the Situation, in which it held that victims' rights under Article 68(3) of the Statute are not limited to judicial proceedings, and that certain victims' rights on communication and information already exist at the preliminary examination stage (which was the status of the Palestine situation at the time); Decision on Information and Outreach for the Victims of the Situation, *Situation in the State of Palestine*, ICC-01/18-2, PTC I, ICC, 13 July 2018, paras 10, 11. It consequently ordered that certain outreach and information activities towards victims be conducted, paras 14ff.

89 Rule 85(a) of the RPE. Rule 85(b) referring to juridical persons is more restrictive in referring to harm to property only.

of victims that had submitted victim application forms pursuant to Regulation 86 of the Regulations of the Court.[90] Yet, in 2008 the Appeals Chamber issued an important ruling, clearly distinguishing the investigation conducted by the Prosecutor from judicial proceedings, and holding that the participation of victims at the stage of a situation can take place only within the context of judicial proceedings (including on issues affecting investigations), and only 'provided their personal interests are affected by the issues arising for resolution'.[91] Subsequent Pre-Trial Chambers have therefore not granted participatory rights to victim applicants at the situation stage unless there was a judicial proceeding in which they would be able to participate.[92] Chambers also provided examples of such proceedings potentially triggering victim participation.[93] Importantly, Chambers ordered the VPRS to collect and store relevant applications, and to transmit these in case specific proceedings arose.[94] In addition, the Registry was given the task to explain the system to victim communities, in order to provide clarity and manage victims' expectations.

The practice in the more recent years has solidified the Appeals Chamber's 2008 ruling that there is no general right of victims to participate at the investigation stage. Importantly, Registry messaging to victim groups, NGOs and other interlocutors has tried to underline this general premise. Messaging has been all the more difficult in the aftermath of Article 15(3) or 18(2) proceedings, where victims had just been enabled to partake in a judicial process, only

90 E.g. Décision sur les demandes de participation à la procédure de VPRS 1, VPRS 2, VPRS 3, VPRS 4, VPRS 5 et VPRS 6, *Situation in the Democratic Republic of the Congo*, ICC-01/04-100-Conf-Exp, PTC I, ICC, 17 January 2006; a public redacted and corrected version in English: ICC-01/04-101-tEN-Corr. See references to ensuing decisions of the Chamber, para. 3, fn 7–9.

91 Judgment on victim participation in the investigation stage of the proceedings in the appeal of the OPCD against the decision of Pre-Trial Chamber I of 7 December 2007 and in the appeals of the OPCD and the Prosecutor against the decision of Pre-Trial Chamber I of 24 December 2007, *Situation in the Democratic Republic of the Congo* ICC-01/04-556, AC, ICC, 19 December 2008 ("AC Judgment on Victim Participation"), paras 43–47, 56, 57.

92 E.g. Decision on victims' participation in proceedings relating to the situation in the Democratic Republic of the Congo, *Situation in the Democratic Republic of the Congo*, ICC-01/04-593, PTC I, ICC, 13 April 2011, para. 9, and concurring Decision on Victim's Participation in Proceedings Related to the Situation in Libya, *Situation in* Libya, ICC-01/11-18, PTC I, ICC, 24 January 2012. See also Decision on Victims' Participation in Proceedings Related to the Situation in the Republic of Kenya, *Situation in the Republic of Kenya*, ICC-01/09-24, PTC II, ICC, 3 November 2010.

93 Decision on victims' participation in proceedings relating to the situation in the Democratic Republic of the Congo (n 92) para. 10.

94 See e.g. ibid., para. 11; AC Judgment on Victim Participation, paras 46ff.

to be told that their representation—including the form submitted—would not lead to participatory status, be that during the investigation or potential ensuing judicial proceedings against one or more accused persons. At the same time, consistent VPRS messaging with its interlocutors has had the beneficial effect that expectations were properly managed, even if the message is sometimes received with a level of disappointment. Continued interaction with relevant victim networks across the situations has helped to retain engagement with the Court and has proven instrumental if and when cases were brought forward. Victim communities could be reached out to more speedily and effectively. However, the length of investigations in a given situation will eventually influence the engagement of victim communities with the Court, as their patience may be limited due to continued suffering and victimisation. Examples in point are Afghanistan, Myanmar/Bangladesh or most recently Ukraine, where victims find themselves in ongoing armed conflict.

### 3.4 *The Facilitation of Victim Participation at the Case Stage*

The victim participation system needs to strike a fair balance between victims' right to enjoy an effective access to ICC proceedings with sufficient protection,[95] and the right of the accused to a fair, expeditious and impartial trial. In order to achieve a fair balance between these requirements, there is a specific need for consistency in the jurisprudence on the principles applicable to victims' participation—including the manner in which victims' applications to participate are dealt with. Since victims' participatory rights concentrate on judicial proceedings against one or more accused persons at the case stage, focus shall be placed that stage in the following.

#### 3.4.1 Timing of Registry Engagement with Victims

As of the moment that the Pre-Trial Chamber issues a warrant of arrest or a summons to appear (following the Prosecutor's request) pursuant to Article 58 of the Statute, victims whose harm originates from the charges described therein can in theory apply to participate in relevant proceedings. However, experience has shown that two key considerations need to be factored in: first, there often lies a considerable amount of time between the issuance of a warrant and the actual start of pre-trial proceedings pursuant to article 60 of the Statute (i.e. with the surrender of the person to the Court).[96] Second, and

95 Article 68(1) and 68(3) of the Rome Statute.

96 On the question presently before Pre-Trial Chamber II whether to hold pre-trial confirmation proceedings in the absence of the suspect in the case of *Kony et al.*, see, Public Redacted Version of the 'Prosecution's Request to Hold a Hearing on the Confirmation

often due to the lapse of time, charges contained in the original warrant may undergo substantial amendments if and when initial/confirmation proceedings under Articles 60 and 61 of the Statute actually commence. It has been considered that if the Registry were to commence a full-fledged victim application process at the issuance of a warrant under Article 58, probable effects on victims' expectations could be detrimental if relevant suspects remain at large for many years or are not apprehended at all. Victims would be reached out to through information sessions and requested to provide accounts of traumatic events, while the continuation of the process would remain entirely unclear. In addition, the administration of a victim application process in a case requires substantial resources of the Registry, both at headquarters and in the field. The VPRS, as per its mandate the lead entity in this process, operates under heavy strain with its less than 20 staff, as it has to service all situations and cases before the Court simultaneously. The practice has therefore become to actively engage with potential victim communities only upon apprehension of a suspect, i.e. when the continuation of confirmation proceedings can be predicted with certainty.

The panel of Independent Experts recommended in its 2020 report that the VPRS collection of applications 'should commence earlier than at present; [...] the date of commencement should be advanced to the point of issue of an arrest warrant or a summons to appear'.[97] This recommendation is motivated by the observation that in many cases the amount of participating victims in a case is significantly inferior to the amount of potential participants, simply for lack of time to collect, assess and submit victim applications.[98] Yet, the IER Report seems to operate on the assumption that a suspect is apprehended shortly after issuance of a warrant—in which case the recommendation of a speedy commencement of the victim application process is indeed imperative. Where an arrest is uncertain, however, considerations of expectation management, the principle of do-no-harm in regard to victims (potential of re-traumatisation) and good management of resources militate against such an approach. Particularly the point on resources merits one last observation: coming back to the underlying premise of many delegations at the PrepComm—'accept victim participation if not overly resource-intense'—, the decision to

---

of Charges against Joseph Kony in his Absence', *Kony et al., Situation in Uganda*, ICC-02/04-01/05-446-Red, PTC II, ICC, 24 November 2022.

97 IER Report, para. 852 and Recommendation 337, at 287.

98 An example would be the *Ongwen* proceedings in the Uganda situation, where a great number of victim applicants could not partake in the application procedure before the cut-off date at the start of trial.

commence active collection of victim applications concomitant to a suspect's initial appearance before the Pre-Trial Chamber would seem to be the most effective use of resources if one does not want to majorly expand the victim-related capacity of the Registry.

In addition, since 2021, Registry advocacy across cases in recent years[99] has moved Chambers to extend the time provided to the VPRS to collect and submit victim applications from the cut-off date at the start of trial to the end of the Prosecution case.[100] This translates generally into more than a year that was gained to collect and transmit victim applications for participation in the proceedings—and reparations.[101]

### 3.4.2 The Victim Application Process at the Case Stage

The Registry process of collection of victims' applications to participate in the proceedings (Rule 89(1) and regulation 86 of the Regulations of the Court) and/or to request reparations (Rule 94 of the RPE) has proven to be a complex endeavour. One question - that has led to a series of different—more *and* less cumbersome—standard victim application forms - has been when to collect *reparation-related* information from victims. The use of a 17-and later 7-page long application form soliciting information for participation *and* reparations proved user-unfriendly in the field and difficult to process at headquarters.[102] This was flanked by an unwieldy work distribution between Registry and Chambers, with Chambers' legal staff scrutinising every single application form received from the Registry, and Chambers consequently

99 E.g. Public redacted version of Annex II to the Registry Submissions in View of the Upcoming Status Conference in accordance with 'Order scheduling first status conference' (ICC-02/05-01/20-451), *Abd-Al-Rahman, Situation in Darfur, Sudan*, ICC-02/05-01/20-462-AnxII-Red, PTC I, ICC, 1 September 2021, para. 24–26. In previous cases, said VPRS advocacy had already led to Chambers ruling favourably on the request (end of Prosecution case): Decision Setting the Commencement Date of the Trial, *Yekatom and Ngaïssona, Situation in the Central African Republic II*, ICC-01/14-01/18-589, TC V, ICC, 16 July 2020, para. 20; Decision on request for extension of deadlines for the final transmission of victim applications for participation at trial, *Al Hassan, Situation in the Republic of Mali*, ICC-01/12-01/18-880 13.

100 See Chambers Practice Manual, para. 97(iii) as of the 5th edition (2021); in the 4th edition (2019), the relevant paragraph (para. 98(iv)) still set the final time limit for victim application submission to Chambers to 'sufficiently before the commencement of the trial'.

101 Since 2016 and starting at the pre-trial phase in the *Al Hassan* case, the VPRS collects victim applications on a combined form regarding victim participation and reparations. This approach has the major benefit that by the end of trial proceedings, the VPRS is in possession of a host of reparation-related information from potential beneficiaries which in turn are expected to accelerate potential reparation proceedings significantly.

102 In this sense also IER Report, para. 844; Wyngaert (n 17) 481, 482.

issuing individual rulings per application. In cases with potentially thousands of participating victims this approach proved non-viable from a resource perspective. In 2013, the Single Judge of Pre-Trial Chamber II sought to streamline the victim application process, including the victim application form and admission process.[103] Consequently, in the *Ntaganda* – and subsequently the *Ongwen* proceedings (2015)[104] -, the Registry applied a drastically shortened two-page application form which *ex*cluded any specific questions regarding reparations apart from the indication whether or not the applicant *also* intends to request reparations should there be a conviction.[105] This form, however, proved problematic when the two cases entered the reparation phase; when the Chamber solicited reparation-related information from the Registry (e.g. specific damages subject to restitution; resulting needs from harm suffered; victims' potential preferences in terms of reparative measures), none of this had been collected.[106] Finally, the wording of Rule 89(1) of the RPE added a layer of complication to the process: the rule describes that as a default, copies of victim applications shall be provided to the Prosecutor and the Defence, for them to be able to challenge participation requests as appropriate. Yet, in order to fulfil its protective duty towards victims, the Registry had to apply redactions to these forms, leading to thousands of pages requiring redactions. These redactions concerned any and all identifying information, requiring thorough assessment and application of redactions in an individualised fashion. With the receipt of thousands of forms per case, this requirement proved extremely resource-intense—for both Registry and Chambers.[107] At the same time it incited the parties to use the forms as material to either generate or rebut evidence, thus pulling victim statements into the litigious process as material potentially falling under Rule 77 of the RPE.

103 Decision Establishing Principles on the Victims' Application Process, *Ntaganda, Situation in the Democratic Republic of the Congo*, ICC-01/04-02/06-67, PTC II, ICC, 28 May 2013, paras 3, 17 ff.

104 Decision Establishing Principles on the Victims' Application Process, *Ongwen, Situation in Uganda*, ICC-02/04-01/15-205, PTC II, ICC, 4 March 2015.

105 Annex to Decision Establishing Principles on the Victims' Application Process, *Ntaganda, Situation in the Democratic Republic of the Congo*, icc-01/04-02/06-67-ANX, PTC II, ICC, 28 May 2013; Annex to Decision Establishing Principles on the Victims' Application Process, *Ongwen, Situation in Uganda*, ICC-02/04-01/15-205-Anx, PTC II, ICC, 4 March 2015.

106 An additional, albeit slightly minor point is that victims are free before the ICC to claim participation *or* reparations *or* both—see Rule 89(1) and 94 of the RPE and Regulations 86 and 88 of the Regulations of the Court. The short two-page form did not fulfil the requirements of the 'standard reparation form' as stipulated in Regulation 88 of the Regulations of the Court as a form required to be at victims' disposition.

107 Similarly Wyngaert (n 17) 482.

In the *Kenya* situation with two multi-accused cases before the Chambers in 2011, the Court was faced with very large numbers of potential victims. In an attempt to make the victim application process manageable, the Trial Chambers of the two cases devised a system whereby only victims who sought to address the Chamber individually and directly were required to submit an application pursuant to Rule 89(1) of the RPE and Regulation 86 of the Regulations.[108] All other victims could register with the Registry following a process where the Registry would not even apply a *prima facie* Rule 85 test or require much more than the personal registration information.[109] This approach however faced the problem that the ICC regulatory framework points to an individualised process of victim participation, not least to render the experience meaningful for the victim (although the Registry also received positive feedback from victims as being well informed by their legal representative residing in the field).[110] The onus of verification whether victims seeking to participate also fulfil the Rule 85 requirements rests with the Court (and not the victims' assigned legal representative, as in the *Kenya* cases), not least with a view to potential future reparations: where the convict is ordered to repair the harm of a victim directly as per Article 75 of the Statute, the causal link between the convict's conduct and the victim's harm needs to be judicially determined;[111] in other words, time saved in skipping the Rule 85 assessment at (pre-)trial may become potential delay added at the reparations stage.

108 At first, Pre-Trial Chambers ordered the Registry to carry out the victim application collection process based on the 7-page standard application form at the time; First Decision on Victims' Participation in the Case, *Muthaura, Kenyatta and Ali, Situation in Kenya*, ICC-01/09-02/11-23, PTC II, ICC, 30 March 2011 and the identical approach by the same Chamber in Decision on Victims' Participation at the Confirmation of Charges Hearing and in the Related Proceedings, *Ruto and Sang, Situation in the Republic of Kenya*, ICC-01/09-01/11-17, PTC II, ICC, 8 August 2011.

109 Decision on victims' representation and participation, *Ruto and Sang, Situation in the Republic of Kenya*, ICC-01/09-01/11-460, TC V, ICC, 9 October 2012, para. 25 and Section IV; and the parallel decision in Decision on victims' representation and participation, *Kenyatta, Situation in Kenya*, ICC-01/09-02/11-498, TC V, ICC, 3 October 2012, para. 25 and Section IV.

110 Seeing the *Kenya* approach as a viable model if victims' legal representatives are well supported: A Sehmi, '"Now that we have no voice, what will happen to us?": Experiences of Victim Participation in the Kenyatta Case' (2018) 16(3) *Journal of International Criminal Justice* 571–591.

111 Arguably, the judicial determination *by a Chamber* does not have to extend to *every individual* potential beneficiary; if the Chamber is minded to provide sufficiently specific guidance as to the relevant requirements/proof, the beneficiary verification can be carried through by the Registry, and the Chamber would solely remain an instance of legal recourse.

With the beginning of pre-trial proceedings in the *Ntaganda* case in 2013, the Pre-Trial Chamber accepted a Registry proposal to use a drastically shortened standard victim application form, focusing on information required for a victim's participation in proceedings only (and thus not soliciting any reparation-related information).[112] A similar form was accepted soon thereafter in the *Ongwen* case. This form, used in the *Ntaganda* and *Ongwen* proceedings throughout, has remained on the ICC website until 2023 as the standard form for victims to use if they wish to send their application at the investigation stage of a situation, i.e. absent a case.[113] The use of the shortened form in the aforementioned cases decidedly marked progress, in terms of user-friendliness and processing speed at the pre-trial and trial stages. Yet, for reparations in these same cases, the form turned out to be less useful, as shall be addressed further below.

#### 3.4.2.1 *The ABC Approach of Victim Application Assessment*

In addition, at the trial stage in the *Ntaganda* case, the VPRS proposed for the first time a reformed and streamlined admission process of victim applications before the Chamber:[114] victim applications are subdivided into three groups, namely those who clearly qualify as victims (Group A), those who clearly do not qualify as victims (Group B); and those for whom the Registry could not make a clear determination (Group C). Groups A and B are remitted only to the Chamber excluding the parties, with Group C forms being the only ones shared with the parties.[115] For Groups A and B, barring a clear error in the Registry's assessment, the Chamber would ratify the assessments regarding these applicants through a decision.

---

112 Decision Establishing Principles on the Victims' Application Process, *Ntaganda, Situation in the Democratic Republic of the Congo*, ICC-01/04-02/06-67, PTC II, ICC, 28 May 2013 (with the form as an annex to the decision).

113 This form does not contain any specific questions relating to reparations (apart from the choice what process the victim is applying for in Question 1) as the collection of such information at the situation stage—where it is all but clear if and when a case materializes—could be considered too early; it may raise victims' expectations and at the same time most certainly render outdated information by the time potential reparations were to ensue. See the form (in different languages, alongside guidelines how to fill in the form) at <https://www.icc-cpi.int/about/victims>.

114 Registry submission pursuant to 'Order Scheduling a Status Conference and Setting a provisional Agenda', *Ntaganda, Situation in the Democratic Republic of the Congo*, ICC-01/04-02/06-350, TC VI, ICC, 14 August 2014.

115 Decision on victims' participation in trial proceedings, *Ntaganda, Situation in the Democratic Republic of the Congo*, ICC-01/04-02/06-449, TC VI, ICC, 6 February 2015, para. 24.

This effectively reduced the amount of application forms shared with the parties to a small number of forms where the Registry is not able to make a clear determination whether the application is within or without the (temporal, geographic or subject-matter) scope of the case. This approach had multiple benefits: it reduced litigation only to those forms and matters that really require the parties' attention and the Chamber's ruling; it massively decreased the resource impact of processing forms for the Registry as redactions have to be applied only to a fraction of the forms received; it dissuaded the parties from considering victim applications as potential evidentiary (or lead) material,[116] and arguably also saved their resources, heavily reducing forms to be reviewed; and it increased Registry capacity to collect and process victim forms by a margin, thus actually allowing a much higher number of victims access to the proceedings. After successful testing of the processing scheme, the Registry proposed this novel approach also in other cases, both at pre-trial and trial. As an effect, the so-called 'ABC approach' has now become common practice throughout all cases before the ICC.[117]

In the *Said* case in the CAR II situation, in 2021 the Defence brought its doubts before the Appeals Chamber whether the ABC approach is not in violation of Rule 89(1) of the RPE.[118] The latter states that by default, 'the Registrar

116 Victim statements of dual status witnesses (i.e. witnesses that are *also* participating victims) are disclosed amongst the parties and have been used as 'prior statements' pursuant to Rule 76(1) of the RPE. Yet, ICC jurisprudence has underlined that 'victim applications are primarily intended as a procedural mechanism to participate in proceedings', and not as evidence: *Ntaganda* Decision on victims' participation in trial proceedings (n 99) paras. 36, 40.

117 Ibid., para. 24 and paras 29–33; Decision Establishing the Principles Applicable to Victims' Applications for Participation, *Al Hassan, Situation in the Republic of Mali*, ICC-01/12-01/18-37-tENG, PTC I, ICC, 24 May 2018 para. 59; Decision Establishing the Principles Applicable to Victims' Applications for Participation, *Yekatom and Ngaïssona, Situation in the Central African Republic II*, ICC-01/14-01/18-141, PTC II, ICC, 5 March 2019, para. 41; Decision on the procedure for the admission of victims to participate in proceedings for the purposes of trial, *Al Hassan, Situation in the Republic of Mali*, ICC-01/12-01/18-661, TC X, ICC, 12 March 2020, para. 1; Order Scheduling First Status Conference, *Yekatom and Ngaïssona, Situation in the Central African Republic II*, ICC-01/14-01/18-459, TC V, ICC, 19 March 2020, para. 8(iv); Decision establishing the principles applicable to victims' participation and representation during the Confirmation Hearing, *Abd-Al-Rahman, Situation in Darfur, Sudan*, ICC-02/05-01/20-259, PTC II, ICC, 18 January 2021, para. 34; Decision on victims' participation and legal representation in trial proceedings, *Abd-Al-Rahman, Situation in Darfur, Sudan*, ICC-02/05-01/20-494, TC I, ICC, 19 October 2021, para. 15; Order on the conduct of the confirmation of charges proceedings, *Mokom, CAR II Situation*, ICC-01/14-01/22-62, PTC II, ICC, 27 June 2022, paras 40 ff.

118 A similar litigation before the *Abd-Al-Rahman* Trial Chamber was decided by the latter in confirming the ABC approach, and leave to appeal was denied.

shall provide a copy of the application to the Prosecutor and the defence'. On 14 September 2021, the Appeals Chamber ruled that the ABC approach is 'in principle an adequate tool to ensure the fairness and expeditiousness of the proceedings, while at the same time respecting the rights of both the accused and the victims'.[119] The Chamber motivated this ruling through the judicial duty to protect the victims' safety, well-being, dignity and privacy under Article 68(1) of the Statute, which needs to be weighed against the rights of the defendant.[120] However, the Appeals Chamber also remarked that "in cases where the number of victims' applications is expected to remain low, the interest of the suspect or accused in receiving copies thereof and replying thereto may outweigh the benefits gained by the implementation of the A-B-C Approach".[121] And indeed, as an exception to the rule, the *Said* case on trial has seen a slight modification of the ABC approach following the Appeals Chamber ruling: due to the small and confined set of charges[122] and an accordingly small group of participating victims, the ABC approach has been retained, yet modified: the Registry is to apply the general ABC logic of application assessment, but then to transmit Group C *and A* (*ie applications considered by the Registry as inside the scope of the case*) applications to the parties, with the necessary redactions, for their observations.[123]

Still, the ABC approach has crystallised as the general standard to be applied: it is outlined as such in the most recent version of the Chambers Practice Manual,[124] after being considered appropriate also by the Independent Experts in their 2021 Report.[125] Also the current landscape of cases before

119 Judgment on the appeal of Mr Mahamat Said Abdel Kani against the decision of Pre-Trial Chamber II of 16 April 2021 entitled 'Decision establishing the principles applicable to victims' applications for participation', *Said, Situation in the Central African Republic II*, ICC-01/14-01/21-171 OA2, AC, ICC, 14 September 2021 ('*Said* Appeals Judgment'), para. 82.

120 *Said* Appeals Judgment, paras 67, 81. The Appeals Chamber stressed that chambers have been afforded a high degree of discretion in terms of how to organise the victims application process and that any decision on the most appropriate system must always be case-specific, based on objective information and the result of a proper balancing of all interests at stake, *Said* Appeals Judgment, paras 63–65.

121 *Said* Appeals Judgment, para. 82.

122 Decision on the Confirmation of Charges, *Said, Situation in the Central African Republic II*, ICC-01/14-01/21-218-Red, PTC II, ICC, 9 December 2021; Public Redacted Version of 'Prosecution's Trial Brief', ICC-01/14-01/21-359-Conf, dated 13 June 2022, *Said, Situation in the Central African Republic II*, ICC-01/14-01/21-359-Red, TC VI, ICC, 28 July 2022.

123 Decision on matters relating to the participation of victims during the trial, *Said, Situation in the Central African Republic II*, ICC-01/14-01/21-278, TC VI, ICC, 13 April 2022, para. 16.

124 Chambers Practice Manual (n 48) para. 96(iv)–(xi), 97.

125 IER Report, para. 849.

Chambers seems to confirm that in general, victim numbers will be sufficiently high to consider that the ABC approach will continue to be the rule. In conclusion, the invention, application and litigation of the ABC approach can be seen as a showcase example how an important reform initiative in ICC proceedings has been launched and solidified in its operational structure—leading to notable efficiency gains.[126] This does not mean that the ABC approach is the *non plus ultra*; other approaches may be as valid and the Court should remain open to discussions. At the same time, the ABC approach may represent a general victim admission system that can be easily exported to *other* international criminal justice systems,[127] thus leading to a standard transcending the ICC system.

Former ICC Judge Christine Van den Wyngaert lamented in an academic contribution in 2011 that the victim application transmission process is labour- and resource-intense and cumbersome.[128] With the ABC approach in place, the Court has addressed and allayed Judge Van den Wyngaert's concerns.

#### 3.4.2.2 *The New Combined Form*

In 2017, the VPRS proposed another reform initiative alongside the continued application of the ABC approach across cases: in the *Al Hassan* pre-trial proceedings, it re-introduced a combined, albeit streamlined victim application form for participation in the proceedings and reparations.[129] The new form, building on the streamlined *Ntaganda* and *Ongwen* form as the 'front end', seeks further information from the victim relevant to reparations on an

126 The latest ruling by the Appeals Chamber in the *Ntaganda* case provides a slight retrogressive step from the non-disclosure of individual victim applications where it holds that for 'at least a sample of applications for reparations, the Defence must be able to challenge this information by means of reviewing the applications and making representations thereon', Judgment on the appeals against the decision of Trial Chamber VI of 8 March 2021 entitled 'Reparations Order', *Ntaganda, Situation in the Democratic Republic of the Congo*, ICC-01/04-02/06-2782 (A4 A5), AC, ICC, 12 September 2022, para. 363 (including the peculiar reference in fn 758 to rule 94(2) of the RPE—the latter only requiring the Registry 'notification of the [reparation] request' to the Defence, and *not* the transmission of the application).

127 The ABC approach has already been adopted by the Kosovo Specialist Chambers: *see* Framework Decision on Victims' Applications, *The Prosecutor v. Hashim Thaci, Kadri Veseli, Rexhep Selimi, and Jakup Krasniq*, Pre-Trial Judge, KSC-BC-2020-06, 4 January 2021, paras. 28 ff.

128 Wyngaert (n 17) 481, 482.

129 Registry Observations on Aspects Related to the Admission of Victims for Participation in the Proceedings, *Al Hassan, Situation in the Republic of Mali*, ICC-01/12-01/18-28, PTC I, ICC, 9 May 2018.

additional two pages. This new standard form clearly outlines *all* options and combinations to applying victims. After approval by the *Al Hassan* Pre-Trial Chamber[130] and successful testing throughout the proceedings, the new combined form has equally become part and parcel of the VPRS victim application collection and transmission system across cases.[131]

The key argument *against* the solicitation of reparations-related information remains (i) the risk of raised expectations; and (ii) the risk of outdated information if/when it finally comes to the implementation of reparations. Yet, experience has shown that once judicial proceedings against an individual commence before the ICC, victim communities are fully cognisant of their options before the ICC, namely regarding reparations. What's more, recent Registry policy to proactively discuss the matter with victim communities from the pre-trial stage onwards has helped to dispel misconceptions and *properly* manage expectations in outlining the many steps and preconditions leading to them. Furthermore, at the time reparation proceedings commence, victims would be represented by their legal representatives; the latter would then be in a position to seek and provide updated information from their clients.[132] Also, the Trust Fund for Victims' access to key reparation information, and notably the desired form of reparation, may be highly conducive to well-modeled reparation measures to victim communities – be they individual or collective.

Recent Registry practice follows the above logic. The VPRS collection of reparation-related information from victims commences at pre-trial and continues throughout the entire trial proceedings. This was first requested by VPRS and then encouraged by the Trial Chamber in the *Al Hassan* case,[133] followed and further detailed in the *Said*[134] and *Abd-Al-Rahman*[135] proceedings, and

130 See the Pre-Trial Chamber's approval decision of the Registry approach: Decision Establishing the Principles Applicable to Victims' Applications for Participation, *Al Hassan, Situation in the Republic of Mali*, ICC-01/12-01/18-37-tENG, PTC I, ICC, 24 May 2018.

131 See fn 117.

132 At the same time, experience in the *Bemba* case has shown that the dynamic situation on the ground may make access to victim communities difficult throughout prolonged periods of time. To collect an aggregate amount of reparation-related information during trial enables the Registry to provide at least mapping data to the Chamber at the end of trial—which may significantly accelerate the preparatory phase of reparations.

133 *Al Hassan* Decision on request for extension of deadlines for the final transmission of victim applications for participation at trial (n 99) para. 15.

134 *Said* Decision on matters relating to the participation of victims during the trial (n 123) paras 86–90.

135 Second decision on the admission of victims to participate in trial proceedings, *Abd-Al-Rahman ('Ali Kushayb'), Situation in Darfur, Sudan*, ICC-02/05-01/20-761, TC I, ICC, 3 October 2022 ('*Ali Kushayb* Second Decision'), paras 13–20.

endorsed more recently by the Appeals Chamber.[136] The crucial benefit of this process is that if a trial proceeding ends in a conviction, the Registry will be in a position to: (i) provide information on victims who participated at trial and may, depending on the scope of conviction, qualify for reparations; (ii) produce an approximate total number of direct and indirect victims that may qualify as potential beneficiaries of reparations; and (iii) report on the different types of harm the potential beneficiaries have suffered.[137] This will enable the Chamber to speedily issue a reparations order upon which the Trust Fund for Victims will be able to immediately commence implementation activities as no – or minimal – further victim identification is required—the latter having been one major reason for years of delay in reparation implementation in the *Lubanga, Katanga* and *Al Mahdi* proceedings.

#### 3.4.2.3 *Form Collection beyond the Start of Trial*

In the first cases before the ICC, the cut-off date for victims to come forward and apply for participation in the proceedings differed across the cases, from the commencement of the evidence hearing (*Katanga*) to a later date well into the presentation of evidence of the parties (*Lubanga, Bemba*).[138] The 2016 edition of the Chambers Practice Manual finally regulated the matter in order to create a common practice across Chambers; however, it took a rather restrictive approach in stipulating that '[t]he Trial Chamber sets a final time limit, sufficiently before the commencement of the trial, for the transmission of any

136 *Ntaganda* Judgment on the appeals against the decision of Trial Chamber VI of 8 March 2021 entitled 'Reparations Order' (n 126) paras 9, 340.

137 See e.g. *Ali Kushayb* Second Decision, para. 18.

138 Decision on the treatment of applications for participation, *Katanga, Situation in the Democratic Republic of the Congo*, ICC-01/04-01/07-933-tENG, TC II, ICC, 27 February 2009 and Order on the Request by the Registry for the Extension of a Time Limit (regulation 35 of the Regulations of the Court), *Katanga, Situation in the Democratic Republic of the Congo*, ICC-01/04-01/07-1087, TC II, ICC, 1 May 2009, ordering the transmission of all victim forms well before the start of trial (24 November 2009); in *Lubanga*, in contrast, the Trial Chamber accepted victim application transmissions throughout the trial, see only Order on the applications by victims to participate and for reparations, *Lubanga, Situation in the Democratic Republic of the Congo*, ICC-01/04-01/06-2838, TC I, ICC, 27 January 2012 (at the time this order was issued, the Chamber was already in deliberation for the article 74 judgment). Finally, also in *Bemba*, Trial Chamber III accepted the transmission of victim application forms well into the trial proceedings (which commenced on 22 November 2010), see Decision on 799 applications by victims to participate in the proceedings, *Bemba, Situation in the Central African Republic*, ICC-01/05-01/08-2401, TC III, ICC, 5 November 2012.

further application by victims', thus following the *Katanga* approach.[139] While having a standardising effect across cases and helpfully allocating the individual assessment of applications with the Registry (thus taking an immense burden off the Chamber's shoulders), the provision also led to unsatisfactory outcomes in terms of numbers of participating victims, since this often provided the Registry with a short time window to collect and process victim applications—a lesson learnt from the *Lubanga* and, notably, *Bemba* cases. As a result, in both the *Ntaganda* and *Ongwen* cases, at the start of trial there were large numbers of potential victim participants that stayed outside the process, due to a lack of time for the Registry to assess and transmit to the Chamber.

Starting in the *Al Hassan* proceedings in 2017, the Registry (VPRS) suggested alongside its ABC approach and the new standard combined application form a digression from the time limit stipulated in the Chambers Practice Manual. It motivated the digression with case-specific challenges to generate representative numbers of victim participation forms while following due process and informing victims in the field properly of their choices. This logic turned out to be true not just for the *Al Hassan* proceedings, but all current cases in the CAR II situation, the *Abd-Al-Rahman* trial in the Darfur situation, and in all likelihood any future proceeding before the ICC. Following the successful VPRS requests across cases in the years following 2017 and various Chambers adjusting time limits against the—restrictive—wording of the Manual, the 2022 edition of the Chambers Practice Manual set the final time limit to 'the end of the Prosecutor's presentation of evidence'.[140] This is a fortunate adjustment as it provides the Registry with the entirety of the Prosecution case to continue its collection of victim applications.

Finally, Registry requests for exceptional extensions of the final time limit until the end of the Victims' case in the *Abd-Al-Rahman* proceedings, motivated by specific in-country security and infrastructural challenges, were granted by the Trial Chamber.[141] It would be fortuitous for the victim participation regime at the ICC if what is an exceptional arrangement in the *Abd-Al-Rahman* case became a general practice across cases – and if the application deadline could indeed extend until the end of the trial phase.[142] Victims'

139 Chambers Practice Manual (version of 1 February 2016) Section C, I., 28, available at: <https://www.icc-cpi.int/about/judicial-divisions/chambers-practice-manual>.

140 Chambers Practice Manual (version of 25 March 2022) para. 97(iii).

141 *See most lately* Decision on the Second Registry's Request to Extend the Time Limit to Submit Victim Applications for Participation, *Abd-Al-Rahman, Situation in Darfur, Sudan*, ICC-02/05-01/20-943, TC I, ICC, 16 May 2023.

142 *See* Public redacted version of 'Registry Request for Extension of Time Limit to Submit Victim Applications for Participation', *Abd-Al-Rahman, Situation in Darfur, Sudan*, ICC-02/05-01/20-838-Red, REGISTRY, ICC, 22 December 2022.

legitimate interest in participating in the proceedings continues throughout the presentation of evidence in the courtroom, where legal representatives interact—quite actively—on their behalf until the end of trial. With the ABC approach in place, the burden on the parties is minimal and neither the fairness not the expeditiousness of the proceedings are impacted negatively while providing a more comprehensive—and meaningful—space for victims to partake in ICC proceedings.

### 3.4.3 Conclusion

Judges Fulford and Van den Wyngaert conceded in their observations more than 10 years ago that even prior to the aforementioned reform initiatives, the victim application process did not have a delaying effect on proceedings.[143] Also the IER Report noted that no tangible evidence could be found that the 'present victim participation scheme in any of its aspects and features has a detrimental effect to the speediness of the criminal process or (fair trial) rights of the Defence'.[144] To the contrary: the ABC process, alongside the combined victim application form and the extended timeframe for information collection from victims have provided major standardisation and efficiency gains of the process in the past years. This has led to a more inclusive participation scheme as more victims got quicker access to the proceedings through their legal representative. In addition, the enhanced Registry collection of reparation-related information during the trial phase will have a major accelerating effect on the implementation of reparation awards.

## 3.5 *Victims' Access to Proceedings at Reparation Stage*

The Statute and the Rules are clear in that a victim is free to claim reparations also without having participated in proceedings at trial. There are impressive examples in the ICC's jurisprudence of heavy increases in numbers of reparation beneficiaries versus victims participating at the trial phase of the same case; the *Lubanga* and *Al Mahdi* proceedings have seen lengthy exercises of additional victim identification during the reparation phases.[145] In both cases, the victim

143 Fulford (n 13) 222; Wyngaert (n 17) 494ff.

144 IER Report, para. 843.

145 *Lubanga:* at trial: 129 participating victims, see Judgment pursuant to Article 74 of the Statute, *Lubanga, Situation in the Democratic Republic of the Congo*, ICC-01/04-01/06-2842, TC I, ICC, 14 March 2012, para. 15; in reparation proceedings, the number of eligible beneficiaries is at 1,546 individuals. In the *Al Mahdi* guilty plea proceedings, the number of participating victims at the time of issuance of the trial judgment and sentence was at 8: Judgment and Sentence, *Al Mahdi, Situation in the Republic of Mali*, ICC-01/12-01/15-171,

identification processes were based on forms to solicit relevant information in a standardised fashion. As the information collection was thus individualised, it enabled the Trust Fund for Victims to implement individual (in *Al Mahdi*)[146] as well as well-designed collective reparation programmes (*Lubanga*)[147] pursuant to relevant Chambers' orders. However, the aforementioned cases have seen three markedly different processes in terms of actors involved in the victim identification and verification exercises (i.e. between the Trust Fund for Victims, the VPRS and the legal representatives of victims), and all processes proved to be very lengthy.

In the *Ntaganda* and *Ongwen* reparation proceedings, at the time of writing relevant reparation orders have not yet become final.[148] In both cases, it is certain that the actual amount of potential reparation beneficiaries quite drastically surpasses the numbers of victims who participated in the judicial proceedings.[149] Yet, *exact* numbers, including victims' whereabouts are very challenging to get to, not just due to the lapse of time and migration of victim communities over the years, but also—at least for the *Ntaganda* proceedings—due to security constraints. It is not clear how potential reparation beneficiaries will be able to enter the relevant proceedings and/or benefit from reparation programmes—a daunting task for the Trust Fund for Victims.

---

TC VIII, ICC, 27 September 2016, para. 6; the number of potential reparation beneficiaries to date (8 February 2023) is at 1,218. However, in *Katanga*, the number of participating victims at trial was 366, see Judgment pursuant to article 74 of the Statute, *Katanga, Situation in the Democratic Republic of the Congo*, ICC-01/04-01/07-3436-tENG, TC II, ICC, 7 March 2014, para. 36; on reparations, it was reduced by the Chamber to 297 (due to the slightly more onerous standard of proof).

146 Reparations Order, *Al Mahdi, Situation in the Republic of Mali*, ICC-01/12-01/15-236, TC VIII, ICC, 17 August 2017, paras 91ff, 104.

147 See, with the procedural history in the body of the decision, Version publique expurgée de la Décision faisant droit à la requête du Fonds au profit des victimes du 21 septembre 2020 et approuvant la mise en oeuvre des réparations collectives prenant la forme de prestations de services, *Lubanga, Situation in the Democratic Republic of the Congo*, ICC-01/04-01/06-3495-Red, TC II, ICC, 4 March 2021.

148 In *Ntaganda*, an initial Reparation Order by Trial Chamber VI of 8 March 2021 has been successfully appealed (*see* Judgment on the appeal against the decision of Trial Chamber VI of 8 March 2021 entitled 'Reparations Order', *Ntaganda, Situation in the Democratic Republic of the Congo*, ICC-01/04-02/06-2782, APPEALS CHAMBER, ICC, 12 September 2022). An amended reparation order by Trial Chamber II ('Public Redacted Version of Addendum to the Reparations Order of 8 March 2021, ICC-01/04-02/06-2659', ICC-01/04-02/06-2858-Red, of 14 July 2023) is presently under appeal.

149 See e.g. the Registry's Mapping Report and Submission on Reparations, *Ongwen, Situation in Uganda*, ICC-02/04-01/15-1919, TC IX, ICC, 6 December 2021, Annex I: at trial, altogether 4,095 victims participated, while it is suggested that a multiple of that will be potential reparation beneficiaries.

It follows that in terms of victims' access to reparation (proceedings), further optimisation of processes may be opportune. As mentioned elsewhere, the Trial Chambers in *Al Hasan, Said* and *Abd-Al-Rahman* instructed the Registry (VPRS) to collect a maximum of information of potential reparation beneficiaries during the trial phase. This will go a long way in having a wealth of reparation-related information, notably on (i) the approximate total number of potential beneficiaries, (ii) types of harm, (iii) needs and (iv) criteria of potential prioritisation, ready for the relevant Chamber to issue a speedy reparations order not long after the judgment pursuant to Article 74 of the Statute.[150] Ideally, further beneficiary identification will not be necessary[151] and the Trust Fund for Victims will be able to commence implementation of reparations months after the verdict.

## 4 Victims' Participatory Rights—through Legal Representation

The Statute provides only limited guidance on the way how victims bring their views and concerns to the attention of the judges (and in fact the parties); Article 68(3) of the Statute merely suggests that '[s]uch views and concerns may be presented by the legal representatives of the victims where the Court considers it appropriate', with a reference to concretising norms in the RPE.

The RPE would thus ideally answer two sets of questions: the first pertaining to the legal representation, including what it entails (i.e. team strength), how it is chosen, who gets to choose, who pays, what qualifications relevant individuals would have to have. The second set of questions relates to the procedural tools and vehicles that are provided to victims to express their views and concerns through their legal representatives throughout the proceedings.

Both the actual means of participation and the choice of who represents victims in the courtroom have a direct impact on how the

150 As in *Ntaganda,* the VPRS would naturally be the Registry office to assess participating victims' eligibility for reparations based on the charges subject to conviction for a seamless onward transfer of dossiers from participation to reparations; see Registry's First Report on Reparations, *Ntaganda, Situation in the Democratic Republic of the Congo*, ICC-01/04-02/06-2602, TC VI, ICC, 30 September 2020 (with relevant Annexes).

151 A VPRS-led residual/exceptional victim identification mechanism could be established *after* a reparation order becomes final (*see* Recommendation R336 of the IER Report, and as recently endorsed by the Plenary of ICC Judges in June 2023), in coordination with the Trust Fund for Victims. Identification and vetting of additional beneficiaries during the reparation phase has added years to the length of proceedings in *Lubanga* and *Al Mahdi* and should ideally be avoided in the future.

victims—individually—experience the quality of their interaction with the ICC, i.e. whether it is meaningful to them or not.[152] In both areas, ICC legislation and jurisprudence have attempted to transform the concept into sensible and viable practice.

### 4.1 *Internal vs. External Legal Representation*

The main provision regulating victims' legal representation is Rule 90 of the Rules. The concept is actually quite clear: as a key tenet, a victim shall be free to choose a legal representative (para. 1). However, where there is a group of victims (which unsurprisingly turns out to be the ICC's operative reality), said group will be represented by a 'common legal representative' (para. 2).[153] While the right to choose remains *a priori* with the victims, it shifts over to the Court where victims lack the necessary means to pay for a common legal representative (para. 5). As to the pool of potential legal representative of victims, the Registry maintains a list of counsel external to the ICC who all satisfy certain minimum (legal) requirements to appear in court (see reference in para. 2). In addition, through the Regulations of the Court, the ICC judges established in the early years of the Court the 'Office of Public Counsel for Victims' ('OPCV'); pursuant to Regulation 81(4)(e) of said regulations, counsel of the OPCV may '[represent] victims throughout the proceedings, on the instruction or with the leave of the Chamber, when this is in the interests of justice'. While OPCV counsel and support staff are funded as Court staff through the ICC's regular budget, external counsel are not incorporated in the staffing structure and paid through a legal aid disbursement system. The latter also defines the remunerated team strength of the relevant victim representatives' team.[154] While

152 It is noted that while representing the ultimate performance indicator for the ICC Registry's victim functions, it is inherently difficult to measure, not least as the experience is of a subjective nature; in addition, the level of meaningfulness will by many victims be measured by their expectations—and receipt—of reparations in case these ensue under Article 75 of the Statute. Sadly, the level of meaningfulness and satisfaction of victims from their participation in criminal proceedings alone will therefore remain difficult to measure, in turn making it at times difficult to discern where and how exactly the system needs to improve.

153 Where certain victims cannot be grouped in a single group due to diverging or indeed conflicting interests (think of child soldiers and victims of child soldier attacks in the same case), multiple victim groups are represented by separate counsel in the proceedings, e.g. the *Yekatom/Ngaissona; Ntaganda; Mokom* cases.

154 The legal aid system is governed by a legal aid policy, see Registry's single policy document on the Court's legal aid system, ICC-ASP/12/3, 4 June 2013 (Twelfth Session of the ASP); the policy is presently under review, see Report of the Bureau on legal aid, ICC-ASP/21/26, 29 November 2022 (Twenty-first Session of the ASP).

the OPCV insofar enjoys more liberty to deploy resources on relevant cases, its *de facto* size as per the ICC's annual budget keeps resources tight and staff work on multiple cases simultaneously.

Unlike the application process for victims to access ICC proceedings, the legal representation of victims has to date not brought forward trends or similar practices across cases that could lend themselves to any form of standard practice. The present landscape of victims' legal representation across on-going cases provides the full universe of options foreseen by the applicable legal framework: cases where victim groups are represented by external legal representatives (*Al Hassan; Abd Al Rahman; Mokom*); proceedings where solely OPCV represents victims, be that in a single group (*Said*) or different victim groups (*Ntaganda*); and trials where counsel from OPCV represents victims alongside external counsel in a joint group (*Yekatom/Ngaïssona*).

There has been criticism over the years that the wording of Rule 90(1) of the Rules is too ambitious in light of the ICC's actual budgetary capacity: that victims' individual choice of counsel, as postulated in said provision, is unrealistic as there will: (i) always be—large—groups of victims; and (ii) never be victim groups financially capable to afford their own chosen counsel in the proceedings. The facts underlying the aforementioned criticism turn out to be true. All cases presently before ICC Chambers have *common* legal representation; and two instances where victims' chosen counsel did initially not request financial assistance from the Registry pursuant to Rule 90(5) of the Rules, the regime at trial had turned into victim counsel fully funded by the ICC.[155] However, this reality does not necessarily render the key tenet of Rule 90(1) invalid; rather, the different constellations of victims' legal representation in past in current cases at the ICC, but also regimes at the Extraordinary Chambers in the Courts of Cambodia, the Special Tribunal for Lebanon or the Kosovo Specialist Chambers lend themselves to a stock-taking and (joint?) brainstorming. Gathering more data on victims' level of satisfaction with the relevant options may help in assessing whether there is *one* best practice. With some minor adjustments of the institutional line-up of the Registry, interesting solutions can be found—which, however will be part of a separate analysis; the present contribution merely seeks to flag the challenge.

Another challenge to flag in passing is the Pre-Trial Chambers' timing on the designation of victims' legal representatives. Present practice that relevant decisions are issued only shortly before the hearing on the confirmation of charges effectively provides counsel with too little time to properly consult victims and

155 See *Ntaganda* and *Abd Al Rahman* proceedings.

represent them more forcefully at the pre-trial stage. An item to be tackled by (Pre-Trial) Chambers and the Registry in future proceedings.

### 4.2 *Procedural Tool Kit of Legal Representatives*

The effectiveness of victims' legal representation (as well as the clients' experience of their participation) is heavily influenced by the repertoire of procedural tools to interact in the proceedings. This is partly governed in the RPE, in particular Rule 91.[156] Rule 131(2) adds to this in providing victims with access to the case record. Yet, the exact set of participatory rights remains in the prerogative of the respective chamber.[157] Jurisprudence in the different cases before the ICC has carved out a rather comprehensive set of victims' participatory rights, with minor differences between the cases.[158] As a fundamental premise, it is for the judges to find the just equilibrium between giving the most meaningful rights to the participating victims and, on the other hand, avoiding prejudice to the rights of the accused or to the fair and impartial conduct of the proceedings.[159] The guiding principle has been throughout that the victims' personal interests have to be affected to invoke relevant participatory

---

156 Rule 91 grants legal representatives (i) participation in hearings; (ii) the right to make oral and written submissions; (iii) the questioning of witnesses, an expert or the accused (upon application to the Chamber); (iv) the introduction of documents. For an early discussion of the applicable legal framework to victims before the ICC see Decision on victims' participation, *Lubanga, Situation in the Democratic Republic of the Congo*, ICC-01/04-01/06-1119, TC I, ICC,18 January 2008, paras 20ff.

157 Pursuant to Rule 89(1) of the Rules, the Chamber shall specify 'the proceedings and manner in which participation is considered appropriate', in keeping with Article 68(3) of the Rome Statute (as 'determined to be appropriate by the Court'); see also similar language in Rule 91(3)(b) of the ICC Rules and Regulation 24(2) of the Regulations of the Court.

158 See e.g. Judgment on the appeals of The Prosecutor and The Defence against Trial Chamber I's Decision on Victims' Participation of 18 January 2008, *Lubanga, Situation in the Democratic Republic of the Congo*, ICC-01/04-01/06-1432, AC, ICC, 11 July 2008; *Kenyatta* Decision on victims' representation and participation (n 94); Decision on contested victims' applications for participation, legal representation of victims and their procedural rights, *Ongwen, Situation in Uganda*, ICC-02/04-01/15-350, PTC II, ICC, 27 November 2015, paras 27ff, and Public Redacted Version of Decision on the Legal Representatives for Victims Requests to Present Evidence and Views and Concerns and related requests, *Ongwen, Situation in Uganda*, ICC-02/04-01/15-1199-Red, TC IX, ICC, 6 March 2018, fn 22 and paras 17–23, 78–83; *Ntaganda* Decision on victims' participation in trial proceedings (n 115) (followed up by multiple decisions further qualifying the applicable regime of victim participation).

159 See Rule 89(1), 91(2), (3)(b) of the ICC Rules; *Ongwen* Decision on contested victims' applications for participation, legal representation of victims and their procedural rights (n 139) para. 28.

rights. Of note, judges have underlined that victims shall not take a 'Prosecutor *bis*' role: attempts by victims' legal representatives to provide evidence on the crimes charged or the accused's role in their commission where the Prosecutor failed to do so are not acceptable.[160] While victims' procedural rights already exist during the pre-trial phase[161], the more relevant participatory regime—including a more inclusive access to the (confidential) case file and (closed) sessions, as well as the right to test, question and adduce[162] evidence—applies at trial.[163] Chambers issue directions on the conduct of proceedings at the outset of trial, which also address the legal representatives' rights and role.[164] Since the early stages of the ICC's existence, Chambers have established a practice whereby victims are also given their own time in the courtroom to present views and concerns and/or to call witnesses,[165] between the presentation of the Prosecutor's and the Defence evidence.

While minor discrepancies continue to exist across cases in terms of the victims' legal representatives' procedural rights and duties, the broad lines can be considered as sufficiently established and tested in practice. A body of

---

160 *Ongwen* Public Redacted Version of Decision on the Legal Representatives for Victims Requests to Present Evidence and Views and Concerns and related requests (n 139) fn 27; see also Directions on the conduct of proceedings, *Abd-Al-Rahman ('Ali Kushayb'), Situation in Darfur, Sudan*, ICC-02/05-01/20-478, TC I, ICC, 4 October 2021 (*'Ali Kushayb* Directions of Conduct'), para. 36; *Lubanga* Judgment on the appeals of The Prosecutor and The Defence against Trial Chamber I's Decision on Victims' Participation of 18 January 2008 (n 158) para. 93.

161 As mentioned above, the *timing* of victims' exercise of participatory rights is subject to possible improvement through earlier assignment of victim counsel.

162 Usually upon request and leave granted by the Chamber, see e.g. *Ali Kushayb* Directions of Conduct, para. 19(ii).

163 See for a comprehensive overview also of key jurisprudence: Office of Public Counsel for Victims (OPCV), *Representing Victims before the International Criminal Court: A Manual for legal representatives* 5th edn (ICC-OPCV-MLR-005/19_ENG, OPCV ICC 2019) <https://www.icc-cpi.int/sites/default/files/manual-victims-legal-representatives-fifth-edition-rev1.pdf> accessed 28 March 2023.

164 See e.g. *Ali Kushayb* Directions of Conduct; Initial Directions on the Conduct of the Proceedings, *Yekatom and Ngaïssona, Situation in the Central African Republic II*, ICC-01/14-01/18-631 TC V, ICC, 26 August 2020; Initial Directions on the Conduct of the Proceedings, *Ongwen, Situation in Uganda*, ICC-02/04-01/15-497 TC IX, ICC, 13 July 2016; Directions on the conduct of the proceedings, *Gbagbo and Blé Goudé, Situation in the Republic of Côte d'Ivoire*, ICC-02/11-01/15-205,TC I, ICC, 3 September 2015.

165 As to the modalities, see e.g. Second order regarding the applications of the legal representatives of victims to present evidence and the views and concerns of victims, *Bemba, Situation in the Central African Republic*, ICC-01/05-01/08-2027, TC III, ICC, 21 December 2011, para. 12.

relevant jurisprudence has further solidified the system. Remaining questions whether victims should have more influence on the Prosecutor's investigations and charging go back to the institutional design of the ICC system and are therefore less an issue of practice *within* that design.

## 5 Conclusion

Similar to the more technical and administrative aspects of the victim participation regime at the ICC, it can be safely concluded that regarding the procedural toolkit of victims how to engage in the courtroom, an aggregate amount of standardization has been achieved. On the issue who is to represent victims—ICC-internal or external counsel or both—there is a diverse field of options which invites for further analysis. Yet, in its diverse constellations, legal representation of victims has by and large been effective. Of note, former ICC Judge Van den Wyngaert's fears that victims' participation in the proceedings will lead to fairness issues or unreasonable delays in the process[166] have not materialized. Similarly, feedback from victim communities across ICC situations and cases has provided evidence that their participation in relevant processes is by and large felt to be meaningful—thus allaying another key concern raised by the Judge.[167] Also with regards to the cost of victims' access to the Court including their representation in the proceedings, the victim participation system of the ICC seems to be a sensible investment: taking together the annual allocation of legal aid funds for victim representation[168] as well as the budgets of OPCV and VPRS, one arrives at just over 5% of the ICC's annual budget.[169] The Victim participation regime at the ICC is thus amongst the most economic 'cornerstone achievements' of the Rome Statute for the emerging international criminal justice framework.

---

166 Wyngaert (n 17) 487, 493, 495. It is noted that the main case for delay cited by the Judge referred to the Chamber's assessment of victim application forms (ibid., 493), which, as demonstrated above, has been subject to reform and streamlining since.

167 Wyngaert (n 17) 495.

168 Approx. 3,5 million EUR as per the ASP Report of the Bureau on legal aid, ICC-ASP/21/26 (n 154) para. 35.

169 For 2023, the ICC's approved annual budget is at €169,649,200, see Resolution of the Assembly of States Parties on the proposed programme budget for 2023, the Working Capital Fund for 2023, the scale of assessment for the apportionment of expenses of the International Criminal Court, financing appropriations for 2023 and the Contingency Fund, ICC-ASP/21/Res.1, 9 December 2022 (Ninth Plenary Meeting of the ASP), para. 3.

In light of all of the above, particularly a closer look at the system enabling victims' access to the Court, but also the representation regime show that a number of cornerstone achievements have been made particularly in recent years with increased caseload before the Chambers. Standardisation and thoughtful application/interpretation of the legal framework have led to a well-balanced system which, while obviously open to further improvements, fulfils the postulate of its creators: a meaningful and efficient victim participation regime in harmony with the rights of the Defence to a fair and expedited process—and at an affordable cost. As highlighted, a number of challenges remain; but expressed differently, this only means that further improvements are waiting to be designed and put in action.

# PART 5

## *Cooperation and Complementarity*

CHAPTER 15

# Behind the Scenes: the Essential Role of Cooperation in an Effective Trial

*Peter Lewis*

## 1 Introduction

All the International Criminal Court has achieved over the last two decades has only been made possible by the cooperation it has received from its States Parties and other stakeholders to support its judicial and investigative roles.[1] As we look to the future and the new situations the Court will be facing, with higher degrees of complexity and much larger scales of operation, the challenges for securing cooperation will be greater than ever. I want to illustrate how important cooperation is by taking you 'behind the scenes' of the work at the Court—with three concrete examples. Firstly, I will stress the essentiality of diplomatic cooperation in order to implement a warrant of arrest. I will, then, zoom in on the importance of protection of witnesses, and how this can be reached only when there are strong ties with States Parties. Lastly, I will explain how collaboration with States is crucial to enhancing victims' participation, and consequently, achieving reparations.

## 2 Arrest[2]

The open 'picture' is a simple process: a person has been arrested in a country following a warrant of arrest issued by the Judges of the ICC at the request of the Prosecutor. In line with Part 9 of the Rome Statute,[3] the relevant national

1 See, for instance, the latest annual report on cooperation to the Assembly of States Parties, Report of the Court on Cooperation ICC-ASP/20/25, 29 October 2021 (Twentieth Session of the ASP).

2 ICC, 'Arresting ICC suspects at large: Why it matters; What the Court does; What States can do', January 2019 <https://www.icc-cpi.int/sites/default/files/bookletArrestsENG.pdf> accessed 30 March 2023.

3 'International Cooperation and Judicial Assistance', Part 9 of the of the Rome Statute of the International Criminal Court (signed 17 July 1998, entered into force 1 July 2002) 2187 UNTS 3.

 | DOI:10.1163/9789004529939_016

authorities implement the warrant of arrest, following a cooperation request transmitted by the ICC Registry. The Registry then sends in a team to the country to organize the transfer with the authorities. The Registry team boards an aircraft to a place often far away, together with security staff, a medical officer, an interpreter and cooperation advisers, to ensure that the procedure goes as smoothly as possible. They will spend a few days in the country and then return with the suspect on board.

'Behind the scenes' in the months and (sometimes) years preceding the arrest, the image is much more complicated. As soon as a warrant of arrest is issued, the Suspects At Large Working Group—composed of cooperation advisers, Registry analysts and investigators from the Office of the Prosecutor—starts collecting information on the suspect's whereabouts, conducts security and political analyses, and consults with the Chamber to elaborate medium-and short-term strategies and optimize the chance of arrest. Our efforts can last for years as warrants of arrest are valid for life and the political context constantly evolves. We work closely with the countries through our focal points. These focal points come to The Hague once a year thanks to the grant we receive from the European Commission to strengthen cooperation.[4] When an opportunity for arrest is identified, a delegation is sent as discreetly as possible. Upon arrest, the person will see a national judge and will then be transferred by air, most of the time, to the Netherlands. There is no publicity until the person arrives safely at the Detention Centre in The Hague.

Depending on the suspect and the situation at stake, various strategies may be put in place and the support of different stakeholders may also be sought. For example, if the United Nations are in the area, we will often contact them for security and logistical support.[5] In certain cases, the assistance of Interpol is requested to issue red notices against ICC suspects.[6]

4 See, for instance, 'Seminar on Cooperation in The Hague with national focal points', 21 January 2019 <https://www.icc-cpi.int/about/cooperation/seminar-cooperation-hague-national-focal-points> accessed 30 March 2023.

5 'Negotiated Relationship Agreement between the International Criminal Court and the United Nations', entered into force 4 October 2004, Resolution ICC-ASP/3/Res.1, 7 September 2004 (Third Plenary Meeting of the ASP) <https://www.icc-cpi.int/news/negotiated-relationship-agreement-between-international-criminal-court-and-united-nations> accessed 30 March 2023.

6 Interpol, 'View Red Notices' < https://www.interpol.int/How-we-work/Notices/View-Red-Notices> accessed 14 December 2022.

Although all States Parties have a duty to cooperate under Part 9 of the Rome Statute,[7] experience has shown that constant follow-up by the Court is necessary to ensure that the execution of warrants remains a priority for the requested States and that updated information is available. An arrest is, therefore, the result of a combination of efforts made by several States that provide intelligence and operational capabilities, international organizations and individuals. The cooperation of States via diplomatic support is also essential.

What is clear is that without this cooperation there would be no arrest, no trial, and no end to impunity. As at the time of writing, 14 defendants are still at large.[8] Greater support and cooperation from all relevant actors in executing these warrants of arrest is much needed.

## 3 Witnesses[9]

The adequate protection of witnesses is imperative to the successful functioning of any judicial process.[10] This is especially true for the ICC, where the nature of the criminal cases necessitates oral evidence and witness testimonies.[11]

The ICC believes in a holistic approach: the responsibility to protect witnesses and victims lies with the Court as a whole. The statutory framework of the Court shows that the Court has a duty to take appropriate measures to protect the safety, physical and psychological well-being, dignity and privacy of victims and witnesses, as stipulated by article 68(1) of the Rome Statute. The Rules of Procedure and Evidence further stipulate that the Victims and Witnesses Section (hereinafter referred to as 'the Section' or 'the VWS'), a neutral service provider located within the Registry, shall provide witnesses,

---

7 See, in particular, Article 86 of the Rome Statute: 'States Parties shall, in accordance with the provisions of this Statute, cooperate fully with the Court in its investigation and prosecution of crimes within the jurisdiction of the Court'.

8 ICC webpage on defendants at large <https://www.icc-cpi.int/defendants?f%5B0%5D=accused_states%3A329> accessed 14 December 2022.

9 ICC, 'Cooperation agreements' <https://www.icc-cpi.int/sites/default/files/Cooperation_Agreements_Eng.pdf> accessed 30 March 2023.

10 C Mahony, *The justice sector afterthought: Witness protection in Africa* (Pretoria: Institute for Security Studies 2010) and S Glušcic et al., *Protecting witnesses of serious crime: Training manual for law enforcement and judiciary* (Strasbourg: Council of Europe Publishing 2006).

11 International Bar Association, 'Witnesses before the International Criminal Court; An International Bar Association International Criminal Court Programme report on the ICC's efforts and challenges to protect, support and ensure the rights of witnesses', July 2013, 14, available at <www.ibanet.org/document?id=July-2013-Witnesses-before-ICC> accessed 30 March 2023.

victims who appear before the Court, and others who are at risk on account of testimony given, with adequate protective and security measures and formulate long-and short-term plans for their protection. The Section is also mandated to recommend to the organs of the Court the adoption of protective measures and assist witnesses when they are called to testify before the Court and victims when they are at risk because of their participation in the proceedings.

This could, for instance, translate into what one can see when following the live streaming of a hearing at the ICC: a witness whose identity is protected through distortion (face pixelated and voice modified). This would be the result of a decision by a Chamber to protect the anonymity of the witness vis-à-vis the public. But what if such in-court protective measures are not sufficient to ensure the protection of ICC witnesses? What is going on behind the scenes and why is the cooperation of States absolutely essential when it comes to ensuring the protection of witnesses and victims at risk on account of their interaction with the Court?

The VWS has a variety of protective measures at its disposal to ensure the protection of persons at risk.[12]

Those protective measures must be proportionate to the level of risk a person is facing. The VWS, therefore, conducts expert protection assessments independently of the calling parties to evaluate the level of threat and associated risk to witnesses and victims due to their interaction with the Court. In many cases, keeping the interaction between the person and the Court confidential is sufficient to avoid exposure. When this is not sufficient, then the next level of protection would involve the implementation of local protective measures or the provision of assistance to the person at risk to move from one part of the country to another.[13]

When none of the above sufficiently mitigate the risk to the witness or victim, inclusion in the Court's Protection Programme (the 'ICCPP') is considered.[14] Such inclusion is a measure of last resort implemented in extreme cases and only when there is no other option available and adequate to ensure the safety of the witness or victim.

Why? Because international relocation is an intrusive process that creates a significant disturbance to the lives of the person at risk and their family members. They would have to leave their country, job, friends and social network,

12 See Regulations 92 to 96 of the Regulations of the Registry, ICC-BD/03-03-13, approved by the Presidency on 6 March 2006 ('RoR').

13 See definition of assisted move in Regulation 95 of the RoR.

14 See Regulation 96 of the RoR.

learn a new language, and familiarize themselves with a new culture and climate.

The VWS is, therefore, inclined to try alternative solutions that would not require such drastic changes in the witness's or victim's life, and to implement less stringent measures whenever possible.

The Registry is mandated to negotiate relocation agreements on behalf of the Court, and to secure the cooperation of States in the highly sensitive area of witness protection and international relocation.

Without this cooperation, there would be a potential loss of crucial evidence and witnesses at trial, essential to deliver justice. Unfortunately, despite the tremendous efforts being made by the Registry in that respect, the number of States Parties agreeing to welcome witnesses and victims on their territories is very limited. Of the 123 States that are party to the Rome Statute, only slightly more than 20 have signed a relocation agreement with the Court or have indicated that they would be open to receiving witnesses on their territories.

Unlike States, the ICC does not have a territory or governmental services, such as schools, hospitals and police forces. This makes the work of the ICC Protection Programme much more difficult than the work of a national witness protection programme that can rely on other national services. The cooperation of States is, therefore, critical in order for the Court to succeed and provide persons at risk with the safe haven they need to be able to testify or participate in the judicial process without putting their lives in jeopardy.

International relocation is not always needed and only a minority of witnesses will be moved across borders, but when it *is* needed, it is essential to implement the relocation before the risks materialize. The ICC fully relies on the States Parties' willingness to accept witnesses and victims at risk on their territories and to provide them with a place to stay to start rebuilding their lives.

This willingness, which forms the basis of the ICC protection system, is often lacking on the part of the States, leading to witnesses and victims being placed in challenging situations. When the Registry is not able to secure a relocation country, protected individuals are temporarily moved to a location where they may stay for only a limited period of time. These temporary situations tend to unreasonably extend. In 2021, it took the Registry around 550 days from the moment a decision was made to include a person at risk in the ICCPP until the day a State would accept the person for relocation. By the end of 2022, more than 700 days were needed for the same purpose. These prolonged temporary situations have a disastrous impact on witnesses' and victims' lives and psychological welfare as they are unable to resume a normal life, provide for their families and make plans for their future and the future of their children.

Considering the challenges ahead, it is essential that States' cooperation in the area of witness protection is further enhanced to allow the Registry to fulfil its mandate and provide persons at risk with the security they need to participate in the judicial process.

## 4 Victim Participation and Reparations

The Registry assists victims of crimes under the jurisdiction of the ICC in gaining access to the Court and to relevant judicial proceedings. It is also a key enabler for victims' access to reparations in case of a conviction. The key provisions governing its work are articles 68(3) (victim participation) and 75 (reparations) of the Rome Statute. The Victims Participation and Reparations Section ('the Section' or 'the VPRS') of the Registry acts as the entry point and key facilitator for victim applications for participation in the judicial proceedings and reparations.

The Registry's victim participation functions require operations both at the seat of the Court and in the field, all led and carried out by the VPRS. Field activities aim at enabling victims to be informed of their rights regarding participation in ICC proceedings, reparations and legal representation in the courtroom. To this end, specially trained Registry staff meet victims on the ground and create the first link between them, their harm and the ICC proceedings addressing this harm. Specialized Registry staff are versed in specific techniques for interviewing vulnerable victims, and victim safety and security issues. The first contact with victims is an often overlooked yet essential feature of Registry victim care. Only if a victim properly understands what the ICC proceedings are and represent for the victim personally will that victim be in a position to make an informed decision about whether or not he or she wants to participate in proceedings. This is also where cooperation with States and international and regional organizations comes to the fore as an essential enabler: the more support the Registry staff encounter on the ground in terms of access and technical and logistic assistance, the more effective their activities will be.

At the seat of the Court, the VPRS analyses and logs victim applications for participation and reparations and all other related documents received from victims. The Section transmits the applications to the Chambers, alongside reports with its legal analysis and recommendations across all cases and situations before the ICC. Access to relevant victim data is governed exclusively by Chambers' decisions across all situations and cases. Yet the relevant database, alongside the rather complex IT structure of the system to generate appropriate reports for the Chambers, is administered by the VPRS. In total, around 16,000 victims have been and are participating in ICC proceedings to date.

The victim function of the Registry has managed to shape the Chambers' decision-making in many technical aspects of victim participation in the proceedings, notably the application process and legal analysis of victims' applications received. Over time, the Registry has developed an effective system of application collection, analysis and reporting, which has been a major efficiency gain for Chambers, as VPRS legal services now carry out the key analysis of thousands of victims' submissions across the proceedings. The Section's most recent application assessment and reporting practice across cases before the ICC was adopted in the Chambers Practice Manual in February 2022.[15]

But Registry engagement in bringing the victims' views and concerns into the courtroom transcends the mere mechanical collection, assessment and reporting on victim applications. Registry-led discussions with, and suggestions to, Chambers in various cases over the past years have produced sensible and meaningful Registry-led victim consultation processes from the very early to the later stages in proceedings. For instance, in the collection of victims' views and concerns under Article 15(3) of the Rome Statute, when the Prosecutor seeks to open an investigation *proprio motu*, the Registry has managed to significantly extend its timeline to collect victims' views from the general default of 30 days pursuant to regulation 50(1) of the Regulations of the Court. Civil society has played an important role in ensuring that victims' voices actually reached the Registry and could be collected and reported to Chambers in these processes. Think of highly sensitive environments like the Philippines, Myanmar or Afghanistan, where local victims' rights advocates provided key means for victims to express their needs, views and fears. Registry staff established secure links with these actors and provided training and information with a view to integrating highly vulnerable victim groups via their representatives in a safe and secure manner. Here, again, a broader consideration of cooperation is of the essence: any and all Registry field activities depend on State support to obtain the relevant accesses for ICC staff and on support from other international and regional actors in order to reach affected communities in a safe and secure manner.

Similarly, for victim consultation exercises in admissibility challenge proceedings under Article 18 of the Rome Statute, the Section's groundwork has steadily improved over the years in bringing an ever more complete yet diverse

15 Chambers Practice Manual, version of 25 March 2022 <https://www.icc-cpi.int/about/judicial-divisions/chambers-practice-manual> accessed 30 March 2023.

display of the victims' views and concerns to the attention of the ICC Judges. Registry reports in situations like the Philippines, Afghanistan and—presently ongoing—Venezuela provide a key platform for the unfiltered communication of victims' views and concerns, reported in a neutral manner. Without the interaction and support of a whole range of external actors, the ICC success rate would be far more limited.

As regards reparations, the Registry has established a number of key functions in its interaction with different Chambers on the matter. In the more recent jurisprudence, Chambers have increasingly called upon VPRS services for the identification of potential reparation beneficiaries as well as eligibility assessments; this request is sensible as these workflows are broadly similar to the Section's victim identification activities for the purpose of victim participation earlier in the proceedings. Recent jurisprudence has certified Registry efforts to gain a maximum of reparation-related information from victims by the end of the trial proceedings with a view to an expedited reparation procedure in case of a conviction. As with the Registry efforts in the field to collect victim data for participation in proceedings, State and other support will be crucial for the amount and breadth of information that can be collected in the field. And in many instances, the system works well: as an illustration, in 2021 alone, 3,844 forms requesting reparations were received across the proceedings.[16] In addition, the Trust Fund for Victims has been delivering critical activities as part of its reparations plans in various situations, including in the Democratic Republic of the Congo and in Mali.[17]

Yet, the Registry also faces complex realities on the ground which often render operations complicated, particularly from the standpoint of victims' access to reparative justice. As is so often the case, State-funded reparation or compensation mechanisms for victims of conflict-related violence may not always be implemented in a post-conflict situation due to infrastructural weaknesses and absence of funds. In addition, the conflict may still be ongoing or a new conflict may have started. Not only will there be little possibility to consider any joint initiatives or support from the authorities in question, but also—on

16 Reparations were also requested in 1,524 applications to participate in the *Yekatom/Ngaïssona* case and in 1,568 applications in the context of the *Al Hassan* proceedings. In reparation proceedings in the *Lubanga* case, 1,335 forms were received, processed, analysed and reported upon. Similarly, in reparations proceedings in the *Al Mahdi* case, altogether 606 forms were processed.

17 Report to the Assembly of States Parties on the projects and the activities of the Board of Directors of the Trust Fund for Victims for the period 1 July 2020 to 30 June 2021, ICC-ASP/20/14, 8 September 2021 (Twentieth Session of the ASP).

the technical and logistical level—we will not be able to travel to the relevant locations or remain there without UN support, let alone undertake reparation implementation activities under the stewardship of the Trust Fund for Victims.

Without State cooperation the missions to prepare for reparations orders as well as to implement measures through the Trust Fund will simply not take place and that may affect the ability to deliver the reparations.

## 5 Brief Outlook

Looking to the future, the new situations the Court is facing provide significant new challenges—their scale in itself is already a challenge. The work of the Court will be more geographically spread across the world, into new continents, where new cooperation partnerships will be required, and where we may also have to deal with new forms of risk—for instance, in terms of the capabilities of the relevant threat actors in place.

Therefore, looking at the twenty years ahead, there will certainly be some rather challenging times in terms of cooperation. But the staff of the Court are highly skilled and determined, and I am sure they will rise to the challenge.

CHAPTER 16

# Crystallizing Complementarity: a New Gambit?

*Priya Pillai*

## 1 Introduction

Complementarity is often described as the "cornerstone" of the Rome Statute.[1] It is no exaggeration to suggest that it was a significant incentive and compromise, needed for more States to sign onto the obligations of the Rome Statute.[2] However construed, it was a reassurance of the preservation of State sovereignty, of the International Criminal Court (ICC) being a court of last resort, and the ability of States to exert a degree of control over situations which could potentially result in international legal scrutiny by the ICC.

From these initial (not so humble) beginnings, the concept of complementarity has not remained static. Apart from a narrow conception of complementarity in relation to admissibility, other functions such as the promotion of effective prosecutions, a better division of labour between the ICC and domestic jurisdictions, as well as cooperation and sharing best practices are envisaged.[3] In its latest iteration, the Prosecutor of the International Criminal Court is putting in place agreements with (Situation) State Parties, with complementarity and cooperation at their core. In crystallizing this approach in the form of such agreements, how do these developments speak to the broader dynamics and implications of complementarity, if at all?

The aim of this chapter is not to address the *minutiae* of complementarity and all that it entails, but to address specific issues that may be affected by these agreements. There are three aspects of complementarity that highlight inherent tensions, which may be impacted by the agreements being entered into: the first relates to a jurisdictional threshold for the purposes of the Rome

1 Cooperation Agreement between the Office of the Prosecutor of the International Criminal Court and the Government of Colombia, 28 October 2021, Preamble para. 4. ('Colombia ICC Cooperation Agreement'), <https://www.icc-cpi.int/sites/default/files/itemsDocuments/20211028-OTP-COL-Cooperation-Agreement-ENG.pdf> accessed 23 January 2023.

2 W Burke-White, 'Proactive Complementarity: The International Criminal Court and National Courts in the Rome System of International Justice' (2008) 49 *Harvard International Law Journal* 53, 64-65.

3 C Stahn, 'Revitalizing Complementarity a Decade after the Stocktaking Exercise,' Policy Brief Series No. 115 (2020), <https://www.toaep.org/pbs-pdf/115-stahn/> accessed 15 April 2023.

 | DOI:10.1163/9789004529939_017

Statute, as opposed to an obligation on states; the second relates to overly restrictive interpretation of complementarity; and the third is that it is neo-colonial, a criticism partly linked to the restrictive interpretation of complementarity. This contribution will briefly sketch these issues, then assess the new agreements entered into by the Office of the Prosecutor of the International Criminal Court (OTP), querying if and to what extent the agreements might have an impact on the aspects highlighted, concluding with reflections based on this new practice.

## 2 Tensions Inherent in Complementarity

At the outset, it is important to be clear that the principle of complementarity, as envisaged by the Rome Statute, is a pre-requisite for admissibility, with the national jurisdiction paramount. By the terms of Article 17, the national jurisdiction retains its primacy with a case/situation inadmissible at the ICC *unless* the state is unwilling or unable to genuinely undertake an investigation or prosecution. Other factors precluding the exercise of jurisdiction include a decision by national authorities not to prosecute, conduct of a trial for the same conduct, and the case being of insufficient gravity, thereby not needing further action.

It is argued that such a threshold does not necessarily translate into a legal obligation in the Rome Statute on states to prosecute those alleged to have committed international crimes, but merely provides for the primacy of national jurisdiction.[4] Complementarity is viewed as a bar to the exercise of jurisdiction of the ICC – a requirement for admissibility – but does not place an obligation to ensure a domestic framework to prosecute.[5] However, the argument to the contrary is that taking the Rome Statute as a whole – and "duty" of the state to exercise criminal jurisdiction in its preamble – encompasses the interpretation that based on Article 17 as well as the principle of *aut dedere aut judicare,* this legal obligation does exist.[6] This has been buttressed

4 D Tladi, 'Complementarity and cooperation in international criminal justice – Assessing initiatives to fill the impunity gap', Institute for Security Studies Paper 277, November 2014, p. 3.

5 International Criminal Court – Office of the Prosecutor, Informal Expert Paper: The principle of complementarity in practice (2003) ('Informal Expert Paper'), <https://www.icc-cpi.int/sites/default/files/RelatedRecords/CR2009_02250.PDF> accessed 23 January 2023.

6 Informal Expert Paper, 19.

by various organs of the ICC, as well as by case law before the Court including the Kenyan admissibility cases.[7]

However, while there are still competing views on the existence of this obligation, can the recent agreements entered into by the ICC Prosecutor affect the argument and tip the scales? Are the agreements entered into in relation to complementarity an incremental step towards greater clarity regarding a binding obligation on states?

It is also important to note that the principle of complementarity runs through the different phases of any given situation – the assessment is made at the stage of a preliminary examination, as well as an investigation. It is an ongoing process, at the situational phase and the case phase.[8] Multiple situations before the court have necessitated addressing questions of complementarity, from preliminary examinations, to requests for deferral, as well as a continuous assessment at the investigation stage. The approach of the court, in so far as it may impact the assessment of Article 17 and its application, is examined briefly from the perspective of *other* forms of accountability, as well as the implications for the national system of justice.

Thus far, the interpretation by the Court in matters of admissibility has been fairly restrictive. The Court has determined that the conduct in question being examined by the state must be 'substantially the same' as that before the ICC.[9] Furthermore, that investigations must be conducted with a 'view to criminal prosecutions'.[10] This was reiterated in a recent decision relating to the Philippines situation, where the pre-trial chamber was assessing compliance with the principle of complementarity.[11] The pre-trial chamber looked into non-criminal and administrative procedures, including the writ of amparo and internal police procedures in relation to the 'war on drugs' and determined these as not amounting to 'tangible, concrete and progressive investigative

7 ICC, *Prosecutor v. Francis Kirimi Muthaura, Uhuru Muigai Kenyatta and Mohammed Hussein Ali,* Public Decision on the Application by the Government of Kenya Challenging the Admissibility of the case Pursuant to Article 19(2)(b) of the Statute, ICC-01/09-02/11, 30 May 2011, para. 40.

8 Burke-White (n 2).

9 *Prosecutor v. Saif Al-Islam Gadaffi,* Judgment on the appeal of Libya against the decision of Pre-Trial Chamber I of 31 May 2013 entitled "Decision on the admissibility of the case against Said Al-Islam Gadaffi", 21 May 2014, ICC-01/11-01/11-547-Red, para. 72.

10 *Situation in the Islamic Republic of Afghanistan,* Decision pursuant to article 18(2) of the Statute authorising the Prosecution to resume investigation, ICC-02/17-196, 31 October 2022 ('Afghanistan Article 18 Determination').

11 *Situation in the Republic of the Philippines,* Public Redacted Version of "Authorization pursuant to Article 18(2) of the Statute to resume the investigation", ICC-01/21, 26 January 2023.

steps carried out with a view to conducting criminal proceedings.'[12] These thresholds have been determined and reiterated by the Appeals Chamber of the Court, including in the *Katanga* case.[13]

The interpretation as determined by the Court can also have another consequence – giving rise to concerns regarding the 'judging' of national jurisdictions and the allegations of a neo-colonial or a Western lens when making this assessment.[14] This extrapolation does not flow necessarily from these decisions by the Court, but such perceptions can be hard to dislodge, once they take hold.

These concerns were front and centre, for instance, in the course of arguments at the Philippine Supreme Court on the constitutionality of the withdrawal of the Philippines from the Rome Statute. When dealing with the arguments relating to Article 17 and complementarity, the Solicitor General of the Philippines raised the prospect of 'interference of foreigners' in the domestic and legal affairs of the country and in a system of justice that he averred was working well. The fears of the bench – of the Philippine judiciary being deemed 'second class' and the entire legal system being maligned as a consequence of it being deemed 'unwilling or unable' to prosecute cases per the Rome Statute – was articulated clearly in the courtroom.[15]

While there are particular aspects of complementarity that could certainly give rise to these concerns, often, it is used as a cloak for state inaction, or worse, complicity in the commission of atrocity crimes. While certainly a more

---

12 *Situation in the Republic of the Philippines*, Public Redacted Version of "Authorization pursuant to Article 18(2) of the Statute to resume the investigation", ICC-01/21, 26 January 2023, paras. 47-48.

13 *The Prosecutor v. Germain Katanga and Mathieu Ngudjolo Chui*, Judgment on the Appeal of Mr. Germain Katanga against the Oral Decision of Trial Chamber II of 12 June 2009 on the Admissibility of the Case, ICC-01/04-01/07-1497 (25 September 2009) ('Katanga Admissibility Judgment').

14 K M Clarke, 'Negotiating Racial Injustice – How International Criminal Law Helps Entrench Structural Inequality', *Just Security*, 24 July 2020, <https://www.justsecurity.org/71614/negotiating-racial-injustice-how-international-criminal-law-helps-entrench-structural-inequality/> accessed 15 April 2023; N Sekhon, 'Complementarity and Post-Coloniality' (2013) 27 *Emory International Law Review* 799.

15 Arguments at the Philippines Supreme Court delved into the question of complementarity, over three days of the hearings. For an assessment based on court room observations in the Supreme Court as the arguments unfolded on 28 August, 4 September and 9 October 2018, see P Pillai, 'Withdrawal from the International Criminal Court: "Much Ado about Nothing" at the Philippine Supreme Court? (Part 1)' (*Opinio Juris*, 18 October 2018)<http://opiniojuris.org/2018/10/18/withdrawal-from-the-international-criminal-court-much-ado-about-nothing-at-the-philippine-supreme-court-part-i/> accessed 1 February 2023.

robust and nuanced understanding of complementarity is called for, we should not lose sight that the invocation of state sovereignty and allegations of colonialism must not serve to derail the endeavour for justice and accountability.

## 3 "Complementarity in Action": Agreements as a New Approach?

The Prosecutor of the ICC has, since 2021, entered into agreements for cooperation, with complementarity as the core of the commitments. While the agreements entered into so far are in varied political and legal contexts, it is important to assess what they may mean to the Court going forward, as well as to other situations. But first, a brief overview of the underlying legal basis of these agreements, the substance of the agreements and what they entail for the parties, as well as the potential consequences, intended and unintended.

The legal basis for such agreements is captured in the language of some of the agreements themselves, to a varying degree. The relevant articles in the Rome Statute that would provide the legal basis for such agreements encompass the principle of complementarity, emanating from Articles 15, 17, 18 & 19, as well as those that relate to Part 9 of the Rome Statute relating to cooperation, such as the general duty to cooperate per Article 86, as well as Article 88 and Article 93. While Article 54 relates to investigations, this is directly relevant to some situations in which agreements are entered into at this stage, but also more broadly to the discretion and powers of the Prosecutor.

For the first time since the establishment of the Court, the OTP in 2021 entered into an agreement on cooperation and complementarity with the Colombian government.[16] A significant move, this buttressed the decision by the Prosecutor to end the preliminary examination into the Situation in Colombia, 17 years in the making. This was not without criticism at the time, given the nascent proceedings relating to the Colombian transitional justice process.[17] It also came on the heels of the call for consultations relating to a 'benchmarking' exercise by the previous Prosecutor, in order to inform a decision whether to conclude the preliminary examination or progress to an investigation.[18]

---

16 Colombia ICC Cooperation Agreement (n 1).

17 Human Rights Watch, 'Colombia: Letter to the Prosecutor of the International Criminal Court', 30 September 2021, <https://www.hrw.org/news/2021/10/14/colombia-letter-prosecutor-international-criminal-court>, accessed 15 February 2023.

18 ICC OTP, 'Situation in Colombia – Benchmarking Consultation' (15 June 2021) <https://www.icc-cpi.int/sites/default/files/itemsDocuments/20210615-COL-Benchmarking-Consultation-Report-eng.pdf>, accessed 15 February 2023. The Office of the Prosecutor also

With the signing of the cooperation agreement, the reasons for the agreement articulated by the Prosecutor included "positive complementarity in action".[19] The Cooperation Agreement is also clear, in Article 6, that the Prosecutor

> may reconsider its assessment of complementarity in light of any significant change in circumstances, including any measures that might significantly hamper the progress and/or genuineness of relevant proceedings and the enforcement of effective and proportionate penal sanctions of a retributive and restorative nature; initiatives resulting in major obstructions to the mandate and/or proper functioning of relevant jurisdictions; or any suspension or revision of the judicial scheme set forth in the peace agreement in a manner that might delay or obstruct the conduct of genuine national proceedings.[20]

The agreement therefore encapsulates a failsafe, i.e., a resumption of the work of the Prosecutor based on a range of circumstances which may arise, left to the assessment of his office. However, it is unclear whether this threat of resumption will serve as sufficient leverage akin to that of an already open preliminary examination, in encouraging progress at the domestic level. There is also another significant aspect of this agreement. The courts in Colombia established to address the ongoing legacy and crimes of the civil war – the 'Special Jurisdiction for Peace' (SJP) based on the negotiated peace agreement[21] – are clearly identified within the Colombia ICC Cooperation Agreement as part of

---

has a policy on Preliminary Examinations, *see*, ICC OTP, 'Policy Paper on Preliminary Examinations' (November 2013).

19 "In light of this, the Prosecutor has determined that the preliminary examination must be closed. The absence of a preliminary examination does not, however, mean an end to the Office's engagement with Colombia or its support to the accountability processes underway. To the contrary, it marks the beginning of a new chapter of support and engagement – an example of positive complementarity in action." See, ICC, 'ICC Prosecutor, Mr Karim A. A. Khan QC, Concludes the Preliminary Examination of the Situation in Colombia with a Cooperation Agreement with the Government Charting the next Stage in Support of Domestic Efforts to Advance Transitional Justice' (28 October 2021) <https://www.icc-cpi.int/news/icc-prosecutor-mr-karim-khan-qc-concludes-preliminary-examination-situation-colombia> accessed 26 January 2023.

20 Ibid.

21 'Final Agreement to End the Armed Conflict and Build a Stable and Lasting Peace between the Government of Colombia and the FARC-EP', <https://www.peaceagreements.org/wview/1845/Final%20Agreement%20to%20End%20the%20Armed%20Conflict%20and%20Build%20a%20Stable%20and%20Lasting%20Peace> accessed 10 January 2023.

the progress achieved in accountability and in particular, noted for its 'positive role'.[22] The SJP is a different and complex legal mechanism, in the manner in which it is structured as well as in the way in which the SJP functions in the context of the Colombian legal system.[23] In this agreement, there is a recognition – beyond the more restricted approach by pre-trial chambers so far in their interpretation – that could broaden the meaning of complementarity, with a new non-traditional court harnessing restorative and retributive approaches within a domestic jurisdiction, fulfilling the test of complementarity. However, this development is not without concerns, in so far as the task of the SJP is still fraught and it faces serious obstacles in its path, political as well as legal.[24]

Another situation that warrants further examination is that of Venezuela, where the Office of the Prosecutor has also entered into an MOU.[25] The situation is open, and unlike the Colombia situation, there is no indication of this step shutting down the work of the Prosecutor. Instead, the Prosecutor has determined the commencement of an investigation subsequent to a preliminary examination, which however is disputed by Venezuela (and is also captured in the language of the MOU). Article 4 of the MOU states that the parties agree, 'To work to ensure that the principle of complementarity has adequate and meaningful effect.' The referral and investigation in Venezuela situates the MOU as an effort to ensure cooperation.[26] The terminology of the

---

22 Preamble para. 6, p. 2, Colombia ICC Cooperation Agreement.

23 Website of the Special Jurisdiction for Peace: <https://www.jep.gov.co/Paginas/casos.aspx> accessed 19 February 2023. For a detailed analysis of the SJP and its legal structure and powers, see M C Correa Florez, A F Martın Parada and J F Soto Hoyos, 'Punishment and pardon: The use of international humanitarian law by the Special Jurisdiction for Peace in Colombia' (2022) 104 *International Review of the Red Cross* 919, 1199–1221.

24 J Pappier and L Evenson, 'ICC starts next chapter in Colombia but will it lead to justice' (*EJIL:Talk!*, 15 December 2021) <https://www.ejiltalk.org/icc-starts-next-chapter-in-colombia-but-will-it-lead-to-justice/>, accessed 15 February 2023. See also A Morales, 'The rocky road to peace II: additional challenges at the Special Jurisdiction for Peace in Colombia' (*EJIL:Talk!*, 12 May 2022) <https://www.ejiltalk.org/the-rocky-road-to-peace-ii-additional-challenges-at-the-special-jurisdiction-for-peace-in-colombia/>, accessed 15 February 2023.

25 Memorandum of Understanding between the Bolivarian Republic of Venezuela and the Office of the Prosecutor of the International Criminal Court (3 November 2021) <https://www.icc-cpi.int/sites/default/files/itemsDocuments/otp/acuerdo/acuerdo-eng.pdf> accessed 26 January 2023. ("Venezuela ICC MoU").

26 'My Office will support any sincere and meaningful effort undertaken by the Venezuelan Government to reform and revitalise the justice and penal system in order to enable genuine accountability in Venezuela for the victims of alleged crimes. The principle of complementarity is the foundation of the Rome Statute system and it remains an important principle during the investigation stage.' See, ICC, 'ICC Prosecutor, Mr Karim A.A. Khan QC, Opens an Investigation into the Situation in Venezuela and Concludes Memorandum of

MOU includes the language that Venezuela will adopt 'all necessary measures to ensure the effective administration of justice, in accordance with international standards.'[27] In the words of a commentator, this MOU may be viewed as 'a game that we've seen elsewhere where repressive governments want to show that they're doing something about cases so that they can avoid the investigation and the international scrutiny.'[28] However, the OTP also opened an office in the country a few months later, perhaps in part due to the political engagement exemplified by this MOU.[29] The Venezuela situation is complicated and rife with the potential to backfire. But this is perhaps a necessary gamble to continue keeping the pressure on the government, towards some form of redress, be it domestic or international.

The most recent agreement entered into by the Prosecutor is with Guinea, with the closure of the preliminary examination, based on the willingness and ability of the national authorities to move forward with investigations and prosecutions.[30] This agreement was signed in conjunction with the start of a landmark national trial – relating to a massacre and assaults at the national stadium in Conakry in 2009 – an emblematic case for the country.[31] The need to make progress in domestic proceedings was emphasized, as was the need to assess complementarity on a rolling basis.[32] That the preliminary examination

---

Understanding with the Government' (5 November 2021) <https://www.icc-cpi.int/news/icc-prosecutor-mr-karim-aa-khan-qc-opens-investigation-situation-venezuela-and-concludes> accessed 26 January 2023.

27 Article 1, Venezuela ICC MoU.

28 T Broner, quoted in J Anderson, 'Venezuela and the ICC: Who's Fooling Who?' (*JusticeInfo.net*, 19 November 2021) <https://www.justiceinfo.net/en/84481-venezuela-icc-who-is-fooling-who.html> accessed 26 January 2023.

29 'International Criminal Court Opens Office in Venezuela', *NBC News* (1 April 2022) <https://www.nbcnews.com/news/latino/international-criminal-court-opens-office-venezuela-rcna22546> accessed 26 January 2023.

30 Memorandum of Understanding between the Republic of Guinea and the Office of the Prosecutor of the International Criminal Court, 28 September 2022, <https://www.icc-cpi.int/sites/default/files/2022-09/2022-09-29-mou-icc-guinea-ns-eng.pdf> accessed 26 January 2023.

31 Human Rights Watch, 'Bloody Monday – The September 28 Massacre and Rapes by Security Forces in Guinea', (17 December 2009) <https://www.hrw.org/report/2009/12/17/bloody-monday/september-28-massacre-and-rapes-security-forces-guinea> accessed 15 February 2023.

32 "As I have previously stated, an assessment of complementarity should not, and cannot, be postponed indefinitely pending the completion of all possible domestic proceedings. To the contrary, the Statute and the Court's case law are clear that the admissibility assessment must be carried out on the basis of the facts as they exist". ICC, 'Statement by ICC Prosecutor Karim A.A. Khan KC Regarding the Opening of the Trial Related to Events of 28 September 2009 in Guinea, Signature of Agreement with Transitional Government on

could be reopened and could progress to a full-fledged investigation, in case of "any attempt to shield the accused" or inconsistency with the Rome Statute obligations, was reiterated, as in the other agreements.[33] In light of the context and circumstances in Guinea, with the transitional government supportive of accountability efforts for the past regime as well as the relatively narrow focus of proceedings, there is perhaps a clearer trajectory for the implementation of such an agreement, and the potential for a satisfactory outcome.

On a plain reading of the agreements, there are a few aspects to highlight. The first is the emphasis on cooperation and complementarity, with the discretion clearly retained by the Prosecutor to reverse course should the occasion arise, with examples of such possible instances. This still begs the question – as raised in the Colombian context – whether the threat of potential reopening of an examination or investigation retains the same pressure that may be brought to bear, compared to an active preliminary examination or investigation. This also leads to the question of completion strategies and the potential pathway to such agreements. Another aspect relates to the different stages and types of engagement of the Prosecutor in these situations – from closure of a particular phase (Colombia and Guinea) to moving to an investigation in another (Venezuela) – clearly all are amenable to such agreements, with potentially different strategies as well as aims, based on the situation and context. But also, it is worth noting the missing contexts that could benefit from such agreements – while there is an agreement in place for Sudan (which does not seem to be publicly available),[34] the situation in Afghanistan seems to be a noticeable omission. Clearly, it is part of the internal workings of the OTP in determining which context to enter into such an agreement, with the calculus of cost-benefit and questions of a strategic nature. However, perhaps greater clarity, externally communicated, in relation to the criteria and context for such agreements would bring consistency to this newly evolving practice.

---

Complementarity and Closure of the Preliminary Examination' <https://www.icc-cpi.int/news/statement-icc-prosecutor-karim-aa-khan-kc-regarding-opening-trial-related-events-28-september> accessed 26 January 2023.

33 ICC, 'Statement by ICC Prosecutor Karim A.A. Khan KC Regarding the Opening of the Trial Related to Events of 28 September 2009 in Guinea, Signature of Agreement with Transitional Government on Complementarity and Closure of the Preliminary Examination' <https://www.icc-cpi.int/news/statement-icc-prosecutor-karim-aa-khan-kc-regarding-opening-trial-related-events-28-september> accessed 26 January 2023.

34 ICC, 'Statement of ICC Prosecutor, Karim A.A. Khan QC, to the United Nations Security Council on the Situation in Darfur, pursuant to Resolution 1593 (2005)', 17 January 2022 <https://www.icc-cpi.int/news/statement-icc-prosecutor-karim-aa-khan-qc-united-nations-security-council-situation-darfur> accessed 26 January 2023.

## 4 Potential Implications of Complementarity Agreements

The crystallization of complementarity in the form of these agreements leads to a few assessments, relating to the tensions inherent in complementarity as described previously, as well as broader implications.

The first one as relates to the broader goal of these agreements, as imagined from the perspective of the Court – to put the onus on the state as envisaged by the Rome Statute. And while these agreements emanate directly from the Rome Statute, they also form an independent source of legal obligation. To put it another way, they may be viewed as a layer onto the obligations already in place by the Rome Statute. The legal obligations crystallized in these agreements are tangible and have the value of additional clarity. For instance, there would be no surprise in case of reopening of a preliminary examination or an investigation based on the factors encapsulated in the agreement – more legal certainty, and that is something to be welcomed by states. However, from the perspective of states, signing onto such agreements may also be a tactic by some to indicate willingness and the intention to undertake particular actions, but which they may not necessarily follow through on. An open question relates to how these agreements are to be monitored and how is compliance assessed? There have been difficulties in ensuring cooperation in many situations as well as the lack of provision of information to the OTP by states. As a result, there would need to be clear standards to make an assessment of non-compliance as well as timelines – with the potential consequence being reverting to the preliminary examination or investigation stage. What, if anything else, might work as a potential sanction for non-compliance?

Notwithstanding the intentions behind entering into these agreements, the consequences of these agreements may be greater in the longer term than immediately obvious. National jurisdictions should be the drivers of justice and accountability, and these agreements only serve to emphasize such an approach. Furthermore, practice based on these agreements will have an impact on interpretation. They may very well be the additional building blocks in the crystallization of the legal obligation of the state in the exercise of criminal jurisdiction. The Vienna Convention on the Law of Treaties emphasizes the importance of any 'subsequent agreements' or 'subsequent practice' in the interpretation of treaties – directly applicable here.[35]

35 Article 31 ("General Rule of Interpretation"), Vienna Convention on the Law of Treaties; see also Informal Expert Paper, 26.

More broadly, the entering into of these agreements hint at a broader engagement with transitional justice mechanisms, albeit with a prosecution/criminal process focus. While alternative forms of justice are envisaged by Article 53 relating to the interests of justice, there is a need to look into this from the perspective of complementarity – factors to take into account include persons most responsible, international legitimation such as by the Security Council, among others.[36] There has been hesitation in broadening the scope of what types of legal institutions could be considered in the context of complementarity, and this may be a start to a more holistic view, especially given the imprimatur of a legal agreement. The clear reference to and inclusion of the SJP in the Colombia ICC Cooperation Agreement, as well as to 'the ordinary justice system' (Article 1) indicates a willingness to consider legal processes that may be different from the norm and in a transitional context, as part of the matrix of what makes up complementarity. This also indicates that evolving practice may emanate from different organs of the Court, which may be in conflict.

Another way to view these agreements relates to the potential to undercut allegations regarding the 'neo-colonial' approach of the court. It may be argued that these agreements re-emphasize that the onus is in fact on the state and not the Court. States undertake these obligations freely and pursuant to the idea of the primacy of the national jurisdiction. In a sense, the emphasis on cooperation as well as capacity-building (however this is defined and implemented) in these agreements may dilute the arguments of neo-colonialism.[37] But context is of course key to any such assessment, and this argument is still subject to any particularly onerous conditions on states that may be encapsulated in subsequent agreements.

At the very least, these developments in the form of agreements indicate a move away from a narrower conception of complementarity; an inclusion of domestic processes that fall within the rubric of transitional justice processes, and an acknowledgement of the array of legal tools available; pragmatism in the signing of agreements but also some idealism in the hope of significant progress. As the agreements are all relatively recent, their longer-term impact on the questions canvassed here relating to complementarity remains to be seen.

---

36 Informal Expert Paper, 22.

37 *See*, Article 3, Colombia ICC Cooperation Agreement, which states, 'The Office of the Prosecutor commits to continue supporting Colombia's accountability efforts within its mandate and means.'

CHAPTER 17

# Making Space for Victims in the ICC's Evolving Complementarity Regimes

*Lorraine Smith-van Lin and Fiona McKay*

## 1 Introduction

One of the much-lauded innovations of the Rome Statute establishing the International Criminal Court (ICC or the Court) and the Rome Statute system is the right of victims to participate in proceedings before the Court and to be awarded reparations. However, while the ICC has a mandate to try international crimes including genocide, war crimes, crimes against humanity and the crime of aggression, it exercises jurisdiction based on the principle of complementarity, through which national states have primary jurisdiction to investigate and prosecute international crimes with the ICC acting as a court of last resort. Complementarity is enshrined in the preamble to the Rome Statute[1] and in several of the provisions including Articles 17, 18 and 19 of the Statute; but the interpretation and application of complementarity as both a legal and policy concept has evolved considerably over the life of the Court. Thus, besides the legal, technical notion of complementarity as an admissibility criterion under Article 17, the Office of the Prosecutor (OTP) has also actively implemented a more relational notion of complementarity, termed 'positive complementarity', which speaks to burden-sharing, cooperation and collaboration between the Court and States in which the former supports and builds the latter's capacity to prosecute Rome Statute crimes. States and civil society also have their own role to play in strengthening domestic justice systems' ability to prosecute these crimes and maximise the Statute's catalytic effect.

This idea of burden-sharing and collaboration between the Court on the one hand and States on the other is key to closing the impunity gap, since the ICC's strategy is to focus only on perpetrators who bear the greatest responsibility for the most serious crimes. This strategic focus implies that mid and

1 Paragraph 10 of the Preamble of the Rome Statues states that 'Emphasizing that the International Criminal Court established under this Statute shall be complementary to national criminal jurisdictions'. Rome Statute of the International Criminal Court (signed 17 July 1998, entered into force 1 July 2002) 2187 UNTS 3.

 | DOI:10.1163/9789004529939_018

lower level perpetrators may fall outside of the Court's prosecutorial net but should be prosecuted at the national level. Beyond the sharing of the prosecutorial burden, the complementarity principle may also be invoked as the basis for the ICC's deferral of jurisdiction to a State that is able and willing to prosecute the crimes. Thus, for example, national authorities in Libya, Afghanistan and the Philippines have contested the Court's jurisdiction and sought to demonstrate that they are prosecuting the relevant crimes themselves, while the Prosecutor, after a protracted preliminary examination in each case, has deferred investigations and prosecutions of crimes within their jurisdiction to Guinea and Colombia. This deference to national authorities with ICC oversight can potentially build the capacity of national prosecution and judicial authorities to investigate and effectively prosecute international crimes.

Complementarity is also beneficial for victims in their quest for accountability and truth, because national investigations and prosecutions of international crimes are physically closer to victims and affected communities and are potentially more capable of delivering broader and more meaningful justice. However, the Rome Statute's comprehensive approach to victims' rights in its proceedings is not always mirrored in national proceedings, and conversely, by insufficiently engaging with victims, ICC proceedings do not always benefit from the wealth of field experience and situational knowledge which victims, their legal representatives and civil society organisations that work with them can bring to the Court.

In 2022, the ICC celebrated its 20th anniversary. The Court's officials and staff, together with diplomats, civil society organisations, academics and supporters met to celebrate the accomplishments of this important institution. Victims were talked about during the anniversary event but they were noticeably absent from the room. Regrettably, the Court's approach to the role of victims in the context of its complementarity regime could follow a similar course, if not carefully managed.

This chapter will make the argument for more space for victims within the context of the ICC's complementarity regime. We focus our arguments specifically on their role in the context of 'positive' complementarity and in relation to victim rights in deferral proceedings under Article 18 of the Statute. The chapter will first examine the procedural rights of victims at the ICC, including at the preliminary examination and investigation stages of proceedings; second, we will examine the extent to which victims have been permitted to participate in Article 18 proceedings relating to the deferral of investigations based on complementarity; third, we review opportunities for ensuring victims' rights in the context of 'positive complementarity' and 'reparative complementarity' and propose a more 'circular' approach to complementarity;

and fourth, we explore complementarity from the perspective of States, highlighting challenges and opportunities in prosecuting Rome Statute crimes. The chapter concludes with recommendations for improving outcomes for victims and strengthening domestic justice processes through the efforts of multiple actors, including the ICC, under the complementarity principle.

## 2 Background and Overview of Victims' Rights at the ICC

The recognition given to victims at the ICC as compared to previous international criminal tribunals is considered one of the major advances of the Rome Statute. The Statute establishes rights for victims to participate in proceedings through legal representatives,[2] to information, to protection and support[3] and to apply for reparation administered through the Trust Fund for Victims in case of a conviction.[4] While only outlined in embryo in the Statute, these have evolved and taken shape through the Court's practice and are now well-established aspects of the Court's law and procedure.

The rationale for such attention to victims in the Rome Statute system came from a desire for the Court to be seen to be delivering justice in a broader sense than just criminal prosecution.[5] During the negotiation of the Statute, the inclusion of comprehensive victim rights provisions was significantly influenced by extant criticism of the ad hoc international criminal tribunals for Rwanda and former Yugoslavia which did not provide for victims to participate in proceedings or seek reparation, and had minimal outreach programmes. Shutting victims out of their proceedings was causing frustration, alienation, and lack of investment in the mission of those tribunals on the part of victimised communities.[6] At the time, enhanced rights for victims of crime were also

---

2 See Article 68(3) which states 'Where the personal interests of the victims are affected, the Court shall permit their views and concerns to be presented and considered at stages of the proceedings determined to be appropriate by the Court and in a manner which is not prejudicial to or inconsistent with the rights of the accused and a fair and impartial trial'.

3 See Article 68(1) which states 'The Court shall take appropriate measures to protect the safety, physical and psychological well-being, dignity and privacy of victims and witnesses'.

4 See Article 75(2) which states 'The Court may make an order directly against a convicted person specifying appropriate reparations to, or in respect of victims, including restitution, compensation and rehabilitation'.

5 C Muttukumaru, 'Reparations to Victims' in R S Lee (ed.), *The International Criminal Court: The Making of the Rome Statute: Issues, Negotiations and Results* (Brill Nijhoff 1999) 264.

6 D Donat-Cattin, 'Article 68: Protection of the victims and witnesses and their participation in the proceedings' in O Triffterer (ed.), *Commentary on the Rome Statute of the International Criminal Court* (CH Beck/Hart/Nomos 1999) 871.

gaining traction internationally, with the adoption of instruments such as the UN Declaration of Basic Principles of Justice for Victims of Crime and Abuse of Power[7] and the Basic Principles and Guidelines on the Right to a Remedy and Reparation for Victims of Gross Violations of International Human Rights Law and Serious Violations of International Humanitarian Law.[8]

Victims, supported by civil society and legal representatives, have taken full advantage of the procedural role established under the Rome Statute framework at different stages of proceedings. Victims have submitted representations on whether the judges should authorise the Prosecutor to open an investigation (approximately 6,220 in the Afghanistan procedure),[9] and have also participated in proceedings relating to jurisdiction and admissibility.[10] In cases that have reached trial, numbers of participating victims have ranged from several hundred in the first two cases (129 in *Lubanga* and 366 in *Katanga*) to several thousand in some subsequent cases (4,107 in *Ongwen*). Reparations proceedings have occurred in five cases (*Lubanga, Katanga, Ntaganda, Al Mahdi* and *Ongwen*).

Mindful of the rationale for including a meaningful voice for victims in the ICC's legal framework, the Court's legitimacy and impact has continued to be seen as at least partly dependent on the success of the victims' role and the legitimacy of outcomes for victims. Beyond the benefits to victims themselves, victim participation has enriched the proceedings and provided contextual understanding of the issues, which is very important given the distance of the ICC from the situation countries. Judge Adrian Fulford, the presiding judge of the ICC's first trial of Thomas Lubanga, noted afterwards that in his experience, the involvement of victims had not greatly added to the length of the case, and their submissions and questioning had been focused, succinct and seemingly relevant to the issues in the case.[11] The right to reparations is also a critical way in which the ICC acts to repair the harm suffered by victims of

7 UNGA 'Declaration of Basic Principles of Justice for Victims of Crime and Abuse of Power' (29 November 1985) UN Doc A/RES/40/34.

8 UNGA 'Basic Principles and Guidelines on the Right to a Remedy and Reparation for Victims of Gross Violations of International Human Rights Law and Serious Violations of International Humanitarian Law' (16 December 2005) UN Doc A/RES/60/147.

9 Annex I-Red to the Final Consolidated Registry Report on Victims' Representations Pursuant to the Pre-Trial Chamber's Order ICC-02/17-6 of 9 November 2017, *Situation in the Islamic Republic of Afghanistan*, ICC-02/17-29-AnxI-Red, PTC III, ICC, 20 February 2018, para. 28.

10 For instance, the Office of Public Counsel for Victims (OPCV) was appointed to represent victims following Libya's admissibility challenge under Article 19.

11 A Fulford, 'The Reflections of a Trial Judge' (2011) 22 *Criminal Law Forum* 215–223. See also the chapter by Ambach.

crimes within the Court's jurisdiction. In its Reparations Order in the first case, Lubanga, the Trial Chamber noted:

> The reparation scheme provided for in the Statute is not only one of the Statute's unique features. It is also a key feature. The success of the Court is, to some extent, linked to the success of its system of reparations.[12]

A study of over 600 victims in four ICC situation countries found that victims had a strong interest in reparations and that this was a key motivation for wanting to participate in proceedings.[13]

However, the path to an effective and meaningful system of victim participation and reparations at the ICC has not been paved with roses. Inconsistent judicial decisions, limited outreach and restricted participatory rights at the preliminary examination and investigation stages, have led to frustration amongst victims and disillusionment with the idealistic notion of the ICC as a victim-centred court. The expert panel in the Independent Expert Review of the ICC commissioned by the Assembly of States Parties in 2019 were told that 'victim participation was overly complex, bureaucratic, inconsistent, and far removed from the reality many victims find themselves in'.[14] This frustration has not been limited solely to participation, but has permeated the victims' experience of reparations at the Court. As we argue further in this chapter, a more expansive approach to victim participation will better serve the interests of the Court and is consistent with the principle of complementarity under the Statute.

## 3 Complementarity and Victim Participation in Article 18 Proceedings

The ICC and the Rome Statute system is based on the principle of complementarity, which essentially governs the exercise of the Court's jurisdiction.[15]

According to Stahn, complementarity has at least four functions:

---

12 Order for Reparations, *Lubanga, Situation in the Democratic Republic of the Congo*, ICC-01/04-01/06-3129-AnxA, AC, ICC, 3 March 2015, para. 3.

13 S Cody et al., 'The Victims' Court: A Study of 622 Victim Participants at the International Criminal Court' (2015).

14 Review of the International Criminal Court and the Rome Statute System, ICC-ASP/18/Res.7, 6 December 2019 (Ninth Plenary Meeting of the ASP).

15 OTP, Informal Expert Paper, 'The principle of complementarity in practice' (1 April 2009), 3.

> To protect sovereignty, by reaffirming the primary role of States in exercising criminal jurisdiction over international crimes; to promote effective investigation and prosecution, by encouraging states to make genuine efforts to hold perpetrators accountable in line with their duty to investigate and prosecute crimes; to facilitate a certain division of labour between different layers of jurisdiction, i.e. by resolving conflicts of jurisdiction and limiting cases that come before the ICC; and to stimulate cooperation.[16]

In a technical legal sense, complementarity informs the admissibility criteria defined in Article 17 for determining whether national states or the ICC should exercise jurisdiction over specific crimes. At the initial stages this assessment is made by the Prosecutor, and Judges make a judicial assessment under the procedures set out in Articles 18, 19 or 53. Only where there are no domestic proceedings or States are unable or unwilling to genuinely investigate and prosecute crimes in their own jurisdictions would the ICC be empowered to act. Thus, according to Bergsmo, Bekou and Jones, the principle of complementarity 'ensures [the] international rule of law by creating an interdependent, mutually reinforcing international system of justice'.[17]

The Rome Statute system envisages various circumstances in which matters relating to jurisdiction and admissibility might come before the judges for adjudication. Some of these provisions have given rise to considerable litigation as regards the status of victims in such proceedings and the standing of victims' legal representatives to present views and concerns. However, in relation to deferral proceedings under Article 18, the Statute is silent concerning the role that victims may play, leaving the matter to judicial and prosecutorial discretion.

Article 18 of the Statute allows a state to challenge the Court's exercise of jurisdiction where the Prosecutor has decided to initiate an investigation, the precursor to opening a case against one or more individuals. According to Article 18(1), the Prosecutor must notify states which would normally exercise jurisdiction of his intention to commence an investigation and defer to the state's investigation if they are exercising jurisdiction with respect to the same

16 C Stahn, 'Fair and Effective Investigation and Prosecution of International Crimes Inventory and State-of-the-Art: Context, Cluster 1 and Cluster 2' (International Nuremberg Principles Academy) 5.

17 M Bergsmo, O Bekou, O, and A Jones, 'Complementarity after Kampala: Capacity Building and the ICC Legal Tools' (2010) 2 *Goettingen Journal of International Law* 791, 796.

criminal acts.[18] If the Prosecutor objects to the State's request for deferral, s/he can apply to the Pre-Trial Chamber (PTC) for authorization to initiate the investigation.[19] Any deferral will remain under review by the Prosecutor, to assess the genuineness of the purported investigation as defined in Article 17. Unlike Article 19, Article 18 does not provide specifically for victims to participate in any proceedings, but Rule 55 of the Rules of Procedure and Evidence (RPE) provides that the PTC shall decide on the procedure to be followed.

The deferral provision under Article 18 applies whether the situation has been referred to the Court by a State party pursuant to Article 13(a) or the Prosecutor initiates an investigation *propio motu* pursuant to Article 13(c) and 15.[20] Applying the principle of complementarity in relation to determinations under article 15(4) and article 18 ensures that the issues of jurisdiction and admissibility can be determined at the earliest stage of proceedings.[21]

The Court's jurisprudence in relation to Article 18 has tended to narrow the role of the PTC and expand the discretionary power of the Prosecutor.[22] At the same time, while the practice of the ICC in relation to the participatory rights of victims at pre-trial and trial stages is relatively well-developed, the role and rights of victims at the preliminary examination and investigation stages are less clear.[23] The manner in which the rights and participation of victims were addressed in the context of the deferral request under Article 18 in the situation in the Islamic Republic of Afghanistan ('Afghanistan') and the Prosecutor's request to resume investigations, provide a useful context for analysis of this issue.

### 3.1 *The Afghanistan Situation*

The preliminary examination by the OTP into alleged crimes committed in the situation in the Islamic Republic of Afghanistan (Afghanistan) was made public in 2007. The PTC's failure to authorize the Prosecutor to investigate was subsequently overturned by the Appeals Chamber (AC) in March 2020. A month

18 Article 18(1). This is in contrast to Article 19 which deals with challenges to jurisdiction or admissibility by a state or a suspect or accused person, after a case has been opened.

19 See Article 18(2).

20 See Article 18(1).

21 L Chigowe, 'The ICC and the situation in Afghanistan: A critical examination of the role of the Pre-Trial Chambers in the initiation of investigation proprio motu' (2022) 35(3) *Leiden Journal of International Law* 699, 716.

22 Ibid., 717.

23 International Federation for Human Rights, 'Whose Court is it? Judicial Handbook on victims' rights at the International Criminal Court' (April 2021) <https://www.fidh.org/IMG/pdf/fidh_whose_court_is_it_en.pdf> accessed 12 April 2023.

after the investigation was authorized, the Government of Afghanistan submitted a request seeking a deferral under Article 18(2) (on the basis that the state is investigating or has investigated its nationals or others within its jurisdiction with respect to those criminal acts).[24] The Prosecutor agreed to defer while considering the request, and proceeded to engage with the then Afghan authorities.

After a year, frustrated at the apparent absence of a conclusion of the Prosecutor's review as well as the lack of public information on the part of the Court, several lawyers who had represented victims during the Article 15 proceedings (in which the PTC and then the Appeals Chamber decided on the Prosecutor's request for authorisation to open an investigation proprio motu), filed requests asking the PTC to order the Prosecutor to provide more information on his review of the deferral request and to set a time limit for the review.

This gave rise to a number of submissions and decisions on the role of the Chamber in relation to deferral decisions, as well as whether victims had standing to approach the Chamber. The Chamber found that the power to review deferral requests and to decide whether, and to what extent, to provide information about the procedure to potential victims and the general public was exclusively within the discretion of the Prosecutor and there was no legal basis for it to interfere with his review of the deferral request, and consequently, no procedural standing for "potential" victims at this stage.[25] Even after the Prosecutor himself requested authorization to resume the investigation, the Chamber rejected attempts by victims' legal representatives to submit observations on the scope of that request, and citing concerns about the 'efficient and orderly conduct of proceedings' and 'disruptive potential' of victims being authorised to submit requests at all times, instructed the Registry to refrain from filing on the record any document received from anyone other than the Prosecutor or a state, who were the only parties permitted to seize the Chamber in relation to a deferral request.[26] While the Chamber decided

24 Letter dated 26 March 2020 from the Embassy of the Islamic Republic of Afghanistan to Prosecutor Bensouda, contained in Annex 1 to the Notification to the Pre-Trial Chamber of the Islamic Republic of Afghanistan's letter concerning article 18(2) of the Statute, *Situation in the Islamic Republic of Afghanistan*, ICC-02/17-139-Anx1, PTC II, ICC, 16 April 2020.

25 Decision regarding applications related to the Prosecution's 'Notification on status of the Islamic Republic of Afghanistan's article 18(2) deferral request', *Situation in the Islamic Republic of Afghanistan*, ICC-02/17-156, PTC II, ICC, 3 September 2021, paras 23 to 25.

26 Decision on submissions received and order to the Registry regarding the filing of documents in the proceedings pursuant to articles 18(2) and 68(3) of the Statute, *Situation*

to nevertheless allow the views and concerns of "potential" victims to reach the Chamber, rather than allowing submissions by their legal representatives it instructed the Registry to receive and transmit victim representations to the Chamber.[27]

In our view, the Chamber should have adopted a more expansive and inclusive approach to the participation of victims in the Article 18 proceedings as envisaged by Article 68(3) of the Statute. Article 68(3) has been interpreted by the AC as including the right of victims to participate in judicial proceedings at the investigation stage. In the situation in the Democratic Republic of Congo (DRC), the AC held that: "[…] Article 68 (3) of the Statute is treated as a hybrid provision, allowing the participation of victims in any matter dealt with by the Statute, *including investigations.* […] Victims are not precluded from seeking participation in any judicial proceedings, including proceedings affecting investigations, provided their personal interests are affected by the issues arising for resolution."[28]

Thus, in addition to the right to make representations, the Chamber should have exercised its discretion to allow victims to make filings on the record through their legal representatives provided that their personal interests were affected. Contested issues of whether the ICC or a State should investigate a matter involve complex legal questions with potentially far-reaching implications for victims, and directly affects their personal interests. Excluding them from direct participation is contrary to the victim-centred raison d'être of the Rome Statute. The Afghanistan Article 18[29] approach to victim participation has commenced a worrying trend which has since been replicated in similar proceedings in the Philippines[30] and Venezuela situations.[31]

---

*in the Islamic Republic of Afghanistan*, ICC-02/17-171, PTC II, ICC, 8 November 2021, para 13.

27 Ibid., para. 14.

28 Appeals Chamber, Judgment on victim participation in the investigation stage of the proceedings in the appeal of the OPCD against the decision of Pre-Trial Chamber I of 7 December 2007 and in the appeals of the OPCD and the Prosecutor against the decision of Pre-Trial Chamber I of 24 December 2007, ICC-01/04-556-tARB, 19 December 2008, para. 56.

29 Pre-Trial Chamber II *Situation in the Islamic Republic of Afghanistan* Decision (n 26).

30 Order inviting observations and victims' views and concerns, *Situation in the Republic of the Philippines*, ICC-01/21-47, PTC I, ICC, 14 July 2022.

31 Order inviting observations and views and concerns of victims, *Situation in the Bolivarian Republic of Venezuela I*, ICC-02/18-21, PTC I, ICC, 18 November 2022.

## 4 Positive Complementarity and Opportunities for the Court to Promote Victims' Rights

The second sense in which the concept of complementarity has evolved at the Court is as a tool for encouraging and supporting national systems to prosecute Rome Statute crimes themselves. As the ICC AC puts it: 'the complementarity principle, as enshrined in the Statute, strikes a balance between safeguarding the primacy of domestic proceedings vis-à-vis the International Criminal Court on the one hand, and the goal of the Rome Statute to 'put an end to impunity' on the other hand'.[32] In practice, it has proved challenging to find this balance. Since the early days of the Court's existence, there has been debate about the extent to which the Court, and specifically the Prosecutor, should aim to maximise the Court's impact by proactively engaging with national authorities and encouraging and/or supporting them to prosecute cases, a strategy known as 'positive complementarity'.[33] An expert group convened by the Court in 2003 identified this as a guiding principle, concluding that the principle of complementarity—which could be achieved through such things as exchange of information, evidence sharing and technical advice—could magnify the effectiveness of the ICC beyond what it would achieve through its own prosecutions.[34] The first Prosecutor espoused this approach and sought to build into his strategy a 'carrot and stick' approach based on the idea that the threat of ICC intervention would motivate states to commence prosecutions themselves.[35] An OTP policy paper issued in 2013 noted that 'a significant part of the Office's efforts at the preliminary examination stage is directed towards encouraging States to carry out their primary responsibility to investigate and prosecute international crimes'.[36]

Some States Parties have been consistently sceptical of this approach, expressing concern that it would drain resources and distract the Court from its core functions. States considered that the Court's role in strengthening national systems should be limited; and complementarity-related activities should not add to the functions of the Court, which is 'not a development

32 Judgment on the Appeal of Mr. Germain Katanga against the Oral Decision of Trial Chamber II of 12 June 2009 on the Admissibility of the Case, *Katanga, Situation in the Democratic Republic of the Congo*, ICC-01/04-01/07-1497, AC, ICC, 25 September 2009.

33 Informal Expert Paper, 'The Principle of Complementarity in Practice', OTP ICC (2003), paras 3, 6 and 10–13.

34 Ibid.

35 K A Marshall, 'Prevention and Complementarity in the International Criminal Court: A Positive Approach' (2010) 17(2) *Washington College of Law Human Rights Brief* 21–26.

36 ICC OTP, 'Policy Paper on Preliminary Examinations' (1 November 2013), para. 100.

agency'.[37] In 2021, in reporting on the conclusions of the ASP's Working Group on Complementarity, the Bureau again recalled the Court's limited role in strengthening national jurisdictions.[38]

Positive complementarity was also a key part of the policy of Fatou Bensouda, the second Prosecutor, who stated that 'it has always been my conviction that the goals of the Rome Statute are best served by States executing their own primary responsibility to ensure accountability at the national level.'[39] Bensouda was however criticised for having too many situations under preliminary examination, for too long, under her watch.

Since assuming office in 2021, Prosecutor Khan has prioritised the clearing of the preliminary examination backlog amidst concern from various actors including the experts who conducted the Independent Expert Review of the ICC.[40] His approach to positive complementarity appears to be based on a 'justice partnership' model, where collaboration is formalised in written agreements with national states encouraging and actively supporting national prosecutions.

Indications of Prosecutor Khan's approach emerged in statements to the UN Security Council on the Libya situation and in relation to the situations in Guinea and Colombia. In his report on Libya in April 2022, the Prosecutor said he was looking for close engagement and partnership, and a more systematic and structured approach to interactions with the Libyan authorities including how to assist them technically. He announced his intention to develop an MOU with Libya, establish benchmarks and a basis for collaboration. 'The Court should not be the only beneficiary of the information it collects,' he stated, 'and in these types of crimes, it's hubris to think that the ICC or any national authority can act alone in dealing with genocide, crimes against humanity or war crimes.'[41]

---

37 Report of the Bureau on Stocktaking: Complementarity: Taking stock of the principle of complementarity: Bridging the Impunity Gap, ICC-ASP/8/51, 18 March 2010 (Resumed Eighth Session of the ASP) ('ASP Report of the Bureau on Stocktaking'), paras 4 and 42–45.

38 Report of the Bureau on Complementarity, ICC-ASP/20/22, 6 December 2021 (Twentieth Session of the ASP), paras 6 and 61.

39 ICC OTP, Statement of the Prosecutor, Fatou Bensouda, on the conclusion of the preliminary examination of the situation in Nigeria, (11 December 2020), < https://www.icc-cpi.int/news/statement-prosecutor-fatou-bensouda-conclusion-preliminary-examination-situation-nigeria> accessed 30 April 2023

40 See for example, Independent Expert Review of the International Criminal Court and the Rome Statute System: Final Report—30 September 2020, icc-asp/19/16, 9 November 2020 (Nineteenth Session of the asp) ('Independent Expert Review Final Report'), paras. 719-736.

41 Statement of the ICC Prosecutor to the UN Security Council presenting his twenty-third report pursuant to UNSCR 1970 (2011), 'ICC Prosecutor, Karim A.A. Khan QC, outlines

Moving quickly to cement this cooperative approach, Prosecutor Khan signed MOUs with states to serve both as a benchmark for how he will assess whether the state is actually prosecuting the relevant crimes, and as a commitment to specific actions by both parties. The Prosecutor concluded a Cooperation Agreement with Colombia in April 2021,[42] and in September 2022, in a sign of an evolving approach, a more comprehensive MOU with the national authorities of Guinea. In the MOU, the Prosecutor committed to support Guinea's accountability efforts including through knowledge transfer, exchange of best practices and technical support. Guinea in turn made seven commitments, which included ensuring outreach and communication to objectively inform the public of developments; ensuring safety and security of participants appearing before the judges, in particular victims and witnesses; and providing support and assistance to victims and witnesses appearing in the trial, including through psychological support and familiarisation.[43] The MOU included indicators the OTP would use for assessing whether Guinea continued to satisfy complementarity going forward. An MOU in similar terms was concluded with the DRC in June 2023.

The Guinea MOU sets a significant precedent, with far-reaching provisions which commit the national State to providing protection and support for victims in domestic proceedings. While a 'one-size fits all' approach for all situations would be inappropriate , the inclusion of provisions designed to protect the rights and interests of victims and survivors in this, and presumably future MOUs is welcomed, and consistent with the OTP's own internal policy on victims.[44] On the other hand, MOUs are a two-edged sword which could also potentially undermine the rights of victims. By signing an MOU, the OTP is effectively signalling that it will not pursue a preliminary examination into potential crimes committed in a State. This decision could jeopardise efforts by victims and affected communities to seek justice in very fragile contexts.

---

renewed approach to investigations in the Situation in Libya to the United Nations Security Council' (29 April 2022) <https://www.icc-cpi.int/news/icc-prosecutor-karim-aa-khan-qc-outlines-renewed-approach-investigations-situation-libya> accessed 30 April 2023.

42 ICC OTP, 'Cooperation Agreement between the Office of the Prosecutor of the International Criminal Court and the Government of Colombia' (28 October 2021).

43 Memorandum of Understanding between The Republic of Guinea and the Office of the Prosecutor of the International Criminal Court, OTP ICC, 28 September 2022.

44 ICC OTP, Office of the Prosecutor Policy Paper on Victims' Participation, (April 2010), <https://www.icccpi.int/sites/default/files/iccdocs/otp/Policy_Paper_on_Victims_Participation_April_2010.pdf. > accessed 28 July 2023

In Colombia, for example, Human Rights Watch criticised the Prosecution's decision to end the preliminary examination. In their view, given the fragile transitional justice system in Colombia, 'the ICC's decision to step back now raises concerns that it could undermine victims' access to justice.'[45]

The OTP has previously been criticised for adopting what we term a 'neo-colonialist'approach to complementarity by actively distancing itself from domestic processes, and failing to properly understand the contexts in which it operated, and thus actively undermining complementarity in all senses in which the term is understood.[46] In his study on the ICCs work in Africa, Phil Clark found that prosecutorial choices and methods of engagement with affected communities by multiple parts of the Court had weakened its ability to bring effective prosecutions and to gain legitimacy as partners in delivering justice in the eyes of affected communities.[47] It is crucial that the partnership model being pursued by the current Prosecutor is not solely focused on government officials and high-level justice actors, but adopts a victim-centred approach which includes engagement with civil society actors and groups from affected communities.

Ultimately, advancing victims' interests and delivering justice to affected communities through positive complementarity is not the sole purview of the Prosecutor. Other Court actors, including those involved in outreach, victim participation and reparations also have a crucial role to play. Civil society organisations have also regularly drawn attention to shortcomings in how different organs of the ICC engage in situations under investigation, and the impact this has on victims and affected communities.[48]

We are mindful of the concerns that the Court itself lacks sufficient resources to actively strengthen and support national courts, and that this is arguably beyond the scope of its mandate. However, a creative and structured approach

---

45 Human Rights Watch, 'The ICC Starts Next Chapter in Colombia: Will it Lead to Justice' (December 16, 2021) <https://www.hrw.org/news/2021/12/16/icc-starts-next-chapter-colombia> accessed 28 July 2023

46 P Clark, *Distant Justice, The Impact of the International Criminal Court on African Politics* (Cambridge: Cambridge University Press, 2018) 302.

47 Ibid., 148–149.

48 See for example International Federation for Human Rights and Kenya Human Rights Commission, 'The victims' mandate of the International Criminal Court: disappointments, concerns and options for the way forward: Observations and recommendations for the Independent Expert Review' (June 2020) <https://www.khrc.or.ke/mobile-publications/civil-political-rights/219-the-victims-mandate-of-the-international-criminal-court-disappointments-concerns-and-options-for-the-way-forward/file.html>accessed30April 2023.

to complementarity that is coordinated with other actors (states, international organisations, regional mechanisms, donors and civil society) which looks for less resource-intensive opportunities for knowledge sharing on the part of Court staff, alongside more resource intensive capacity building by other actors, is feasible.Complementarity is not just about burden sharing, but about working in partnership, including with victims organisations, to change the legal landscape.

We do not see complementarity as a one-way, top-down model whereby the ICC standards are always the gold standard for local processes. We strongly advocate the importance of local contextual understanding and this is where victims come in. The Rome Statute system will be more effective if there is a flow of learning and information from both sides and mutual respect, through a more 'circular complementarity'. Given the nature of the crimes within the ICC's jurisdiction, the ICC will likely be the venue of choice for prosecuting grave crimes that cannot or will not be prosecuted at the national level. The voices calling on all organs of the Court to do much more to understand and engage with the contexts where it is operating have become increasingly loud and insistent.[49] Ensuring a continuous flow of information and knowledge sharing between the OTP, victims and affected communities-through circular complementarity- can only strengthen national and international investigations and bolster the ICC's legitimacy.

## 5 Reparative Complementarity

Beyond investigations and prosecutions, complementarity is also relevant to reparations, a crucially important issue for victims. The reparations process at the Court is administered by the Trust Fund for Victims (Trust Fund) which has a dual mandate: to support the implementation of judicial reparations awards;[50] and to apply funds for the benefit of victims, its so-called assistance mandate.[51] However, the system of reparations at the ICC has not functioned optimally, characterised by inefficiency and delay. The Independent Expert Review found that the Court's conceptual and procedural processes for reparations were 'laden with complexity and uncertainty, which gravely affects the

49 Independent Expert Review Final Report (n. 40), Recommendations 293–298.

50 See Article 79 and Rule 98 (1–4), Rules of Procedure and Evidence of the International Criminal Court, PCNICC/2000/1/Add.1, adopted 9 September 2002 by the ASP, ICC-ASP/1/3, 3–10 September 2002 (First Session of the ASP).

51 See Rule 98(5), Rules of Procedure and Evidence.

victims' rights to meaningful participation and reparations'.[52] Nevertheless, for some victims in conflict affected situations, the ICC's reparations programme has been the only hope for obtaining redress for the harm that they have suffered. Several states have no reparations framework, while others are in the embryonic stages with little political will to move them forward. However, there are some states that have latent national reparations programmes and other global initiatives, such as the Global Survivors Fund, work to support the provision of reparations for conflict-affected sexual violence survivors.[53]

Some commentators who have reviewed the Court's experience in delivering reparations in its first cases have urged that it must take care to avoid the pitfall of operating in isolation from other reparations practices in the state. The Court itself has a narrow mandate and limited resources for reparation, they argue, and consequently should adopt an approach of 'reparative complementarity' aimed at maximising the positive impact the Court can have for victims by working as part of a landscape of international and domestic responses to reparation for victims.[54]

The independent experts recommended that consideration should be given to 'the potentiality of Court-ordered reparations to feed into and reinforce national reparative justice and reparations efforts'[55] requiring reinforcement of collaboration with relevant States and 'more determined and resolute efforts' to invite and solicit cooperation from credible and competent partners.[56] Because its role goes wider than specific cases before the Court and it is able to use its assistance mandate to benefit all victims of Rome Statute crimes within ICC situations, the Trust Fund has greater scope for even wider impact.

At the same time, there is also a role for the Court to encourage states to build their reparative justice framework to complement what it is doing. Reparations for Rome Statute crimes is an important element of the ICC framework that is absent from many domestic legal systems and an important issue for victims. States should be encouraged to either amend their laws to include reparations provisions or to develop national reparations programmes when considering how to implement the Rome Statute. Such steps could be particularly urgent in post-conflict contexts where other restorative justice processes,

52 Independent Expert Review Final Report (n 40) para. 879.

53 Available at <https://www.globalsurvivorsfund.org/> accessed 30 April 2023.

54 L Moffett and C Sandoval, 'Tilting at Windmills: Reparations and the International Criminal Court' (2021) 34 *Leiden Journal of International Law* 749.

55 Independent Expert Review Final Report (n 40) Recommendation 353.

56 Ibid., paras 930 and 932.

such as transitional justice mechanisms, are ongoing. Thus, beyond being seen as a catalyst for retributive justice, positive complementarity has the potential to catalyse or strengthen restorative justice mechanisms in national systems.[57]

## 6 Practical Challenges and Opportunities regarding Victims' Rights and Complementarity at the National Level

It would be remiss of us to examine positive complementarity solely through the lens of the Court and the OTP, without an examination of some of the practical challenges and opportunities that States deal with in seeking to prosecute Rome Statute crimes, including in relation to national implementing legislation and in applying the Rome Statute framework on victims. These should be borne in mind by all those wishing to contribute to maximising the multiplier effect of the Statute.

Prosecution of international crimes domestically under the principle of complementarity helps to bring justice closer to victims and affected communities, and the visibility of the justice process, given the ICC's distance away in the Hague, helps to increase 'buy-in' and process legitimacy among affected communities, enhancing its restorative impact.[58] Nevertheless, while there are clear advantages to prosecuting international crimes domestically, there are undoubtedly significant challenges which stymie the efforts of some States to do so effectively. These are often due to major capacity and infrastructural challenges, particularly in post-conflict countries.[59] Despite having the will and intent to end impunity, some States simply lack resources, expertise and capacity and a functional and independent judiciary to do so.[60]

A strong national framework is critical for positive complementarity to be effective. As Bergsmo et al. opine:

57 Experience has shown, however, that states do not find it easy to develop comprehensive reparations schemes. The DRC and Uganda, both countries with Rome Statute crimes prosecuted by the ICC as well as in national courts, have been discussing establishing national reparations programmes for years without conclusion. The ICC has issued reparations awards in cases from both countries, necessarily limited to the crimes charged and that the respective Accused were convicted of, and the ICC Trust Fund for Victims has been active in both places. There seems to us to be scope for greater collaboration—both on the part of different organs of the Court and other actors—to achieve a means of delivering reparations to all victims of Rome Statute crimes from those conflicts.

58 Bergsmo, Bekou, and Jones (n 17), 800.

59 ASP Report of the Bureau on Stocktaking (n 37), para. 9.

60 Ibid.

> For positive complementarity to work, it is not enough to rely on the OTP to steer national processes towards more investigations and prosecutions. Although such encouragement is influential, it runs the risk of becoming a paper exercise if there is no strong national framework in place enabling States to exercise criminal jurisdiction. It was clear, even prior to shaping the agenda for the Review Conference, that if positive complementarity was to succeed, a more systematic approach towards empowering national legal orders was needed.[61]

Domestic implementation of Rome Statute crimes helps to provide the framework that is critically important for equipping states to successfully investigate and prosecute international crimes and includes several benefits such as the 'strengthening of the domestic criminal justice systems and updating offences and principles of criminal responsibility' among others.[62] However, guidelines issued by various bodies on how states should implement the Rome Statute in national legislation tend to address some, but not all, the rights afforded to victims under the Statute and the practice of the ICC. They tend to call for inclusion of provisions to enable cooperation with the ICC on matters such as victim and witness protection and seizure of assets associated with crime,[63] but most do not recommend that states adopt such provisions in their national proceedings, or that they address other matters such as victim participation, reparation or outreach. There are some exceptions: for instance, the Amnesty International guide recommends that states provide in their national law for reparations for all victims of crimes under international law in accordance with international standards,[64] and the International Bar Association's guide for States Parties includes recommendations that states ensure victims are provided with effective support to participate in national criminal proceedings, and are able to access full and effective reparations before national courts or administrative mechanisms.[65]

---

61 Bergsmo, Bekou, and Jones (n 17) 796.

62 See Stahn (n 16) 12.

63 See The Commonwealth, 'Model Law to Implement the Rome Statute of the International Criminal Court' (2017) <https://production-new-commonwealth-files.s3.eu-west-2.amazonaws.com/migrated/key_reform_pdfs/P15370_ROL_Model_Rome_Statute.pdf>accessed 30 April 2023.

64 Amnesty International, 'International Criminal Court: Updated checklist for effective implementation' (6 May 2010) <https://www.amnesty.org/en/documents/ior53/009/2010/en/> accessed 30 April 2023.

65 International Bar Association, 'Strengthening the ICC and the RS System: A guide for States Parties' (2021), Recommendations 67 and 68 <https://www.ibanet.org/document?id=ICC-Report-Rome-Statute-October-2021> accessed 30 April 2023.

While this gap is understandable given that the Rome Statute does not oblige states to adopt its provisions on protection, participation and reparation, or its practice to conduct outreach, the fact that some drafters of guides have found solid bases in international law and best practices for recommending at least some of these rights points the way for others. We would encourage all those providing guidance to states on Rome Statute implementing legislation to demonstrate how states could give full effect to the rights afforded to victims under the Statute.

Legislation is only a starting point, and states may face other practical and procedural challenges in implementing the Rome Statute framework when it comes to actual investigations and prosecutions. The example of the International Crimes Division (ICD) in Uganda illustrates the kinds of challenges that national states may face. Despite being hailed as the first case based on the principle of complementarity, the ICD's trial against Thomas Kwoyelo, a former combatant in the rebel group Lord's Resistance Army charged with war crimes and crimes against humanity, initially struggled with with a lack of clear procedural rules or guidelines governing victim participation in international criminal cases.[66] Adopting Rules of Procedure and operationalising this unfamiliar procedure, in a common law system in which victim participation is unknown, proved extremely challenging in a context where Court actors and judges had limited knowledge of the procedures, and amidst limited resources including for legal aid and outreach to victims. Support from NGOs and external experts familiar with the ICC victim participation regime on which the ICDs Rules were based, was essential in enabling the ICD to manage the situation. Supporting national legal systems to apply new and unfamiliar procedures such as victim participation in domestic proceedings, presents an opportunity for complementarity to work.

## 7 Conclusion

Our review of victims' role in the complementarity regime of the ICC—specifically in relation to deferral proceedings and under 'positive'

66 See Redress 'Ugandan International Crimes Division (ICD) Rules 2016, Analysis on Victim Participation Framework' (2016) <https://redress.org/wp-content/uploads/2017/12/1608REDRESS_ICD-Rules-Analysis.pdf> accessed 30 April 2023; Uganda Law Society, 'The International Crimes Division of the High Court of Uganda: Towards Greater Effectiveness' (2018) <https://www.kpsrl.org/sites/default/files/2019-01/2%20-%20Research%20Report%20on%20the%20International%20Crimes%20Division.pdf> accessed 30 April 2023.

complementarity—points to a need for increased focus on the rights and interests of victims. In relation to deferral proceedings under article 18, we consider that the PTCs should adopt an expansive, victim-centred view of the role and rights of victims at this stage which is consistent with other statutory provisions including article 68(3) and article 21(3). Chambers should allow victims to make submissions on the record including through their legal representative and the Prosecutor and the Registry should ensure that victims are consulted and fully informed at this stage of the process. This can only strengthen the effective investigation and prosecution of cases rather than undermine them. The approach to positive complementarity has had mixed results at the Court under previous prosecutors. Prosecutor Khan's current emphasis on burden-sharing and collaborative justice partnership seems to concretely focus on supporting domestic prosecutions and includes progressive provisions concerning protection and support for victims in the MOUs. But in our view, it could still go much further particularly in relation to victims and their role and rights in investigations and prosecutions in domestic proceedings.

We propose that it is time for complementarity to come full circle. Notions of complementarity at the Court should continue to evolve to become a mutually reinforcing, symbiotic relationship between the ICC and States on the one hand, and where the ICC more actively engages with and learns from victims and those with situational expertise on the other. There is much that the ICC can and should learn from victims and national actors which could enhance its approach to investigations and prosecutions. In our view, a circular approach to complementarity is a better, more holistic approach to prosecuting international crimes. This approach to complementarity is an opportunity for all organs of the Court to work to support national prosecutions of Rome Statute crimes. It is not a matter only for the OTP. Indeed, in some instances, we have suggested that different parts of the Court should consider whether there is more they could do to engage with other justice processes, both to pass on their experience and to learn from others.

Given the well-established rights of victims before the ICC, the relative absence of victims in complementarity proceedings and policies is anomalous, in light of the obvious convergence between the objectives of complementarity and the centrality of victims in the quest for justice and accountability. Ensuring that victims' interests are included within evolving iterations of the complementarity principle will help build support for the Court and enhance its impact, in keeping with Rome Statute principles. True complementarity must make space for victims, wherever accountability is pursued.

CHAPTER 18

# National Implementation of the Rome Statute as a Critical Precondition for Complementarity and Cooperation

*Olympia Bekou*

## 1 Introduction*

Since becoming operational on the 1st of July 2002, the International Criminal Court (hereinafter, ICC or the Court) has morphed into a fully-fledged institution which occupies a central role in the fight against impunity. In recent years, the Court has faced significant political attacks on its identity from both within and outside its membership and its independence and impartiality have been questioned. The ICC's operation has been the subject of increased scrutiny and has attracted much criticism.

The 20th anniversary of the entry into force of the Rome Statute of the International Criminal Court[1] provides an important opportunity to reflect on whether the promise to deliver justice that the Rome system has been founded upon, has materialised. This important milestone is also an opportune moment to look to the future and ensure the continued relevance of this permanent institution.

This important anniversary in the life of the ICC comes at a time of crisis, with the international community having to prioritise the rise in situations where the ICC's work is relevant against the demand on ever shrinking resources. The increasing number of ongoing instances of mass atrocity that may need to be investigated are testing the ability of International Law to respond to such situations and are putting an unprecedented strain on the international criminal justice order. The ICC has a key role to play, and, despite the unforeseen expansion of its workload following the war in Ukraine,[2] it must fulfil its mandate in

* I would like to thank Sara Ciucci for her research assistance. All errors and omissions remain mine alone.

1 The Rome Statute of the International Criminal Court (signed 17 July 1998, entered into force 1 July 2002) 2187 UNTS 3 ('Rome Statute').

2 On 2 March 2022, the ICC's Prosecutor Karim Khan announced the opening of an investigation into the Situation in Ukraine encompassing allegations of war crimes, crimes against humanity or genocide committed on any part of the territory of Ukraine by any person from

 | DOI:10.1163/9789004529939_019

every situation under its jurisdiction.[3] Bringing justice to victims and affected communities worldwide, within the parameters of the system created by the Rome Statute, is key.

## 2 Complementarity

The Rome Statute system is built upon two fundamental pillars: complementarity and cooperation. Under complementarity,[4] it is acknowledged that the ICC is not intended to replace or displace national courts.[5] Rather, it co-exists with national courts and operates as a court of last resort. This, in turn, means that primary responsibility to investigate and prosecute core international crimes rests with States,[6] and the ICC only intervenes when States are 'unwilling' or 'unable' genuinely to do so.[7]

To this end, the principle of complementarity in the Statute, is designed to ensure that cases are heard at the appropriate level—be it at the ICC or before national courts. Complementarity therefore both respects sovereignty and harnesses the advantages trials before national courts have to offer. One such advantage is easier access to evidence and witnesses, given the geographical proximity to the location where the crimes have been committed.

Moreover, complementarity brings judicial proceedings closer to the people it concerns.[8] Investigations and prosecutions conducted at the domestic level can facilitate the easier participation of victims and members of the affected communities during proceedings.[9] The involvement of local personnel might also ensure the use of local languages and higher respect for local cultural

21 November 2013 onwards. See International Criminal Court, 'Ukraine', <https://www.icc-cpi.int/ukraine> accessed 17 October 2022.

3 See International Criminal Court, 'Situations Under Investigation', <https://www.icc-cpi.int/situations-under-investigations> accessed 17 October 2022.

4 See C Stahn and M El Zeidy (eds), *The International Criminal Court and Complementarity: From Theory to Practice* (Cambridge: Cambridge University Press, 2011).

5 International Criminal Court, Paper on some policy issues before the Office of the Prosecutor, Office of the Prosecutor, September 2003 <https://www.icc-cpi.int/sites/default/files/NR/rdonlyres/1FA7C4C6-DE5F-42B7-8B25-60AA962ED8B6/143594/030905_Policy_Paper.pdf> accessed 11 July 2022.

6 Strengthening the International Criminal Court and the Assembly of States Parties, ICC-ASP/20/Res.5, 9 December 2021, (Eighth Plenary Meeting), para. 132.

7 Article 17 of the Rome Statute.

8 M Bergsmo, O Bekou, A Jones, 'Complementarity After Kampala: Capacity Building and the ICC's Legal Tools' (2010) 2 *Goettingen Journal of International Law* 791, 800.

9 Ibid.

practices.[10] Moreover, complementarity can also promote deterrence through fostering greater visibility of accountability efforts at the national level.[11]

In addition, as the ICC cannot process each and every case that arises from the commission of mass atrocity,[12] complementarity helps allocate finite resources effectively. Given the distance of the Court from the place where the alleged crimes have been committed, and the complexity and volume of evidence associated with cases heard before it, ICC proceedings are likely to take longer. By contrast, national proceedings can be faster and less costly.[13] However, national jurisdictions must have the capacity to investigate and prosecute. Ensuring that domestic capacity exists is therefore key, given the ICC's own capacity limitations.

## 3 Cooperation

Even where the ICC were to step in and take over proceedings owing to complementarity, States retain a significant role. For example, the Court does not have its own police force[14] or an enforcement mechanism to collect evidence or arrest and surrender individuals. It, therefore, largely relies upon the cooperation of national authorities to effectively carry out its functions. State

10 Ibid.

11 E A Witte, 'Putting Complementarity into Practice: Domestic Justice for International Crimes in DRC, Uganda, and Kenya' (Open Society Foundations, 2011), 5 <https://www.justiceinitiative.org/uploads/9cfa63af-e78c-483d-b9ad-60e0b1beb8a2/putting-complementarity-into-practice-20110120.pdf> accessed 17 October 2022.

12 J H Anderson, 'The ICC in Times of Budget Crunch' (*Justice Info*, 13 December 2021), <https://www.justiceinfo.net/en/85475-icc-times-budget-crunch.html> accessed 17 October 2022. Also see Proposed Programme Budget for 2022 of the International Criminal Court, ICC-ASP/20/10, 16 August 2021 (Twentieth Session of the ASP).

13 Parliamentarians for Global Action, 'Explanatory Note on the Significance of Effective and Full Implementation of the Rome Statute of the International Criminal Court' <https://www.pgaction.org/pdf/2022/explanatory-memo-significance-rome-statute.pdf> accessed 17 October 2022.

14 The first president of the International Criminal Tribunal for the Former Yugoslavia (ICTY)—Judge Antonio Cassese—described the ICTY in a manner that is also true of the ICC: '[The Tribunal] remains very much like a giant without arms and legs—it needs artificial limbs to walk and work. And these artificial limbs are state authorities. If the cooperation of states is not forthcoming, the [Court] cannot fulfil its functions'. See A Cassese, 'On the Current Trends towards Criminal Prosecution and Punishment of Breaches of International Humanitarian' (1998) 9(1) *European Journal of International Law* 2, 13.

cooperation is also required to secure the presence of the accused in Court, given that the Rome Statute does not allow for trials *in absentia*.[15]

However, in the aftermath of mass atrocity, when national systems break down and are unable to carry out domestic investigations, having the ability to cooperate with ICC requests, is not always a given. Yet, States are still required under the Statute to cooperate fully with the Court. This is also true even when they are unwilling to genuinely investigate or prosecute core international crimes—the so-called complementarity paradox, and a major flaw in the system.[16]

Putting the legal requirements of the Rome Statute system to one side, with an increasing number of countries mounting political attacks against the Court or challenging its integrity in the face of recent activities, political support is vital to support the Court in fulfilling its mandate and to increase States' cooperation with ICC requests.[17] When political support for the Court is high, so too is the level of cooperation with its requests. Conversely, when a State withdraws political support, cooperation levels fall.[18] Therefore, although States are under a general obligation to cooperate with the Court,[19] non-cooperation remains a significant challenge for the ICC, hindering its effective functioning.

## 4 The Key Role of Implementing Legislation

Having briefly examined the role played by complementarity and cooperation in the ICC regime, let us now turn to how States can fulfil their obligations under the Statute. To enable States to investigate and prosecute core international crimes domestically, enacting legislation implementing the provisions of the Rome Statute—fully and effectively—in their respective national legal systems is key. Implementation fulfils a dual purpose: crucially, it enables States to exercise primary jurisdiction over core international crimes, as envisaged

15 Article 63 of the Rome Statute.

16 P Benvenuti, 'Complementarity of the International Criminal Court to National Jurisdiction' in F Lattanzi and W A Schabas (eds), *Essays on the Rome Statute of the International Criminal Court* (Vol. 2, Il Sirente, Ripa Fagano Alto 1999) 21.

17 O Bekou, 'European Parliament Briefing: The Role of the ICC since its Foundation and Possible Scenarios for the Future: Political Support and Cooperation by States' (European Parliament, 2021), 2–3 <https://www.europarl.europa.eu/RegData/etudes/STUD/2021/653659/EXPO_STU(2021)653659_EN.pdf> accessed 17 October 2022.

18 Ibid., 5.

19 Article 86 of the Rome Statute.

by the principle of complementarity, and it facilitates State compliance with cooperation requests made by the Court.

Whilst it is true that the Rome Statute does not expressly require the enactment of national implementing legislation with respect to the core crimes and procedures, and the decision to implement is left at the discretion of each State, implementation is indispensable to meeting the 'duty of every State to exercise its criminal jurisdiction over those responsible for international crimes', enshrined in the Preamble of the Rome Statute.[20]

The widespread practice of State Parties of enacting implementing legislation clearly demonstrates that many States choose to do so. The Dutch Explanatory Memorandum on the substantive implementation stated that 'although not expressly provided for in the Statute, the majority of States were always of the opinion that the principle of complementarity entails that States parties to the Statute are obliged to criminalise the crimes that are subject to the International Criminal Court's jurisdiction in their national laws'.[21]

Implementing legislation is a precursor to national criminal justice systems being able to investigate and prosecute core international crimes. It enables the strengthening of national criminal justice systems and the rule of law and ensures the practical application of the choice made by the adoption of complementarity to give primacy to domestic proceedings over international crimes. Removing obstacles and building national capacity to enable investigations and prosecutions could lead to reducing the number of self-referrals made to the ICC and also fewer cases becoming admissible before the ICC. Conversely, the absence of implementing legislation has the potential to undermine the promise of complementarity and the effective functioning of the ICC system, as any cases that may arise would have to be tried as ordinary crimes, which lack the stigma attached to core international crimes and may not provide full coverage of the punishable acts or modes of liability.

Implementing legislation is also indispensable in discharging a State's cooperation obligations and minimising the possibility of refusing to execute ICC cooperation requests. Unlike the crimes where there is no specific provision requiring States to adopt legislation, State Parties are under an obligation to cooperate fully with the Court.[22] Moreover, Article 88 requires States to ensure

20 Preamble of the Rome Statute, para 6.

21 J K Kleffner, 'The Impact of Complementarity on National Implementation of Substantive International Criminal Law' (2003) 1(1) *Journal of International Criminal Justice* 86.

22 Article 86 of the Rome Statute.

that there are procedures available under their national laws for all forms of cooperation.[23]

Having procedures available under domestic law facilitates the identification of the competent national authorities entrusted with executing cooperation requests and ensures direct communication and cooperation between these authorities and their counterparts at the ICC.[24] Although cooperation mechanisms covering extradition may be already in place under existent national frameworks, these should not be relied upon by States when dealing with the ICC without careful consideration, given the considerable difference in the cooperation regime under the Rome Statute.[25] Existing national legal frameworks on cooperation must, therefore, be reviewed and, if not adequate or suitable, amended to be able to take on cooperation requests under the Rome Statute. Having the right procedures in place that enable States to execute ICC cooperation requests is essential for the success of the Rome system of justice.

## 5 Trends on Implementing Legislation

The entry into force of the Rome Statute acted as a catalyst for implementation, triggering a wave of incorporation of the core international crimes found in the Statute into domestic law. Several States had already criminalised genocide and war crimes in their national legal systems before the coming into force of the Rome Statute. The definition of genocide which has remained unchanged since the adoption of the Convention on the Prevention and Punishment of the Crime of Genocide in 1948[26] had led to the inclusion of the crime of genocide in domestic laws of many States and the four Geneva Conventions and Additional Protocols I and II[27] had laid the basis for the incorporation of

23 Article 88 of the Rome Statute.

24 Article 87(1)(a) of the Rome Statute makes clear that States should designate the authority competent to receive cooperation requests by the Court.

25 According to Article 102 of the Rome Statute, it exists a clear distinction between requests relating to the ICC cooperation, such as the concepts of 'surrender' of a person to the Court, and 'extradition' to other States.

26 Convention on the Prevention and Punishment of the Crime of Genocide (adopted 9 December 1948, entered into force 12 January 1951) 78 UNTS 277.

27 Geneva Convention (I) for the Amelioration of the Condition of Wounded, Sick and Shipwrecked Members of Armed Forces in the Field (adopted 12 August 1949, entered into force 21 October 1951) 75 UNTS 31; Geneva Convention (II) for the Amelioration of the Condition of Wounded, Sick and Ship-wrecked Members of Armed Forces at Sea (adopted 12 August 1949, entered into force 21 October 1950) 75 UNTS 85; Geneva

provisions on war crimes. The adoption of the Rome Statute provided, however, the impetus for those States that had not yet incorporated those crimes into their national laws to do so. It also incentivised the adoption of new provisions, particularly with regard to crimes against humanity.

In the 20 years since the adoption of the Rome Statute, numerous States have stepped up their efforts to fight impunity and have made sure that they can exercise jurisdiction in line with the complementarity principle by adopting legislation explicitly implementing the ICC regime. Complementarity has functioned as a strong incentive for implementation, and has acted as a jurisdictional safety pin, empowering States to investigate and prosecute crimes within the jurisdiction of the Court, keeping the ICC away.

However, challenges remain. A considerable number of states that have ratified the Rome Statute have not yet taken action in this regard. At the time of writing, only a little over half of all State Parties have at least partially adopted domestic implementing legislation giving meaning to complementarity, i.e., through incorporating the four core crimes.[28]

Moreover, the status of implementation amongst State parties continues to be far from uniform. Even among those States that have enacted legislation, differences in approaches exist, as wide discretion is afforded when carrying out the implementation task. The Rome Statute does not dictate nor favour a particular implementation approach. Some States, like Ireland, Samoa and Uganda, have enacted a single comprehensive act covering all relevant provisions that need to be implemented.[29] This covers all international criminal law matters in a stand-alone piece of legislation. Other States have incorporated the relevant elements into pre-existing legislation by amending their criminal law and criminal procedure codes. This approach has been chosen where some elements are already covered by national legislation and a substantial re-formulation is not required.[30] For instance, Norway, Senegal and Spain have

Convention (III) relative to the Treatment of Prisoners of War (adopted 12 August 1949, entered into force 21 October 1950) 75 UNTS 135; Geneva Convention (IV) relative to the Protection of Civilian Persons in Time of War (adopted 12 August 1949, entered into force 21 October 1950) 75 UNTS 287.

28 National Implementing Legislation Database, accessible at <https://demo.hrlc.net/en/> accessed 30 April 2023.

29 Case Matrix Network, 'Implementing the Rome Statute of the International Criminal Court' (September 2017), 18 <https://www.legal-tools.org/en/doc/e05157/> accessed 19 July 2022.

30 Ibid.

all followed this approach.[31] Lastly, a combination of both these approaches may also be employed, such as in the case of Canada.[32]

Several States have replicated the exact wording of the Rome Statute or made explicit reference to the relevant provisions of the Rome Statute. The "replication method" has been followed, for instance, by Australia, Belgium, Georgia, Kenya, Malta, New Zealand, South Africa and Trinidad and Tobago.[33] Austria, Ireland, the Republic of Korea, Uganda and the United Kingdom have instead embodied the 'reference method'.[34] Both these approaches require few resources and little expert knowledge of international criminal law. They also ensure clarity, predictability, and compliance with the principle of legality, by setting forth the criminalised conducts and the applicable penalties.

Other States have incorporated international crimes into their national systems using different terms, by reformulating, rephrasing and redrafting the way conducts have been criminalised in the Rome Statute. Nevertheless, some States have adopted more restrictive definitions, leaving possible gaps in implementation. For instance, recognising fewer protected groups in the domestic definition of genocide.[35] Conversely, others have employed broader definitions and criminalised wider conducts, adapting their national legislation to more expansive definitions found in general international law or other applicable treaties, as well as new developments in customary international law. For instance, some States have expanded the protected groups in their domestic definitions of genocide to include political or social groups.[36] Others have also included some conducts that have been omitted during the negotiations of the Rome Statute, for example, the prohibition on the use of chemical and biological weapons among war crimes.[37] When this leads to an increased number of perpetrators being brought to justice, expanding the definitions

31 Ibid.

32 Canada has enacted a specific piece of legislation implementing the core international crimes—the Crimes against Humanity and War Crimes Act entered into force on 29 June 2000. In addition, the already existing legislation on extradition has been amended to include the ICC cooperation regime.

33 Case Matrix Network 'Implementing the Rome Statute of the International Criminal Court' (n 29) 22.

34 Ibid.

35 For instance, Bolivia and Paraguay omit racial groups; El Salvador omits ethnical groups; and Nicaragua omits both racial groups and national groups. See Case Matrix Network 'Implementing the Rome Statute of the International Criminal Court' (n 29) 26.

36 Colombia, Costa Rica, Ethiopia, Ivory Coast, Panama and Poland include political groups; Estonia, Latvia and Peru include social groups; while Lithuania and Switzerland include both political and social groups.

37 For instance, Argentina, Ecuador and Germany.

could be welcome. However, it is equally important to assess how this is used in practice, as the risk of excessively broadening the spectrum of the most serious crimes and diluting the stigma inherently attached to them and, consequently, weakening the application of these provisions, remains.

In addition to implementing the core internal crimes, several State Parties have also amended or enacted domestic legislation to cover procedural aspects and facilitate compliance with the obligation to cooperate fully with the Court. States have consistently designated either the Minister of Justice or the Minister of Foreign Affairs as competent authorities in charge of executing cooperation requests made by the Court.[38] They have also specifically provided national provisions for most of the forms of cooperation specified in the Rome Statute: arrest and surrender of persons to the Court,[39] competing requests,[40] provisional arrest,[41] and other forms of cooperation.[42] Although cooperation provisions have generally been incorporated into national legislation in a manner consistent with the Rome Statute, less than half of the State Parties have—at the time of writing—adopted legislation enabling cooperation with the Court.[43]

## 6 Some Recommendations on Implementation

A comprehensive legislative framework implementing the Rome Statute must, at a minimum, incorporate substantive provisions explicitly criminalising genocide, crimes against humanity, war crimes and aggression. As the most serious crimes of concern to the international community as a whole, core international crimes hold a distinctive stigma and significance and this needs

38 See Cooperation and Judicial Assistance Database, 'Competent National Authority' <https://cjad.nottingham.ac.uk/en/keyword/203/> accessed 30 April 2023.

39 For instance, South Africa has provided a detailed procedure for the arrest and surrender of persons.

40 States have widely incorporated the provision on competing requests by replicating or referring to Article. For instance, while an extensive formulation has been adopted by New Zealand, Mauritius only referred to the Statute. See Case Matrix Network 'Implementing the Rome Statute of the International Criminal Court' (n 29) 88–89.

41 Differences in the way Article 92 has been implemented however exist. While some States—such as Samoa have adhered to the 60-day time limit imposed by the ICC Rule of Procedure and Evidence, others—for instance, Canada—have provided for a broader time limit.

42 See Case Matrix Network, 'Implementing the Rome Statute of the International Criminal Court' (n 29) 92–98.

43 Cooperation and Judicial Assistance Database, 'Competent National Authority' (n 38).

to be reflected in national legislation. It may be that prosecuting a conduct as an ordinary crime—such as murder, rape or theft—does not render the State automatically 'unwilling or unable'. However, such prosecutions may not be able to reflect the nature, gravity and scale of core international crimes fully.

There might not be an equivalent ordinary law provision which is able to perfectly capture the conduct criminalised in the Rome Statute. A narrower range of conducts is indeed likely to be punishable as ordinary crimes compared to what is envisaged in the Statute.[44] For instance, not all forms of persecution as a crime against humanity or all of the war crimes may be covered by ordinary criminal law provisions. The same holds true for all modes of liability including, commonly, command responsibility. Moreover, the sentencing framework for ordinary crimes may be inadequate to meet the seriousness of conducts constituting core international crimes,[45] and can undermine the deterrent effect of preventing the commission of further crimes in the future. Therefore, recognising the international character of the core crimes in the Rome Statute, as opposed to considering them as ordinary offences, is a choice for States to make.

Alongside incorporating the definitions of crimes, the ability of States to effectively investigate and prosecute core international crimes depends also on the jurisdictional reach they envisage. States are free to choose the heads of jurisdiction they wish to pursue. Exercising jurisdiction based on territoriality as well as active and passive nationality is common, and in line with the Statute.[46] Pre-existing provisions contained in criminal codes or codes of criminal procedure might already provide for such jurisdiction. However, a broader approach that includes universal jurisdiction—that is exercising jurisdiction before national courts irrespective of where the crime has been committed, owing to the heinous nature of the crimes—can also help reduce the impunity gap, enabling States with interest and resources to step in.[47] Nevertheless, the pure form of universal jurisdiction, which enables a State to exercise jurisdiction over a crime without requiring the presence of the accused in its territory, is still rarely practiced.[48]

44 Kleffner (n 21) 99.

45 Ibid., 97.

46 See Case Matrix Network, 'Implementing the Rome Statute of the International Criminal Court' (n 29) 51.

47 See P Gaeta, 'The Need Reasonably to Expand National Criminal Jurisdiction over International Crimes' in Antonio Cassese (ed.), *Realizing Utopia: The Future of International Law* (Oxford University Press, 2012), 597.

48 For instance, Section 8(1)(c)(iii) of the New Zealand International Crimes and International Criminal Court Act of 2000 is one of the few legislations that provides for the wider form of universal jurisdiction. See M El Zeidy, 'Universal Jurisdiction in Absentia: Is it a

Moreover, whilst the principle of complementarity does not dictate how cases are to be tried before domestic courts, nor does it expect an ICC-style trial at the domestic level, State Parties ought to give due consideration to the general principles of customary international law found in the Statute.[49] Enacting national legislation that encompasses all forms of criminal responsibility recognised in the Rome Statute, including the irrelevance of official capacity, the doctrine of command responsibility and the inadmissibility of the defence of superior orders, are key.[50] Similarly, the non-applicability of statutes of limitations should also be included.[51] The absence of bars to investigate and prosecute core international crimes is crucial for the effectiveness of the international criminal justice system.

Lastly, no trial can succeed without getting hold of the accused and providing evidence to prove their guilt or innocence. Domestic provisions must be in place to arrest and surrender individuals at the request of the Court, to collect evidence, hand over documents and facilitate the appearance of experts and witnesses—and also to give meaning to the full range of other forms of cooperation specified in the Statute.

In addition, ratifying and implementing the Agreement on Privileges and Immunities (APIC)[52] and signing bilateral or multilateral agreements on mutual legal assistance, extradition and judicial cooperation are also important. Encouraging States to do so, ought to be a priority.

## 7 Looking to the Future

The availability of a domestic framework implementing the full gamut of the Rome Statute does not—*on its own*—ensure greater accountability at

Legally Valid Option for Repressing Heinous Crimes?' (2003) 37(3) *International Lawyer* 835–862, 844. For a comprehensive list of Universal Jurisdiction practice see TRIAL International, 'Universal Jurisdiction Annual Review 2022: Universal Jurisdiction, an Overlooked Tool to Fight Conflict-Related Sexual Violence' (2022) <https://trialinternational.org/wp-content/uploads/2022/03/TRIAL_International_UJAR-2022.pdf> accessed 17 October 2022.

49 Parliamentarians for Global Action, 'Explanatory Note on the Significance of Effective and Full Implementation of the Rome Statute of the International Criminal Court' (n 13).

50 Ibid.

51 See Case Matrix Network, 'Implementing the Rome Statute of the International Criminal Court' (n 29) 61.

52 Agreement on the Privileges and Immunities of the International Criminal Court (APIC), ICC-ASP/1/3, 3–10 September 2022 (First Session of the ASP) (entered into force 22 July 2004).

the national level, nor does it guarantee compliance with ICC cooperation requests. A lot rests on political will. It is therefore of pivotal importance that laws and procedures are applied in practice by legislative, executive and judicial authorities to particular cases.

All State Parties must rise to the implementation challenge. This requires, for example, legislators to play their role in fostering implementing legislation and State leadership to sign bilateral cooperation agreements with the Court. However, the challenges of the implementation task must not be underestimated. Alongside the need for political will, drafting and enacting implementing legislation on international criminal law is a complex and time-consuming process. It generally requires long-term efforts and the mobilisation and action of several state bodies, interest groups and experts, as well as civil society.[53] It is also an unfamiliar and challenging process for the majority of drafters at the domestic level. Not all States, particularly, post-conflict or transitioning States, have the necessary resources and expertise to do so. They might lack funding and institutional capacity, which might have been destroyed or damaged as a result of an armed conflict.[54] Inherent difficulties within domestic legal systems—for instance, certain constitutional provisions or pre-existing national laws which need to be reviewed, such as statutes of limitations, amnesties and immunities for national officials, constitute possible hurdles.[55]

It is then necessary to remove such obstacles and provide assistance to those States that require it. Over the past 20 years, the concept of positive complementarity has been developed to help build national capacity and increase the ability of States to conduct genuine investigations and prosecutions. Positive complementarity must involve 'any cooperation with national or regional criminal jurisdictions aimed at enhancing the capacity and willingness of

53 ICRC Advisory Service on International Humanitarian Law, 'Preventing and Repressing International Crimes: Towards an "Integrated" Approach Based on Domestic Practice' (Vol. I, International Red Cross, 2020), 45.

54 For example, for the challenges faced by Rwanda in delivering justice in the aftermath of the genocide, see Human Rights Watch, 'Justice Compromised: The Legacy of Rwanda's Community-Based Gacaca Court' (2011) <https://www.hrw.org/report/2011/05/31/justice-compromised/legacy-rwandas-community-based-gacaca-courts> accessed 17 October 2022. Or for Afghanistan, see A Wardak, 'A Decade and a Half of Rebuilding Afghanistan's Justice System: An Overview' (Van Vollenhoven Institute, 2016) <https://www.universiteitleiden.nl/binaries/content/assets/rechtsgeleerdheid/instituut-voor-metajuridica/afghanistans-justice-system-vs-2016.10.04.pdf> accessed 17 October 2022.

55 See Council of Europe, Venice Commission, Second Report on Constitutional Issue raised by the Ratification of the Rome Statute of the International Criminal Court, CDL-AD(2008)031, 4 November 2009.

those jurisdictions to investigate and prosecute crimes within the ICC's subject-matter jurisdiction'.[56]

The positive approach to complementarity that emerged from the Kampala Review Conference encouraged a range of activities to strengthen domestic courts and enable them to conduct genuine national investigations and prosecutions.[57] The Court has an active role to play in promoting domestic capacity building in order to enhance the capacity of national judicial systems to carry out the investigation and prosecution of international crimes themselves. The positive approach to complementarity adopted by the Office of the Prosecutor, exemplified in the cooperation agreements signed with Colombia and Venezuela,[58] is a step in the right direction.

Similarly, the Assembly of States Parties to the Rome Statute for the International Criminal Court (ASP) has 'resolve[d] to continue and strengthen, within the appropriate fora, effective domestic implementation of the Rome Statute, to enhance the capacity of national jurisdictions to prosecute the perpetrators of the most serious crimes of international concern'.[59] It also 'urges States Parties to the Rome Statute that have not yet done so to adopt such legislative [implementing legislation] and to set up effective procedures and structures so as to ensure that they can fully meet their obligation under the Rome Statute regarding cooperation and judicial assistance'.[60] The ASP has a key role in facilitating discussions between States to accelerate the pace of national implementation processes in those States that have not yet done so.

States can also draw upon and find inspiration in examples of implementing laws enacted by others, as legislation that has been in force for a considerable number of years is likely to have already been subject to scrutiny and, potentially, even amended accordingly. Existing support includes the ICC's Legal Tools Project, which contains freely available databases on

---

56 International Law Association, Committee on Complementarity, 'The Lisbon Conclusions and Recommendations on Complementarity', Resolution 04/2022, <https://www.ila-hq.org/en_GB/documents/resolution-4-complementarity-committee-final-1> accessed 26 July 2022.

57 Draft Resolution on Complementarity, ICC-ASP/8/Res.9, Annex VII, 11 June 2010 (Tenth Plenary Meeting of the ASP).

58 OTP, Cooperation Agreement between the Office of the Prosecutor of the International Criminal Court and the Government of Colombia (28 October 2021); Memorandum of Understanding between the Bolivarian Republic of Venezuela and the Office of the Prosecutor of the International Criminal Court (21 November 2000).

59 Report of the Bureau on Complementarity, ICC-ASP/20/22, 6 December 2021 (Twentieth Session of the ASP), para. 2.

60 Resolution on Cooperation, ICC-ASP/20/Res.2, 9 December 2021 (Eighth Plenary Meeting of the ASP), para. 7.

implementing legislation and cooperation—the National Implementing Legislation Database (NILD)[61] and the Cooperation and Judicial Assistance Database (CJAD).[62] The two databases enable States to compare the different approaches on implementing legislation that have been employed by different jurisdictions and to model their national legislation following that of systems with similar features.

## 8 Concluding Observations

While marking the 20-year anniversary, and looking to the future, it is clear that the ICC remains at the centre of the system of accountability for core international crimes. It is the international community's only criminal justice institution with a global outlook. There remains a strong link with domestic justice as, pursuant to the ICC's principle of complementarity, the Rome Statute system encourages genuine and fair justice efforts closer to where the crimes have taken place.

The longevity of the ICC rests greatly on the success of the complementarity regime. States are strongly encouraged to adopt implementing legislation as a first step towards being willing and able to investigate and prosecute core international crimes. Conversely, gaps in national legislation adversely affect the complementary role of the Court, shielding perpetrators from being brought to justice and rendering cases admissible before the ICC. In addition, the success of the Rome Statute system is also significantly influenced by the ability and willingness of States to cooperate fully with the ICC in its investigations and prosecutions. National implementing legislation provides the legal basis for giving full effect to cooperation requests originating at the Court.

As with complementarity, the ability of States to cooperate with the Court is inextricably linked with the domestic implementation of the Statute's provisions into the national sphere. Implementing the Statute is of paramount importance for the future of the ICC. Political support is also needed.

Twenty years after the entry into force of the Rome Statute, significant progress has been made in supporting the Court to fulfil its mandate. This is not

61 National Implementing Legislation Database, accessible at <https://demo.hrlc.net/en/> accessed 30 April 2023.

62 Cooperation and Judicial Assistance Database, accessible at <https://cjad.nottingham.ac.uk/en/> accessed 30 April 2023.

the end of the road, however. It is vital to urge those States that have not yet implemented the Statute to take that important step and to do so fully in order for the promise of complementarity to be materialised and for cooperation to be supported. The future of the ICC rests on this.

# PART 6

## *Confronting Institutional Challenges*

CHAPTER 19

# The Gap: Gender and Geographical Imbalance at the ICC, 20 Years on

*Angela Mudukuti*

> When we're talking about diversity, it's not a box to check. It is a reality that should be deeply felt and held and valued by all of us.
>
> AVA DUVERNAY

∴

## 1 Introduction

Many impactful events related to gender and geographical balance took place 20 years ago—for example, the FIFA Men's World Cup was hosted jointly by South Korea and Japan, first time it was not held in Europe or the Americas and Halle Berry became the first African American woman to win the Oscar for Best Actress. 20 years ago, the Rome Statute also entered into force giving birth to the International Criminal Court (ICC), an institution that should also be diverse including gender and geographical balance.

The ICC, the only permanent international criminal court, is an essential part of the international criminal justice landscape. Its inception signalled hope for justice, accountability and even deterrence. The Rome Statute has been referred to as 'a high act of international creativity'[1] and the moment it was finalised it was seen as an 'international epiphany'[2] Unfortunately, the Court itself has a history coloured by both success and failure. One of the most

1 F Benedetti and J L Washburn, 'Drafting the International Criminal Court Treaty: Two Years to Rome and an Afterword on the Rome Diplomatic Conference' (1999) 5 *Global Governance* 1–37, 2.

2 J Washburn, 'The Negotiation of the Rome Statute for the International Criminal Court and International Lawmaking in the 21st Century' (1999) 11 *Pace International Law Review* 361.

 | DOI:10.1163/9789004529939_020

troubling failures of the Court has been the lack of gender and geographical balance on staff[3] which has had adverse impacts on the work of the ICC.

## 2 Sign of Times

Globally there has been a much-needed awakening about the need for genuine diversity, equity and meaningful inclusion. The #MeToo movement, created by survivor and activist Tarana Burke, started an important wave for change. It was designed to help survivors of sexual violence and sexual harassment. It gave many women and other targeted groups a voice and a platform to speak against sexual violence in a variety of industries including Hollywood. Sexual violence and harassment are inextricably linked to patriarchy and male dominance. As written by Suzanne Moore[4] who advocates for an analysis of patriarchy in order to understand sexual violence, 'with no understanding of patriarchy, we are stuck' and failing to meaningfully include women in all levels and structures of society results in male dominated, patriarchal spaces that give rise numerous forms of harm. The same applies to the workplace.

Gender is not where the conversation should end as one cannot speak about gender without talking about race and geographical diversity in international spaces. A truly intersectional and impactful approach behoves us to advocate for both these causes in tandem. The devastating consequences of racism around the world, including the murder of African American George Floyd in May 2020, which spurred on the Black Lives Matter movement have been catalysts for much need change particularly in the Global North.[5] In the 21st century international workspaces that are dominated by white men from the global north are patently unacceptable and unsustainable. The centrepiece of the international criminal justice landscape, the ICC should not be exempt from scrutiny and pressure that will hopefully result in consequential change. As there is no publicly available race disaggregated data from the ICC, this chapter will use figures based on geographical representation to highlight the lack of

3 Gender balance and geographical representation with regard to elected officials also needs significant improvement but will not be covered in this chapter.

4 S Moore, 'What connects rape in war, domestic violence and sexual harassment? Patriarchy' (*PeaceWomen*, 18 October 2017) <https://peacewomen.org/resource/what-connects-rape-war-domestic-violence-and-sexual-harassment-patriarchy> accessed 30 April 2023.

5 J Silverstein, 'The global impact of George Floyd: How Black Lives Matter protests shaped movements around the world', *CBS News* (4 June 2021) <https://www.cbsnews.com/news/george-floyd-black-lives-matter-impact/> accessed 30 April 2023.

diversity and representation at the Court. Admittedly, race and geographical representation do not necessarily align in every case but looking generally at Court staff and numbers pertaining to geographical representation, a correlation and pattern does indeed emerge.

## 3 The Numbers

From the beginning, the issues of gender and geographical representation have been on the radar at the Court and as early as 3 December 2005, the Assembly of States Parties (ASP) adopted a resolution[6] which states as follows, '[t] he Assembly of States Parties, [...] Decides to invite the Bureau, in consultation with the Court, to submit proposals to improve equitable geographical representation and gender balance in the recruitment of staff members'.[7] Despite this awareness, progress has been slow.

The first report from the Bureau on Geographical Representation and Gender Balance in the Recruitment of Staff of the ICC (hereafter the GRBB report) issued in 2007 shows the imbalance in gender and geographical balance.

As of 1 May 2007, 18.14% professional staff were from African States; 6.37% from Asian States; 7.84% from Eastern European States; 11.27% from Latin American and Caribbean States; 56.37% for the group of Western European and other States (WEOG).[8]

At the very senior level of staff, Director level (D1)—there was one person from GRULAC[9] and four from WEOG. Moving down to P5 level, there were three Africans, one Asian, two people from GRULAC and 14 from WEOG.

At the P4 level there were five from Africa, one from Asia, from from Eastern Europe, five from GRULAC and 20 from WEOG.

At the P3 level there were 13 from Africa, two from Asia, three from Eastern Europe and 33 from WEOG. At P2 level, 13 Africans, eight Asians, eight Eastern Europeans, five people from GRULAC and 39 from WEOG.

6 Strengthening the International Criminal Court and the Assembly of States Parties, ICC-ASP/4/Res.4, 3 December 2005 (Fourth Plenary Meeting of the ASP), para. 23.

7 Report of the Bureau on geographical representation and gender balance in the recruitment of staff of the International Criminal Court, ICC-ASP/6/22, 24 October 2007 (Sixth Session of the ASP), para. 1.

8 Ibid., para. 17.

9 Report of the Bureau on geographical representation and gender balance in the recruitment of staff of the International Criminal Court: Addendum, ICC-ASP/6/22/Add.1, 25 October 2007, Annex X.

Finally, at P1 level there were two Africans, one Asian, three Eastern Europeans, two people from GRULAC and five people from WEOG.

Not only were more than half of the staff at the ICC from WEOG but they also held the vast majority of the senior roles. Fast forward to 2021, not much has changed.

As of 31 July 2021, out of 473 professional staff at the ICC, 256 are from WEOG, 31 from Asia, 33 from Latin America and Caribbean countries, 77 from Africa and 45 from Eastern Europe. As in 2007, more than half of the professional staff at the ICC are from WEOG.[10]

Compounding the problem currently, same as it was in 2007, is that nationals from WEOG also hold the most senior positions currently. WEOG nationals hold: 55.6% of D1 positions; 72% of P-5 positions; and 56% of P4 positions.[11]

The statistics regarding gender also leave a lot to be desired. As of 1 May 2007, there were 468 established posts[12] at the ICC and 43.70% were held by females and 56.30% were held by males.[13] On the surface that distribution, whilst imperfect does not raise extreme alarm however, when one digs deeper cause for alarm is apparent as women held more junior professional staff positions. There were 203 professional staff and at D1 level there was one woman (20%) and four men (80%). At P5 level, there were six women and 14 men, meaning 70% of P5s were men. At P4 level, 14 women (42%) 19 men (58%). At P3 20 women (34%) and 39 men. (66%). P2 31 women held 42% of the positions and men had 42 which is 58%. In the lowest position the balance tips P1 9 women (69%) 4 men (31%).[14]

As the Hague Working Group found 'most female staff are concentrated in lower-level professional posts (P-1 to P-3) and this may result in them having less opportunity to participate and influence the fora and structures where crucial decisions are made on a day-today basis regarding the substantive work of the Court.'[15]

Despite the Court establishing a 5 and 10-year plan which sought to address gender equity,[16] the 2021 statistics show little progress.

---

10 Report of the Bureau on equitable geographical representation and gender balance in the recruitment of staff of the International Criminal Court, ICC-ASP/20/29, 29 November 2021 (Twentieth Session of the ASP).

11 Ibid., para. 17.

12 This includes General Service staff, language staff and GTA.

13 Report of the Bureau on geographical representation and gender balance in the recruitment of staff of the International Criminal Court (n 7) para. 24.

14 Ibid.

15 Ibid., para. 28.

16 Ibid., para. 29.

As of 31 July 2021, female staff comprised 48.1% of the Court's professional staff, which is more than the 2007 figures, while male staff comprised 51.9%. However, the imbalance at the top which is where all the critical decision making is done remains with only 11.1% of female staff at the D-1 level, 27.5%at the P-5 level, 38.1% at the P-4 level, and 46% at the P-3 level.[17] Compared to 2007 gender representation at the top has taken a turn for the worst except in the P3 and P5 category where we see an increase in female staff at that level.

The overall numbers are concerning and the balance of power in terms of gender and geographical representation shows that the ICC has a long way to go to achieve the balance that will ultimately improve its internal and external operations.

## 4 Corollaries of Poor Gender and Geographical Representation

The overall numbers are concerning and the balance of power in terms of gender and geographical representation shows that the ICC has a long way to go to achieve the balance that will ultimately improve its internal and external operations.

### 4.1 *Workplace Culture*

In December 2019, a group of Independent Experts, were mandated by the Assembly of States Parties (ASP) to review the entire Rome Statute system and develop concrete actionable recommendations 'aimed at enhancing the performance, efficiency and effectiveness of the Court and the Rome Statute system as a whole.'[18] They produced a detailed report based on access to court documents, interviews with current and former ICC officials, staff and external defence and victims' representatives, heads of Court organs, the ICC Staff Union Council, States Parties, ASP representatives and bodies, NGOs and academics and provided a set of recommendations to address some of the challenges.

The Independent Expert Review report[19] shed light on the internal environment at the ICC including sexual harassment which, as highlighted above,

17 Report of the Bureau on geographical representation and gender balance in the recruitment of staff of the International Criminal Court (n 10) para. 12.

18 Review of the International Criminal Court and the Rome Statute system, ICC-ASP/18/Res.7, 6 December 2019 (Ninth Plenary Meeting of the ASP).

19 Independent Expert Review of the International Criminal Court and the Rome Statute System: Final Report—30 September 2020, ICC-ASP/19/16, 9 November 2020 (Nineteenth Session of the ASP) ('IER Report').

cannot be divorced from the gender imbalance and patriarchy. The Experts 'heard a number of accounts of sexual harassment, notably uninvited and unwanted sexual advances from more senior male staff to their female subordinates. Female interns seemed to be particularly vulnerable to such approaches.'[20] There are many strategies to combat this predatory behaviour but if there were more women at the institution and more women in managerial positions it would go a long way towards reducing sexual harassment and improving an office culture that perpetuates such behaviour. As pointed out by the Experts, '[w]hile women as individuals are not necessarily more inclusive or less confrontational in their work practices than male colleagues, experience in other organisations suggests that when the composition of management approaches parity between women and men, the overall culture of the office becomes more collaborative and is less tolerant to bullying behaviour.'[21]

The office culture at the ICC is as reported by the Experts, is one where men in senior leadership 'exert enormous weight and influence not merely over the substantive work of the Court and how it is organised, but over recruitment, placements and other staffing decisions that impact officers at all levels.'[22] Momentum generated by the #MeToo movement and other global developments have seen sexual harassment finally receive warranted international attention, the ICC cannot afford to be sustain an environment and workplace culture that allows sexual harassment to proliferate.

### 4.2 *Approach to Investigations, Prosecutions and Adjudication*

Externally, the poor geographical and gender representation has affected how cases are approached, investigations and prosecutions conducted and the adjudication of cases. Investigations carried out in the global south led by predominantly white men from the global north have led to a failure to apply an intersectional approach which would better reflect the harm suffered by victims and survivors which would in turn ultimately lead to appropriately tailored accountability. For example, having an all-white, all male investigative team interviewing female victims of sexual violence may not lead to the same results as having a more diverse team handling different aspects of the investigation. According to Phil Clarke's 2016 interviews with OTP officials, at that point, the OTP 'used only investigators who [were] not nationals of the situation countries in question. Despite eight of the ICC's nine situations being in Africa, only a handful of OTP investigators are even African, with most coming

20 Ibid., para. 209.
21 Ibid., para. 212.
22 Ibid., para. 205.

from western Europe, North America and Australia.'[23] Having staff who have little or no understanding of social and cultural norms relevant to the situation they are working on has a detrimental effect on evidence collection and analysis. That ultimately hinders the OTP's ability fully grasp the depth and breadth of the harm suffered by the constituents it seeks to serve-the victims and survivors.

Which charges are filed and which ones are not is deeply influenced by the outcomes of the investigation and therefore, failures there will be reflected in the prosecution strategy as well.

Though elected officials are not the focus of this contribution, the bench (and the legal officers who play an integral role in the work of the ICC judges) remains a useful example. Men and women are likely to approach judicial adjudication differently, which means that a homogeneous bench and in this case, staff is inherently biased.[24] Women and men may also view situations in different ways, for example, Judge Navanethem Pillay, the only woman on a panel hearing Jean Paul Akayesu's at the International Criminal Tribunal for Rwanda, is credited with vigorously questioning witnesses about sexual violence, which ultimately brought about the first conviction of an individual for rape as a crime against humanity and genocide founded on rape.[25]

Whilst men can be gender sensitive, the lived experience of different women can only be brought to the fore by women themselves. The same logic applies to geographical balance—people from different legal traditions, races and cultures bring to bear that expertise that is unique to them. The ICC can only benefit by having a genuine balance in terms of geographical representation and gender on staff.

### 4.3 *Legitimacy and Legacy*

Failure to have a gender balanced and geographically representative court has already affected the Court's legitimacy and by extension its legacy. It will continue to do so unless the imbalance is addressed. Writing specifically about gender representation, Grossmann reflects that 'it affects both the normative and sociological legitimacy of international courts'[26] and the same applies to

23 P Clark, *Distant Justice: The Impact of the International Criminal Court on African Politics* (Cambridge: Cambridge University Press, 2018) 67.

24 N Grossman, 'Shattering the Glass Ceiling in International Adjudication' (forthcoming 2016) 56(2) *Virginia Journal of International Law*, 7.

25 Ibid.

26 Ibid., 6.

geographical representation. For example, the under prosecution[27] of sexual and gender-based violence at the ICC has raised questions about its effectiveness and whether it has failed to serve women and girls who are more often than not, victims of these crimes.[28]

The allegations of the Court targeting Africans,[29] whether one believes it to be true or not, has been used to question the court's legitimacy and even raised concerns about the withdrawal of African states from the Rome Statute. Having predominantly all white, all male, leadership from the Global North has only fanned the flames.

## 5 How We Got Here

In order to adequately address the imbalance, understanding its structural and root causes is necessary. The gender imbalance is steeped in a long history of sexism, patriarchy and male hegemony that continues to affect institutions like the ICC. Including but not limited to, men who only hire other men, men who refer jobs and opportunities to their male peers, men who do not think women suitably qualified for jobs in international criminal law, or work environments that do not cater for the needs of women for example safe, clean, private spaces to breastfeed or use a breast pump.

The geographical imbalance has structural causes including,

> [i]n accordance with resolution ICC-ASP/1/Res.10, the Court's selection of staff in the Professional category is guided by a system of desirable ranges based on that of the United Nations. The desirable ranges, or in other words percentages, are calculated by considering three factors: the total number of States Parties, a State's financial contribution to the

27 E Y Oskarsdottir, 'The Gendered Politics Behind the International Criminal Court' (*E-International Relations*, 30 July 2020), 2 <https://www.e-ir.info/2020/07/30/the-gendered-politics-behind-the-international-criminal-court/> accessed 30 April 2023.

28 Men can also be victims of sexual violence.

29 F Kuwonu, 'ICC: Beyond the threats of withdrawal' (*Arica Renewal*, 2017) <https://www.un.org/africarenewal/magazine/may-july-2017/icc-beyond-threats-withdrawal> accessed 30 April 2023. Kamari Clarke asks the question 'Why Africa' and discusses structural inequalities in international criminal law that have contributed to an imbalance in the geography of the Court's docket. See K M Clarke, 'Negotiating Racial Injustice: How International Criminal Law Helps Entrench Structural Inequality' (*Just Security*, 24 July 2020) <https://www.justsecurity.org/71614/negotiating-racial-injustice-how-international-criminal-law-helps-entrench-structural-inequality/> accessed 30 April 2023.

> budget and its population size. These factors are attributed with weights that determine the outcome. At present, substantial weight is given to membership (40%), which is equal for each State Party, *the greatest importance is given to the State's contribution* (55%) and the final 5% is determined according to the population size of the country (United Nations model 40-55-5).[30] (emphasis added).

As of 2021, this has not changed, '[a]s decided by the Assembly, the system of desirable ranges applied by the Court is based on the system of the United Nations. The ranges are calculated on the basis of a State's financial contribution to the budget of the Court and of a state's population size, both criteria in relation to the total membership of the Rome Statute.'[31]

Therefore, states that provide more financial support are more likely to have their nationals hired at the ICC. This is a flaw inherited from the UN system and it must be reconsidered given that it clearly privileges those who come from wealthy states. This is neither fair nor merit based. Given the geopolitical realities, including the aforementioned accusations of the ICC 'targeting' African states[32] (which has been linked to the number of African accused and the fact that influential nations in the global north are not all signatories of the Rome Statute) staffing the Court at its highest levels with only global northers perpetuates this perception and gives credence to allegations of neo-colonialism[33] and white supremacy.[34] The fact that multilateral institutions have been organised in this way in the past is deeply problematic and maintaining this system falls gravely short of the demands of our time. It serves to reinforce barriers to entry and compounds entrenched discrimination already felt and experienced by those who come from less economically wealthy countries who are qualified and more than capable of performing at the highest levels.

30 Report of the Bureau on geographical representation and gender balance in the recruitment of staff of the International Criminal Court (n 7).

31 Report of the Bureau on geographical representation and gender balance in the recruitment of staff of the International Criminal Court (n 10) para. 2.

32 K Allen, 'Is this the end for the International Criminal Court', *BBC News* (24 October 2016) <https://www.bbc.com/news/world-africa-37750978> accessed 30 April 2023.

33 Kamari Clarke refers to the ICC as.

34 See Clarke (n 29).

## 6 Changing the Status Quo

Addressing the imbalance must come in a way that is intersectional in nature. For example, populating the court with white women from the global north may help with gender balance but it completely ignores the geographical representation issues. The situation must also be addressed with a sense of urgency because the longer it lasts, the wider the gap. The Court is not oblivious to the issues and its efforts to address the gender and geographical imbalance have been documented.

### 6.1 *Court Efforts to Improve Gender Balance*

For example, mentoring programmes for women designed to support women 'in strengthening professional networks and defining and pursuing career aspirations with the coaching and support of an experienced mentor' have been established.[35] A Gender Equality Focal Point was appointed in March 2021, and their mandate was to 'assist the Court's Leadership in their efforts to strengthen gender related policies across the Court and to address issues related to employment conditions of women in the institution, including gender balance at all levels of employment. The Focal Point's key functions include monitoring the Court's progress in strengthening gender equality; advocating on issues impacting women and gender; providing individual counselling; raising greater awareness through training programmes, workshops and events; and advising on gender parity targets.'[36]

In December 2022 the Court launched its Strategy on Gender Equality and Workplace Culture (GEWC) and it seeks to address some of the findings and recommendations made by the IER as well as the relevant gaps and needs identified in the ICC staff engagement surveys.[37] The GEWC Strategy has three key pillars: safe and inclusive workplace culture and processes; personal and professional life integration; gender parity & equal opportunities.[38] This is an important step and is definitely setting the Court on an appropriate trajectory but as always implementation will be key as that will determine whether the

35 Report of the Bureau on geographical representation and gender balance in the recruitment of staff of the International Criminal Court (n 10) para. 13.

36 'International Women's Day: ICC appoints Focal Point for Gender Equality', ICC Press Release (8 March 2021) <https://www.icc-cpi.int/news/international-womens-day-icc-appoints-focal-point-gender-equality> accessed 30 April 2023.

37 ICC, Strategy on Gender Equality and Workplace Culture for the International Criminal Court (2022), 4 <https://www.icc-cpi.int/sites/default/files/2022-12/gender-strategy.pdf> accessed 30 April 2023.

38 Ibid., 11.

situation improves or deteriorates. Other initiatives include the Prosecutor, President and Registrar of the Court joining the Gender Champion Leadership Network.[39]

Whilst all these initiatives are important, more can and should be done. The first document[40] formally adopted by the UN Human Rights Council in 2021 on gender balance, entitled, 'Current levels of representation of women in human rights organs and mechanisms: ensuring gender balance Report of the Human Rights Council Advisory Committee'[41] provides recommendations that should be considered in the context of the ICC. For example, establishing mandatory targets to improve female representation, holding decision makers accountable for achieving this target including requiring an explanation when targets are not met; having selection committees/hiring teams that are diverse; and advertising jobs using gender-neutral and inclusive language that will attract gender-diverse candidates.[42] There is a need for formal equality, substantive equality and transformative gender equality and progress must be made in the next 20 years.

### 6.2 *Further Measures to Improve the Situation*

In relation to both gender and geographical balance, the most urgent change required is term limits for staff. As indicated above, men and mostly people from the Global North hold high level positions in the Court without term limits. According to the Experts, 44% of D-1 staff and 23% of P-5s have been at the Court for more than 10 years whilst 33% of D-1s and 41% of P-5s have been at the Court for between 5–10 years.[43] This means that men, and people from the Global North stay in their coveted high powered positions and promotion of women and people from regions outside of WEOG is mostly impossible until these positions become vacant.

---

39 Report of the Bureau on geographical representation and gender balance in the recruitment of staff of the International Criminal Court (n 10) para. 13.

40 M N Leoni, 'Symposium on Gender Representation: The GQUAL Campaign—Witnessing Change on Gender Balance in International Bodies' (*Opinio Juris*, 4 October 2021) <https://opiniojuris.org/2021/10/04/symposium-on-gender-representation-the-gqual-campaign-witnessing-change-on-gender-balance-in-international-bodies/> accessed 30 April 2023.

41 Current levels of representation of women in human rights organs and mechanisms: ensuring gender balance, Report of the Human Rights Council Advisory Committee, Human Rights Council, Forty-seventh Session, (21 May 2021) UN Doc A/HRC/47/51.

42 Ibid., para. 75.

43 IER Report (n 19) para. 248.

The Experts recommended a tenure system be introduced for new recruitments in P-5 and Director Level positions.[44] Citing international organisations that operate in this manner, the Experts pointed to the Hague based Organisation for the Prohibition of Chemical Weapons which has a maximum 7-year terms for all its officers, the Organisation for Security and Cooperation in Europe, the International Atomic Energy Agency which have a maximum of five years.[45] The Experts recommend something between the five-year term of the Registrar, and the nine-year terms of the judges and prosecutor.[46] Whilst this is a progressive recommendation it should apply to current position holders, not just new recruitments.

In the Court's 2021 'Overall Response of the International Criminal Court to the "Independent Expert Review of the International Criminal Court and the Rome Statute System—Final Report" Preliminary Analysis of the Recommendations and information on relevant activities undertaken by the Court' (hereafter Overall Response),[47] the resistance to a system of tenure was apparent specifically with regard to the OTP which indicated that, due to the length of trials and cases at the ICC, losing a senior trial lawyer would result in, '[t]he loss of the skill, experience, case and situation knowledge, and personal commitment to the mission possessed by the senior lawyer … [which] would be detrimental to OTP operations.'[48] Strain on limited financial resources due to frequent recruitment and the risk of increasing the, 'vulnerability members of such organisations might otherwise feel, if their ability to make decisions independently of public and political opinions, as career public servants, were not protected.'[49]

These concerns warrant due consideration, however, they cannot be used to prevent introducing a system of tenure which is vital if there ever is to be more balanced leadership on staff at the ICC. A response that balances these concerns with the need for change must be implemented.

44 Ibid., para. 249.

45 Ibid.

46 Ibid.

47 Overall Response of the International Criminal Court to the 'Independent Expert Review of the International Criminal Court and the Rome Statute System—Final Report': Preliminary Analysis of the Recommendations and information on relevant activities undertaken by the Court, ICC-ASP/20/2, 11 June 2021 (Twentieth Session of the ASP).

48 Ibid., para. 236.

49 Ibid., para. 237.

## 7 Conclusion

Gender and geographical representation cannot remain largely the same as it was 20 years ago. The ICC must move with the times and ensure diversity on staff as this will guarantee that a whole range of lived experiences are utilised in the delivery of justice. Improving the gender balance and geographical representation will lay to rest some concerns about legitimacy, bias and could have a very positive impact on the internal work culture. It is time to make sure the Court is staffed and led by people from different walks of life and hopefully 20 years from now the Court will be where it should be—gender balanced and with significantly better geographical representation.

CHAPTER 20

# Funding the ICC for Its Third Decade

*Stuart Ford*

## 1 Introduction*

The International Criminal Court (ICC) is an international organization that was established by states to 'end impunity' for the 'most serious crimes of concern to the international community' and ensure 'lasting respect for and the enforcement of international justice.'[1] Like most international organizations, its members are states.[2] Within the ICC system, these are referred to as State Parties. The State Parties meet together as the Assembly of States Parties (ASP),[3] which serves as the governance and oversight body for the ICC.[4] As part of its role, the ASP 'consider[s] and decide[s] the budget for the Court.'[5] Once a budget has been adopted, the State Parties are obligated to make contributions to cover their portion of the budget.[6] The contributions are then collected and distributed to the various organs of the Court according to the budget.

The process of deciding on the budget for any given year begins with a proposed budget that is created by the court.[7] A body of independent finance experts created by the ASP called the Committee on Budget and Finance (CBF)[8] then reviews the proposed budget and compiles a report for the ASP

---

* This chapter represents the views of the author and not those of the Coalition for the International Criminal Court or Human Rights Watch.

1 See Rome Statute of the International Criminal Court (signed 17 July 1998, entered into force 1 July 2002) 2187 UNTS 3 ('Rome Statute'), Preamble.

2 See Rome Statute, Arts. 125–126.

3 See Rome Statute, Art. 112(1).

4 See Rome Statute, Art. 112.

5 See Rome Statute, Art. 112(2)(d).

6 See Rome Statute, Art. 115. See also ibid., Art. 117 (describing how the states' contributions are calculated).

7 See e.g., Proposed Progamme Budget for 2023 of the International Criminal Court, ICC-ASP/21/10, 19 August 2022 (Twenty-first Session of the ASP).

8 The CBF was established by Resolution ICC-ASP/1/Res.4. It was created for the purpose of providing 'budgetary and financial review and monitoring of the resources of the International Criminal Court.' Establishment of the Committee on Budget and Finance, ICC-ASP/1/Res.4, 3 September 2002 (First Plenary Meeting of the ASP).

 | DOI:10.1163/9789004529939_021

that contains recommended changes to the court's proposed budget.[9] The ASP considers the proposed budget and the CBF report and then decides on the budget for the upcoming year during its annual meeting.[10] The ASP has tended to follow the recommendations in the CBF report, but is not required to do so.[11]

While NGOs play no formal role in the ICC's budget process, many NGOs attend the annual meeting of the ASP where they can lobby the States Parties and officials from the Court.[12] NGOs also publish various articles that are designed to influence the budget process.[13] For example, in advance of the 2023 budget discussions, Human Rights Watch put out a 'Briefing Note' criticizing the ASP for failing to provide the court with adequate resources and urging the ASP to 'reject arbitrary approaches, including a strict zero-nominal growth approach' and instead to provide the court with sufficient resources to 'fulfill its mandate robustly and consistently across [all] situations.'[14]

## 2 The 2023 Budget

In its proposed 2023 budget, the ICC asked the ASP for 186 million Euros, which represented an increase of 22 million Euros over its 2022 budget of 154 million Euros.[15] This was a proposed increase of 20%.[16] This is a striking figure. Some members of the ASP have been pushing for the past decade to freeze the

9 See, e.g., Report of the Committee on Budget and Finance on the work of its thirty-ninth session, ICC-ASP/21/15, 29 November 2022 (Twenty-first Session of the ASP).

10 See e.g., Resolution of the Assembly of States Parties on the proposed programme budget for 2023, the Working Capital Fund for 2023, the scale of assessment for the apportionment of expenses of the International Criminal Court, financing appropriations for 2023 and the Contingency Fund, ICC-ASP/21/Res.1, 9 December 2022 (Ninth Plenary Meeting of the ASP) (approving the 2023 programme budget of 173 million Euros).

11 See J O'Donohue, 'Financing the International Criminal Court' (2013) 13 *International Criminal Law Review* 269, 276.

12 See S Ford, 'How Much Money Does the ICC Need?' in C Stahn (ed.), *The Law and Practice of the International Criminal Court* (Oxford University Press 2015) 90.

13 Ibid.

14 See Human Rights Watch, 'Briefing Note for the Twenty-First Session of the International Criminal Court Assembly of States Partie' (22 November 2022) <https://www.hrw.org/news/2022/11/22/human-rights-watch-briefing-note-twenty-first-session-international-criminal-court> accessed 30 April 2023.

15 See Proposed Programme Budget for 2023 of the International Criminal Court – Executive Summary, ICC-ASP/21/INF.2/Rev.1, 30 September 2022 (Twenty-first Session of the ASP), para. 34.

16 Ibid.

ICC's budget, a so-called "zero growth" budget.[17] Perhaps in response to these pressures, in recent years, the court has been proposing quite small annual increases. For example, in 2018, the court asked for an increase of 4.4%.[18] In 2019, the court proposed an increase of 2.6%.[19] In 2020, it proposed an increase of just 1.6%,[20] and then in 2021, the court actually proposed a reduction in its budget of 0.5%.[21] This pattern changed in 2022, when the court asked for an increase of nearly 10%.[22] And then, this year, it asked for an increase of 20%.[23] Why the sudden request for such a large increase?

Part of the requested increase is being driven by what the Court delicately calls 'worldwide inflationary pressures.'[24] This is a reference to the effect of Russia's invasion of Ukraine, which has caused a sharp rise in global inflation.[25] This has resulted in an increase in the cost of goods and services that the court needs to operate.[26] But, more importantly, it has also caused an increase in salaries,[27] which represent the largest driver of costs at the ICC.[28]

---

17 See Ford (n 12) 85. See also Human Rights Watch (n 14) (noting that 'an insistence by some states parties on a strict, zero nominal growth approach to setting the court's budget has been a key factor in distorting budget negotiations away from discussion of the real investment needed at the court').

18 See Proposed Programme Budget for 2018 of the International Criminal Court, ICC-ASP/16/10, 11 September 2017 (Sixteenth Session of the ASP), para. 1.

19 See Proposed Progamme Budget for 2019 of the International Criminal Court, ICC-ASP/17/10, 1 August 2018, (Seventeenth Session of the ASP), para. 5.

20 See Proposed Programme Budget for 2020 of the International Criminal Court – Executive Summary, ICC-ASP/18/INF.3, 17 July 2019 (Eighteenth Session of the ASP), para. 3.

21 See Proposed Programme Budget for 2021 of the International Criminal Court – Executive Summary, ICC-ASP/19/INF.3, 15 July 2020 (Nineteenth Session of the ASP) para. 2.

22 See Proposed Programme Budget for 2022 of the International Criminal Court – Executive Summary, ICC-ASP/20/INF.3, 21 July 2021 (Twentieth Session of the ASP), para. 1.

23 See above text accompanying note 16.

24 See Proposed Programme Budget for 2023 of the International Criminal Court (n 15) para. 27.

25 See J Siemplenski Lefort, 'Ukraine economic shock' European Investment Bank, 14 June 2022 <https://www.eib.org/en/stories/ukraine-trade-inflation> accessed 30 April 2023; D Caldara et al., 'The Effect of the War in Ukraine on Global Activity and Inflation' Board of Governors of the Federal Reserve System, 27 May 2022 <https://www.federalreserve.gov/econres/notes/feds-notes/the-effect-of-the-war-in-ukraine-on-global-activity-and-inflation-20220527.html> accessed 30 April 2023.

26 See Proposed Programme Budget for 2023 of the International Criminal Court (n 15) para. 27.

27 Ibid., para. 28.

28 For example, the OTP, which is the largest organ within the court, spends more than 90% of its budget on staff costs. Ibid., para. 45 (showing the staff and non-staff costs of the OTP).

As a result, nearly 40% of the court's increase in its requested budget is caused by inflation.[29]

The rest of the requested increase is driven by what the court describes as a significant increase in the volume of its work.[30] The court says that its "overriding objective" is to achieve 'an effective, efficient, and universal system of international justice' and that it will do so by 'independently conduct[ing] fair and expeditious investigations and trials.'[31] In effect, while the overall goal of the ICC is ending impunity and promoting an effective system of international criminal justice,[32] the principal work of the court involves investigations, trials, and appeals.[33] Conducting those investigations, trials, and appeals requires sufficient resources.

In 2023, the Office of the Prosecutor (OTP) will be participating in a number of pre-trial proceedings, trials, and appeals,[34] but its investigations remain the most resource-intensive part of its work.[35] The OTP will be operating in sixteen geographically distinct 'situations,'[36] while also conducting three additional preliminary examinations.[37] This is a significant workload and the OTP

29 Ibid., para. 28.

30 Ibid., para. 2 (claiming that the court's proposed budged focuses on 'the resources required to appropriately respond to the increasing demands for justice around the world' and represents 'a significant shift in the scope of its activities, both in terms of volume and complexity'); ibid., para 4 (noting the 'significant and increasing volume of demands for intervention by the Court'). See also J H Anderson, 'Can 2023 Be the Booster Year for the ICC Budget?' (*Justice Info*, 2 December 2022) <https://www.justiceinfo.net/en/109715-2023-booster-year-icc-budget.html> accessed 30 April 2023 (noting that the Court was facing an unprecedented level of activity including the continuation of two trials, the start of three new trials, several new arrest warrants, and two new investigations).

31 See Proposed Programme Budget for 2023 of the International Criminal Court (n 15) para. 19.

32 See above text accompanying note 1.

33 See S Ford, 'A Hierarchy of the Goals of International Criminal Courts' (2018) 27(1) *Minnesota Journal of International Law* 179, 182–183, 186 (highlighting the distinction between a court's overall goals – the effect it is supposed to have on the outside world – and its outputs – the day to day work the court engages in that is supposed to lead to the accomplishment of its goals). See also Y Shany, 'Assessing the Effectiveness of International Courts: A Goal-Based Approach' (2012) 106(2) *American Journal of International Law* 225, 248.

34 See Proposed Programme Budget for 2023 of the International Criminal Court (n 15) para. 20. See also below, text accompanying notes 45–49 (describing the expected workload of Chambers in 2023).

35 Ibid., para. 21.

36 Ibid., para. 5.

37 Ibid.

does not believe that it has the necessary resources to carry out its mandate.[38] It needs additional resources, particularly additional personnel.[39] The OTP needs additional investigators and analysts to assist with evidence collection and analysis,[40] and additional forensic capacity, particularly in relation to the situation in Ukraine.[41] The Court also plans to open a number of new field offices in 2023,[42] and the OTP needs additional staff so that it can deploy personnel 'close to or in situation countries wherever possible.'[43] As a result, the OTP asked for an increase in its budget of 26.6%.[44]

The ICC also predicted a significant increase in the workload of the various Chambers. The Court anticipates that three trials will take place during 2023 and two additional cases will be at the deliberation stage, requiring the 'simultaneous use of the three courtrooms with the corresponding support capacity' throughout the year.[45] The Court also stressed the complexity of its cases compared to 'most domestic proceedings.'[46] The large number of ongoing trials will also result in an increase in the number of people in detention, with an attendant increase in costs.[47] The Court also expects at least one confirmation of charges proceeding as well as five reparations proceedings.[48] Finally, the Appeals Chamber is expected to hear final appeals from two cases as well as "a number of interlocutory appeals in pending situations and cases."[49] As a result of this increasing workload, the Court requested a 22% increase in the budget for Chambers.[50]

---

38 Ibid., para. 22 ('The OTP does not presently benefit from sufficient resources in order to effectively discharge its mandate with respect to the range of situations [in which] it is currently engaged.').

39 Ibid., para. 23 (noting that 'it is critical that the [OTP] is able to strengthen its staff capacity').

40 Ibid., para. 39.

41 Ibid.

42 Ibid., para. 43.

43 Ibid., para. 39.

44 Ibid., para. 38.

45 Ibid., para. 13.

46 Ibid., para. 14 (noting that the ICC's cases are 'exceptionally complex' because of the 'number of witnesses, volume of evidence, and number of languages involved, coupled with the need for security on the ground and cooperation with national jurisdictions'). See also S Ford, 'Complexity and Efficiency at International Criminal Courts' (2014) 29 *Emory Internationa Law Review* 1 (noting that trials at international criminal courts are much more complex than most domestic trials).

47 See Proposed Programme Budget for 2023 of the International Criminal Court (n 15) para. 18.

48 Ibid., paras. 15–16.

49 Ibid., para. 17.

50 Ibid., para. 37.

The Registry supports the work of both the OTP and the Chambers. Thus, it is not surprising that it also requested a significant increase in funding in 2023.[51] This increase was driven largely by the need to support the increased workload of Chambers[52] and the OTP's investigative activities.[53] The Registry argued that it had worked to 'carefully assess ways to enhance and sustain its long-term capacity,' that it requested additional funds 'only after all possible steps . . . have been undertaken to contain the additional requirements,' and that it had been able to reduce its request by nearly 4 million Euros by identifying 'reductions,' 'savings and efficiencies.'[54]

The ICC will be supporting eleven defence teams through legal aid payments during 2023,[55] but proposed no budget increase for them.[56] This came amidst criticism of the Court by those working on defence teams.[57] Defence personnel have no formal contract, have few protections against workplace misconduct, do not get sick leave or vacation time, are not exempt from taxation (unlike employees of the Court), and have not had a cost of living increase in years, with the result that they make approximately 30% less than their counterparts in the OTP.[58] Some defence staff went on strike during the most recent meeting of the ASP to protest their working conditions.[59] They were subsequently barred from the ASP meeting.[60] The International Criminal Court

51 Ibid., para. 46 (noting that the Registry requested a 17.9% increase in funding compared to 2022).

52 Ibid., paras 47–48. See also above text accompanying notes 45–49.

53 See Proposed Programme Budget for 2023 of the International Criminal Court (n 15) paras 47, 49.

54 Ibid., para. 50.

55 See Proposed Programme Budget for 2023 of the International Criminal Court (n 15) para. 494.

56 Ibid., Table 22 (noting that the Court was proposing defence spending of 5.19 million Euros, almost exactly the same as what had been budgeted in 2022). The CBF subsequently recommended reducing legal aid spending by a further 180,000 Euros, mainly by reducing 'resources allocated to Ad-hoc counsel.' See Report of the Committee on Budget and Finance on the work of its thirty-ninth session (n 9) paras 124–125.

57 See Anderson (n 30) (noting that the lead counsel one of the Central Africa cases had called for respect and fair treatment for defence teams).

58 See C Dinney, 'EU Dispatch: ICC legal defence staff launching historic strike over labour rights, pay disparity' (*Jurist*, 2 December 2022) <https://www.jurist.org/news/2022/12/eu-dispatch-icc-legal-defence-staff-launching-historic-strike-over-labor-rights-pay-disparity/> accessed 30 April 2023.

59 See 'Bitterness after striking ICC support staff barred from ASP' *Irish Legal News* (6 December 2022) <https://www.irishlegal.com/articles/bitterness-after-striking-icc-support-staff-barred-from-asp> accessed 30 April 2023.

60 Ibid.

Bar Association has argued that the poor working conditions of defence staff 'compromises fair trial rights and the principle of equality of arms.'[61] The ASP has acknowledged that the 'quality of justice' at the ICC depends on having defence counsel who can 'perform the roles effectively and independently,'[62] and has had discussions about how to 'improve the working conditions' of defence team members and about '[r]emuneration of external defence' team members,[63] so it is disappointing that the concerns of the defence teams were not addressed in the 2023 budget.

Most other organs of the court requested relatively modest increases,[64] with the notable exception being the Secretariat for the Trust Fund for Victims (SFTV).[65] While the SFTV is a relatively small organ overall, it requested a 37.8% increase in its budget for 2023.[66] This was driven largely by increasing the number of personnel in the SFTV to improve its 'reparations implementation' capacity.[67] The organ also noted that it was planning on improving 'operational expertise, internal organization, and governance improvements' and that this would lead future savings and the organ's ability to handle a 'significant increase' in its workload in the future.[68]

In response to the Court's proposed budget, the ASP's Committee on Budget and Finance (CBF) conceded that the Court was facing high levels of inflation and an increased workload that justified an increase in its budget.[69] The CBF did, however, recommend some changes to the court's budget to save money. For example, Chambers requested 11 new P-2 positions,[70] but the CBF recommended abolishing 5 P-3 positions that had been vacant for some time and using the money saved to fund the P-2 positions the court requested.[71] The

61 Ibid.

62 See Report on the Constitution and Activities of the International Criminal Court Bar Association, ICC-ASP/21/23, 18 November 2022 (Twenty-first Session of the ASP), Executive Summary.

63 See Report of the Bureau on legal aid, ICC-ASP/21/26, 29 November 2022 (Twenty-first Session of the ASP), para. 18.

64 See Proposed Programme Budget for 2023 of the International Criminal Court (n 15) para. 34 (containing a table showing the percentage increases requested by organ of the court).

65 Ibid.

66 Ibid., para. 54.

67 Ibid., para. 55.

68 Ibid.

69 See Report of the Committee on Budget and Finance on the work of its thirty-ninth session (n 9) paras 5–6.

70 Ibid., para. 15.

71 Ibid., para. 21.

CBF also recommended reducing some of the staff requests made by the OTP[72] and Registry.[73] The CBF justified reducing the Registry's travel budget by pointing to the 'new hybrid ways of working' that the Court developed during the COVID pandemic to 'successfully perform various activities remotely including witness interviews and testimonies.'[74] More generally, the CBF identified small savings in a number of places.[75] Ultimately, the CBF identified about 7 million Euros in reductions, but still recommended that the ASP approve a budget increase of more than 24 million Euros in 2023.[76]

The ASP then made some further reductions and eventually agreed on a budget of 173 million Euros for the Court,[77] which still represents a 12% increase over the 154 million Euros approved in 2022.[78] So, while the Court was ultimately given less than it asked for,[79] it still received an increase of nearly 20 million Euros. Even taking into account the additional costs of inflation,[80] this was a significant increase in the resources being given to the Court.

---

72 See, e.g., ibid., para. 32 ('The Committee was of the view that the workload and functions of four GTA positions could be met by existing staff"); ibid., para. 37 ('The Committee was of the view that the workload and functions of Special Assistant to the Deputy Prosecutor [...] could be met by existing staff.'); ibid., para. 41 ('The Committee was of the view that the workload and functions of one GTA position Assistant to the Deputy Prosecutor [...] could be met by existing staff.').

73 Ibid., paras 74–77, 75 (declining to add three new permanent positions because the 'Committee was of the view that the additional workload in the Office of the Registrar [...] could be carried out by existing approved human resources'). See also ibid., paras 87–90 (recommending approval of fewer security officers than the court had requested partly because 'a number of staff at the Court prefer to work from home' which reduced the need for security personnel).

74 Ibid., paras 111–114, 112.

75 See e.g., ibid., paras 124–125 (reducing the budget for legal aid for defendants from 5.2 million to 5 million Euros); ibid., paras 126–129 (reducing the budget for legal aid for victims by 120,000 Euros out of a total budget of 2.2 million Euros).

76 Ibid., 4.

77 See Resolution ICC-ASP/21/Res.1 (n 10) 1.

78 See Resolution of the Assembly of States Parties on the proposed programme budget for 2022, the Working Capital Fund for 2022, the scale of assessment for the apportionment of expenses of the International Criminal Court, financing appropriations for 2022 and the Contingency Fund, ICC-ASP/20/Res.1, 9 December 2021 (Eighth Plenary Meeting of the ASP), 1.

79 The court had initially asked for a budget of 186 million Euros. See above text accompanying note 15.

80 See above, text accompanying notes 24–29.

## 3 Other Financial Concerns

In addition to considering the Court's proposed 2023 budget, the CBF identified some other issues that could have financial implications for the ICC. One concern the CBF raised was that the new positions the Court was asking for represented not just costs in 2023, but long-term costs that would presumably continue into future years.[81] This did not stop the CBF from recommending the creation of new positions, but it did not recommend giving the Court all the new staff members it asked for.[82] The CBF also raised concerns about the cost of maintaining the Court building. To save costs, the Court shifted in 2022 to a policy of 'limiting the replacement of components' to when 'they break or show signs of imminent breakdown.'[83] The CBF noted that this policy was unsustainable and that the Court had millions of Euros of backlogged maintenance requirements.[84] The CBF recommended 'a fully impartial evaluation of the building and the establishment of a medium-and long-term [capital replacement] plan'[85] but acknowledged that funding this would 'require a commitment to reliable long-term funding from States Parties.'[86]

The CBF was also very concerned about the status of payments by States Parties.[87] The CBF recognized that this was not a new problem and that there had often been states who paid late or did not pay their share of contributions to the ICC's budget.[88] But by the end of 2022, states owed the court more than 44 million Euros in past due payments.[89] A crisis was only averted at the end of 2021 when a number of states made early payments on their 2022 contributions, but this exacerbated the shortfall in 2022 as money that was meant to pay the Court's 2022 expenses was used in 2021.[90] The CBF warned that unless

81 See Report of the Committee on Budget and Finance on the work of its thirty-ninth session (n 9) 4.
82 See above, text accompanying notes 70–73.
83 See Report of the Committee on Budget and Finance on the work of its thirty-ninth session (n 9) para. 157.
84 Ibid., para. 158.
85 Ibid., para. 159.
86 Ibid., para. 160.
87 Ibid., paras. 210–216.
88 Ibid., para. 212, Table 8.
89 Ibid., para. 211. The countries with the largest arrears were Brazil (22 million Euros), Venezuela (13.4 million Euros), Argentina (4 million Euros), and Mexico (3.5 million Euros). Ibid., 49–50, Annex II.
90 Ibid., para. 212.

states made their payments on time, 'a significant cash shortfall would occur.'[91] In effect, the Court is in danger of running out of money to pay its bills.

Of course, the CBF cannot force countries to pay their arrears, but it did recommend that 'the Assembly explore additional means of encouraging the timely payment of contributions' and suggested that 'the inability to present candidates for elected positions should be seriously considered.'[92] The ASP declined to make eligibility for elected positions contingent on payment of dues, instead 'urg[ing] all States Parties to pay their assessed contributions in full and on time' and offering 'voluntary and sustainable payment plans' for states that face 'significant economic hardship.'[93]

The CBF was also concerned about two decisions taken by the Prosecutor during 2022 that could have financial implications. In the first decision, the Prosecutor had announced that he would establish a trust fund to which states could contribute.[94] The trust fund would be used to 'enhance the efficiency and effectiveness' of the OTP.[95] The CBF was informed that the Prosecutor had already secured a commitment of more than 7 million Euros from the EU to develop a 'modern, efficient evidence management system' and 'run it until it could be taken over by regular staff.'[96] In the second decision, the Prosecutor called for the 'secondment of investigative personnel from States Parties to support him in coping with the increased workload for all the situations.'[97] By late 2022, 'a total of 74 national experts from judicial, military and law enforcement agencies were committed by States Parties on a secondment basis.'[98]

The CBF was concerned both that these initiatives would undermine the independence of the Court and that they would result in long-term costs that would be borne by the Court. Ultimately, the CBF's concerns appear to have been assuaged. The Court noted that any donations to the trust fund would be subject to regulation by the Registrar, who has the obligation to ensure that their use does not affect the independence of the Court.[99] In addition, funds are to be used at the 'sole discretion' of the Prosecutor and cannot be

91 Ibid.
92 Ibid., para. 216.
93 See Resolution ICC-ASP/21/Res.1 (n10) 3.
94 See Report of the Committee on Budget and Finance on the work of its thirty-ninth session (n 9) para. 239.
95 Ibid., para. 242.
96 Ibid., paras. 243–245, 245.
97 Ibid., para. 239.
98 Ibid., para. 254.
99 Ibid., para. 249.

earmarked for certain investigations or situations.[100] The CBF concluded that the trust fund did not undermine the Court's independence, nor did it create any 'direct or indirect financial liability' for the Court.[101] With respect to the secondment of personnel, the CBF noted that they provided a 'short-term injection of specialized resources' where needed[102] but reported to the OTP and were 'required to sign an Oath of Office' committing them to 'avoid any action' which would adversely affect their 'integrity, independence and impartiality.'[103] The CBF took no action on the Prosecutor's initiatives, simply asking to be updated about them in May 2023.[104] This appears to serve as tacit acceptance of the Prosecutor's new initiatives, although the CBF will continue to monitor the situation.

Some people outside the Court, however, have raised concerns about the OTP's use of the trust fund and the secondments. One concern is that soliciting donations for a voluntary trust fund is not a sustainable funding model.[105] Enthusiasm and support for the Court will likely wax and wane over time, but its budget needs are not likely to fluctuate in time with state enthusiasm. Another concern is that adding capacity to the OTP through the trust fund and secondments could lead to new investigations, new arrest warrants, and new trials. At that point, it would generate additional work for the other organs of the Court, which would have to be funded somehow. Thus, even if it the OTP's decisions do not increase the ICC's budget now, they might well necessitate budget increases in the future.[106] Finally, there have been concerns that the influx of donations and secondments linked to the Ukraine investigation may lead to further politicization of the Court's investigations.[107] Indeed, it is possible that the new resources will be used by the OTP to strengthen the Ukraine investigation while allowing other investigations to languish. This would contribute to perceptions of the Court as biased and politicized.[108] On

---

100 Ibid., para. 250.

101 Ibid., para. 251.

102 Ibid., para. 256. The CBF noted, for example, that ten investigators had been seconded to the OTP to work on the investigation into the situation in Ukraine. Ibid.

103 Ibid., para. 255.

104 Ibid., para. 257.

105 See Anderson (n 30).

106 Ibid.

107 Ibid.

108 See, e.g., S Ford, 'Can the International Criminal Court Succeed? An Analysis of the Empirical Evidence of Violence Prevention' (2020) 43 *Loyola Los Angeles Intenrational and Comparative Law Review* 101, 102 (2020) (noting that the Court has been accused of having an anti-African bias by both critics and some African states).

the other hand, if the new resources allowed the OTP to bolster some of the investigations that have seemed to be under-resourced, then it might actually combat perceptions of bias. Ultimately, it is too early to tell how the additional resources will affect the OTP's investigations and perceptions of the Court's legitimacy.

The ASP raised a concern of its own in its 2023 budget resolution. It noted "with concern" that "expenses incurred by the Court due to referrals by the United Nations Security Council have been borne exclusively by the States Parties."[109] The Rome Statute contains a provision that allows the Security Council to refer matters to the Court,[110] and it was anticipated that when the Security Council made a referral, the United Nations would fund the resulting investigation and trials.[111] While the Security Council has referred two situations to the Court (Darfur and Libya),[112] the United Nations had not paid for any of the Court's expenses, which totaled more than 83 million Euros by the end of 2022.[113] While the Court cannot force the United Nations to pay, the ASP encouraged the member states to 'continue discussions on a possible way forward,' and instructed the Court to 'continue including this matter in its institutional dialogue with the United Nations.'[114]

Finally, the ASP indicated that it did not expect another significant increase in spending in 2024. It instructed the court to prepare a 'sustainable budget proposal for its 2024 programme budget,'[115] but stressed the 'utmost importance of achieving economies of scale, streamlining activities, identifying potential duplications, and promoting synergies' between different organs of the Court.[116] The ASP concluded by warning the Court that additional funding would only be available 'when necessary for the purpose of mandated

109 See Resolution ICC-ASP/21/Res.1 (n 10) 10.
110 See Rome Statute, Art. 13(b) (granting the Court jurisdiction when such crimes are 'referred to the Prosecutor by the Security Council acting under Chapter VII of the Charter of the United Nations').
111 See Rome Statute, Art. 115(b) (noting that expenses of the Court would come from '[f]unds provided by the United Nations, subject to the approval of the General Assembly, in particular in relation to the expenses incurred due to referrals by the Security Council').
112 See UN Security Council Resolution 1970 (26 February 2011) UN Doc S/Res/1970 (referring the situation in Libya to the ICC); UN Security Council Resolution 1593 (31 March 2005) UN Doc S/Res/1593 (referring the situation in Darfur to the ICC).
113 See Resolution ICC-ASP/21/Res.1 (n 10) 10.
114 Ibid.
115 Ibid., 7.
116 Ibid., 8.

activities and after all possible steps have been taken to finance such increases through savings and efficiencies.'[117]

## 4 Conclusion

The ICC's 2023 budget is 173 million Euros, which represents a 12% increase over its 2022 budget.[118] This is a significant departure from the last five years, when ICC budgets were relatively flat year to year.[119] The size of the increase is primarily the result of two factors: 1) a substantial increase in inflation that has raised the costs of goods, services and personnel; and 2) a continuing increase in the Court's workload.[120] The sharp rise in inflation is largely the result of Russia's invasion of Ukraine and entirely out of the Court's control,[121] while 2023 is set to be one of the Court's busiest years.[122] It will have three trials going on at the same time, as well as numerous proceedings before both the Pre-Trial Chamber and the Appeals Chamber.[123] It is currently involved in sixteen different situations, plus the Prosecutor is conducting three preliminary examinations, which may turn into new investigations.[124] The size of the increase in the Court's 2023 budget sets it apart from the trend over the last five years but appears to be justified by the Court's increasing workload.

The ASP is not particularly happy about the growth in the budget and hopes that it will not happen again in 2024,[125] but ultimately the Court's budget is driven by the resources necessary to achieve its mandate.[126] This Court needs adequate resources to carry out its investigations, trials, and appeals. Thus, if the Court's workload continues to increase then its budget will probably increase as well. Indeed, NGOs have warned against framing the increase in the 2023 budget as exceptional and urged the ASP to continue increasing the Court's budget in future years.[127]

---

117 Ibid., 7.
118 See above, text accompanying notes 77–78.
119 See above, text accompanying notes 19–21.
120 See above, text accompanying notes 24–50.
121 See above, text accompanying note 25.
122 See above, text accompanying notes 34–50.
123 See above, text accompanying notes 45–50.
124 See above, text accompanying notes 34–38.
125 See above, text accompanying notes 115–117.
126 See above, text accompanying notes 31–33.
127 See Human Rights Watch (n 14) (warning that 'States parties should avoid language suggesting that any budget increase [...] is exceptional' and urging states to provide 'adequate investment [...] to permit the court to fulfill its mandate' and move towards 'longer-term

To put things in a broader perspective, this is the largest budget the ICC has ever received.[128] Figure 20.1 shows that there has been an increase in the ICC's budget over time, but that increase has not been linear. There have been periods of greater growth, particularly during the early years of the court (2002–2007) and during the period between 2013 and 2016.[129] At the same time, there have also been periods of relatively slow growth, like the period between 2009 and 2012 and again between 2017 and 2021.[130] In fact, in two years (2011 and 2021), growth was either zero or negative. Even against this broader backdrop, however, 2023 stands out. It represents the largest percentage increase in the court's budget since the early years (2002–2007) when the court was getting itself established.

In addition to reviewing the Court's 2023 budget, this chapter has also identified several long-term trends or innovations that have financial implications. Not all of these, however, represent significant financial risks. The Prosecutor's decisions to create a trust fund to support its work and accept experts on secondment appear to be innovations that will allow the OTP to increase its capacity while not giving up its independence or increasing the Court's budget in the short term.[131] Having said that, concerns have been raised about both of those decisions by some people outside the court.[132] Critics are particularly concerned that if voluntary contributions result in the prioritization of certain investigations over others this could lead to further politicization of the Court's work.[133] It is too early to tell whether the critics' concerns are valid, but both decisions warrant further scrutiny in the coming years.

The UN's failure to pay the costs associated with Security Council referrals clearly frustrates the ASP,[134] but those costs are included in the ICC's regular budgets and do not pose a long-term threat to the Court unless the number of

---

sustainability for the court's work'). See Anderson (n 30) (noting that many people would like to see a 'multi-year commitment from states' to increasing the budget that would 'remove some of the unpredictability of the annual process').

128 See below Figure 20.1 for a chart of the ICC's budgets over time. The data for Figure 20.1 comes from the budget resolutions adopted by the ASP at the end of every annual session of the ASP. This budget resolutions can be found at the ASP's website: <https://asp.icc-cpi.int/resolutions/sessions>. The data has not been adjusted for inflation.

129 See below Figure 20.1. See also Ford (n 12) 86 (noting in Figure 5.1 that the ICC's inflation adjusted spending grew rapidly during the early years of the Court).

130 See below Figure 20.1. See also Ford (n 12) 86 (noting in Figure 5.1 that the ICC's inflation adjusted spending was also relatively flat in the period 2009–2013).

131 *See supra* text accompanying notes 94–104.

132 *See supra* text accompanying notes 105–108.

133 *See supra* text accompanying notes 107–108.

134 *See supra* text accompanying notes 109–114.

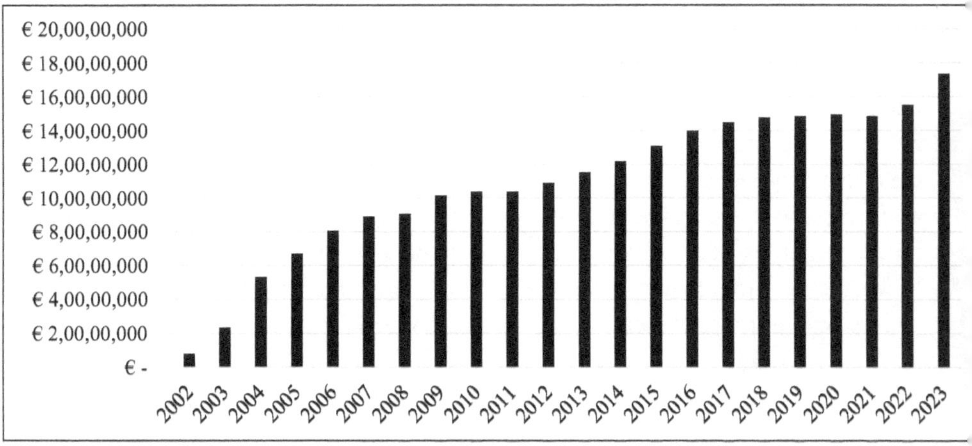


FIGURE 20.1 ICC programme budgets

Security Council referrals were to sharply increase. Given the current deadlock in the Security Council between those Permanent Members that support the ICC and those that do not,[135] a large number of new referrals seems unlikely.

There are, however, some potentially problematic long-term financial risks. The Court has delayed a lot of long-term maintenance and shifted to a policy of only replacing things when they break, which has resulted in millions of Euros of backlogged maintenance requirements.[136] As the CBF has noted, this is not a sustainable policy. Deferring maintenance requirements will only make the problems worse over time. The court needs a long-term capital replacement plan and the ASP needs to commit to fund such a plan.[137] Unfortunately, the most the ASP could do was note the CBF's recommendation and reiterate the need for any capital replacement plan to be "fully justified and limited only to those elements which are absolutely necessary."[138] Thus, it appears the Court will be putting off its long-term maintenance problems for another year.

Finally, and most worryingly, the Court has a serious problem getting members of the ASP to pay their contributions.[139] The ICC spends money on the

135 *See* Stuart Ford, *The ICC and the Security Council: How Much Support Is There for Ending Impunity?*, 26 INDIANA INT'L & COMP. L. REV. 33 (2016) (describing how the Permanent Members of the Security Council are deadlocked over support for the ICC).

136 *See supra* text accompanying notes 83–86.

137 *See supra* text accompanying notes 85–86.

138 *See* Resolution ICC-ASP/21/Res.1, dated 9 Dec. 2022, at page 4.

139 It should be noted that a relatively small number of countries account for the bulk of the arrears. *See supra* note 89. Most countries are not in arrears.

assumption that the funds allocated in the budget will be available, but in recent years the amount in arrears has become so substantial that the Court risks running out of money before the end of the fiscal year.[140] The CBF uses bland language ("a significant cash shortfall would occur") to describe a very serious problem.[141] If the Court were to run out of money midway through the year, it could have serious consequences. The Court would not be able to pay salaries or pay for vital services like travel or interpretation/translation services. This could cause the entire Court to shutdown, at least temporarily. It is likely that the ASP would step in with emergency funding, but the arrears issue appears to be the most significant long-term financial risk to the operation of the Court. The CBF has proposed imposing penalties on states that are in arrears, but so far, the ASP has been largely content to urge states to pay, although it did offer states who were in arrears payment plans.[142] It is unlikely this will solve the problem.

---

140 *See supra* text accompanying notes 87–91.

141 *See supra* text accompanying note 91.

142 *See supra* text accompanying notes 92–93.

CHAPTER 21

# 'Nor Is It Neutral': New Technologies and the International Criminal Court

*Alexa Koenig and Lindsay Freeman*

## 1 Introduction

In 1986, historian Melvin Kranzberg published his 'six laws of technology' in a now-seminal presidential address.[1] Today, his 'first law' is widely regarded as a truism: that the introduction of new technologies into a field of practice is neither inherently good nor bad, but nor is it neutral. Ultimately, what matters is what one does with those new technologies. What also matters is recognizing that despite the positive or negative intent of the user, the introduction of new technologies *always* has an effect.

Some of these effects will be anticipated, others unintended. Nowhere has this proven more true than in the field of international criminal justice, and–even more specifically–in the operations of the International Criminal Court (ICC or Court). In this essay, we focus on the activities of the ICC, with an emphasis on the Office of the Prosecutor (OTP or Office), to outline three ways in which digital technologies have been and are increasingly impacting investigations and prosecutions. We also consider trends that we anticipate will have a growing impact on the Court's operations. Specifically, we assess 1) the benefits digital technologies have provided (and are increasingly providing) with regards to conducting international criminal investigations; 2) the limitations of and challenges to their use; and 3) the ways in which digital technologies are enabling crimes within the jurisdiction of the Court.

As Chief Prosecutor Karim Khan noted in his address marking the Court's 20th anniversary, '[T]his is ... a moment to pause, to reflect, and to try to refresh the process of international justice,' as well as 'to try to speed up and improve the quality and delivery of international justice.'[2] This moment presents an opportunity for the ICC to build off its past two decades of experimentation

1 M Kranzberg, 'Technology and History: "Kranzberg's Laws"' (1986) 27 *Technology and Culture* 544.

2 'ICC Prosecutor's Statement on the Court's 20th Anniversary' <https://www.youtube.com/watch?v=Xygnof-ursA> accessed 7 December 2022.

 | DOI:10.1163/9789004529939_022

with digital technologies, and identify lessons learned that can significantly advance the practice of international criminal law. To support that advancement, this essay opens with a brief history of the OTP's engagement with digital technologies, focusing on the ways in which they have benefited the Office's work. In Part 2, we turn to the limitations and challenges of digital technologies. In Part 3, we outline emerging trends in the use of digital technologies in warfare that will unquestionably impact the composition of the battlefield and the means and methods by which international crimes are committed. We conclude with a reflection on the future.

## 2 Historical Background and the Benefits of Digital Technologies

In 2011, as the ICC's ten-year anniversary was looming, the Office of the Prosecutor was struggling to advance its cases–and the world was watching. A handful of cases had failed to proceed past the confirmation of charges phase of the proceedings. The question outside observers were asking was 'why?'

A number of organizations set about trying to answer that question. One was the Human Rights Center at UC Berkeley School of Law (where we both work), which sent a doctoral candidate to the Court. She reviewed and analyzed thousands of pages of documents and came back with an interesting answer. According to her research, the judges were asserting that the prosecution was over-relying on witness testimonies and open source information such as media articles, United Nations reports, and reports from non-governmental organizations. The judges admonished the prosecution for relying on these secondary sources without introducing the corroborating evidence necessary to meet its burden of proof.[3] The overreliance on witnesses was particularly problematic in the ICC's early cases, when investigators were faced with issues around the conduct of intermediaries and witnesses who were found to lack credibility. Together these challenges highlighted the need for more documentary and physical evidence.

---

3 For more on this history, see Human Rights Center at Berkeley School of Law, 'Beyond Reasonable Doubt: Using Scientific Evidence to Advance Prosecutions at the International Criminal Court: 23–24 October 2012 Workshop Report' (2012), 1; A Koenig, 'Open Source Evidence and Human Rights Cases: A Modern Social History' in S Dubberley, A Koenig and D Murray (eds), *Digital Witness: Using Open Source Information for Human Rights Investigation, Documentation and Accountability* (University of Oxford Press 2020).

That critique launched a decade of internal and external efforts to improve the quality of OTP investigations.[4] Many in the OTP acknowledged the need to exploit diverse sources of information more efficiently and effectively—a need of increased importance given the quickly expanding digital information environment.[5] This new information ecosystem included images and videos captured by smartphones and first-hand accounts shared on social media platforms such as Facebook and YouTube. These peer-to-peer information sharing platforms created a new form of open source information from primary sources like eyewitnesses and first responders recording, for example, the aftermath of a bombing or the killing of civilians. Satellite imagery, which became commercially available in 2000,[6] aerial footage from drones, and CCTV also became rich sources of digital data, providing visibility into places for which investigators struggled to gain access. In recent years, machine learning-based technologies have offered investigators more efficient methods for analyzing large data sets. For example, natural language processing has increasingly facilitated the review of sizable document collections, while object recognition has

4 See, e.g., X Agirre Aranburu and others (eds), *Quality Control in Criminal Investigation* (Torkel Opsahl Academic Epublisher 2020).

5 See OTP ICC, 'Strategic Plan 2016–2018' (6 July 2015). For example, strategic goal three focused on improving the quality of preliminary examinations, investigations and prosecutions, in part by 'increasing its ability to collect different forms of evidence other than witness statements through continually enhancing its scientific and technology-related capabilities.' Similarly, strategic goal four aimed at further adapting 'the Office's investigative and prosecutorial capabilities and network to the scientific and technological environment in which it operates.' See also ICC OTP, 'Strategic Plan 2019–2021' (17 July 2019) which, for example, noted the importance of science and technology to the Office's work, including as examples the *Al Mahdi* and *Al-Werfalli* cases. The Office also stated the importance of a handful of outside partners to expand their capacity, and acknowledged the role of both the Office's Scientific and Technology Advisory Boards in expanding their capacities. See, Strategic Plan 2019–2021.

6 For an overview of the limitations, challenges and opportunities afforded by satellite imagery in the investigation and prosecution of international crimes, see, e.g., K M Clarke and S Kendall, '"The Beauty … Is That It Speaks for Itself": Geospatial Materials as Evidentiary Matters' (2019) 23 *Law Text Culture* 91; T Harris et al., 'Geospatial Evidence in International Human Rights Litigation: Technical and Legal Considerations' (*American Association for the Advancement of Science*, 2018); 'Satellite Imagery as Evidence for International Crimes' (*Coalition for the International Criminal Court*, 23 April 2015) <https://www.coalitionfortheicc.org/news/20150423/satellite-imagery-evidence-international-crimes> accessed 7 December 2022 (noting four now large historic challenges for the ICC as including 'the limited availability of appropriate imagery data; restricted budgets and cognitive bias of external organizations conducting the analysis; no accepted forensic standards and methodologies; and a lack of familiarity of judges with this kind of evidence').

streamlined the analysis of voluminous image collections. While imperfect, such tools increasingly augment the work of OTP analysts and investigators.[7]

In 2013, the OTP created a cyber unit within its Forensic Science Section to handle digital forensics and analysis as more of this evidence became relevant to active investigations.[8] Given the Office's relatively small budget compared with the size of its global mandate, the OTP benefited from a number of strategic partnerships and alliances, including the establishment of a Scientific Advisory Board that could guide the Office's handling of scientific evidence and a Technology Advisory Board, to help keep the Office on top of emerging trends in information management, communications security, and online investigations.[9]

The Court's second decade produced progress marked by multiple milestones, including the first case to use call data records as evidence (*Bemba et al*),[10] the first arrest warrant to use social media videos as evidence (*Al Werfalli*),[11] and the first trials to feature a geolocation report with testimony from the analyst (*Al Mahdi* and *Al Hassan*).[12] Facilitated by a series of workshops, such advancements included the hiring of people with specialized expertise in digital forensics, video forensic analysis, and geospatial analysis.[13] The OTP evolved from passive actor to pioneering innovator as it engaged external partners to provide pro bono advice and in-kind tools to enhance its work.

---

7 For an overview of the Court's use of digital evidence see L Freeman and R Vazquez Llorente, 'Finding the Signal in the Noise: International Criminal Evidence and Procedure in the Digital Age' (2021) 19 *Journal of International Criminal Justice* 163.

8 A Koenig et al., 'Digital Fingerprints: Using Electronic Evidence to Advance Prosecutions at the International Criminal Court' (*Human Rights Center at Berkeley School of Law*, 2014); N Mehandru and A Koenig, 'Open Source Evidence and the International Criminal Court' (2019) *Harvard Human Rights Journal* (online) <https://harvardhrj.com/2019/04/open-source-evidence-and-the-international-criminal-court/> accessed 7 December 2022; B Duerr, 'Can Smartphones help ICC investigators?' (*Justice Hub*, 15 September 2015) <https://justicehub.org/article/can-smartphones-help-icc-investigators/> accessed 7 December 2022.

9 Strategic Plan 2019–2021 (n 5).

10 Decision Pursuant to Article 61(7)(a) and (b) of the Rome Statute on the Charges of the Prosecutor Against Jean-Pierre Bemba Gombo, *Bemba, Situation in the Central African Republic*, ICC-01/05-01/08-424, PTC II, ICC, 15 June 2009.

11 *Prosecutor v Mahmoud Mustafa Busayf Al-Werfalli*, ICC-01/11-01/17.

12 *Prosecutor v. Ahmad Al Faqi Al Mahdi*, ICC-01/12-01/15; *Prosecutor v. Al Hassan Ag Abdoul Aziz Ag Mohamed Ag Mahmoud*, ICC-01/12-01/18.

13 *Prosecutor v. Ahmad Al Faqi Al Mahdi*, ICC-01/12-01/15, opening statement.

Over the past twenty years, the integration of digital technologies into its operations has been one of the greatest areas of advancement for the OTP. The Office's innovations were complemented by tremendous growth and maturation within the international justice sector. With the development of new manuals (for example, from the Public International Law and Policy Group)[14] and training programs on international criminal investigations (from organizations like the Institute for International Criminal Investigations and Justice Rapid Response), nongovernmental organizations' investigations also became more sophisticated, producing professional work product to the OTP's benefit. Thus, a global community of court and non-court investigators–working in local, regional, national and international jurisdictions–similarly benefited from a rapidly-maturing understanding of how new technologies fit into investigative practice.[15]

Today, investigators collect digital information from various sources, including electronic devices, the internet, telecommunications service providers, internet service providers and other third-parties. They also generate digital evidence in the course of their investigation by, for example, digitally mapping crime scenes or working with national law enforcement to intercept wire communications. In addition, a number of methods have emerged for analyzing digital devices. Digital forensics is now an umbrella term for a host of specialized practices: computer forensics, network forensics, mobile forensics, memory forensics and cloud forensics.[16] The oldest and most established method among these forensic processes is the analysis of computers and other electronic devices, for which there are recognized standards and procedures,[17] whereas protocols for newer technologies like cloud computing are earlier in their development.

One area of practice that has witnessed particular growth and attention over the past decade is digital open source investigations. In recent years, significant progress has been made in establishing international standards

---

14 See, e.g., Field Guide for Civil Society Documentation of Serious Human Rights Violations, PILPG (2016) and Handbook on Civil Society Documentation of Serious Human Rights Violations, PILPG (2016).

15 See M Pollitt et al., 'A Framework for Harmonizing Forensic Science Practices and Digital/Multimedia Evidence,' Organization of Scientific Area Committees for Forensic Science (January 2018) <https://serval.unil.ch/resource/serval:BIB_32FB580596A3.P001/REF.pdf> accessed 7 December 2022.

16 See, e.g., P Reedy, 'Interpol review of digital evidence 2016–2019' (2020) 2 *Forensic Science International* 489.

17 NIST, SWGDE.

for conducting digital investigations, including the development of the OTP's *Manual on Online Intelligence and Investigations* and the publication of the *Berkeley Protocol on Digital Open Source Investigations*.[18] The OTP has benefited from the innovation of and partnership with external organizations, ranging from new methods of finding information online, to its analysis (including assessing its authenticity and reliability), to its presentation in court. In turn, the Office has offered critical use cases, and enabled new tools–like the *Berkeley Protocol*–to be tested against their own internal procedures, providing invaluable information for external groups, and advancing their complementarity function.

The Office's expanded ability to identify, ingest, analyze and present digital information with other categories of evidence (such as physical and testimonial) is a perfect example of the iterative learning that can come from investigation teams collaborating with external organizations–and vice versa, as those external partners grow to better understand the Court's practical challenges.

Today, those efforts are maturing. Just one example of how far this community has collectively come is the proposal for a conflict-agnostic mechanism–modeled after those created to collect and preserve evidence of atrocities in Syria, Myanmar and Iraq–that could complement the investigation and prosecution functions of the International Criminal Court.[19] Such an institution would help fill the preservation gap between the ephemerality of digital data and the relatively long lags before the ICC and other investigative teams have jurisdiction and/or the practical ability to investigate atrocities. Such a mechanism also has tremendous potential to help the ICC and other investigators avoid some of the disclosure challenges that accrue with acquiring mammoth digital data sets themselves. Instead of siphoning up massive amounts of data, they should be able to make targeted requests for relevant information that will better fit their budgets and their needs.

---

18 'Berkeley Protocol on Digital Open Source Investigations: A Practical Guide on the Effective Use of Digital Open Source and Information in Investigating Violations of International Criminal, Human Rights and Humanitarian Law' (*UN Human Rights Office and Human Rights Center at Berkeley School of Law*, 3 January 2022); R Hamilton and L Freeman, 'The Criminal Court's Ukraine Investigation: A Test Case for User-Generated Evidence' (*Just Security*, 2 March 2022) <https://www.justsecurity.org/80404/the-intl-criminal-courts-ukraine-investigation-a-test-case-for-user-generated-evidence/> accessed 7 December 2022.

19 F D'Alessandra et al., 'Anchoring Accountability for Mass Atrocities: The Permanent Support Needed to Fulfil UN Investigative Mandates' (*Blavatnik School of Government and University of Oxford*, 2022).

Finally, experimentation and innovation are producing creative new forms of visualization of relevant digital information. These visualizations are being used for various functions in the investigation and prosecution lifecycle. Just a few examples include innovations like the interactive digital platform developed by SITU Research for the *Al Mahdi* case and now used in the *Al Hassan* case.[20] This form of sharing and relating disparate pieces of visual evidence (including both closed and open source photographs, videos, satellite imagery and drone footage), has expanded over the last handful of years to produce new forms of storytelling, including walking various audiences through the 3D digital reconstruction of mass graves. Such reconstructions are being increasingly used as demonstrative 'evidence,'[21] not only helping judges and other fact-finders understand when, where and how atrocities unfolded, but to aid the interviewing of witnesses about their experiences.[22]

## 3 The Challenges and Limitations of Digital Technologies

While new technologies provide undeniable benefits, they also have serious limitations and introduce new challenges into investigative processes.[23] For example, to utilize digital technologies in the ways described above, the ICC needs adequate resources, appropriate infrastructure, qualified personnel, and continuous training on new tools and techniques for all staff. However, restricted budgets, cumbersome procurement procedures, and lengthy hiring processes make it almost impossible for the Court to keep up with technological innovation. There is undoubtedly progress, but it is nevertheless valuable to examine some of the problems that new initiatives like the Trust Fund for

20 See SITU Research, 'ICC Digital Platform: Timbuktu, Mali' <https://situ.nyc/research/projects/icc-digital-platform-timbuktu-mali> accessed 7 December 2022.

21 Demonstrative evidence is not considered 'real' evidence, but an aid for explaining or illustrating actual evidence, such as witness testimonies or physical evidence. For more on crime scene reconstructions as a form of demonstrative evidence, see S Zarmsky, 'Why Seeing Should Not Always Be Believing: Considerations Regarding the Use of Digital Reconstruction Technology in International Law' (2021) 19 *Journal of International Criminal Justice* 213.

22 See, e.g., Forensic Architecture and its discussion of 'situated testimonies,' which use '3D models of the scenes and environments in which traumatic events occurred to aid in the process of interviewing and gathering testimony from witnesses to those events.' Forensic Architecture, 'By Methodology: Situated Testimonies' <https://forensic-architecture.org/methodology/situated-testimony> accessed 7 December 2022.

23 See, e.g., A Koenig and L Freeman, 'Cutting-Edge Evidence: Strengths and Weaknesses of New Digital Investigation Methods in Litigation' (2022) 73 *Hastings Law Journal* 1233.

Advanced Technology and Specialized Capacity are seeking to solve.[24] The volume of digital information poses significant challenges with regards to storage, security, and scale, while the ways in which digital content can be manipulated and endlessly reproduced raises concerns about the ability of investigators to authenticate digital items and verify the information they contain. Thus, the Court needs quality control mechanisms to ensure the authenticity of each piece of digital evidence and the accuracy of the findings of any analysis of digital evidence, even when tools are necessary to supplement human review.

### 3.1 *Budget, Procurement, Hiring and Training*

Since the birth of the ICC, barriers to modernization have ranged from an historically complicated budget process and a lack of transparency and predictability in funding,[25] to insufficient resources for meeting investigatory needs. Such needs have included the hiring of personnel with technical skills, training for existing and future staff, and securing necessary hardware and software.[26]

As with all bureaucratic institutions, procurement of new software can be time consuming. This is especially true in international organizations adhering to the UN's strict procurement rules. Unfortunately, when it comes to working with new technologies–and especially with digital data–time is of the essence. Even a couple years' time can render critical tools obsolete. This leaves the international criminal justice field with a 'preparing for the future' problem. Through various advisors, and through their own diligence and research, prosecution and defense teams must stay abreast of current developments and future trends, and ideally, get as far ahead of those developments as possible.

Investigators and lawyers also need continuous training, both to maximize the efficient and effective use of digital technologies, and to understand their limitations. This training must be ongoing, as digital platforms and products are constantly changing, reflecting the dynamic nature of a modern court's operating environment. For example, social media platforms are regularly modifying the ability for users to access data and to know what to request through formal evidence collection processes; new tools and methods are constantly being developed by civil society to better exploit these and other

---

24 See the chapter by Karim Khan in this volume.

25 Independent Expert Review of the International Criminal Court and the Rome Statute System: Final Report—30 September 2020, ICC-ASP/19/16, 9 November 2020 (Nineteenth Session of the ASP), 106 <https://asp.icc-cpi.int/sites/asp/files/asp_docs/ASP19/IER-Final-Report-ENG.pdf> accessed 7 December 2022.

26 Koenig et al., 'Digital Fingerprints' (n 8) 3–4, 8 (noting limitations in the Court's funding and staff and their impact on the OTP's ability to 'produce quality digital evidence').

platforms. While it is essential to have one or more members of an investigation team stay on top of these constantly shifting developments, these individuals must be able to bring those insights back to other team members so as not to silo any insights and to provide their team with a baseline understanding of technological advancements. Issues such as cyber security should be seen as the responsibility of each individual in the office, not the responsibility of one IT professional.

While traditional investigators can be trained in a broad swath of digital investigation techniques, there are times when specialized expertise will be required, for example, geospatial analysts, video forensics experts, or digital forensic experts. Much of this expertise can be accessed through external partnerships and services such as the Netherlands Forensic Institute, which has had a long-standing relationship with the ICC.

However, as the amount of digital evidence increases, the prosecution will need in-house expertise to fulfill some of these functions. The changing nature of the information environment, as well as the changing nature of armed conflict, as discussed below, requires hiring for new job profiles. The OTP in particular will need a combination of specialized experts and 'jacks of all trades' who can translate and coordinate between areas of expertise. This might require a fundamental re-thinking of an investigation team and the types of professional profiles that should be brought into the international justice field. When it comes to digital evidence, there is an increasing need for lawyers who deeply understand the relevant technologies, and digital analysts and investigators who understand the law, especially the Court's rules of procedure and evidence.

### 3.2 *Scale, Storage and Security*

While the internet contains more relevant information than lawyers and investigators may realize, new digital investigation methods necessitate careful awareness by prosecution, defense and judges of the limitations in accessing and meaningfully analyzing the wealth of available information. Potentially relevant digital information can easily number into the terabytes. Scraping social media platforms for relevant data can result in overwhelmingly large data sets that require comparably large repositories and sophisticated information management systems. Collecting data in bulk can also raise challenges for the prosecution with regards to disclosure obligations, given that it may be difficult if not impossible to know the full scope of what they have, including both incriminating and potentially exonerating information.

As the prosecution takes on more cases, each with a growing volume of digital information, the Court will need significantly more secure storage space, which can come with a substantial cost. While there are solutions offered by industry leaders, the ICC should be careful about the degree to which it relies on the private sector, which runs on a very different incentive structure.

Like many other international organizations, the Court is currently grappling with a transition to cloud computing. Rather than owning and maintaining its own servers, the ICC is moving its data to cloud services, likely those run by large multinational corporations like Microsoft, Google or Amazon. Cloud-computing offers huge benefits in terms of convenience and access to data, but also has concerning drawbacks around security and privacy. The use of these services places a tremendous amount of trust in for-profit businesses to act as responsible third-party custodians.

### 3.3 *Authenticity, Accuracy and Bias*

One of the biggest challenges is ensuring the authenticity, accuracy and reliability of digital open source data, especially given the prevalence of misinformation and disinformation found online. As noted in one article on open source information, '[such] evidence requires corroboration and triangulation from multiple sources to piece together what it might prove. It may also require an expert witness to explain what it is, and what it means.'[27] Errors can arise at various stages of the collection and analysis process,[28] and–especially with visual information–can be amplified by investigators' propensity to trust their ability to interpret visual data in ways that may not hold up under scrutiny.[29]

Because of the risks, one of the methodological principles underpinning the Berkeley Protocol is accuracy. This principle underscores the 'methodological and ethical imperative to ensure the accuracy–and thus the quality–of investigations by only relying on credible materials.' To ensure credibility, it's critical that investigators and analysts be trained in (and deploy) multiple working hypotheses and use peer review as a check on their work, as well as engage in ongoing training in digital verification and related analytical methods.

Finally, digital information and analysis by machines are subject to both overt and covert biases. As author Judith Martin has claimed, 'Many people mistakenly think a new technology cancels out an old one.' It's easy, given the digital information age we're living in, to increasingly overvalue the possibilities of digital evidence to an investigation, just as it's possible to undervalue it. Ultimately, the Office, like all investigation teams, needs to triangulate

---

27 K Hiatt, 'Open Source Evidence on Trial' (2016) 125 *Yale Law Journal* 323.

28 Koenig and Freeman, 'Cutting-Edge Evidence' (n 25).

29 Y Granot et al., 'In The Eyes of The Law: Perception Versus Reality in Appraisals of Video Evidence' (2018) 24 *Psychology, Public Policy, and the Law* 93.

digital evidence with other types of evidence. Many investigators who were interviewed for a study on the use of digital open source evidence in sexual violence investigations expressed a serious concern that the introduction of digital open source evidence in a variety of international criminal cases would distort what judges value when weighing evidence, and that the judges would increasingly weigh digital evidence more heavily than witness testimony, or begin to expect videos, photographs and other information shared online in ways that make some difficult-to-prosecute cases even harder.[30] Ideally, all investigation planning will seek to fully exploit available physical, digital and testimonial evidence.

Digital investigations are affected by both machine and human biases that can distort the findings of an investigation if not properly mitigated.[31] In the course of digital investigations, the prosecution must adjust for which potential sources have access to the internet and which do not. As has been well documented, access can vary significantly by age, gender, and geography.[32] Access may also be affected by internet blackouts, a commonly used tool of governments to limit what witnesses and others can post online. In addition, investigators can easily fall prey to algorithmic bias, especially if precautions are not taken to counteract these biases. For example, setting a VPN to California will yield very different results in an online search than setting a VPN to Moscow when conducting investigations relevant to the recent invasion of Ukraine, as will searches in different languages. In addition, varying patterns of social media use and browser history will effect what information is available on each platform and to each user. For example, as noted by Matthew Ford, a senior lecturer of war studies at the Swedish Defence University, 'of the over 320 million Twitter users, the greatest number are in the US and Japan while Russia isn't even in the top 20 … By contrast, Russians make use of VKontakte and OK, while Ukrainians use Telegram.'[33] All of this variability must be carefully considered and documented during investigation planning.

Finally, the scale and nature of the internet mean that human biases can be readily indulged, finding information that corroborates an initial theory of

30 A Koenig and U Egan, 'Power and Privilege: Investigating Sexual Violence with Digital Open Source Information' (2021) 19 *Journal of International Criminal Justice* 55.

31 Y McDermott, A Koenig and D Murray, 'Open Source Information's Blind Spot: Human and Machine Bias in International Criminal Investigations' (2021) 19 *Journal of International Criminal Justice* 85.

32 Ibid.

33 M Ford, 'The Smartphone as Weapon part 1: the new ecology of war in Ukraine' (*Academia.edu*, 2022) 8 <https://www.academia.edu/75845985/The_Smartphone_as_Weapon_part_1_the_new_ecology_of_war_in_Ukraine> accessed 7 December 2022.

a case, without identifying opposing information; even more than with traditional forms of investigation, investigators must deploy multiple working hypotheses, peer review and other safeguards to protect against the risks. These challenges are not exhaustive, but just a few examples of the difficulties that motivate the need for careful planning of processes and practices to counter the hurdles that new technologies engender.

## 4 The Use of Digital Technologies to Enable International Crimes

Digital tools are being used not just to investigate international crimes, of course, but also to perpetrate them. Innovations in both commercial civilian technologies and military technologies will inevitably be exploited by malicious actors. Digital technologies can enable or facilitate the commission of international crimes in overt ways–for example, using weaponized drones to commit extrajudicial killings–or in subtler ways–for example, hacking an individual's phone to identify and locate an assassination target. Of course, several of the applications of these technologies are permissible during armed conflicts and do not necessarily constitute international crimes, but when they are used to target or disproportionately affect civilians, the Court has a responsibility to hold perpetrators accountable. As digital technologies become more sophisticated and accessible to a wider range of actors, the OTP must advance its cyber investigative capacity and its ability to both ingest and analyze relevant digital evidence.

The Office also must understand these dynamics in the changing nature of warfare, including the types of technologies being deployed on the battlefield, how they work, how they are being used, who is using them and how their use might affect military affairs. The following briefly highlights three key areas in which new technologies are already influencing the way wars are waged, the way war crimes are investigated, and the application of international law to modern warfare.

### 4.1 *The Impact of the Internet on Information Warfare*

Information warfare is as old as war itself, but it has evolved as new information and communications technologies emerge: from paper pamphlets, to the radio, to films and television, to social media. Matthew Ford, mentioned earlier, has established the term 'Radical War' to reference 'the immediate and ongoing interaction between connected technologies, human participants and the politics of violence.'[34] He has explained in a series of papers how such connected devices, and especially smartphones, 'are shaping what we call the new war ecology.'[35] This enhanced role of digital tools in armed conflicts necessitates that the OTP and other accountability mechanisms deeply understand how those tools are being used, the legality of their use, and how the use of those tools may be effectively investigated. Below, we touch on three (non-exhaustive) developments that are likely to be of increasing concern to the court: the need to assess the use of the smartphone as a weapon; to investigate and establish responsibility for the use of autonomous and other weapons that enable remote attacks; and to prosecute cyber attacks as violations of international humanitarian law, as well as other international crimes within the court's jurisdiction.

Over the last twenty years, the proliferation of the smartphone has been astounding, growing from approximately 30,000 users in 1994 to close to 4 billion in 2021.[36] Approximately 75% of people surveyed across 18 advanced economies recently reported owning a mobile phone, with most being smartphones.[37] Given that the majority of the world's humans now carry at least one smartphone at any given time,[38] such connected devices have become increasingly relevant to the perpetration and investigation of war crimes, crimes against humanity, genocide, and the crime of aggression.

The adept application of social media by terrorist groups like ISIS for recruitment and indoctrination purposes has provoked new approaches to counter-terrorism focused on removing harmful content from social and mobile media platforms. Evidence of information operations that utilize smartphones and social media to distribute and amplify or micro-target online messaging will include the content itself, information about the poster, and information about receivers. For example, investigators will want to track the spread of disinformation or misinformation by tracing to the original post, if possible, and following the chain of retweets and reposts.

---

34 M Ford and A Hoskins, *Radical War Data: Attention and Control in the Twenty-First Century* (Oxford University Press 2022) 11.

35 Ibid., 1.

36 'Strategy Analytics: Half the World Owns a Smartphone' (*BusinessWire*, 24 June 2021) <https://www.businesswire.com/news/home/20210624005926/en/Strategy-Analytics-Half-the-World-Owns-a-Smartphone> accessed 7 December 2022.

37 R Wike and others, '3. Internet, Smartphone and Social Media Use' (*Pew Research Center*, 6 December 2022) <https://www.pewresearch.org/global/2022/12/06/internet-smartphone-and-social-media-use-in-advanced-economies-2022/> accessed 7 December 2022.

38 'Strategy Analytics' (n 38).

### 4.2 *Military Cyber Operations and Cyberattacks*

In April 2007, targeted cyberattacks disabled government networks and online banking in Estonia.[39] The notorious incident, attributed to Russia, marked the first significant state-on-state confrontation in the cyber domain.[40] The following year, Russian cyberattacks took down Georgian websites in coordination with the invasion of South Ossetia.[41] In December 2015 and 2016, amid an illegal annexation, Ukrainian networks fell victim to more sophisticated and damaging cyberattacks, which temporarily shut down Kyiv's electrical grid.[42] Today, Russian cyberattacks continue to be widespread and aggressive, targeting the United States with high-profile information operations—like the DNC hack—and cyber operations—like the SolarWinds hack.[43] Most troublingly, Russia is not alone in its adoption of these methods. China recently compromised over 100,000 Microsoft Exchange servers, flooded Hong Kong social media with disinformation, and escalated military pressure on Taiwan by flying two dozen warplanes in its airspace and, allegedly, intensifying cyberattacks on the small island's computer networks to an estimated 20 million to 40 million per month.[44] In 2022, Iran crippled the digital infrastructure of Albania to such a degree that there was consideration of invoking Article 5 of NATO.[45]

Over the past two decades, more than 40 states have established some type of military cyber command, and at least a dozen other states have indicated their desire to follow suit.[46] In the United States, every division of the armed

---

39 M Lesk, 'The New Front Line: Estonia under Cyberassault' (2007) 5 *Institute of Electrical and Electronics Engineers Security & Privacy* 76.

40 S Herzog, 'Revisiting the Estonian Cyber Attacks: Digital Threats and Multinational Responses' (2011) 4 *Journal of Strategic Security* 49.

41 A Kozlowski, 'Comparative Analysis of Cyberattacks on Estonia, Georgia and Kyrgyzstan' (2014) 3 *European Scientific Journal* 1.

42 D E Whitehead et al., 'Ukraine Cyber-induced Power Outage: Analysis and Practical Mitigation Strategies' (2017) *70th Annual Conference for Protective Relay Engineers, Institute of Electrical and Electronics Engineers* 1.

43 M Poznansky, 'Confronting Cyber Threats: Challenges and Opportunities' (*Modern War Institute*, 26 July 2021) <https://mwi.usma.edu/confronting-cyber-threats-challenges-and-opportunities/> accessed 7 December 2022.

44 E Cheung, W Ripley, and G Tsai, 'How Taiwan is Trying to Defend against Cyber World War III,' *CNN* (23 July 2021) <https://www.cnn.com/2021/07/23/tech/taiwan-china-cybersecurity-intl-hnk/index.html> accessed 7 December 2022.

45 See, e.g., M Miller, 'Albania Weighed Invoking NATO's Article 5 over Iranian Cyberattack' *Politico* (5 October 2022) <https://www.politico.com/news/2022/10/05/why-albania-chose-not-to-pull-the-nato-trigger-after-cyberattack-00060347> accessed 7 December 2022.

46 M Smeets, 'Building a Cyber Force is Even Harder than You Thought' (*War on the Rocks*, 12 May 2022) <https://warontherocks.com/2022/05/building-a-cyber-force-is-even-harder-than-you-thought/> accessed 7 December 2022.

forces from the navy to the air force has its own cyber unit. In Russia, at least three government divisions–the FSB, GRU, and SVR–exercise cyber capabilities. While most 'cyber superpowers' are not States Parties to the Rome Statute and therefore fall beyond the Court's jurisdiction, it is inevitable that one day the ICC Prosecutor will have to take on the issue of war crimes committed through cyber means and methods.

In fact, the OTP already has jurisdiction over one situation in which offensive cyber operations on critical civilian infrastructure could amount to war crimes. When Russia invaded Ukraine on February 24, 2022, the Kremlin's aggression was not only kinetic, but also digital. In coordination with armed forces moving into Ukraine's sovereign territory, a cyberattack targeted broadband internet access, disabling modems that communicate with global internet provider Viasat's satellite network and disrupting Ukrainian command and control during the invasion.[47] The consequences of these actions extended far beyond military objectives, impacting civilian infrastructure in European countries including the disruption of emergency health services in France, and disturbance of wind turbines in Germany. Since then, the cyber domain has been an active battleground in the situation in Ukraine.

In August 2021, the Permanent Mission of Liechtenstein to the United Nations published a ground-breaking report on the application of the Rome Statute of the International Criminal Court to cyberwarfare with support from ten States Parties and contributions from a group of expert advisors.[48] Around the same time, the Human Rights Center at the University of California Berkeley School of Law independently initiated an investigation into Russian cyberattacks against Ukraine's critical infrastructure in the context of the armed conflict that has been ongoing since 2014.[49] Since then, the Berkeley Human Rights Center has been monitoring, documenting and investigating offensive cyber operations in the Russo-Ukraine conflict for the first time through an international criminal law lens.

While military legal advisers, academics and other experts in international humanitarian law have been grappling with the application of the laws of

47 'Case Study: Viasat' (*Cyber Peace Institute*, June 2022) <https://cyberconflicts.cyberpeaceinstitute.org/law-and-policy/cases/viasat> accessed 7 December 2022.

48 The Permanent Mission of Liechtenstein to the United Nations, 'The Council of Advisers' Report on the Application of the Rome Statute of the International Criminal Court to Cyberwarfare' (August 2021) <https://www.regierung.li/files/medienarchiv/The-Council-of-Advisers-Report-on-the-Application-of-the-Rome-Statute-of-the-International-Criminal-Court-to-Cyberwarfare.pdf> accessed 7 December 2022.

49 See A Greenberg, 'The Case for War Crimes Charges Against Russia's Sandworm Hackers' (*WIRED*, 12 May 2022) <https://www.wired.com/story/cyber-war-crimes-sandworm-russia-ukraine/> accessed 7 December 2022.

armed conflict to the cyber domain for many years now, very little has been written about how these conversations translate to the international criminal law context in which charges of war crimes are litigated against responsible individuals. As State-run military operations look less like war, and more like coordinated criminal endeavors, it is appropriate and overdue to contribute the international criminal law perspective to ongoing conversations about protecting civilians and civilian infrastructure in cyberspace.

### 4.3 *Unmanned Vehicles, Autonomous Systems and AI*

Militaries around the world are increasingly removing personnel from the vehicles used to transport weapons and goods, to render attacks, and to defend critical infrastructures. This is true of vehicles that travel by air, land and sea. Such remote control of military operations changes the calculus of risk and reward in ways that could radically change the footprint of war. It also means that the digital domain will be a critical evidence collection space for war crimes investigators. Such investigators will need to know what traces are left behind, and may need new skills and new forms of documentation to prove the elements of crimes, as well as the applicable modes of liability of the responsible perpetrators. The question of individual criminal responsibility becomes even more complex when remote tools are used to carry out military tasks that have traditionally been in the purview of humans. While fully autonomous weapons are banned, at least for the time being, there is a growing risk of deployment of semi-autonomous weapons, in which algorithms determine targets.[50] According to the International Committee of the Red Cross, such weapons are those 'that select and apply force to targets without human intervention,' and are activated by people who 'do not know specifically who or what it will strike, nor precisely where and/or when that strike will occur.'[51] A body of practice needs to emerge with regards to how to document and

50 For an overview of some of the new fact-finding and accountability challenges raised by autonomous weapons, see, e.g., Human Rights Watch, 'Mind the Gap: The Lack of Accountability for Killer Robots' (9 April 2015) <https://www.hrw.org/report/2015/04/09/mind-gap/lack-accountability-killer-robots> accessed 7 December 2022; T Chengeta, 'Accountability Gap: Autonomous Weapon Systems and Modes of Responsibility in International Law' (2016) 45 *Denver Journal of International Law & Policy* 1; M Taddeo and A Blanchard, 'Accepting Moral Responsibility for the Actions of Autonomous Weapons Systems–A Moral Gambit' (2022) 35 *Philosophy & Technology* 77.

51 International Committee of the Red Cross, 'What You Need To Know about Autonomous Weapons' (26 July 2022) <https://www.icrc.org/en/document/what-you-need-know-about-autonomous-weapons> accessed 7 December 2022.

establish legal responsibility for such attacks. The ICC is well poised to help develop such processes and any accompanying jurisprudence.

One relevant technology is unmanned vehicles, also known as drones. Today, drones are used by both state and non-state actors, and can serve intelligence, surveillance, reconnaissance, delivery, combat and other functions. Reconnaissance drones provide 'aerial surveillance of individuals, troop movements and military sites,' giving military groups vital information to inform strategy and target military actions.[52] The rapid increase of commercial drone production in the last few years has made drone technology more accessible for non-state actors.[53] Extremist groups such as the Islamic State have used these commercial drones as weapons, to create propaganda, and to surveil enemy positions.[54]

Current research and development of drones concentrates heavily on automation, specifically enhancing a drone's ability to automatically perform a narrow task that the user has programmed for it,[55] such as following a specific, pre-programed flight path.[56] Refinements in predictive analytics and artificial intelligence aim to advance drone autonomy.[57] Many researchers have focused on employing deep learning technology as part of the process to improve autonomy.[58] Such deep learning, a form of 'artificial intelligence, aims at enabling machines to replicate human behaviour.'[59] Because algorithms form the basis of artificial intelligence, courts will need to understand the algorithms deployed in these processes. However, machine learning processes are essentially black boxes, meaning that it can be difficult if not impossible to know why a machine has come to a certain decision.

52 W Zwijnenburg and A Jansen, 'Violent Skies: How Lethal Drone Technology is Shaping Contemporary Warfare' (*PAX for Peace*, August 2020) 1, 21 <https://paxforpeace.nl/media/download/paxviolentskies_0.pdf> 7 December 2022.

53 Ibid.

54 Ibid.

55 T McClean, 'The Path from Automation to Autonomy Is Swarming with Activity' (*Forbes*, 1 April 2021) <https://www.forbes.com/sites/forbestechcouncil/2021/04/01/the-path-from-automation-to-autonomy-is-swarming-with-activity/?sh=288a2ae53716> 7 December 2022.

56 B Wilson et al., 'Small Unmanned Aerial System Adversary Capabilities' (RAND 2020) 31.

57 Ibid.

58 T Lee, S Mckeever and J Courtney, 'Flying Free: A Research Overview of Deep Learning in Drone Navigation Autonomy' (2021) 5 *Drones* 1.

59 M van Rijmenam, 'Algorithms Are Black Boxes, That Is Why We Need Explainable AI' (*Medium*, 4 September 2019) <https://markvanrijmenam.medium.com/algorithms-are-black-boxes-that-is-why-we-need-explainable-ai-72e8f9ea5438> accessed 7 December 2022.

Addressing these developments will require a coordinated and complementary effort by the OTP and other actors in the international justice field, including investigators and prosecutors in other jurisdictions, academic researchers, legal practitioners, technologists, and members of civil society.[60] Several advancements in communication, collaboration and coordination spotlight how far the international justice community has come–as a community of practice–over the past two decades, triggered by both the growing process and the growing pains of the International Criminal Court.[61] These include experiments at creating evidentiary mechanisms with specialized expertise on the identification, preservation, analysis and visualization of digital information; a better understanding of the technologies that can be used to establish the chain of custody of digital content; and the development of infrastructures for the ingestion and sharing of digital data.

Finally, still on the horizon–but coming quickly into view–is the use of virtual reality, augmented reality and other immersive technologies as demonstratives, for witness interviewing, and other accountability-related functions.[62] These emerging uses of advanced digital technologies offer significant promise for the efficiency and efficacy of international criminal investigations, as well as raise new concerns that are worthy of extensive future research.

## 5 Conclusion

Over the past decade, the ICC has increasingly embraced the exploitation of new technologies in investigations, case building, and the presentation of evidence in the courtroom. Today, the OTP is emerging as a leader in the use of new technologies–both procedurally, to enhance investigations and prosecutions,

---

60 See Carsten Stahn, *A Critical Introduction to International Criminal Law* (Cambridge University Press 2019) (noting the multidisciplinarity underpinning the evolution of international criminal law, and stating that '[m]any of the relevant debates about international criminal law do not arise from conversations among lawyers, or endless doctrinal disputes over legal concepts, but rather from engagement with other disciplinary standpoints or critiques'). Ibid., xiiii.

61 See, e.g., A Koenig, 'From "Capture to Courtroom": Collaboration and the Digital Documentation of International Crimes in Ukraine' (2022) 20(4) *Journal of International Criminal Justice* 1 (noting the various collaborations that have emerged to advance the identification, collection and analysis of digital data in the context of Ukraine).

62 See, e.g., Forensic Architecture, 'Situated Testimony' (n 22); SITU Research Website <https://situ.nyc/research> accessed 7 December 2022.

and substantively, to investigate and prosecute new types of crimes. To maintain this momentum, the Court and its States Parties should continue to carefully assess any amendments that may be needed to the Rome Statute and the ICC Rules of Procedure and Evidence,[63] as well as the functionalities available internally and in collaboration with external partners. They will also need to secure the budgets necessary to keep up with these developments. Ultimately, perhaps in no other area of its functioning is the ICC better positioned to fulfill its complementary function than in helping to disseminate its lessons learned with regards to the use of digital technologies with other critical players in the quest for justice.

63 For relevant recommendations, see Freeman and Llorente, 'Finding the Signal' (n 7).

CHAPTER 22

# Is the International Criminal Court Succeeding in Providing Justice to Victims?

*Carla Ferstman*

## 1 Introduction[1]

Throughout and continuing to this day, I, together with many others in civil society, have advocated for the recognition of victims' rights in the ethos, the procedures and the practice of the Court.[2] The ICC, we argued then and still maintain, needed to both reflect and fulfil a new vision of international criminal justice[3] that was physically and conceptually closer to the people international justice was intended to serve.[4] Central to those the Court was supposed

1 I have been involved with the ICC project from early on, having attended the bulk of the Preparatory Commission meetings after the ICC Statute was adopted and the meetings of the Assembly of States Parties. This was in my then capacity as Director of REDRESS, an organisation devoted to promoting the rights and interests of victims of torture and related international crimes.

2 Some of the early advocacy work and positions on victims' rights are reflected in: REDRESS, 'Promoting the right to reparation for survivors of torture: What role for a permanent international criminal court?' (1997); Preparatory Commission of the ICC, 'Report on the International Seminar on Victims' Access to the International Criminal Court', UN Doc. PCNICC/1999/WGRPE/INF/2 (6 July 1999); Victims' Rights Working Group (VRWG), 'Strategy Meeting on the Development of Structures and Procedures for Victims at the International Criminal Court 6–7 December 2002: Summary Of Proceedings And Final Recommendations' (2003) <https://redress.org/wp-content/uploads/2018/01/VRWGsumprocfinrec67122002.pdf> accessed 30 April 2023.

3 The early debates on the inclusion of victims' rights in the ICC Statute and Rules of Procedure and Evidence are summarised in: C Muttukumaru, 'Reparations to Victims' in R S Lee (ed.), *The International Criminal Court: The Making of the Rome Statute: Issues, Negotiations, Results* (Brill Nijhoff 1999) 262–264; D Donat Cattin, both chapters 'Article 68' and 'Article 75' in O Triffterer (ed.), *Commentary on the Rome Statute of the International Criminal Court. Observers' notes, Article by Article* (CH Beck/Hart/Nomos, 1999); C Jorda, J de Hemptienne, 'The Status and Role of the Victim' in A Cassese, P Gaeta, J R W D Jones, *The Rome Statute of the International Criminal Court: A Commentary* (Oxford University Press 2002), Vol II, Ch 32; T van Boven, 'Victims rights and interests in the International Criminal Court', in J Doria et al. (eds), *The Legal Regime of the ICC: Essays in Honour of Prof. I.P. Blishchenko* (Brill Nijhoff 2008) 895–906.

4 See, Donat Cattin, 'Article 68', ibid.

 DOI:10.1163/9789004529939_023

to serve are victims. Indeed, we argued, there was a need to move from a largely perpetrator-centred, retributive notion of justice to a more inclusive vision that recognised not only the dignity and agency of victims but afforded a form of justice that was reparative and empowering to them.[5]

The Preamble of the ICC Statute is mindful that 'millions of children, women and men have been victims of unimaginable atrocities that deeply shock the conscience of humanity'.[6] Thus, the suffering of victims was clearly in the minds of the drafters when the Statute was adopted. The importance of treating victims with dignity and respect and engaging them in proceedings is reflected in Article 68 of the ICC Statute. This fundamental requirement has also been underscored in the policy statements of the Office of the Prosecutor,[7] the Board of Directors of the Trust Fund for Victims[8] and the Office of Public Counsel for Victims,[9] among others.[10] Nevertheless, given the novelty of the

---

5 Y Danieli, 'Preliminary reflections from a psychological perspective', in T van Boven et al. (eds), *The Right to Restitution, Compensation and Rehabilitation for Victims of Gross Violations of Human Rights and Fundamental Freedoms*, Netherlands Institute of Human Rights, Special issue No. 12 (1992) 196–213; Y Danieli, 'Massive trauma and the healing role of reparative justice: an update', in C Ferstman and M Goetz (eds), *Reparations for victims of genocide, war crimes and crimes against humanity: systems in place and systems in the making* 2nd revised edn (Brill Nijhoff 2020) 38–85.

6 Rome Statute of the International Criminal Court (signed 17 July 1998, entered into force 1 July 2002) 2187 UNTS 3 ('ICC Statute').

7 The Office of the Prosecutor, for instance has recognised that 'victims bring a unique and necessary perspective to the activities of the ICC and contribute to fair and efficient trials'; 'victims' participation in proceedings before the Court is an essential feature of the Rome system and an important contribution to international justice.' ICC OTP, 'Policy Paper on Victims' Participation' (April 2010), 1, 5.

8 On behalf of the Board of Directors of the Trust Fund, Archbishop Tutu described the meaning of assistance to victims: '[W]hen a country, a nation, the international community says, symbolically "we cannot compensate you but we want to show that we care, we want to show you that we hope that this small thing that we do for you will somehow pour balm on your wounds and help those wounds to heal."' Archbishop D Tutu, 'Statement by His Eminence Archbishop Desmond Tutu on behalf of the Board of Directors of the Trust Fund for Victim', Video Statement at the Ceremony Marking their First Meeting (The Hague, 22 April 2004).

9 OPCV, *Representing Victims before the International Criminal Court: A Manual for legal representatives* 5th edn (ICC-OPCV-MLR-005/19_ENG, OPCV ICC 2019) <https://www.icc-cpi.int/sites/default/files/manual-victims-legal-representatives-fifth-edition-rev1.pdf> accessed 28 March 2023; P Massida, 'The Participation of Victims Before the ICC: A Revolution Not Without Challenges', in R Jasini and G Townsend (eds), *Advancing the Impact of Victim Participation at the International Criminal Court: Bridging the Gap Between Research and Practice* (ESRC, online, 30 November 2020), 33. She identifies victim participation as 'one of the main innovations of the Statute of the International Criminal Court'.

10 Report of the Court on the Strategy in Relation to Victims, ICC-ASP/8/45, 10 November 2009 (Eighth Session of the ASP).

burgeoning ICC framework with respect to victims, and the many different perspectives, experiences and legal traditions at play, not all court officials, states, civil society groups and other interlocutors, not least victims themselves, had the same vision or understanding of what 'justice to victims' was supposed to mean. Much of this divergence in views and perspectives remains twenty years after the entry into force of the Statute.

In my own view, the crimes coming within the jurisdiction of the Court were always going to dictate the kind of approach that was needed—both their substance (the types of harms they engender) and their scale. The fact of significant numbers of victims with physical, psychological and material harms that are extensive, lifelong and often multigenerational is part and parcel of the nature of the crimes over which the ICC has jurisdiction and the necessary starting point from which one considers how the ICC may fulfil its mandate towards victims and whether that fulfilment is meaningful or effective. Yet, there were and continue to be different views about purpose, methods, and approach.[11] Naturally, it can be difficult to implement something that means different things depending upon who one asks.

## 2 What Is Justice to Victims?

Is justice to victims about striking the right balance between victim and defence rights? Is it acknowledging that behind each investigation, each case, each proceeding—there are people, individuals of all genders, communities, young people, old people who have suffered unimaginable atrocities? Is the act of acknowledgment enough? Should justice to victims be real, tangible, practical or are we really speaking philosophically or symbolically? Who should

11 I assess some of these competing visions in C Ferstman, 'The ICC as a Tool for Social Transformation? Challenges and Prospects for Addressing Victims' Right', in W J M van Genugten, M P Scharf, and S E Radin (eds), *Criminal Jurisdiction 100 Years after the 1907 Hague Peace Conference: 2007 Hague Joint Conference on Contemporary Issues of International Law* (Springer 2009) 286–293. See also, on different perspectives on the value of victim participation, M Hirst, 'Valuing victim participation: why we need better systems to evaluate victims' participation at the ICC', in FIDH, *Victims at the Center of Justice from 1998 to 2018: Reflections on the Promises and the Reality of Victim Participation at the ICC* (2018), 81. On competing approaches to reparations, see additionally, C Ferstman, 'Reparations at the ICC: The Need for a Human Rights Based Approach to Effectiveness', in C Ferstman and M Goetz (eds), *Reparations for victims of genocide, war crimes and crimes against humanity: systems in place and systems in the making* 2nd revised edn (Brill Nijhoff 2020) 469–472.

really be answering the question whether the ICC is succeeding in providing justice to victims?

Perhaps 'success', 20 years after the ICC has been established, with the key texts all recognising the importance of victim participation and of fostering the dignity and inclusion of victims in matters that affect them,[12] would have been to recognise that there are clear interlocutors from within the communities that have suffered most who could properly canvass the issues around whether the ICC is succeeding in providing justice to victims. Victims and the communities in which they live have clear views on these issues, and it is important not only to provide them the space to articulate such views but to listen to them. Pablo de Greiff, as then UN Special Rapporteur on Truth, speaking about transitional justice measures but making arguments which have equal resonance for international criminal justice processes:

> The participation of victims [...] always provides a poignant reminder of the fact that the choices necessary for the adoption of an effective and sustainable [...] policy are not merely technical in nature, but are intended to both manifest and sustain the dignity and worth of all concerned. In this respect, [it] ... is not merely an exercise in institutional design. Given the increased professionalization and standardization of the field, it is always good to be reminded of this. The presence of victims, their narratives of pain and loss but also of endurance, offers this indispensable reminder, and is an important source of motivation.[13]

As was confirmed by Pre-Trial Chamber I in relation to the Palestine situation, 'it is worth recalling that victims also have the right to provide information to, receive information from and communicate with the Court, regardless and independently from judicial proceedings, including during the preliminary examination stage.'[14] In order to give effect to these rights, the Chamber called on the Registry to 'establish a continuous system of interaction between the Court and victims, residing within or outside of Palestine'.[15] Similarly, Pre-Trial

12 Art. 68(3) ICC Statute; Arts 4, 6, UNGA 'Declaration of Basic Principles of Justice for Victims of Crime and Abuse of Power' (29 November 1985) UN Doc A/RES/40/34.

13 Report of the Special Rapporteur on the promotion of truth, justice, reparation and guarantees of non-recurrence, Human Rights Council, Thirty-fourth session, UN Doc A/HRC/34/62 (27 December 2016), para. 83.

14 Decision on Information and Outreach for the Victims of the Situation, *Situation in the State of Palestine*, ICC-01/18-2, PTC I, ICC, 13 July 2018, para. 10.

15 Ibid, para. 14.

Chamber III indicated in the context of the Situation in the People's Republic of Bangladesh/Republic of the Union of Myanmar that giving meaningful effect to the obligation under Article 68(3) of the ICC Statute to permit victims' views and concerns to be presented and considered at stages of the proceedings is premised 'on the victims having access to complete and accurate information about their role at the Court during the various stages of the proceedings.'[16]

The Independent Expert Review of the ICC has noted in this respect that the ability to reach victims 'is not the result of the application procedure, but depends on other factors, including the steps taken to reach out to victim communities to alert them to the interest of the Court and ensure that they are fully informed of their rights as victims, and the extent to which these steps are successful in the face of various obstacles and communication difficulties';[17] '[o]utreach facilitates and enables victims to enjoy and exercise their rights and the Court to fulfil its duties'; 'victims also have the right to provide information to, receive information from and communicate with the Court, regardless and independently from judicial proceedings.'[18] As it was affirmed as part of the stock-taking exercise on victims and affected communities held in the context of the Review Conference of the Assembly of States Parties in 2010, 'access to justice is fundamental for victims to realise their right to a remedy. [...] outreach [is] a process for "establishing sustainable, two-way communication between the Court and communities affected by situations that are the subject of investigations or proceedings. It aims to provide information, promote understanding and support for the Court's work, and to provide access to judicial proceedings."'[19]

Another question which might be posed, 'is providing justice to victims even possible?' Given the daunting nature and scale of the crimes, should we all just give up and go home? Is justice to victims a realistic benchmark? My

16 Order on Information and Outreach for the Victims of the Situation, *Situation in the People's Republic of Bangladesh/Republic of the Union of Myanmar*, ICC-01/19-28, PTC III, ICC, 20 January 2020, para. 7.

17 Independent Expert Review of the International Criminal Court and the Rome Statute System: Final Report—30 September 2020, ICC-ASP/19/16, 9 November 2020 (Nineteenth Session of the ASP) ('IER Report') para. 849.

18 *Bangladesh/Myanmar*, Order on Information and Outreach for the Victims of the Situation (n 16) para. 7.

19 Review Conference of the Rome Statute, 'The impact of the Rome Statute system on victims and affected communities', RC/ST/V/INF.4 (30 May 2010) para. 28, referring to ICC, 'Integrated Strategy for External Relations, Public Information and Outreach' <https://www.icc-cpi.int/sites/default/files/ICCPIDSWBOR0307070402_IS_En.pdf> accessed 30 April 2023 (hereafter 'Integrated Strategy').

view on this is that for crimes involving serious physical harm or mental suffering there is probably no such thing as 'full' justice—justice that properly and fully responds to all the different harms suffered, in the sense of *restitutio ad integrum*, to as far as possible, wipe out all the consequences of the illegal act and re-establish the situation which would, in all probability, have existed if that act had not been committed.[20] Indeed, it is recognised that there can be no 'going back' with such types of crimes. As Shelton has argued, '[a]lthough restitution is the preferred remedy, it is not possible for many types of human rights violations. An order of restitution would be futile, for example, after violations of the right to life, torture and other physical or mental abuse'.[21]

The types of crimes which come before the ICC transform victims so fundamentally that there is no way to simply 'go back' to what was before or to undo the kinds of acts that encompass genocide, crimes against, humanity, war crimes or aggression. Reparation is much more about getting as close as is possible to 'full' justice for victims, to adopt measures to guarantee infringed rights, repair the damages caused and afford compensation.[22] The Court should also assist victims to move forward with their lives in dignity. Thus, anything less than the possibility of realising 'full' justice does not open up the opportunity for decision-makers and policymakers to decide that anything will be adequate—to simply choose from within the toolbox of options and make it symbolic to give some appearance of justice. That would be inadequate, even though symbols are certainly still important.

Certainly the ICC has had an impact on victims and affected communities, and some of this impact has been evaluated.[23] So when thinking about justice

20 *Case Concerning the Factory at Chorzów (Germany v Poland)* (Merits) PCIJ Rep Series A No 17, 21; *Armed Activities on the Territory of the Congo (Democratic Republic of the Congo v Uganda)* (Judgment, Reparations), 9 February 2022, ICJ, para. 69; Art. 31, ILC, Articles on the Responsibility of States for Internationally Wrongful Acts, 'Report of the International Law Commission on the work of its 53rd session' (23 April–1 June and 2 July–10 August 2001) UN Doc A/CN.4/SER.A/2001/Add.1 (2001).

21 D Shelton, *Remedies in International Human Rights Law* 3rd edn (Oxford University Press 2015) 298.

22 Reparations Order, *Ntaganda, Situation in the Democratic Republic of the Congo*, ICC-01/04-02/06-2659, TC VI, ICC, 8 March 2021, para. 83, citing with approval the Inter-American Court of Human Rights judgment: *Atala Riffo and daughters v. Chile*, Judgment (Merits, Reparations, and Costs) IACHR Series C No 239 (24 February 2012), para. 241.

23 See e.g. VRWG, 'The Impact of the Rome Statute System on Victims and Affected Communities' (April 2010) <https://redress.org/wp-content/uploads/2018/01/Apr-10-The-Impact-of-the-Rome-Statute-System-on-Victims.pdf> accessed 30 April 2023. See also, A Koenig, E Stover, S Cody and M Balthazard, 'The Victims' Court? A Study of 622 Victim Participants at the International Criminal Court' (Human Rights Center, UC Berkely, 2015) <https://humanrights.berkeley.edu/sites/default/files/publications/vp_report_2015_full_rev_b-4.pdf>

for victims, the question is 'what should the Court and those who support its mission be aiming for'?

## 3 Realising Victims' Rights

To my mind, the ICC should be focusing its attention on realising victims' rights;[24] serving as a catalyst for and fostering a process that leads to victims' empowerment and gives space to victims' unfiltered voices. We should be recognising that for justice for victims to happen, we (those involved in the international justice project whether inside or outside of the Court), need to make space for victims, and we need to be prepared to be transformed by the act of giving space to victims. We must stop thinking we have achieved something when victims finally understand the Court's limitations and the boxes they need to fit into and the hoops they need to jump through, to engage with the Court.[25] Also, we must stop thinking we have achieved anything meaningful when we take decisions on their behalf because we think somehow, we know better what their needs are, what their priorities are, and what risks they face by engaging with the Court. We must realise that—it is us that need to evolve, not the victims. We also need to become more accountable to victims for the

accessed 30 April 2023; Independent Panel of experts report on victim participation at the International Criminal Court (July 2013) <https://redress.org/wp-content/uploads/2017/12/July-Independent-Panel-of-experts-report-on-victim-participation-at-the.pdf> accessed 30 April 2023; G Mettraux et al., 'Victims Participation before the ICC', in *Expert Initiative on Promoting Effectiveness at the International Criminal Court,* 175–201 <https://dickinsonlaw.psu.edu/sites/default/files/2019-10/Groome-ICC-Expert-Report-Dec-2-2014.pdf> accessed 30 April 2023; FIDH, 'Victims at the Center of Justice from 1998 to 2018: Reflections on the Promises and the Reality of Victim Participation at the ICC' (2018) <https://www.fidh.org/IMG/pdf/droitsdesvictimes730a_final-2.pdf> accessed 30 April 2023.

24 See generally, Ferstman, 'Reparations at the ICC: The Need for a Human Rights Based Approach to Effectiveness' (n 10).

25 FIDH, 'Enhancing Victims' Rights before the ICC: A View from Situation Countries on Victims' Rights at the International Criminal Court' (2013); Independent Panel of experts report on victim participation at the International Criminal Court (July 2013); Mettraux et al. (n 22); FIDH, *Victims at the Center of Justice from 1998 to 2018: Reflections on the Promises and the Reality of Victim Participation at the ICC* (n 22). See also, R Clements, 'From bureaucracy to management: The International Criminal Court's internal progress narrative' (2019) 32(1) *Leiden Journal of International Law* 149–167.

steps we take or do not take, and for how long it takes us, to take any steps at all.[26]

This is quite fundamental I think though it does not need to be revolutionary.

It simply means that there must be more latitude, more room, more space to be truly inclusive, to not only ensure that victims understand and are informed about what is happening, but also to allow the procedures to be informed and to transform to adjust to their realities and to what they find meaningful: whether it is timeframes, application processes, protective measures, rights of audience, assistance and support, access to reparations or the forms and content of reparations. Neither the procedure nor the substance of victim engagement should be enslaved by bureaucratic people or bureaucratic rules.[27]

This is not to say that none of this is not already happening or that these concerns are not known or acknowledged. The Court is in a different place today than it was a decade ago, and that was a different place from when it started, but there is still room for improvement.

26 The ICC's most recent report on its performance provides limited, mainly quantitative information on victim participation and reparations. See '2021 Report of the Court on Key Performance Indicators' (ICC, 2021), 43–45. Hirst (n 11) explains that '[u]nfortunately, the Court's PKIs in this area fall a long way short of the framework for monitoring and evaluation which is required. Only three of the indicators actually relate to participating victims (as opposed to reparations, outreach, or—rather bizarrely—witnesses assisted by duty counsel). These are: (1) the number of victims participating by the phase of proceeding in each ongoing case; (2) the number of victims in each case represented by external counsel versus OPCV; and (3) the number of field "trips" undertaken by legal representatives of victims in each ongoing case. It must be immediately apparent that these three indicators surely cannot be sufficient to enable any real evaluation of victim participation. They are so limited and arbitrary that it appears they have been chosen by reference to what quantitative data was available, rather than what information is most relevant to assessing victim participation. The three indicators ignore entire areas of victim participation (such as participation outside the context of an active case).'

27 On the bureaucratic tendencies of victim participation and reparations see: IER Report (n 17) para. 858, which while recognising the inevitability of a certain level of bureaucracy, notes that 'Complicated and inconsistent application processes are said to have undermined meaningful victim participation before the Court and that is said still to be the situation in spite of the developments in that area narrated above. One experienced counsel recognised the efforts being made by Chambers to move towards a model that would be workable for all cases, particularly those with very large interested victim numbers, and reserved their harshest comments for the Registry where, he said, "effective victim participation encounters its greatest inefficiencies and obstacles"'.

## 4 Some Specific Areas for Improvement

I will highlight several areas where I think there is room for change.

### 4.1 *Victim Participation at the Preliminary Examination, Investigation, Pre-confirmation and Confirmation of Charges Phases*

Victims have distinct interests in prosecutorial strategy. As the Single Judge indicated in the *Katanga case*,

> the interests of victims go beyond the determination of what happened and the identification of those responsible, and extend to securing a certain degree of punishment for those who are responsible for perpetrating the crimes for which they suffered harm. These interests—namely the identification, prosecution and punishment of those who have victimised them by preventing their impunity—are at the root of the well-established right to justice for victims of serious violations of human rights, which international human rights bodies have differentiated from the victims' right to reparations.[28]

Victims will have an interest *inter alia*, in decisions whether to proceed with an examination or an investigation, decisions not to proceed with an investigation or not to bring charges, or a decision to stay an investigation or prosecution. All these decisions impact on the capacity of the ICC to deliver justice. As victims explained when they sought to review the decision of the then Prosecutor to cease active investigations in Kenya,

Many victims were killed, and in fact one of us had to carry the head of her dead husband from Nakuru so that she could bury it. Her husband was killed during PEV. Do you know how traumatising that is? Another lady's husband was killed in their house. These women are suffering and their only hope was the ICC. You are now informing us that the case has been terminated, do you want us to kill ourselves also? (*Halafu unatuáfembia case imeisha, unataka hata sisi tujiue?*) [...] Will the Court at least allow us to give our opinions in regards to this termination? There is so much we have to tell the Court and we feel they should listen to our grievances.[29]

---

28 Decision on the Set of Procedural Rights Attached to Procedural Status of Victim at the Pre-Trial Stage of the Case, *Katanga, Situation in the Democratic Republic of the Congo* ICC-01/04-01/07-474, PTC I, ICC, 13 May 2008, paras 38–39, and more broadly, paras 31–44.

29 Victims' request for review of Prosecution's decision to cease active investigation, *Situation in the Republic of Kenya*, ICC-01/09-154, PTC II, ICC, 3 August 2015, Annex 1: Victims' Views and Concerns, which is described as an illustrative set of views and concerns expressed

For victims to participate in a particular proceeding, they would have to demonstrate that their personal interests are engaged by that proceeding. For the most part (and noting the wider approaches taken in respect of the Myanmar and Palestine situations),[30] this requirement has been narrowly interpreted during the earliest phases of prosecutorial engagement. Successive Chambers have interpreted the preliminary examination and investigation of a situation as phases which do not constitute 'proceedings' in which victims have any general right to participate.[31] When victims have sought to express views and concerns during those phases, Chambers held that victims' personal interests were not affected by the respective proceedings (when the victims' experiences did not pertain to the charges brought by the Prosecutor), or that for other reasons they lacked legal standing to participate.

When the Prosecutor indicated his plans to re-open only parts of the Afghanistan investigation, victims whose victimisation fell outside what the Prosecutor was seeking to re-open sought to express views and concerns about the failure of the Prosecutor to seek to resume investigations into 'their' crimes. The Pre-Trial Chamber denied the request on the basis of their lack of legal standing to address the Court.[32] In some kind of a 'bone' thrown to the victims, the Chamber, noted that the various applications [which it had just denied] 'seem to stem from potential victims being concerned as to the adequacy of the action and strategy of the Office of the Prosecutor in this matter', and 'reminds the Prosecutor that the duties and obligations as regards victims should indeed inform its investigative and prosecuting action at all stages.'[33]

Similarly, when victims sought to express their views and concerns relating to the decision of the Prosecutor 'not to conduct any further active investigation

---

by 93 Victims communicated in person to the Legal Representative for Victims during meetings with 702 Victims held in Kenya during the period 25 May to 17 June 2015.

30 *Palestine* Decision on Information and Outreach for the Victims of the Situation (n 14); *Bangladesh/Myanmar,* Order on Information and Outreach for the Victims of the Situation (n 16).

31 Judgment on victim participation in the investigation stage of the proceedings in the appeal of the OPCD against the decision of Pre-Trial Chamber I of 7 December 2007 and in the appeals of the OPCD and the Prosecutor against the decision of Pre-Trial Chamber I of 24 December 2007, *Situation in the Democratic Republic of the Congo* ICC-01/04-556, AC, ICC, 19 December 2008, para. 45; Decision on Victims' Participation in Proceedings Related to the Situation in the Republic of Kenya, *Situation in the Republic of Kenya*, ICC-01/09-24, PTC II, ICC, 3 November 2010.

32 Decision on submissions received and order to the Registry regarding the filing of documents in the proceedings pursuant to articles 18(2) and 68(3) of the Statute, *Situation in the Islamic Republic of Afghanistan*, ICC-02/17-171, PTC II, ICC, 8 November 2021.

33 Ibid, para. 15.

at present' in the Kenya situation, the Appeals Chamber determined that, as no formal decision had been taken to close the Kenya investigation (the investigation has simply been stayed, indefinitely), they were told they had no right of audience.[34] At the time of writing, more than seven years after the Appeals Chamber decision was issued, it is clear that the investigation is firmly and permanently closed. There have been no new steps by the Prosecutor to address the cooperation gap with the Government of Kenya or to seek out new avenues to obtain the missing evidence subsequent to that Appeals Chamber decision. However, in denying the application back in 2015, the Appeals Chamber missed out on an important opportunity. It failed to refer the matter back to the Pre-Trial Chamber, nor did it require the Prosecutor to report back after a specified period, nor institute any further monitoring or oversight process to give the Court the opportunity to decide on the evolving status of the matter based on anything other than the Prosecutor's assertion that the investigation could theoretically be reinstituted. Consequently, that Appeals Chamber decision ultimately foreclosed an avenue to provide oversight of prosecutorial discretion and a potential opportunity for victim participation was lost.

A similar challenge arose in the *Lubanga case*. The then Prosecutor had indicated that, despite the narrow indictment relating to the recruitment and enlistment of child soldiers, he was continuing to investigate other potential crimes.[35] However, in June 2006, the Pre-Trial Chamber was informed that the Prosecutor had suspended investigations into other crimes because of security concerns.[36] Despite the significant passage of time since this filing, no new charges were subsequently brought to the attention of the Pre-Trial Chamber, and there is no indication of ongoing investigations.[37]

A further and related issue concerns how successive Chambers have assessed victims' 'personal interests'.[38] For the purpose of victims' participation in any given case, it is necessary that a link between the events described by the victim applicants and the case brought by the Prosecutor against the

34 Decision on the 'Victims' request for review of Prosecution's decision to cease active investigation', *Situation in the Republic of Kenya*, ICC-01/09-159, PTC II, ICC, 5 November 2015, para. 14.

35 Prosecutor's Information on Further Investigation, *Lubanga, Situation in the Democratic Republic of the Congo*, ICC-01/04-01/06–170, OTP, ICC, 28 June 2006, para. 2.

36 Ibid., paras 7, 9, 10.

37 Discussed in C Ferstman 'Limited Charges and Limited Judgments by the International Criminal Court—Who Bears the Greatest Responsibility?' (2012) 16(5) *International Journal of Human Rights* 796.

38 Article 68(3) ICC Statute.

suspect is established.[39] In other words, victims whose victimisation is outside the charges the Prosecutor is seeking to confirm cannot participate in confirmation of charges hearings or other proceedings where the scope of the charges is being discussed.[40] This is the case even though it is such victims that will have the greatest interest in expressing their views and concerns about what they might see as a premature closure of an investigation or particular line of inquiry. Indeed, no submissions which pertain to matters outside of the scope of the charges have been entertained in relation to confirmation of charges or related proceedings.[41]

These various challenges have to do with Chambers' interpretations of statutory provisions in ways that privilege prosecutorial discretion, and at least in the instances highlighted, ignore victims' legitimate interests and the role of the Court to provide a modicum of oversight. In more recent cases Chambers have determined that 'article 68(3) of the Statute and the relevant Rules may and should be at times construed as vesting in a chamber a certain margin of discretion in determining whether, and in what modalities, victims may appropriately be allowed to play a role at certain stages of the proceedings (including before or during the investigation stage), despite the absence of an explicit provision to this effect.'[42] Giving greater space to victims even when the issues they seek to raise involve issues squarely within the remit of the Prosecutor does not reduce prosecutorial discretion, it simply increases the accountability for the exercise of such discretion.

The following steps are recommended:

---

39 Decision on Victims' Participation at the Confirmation of Charges Hearing and in the Related Proceedings, *Ntaganda, Situation in the Democratic Republic of the Congo*, ICC-01/04-02/06-211, PTC II, ICC, 15 January 2014, para. 25.

40 See, e.g. ibid., paras 24–25, 27, 53–54; Decision on the Applications for Participation in the Proceedings of Applicants a/0327/07 to a/0337/07 and a/0001/08, *Katanga, Situation in the Democratic Republic of the Congo*, ICC-01/04-01/07-357, PTC I, ICC, 2 April 2008; Decision on the Applications for Participation in the Proceedings of a/0001/06, a/0002/06 and a/0003/06 in the case of the Prosecutor v Thomas Lubanga Dyilo and the investigation in the Democratic Republic of the Congo, *Lubanga, Situation in the Democratic Republic of the Congo*, ICC-01/04-01/06-228-tEN, PTC I, ICC, 28 July 2006.

41 See, e.g., Decision on Request Pursuant to Rule 103(1) of the Statute, *Lubanga, Situation in the Democratic Republic of the Congo*, ICC-01/04-01/06-480, PTC I, ICC, 26 September 2006.

42 *Afghanistan*, Decision on submissions received and order to the Registry regarding the filing of documents in the proceedings pursuant to articles 18(2) and 68(3) of the Statute (n 31) para. 12, referring to decisions pertaining to the Situation in the State of Palestine; the Situation in the People's Republic of Bangladesh/Republic of the Union of Myanmar; the Situation in the Republic of Kenya; Prosecutor v. Joseph Kony, Vincent Otti, Okot Odhiambo and Dominic Ongwen; Situation in the Republic Democratic of the Congo.

i) Ensure a modicum of legal representation for victims during these early phases. Given the lack of general standing to participate in these phases, funds for outside legal assistance have typically not been made available, which is unfortunate. This limits the options for victims at a time when their interests are certainly engaged and they have the greatest need for counsel. This recommendation aligns with the findings of the Final Report of the Independent Expert Review of the International Criminal Court and the Rome Statute System.[43]

ii) Create more space for judges to hear from victims, formally. In many of the instances cited, victims' legal representatives have sought to identify creative ways to engage the competent Chambers with legitimate concerns, only to be shut down on formal grounds. Chambers should use their *proprio motu* powers more liberally to hear from victims in the interests of justice, even if the Statute and rules of procedure and evidence provide no direct route.

iii) More proactive engagement by competent Chambers on issues pertaining to prosecutorial discretion. While ultimately it will be for the Prosecutor to decide matters within his discretion, it is for the competent Chambers to ensure that cases that arrive before it (and sometimes those that do not) reflect an appropriate exercise of discretion. In respect of the examples cited, whether an investigation or prosecution has been definitively closed should be a decision the Chambers makes on the basis of its factual assessment of the steps actually taken over time, irrespective of the Prosecutor's assertions. In a somewhat analogous set of proceedings, the Central African Republic argued that the Prosecutor's failure to progress the preliminary examination of the situation without undue delay amounted to an implicit decision not to proceed. The Pre-Trial Chamber never addressed this contention in its ruling, and indeed with some further delay, the Prosecutor eventually did proceed with a full-fledged investigation in that situation.[44] However, the Pre-Trial Chamber underscored what it understood to be the Prosecutor's obligation to proceed with timely preliminary examinations, regardless of their complexity.[45] Arguably this same reasoning could apply to the need for the Prosecutor to carry out timely formal investigations. The

43 IER Report (n 17) paras 868–869.

44 OTP, 'Prosecutor Opens Investigation in the Central African Republic' (22 May 2007).

45 Decision Requesting Information on the Status of the Preliminary Examination of the Situation in the Central African Republic, *Situation in the Central African Republic*, ICC-01/05-6, PTC III, ICC, 30 November 2006, 4.

Pre-trial Chamber can only review on its own motion the Prosecutor's exercise of discretion not to proceed when a decision not to proceed is taken solely on the basis of Article 53, paragraph 1(c) or 2(c). Beyond this, it is only when the Prosecutor's initial examination was triggered by a State or Security Council referral, and those parties seek a review of the Prosecutor's exercise of discretion not to proceed, that the Pre-Trial Chamber will be able to embark on a review. Nevertheless, the competent Chamber can as appropriate, determine on the basis of all the evidence before it (as opposed to simply relying on the assertions of the Prosecutor) the basis upon which a decision not to proceed was taken. This may provide more scope for oversight of prosecutorial discretion.

### 4.2 *Finding Additional Ways for Victims to Contribute Views and Concerns*

It is important for the Court to find more effective ways for victims to contribute views and concerns than only, or mainly, through common legal representatives expressing legal arguments in The Hague. Important as the system of common legal representation is, complementing it with more intensive, field-based two-way engagements between victims and judges and other court officials would make victim participation more tangible for many, and modern technology makes this possible.

The Independent Panel of experts report on victim participation at the International Criminal Court stressed that the victim participation process "should offer victims an opportunity to share their experiences in a manner that is meaningful to them".[46] According to the Berkeley study of 622 victim participants, few of the victims they interviewed said that they wanted to participate in person in trials at The Hague, and some felt that such exposure could lead to reprisals.[47] However, some respondents expressed frustration at the lack of feedback from the court during the application process which undermined trust, and insufficient opportunities to speak with legal representatives. Ugandan respondents questioned:

What are victims' representatives telling the judges? Are they telling them what's on their mind or what's on my mind? I know the lawyers can speak about the legal issues, but these legal issues should be framed by local understandings. If the court staff really listens, they will understand our perspectives

46 Independent Panel of experts report on victim participation at the International Criminal Court (July 2013), para. 55.

47 Koenig et al. (n 23) 3.

and can translate them into legal language for the court. But no one is coming to speak with me anymore. It's very hard.[48]

Respondents from the Democratic Republic of the Congo expressed concern that 'a lack of ICC feedback compounded by the slowness of the prosecutorial process caused many victims to doubt their voices had reached The Hague.'[49]

Victims' sense of victim participation does not comprise a divisible marker separate from how they understand access to information, outreach, engagement, reparations and assistance or legal representation in The Hague. There is a natural synergy between these concepts, and they tend to blur, especially since victims' needs are complex and largely unmet for multiple, intersecting reasons. Unmet expectations about the justice process and lack of access to reparations or assistance undermine trust and fuel concerns about the utility of victim participation, according to DRC respondents to the Berkeley study.[50] Lack of results with the progress of investigations and prosecutions have also fuelled concerns amongst Libyan victims: 'Victims are reluctant to be in contact with the ICC because they lack trust in the institution, lack clarity about protection measures in addition to the fact that cases take too much time and still remain unsolved.'[51]

The experience of large-scale transitional justice processes which require outreach to and engagement with victims' communities, such as truth commissions, domestic reparations programmes and claims commissions may offer some lessons about how to engage victims successfully and safely in justice processes in a way that is meaningful and effective to them. These engagements can be important and empowering to victims in and of themselves; they are also important in their ability to foster other justice outcomes, such as effective investigations, prosecutions, reparations and assistance. As Correa, Guillerot and Magarrell have noted,

> Participation that is respectful, knowledgeable, and transparent, and achieved through effective forms of representation, allows victims to feel that they are valued and recognised as rights-holders under the law and as relevant actors in their society. This is particularly important for groups of persons who were victims of violence due to their political

48 Ibid., 33.
49 Ibid., 43.
50 Ibid., 44–46.
51 Lawyers for Justice in Libya, 'Victims' Voices: Participation At The International Criminal Court' (January 2022), 8.

> stance and who demand recognition as political actors, but it is also true for those who were victims because they belonged to populations that were marginalised, discriminated against or made effectively invisible by society. In this way, participation serves not only to add value to measures of restitution, rehabilitation, or compensation, but also as a good in itself by opening the space for debate about how to ensure greater inclusion for victims both socially and politically.[52]

Working with victims' groups or other local interlocutors is usually invaluable to maximise victim participation, though how successful this will be will depend on the extent to which relationships and engagements are built on mutual understanding and trust.

Technological advances in electronic communications and specialist documentation applications[53] have been used in a variety of countries particularly during the COVID pandemic to enable investigations and court proceedings to continue despite national lockdowns. These measures include: recording of telephone or video call statements for victims/survivors; measures to take photographs that can be used as evidence in case of complaints made in police units; virtual working meetings with investigators in order to define priority lines of investigation, identify problems and solutions.[54] While such measures are not without their difficulties and will not be feasible for all situation countries, they are worth exploring and may be usefully adapted to the particular context of the ICC and some situation countries. Making greater use of technology to complement in-person engagements to enable victims to 'e-meet' with legal representatives and/or court officials in local safe hubs, or to address

52 C Correa, J Guillerot and L Magarrell, 'Reparations and Victim Participation: Experiences with the Design and Implementation of Domestic Reparations Programmes', in Ferstman and Goetz (eds) (n 5) 242.

53 E.g., 'MediCapt application, developed to help document sexual violence' (*Physicians for Human Rights*) <https://phr.org/issues/sexual-violence/medicapt-innovation-2/> accessed 30 April 2023.

54 Commission on Crime Prevention and Criminal Justice, 'The impact of COVID-19 on criminal justice system responses to gender-based violence against women: a global review of emerging evidence' UN Doc E/CN.15/2021/CRP.2 (28 April 2021); European Commission, Directorate-General for Justice and Consumers, *Study on the use of innovative technologies in the justice field: final report* (Publications Office, 2020) <https://data.europa.eu/doi/10.2838/585101> accessed 30 April 2023; HiiL, 'Use of digital technologies in judicial reform and access to justice cooperation' (2021) <https://www.hiil.org/wp-content/uploads/2021/11/HiiL-Use-of-digital-technologies-in-judicial-reform-and-access-to-justice-cooperation.pdf> accessed 30 April 2023.

judges through mobile phone or video technology might enhance victims' sense of empowerment through the process.[55]

There is increasing evidence of good practice associated with the use of mobile courts to deliver justice in countries and regions where justice is most elusive, including ICC situation countries. Such methods, possibly in combination with technological options should be scrutinised by the ICC to determine whether any lessons can be learned to bring ICC proceedings closer to victims and affected communities. We are only limited by our limited creativity.

### 4.3 *Reparations*

As is known, the ICC has struggled to deliver reparations that are meaningful, timely or effective. The Independent Expert Review of the International Criminal Court and the Rome Statute System indicated that

> the Court's conceptual and procedural processes for reparations are laden with complexity and uncertainty, which gravely affects the victims' rights to meaningful participation and reparations. The implementation plans and execution of reparations projects have taken and are taking an extensive time to develop, commission and realise. Overall, profound delays exhibit the whole process. Victims, it was asserted to the Experts, wait a lifetime.[56]

The Review has been particularly biting in its assessment of the Trust Fund for Victims' capacity for timely engagement: 'the TFV is neither equipped to trace and locate victims nor to act expeditiously at a stage in a case where there is a need for urgent action to avoid the unnecessary passage of further time before the justice process is completed.'[57]

Reparations, which may include, as appropriate, measures of restitution, compensation, rehabilitation, satisfaction and guarantees of non-repetition, should be proportional to the gravity of the violations and the harm suffered; they should be adequate, effective, and prompt.[58] The ability of the Court to

---

55 UNDP, 'Evaluation of UNDP's Support to Mobile Courts in DRC, Sierra Leone and Somalia' (24 July 2017); A Ferreira, S Loeckx 'Evaluation of the projects: "Enhancing and Protecting the Civic Space" and "Strengthening the Senior Women Protection Advisor: Preventing and Responding to Conflict-Related Sexual Violence in the Democratic Republic of Congo": Evaluation Report', OHCHR (May 2022).

56 IER Report (n 17) para. 879.

57 Ibid., paras 868-869.

58 UNGA, 'Basic Principles and Guidelines on the Right to a Remedy and Reparation for Victims of Gross Violations of International Human Rights Law and Serious Violations

afford reparations is set out in Article 75 of the ICC Statute and trial chambers have regularly ordered reparations following the conviction of perpetrators. The ICC faces some inevitable challenges to afford meaningful and effective reparations. Many of these challenges are structural and are connected to the ICC's limited mandate focused on individual responsibility; that reparations follow what are usually narrowly framed prosecutions and consequently the universe of victims who are eligible for reparations is much narrower than what victims in situation countries would expect; and the often impecunious perpetrators and the limited resources at the disposal of the Trust Fund for Victims.[59] While in its decisions on reparations, various chambers have drawn in a general sense on human rights principles and state practices related to reparations to victims,[60] the reparations orders have more tightly reflected the *sui generis* nature of the Court and have sought, often with great difficulty, to balance the significant needs of victims, with the limited resources and the difficult operating environments in many situation countries to deliver practically reparations to victims.[61]

The starting point with reparations is to centre victims' agency and empowerment, both with assistance projects and court-ordered reparations. This is fundamental, especially where the nature and scale of the crimes makes full reparations impossible. Recognising victims' role in coming up with solutions on what would be most meaningful, and most helpful is in and of itself reparative as it recognises voice, dignity and contributes to empowerment. And, there is a need to recognise that not all victims will be the same, have the same needs or aspirations-large numbers gives no license to ignore this reality. Too often, the ICC has taken a charitable approach with respect to reparations; instead, it should focus on measures which maximise victims' agency and empowerment.

---

of International Humanitarian Law' UN Doc A/RES/60/147 (16 December 2005), paras 11, 15, 18–23.

59 These challenges have been described at length in a variety of academic and policy papers, including the following recent examples: L Moffett and C Sandoval, 'Tilting at Windmills: Reparations and the International Criminal Court' (2021) 34(3) *Leiden Journal of International Law* 749; Ferstman, 'Reparations at the ICC: The Need for a Human Rights Based Approach to Effectiveness' (n 11) 446; O Owiso, 'The International Criminal Court and Reparations: Judicial Innovation or Judicialisation of a Political Process?' (2019) 19(3) *International Criminal Law Review* 505; REDRESS, "No Time to Wait: Realising Reparations for Victims before the International Criminal Court" (2019).

60 See, e.g., Order for Reparations, *Lubanga, Situation in the Democratic Republic of the Congo*, ICC-01/04-01/06-3129-AnxA, AC, ICC, 3 March 2015, Part A: Principles on Reparations.

61 E.g., ibid., Part B: Order for Reparations against Mr Lubanga.

In addition, there is a need to improve timeliness. The time it takes to reach the reparations phase is already inordinate; the reparation phase itself should aim for much greater efficiency in achieving reparative outcomes. A part of the problem appears to be the lack of common purpose between the competent Chambers issuing the reparations order and the Trust Fund for Victims, with the Chambers ordering (as it is mandated to do) the Trust Fund to implement reparations in a particular way, and the Trust Fund or other parties considering that for various operational reasons it is not possible to implement the awards in the way in which the Court envisioned. This has resulted in several cases in a lengthy back-and-forth which has contributed to delays.[62] Furthermore, all of the reparations orders issued to date have resulted in lengthy appeals, with Appeals Chambers referring the matter back to the Trial Chambers with a view to issuing a new reparations order.[63] In the *Ntaganda case*, which concerned events which occurred in 2002–2003, the accused was convicted in 2019 and the Trial Chamber issued its order on reparations in 2021.[64] In September 2022, the Appeals Chamber reversed the findings of the Trial Chamber and remanded the relevant matters it took issue with, which were substantial, back to the Trial Chamber to issue a new reparations order.[65] The lack of common vision on reparations between the Court and the Trust Fund and amongst the ICC judiciary is contributing to delays.

There is also a need to get much better at identifying, seizing and preserving the assets of potential perpetrators for the eventual purpose of reparations.[66]

62 These and related challenges are explored in: Ferstman, 'Reparations at the ICC: The Need for a Human Rights Based Approach to Effectiveness' (n 11) 446.

63 In the *Al Mahdi* case, the Appeals Chamber mainly affirmed the Trial Chambers' reparations order, but in other cases which resulted in reparations, the respective Appeals Chambers referred the matter back to Trial Chambers with more extensive requests for changes. Judgment on the appeal of the victims against the 'Reparations Order', *Al Mahdi, Situation in the Republic of Mali*, ICC-01/12-01/15-259-Red2, AC, ICC, 8 March 2018.

64 *Ntaganda* Reparations Order (n 22).

65 Judgment on the appeal against the decision of Trial Chamber VI of 8 March 2021 entitled 'Reparations Order', *Ntaganda, Situation in the Democratic Republic of the Congo*, ICC-01/04-02/06-2782, TC VI, ICC, 12 September 2022; See also, Order for the implementation of the Judgment on the appeals against the decision of Trial Chamber VI of 8 March 2021 entitled 'Reparations Order', *Ntaganda, Situation in the Democratic Republic of the Congo*, ICC-01/04-02/06-2786, TC II, ICC, 25 October 2022.

66 C Ferstman, 'Cooperation and the International Criminal Court: The Freezing, Seizing and Transfer of Assets for the Purpose of Reparations', in C Ferstman, *Cooperation and the International Criminal Court* (Brill Nijhoff 2016).

While not all perpetrators will have assets, certainly some will, as can already be seen by some of the cases that have come before the Court.[67]

## 5 Conclusion

If all of this is done, will it be possible to say that the ICC is succeeding in providing justice to victims? Perhaps we will indeed be getting closer, but we should bring the victims much more closely into that debate. They will not always say what it is we may want to hear or use the words we might ourselves choose to use, but this is precisely the reason why engaging them is not only important it is crucial—we should not be aiming for an echo chamber to validate the approaches or policies the Court already has in place. The 'we' needs to shift in order to encompass victims. It is us who must change for that to happen.

67 Daley J Birkett, 'Managing Frozen Assets at the International Criminal Court: The Fallout of the *Bemba* Acquittal' (2020) 18(3) *Journal of International Criminal Justice* 765.

# PART 7

## *Looking to the Future*

CHAPTER 23

# The Evolving System of International Criminal Justice

*Muriel Ubéda-Saillard*

## 1 Introduction

Can we predict how the international criminal justice system will evolve? The first instinct of a seasoned observer of international relations would be to doubt it. Since the beginning of the twenty-first century, the world has witnessed a succession of humanitarian, economic, security, health, and environmental crises, which have seriously undermined multilateralism. Confidence in international organizations has been eroded and it is increasingly difficult for them to effectively guarantee the protection of the values and goods common to all humanity—especially as they themselves are partly called into question.

International criminal courts are not immune to nihilistic criticism of their legitimacy. Their detractors invoke, among other reasons: the selectivity of the situations dealt with and the politicization of these courts; the risk of increased destabilization of the state and the peace/justice dilemma; the *de facto* but nonetheless constant impunity of the powerful—whether legitimate or not; or even more broadly the necessary end of legal universalism seen as an instrument of neo-colonialism and the westernization of the world; not to mention the doubts harboured by like-minded states as to the financial cost and relative effectiveness of these courts. These recurring criticisms must be taken seriously because, in order to imagine an evolution of the international criminal justice system that would fight more effectively against impunity, it is necessary to give meaning to its very existence by returning to its *raison d'être* and the causes that legitimately motivated its construction.

The international criminal justice system was born of two convictions of the international community in the face of the unprecedented atrocities committed in the twentieth century: peace had to be established as the 'supreme legal asset'[1] of the international order; and criminal law could contribute to

1 V V Pella, 'La justice pénale internationale' (1945) 23 *Revue de Droit international, de sciences diplomatiques et politiques* 88, 88 ('bien juridique suprême').

 | DOI:10.1163/9789004529939_024

protecting it, as it had done in national orders thanks to the dissuasive, expressive, and restorative values of punishment.[2] The creation of international criminal courts and tribunals by the victorious states of the Second World War, then by the United Nations Security Council, and finally by the broad treaty community of States Parties to the Rome Statute, made it possible to punish crimes that harmed the whole of *societas generis humani* and undermined peaceful coexistence as a whole.

That said, it was clear from the outset that international criminal courts would not be able to judge all individual criminal responsibilities. This is why the rise of universal jurisdiction from the 1990s onwards and the creation of hybrid courts in situation states have been beneficial to the fight against impunity, while allowing national judges to become important actors. However, all these national, hybrid, or international courts have had to face the difficulties inherent in the exercise of their judicial role in an international context. How to establish the materiality of facts in complex situations of mass crimes? How to collect the necessary evidence or arrest suspects in the absence of enforcement powers? In order to avoid these pitfalls, the cooperation of other institutions has been necessary. Today the international criminal justice system can therefore be considered to be composed, in addition to its judicial component, of: international commissions of enquiry, joint investigation teams, and joint structural investigation mechanisms, such as those operating in Syria,[3] Iraq,[4]

---

2 See the authors of the precursors' doctrine, e.g. A Sottile, 'Les criminels de guerre et le nouveau droit pénal international, seul moyen efficace pour assurer la paix du monde' (1945) 23 *Revue de Droit international, de sciences diplomatiques et politiques* 228 and V V Pella, 'Fonctions pacificatrices du droit pénal supranational et fin du système traditionnel des traités de paix' (1947) 51 *Revue Générale de droit International Public* 1 ; For a synthesis, F Mégret, 'International criminal justice as a peace project' (2108) *European Journal of International Law* 835.

3 The International, Impartial, and Independent Mechanism (IIIM), tasked with facilitating investigations into the most serious violations of international law committed in the Syrian Arab Republic since March 2011 and assisting in bringing to justice those responsible, was established by UN General Assembly (UNGA) 'International, Impartial and Independent Mechanism to Assist in the Investigation and Prosecution of Persons Responsible for the Most Serious Crimes under International Law Committed in the Syrian Arab Republic since March 2011' UN Doc A/RES/71/248 (21 December 2016). See its website <https://iiim.un.org> accessed 30 April 2023.

4 The UNITAD Investigative Team, tasked with collecting, preserving, and storing evidence of crimes of genocide, crimes against humanity, and war crimes committed in Iraq by the Islamic State, was established by UN Security Council (UNSC) Res 2379 (21 September 2017) UN Doc S/RES/2379. See its website <https://www.unitad.un.org> accessed 30 April 2023. For a general reflection, see e.g. Z D Kaufman, 'The Prospects, Problems and Proliferation of Recent UN Investigations of International Law Violations' (2018) 1 *Journal of International Criminal Justice* 93.

and Myanmar;[5] international or regional mechanisms for police and judicial cooperation in criminal matters, such as Interpol or Eurojust; actors in peace-keeping and reconstruction operations; and, more broadly, NGOs and other civil society actors involved in the observance of human rights. The construction of this global and composite institutional network is a process that is reconfiguring the conditions for the exercise of sovereignty in criminal matters.[6] To predict how this will evolve is to be aware of its prerequisites (2) and its drivers (3), and to imagine what directions it might take (4).

## 2 Prerequisites for the Evolution of the System of International Criminal Justice

The system of international criminal justice presupposes two things above all: a consensus on the defence of the founding prohibitions of the international community; and the granting of material resources commensurate with the ambitions pursued.

### 2.1 *Belief in a Community of Values*

Over the past seventy years, international criminal courts have fulfilled some of their promise. They have also shown their limitations. The disappointment has been so bitter because the hopes were so high, and these courts have been condemned without appeal because they failed to live up to the standards of exemplarity that they were set. Let us be clear-sighted: whatever they did, they could not meet all the expectations of the parties to the proceedings, the victims, the actors in the peaceful reconstruction of the region, and, more broadly, the international community—all in the context of an international order fragmented between sovereign states with potentially divergent economic and political interests.

In order not to give in to the ontological fatalism that plagues all human endeavours, which are by nature fallible, it is therefore necessary to be humble and to adopt an analytical grid adapted to the characteristics of both the international criminal justice system and the relations between the legal systems

5 An Independent Investigative Mechanism has been established by the UN Human Rights Council, see Situation of human rights of Rohingya Muslims and other minorities in Myanmar, Human Rights Council, Thirty-ninth session, UN Doc A/HRC/39/L.22 (25 September 2018).

6 M Ubéda-Saillard, 'Le lien entre souveraineté et droit de punir' in M Ubéda-Saillard (ed.), *La souveraineté pénale de l'Etat au XXIème siècle: colloque de Lille*, Société française pour le droit international (Paris: Pedone 2018) 19.

in which it is embedded. For example, measuring the effectiveness of the system in terms of its ability to restore social peace in a given region inevitably leads to a negative assessment, which is unjustified because the peace process, while it may be fostered by the criminal process, is in fact dependent on many other political and economic factors that are beyond the control of judges. The success of cooperation with the ICC—another example—should be assessed in relative rather than absolute terms: the failure to arrest one of the accused should not overshadow the handing over of all the others! In reality, the process of building the system of international criminal justice is part of the incremental approach (*'méthode des petits pas'*), which is at the heart of the construction of the European Union. Like any evolutionary process, it is unstable and that is why it should be anchored in respect for fundamental principles such as the independence of justice, the representation of all legal systems, impartiality and the fairness of procedures—with particular vigilance, from this point of view, for the condition of the Defence, which remains the 'poor relation' of international criminal courts and tribunals. The technical (i.e. legal, political, and financial) difficulties encountered by the various actors should not cause us to lose sight of the essential point: the international criminal justice system aims to defend the founding prohibitions of international society, which are based on a 'common conception of evil'[7] specific to humanity as a whole. Any failure to link peace and justice, and to place ethics at the heart of international relations, will seriously jeopardize the chances of sustainable development for human communities.[8]

### 2.2 *The Provision of the Necessary Means*

As we know from Cicero, *Pecunia est nervus belli:* money is the sinews of war. The fight against impunity will not be won without the provision of adequate and sustainable financial resources. In 2015, the Office of the Prosecutor stated that it needed a budget of €60 million to carry out six investigations; in 2022, it must carry out three times that number with a budget that is €10 million less than what it requested at the time.[9] The Defence, the Victims and Witnesses Unit, and the Trust Fund for Victims also need additional resources. From this point of view, the increase in the ICC's budget through exceptional voluntary

7 M Delmas-Marty, 'La paix, de quel droit ?' in F Barret-Ducrocq (ed.), *Imaginer la paix*, Académie universelle des cultures (Grasset 2003) 242.

8 Sustainable Development Goal 16, adopted by the United Nations, aims at securing 'peace, justice and effective institutions'.

9 See in particular Report of the Committee on Budget and Finance on the work of its thirty-seventh session, ICC-ASP/20/15, 8 November 2021 (Twentieth Session of the ASP), para. 59.

contributions, however commendable, is not a sustainable solution to the overall shortfall in the Court's regular budget and the cash flow crisis it is experiencing due to the existence of arrears from States Parties. Moreover, the earmarking of financial support to the Office of the Prosecutor to address certain situations inevitably reinforces the perception of selection bias in investigations and prosecutions,[10] especially when parliamentarians from third states hostile to the Rome Statute[11] encourage criminal prosecutions before the ICC.[12]

Since the economic and financial crisis of 2008, states have naturally sought to better control public spending at both international and national levels.[13] Budgetary orthodoxy is obviously virtuous when it leads to a rationalization of the functioning of international institutions and to the development of a culture focused on results,[14] as it is then synonymous with efficiency. Better transparency of the budgetary process strengthens the trust between states and the international organization, and therefore the legitimacy of the latter. These points were highlighted by the group of independent experts who audited the

10 See Coalition for the ICC, 'Victims could lose out with states' double-standard on International Criminal Court resources' (30 March 2022) <https://coalitionfortheicc.org/news/20220330/OpenLetter_ICCresources> accessed 30 April 2023.

11 On the relationship between the United States and the ICC, see J G Ralph, *Defending the Society of States: Why America Opposes the International Criminal Court and its Vision of World Society* (Oxford: Oxford University Press 2007) and J Fernandez, *La politique juridique extérieure des Etats-Unis à l'égard de la Cour pénale internationale* (Paris: Pedone 2010). Among the most significant elements of the US offensive against the Court are the adoption of the *American Servicemember's Protection Act* 2002 and the *Nethercutt Amendment* 2004, as well as the unilateral extraterritorial sanctions adopted by the US Department of State under President Donald Trump against Prosecutor Fatou Bensouda and the Head of the Jurisdiction, Complementarity and Cooperation Division, Phakiso Mochochoko, due to the opening by the Office of the Prosecutor of an investigation concerning the situation in Afghanistan and potentially involving members of the US armed forces and the CIA; see Executive Order on Blocking Property of Certain Persons Associated with the International Criminal Court, 11 June 2020.

12 See USA, S.Res.531—117th Congress (2021–2022) expressing the sense of the Senate condemning the Russian Federation, President Vladimir Putin, members of the Russian Security Council, the Russian Armed Forces, and Russian military commanders for committing flagrant acts of aggression and other atrocities rising to the level of crimes against humanity and war crimes against the people of Ukraine and others <https://www.congress.gov/bill/117th-congress/senate-resolution/531/text> accessed 30 April 2023.

13 On the criticism of the ICC's 2017 programme budget, see e.g. L Danguy des Déserts, 'La 15ème session de l'Assemblée des États parties, La Haye, 16–24 novembre 2016' (2018) 16 *Droits fondamentaux*, 4.

14 Shifting the Management Paradigm in the United Nations: Implementing a New Management Architecture for Improved Effectiveness and Strengthened Accountability, Report of the Secretary-General, UN Doc A/72/492/Add.2 (21 March 2018), para. 15.

ICC in 2020.[15] That said, the Court's efforts to make optimal use of its resources will not exempt states from a more general reflection on the role of justice in society, its place in public policy, and the corresponding financial means that it should be granted.[16] The ICC is not the only court that requires sufficient financial resources. National units specialized in the exercise of extraterritorial or universal jurisdiction, such as the French *Pôle des crimes contre l'humanité* or the German Central Unit for the Fight against War Crimes and further Offences pursuant to the Code of Crimes against International Law (ZBKV), also need additional resources to carry out their ambitious mission. Any creation of a new specialized body—for example, a permanent international investigation mechanism[17]—will inevitably result in significant expenditure. In other words, the system of international criminal justice has an unavoidable fixed cost that requires political trade-offs on the part of states, in the context of the current constrained economic situation.

## 3 The Drivers for the Evolution of the System of International Criminal Justice

The first driver for the evolution of the international criminal justice system is imagination. We must dare to project ourselves into the realm of *lex ferenda* and invent new procedures and mechanisms that will allow the system to be more efficient and to come closer to the ideal of justice that it embodies. The dream should not, however, be confined to utopia. Rather, it is a matter of identifying in positive law the basis for a dynamic of evolution that can be achieved *in concreto*. In addition to this positive driving force, there must be engine braking, mechanically generated by the system, so to speak, in order to preserve its integrity and prevent it from going astray. Each actor in the system should

15 Independent Expert Review of the International Criminal Court and the Rome Statute System: Final Report—30 September 2020, ICC-ASP/19/16, 9 November 2020 (Nineteenth Session of the ASP), paras. 303ff.

16 The conclusions of the general audit of the French judicial system conducted in 2021–2022 are enlightening from this point of view, Rapport du Comité des Etats généraux de la justice 'Rendre justice aux citoyens' (2021–2022), especially at 100 <https://www.vie-publique.fr/sites/default/files/rapport/pdf/285620.pdf> accessed 30 April 2023.

17 See the proposal by the International Commission of Jurists, 'Options for the Establishment of a Standing Independent Investigative Mechanism (SIIM)' (September 2022) <https://www.icj.org/wp-content/uploads/2022/09/Options-for-the-establishment-of-a-Standing-Independent-Investigative-Mechanism-SIIM-26-September-2022-1.pdf> accessed 30 April 2023.

observe with vigilance and lucidity the pragmatic arrangements with which they are inevitably confronted, due to the power relations and *realpolitik* in which their action is embedded. Faustian pacts inevitably weaken legitimacy.

### 3.1 *Mobilizing the Imagination*

In view of the current challenges facing the international criminal justice system, the imagination could be deployed in three areas of reflection: the identification of responsibilities; the trial of the accused; and the effective reparation provided to victims.

In the first place, with regard to the determination of persons suspected of being responsible for crimes under international law, only individuals are currently liable to be prosecuted in the international order, in accordance with the famous dictum of the Nuremberg judgment—‘Crimes against International Law are committed by men, not by abstract entities, and only by punishing individuals who commit such crimes can the provisions of International Law be enforced’.[18] The principle of individual criminal responsibility has so far not been derogated from in the statutes of international or hybrid criminal courts and is enshrined in Article 25(1) of the Rome Statute. However, multinational companies, as key players in international relations, are quite likely to commit international crimes, particularly because of their complicity with the governments of ‘rogue states’ or criminal organizations. This has been demonstrated in a number of cases before national courts, which are empowered under their domestic law to bring criminal charges against companies,[19] as well as in the reports of the Truth and Reconciliation Commissions in South

---

18 *Judgment of the Nuremberg International Military Tribunal 1946* (1947) 41 AJIL 172, Part 22 447.

19 See for example C Stahn, ‘Liberals vs. Romantics: Challenges of an Emerging Corporate International Criminal Law’ (2018) 50(1) *Case Western Reserve Journal of International Law* 91, and S Geeroms, ‘Corporate Criminal Liability: A Comparative Study’ (1996) 3 *Revenue Internationale de Droit Comapre* 533. Currently, the cases concerning the French group Lafarge are interesting. The Criminal Chamber of the French Court of Cassation recognized, in its three judgments of 7 September 2021, that the cement company could be prosecuted for complicity in crimes against humanity with terrorist groups, including the Islamic State, as a result of its activities in Syria. The text of the judgments is available online <https://www.dalloz-actualite.fr/sites/dalloz-actualite.fr/files/resources/2021/09/19-87031.pdf>, <https://www.dalloz-actualite.fr/sites/dalloz-actualite.fr/files/resources/2021/09/197-87036.pdf>, <https://www.dalloz-actualite.fr/sites/dalloz-actualite.fr/files/resources/2021/09/19-87367.pdf>. In addition, the company accepted the sanctions imposed on it by the US Department of Justice <https://www.justice.gov/opa/speech/assistant-attorney-general-national-security-matthew-g-olsen-delivers-remarks-lafarge>. All accessed 30 April 2023.

Africa and Liberia for example.[20] International law is not intended to govern all conduct of domestic legal subjects, but, like any legal system, it must allow for accountability in the exercise of power, especially if it aims to promote 'a democratic and equitable order'.[21] The voluntary commitment of companies to abide by certain fundamental principles of international law, through the Global Compact,[22] is undeniably a step forward but has the inherent limitations of self-regulation.[23] Moreover, national lawsuits are not a panacea, due to the failure of domestic laws or the 'judicial restraint' practised by the courts.[24]

---

20 'Truth and Reconciliation Commission of South Africa Report' (1998) 4, at 31, 35, and 49. The report is available online <http://www.justice.gov.za/trc/report/finalreport/Volume%204.pdf> accessed 30 April 2023. See also 'Republic of Liberia, Truth and Reconciliation Commission, Volume 3, Appendices, Title III: Economic Crimes and the Conflict, Exploitation and Abuse' (30 June 2009) available online: <http://trcofliberia.org/resources/reports/final/volume-three-3_layout-1.pdf> accessed 30 April 2023. For doctrinal analyses, W A Schabas and S Darcy (eds), *Truth Commissions and Courts, The Tension between Criminal Justice and the Search for Truth* (Kluwer Academic Publishers 2004) and more specifically L A Payne, G Pereira, and L Bernal-Bermúdez, *Transitional Justice and Corporate Accountability from Below: Deploying Archimedes Lever* (Cambridge University Press 2020).

21 Promotion of a democratic and equitable order, Note by the Secretary-General, UN Doc A/74/245 (29 July 2019).

22 Launched in 2000 at the initiative of UNSG Kofi Annan, this pact is based on ten fundamental principles drawn from human rights, labour, the environment, and the fight against corruption. Today it brings together more than 12,000 companies from 160 countries; for more information, see the online site <https://www.unglobalcompact.org/> accessed 30 April 2023. For an analysis, see e.g. H Ascensio, 'Le Pacte Mondial et l'apparition d'une responsabilité internationale des entreprises' in L Boisson de Chazournes and E Mazuyer, *Le Pacte mondial 10 ans après* (Bruylant 2011) 167–84. See also OECD, 'Guidelines for Multinational Enterprises', available on <https://www.oecd.org/investment/mne/> accessed 30 April 2023, and Report of the Special Representative of the Secretary-General on the issue of human rights and transnational corporations and other business enterprises, J Ruggie, 'Guiding Principles on Business and Human Rights: Implementing the United Nations "Protect, Respect and Remedy" Framework', Human Rights Council, Seventeenth Session, UN Doc A/HRC/17/31 (21 March 2011).

23 In this sense, see Resolution adopted by the Human Rights Council '26/9 Elaboration of an international legally binding instrument on transnational corporations and other business enterprises with respect to human rights', Human Rights Council, Twenty-sixth Session, UN Doc A/HRC/RES/26/9 (14 July 2014); also see Report on the seventh session of the open-ended intergovernmental working group on transnational corporations and other business enterprises with respect to human rights, Human Rights Council, Forty-ninth Session, UN Doc A/HRC/49/65 (29 December 2021).

24 One may recall the US Supreme Court's decision in *Kiobel v Royal Dutch Petroleum Co*, to stop the extraterritorial civil jurisdiction of US courts. *Royal Dutch Petroleum Co*, 569 US No 10-1491 S Ct (2013), Opinion of the Court, at 1–2.

Existing international trials of company directors and employees[25] have not yet grasped the full chain of responsibility in its collective dimension. At a time, where management is 'de-humanized' and entrusted to artificial intelligence,[26] the empirical validity of standards should be more in line with the reality they are supposed to govern, guaranteeing the protection of employees but also, and above all, of the populations. Various current developments relating to the consecration of corporate social responsibility bear witness to this awareness.[27] It is therefore difficult to see what could still justify the asymmetry of the criminal status of companies, depending on whether it is considered in national or international law. The possibility of international criminal liability of legal persons, which was originally envisaged by the preparatory work for the Rome Statute,[28] should be seriously debated again.

Secondly, with regard to the capacity of international courts to effectively try the accused, the arrest of suspects is obviously the 'Gordian knot' of the system

25 The responsibility of A Krupp, F Flick, and members of the chemical group I.G. Farben (producer of Zyklon B gas) was the subject of three of the twelve trials held under Control Law No. 10 promulgated in December 1945 by the Allied Control Committee for Germany, see e.g. R K Woetzel, *The Nuremberg Trials in International Law* (Stevens & Sons Limited and Frederick A Praeger, Inc. 1960) and A Reggio, 'Aiding and Abetting in International Criminal Law: The Responsibility of Corporate Agents and Businessmen for "Trading With the Enemy" of Mankind' (2005) 5 *International Criminal Law Review* 623. Concerning Judgment (reasons), *Kayishema et al.*, ICTR-95-1-A, AC, ICTR, 1 June 2001, and Judgment, *Nahimana et al.*, ICTR-99-52-A, AC, ICTR, 28 November 2007.

26 In September 2022, the Chinese company NetDragon websoft named a humanoid robot CEO, 'Ms Tang Yu'; 'AI-powered humanoid robot named CEO of Chinese company in world first', *TimesNow* (7 September 2022) <https://www.timesnownews.com/viral/ai-powered-humanoid-robot-tang-yu-named-ceo-of-chinese-gaming-company-netdragon-websoft-in-world-first-article-94045663> accessed 30 April 2023.

27 See F J Zamora Cabot, L Heckendorn Urscheler, and S De Dycker (eds), *Implementing the U.N. Guiding Principles on Business and Human Rights: Private International Law Perspectives* (Schulthess 2017); C Kessedjian and H Cantú Rivera (eds) *Private International Law Aspects of Corporate Social Responsibility* (Springer 2020).

28 The 1996 Report of the Preparatory Committee expressly referred to such a hypothesis: 'The Court shall be competent to take cognizance of the criminal responsibility of: b) Juridical persons, with the exception of States, when the crimes committed were committed on behalf of such juridical persons or by their agencies or representatives'. Report of the Preparatory Committee on the Establishment of an International Criminal Court, Volume 2 (Compilation of proposals), UNGA, Supplement No. 22A (A/51/22), UN Doc A/51/22 (13 September 1996), 3rd part bis, article B, proposal 2, para. 1, subpara. b, 81. On the eve of the Rome Conference, there were still deep differences between national delegations on this possibility, Report of the Preparatory Committee on the Establishment of an International Criminal Court, Addendum, UN Doc A/CONF.183/2/Add.1 (14 April 1998), 49, fn 3.

of international criminal justice as a whole because, unless it is resolved, the ICC cannot move forward. It highlights the great weakness of the legal and political status of international or hybrid criminal courts, which are paralysed if the accused are not handed over to them. It also gives rise to the temptation to limit prosecutions to intermediate officials, who are easier to apprehend. This drift is obviously dangerous, independently of the principle of discretionary prosecution, because it distances international courts from their *raison d'être*, which is to prosecute the main perpetrators of the crimes committed; those who are supposed to protect their population and yet trample on their social pact; those whom national jurisdictions cannot judge, precisely because of the protection offered by immunities of jurisdiction and execution; those who seem impossible to apprehend—such as those responsible for the current aggression in Ukraine, and who, even if arrested through a change of political regime, would not be systematically transferred to the Court, as the case of former Sudanese President Omar al-Bashir shows.

Two avenues can be explored to address this critical difficulty. The first is to define more effective mechanisms for the execution of arrest warrants for alleged perpetrators of crimes under international law. The choice of the normative vector would obviously be crucial. The treaty route is probably not the most appropriate one for determining bold innovations, since securing a broad consensus generally presupposes a minimalist conception of the treaty provisions. This is probably one of the reasons why the provisions contained in the draft Convention on International Cooperation in the Investigation and Prosecution of the Crime of Genocide, Crimes Against Humanity and War Crimes are very inadequate with regard to the arrest of suspects, even though they are intended to be effective.[29] The decision-making power of the Security Council or at least the bilateral treaty route, which is more flexible and rooted in the traditional reciprocity of international relations, could be mobilized.

The second path leads to the question of failure to appear in court within the hybrid and autonomous international criminal procedure, and to consider the possibility of judging *in absentia* indicted senior officials who voluntarily evade

29 The Mutual Legal Assistance Initiative (MLAI) was launched in 2011 by the Netherlands, Belgium, and Slovenia. The aim is to propose an international treaty on cooperation in criminal matters based on the most modern and effective treaty provisions on mutual assistance and extradition. See the MLAI website <https://www.gov.si/en/registries/projects/mla-initiative/> accessed 30 April 2023. For a commentary, see e.g. A Ijzerman, 'The Initiative for a New Multilateral Treaty for Mutual Legal Assistance and Extradition for Domestic Prosecution of Crimes of Genocide, Crimes against Humanity and War Crimes' (2016–2017) 55(2) *Journal of Military Law and the Law of War* 275.

prosecution and do not want to appear before their judges.[30] Of course, this procedure is not without its drawbacks in terms of the effective defence of the rights of the accused, as witnessed by the trial *in absentia* of Martin Bormann before the Nuremberg Tribunal or the mixed record of the Special Tribunal for Lebanon. But is there really a big difference *in concreto* between the situation of a fugitive indictee and that of an indictee who refuses to appear in the courtroom?[31] How much of an *obligation* is there in the *right* of the accused to be present at trial, in accordance with Article 63 of the Rome Statute? Can the logic of Article 61 of the Statute and Rule 126 of the Rules of Procedure and Evidence, which allow for the confirmation of charges in the absence of the accused, not be taken further? Would the requirement of a *de novo* and *in praesentia* trial of the accused who voluntarily surrenders to justice, after conviction *in absentia*, not be a sufficient guarantee of the highest standards of fair trial? All these questions deserve to be asked again and analysed in the light of the difficulties encountered by international or hybrid criminal courts in fully exercising their judicial role. A conviction *in absentia* would ostracize the accused. A conviction would make it more difficult for the accused to travel and to be a credible and legitimate interlocutor in the exercise of any official international responsibilities. The criminal sanction would ultimately have the same effect as some of the multilateral or unilateral targeted sanctions and restrictive measures that are their equivalent in the EU context.[32] Such a conviction would also reinforce the victims' sense that justice has been done. It would symbolically reinforce the legitimacy of their existence and their distinctiveness, both of which have been flouted by the process of dehumanization, or at least coercion, put in place by the government overthrown.[33]

---

30 In this regard, see the article published in *Le Monde* by B Cotte et al., 'Comment juger les criminels de guerre en France alors la loi pose bien obstacles', 15 April 2022.

31 This was the case for Bosco Ntaganda, Uhuru Kenyatta, and William Ruto for different reasons. The latter had requested not to attend all the hearings because of their 'extraordinary public functions', which led to the adoption of the new Rule 134 quater of the ICC Rules of Procedure and Evidence; for a commentary, see J Fernandez, A-L Chaumette, and M Ubéda-Saillard, 'L'activité des juridictions pénales internationales' (2013) *Annuaire Français de Droit International* 359 and ibid. (2016) 543.

32 On this practice, see C Beaucillon (ed.), *Unilateral/Extraterritorial Sanctions* (Edward Elgar Publishing 2021); N Ronzitti (ed.), *Coercive Diplomacy, Sanctions and International Law* (Brill Nijhoff 2016).

33 This process of dehumanization is revealed in all its horror when reading the memoirs of Holocaust survivors, see e.g. P Levi, *Si c'est un homme* (Gallimard, coll. Pockett, 1988), C Delbo, *Auschwitz et après* (Ed. de minuit 1970, republished 2018), and M Loridan-Ivens, *Et tu n'es pas revenu* (Grasset 2015).

Finally, with regard to reparations to victims, the efforts currently being made to improve the functioning and efficiency of the system should be continued. This means speeding up the compensation procedures, so that those entitled do not have to wait too many years after the conviction of the accused to obtain compensation, as in the *Thomas Lubanga Dyilo* case,[34] or worse, in the *Hissène Habré* case.[35] It is also a question of refining the methods for assessing the number of victims and the harm suffered, in order to put a fair figure on them. The practice of the ICC and even that of the International Court of Justice testify to the great difficulties encountered in this case and the use of experts as an *a priori* ideal solution.[36] Without disputing the very principle, the intervention of experts in international proceedings raises questions about the remaining power of interpretation of judges[37] and more generally about the need to develop an international status for expertise, since it

34 Thomas Lubanga Dyilo was convicted on 14 March 2012 at first instance, and the verdict and sentence were confirmed on appeal on 1 December 2014. The dialogue between the Trust Fund and Trial Chamber II is ongoing in relation to the implementation of the reparations order adopted by the Appeals Chamber in 2015. This includes the form of reparations, the identification of victims, or the admission of additional requests for reparations.

35 The former Chadian dictator, a refugee in Senegal, was sentenced to life imprisonment by the Extraordinary African Chambers on 30 May 2016 for crimes committed between 1982 and 1990. However, the victims did not receive any compensation under the regime of President Idriss Déby, who had driven H. Habré from power. On 19 September 2022, his son, who succeeded him at the head of the country after his death in August 2021, finally decided to pay 10 billion CFA francs to the Fund for Victims after an African Union mission visited the country in the summer of 2022. As a reminder, the victims should receive 82.290 billion CFA francs (or €124 million), F Petit, 'Chadian President promises to compensate Hissène Habré's victims' (*Justice Info*, 14 October 2022) <https://www.justiceinfo.net/en/107774-chad-president-promises-compensate-habre-victims.html/> accessed 30 April 2023.

36 See Public Redacted Version of 'Decision Appointing Reparations Experts and Partly Amending Reparations Calendar', *Al Mahdi, Situation in the Republic of Mali*, ICC-01/12-01/15-203-Red, TC VIII, ICC, 19 January 2017; Public redacted version of 'Decision appointing experts on reparations', *Ntaganda, Situation in the Democratic Republic of the Congo*, ICC-01/04-02/06-2528-Red, TC VI, ICC, 14 May 2020; and *Armed Activities on the Territory of the Congo Democratic Republic of the Congo v. Uganda*) (Order of 8 September 2020) [2020] ICJ Rep 264, and ibid. (Order of 12 October 2020) [2020] ICJ Rep 295, appointing four independent experts.

37 In its judgment of 9 February 2022, the ICJ thus departed from the recommendations of the experts it had appointed on a number of decisive points, *Armed Activities on the Territory of the Congo* (*Democratic Republic of the Congo v Uganda*) (Judgment, Reparations) 9 February 2022.

is called upon, more generally, to take on an increasing role in world governance.[38] Furthermore, it would be useful to identify, in the light of the practice of the various competent institutions, a clear methodology and guidelines for the assessment of damages in the context of mass crimes; for example, should the reference to decisions handed down by the courts of the victims' nationality be systematized in order to compensate damages according to their standard of living?[39] Finally, it would be necessary to devise mechanisms to feed the financial resources dedicated to compensation and to control their effective payment when the latter depends on the national authorities.

### 3.2 *The Refusal to Compromise*

The international criminal justice system is made up of institutions that are diverse in nature, but which are all dependent on their dual legal and political status.[40] The requirement of exemplarity, which is particularly acute for the International Criminal Court, must be reconciled with certain modalities of its operation that may be problematic, such as: the existence of third states, which are not subject to the exercise of its jurisdiction; the discretionary power of states, the Security Council, and the Prosecutor, when they decide whether or not the ICC will exercise its jurisdiction in a given situation;[41] or again, the indispensable cooperation, without which the Court would be like a 'giant with no arms and no legs'[42] since, unlike national courts, it has no *imperium*

---

38 See M Delmas-Marty and J Sopova, 'Humaniser la mondialisation' (2011) Le courrier de l'Unesco 28. See also A Appazov, *Expert Evidence and International Criminal Justice* (Springer 2016).

39 This is how the Inter-American Court of Human Rights and the ICC proceed. For the first one, see *Case of Certi-Hurtado v Peru*, Judgment (Reparations and Costs) IACHR Series C No 78 (31 May 2001), para. 46; *Case of Ivcher Bronstein v. Peru*, Judgment (Merits, Reparations and Costs) IACHR Series C No 74 (6 February 2001), para. 181; Case of *Acevedo Jaramillo et al. v Peru*, Judgment (Preliminary Objections, Merits, Reparations and Costs) IACHR Series C No 144 (7 February 2006), para. 300. See also, Order for Reparations pursuant to Article 75 of the Statute, *Katanga, Situation in the Democratic Republic of the Congo*, ICC-01/04-01/07-3728-tENG, TC II, ICC, 24 March 2017, para. 230; Corrected version of the 'Decision Setting the Size of the Reparations Award for which Thomas Lubanga Dyilo is Liable', *Lubanga, Situation in the Democratic Republic of the Congo*, ICC-01/04-01/06-3379-Red-Corr-tENG, TC II, ICC, 21 December 2017, paras. 256ff.

40 See F Mégret, 'La Cour pénale internationale comme objet politique' and M Ubéda-Saillard, 'La Cour pénale internationale comme objet juridique. A propos de la condition juridique de la Cour' in J Fernandez, X Pacreau and M Ubéda-Saillard (eds), *Commentaire du Statut de Rome* (Pedone 2019) 54 and 83, respectively.

41 Articles 13ff.

42 This is the famous metaphor used by Antonio Cassese, President of the *ad hoc* Tribunal for the former Yugoslavia, in his speech to the United Nations General Assembly, 52nd plenary meeting, UN Doc A/50/PV.52 (7 November 1995), 3. On the fundamental question

and no powers of enforcement. In such a legal context, making the neutrality of the institution the *sine qua non* of its legitimacy inevitably leads to a dead end. The Court and, more broadly, the criminal courts are not exempt from the influence of exogenous and endogenous political factors, which can lead them to oscillate between 'judicial activism' and 'judicial restraint'[43] and to develop a genuine jurisdictional policy. Although justice always relies on power,[44] the compromises made should not lead it to accept its instrumentalization.

From this perspective, two main points to watch out for can be identified. First, the conditions under which a situation is referred to the Court inevitably have an impact on the exercise of its jurisdiction. Self-referral by a situation state may lead to investigations being limited to crimes committed by deposed political opponents.[45] Collective referrals by states outside the situation, as in the case of Venezuela or Ukraine,[46] can also limit the use of the Court as a mere parameter of the foreign legal policy of states. The exercise of national criminal jurisdiction must obviously be encouraged, as part of a positive approach to complementarity, but the capacity and willingness of the state must be strictly analysed by the Court, as shown by the recent decision

of cooperation, see, among others, M Ubéda-Saillard, *La coopération des Etats avec les juridictions pénales internationales* (Thèse dactylographiée soutenue à l'université Paris Nanterre le 4 décembre 2009) and O Bekou and D J Birkett (eds), *Cooperation and the International Criminal Court. Perspectives from Theory and Practice* (Brill Nijhoff 2016).

43 See S C Roach, *Politicizing the International Criminal Court: The Convergence of Politics, Ethics, and Law* (Lanham, MD, Rowman & Littlefield 2006); W A Schabas, 'Prosecutorial Discretion v. Judicial Activism at the International Criminal Court' (2008) 6(4) *Journal of Interntional Criminal Justice* 731.

44 Has there ever been a 'justice of the vanquished', as President Ouattara reminded us, not without a certain cynicism, during a meeting with victims of the Ivorian post-electoral crisis on 12 March 2015, 'Côte d'Ivoire : personne ne sera plus transféré à la CPI, selon Ouattara', (*Jeune Afrique*, 13 April 2015) <https://www.jeuneafrique.com/229061/politique/c-te-d-ivoire-personne-ne-sera-plus-transf-r-la-cpi-selon-ouattara/> accessed 30 April 2023.

45 In this respect, one recalls the criticism levelled at the Office of the Prosecutor during the management of the situation in Côte d'Ivoire, when it was accused of prosecuting only Laurent Gbagbo's supporters, or at the Ivorian authorities for their refusal to hand over Simone Gbagbo to the Court.

46 See Referral of the situation in Venezuela under Article 14 of the Rome Statute submitted by the Republic of Argentina, Canada, the Republic of Colombia, the Republic of Chile, the Republic of Paraguay, and the Republic of Peru (26 September 2018). On 2 March 2002, the Office of the Prosecutor also received referrals of the Situation in Ukraine from 39 ICC States Parties.

in Afghanistan.[47] Secondly, the opening of investigations by the Office of the Prosecutor should allow the Court to embody its universal ambition. Today the African tropism, denounced in its time by the African Union,[48] could well give way to criticism of a European tropism, due to the exceptional means deployed in Ukraine. However, in order to convince reluctant regions, such as the Middle Eastern states, it would be necessary to consider with diligence certain existing (Palestine) or perhaps future (Yemen) situations. The Court's ambition of universality will also require a better representation of legal systems and, from this point of view, the predominance of Common Law and its natural vector, the English language, may be a serious obstacle. All actors in the system of international criminal justice should be aware that they are participating in the construction of a hybrid and autonomous international criminal law, distinct from their national legal culture.[49]

## 4 Pathways to the Evolution of the International Criminal Justice System—Concluding Remarks

Today two major trends are emerging in the construction of the international criminal justice system: the renationalization of the fight against impunity, with states exercising their *ius puniendi*; and hybridization with the 'tailor-made' creation of *sui generis* jurisdictions or investigative mechanisms specifically adapted to the situations they have to deal with.[50] The optimization of the system will be achieved by improving its internal coherence, effectiveness, and efficiency.

---

47 Decision pursuant to article 18(2) of the Statute authorising the Prosecution to resume investigation, *Situation in the Islamic Republic of Afghanistan*, ICC-02/17-196, PTC II, ICC, 31 October 2022.

48 See e.g. K Ambos, 'Expanding the focus of the "African Criminal Court" ' in W A Schabas, Y McDermott, and N Hayes (eds), *The Ashgate Research Companion to International Criminal Law: Critical Perspectives* (Ashgate 2013) 499; C C Jalloh and I Bantekas (eds), *The International Criminal Court and Africa* (Oxford University Press 2018); J-B Jeangène Vilmer, 'L' "Afrique" et la Cour pénale internationale' in Fernandez et al. (n 40) 229.

49 For an interesting reflection on the diffusion of legal cultures, see in particular C P Romano, 'The Americanization of International Litigation' (2003) 1(19) *Ohio State Journal on Disopute Resolution* 89.

50 See the colloquium organized by the Cour de Cassation for the 20th anniversary of the entry into force of the Rome Statute (24 October 2022), whose debates can be listened to online <https://www.courdecassation.fr/agenda-evenementiel/les-20-ans-de-lentree-en-vigueur-du-statut-de-rome> accessed 30 April 2023, and whose proceedings are to be published by Pedone (Paris).

### 4.1 *Improving the System Architecture*

Promoting greater synergy between the elements of the international criminal justice system would undoubtedly help it to function more effectively. Recent developments are proving fruitful and could be taken further. Since the 1990s, the rise of universal jurisdiction has been unstoppable.[51] After Iraq and Syria, the situation in Ukraine seems to have catalysed the involvement of national and regional bodies in the extraterritorial prosecution of crimes, embodying the idea of 'solidarity justice',[52] more than 25 years after the 'territorial compassion'[53] called for by Claude Lombois on the occasion of the prosecution of crimes committed in former Yugoslavia. But it has also, and above all, favoured the extremely rapid deployment of multi-level cooperation and networked complementarity between the various competent institutions. This practice constitutes a laboratory for innovations that could be extended to other situations, with the creation of joint investigation teams, coordination of actors involved through Eurojust,[54] the exploitation of private initiatives in the field of evidence gathering,[55] or the use of structural investigation methods already implemented by the MIII and UNITAD. These 'new-style' investigation mechanisms make it possible to collect not only information and intelligence

---

51 TRIAL, 'Universal Jurisdiction Annual Review 2021. A Year Like no Other? The Impact of Coronavirus on Universal Jurisdiction' (12 April 2021) and 'Universal Jurisdiction Annual Review 2022. Universal Jurisdiction, An Overlooked Tool to Fight Conflict-Related Sexual Violence' (4 April 2022).

52 S Vasiliev, 'The Future of Justice for Ukraine is Domestic' (*Justice Info*, 29 March 2022) <https://www.justiceinfo.net/en/89434-future-justice-for-ukraine-domestic.html> accessed 30 April 2023.

53 C Lombois, 'De la compassion territoriale' (1995) *Revue de science criminelle et de droit pénal comparé* 399.

54 On 25 April 2022, Prosecutor Karim Khan signed a cooperation agreement between the ICC and the JIT, see 'ICC participates in joint investigation team supported by Eurojust on alleged core international crimes in Ukraine', EU, Eurojust Press Release (25 April 2022). Furthermore, on the proposal of the European Commission, the Eurojust Regulation was amended to allow the agency to retain the multitude of evidence collected on Ukrainian territory, to process it, and to ensure its disclosure to national authorities, Regulation (EU) 2022/838 of the European Parliament and of the Council of 30 May 2022 amending Regulation (EU) 2018/1727 as regards the preservation, analysis and storage within Eurojust of evidence relating to genocide, crimes against humanity, war crimes and related criminal offences [2022] OJEU L 148, 1. See more generally the dedicated information site <https://www.eurojust.europa.eu/eurojust-and-the-war-in-ukraine> accessed 30 April 2023.

55 Battlefield evidence collected on the spot by individual initiatives and NGOs is also made available to the investigative services via dedicated web portals, see the websites <https://otppathway.icc-cpi.int/index.html> and <https://warcrimes.gov.ua/> both accessed 30 April 2023.

establishing the materiality of the facts, like the UN commissions of enquiry, but also evidence of the crimes committed, with a view to identifying and prosecuting the individuals bearing criminal responsibility where appropriate. They are developing a hybridity that has already been used at the jurisdictional level with the creation, for example, of the Special Jurisdiction for Peace in Colombia, the Special Criminal Court in the Central African Republic, or the Kosovo Specialist Chambers.[56] These mixed institutions make it possible to respond to the specific challenges of each situation, while at the same time contributing to capacity building and thus to the more general issue of developing the rule of law. They can therefore constitute an interesting intermediate layer between national and international courts.[57]

All of these developments will undoubtedly make the national criminal judge the general law judge of international criminal law and will confine the ICC to its role as a 'guardian', like Themis towering over the system. However, this horizon will only be reached if each state has the will and the capacity to prosecute crimes that harm humanity as a whole, failing which the jurisdiction of international or hybrid courts will probably remain preferable, for peaceful coexistence, to that of the universal jurisdiction of the most powerful states.

### 4.2 *Mobilizing the System for Only the Most Serious Crimes*

The performance of the international criminal justice system should be measured in terms of success, not output. We must question the desire for punishment that is now generally expressed in most legal systems, and which leads in particular to a 'penal over-investment',[58] that is, to an increasing criminalization of behaviour, making criminal law the *prima ratio* and no longer the

56 For more information, see the web portals dedicated to these institutions: <https://www.jep.gov.co/JEP/Paginas/Jurisdiccion-Especial-para-la-Paz.aspx>; <https://cps-rca.com/>; <https://www.scp-ks.org/en> all accessed 30 April 2023.

57 The Central African Special Criminal Court, for example, has primacy over any other national court, but it automatically relinquishes jurisdiction to the ICC if the latter has decided to exercise its jurisdiction, in accordance with Articles 3 and 37 of Organic Law No. 15.003 of 3 June 2015 on the creation, organization and functioning of the Special Criminal Court.

58 Y Cartuyvels, 'Le droit pénal et l'État : des frontières "naturelles" en question' in M Henzelin and R Roth (eds), *Le droit pénal à l'épreuve de l'internationalisation* (LGDJ, Georg, Bruylant 2002) 3–2, 23 ('surinvestissement pénal'). See also G Giudicelli-Delage, S Manacorda, and J Tricot, *Devoir de punir ? Le système pénal face à la protection internationale du droit à la vie* (Paris: Société de législation comparée, 2013).

*ultima ratio*[59] that it should be, by being mobilized only as a last resort, when all other means less prejudicial to freedoms have been exhausted. This excessive recourse to the expressive function of punishment to consolidate the essential principles on which societies are based undoubtedly reflects the difficulties of the 'powers that be' in managing the current crisis of values. It is not without danger, however, in terms of its real or virtual effects on the effectiveness of protected norms.

This raises the question of whether the expansion of the ICC's subject matter jurisdiction would lead to a fragmentation of its efforts, as well as a dilution of the gravity of the crimes that currently fall within its jurisdiction.[60] Not all human rights violations can lead to investigations, as the OTP's annual reports on preliminary examination activities for alleged violations in Cuba, China, or North Korea reveal.[61] The Court's *prima facie* lack of jurisdiction does not, however, prejudge the jurisdiction of human rights bodies. In a holistic view of respect for rights, the actions of one and the other may even be part of a *continuum*, as shown for example by the treatment of the situation in Venezuela.[62]

59 The expression refers to the expression '*ultima ratio regum*'—the last argument of kings—which Louis XIV had engraved on his cannons, thus signifying that armed force was used as a last resort, when all diplomatic and peaceful means had been exhausted.

60 These criticisms have been raised with regard to the emergence of a 'third generation international criminal law', C Kress, 'Actes de terrorisme : nouvelle forme de crime contre l'humanité ?', speech at the colloquium organized on 30 September 2016 by the *Cour de Cassation*, '70 years after Nuremberg. Juger le crime contre l'humanité', the proceedings of which are available on the website: <https://www.courdecassation.fr/agenda-evenementiel/70-ans-apres-nuremberg-juger-le-crime-contre-lhumanite> accessed 30 April 2023. The author was critical of the inclusion of acts of terrorism, committed by organized groups, in the scope of the definition of crimes against humanity, in accordance with certain decisions of the Court, see ICC, Trial Chamber III, *Situation in the Republic of Kenya*, Decision Pursuant to Article 15 of the Rome Statute on the Authorization of an Investigation into the Situation in the Republic of Kenya, *Situation in the Republic of Kenya*, ICC-01/09-19-Corr, PTC II, ICC, 31 March 2010, para. 92, and see also Dissenting opinion of Judge Hans-Peter Kaul; and Judgment pursuant to article 74 of the Statute, *Katanga, Situation in the Democratic Republic of the Congo*, ICC-01/04-01/07-3436-tENG, TC II, ICC, 7 March 2014, para. 1119.

61 See e.g. ICC OTP, 'Report on Preliminary Examination Activities in 2018' (5 December 2018) and ICC OTP, 'Report on Preliminary Examination Activities in 2019' (5 December 2019).

62 The situation in Venezuela I was referred to the Court, in an unprecedented move, by a group of six States Parties on 27 September 2018, after Prosecutor Fatou Bensouda opened a preliminary examination on the basis of 110 communications received earlier that year. For several years, treaty bodies have expressed concern about the respect of human rights in this country, see in particular Compilation prepared by the Office of the United Nations High Commissioner for Human Rights in accordance with paragraph 15 (b) of the annex to Human Rights Council resolution 5/1 and paragraph 5 of the annex to Council

In the light of the serious tensions in international relations today, the instrumentalization of criminal proceedings constitutes a real risk[63] which, if left unchecked, could sound the death knell for the legitimacy of the system of international criminal justice and the hopes that victims have placed in it.

---

resolution 16/21: Bolivarian Republic of Venezuela, Human Rights Council, Twenty-sixth Session, UN Doc A/HRC/WG.6/26/VEN/2 (25 August 2016).

63 The implementation of unilateral or multilateral sanctions can lead to an instrumentalization of mutual assistance and extradition cooperation, as illustrated by the *Meng Whanzou* case, see M Ubéda-Saillard, 'The right to be protected from the criminal enforcement of extraterritorial sanctions: Lessons learned from the Huawei Case' in Beaucillon (n 32) 841–76.

CHAPTER 24

# The International Criminal Court of the Future

*Leila Nadya Sadat*

## 1 Introduction*

Some years ago, the late judge Hans Peter Kaul delivered a lecture entitled "*The International Criminal Court of the Future*."[1] He canvassed the internal and external challenges facing the International Criminal Court and offered several short and longer-term predictions. He opined that, in the future, the Court's work culture and the 'one-court' principle would be well enshrined;[2] that at least by 2040 the United States and China would become parties, with China joining first; he chuckled when he predicted – or perhaps wished – that meetings at the Court would begin on time; and he hoped that the budget would grow and the working methods of the judiciary, registry, office of the prosecutor, and chambers would improve.[3] I think he would have been pleased with many of the recommendations in the Report of the Independent Expert Review commissioned by the ICC's Assembly of States Parties (ASP) to assess the Court's performance,[4] and the strong engagement of the Court's organs and the ASP with the Report.[5] I suspect he would have concerns with the 2023

---

* An earlier version of these remarks was delivered at the Nuremberg Academy on 15 October 2022.

1 Judge Kaul delivered the lecture at the Chautauqua Institution on 28 August 2012 <https://www.youtube.com/watch?v=IrGNctYdsM4> accessed 30 April 2023, and it was subsequently published. H-P Kaul, 'The International Criminal Court of the Future', in W Schabas (ed.), *The Cambridge Companion to International Criminal Law* (Cambridge: Cambridge University Press 2016), 335–352.

2 The 'one-court principle' is a term used, but not defined, to describe the 'different entities within the Court and their leaders acting jointly, as one institution'. Independent Expert Review of the International Criminal Court and the Rome Statute System: Final Report – 30 September 2020, ICC-ASP/19/16, 9 November 2020 (Nineteenth Session of the ASP), 106 <https://asp.icc-cpi.int/sites/asp/files/asp_docs/ASP19/IER-Final-Report-ENG.pdf> accessed 30 April 2023, 14, n 19, (hereinafter 'IER').

3 Kaul (n 1).

4 IER (n 2).

5 Overall Response of the International Criminal Court to the 'Independent Expert Review of the International Criminal court and the Rome Statute System – Final Report', ICC (14 April 2021), paras 21–25, available at <https://asp.icc-cpi.int/sites/asp/files/asp_docs/ASP20/Over

 DOI:10.1163/9789004529939_025

budget given the Court's burgeoning workload. He would undoubtedly have been thrilled by this important volume, dedicated to the twentieth anniversary of the Statute's entry into force.

I evoke Judge Kaul's essay not only to honor his memory, his foresight, and his many contributions to the Court, but as a touchpoint for imagining the ICC of 2032 or 2042, my assigned subject. For in developing strategies to improve the Court's future standing and performance, or enhance its legitimacy and universality, it seems useful to understand – and potentially challenge – the assumptions of the past, considering which proved to be correct and which did not. Many developments over the past two decades have come as a surprise; others, in contrast, were anticipated or successfully predicted. Revisiting the assumptions of 1998 offers insights not only into the world of 2022, but of 2032 and beyond.

A complete treatment of the subject is beyond the scope of this short contribution. Instead, I address some key external and internal trends and factors, viewed from the perspective of a U.S citizen and scholar of the Court who had the opportunity to observe the Statute's negotiation first-hand and has served as a Special Adviser to the Prosecutor since 2012. On the positive side, I conclude that the Court is likely to see slow but continued grown in the number of States Parties; that the judiciary will, by and large, continue to build an important corpus of international criminal law and establish both the underlying theoretical framework of the Statute as well as addressing the elements of specific crimes and procedures; and that the Office of the Prosecutor (OTP) will continue to refine and improve its working methods. The Court's burgeoning docket will also likely inspire growth in accountability measures *outside* the ICC, in the guise of new treaties addressing ICC crimes, including crimes against humanity,[6] enhanced state cooperation,[7] increased use of universal jurisdiction prosecutions, and the establishment of additional special tribunals, regional tribunals, or other specialized courts.

all%20Response%20of%20the%20ICC%20to%20the%20IER%20Final%20Report%20-%20ENG%20-%2014April21.pdf> accessed 30 April 2023.

6 International Law Commission, 'Draft Articles on Prevention and Punishment of Crimes Against Humanity' (2019), adopted by the ILC at its 71st session (A/74/10). On November 18, 2022, the U.N. Sixth Committee adopted a Resolution calling for a two-year process to discuss the Draft Treaty, A/C.6/77/L.4 (awaiting General Assembly approval as of this writing).

7 The Mutual Legal Assistance Initiative has proposed the adoption of a new international convention on mutual legal assistance, to be discussed at a diplomatic conference in Slovenia from 15–16 May 2023. Ministerie van Buitenlandse Zaken, Centrum Voor International Recht, MLA Initiative <https://www.centruminternationaalrecht.nl/mla-initiative> accessed 30 April 2023.

In contrast, I believe that the Court will continue to struggle with State cooperation; failure by the Security Council either to refer or to support referrals; lengthy and sometimes disappointing investigations and trials; and a barrage of outside criticism.[8] In addition, if the United States was the 'self-appointed guardian of the frontiers of sovereignty at Rome',[9] two other Permanent Members of the U.N. Security Council, China and the Russian Federation, have now donned that mantle, asserting sovereignty as guiding principle in international fora, and committing Rome Statute crimes on their territories, and, in the case of the Russian Federation, on the territory of other States. Were all three superpowers to attack the Court in the manner the United States did during the Trump administration it would undoubtedly represent an existential threat to the Court and to global peace and security more generally.

Even assuming global catastrophe is averted, however, it seems unlikely that Xi Jinping's China and Vladimir Putin's Russia will join the ICC anytime soon, although China diligently attends ASP sessions as an observer,[10] and the Russian Federation did so in the past.[11] Conversely, there has been a sea change in U.S. attitudes about the Court resulting from sustained advocacy within the

8 D Robinson, 'Inescapable Dyads: Why the ICC Cannot Win', (2015) 28 *Leiden Journal of International Law* 323; C K Hale, 'Are we a Bigger Problem than we Realize? International Criminal Justice and the Need for Self-scrutiny among (Online) Commentators' (2022) 20 *Journal of International Criminal Justice* 293.

9 L N Sadat and S R Carden, 'The International Criminal Court: An Uneasy Revolution', (2000) 88 *Georgetown Law Journal* 388, 457.

10 This year China congratulated the Court on its twentieth anniversary but noted with 'concern' the Court's jurisdiction in the Bangladesh/Myanmar and Philippines which it suggested may be problematic in light of 'sovereignty and the principle of state consent'. Statement of the Chinese Observer Delegation, 21th (sic) Session of the Assembly of States Parties to the Rome Statute of the International Criminal Court, General Debate, The Hague, 6 December 2022 <https://asp.icc-cpi.int/sites/asp/files/2022-12/ASP21.GD_.CHN_.06.12.pdf> accessed 30 April 2023.

11 See, e.g., Delegations to the Fourth Session of the Assembly of States Parties to the Rome Statute of the International Criminal Court, 28 November – 3 December 2005, ICC-ASP/4/INF.1/Rev.1, 12 December 2005 (Fourth Session of the ASP), available at <https://asp.icc-cpi.int/sites/asp/files/asp_docs/library/asp/ICC-ASP-4-INF1-REV1_FINAL_English.pdf> accessed 30 April 2023, noting the presence of a distinguished Russian Federation delegation. See also B Tuzmukhamedov, 'Russia and the International Criminal Court: From Uncertain Engagement to Positive Disengagement', in A Heinze and V E Dittrich (eds), *The Past, Present, and Future of the International Criminal Court* (Brussels: Torkel Opsahl Academic EPublisher 2021), 733–745 (noting that despite the official repudiation of the Court, Russian representatives, judges, and academics are aware of the Court and sometimes engage with its personnel and activities and Russian teams compete in a Russian language ICC Moot Court Competition and in the Nuremberg Moot Court). Recently, Russia has been highly critical of the Court at the United Nations.

United States by ICC supporters, and the conflict with Ukraine, which has brought it closer to its natural allies in Europe. This could change with a new administration in 2024, but for now the pro-ICC consensus in the United States is bipartisan and strong. Thus, it is envisageable that the United States could join the Court in the next ten or twenty years. That said, U.S. participation may come at the price of further concessions that might erode the Nuremberg principles that serve as the pillars on which the Court's universality rest: no immunity for heads of State and equality before the law. These principles have already been compromised by the adoption of a special rule governing participation of high government officials at trial; by the Kampala amendment's restricted jurisdictional regime; by the African Union in its objections to the Kenya and Sudan situations and the adoption of the (unratified) Malabo Protocol; and, more recently, by European ICC States Parties and scholars advancing the idea of immunity for heads of State, in significant departures from the Rome consensus.

## 2 The External Environment Shaping the Court of 2022 and beyond

The Court is a creature of the global political ecosystem, which has evolved and changed since 1998. The General Assembly declared the 1990s to be 'the decade of international law'.[12] It was a moment of 'Superpower rapprochement',[13] during which states could and did work together to build new institutions and legal regimes, including the International Criminal Court. In contrast, the current decade is one of gridlock and 'colossal global dysfunction', as U.N. Secretary-General Antonio Guterres recently observed.[14] Pandemic, War, Climate Change, Poverty, Hunger, Human Migration, and rising global authoritarianism are stressing the global ecosystem. The Rome Statute was negotiated following the collapse of the Soviet Union in a time of hope in

12 On November 17, 1989, the UNGA adopted Resolution 44/23 declaring the period 1990–1999 as the United Nations Decade of International Law. UNGA, 'United Nations Decade of International Law' UN Doc A/RES/44/23 (17 November 1989).

13 J Thomas, 'The United Nations Decade of International Law', (1991) 3 *African Journal of International and Comparative Law* 386. See also T Hopkins and P D Paton, 'The United Nations Decade of International Law: A Canadian Perspective' (1993) 31 *Canadian Yearbook of International Law* 283.

14 A Guterres, Secretary-General's address to the General Assembly (20 September 2022) <https://www.un.org/sg/en/content/sg/speeches/2022-09-20/secretary-generals-address-the-general-assembly> accessed 30 April 2023.

which emerging structures of power could be seen or glimpsed but had not yet been created.[15] The Rome Conference opened a window of opportunity to establish the last great international institution of the Twentieth Century. Able individuals seized the moment, knowing that the window might suddenly close. They constructed an institution based upon certain working assumptions about State behavior and the institutional framework that would best serve the future Court. What were some of those expectations and assumptions? And do they still hold today?

### 2.1 *The Values the ICC Represents*

During the Rome Conference, the consensus was that it would take decades for the Statute to enter into force with the necessary ratifications. To have it happen in four short years was unexpected and evinces an enthusiasm for the Court and the values it represents. These values include a commitment to human rights and democracy, and a belief that a lack of (criminal) accountability for the commission of grievous crimes fuels cycles of violence and that, conversely, punishment of individuals for their commission is both a moral imperative and a contribution to peace and security. While these values and assumptions have been challenged over the past two decades by States and scholars, they have remained remarkably constant, and continue to be articulated by States Parties, at the ICC ASP and elsewhere.[16] The continued, albeit slow, growth in the number of ratifications and accessions appears to bear this out.

### 2.2 *The Referral System*

The prevailing wisdom regarding the Court's referral system was premised on two assumptions: *First*, that no State would likely refer a situation to the Court; *second*, that the political nature of the Security Council would render it an unreliable partner for the Court. Both assumptions were reasonable based on prior experience and caused civil society and many governments to insist upon an independent prosecutor who could trigger the Court's jurisdiction on his or her own initiative. This latter feature of the Statute engendered significant

15 Sadat and Carden, 'Uneasy Revolution' (n 9), citing R Falk, 'The Grotian Moment: Unfulfilled Promise, Harless Fantasy, Missed Opportunity?' (1997) 13 *International Insights* 3.

16 See., e.g., Statement of Portugal to the Twenty-first Session of the ICC Assembly of States Parties (5–10 December 2022), available at <https://asp.icc-cpi.int/sites/asp/files/2022-12/ASP21.GD_.PRT_.05.12.pdf> accessed 30 April 2023.

opposition during the negotiations[17] and caused States to insert various procedural barriers to investigation and prosecution, some of which have (predictably) slowed the work of the Court. It was also one of the key reasons the United States voted 'no' in 1998.[18]

While worries about the Security Council were well-founded, the State referral mechanism has been a surprising success. As predicted in 1998, the Security Council has had a disappointing track record regarding the ICC. It has referred only two Situations, Darfur, Sudan in 2005 (Resolution 1593),[19] and Libya in 2011 (Resolution 1970),[20] even though others clearly merit referral (such as Syria, which has been subject to multiple Russian and Chinese vetoes).[21] Moreover, the Resolutions referring the Darfur and Libyan situations place the financial burden of those situations on the Court, rather than the Council. Yet, Article 115(b) of the Rome Statute clearly anticipates that the Council will pay for expenses incurred for referrals it sends to the Court,[22] and such seems to have been the negotiators' intent.[23] Both Resolutions exempt the nationals of

---

17 F Benedetti, K Bonneau and J L Washburn, *Negotiating the International Criminal Court: New York to Rome, 1994-1998* (Brill Nihoff 2014), 164–165; Sadat and Carden, 'Uneasy Revolution' (n 9) 400–401.

18 L N Sadat, *The International Criminal Court and the Transformation of International Law* (Brill Nijhoff 2002) 94. The original position of the United States is set out in the Statement of D J Scheffer, Ambassador-at-Large for War Crimes Issues, Before the Committee on Foreign Relations of the U.S. Senate (23 July 1998), available at <https://1997-2001.state.gov/policy_remarks/1998/980723_scheffer_icc.html> accessed 30 April 2023.

19 UNSC Resolution 1593 (31 March 2005) UN Doc S/Res/1593.

20 UNSC Resolution 1970 (26 February 2011) UN Doc S/Res/1970.

21 See, e.g., UNSC Resolution of 22 May 2014, proposing the referral of the situation in the Syrian Arab Republic since 1 March 2011 (13 votes in favor, however, vetoed by China and the Russian Federation), 'Referral of Syria to International Criminal Court Fails as Negative Votes Prevent Security Council from Adopting Draft Resolution', SC/11407 (22 May 2014) UN Department of Public Information <https://press.un.org/en/2014/sc11407.doc.htm> accessed 30 April 2023. See also G Melling and A Dennett, 'The Security Council veto and Syria: responding to mass atrocities through the "United for Peace" resolution' (2017) 57 *Indian Journal of International Law* 285 (noting 8 Russian vetoes relating to the Syrian crisis); J Trahan, *Existing Legal Limits to Security Council Veto Power in the Face of Atrocity Crimes* (Cambridge University Press 2020) 362–302.

22 Rome Statute of the International Criminal Court (signed 17 July 1998, entered into force 1 July 2002) 2187 UNTS 3, Art. 115(b). See W M Reisman, 'On Paying the Piper: Financial Responsibility for Security Council Referrals to the International Criminal Court' (2005) 99 *American Journal of International Law* 615.

23 M H Arsanjani, 'Financing' in A Cassese, P Gaeta, J R W D Jones, *The Rome Statute of the International Criminal Court: A Commentary* (Oxford University Press 2002), 315–329; M Halff, D Tolbert, R Villacis, 'Article 115: Funds of the Court and the Assembly of States Parties' in O Triffterer and K Ambos (eds), *The Rome Statute of the International Criminal Court: A Commentary* 3rd edn (CH Beck/Hart/Nomos 2016) 2253–2266.

non-States Parties from the ICC's jurisdiction, in an extraordinary example of political and selective justice.[24]

On a more positive note, the provision allowing States to refer situations to the Court has proved more useful. At the time of the Statute's negotiation, no State had used the interstate complaint mechanism provided for in human rights treaties,[25] so it was fair to assume they would be unlikely to refer criminal cases. Yet the ICC's first Prosecutor, Luis Moreno Ocampo, unexpectedly invited States to refer situations involving the commission of ICC crimes on their own territories, and they did so in 2004, only two years after the Statute's entry into force. The situation in Uganda[26] and the Democratic Republic of the Congo[27] were first, and others followed including the Central African Republic, Mali, and Palestine. While the self-referrals raised questions about objectivity and selectivity,[28] they ensured that the Office of the Prosecutor (OTP) would have access to crime scenes and evidence, and at least some modicum of State cooperation. This allowed the office to bring charges in a series of cases, many of which have generated important jurisprudence and produced final judgments (or are currently in trial), including *Bemba, Al Hassan, Lubanga, Katanga, Al Mahdi, Mbarushimana, Ngudjolo Chui, Ntaganda,* and *Ongwen.* Regardless of whether the cases resulted in successful convictions (and several did not), they allowed the Court to begin its investigative and judicial activities.

Interestingly, not only did States refer their own situations, but they have referred situations in other States. On September 27, 2018, six States – Argentina, Canada, Chile, Colombia, Paraguay, and Peru – jointly referred the situation in the Bolivarian Republic of Venezuela under the government of President Nicolas Maduro to the Court,[29] requesting that the Prosecutor open

---

24 N Ali, 'Through a Glass Darkly: The ICC, the UNSC and the Quest for Justice in International Law' (2019) 19 *International Criminal Law Review* 669–697.

25 Indeed, as recently as 2018, a leading human rights casebook made the same point. H Hannum, et al., *International Human Rights* 6th edn (Aspen 2018) 681–83.

26 *Situation in Uganda*, International Criminal Court <https://www.icc-cpi.int/uganda> accessed 30 April 2023.

27 ICC –Prosecutor receives referral of the situation in the Democratic Republic of Congo, ICC Press Release (19 April 2004) <https://www.icc-cpi.int/news/icc-prosecutor-receives-referral-situation-democratic-republic-congo> accessed 30 April 2023.

28 See, e.g., P Akhavan, 'Self-Referrals before the International Criminal Court: Are States the Villains or the Victims of Atrocities?' (2010) 21 *Criminal Law Forum* 103–120; W A Schabas, '"Complementarity in Practice:" Some Uncomplimentary Thoughts', (2009) 19 *Criminal Law Forum* 5.

29 'Statement of the Prosecutor of the International Criminal Court, Fatou Bensouda, on the referral by a group of Six States Parties regarding the situation in Venezuela', ICC OTP (27 September 2018) <https://www.icc-cpi.int/news/statement-prosecutor-international-criminal-court-fatou-bensouda-referral-group-six-states> accessed 30 April 2023.

an investigation into the commission of crimes against humanity. The State Party referral arguably did not have much legal effect, because the situation in Venezuela was already in Preliminary Examination. However, it served as a 'formal display of political support',[30] much needed for the OTP to do its work. Likewise, when Prosecutor Khan wished to move the situation in Ukraine from the Preliminary Examination stage to investigation, he invited States to refer the situation to him to avoid having to obtain Pretrial Chamber approval,[31] whereupon thirty-nine States promptly did so on 1 March 2022, followed by four others.[32] This political support has also translated into financial support, not just for Ukraine but for the Court more generally.

Conversely, while the *proprio motu* power of the Prosecutor remains an important driver of ICC investigation and prosecution, it has posed myriad challenges, including a lack of State cooperation. The Kenya situation was the first use of the *proprio motu* power, and the lack of State cooperation ultimately derailed the cases even if the investigation may have produced some salutary effects, as Beth Simmons and others scholars have suggested.[33] Subsequently Burundi[34] and the Philippines[35] withdrew from the Rome Statute faced with

30 N E Ortiz, 'Understanding the State Party Referral of the Situation in Venezuela' (*EJIL:Talk!*, 1 November 2018) <https://www.ejiltalk.org/understanding-the-state-party-referral-of-the-situation-in-venezuela/> accessed 30 April 2023.

31 'Statement of ICC Prosecutor, Karim A.A. Khan QC, on the Situation in Ukraine: "I have decided to proceed with opening an investigation"', ICC OTP (28 February 2022) <https://www.icc-cpi.int/news/statement-icc-prosecutor-karim-aa-khan-qc-situation-ukraine-i-have-decided-proceed-opening> accessed 30 April 2023.

32 *Situation in Ukraine*, Jurisdiction in the General Situation, International Criminal Court <https://www.icc-cpi.int/ukraine> accessed 30 April 2023.

33 H Jo and B A Simmons, 'Can the International Criminal Court Deter Atrocity'?, (2016) 70 *International Organization* 443. For a general summary of the possible deterrent effect of ICC investigations see S Ford, 'Can the International Criminal Court Succeed? An Analysis of the Empirical Evidence of Violence Prevention' (2020) 43 *Loyola Los Angeles Intenrational and Comparative Law Review* 101.

34 Burundi became the first country to withdraw from the Rome Statute by written notification on 27 October 2016, taking effect on 27 October 2017, after the ICC Prosecutor opened a preliminary examination into the situation. On 5 September 2017, the Prosecutor submitted a request to open an investigation *proprio motu*, which was granted by Pre-Trial Chamber III on October 25, 2017, notwithstanding Burundi's withdrawal. Public Redacted Version of 'Decision Pursuant to Article 15 of the Rome Statute on the Authorization of an Investigation into the Situation in the Republic of Burundi', *Situation in the Republic of Burundi*, ICC-01/17-X-9-US-Exp, TC III, ICC, 25 October 2017.

35 Philippine President Duterte withdrew from the Statute on 17 March 2018, effective 17 March 2019, International Criminal Court, *Situation in the Republic of the Philippines* <https://www.icc-cpi.int/philippines#:~:text=While%20the%20Philippines'%20withdrawal%20from,and%20including%2016%20March%202019> (accessed 30 April

investigations launched by the Prosecutor, and although three arrest warrants were authorized in the Georgia situation (also *proprio motu*) and requests for cooperation seeking their surrender to the Court in June 2022,[36] that may not be easy, which is perhaps why Prosecutor Kahn recently closed that investigation.[37]

### 2.3 *Resistance to the Court's Investigations*

All three referral mechanisms have generated a backlash to the Court in certain cases, on the part of States either objecting to the cases or situations *sub judice* or attempting to pressure the Court or undermine its independence. This was a major preoccupation of delegates in the 1990s, who were right to worry but could not have imagined the punishment the Court and especially its Prosecutor might endure in endeavoring to do their job 'without fear or favour',[38] under their statutory mandates.[39] It is fair to say that in the summer of 1998, the article 98 bilateral immunity campaign of the United States of America embarked upon by the administration of George W. Bush in 2000 was not foreseeable.[40] Neither was the U.S. decision to repudiate its signature, nor

---

2023) and efforts inside the country to invalidate the withdrawal have been dismissed by the Philippine Supreme Court. 'Philippines Supreme Court dismisses challenge to Duterte's ICC withdrawal' *Reuters* (16 March 2021) <https://www.reuters.com/article/philippines-icc/philippines-supreme-court-dismisses-challenge-to-dutertes-icc-withdrawal-idUSL4N2LE2JW> accessed 30 April 2023.

36 'Situation in Georgia: ICC Pre-Trial Chamber delivers three arrest warrants', ICC Press Release (30 June 2022) <https://www.icc-cpi.int/news/situation-georgia-icc-pre-trial-chamber-delivers-three-arrest-warrants> accessed 30 April 2023.

37 'The Prosecutor of the International Criminal Court, Karim A.A. Khan, QC, announces conclusion of the investigation phase in the Situation in Georgia', ICC OTP (16 December 2022) <https://www.icc-cpi.int/news/prosecutor-international-criminal-court-karim-aa-khan-kc-announces-conclusion-investigation> accessed 30 April 2023.

38 F Bensouda, '"Without Fear or Favour": Reflections on my term as Prosecutor of the International Criminal Court' (Farewell end of term statement, 15 June 2021) <https://www.icc-cpi.int/sites/default/files/itemsDocuments/20210615-prosecutor-fatou-bensouda-end-of-term-farewell-statement.pdf> accessed 30 April 2023.

39 See, e.g., Rome Statute, Arts. 40(1), 42(1), (3) & (5), and 45.

40 L N Sadat, 'Summer in Rome, Spring in The Hague, Winter in Washington? U.S. Policy Towards the International Criminal Court', (2003) 21 *Wisconsin International Law Journal* 557 (summarizing the bilateral immunity campaign). See also A Bogdan, 'The United States and the International Criminal Court: Avoiding Jurisdiction through Bilateral Agreements in Reliance on Article 98', (2008) 8 *International Criminal Law Review* 1; J Crawford, P Sands, and R Wilde, 'In the Matter of the Statute of the International Criminal Court and in the Matter of Bilateral Agreements Sought by the United States Under Article 98(2) of the Statute' (5 June 2003), <https://www.legal-tools.org/doc/7f2edf/pdf/> accessed 30 April 2023; J Ralph, 'Europe, the United States, and the International Criminal

the punishing U.S. pressure on the OTP to drop the Afghanistan investigation to the extent it implicated U.S. persons or policy. That pressure was so intense that it arguably warped the Court's jurisprudence[41] and resulted in the imposition of punishing sanctions on Prosecutor Bensouda and one of her deputies.[42] Although the sanctions were eventually lifted with the inauguration of a new U.S. President, a shattering precedent was set, and it is not impossible that the Court and its officers might suffer similar attacks in the future from the United States or other States. It is a testament to the States Parties that rallied around the OTP, as well as the personal courage of the Prosecutor and her staff and the support of the entire Court, that she and the Court weathered the storm.

Likewise, the firestorm created by the Kenya cases involving Kenyatta and Ruto and the *Al Bashir* arrest warrants was not envisaged in 1998. As noted earlier, the first ICC Prosecutor invited States to refer situations to him, and all the first self-referrals came from African States Parties. Although commentators sometimes noted with concern that each of the three situations involved an

---

Court' (2007) 151, *in Defending the Society of States: Why America Opposes the International Criminal Court and Its Vision of World Society* 156–163.

41 Pre-Trial Chamber II refused to authorize the investigation on the grounds that it would not be served by 'the interests of justice'. Decision Pursuant to Article 15 of the Rome Statute on the Authorisation of an Investigation into the Situation in the Islamic Republic of Afghanistan, *Situation in the Islamic Republic of Afghanistan*, ICC-02/17-33, PTC II, ICC, 12 April 2019. This decision was described as judicial 'suicide' by others who noted that it appeared to be a response to US pressure. M Simons, R Gladstone and C Rosenberg, 'Hague Court Abandons Afghanistan War Crimes Inquiry' *NY Times* (12 April 2019) <https://www.nytimes.com/2019/04/12/world/asia/icc-afghanistan-.html> accessed 30 April 2023. The decision was reversed on appeal and the investigation authorized. Judgment on the appeal against the decision on the authorisation of an investigation into the situation in the Islamic Republic of Afghanistan, *Situation in the Islamic Republic of Afghanistan*, ICC-02/17-138, AC, ICC, 5 March 2020. That said, Prosecutor Khan has stated he will not focus on U.S. forces in a newly resumed phase of the investigation. 'Statement of the Prosecutor of the International Criminal Court, Karim A.A. Khan QC, following the application for an expedited order under article 18(2) seeking authorization to resume investigations in the Situation in Afghanistan', ICC OTP (27 September 2021) <https://www.icc-cpi.int/news/statement-prosecutor-international-criminal-court-karim-khan-qc-following-application> accessed 30 April 2023.

42 Executive Order on Blocking Property of Certain Persons Associated with the International Criminal Court, 11 June 2020, set out a regime under which individuals could be sanctioned by the United States. On September 2, 2020, Prosecutor Fatou Bensouda and another high-ranking member of the office, Phakiso Mochochoko, were personally sanctioned. H S Anderson, '"Why Them" On the U.S. Sanctions Against Int'l Criminal Court Officials' (*Just Security*, 2 September 2020) <https://www.justsecurity.org/72275/why-them-on-the-u-s-sanctions-against-intl-criminal-court-officials/> accessed 30 April 2023.

African nation, 'African sovereignty' was arguably protected because African leaders had themselves invoked the jurisdiction of the Court, the crimes were substantial and notorious, and government officials were not under investigation, at least not initially. That changed with the indictment and issuance of warrants of arrest against Sudanese President Omar Al-Bashir, however in 2009 and 2010,[43] and the opening of the Kenya Situation by the Prosecutor *proprio motu* in 2010, which resulted in proceedings against another African Head of State, Uhuru Kenyatta.[44] This inflamed the situation between the African Union and the Court.[45]

The African Union responded over the next several years by taking Decisions criticizing the Al-Bashir arrest warrants and requesting its Members to refuse to execute them and amend Article 16 of the Rome Statute to permit the U.N. General Assembly to suspend cases before the Court.[46] The AU also supported Kenya's (unsuccessful) request for a Security Council deferral under Article 16 of the Rome Statute.[47] Although support for formal AU positions on the Sudan and Kenyan situations was not uniform within African States[48] or African civil

43 Decision on the Prosecution's Application for a Warrant of Arrest against Omar Hassan Ahmad Al Bashir, *Al Bashir, Situation in Darfur, Sudan,* ICC-02/05-01/09-3, PTC I, ICC, 4 March 2009 ('First *Al Bashir* Arrest Warrant'). A second warrant was issued adding the crime of genocide. Second Warrant of Arrest for Omar Hassan Ahmad Al Bashir, *Al Bashir, Situation in Darfur, Sudan*, ICC-02/05-01/09-95, PTC I, ICC, 12 July 2010.

44 Kenyatta was elected President *after* he was charged by the ICC.

45 See, e.g., R J. Hamilton, 'Africa, the Court, and the Council in M M DeGuzman and V Oosterveld (eds), *The Elgar Companion to the International Criminal Court* (Elgar 2020), 261; A G Kiyani, 'Re-narrating selectivity' in DeGuzman and Oosterveld (eds) ibid., 307, 309–315.

46 African Union, Assembly, Decision on the Progress Report of the Commission on the Implementation of Decision Assembly/AU/DEC.270 (XIV) on the Second Ministerial Meeting on the Rome Statute of the International Criminal Court (ICC) Doc. Assembly/AU/10 (XV), AU Doc Assembly/AU/Dec.296 (XV) (July 2010).

47 African Union, Assembly, Decision on the Implementation of the Decisions on the International Criminal Court Doc. EX.CL/639(XVIII), AU Doc Assembly/AU/Dec.334(XVI) (January 2011). The African Union urged African States to vote for an amendment to Article 16 of the Rome Statute to allow for the UN General Assembly to defer cases for a year. It reiterated these positions in 2011, see African Union, Assembly, Decision on the Implementation of the Assembly Decisions on the International Criminal Court – Doc. EX.CL/670(XIX), AU Doc Assembly/AU/Dec.366(XVII) (30 June–1 July 2011) and 2012. See African Union, Assembly, Decision on the Progress Report of the Commission on the Implementation of the Assembly Decisions on the International Criminal Court (ICC), AU Doc Assembly/AU/Dec.397(XVIII) (January 2012). African Union, Assembly, Decision on the Implementation of the Assembly Decisions on the International Criminal Court (ICC), AU Doc Assembly/AU/Dec.419(XIX) (July 2012).

48 See, e.g., African Union, Assembly, Decision on the Meeting of African States Parties to the Rome Statute of the International Criminal Tribunal (ICC) Doc. Assembly/AU/

society,[49] the AU continued to press its case. By threatening a mass withdrawal of African States from the ICC,[50] in 2013 it successfully obtained an amendment to the ICC's rules of procedure and evidence to allow '[a]n accused ... who is mandated to fulfill extraordinary public duties at the highest national level may ... request to the Trial Chamber to be excused and to be represented by counsel only; the request must specify that the accused explicitly waives the right to be present at the trial'.[51] In 2014 it amended the proposed Statute of the African Court of Justice and Human Rights in the 'Malabo Protocol' incorporating a provision immunizing Heads of State and government as well as 'senior state officials' from arrest.[52] (As of this writing, only 15 States have signed the Malabo Protocol and none have ratified it).[53] Finally, several members of the African Union, including ICC States Parties, refused to arrest former Sudanese

---

13(SXIII), AU Doc Assembly/AU/Dec.245(XIII) Rev. 1 (July 3, 2009), (Chad entered a reservation to the language deciding that 'AU Member States shall not cooperate pursuant to the provisions of Article 98 of the Rome Statute of the ICC relating to immunities, for the arrest and surrender of President Omar El Bashir of The Sudan.'ibid.); African Union, Assembly, Decision on International Jurisdiction, Justice, and the International Criminal Court (ICC) Doc. Assembly/AU/13 (XXI), n. 2, AU Doc.Assembly/AU/Dec.482 (XXI) (May 2013) (reservation entered by the Republic of Botswana on the entire Decision).

49 See, e.g., Kenyans for Peace with Truth and Justice, Memo Responding to Kenyan Ambassador's Letter to the UNSC on ICC Cases (17 May 2013); Kenyans for Peace with Truth and Justice objected, stating 'allowing certain individuals to absent themselves from the trials on the basis of their status violates the principle of equality before the law'. Kenyans for Peace with Truth and Justice, Statement at the Assembly of States Parties (21 Nov. 2013).

50 The AU position did not appear to be supported by many African States Parties. See, e.g., Statement by Lesotho on Behalf of the African State Parties to the Rome Statute at the Thirteenth Session of the Assembly of States Parties to the Rome Statute (8 December 2014) ('The African Union (AU) repeated calls for noncooperation should not obscure the consistent, active backing for the ICC among African governments and civil society across the African continent.'). African States have also discouraged other African nations from withdrawing from the Rome Statute. See, e.g., Statement by Ghana to the Sixteenth Session of the Assembly of States Parties to the Rome Statute (6 Demeber 2017); Statement by The Gambia at the Sixteenth Session of the Assembly of States Parties to the Rome Statute (6 December 2017). See also 'ICC: African Countries Support Court' CICC Press Release (17 December 2014) (summarizing statements by over a dozen African countries expressing strong support for the Court's work at the 13th Assembly of States Parties).

51 ICC Rules of Procedure and Evidence Rule 134*quater*, adopted by the ICC ASP in 2013. Amendments to the Rules od Procedure and Evidence, ICC-ASP/12/Res.7, 27 November 2013 (Twelfth Plenary Meeting of the ASP).

52 Draft Protocol on Amendments to the Protocol on the Statute of the African Court of Justice and Human Rights, Article 46A *bis*, EX.CL/846(XXV) (June 27, 2014).

53 African Union, Protocol on Amendments to the Protocol on the Statute of the African Court of Justice and Human Rights.

President Omar Al-Bashir on the grounds of his immunity as a sitting Head of State, and contested the applicability of Article 27 of the Rome Statute to nationals of non-States Parties, a challenge that was unanimously rejected by the ICC Appeals Chamber in 2019,[54] but continues to be advanced by some scholars and state officials.[55]

Despite the worry about a "mass withdrawal" of African States and the very real attacks on the Court by the United States, in 2022 we can safely say that Judge Kaul's relatively sanguine appraisal of the likelihood of future State support and even ratification was correct. Only two States have withdrawn from the Statute, and only three have repudiated their signatures: the United States, the Russian Federation, and Israel. Meanwhile, the number of ratifications stands at a healthy 123, with Armenia and Ukraine promising to ratify soon, and other States suggesting they may do the same.

## 3 The Court's Judicial and Investigative Activities

### 3.1 *The Independent Expert Review and the Budget*

The Rome Statute created a complex institution that has experienced significant growing pains as its judicial and prosecutorial activity have increased with time.[56] In December 2019, the ICC ASP commissioned an Independent Expert Review to address many of the perceived and real shortcomings of the Court's operations themselves, including complaints about the work culture, overly long proceedings, fractured and controversial judicial decisions, and disputes

54 Judgment in the Jordan Referral re-Al-Bashir Appeal, *Al Bashir, Situation in Darfur, Sudan*, ICC-02/05-01/09 OA2, AC, ICC, 6 May 2019.

55 See, e.g., D Akande, 'ICC Appeals Chamber Holds that Heads of State have No Immunity under Customary International Law before International Tribunals' (*EJIL:Talk!*, 6 May 2019), available at <https://www.ejiltalk.org/icc-appeals-chamber-holds-that-heads-of-state-have-no-immunity-under-customary-international-law-before-international-tribunals/> accessed 30 April 2023 (labeling the Appeals Chamber's judgment 'stunning', 'deeply misguided', 'dangerous' and 'unwise'). See also Advisory Committee on Public International Law, 'Challenges in prosecuting the crime of aggression: jurisdiction and immunities', No 40 (12 September 2022) available at <https://www.advisorycommitteeinternationallaw.nl/publications/advisory-reports/2022/09/12/challenges-in-prosecuting-the-crime-of-aggression-jurisdiction-and-immunities> accessed 30 April 2023 (asserting that article 27 of the Rome Statute may not 'apply to nationals of third states [...]since they have not agreed to this rule.'), 13.

56 See, e.g., P Ambach and K U Rackwitz, 'A Model of International Judicial Administration? The Evolution of Managerial Practices at the International Criminal Court' (2014) 76 *Law and Contemporary Problems* 119–161.

between organs of the Court over the allocation of authority and resources.[57] The final Report focused on many of the more problematic aspects of the ICC's operations over the past twenty years, some of which were also highlighted by Judge Kaul, and offered 384 recommendations, which have been taken up by the Court's organs and the ASP with great seriousness. That said, a close observer of the 21st Session of the ICC ASP in December 2022 could not help but notice that there is more work to be done in implementing the many of the recommendations of the IER,[58] particularly as regards management, work culture, gender and geographic representation, and the one-court principle.

While the IER was demanding more efficiency and effectiveness, however, the Court's caseload was growing exponentially. Yet many States Parties remain reluctant to provide adequate funding. At the 2022 ICC ASP, Kenya, for example, noted that considering continued management issues at the ICC, and given the impact of drought, war, the Covid-19 pandemic and 'severe economic and inflationary pressures' in the Horn of Africa, it was simply unable to support even the figure of 16% that the Committee on Budget and Finance had proposed (in response to a request of 20% from the Court). In the words of its delegate, 'this is the time to tighten our belts, not loosen them'.[59] Following intense negotiations, the ASP adopted an 11.9 percent increase.[60] The Ukraine

57 IER (n 2) 7, para. 1.

58 The ASP decided to extend to the next session of the ASP the mandate of the Review Mechanism to monitor and assess implementation of Court reform activities. Review of the International Criminal Court and the Rome Statute system, ICC-ASP/21/Res.4, 9 December 2022 (Ninth Plenary Meeting of the ASP).

59 Statement by the Republic of Kenya, The General Debate of the Assembly of States Parties, 21st Session of the Assembly of States Parties to the Rome Statute, 5–10 December 2022, The Hague, available at <https://asp.icc-cpi.int/sites/asp/files/2022-12/ASP21.GD_.KEN_.06.12.pdf> accessed 30 April 2023.

60 The Court requested a 20% increase in its budget, to address additional costs of the Ukraine referral, the zero-increase policy of prior years, and inflation. J Anderson, 'Can 2023 be the Booster Year for the ICC Budget', (*Justice Info*, 2 December 2022) available at <https://www.justiceinfo.net/en/109715-2023-booster-year-icc-budget.html> accessed 30 April 2023. It received approximately 173,234 million Euros, Resolution of the Assembly of States Parties on the proposed programme budget for 2023, the Working Capital Fund for 2023, the scale of assessment for the apportionment of expenses of the International Criminal Court, financing appropriations for 2023 and the Contingency Fund, ICC-ASP/21/Res.1, 9 December 2022 (Ninth Plenary Meeting of the ASP), which was an increase of 11.9 % over the prior year's budget of 154,855 million euros. Resolution of the Assembly of States Parties on the proposed programme budget for 2022, the Working Capital Fund for 2022, the scale of assessment for the apportionment of expenses of the International Criminal Court, financing appropriations for 2022 and the Contingency Fund, ICC-ASP/20/Res.1, 9 December 2021 (Eighth Plenary Meeting of the ASP).

situation has generated significant voluntary contributions to the Court, of both financial support and secondments, but this is a stop gap measure. As Ireland observed during the 2022 ASP plenary debate, 'voluntary contributions are not a sustainable means of funding the Court... [and] can fuel accusations of bias in international law'. For this reason, Ireland urged adoption of a budget that can support the Court's increased activities.[61]

### 3.2 *The Emergence of Crimes against Humanity as Pivotal to Atrocity Crime Prevention*

Inside the Court, one of the most interesting positive developments has been the continued evolution of international criminal law and the emergence of crimes against humanity as the predominant charge invoked in a Court able to work in real time, not just established on an *ad hoc* basis after the fact. In thinking about the preventive dimension of the ICC's functions, one sees that the expansion of the 'peacetime' enforcement of international criminal law by international criminal adjudication has been greatly expanded under the Rome Statute. This was an unexpected outcome of the Rome Statute. As I noted in a study in 2013, unlike prior international criminal tribunals which treated crimes against humanity largely as a variant of or attached to the commission of war crimes, at the ICC, a significant number of situations and/or cases involve *only* crimes against humanity charges.[62] This was the case for the post-election violence in Kenya; allegations of extrajudicial killings in the Philippines; and the allegations made against the government in the Venezuela situation referred to the Court. This has made it possible to intervene early in an 'atrocity cascade', in which a human rights situation deteriorates into international crime, and has made one of the key issues at the ICC determining where the line is between human rights violations and crimes against humanity.[63]

61 Ireland National Statement at the 21st Session of the Assembly of States Parties (December 2022) available at <https://asp.icc-cpi.int/sites/asp/files/2022-12/ASP21.GD_.IRL_.06.12.pdf> accessed 30 April 2023.

62 L N Sadat, 'Crimes Against Humanity in the Modern Age' (2013) 107 *American Journal of International Law* 334–377.

63 I have set out my views on the phenomenon of 'atrocity cascades' in a series of writings and lectures. See, e.g., L N Sadat, 'Little Progress in the Sixth Committee on Crimes Against Humanity', (2022), 54 *Case Western Reserve Journal of International Law* 89–107.

### 3.3 *Growth and Change in the OTP and Development of the Law by Chambers*

With respect to the Prosecutor, the IER focused heavily on issues relating to case and situation selection, priorisation, hibernation, and closure, the need for quality control of evidence and work culture.[64] Having a Court with a truly global reach creates a complexity that was hard to imagine in the summer of 1998. Early disappointments that led to acquittals, evidentiary challenges, and seeming conflict between the bench and the OTP were challenges for the Court's first Prosecutor, and some of these challenges were inherited by its second. The third Prosecutor has declared his intention to 'narrow and deepen' OTP's investigative and prosecutorial activity so as to 'achieve meaningful results', consistent with the recommendations of the IER, and determine 'how resources can be most effectively deployed to deliver the greatest impact for those affected by crimes falling with our jurisdiction globally'.[65] As a consequence, Prosecutor Khan recently closed two longstanding investigations in the Central African Republic and Georgia.[66] As the Court now moves into a third decade, lessons learned, as well as the development of ongoing traditions and practices, will enhance institutional stability and enhanced performance.

If the Prosecutor is the engine of the Court, the jurisprudence – the means by which the Court speaks law to power – is its voice. In 1998, the negotiators did not predict how difficult and important the judicial task would be. There was little precedent from the *ad hoc* international criminal tribunals available and the negotiators' approach to the judicial function evidences 'mistrust in the competence and independence of the judiciary'.[67] This led to the adoption of features of the Rome Statute designed to constrain the judicial function including, complex definitions of crimes, the inclusion of additional 'Elements of Crimes' for each offense, as well as provisions on the Statute's interpretation in Articles 21 and 22. It also led to a new and potentially cumbersome institutional innovation, a Pre-trial Chamber, to serve as a filter for *proprio motu* investigations and confirmation decisions. For this and other reasons, perhaps, fractured opinions and unclear methodology have slowed the Court

64 IER (n 2) 206–262.

65 'The Prosecutor of the International Criminal Court, Karim A.A. Khan QC announces conclusion of the investigation phase in the Situation in the Central African Republic', ICC OTP (16 December 2022) available at <https://www.icc-cpi.int/news/prosecutor-international-criminal-court-karim-aa-khan-kc-announces-conclusion-investigation-0> accessed 30 April 2023.

66 Ibid.

67 J Powderly, *Judges and the Making of International Criminal Law* (Brill Nihoff 2020), 465.

in finding its voice.[68] Yet there have also been important judgments regarding the substantive law of the ICC which constitute a significant achievement of the Institution.

Decisions on child soldiers;[69] rape and sexual slavery;[70] forced marriage and forced pregnancy;[71] the definitions of armed conflict;[72] attacks on cultural property and reparations;[73] and procedures such as guilty pleas,[74] the 'no case to answer' motion,[75] and defenses such as duress and mental defect are important.[76] Less felicitous have been the judgments setting out the elements for establishing modes of liability under article 25 of the Rome Statute, and particularly the adoption of the 'control of the crime' theory by the Court incorporated into article 25(3)(a) of the Statute. These have been confusing to apply, inconsistent with the Statute itself, subject to important judicial dissents, and surprising to those who closely followed the Statute's negotiation.[77]

68 See ibid. Powderly; L N Sadat, 'Meeting Challenges: Politics, Trial Processes, and Early Judicial Work', *in* R H Steinberg (ed.), *The International Criminal Court: Contemporary Challenges and Reform Proposals* (Brill Nijhoff 2020), 319–334.

69 See, e.g., Public Redacted Judgment on the appeal of Mr Thomas Lubanga Dyilo against his conviction, *Lubanga, Situation in the Democratic Republic of the Congo*, ICC-01/04-01/06-3121-Red, AC, ICC, 1 December 2014.

70 Public redacted Judgment on the appeals of Mr Bosco Ntaganda and the Prosecutor against the decision of Trial Chamber VI of 8 July 2019 entitled 'Judgment', *Ntaganda, Situation in the Democratic Republic of the Congo*, ICC-01/04-02/06-2666-Red, AC, ICC, 30 March 2021 (affirming the conviction).

71 Judgment on the appeal of Mr Ongwen against the decision of Trial Chamber IX of 4 February 2021 entitled 'Trial Judgment', *Ongwen, Situation in Uganda*, ICC-02/04-01/15-2022-Red, AC, ICC, 15 December 2022.

72 Decision on Sentence pursuant to Article 76 of the Statute, *Lubanga, Situation in the Democratic Republic of the Congo*, ICC-01/04-01/06-2901, TC I, ICC, 10 July 2012).

73 Judgment and Sentence, *Al Mahdi, Situation in the Republic of Mali*, ICC-01/12-01/15-171, TC VIII, ICC, 27 September 2016.

74 Ibid.

75 The adoption of this procedure has been contentious and its application not yet settled at the Court. See Judgment in the appeal of the Prosecutor against Trial Chamber I's decision on the no case to answer motions, *Gbagbo and Blé Goudé, Situation in the Republic of Côte d'Ivoire*, ICC-02/11-01/15-1400, AC, ICC, 31 March 2021.

76 *Ongwen Appeals Judgment* (n 71).

77 This critique is laid out in L N Sadat and J M Jolly, 'Seven Canons of ICC Treaty Interpretation: Making Sense of Article 25's Rorschach Blot' (2014) 27 *Leiden Journal of International Law* 755. The current system is so complex that Carsten Stahn's excellent volume on the International Criminal Court contains five separate Chapters on Article 25, or ten percent of the book's content. See Carsten Stahn (ed.), *The Law and Practice of the International Criminal Court* (Oxford University Press 2015).

The judges of the future ICC of 2032 and 2042 will undoubtedly find additional opportunities to advance and enhance international criminal law as they continue to adjudicate cases from around the world. They must also protect the rights of the accused. They bear a heavy burden not only to adjudicate in a manner that is efficient, effective, and impartial, but to communicate their rulings in language that can reach a broader public, explaining the law of the ICC to potential perpetrators and providing a sense of satisfaction and solace to victims that feel their claims have been heard and adjudicated. Given the importance of public perception and legitimacy when ruling upon the guilt or innocence of high-ranking individuals, they may wish to curb the tendency towards dissents and separate opinions manifested thus far,[78] allowing the Court to speak with one voice as often as possible, and reserving dissent for rare and critical legal issues[79] in which it is important to appeal 'to the intelligence of a future day'.[80]

### 3.4 *Solidifying the Founding Principles of the Court's Jurisdiction*

If the past two decades have demonstrated that the ICC *can work in practice,* it remains to be seen whether it works *in theory.* Unlike the ICTY, the ICC did not have a '*Tadić* moment' early in its history; that is, a case that set out the fundamental parameters of the Court's jurisdiction and operation, in a comprehensive way.[81] Perhaps this is because it seemed obvious to the negotiators

78 U.S. scholars have noted how dissents have become a troubling feature of U.S. Supreme Court practice due to their overuse and capacity to undermine the Court's legitimacy. J Knight and L Epstein, 'The Norm of Stare Decisis', (1996), 40 *American Journal of Political Science* 1018; C F Hobson, 'Defining the Office: John Marshall as Chief Justice', (2006) 154 *University of Pennsylvania Law Review* 1421. Conversely, the unanimous decisions of the European Court of Justice were often cited as a factor that contributed to its success and legitimacy, although scholars have recently challenged that narrative, suggesting that it may lead to decrease in quality and/or a lack of transparency. R Alford, 'The Inferior Quality of ECJ Decisions' (*Opinio Juris*, 31 October 2007) *available at* <http://opiniojuris.org/2007/10/31/the-inferior-quality-of-ecj-decisions/> accessed 30 April 2023.

79 In an important multi-part study, Nancy Combs has taken up this question in a serious way, finding that the putative benefit of dissents is less than often touted: they rarely later become law (although important counter examples can of course be found including the dissent of Judge Usacka in the Al Bashir genocide case, for example). See N Combs, 'The Impact of Separate Opinions on International Criminal Law', (2021) 62(1) *Virginia Journal of International Law* 1. See also R B Ginsburg, 'The Role of Dissenting Opinions', (2007) 95 *Minnesota Law Review* 1.

80 C E Hughs, *The Supreme Court of the United States* (Columbia University Press 1928), 67–68. Hughes notes that a judge should not be 'swift to dissent' or do so 'because of a lack of that capacity for cooperation which is of the essence of any group action'.

81 Decision on the Defence motion for interlocutory appeal on jurisdiction, *Tadić*, IT-94-1-A, AC, ICTY, 2 October 1995. The *Tadić Appeal* has been described as bold and visionary, and

and the Court's personnel. In 1998, the debates regarding the legality of the ICTY and ICTR's establishment had largely been settled by the ICTY Appeal's Chamber's 1995 decision on jurisdiction. When the ICC Statute was negotiated, it built upon the Nuremberg legacy and the establishment of the *ad hoc* tribunals for Rwanda and the former Yugsolavia. Writing in 1946, Egon Schwelb asked whether the International Military Tribunal at Nuremberg was an 'organ of the community of nations' representing the 'supremacy of international law over municipal law, and the overriding of national sovereignty by this organ of the international community',[82] or an occupation court. Although Schwelb found some evidence that the IMT's authority flowed from Control Council Law No. 10,[83] he nonetheless concluded that the tribunal had the character of an international judicial body, exercising jurisdiction 'on behalf of the international community, which of the relevant time was, and is now, represented for all practical purposes by the United Nations'.[84]

This was not a new idea,[85] although its effective implementation at Nuremberg was a first. The International Criminal Tribunals for the former Yugoslavia (ICTY) and Rwanda (ICTR) were established quickly by the Security

was penned by Antonio Cassese, one of the primary architects of modern international criminal law. M Fan, 'Custom, General Principles and the Great Architect Cassese' (2012) 10 *Journal of International Criminal Justice* 1063.

82 E Schwelb, 'Crimes against Humanity', (1946) 23 *British Yearbook of International Law* 178.

83 Allied Control Council Law No. 10, Punishment of Persons Guilty of War Crimes, Crimes against Peace and against Humanity, 20 December 1945, Official Gazette of the Control Council for Germany, No 3, Berlin, 31 January 1946.

84 E Schwelb (n 82) 210.

85 According to Christopher Hall of Amnesty International, the first draft was a proposal by Gustave Moynier in 1872 for a court to prevent and punish violations of the Geneva Conventions. C K Hall, 'The First Proposal for a Permanent International Criminal Court' (1999) 38 *International Review of the Red Cross* 57. Following that was, of course, was the provisions of the Treaty of Versailles calling for the trial of the Kaiser. W A Schabas, *The Trial of the Kaiser* (Oxford University Press 2018). The first modern draft statutes for an international criminal court emerged in 1924 and 1926 from the International Law Association. See, e.g., International Law Association, *Report of the 34th Conference* (1926), 183. See also the very early and interesting work of Henri Donnedieu de Vabres, the distinguished French law professor who would ultimately serve as a judge on the Nuremberg Tribunal, H Donnedieu de Vabres, 'La Cour Permanente de Justice international et sa vocation en matière criminelle' (1924) 1 *Revue Internationale de Droit Pénal* 175, and his contrast between an imperialist or nationalist approach to international criminal law versus a universalist or cosmopolitan approach. H Donnedieu de Vabres, *Introduction à l'Etude du Droit Pénal International, Essai d'histoire et de critique sur la Compétence Criminelle dans les Rapports avec L'Etranger* (Paris: Recueil Sirey 1922), 458–459. See generally L N Sadat, 'The Nuremberg Paradox' (2010) 58 *American Journal of Internatioanl Law* 151.

Council (rather than by treaty, which the Secretary-General opined would take too long)[86] and like the IMT itself, rested on the idea that international crimes *stricto sensu* were properly the subject of international adjudication. This conception also informed the establishment of the ICC as a universal jurisdiction court, subject to jurisdictional limitations in situations not referred by the Security Council, and other constraints including complementarity, gravity, and other admissibility criteria.[87] The United States argued at Rome that, as a treaty court, the ICC had no judicial authority over the nationals of non-States Parties as those States have not 'delegated' authority to it.[88] This 'delegation theory', and variants thereof, has attracted additional adherents,[89] most recently a committee advising the Dutch government.[90] It has been challenged by other scholars, including this author,[91] and repudiated by the former U.S. Head of Delegation at Rome, Ambassador David Scheffer, who advanced it in

86 Report of the Secretary-General Pursuant to Paragraph 2 of the Security Council Resolution 808 (1993), UN Doc S/25704 (3 May 1993), paras 31–68.

87 Sadat and Carden (n 9) 412–415.

88 T Meron, 'The Court We Want' (November–December 1998) *ASIL Newsletter* (American Society of International Law, Washington, D.C.), 9; M Morris, 'High Crimes and Misconceptions: The ICC and Non-party States' (2001) 64 *Law and Contemporary Problems* 13, 15; D J Scheffer, 'The United States and the International Criminal Court' (1999) 93(1) *American Journal of Internatioanl Law* 12, 18.

89 D Akande, 'The Jurisdiction of the International Criminal Court over Nationals of Non-Parties: Legal Basis and Limits', (2003) 1 *Journal of International Criminal Justice* 618 (finding jurisdiction permissible, but invoking procedural limits upon its exercise under the delegation theory); M A Newton, 'How the International Criminal Court Threatens Treaty Norms', (2017) 49 *Vanderbilt Journal of Transnational Law* 371; T de Souza Dias, 'The Nature of the Rome Statute and the Place of International Law before the International Criminal Court', (2019) 17 J. *Journal of International Criminal Justice* 507, 515. *Cf.* Monique Cormier, 'Delegation of Jurisdiction: The Concepts', in Monique Cormier (ed.), *The Jurisdiction of the International Criminal Court over Nationals of Non-States Parties* (Cambridge University Press 2020).

90 Advisory Committee on Public International Law, 'Challenges in prosecuting the crime of aggression: jurisdiction and immunities' Advisory Report No 40 (12 September 2022), available at <https://www.advisorycommitteeinternationallaw.nl/publications/advisory-reports/2022/09/12/challenges-in-prosecuting-the-crime-of-aggression-jurisdiction-and-immunities> accessed 30 April 2023 (arguing that States 'transfer' their criminal jurisdiction to the ICC).

91 See, e.g, R Cryer, 'The ICC and its Relationship to Non-States Parties' in C Stahn (ed.), *The Law and Practice of the International Criminal Court* (Oxford University Press 2003), 260–280; C Eboe-Osuji, *Not Immune from Punishment* (unpublished manuscript, forthcoming 2023); Sadat, *Transformation of International Law* (n 18) 103–121; M P Scharf, 'The ICC's Jurisdiction over the Nationals of Non-Party States: A Critique of the U.S. Position' (2001) 64 *Law and Contemporary Problems* 67.

the first place.[92] It has not found favor at the Court itself, although sometimes the term 'delegation' is employed by the OTP and Chambers in a non-technical sense. Rather, relying on the jurisprudence of the *ad hoc* international criminal tribunals, and the International Court of Justice, the ICC's judiciary have issued important decisions on the Court's extraterritorial jurisdiction in the Bangladesh/Myanmar situation,[93] on immunities in the *Al Bashir* immunity decision,[94] and on the status of Rome Statute crimes as customary international law in the *Abd-Al-Rahman* judgment.[95]

As Carsten Stahn has written, proponents of the 'delegation' theory of the ICC's jurisdiction have neglected 'univeralist foundations' that do not make the ICC's exercise of jurisdiction contingent upon the 'jurisdictional title' of States;[96] rather, it rests on the *ius puniendi* of the international community as a whole.[97] In a recent essay, I build upon this to show that the Court's jurisdiction cannot be described in a technical sense as having been 'delegated' to the Court by Statutes; rather, it is *conferred upon it* by the States Parties to the Rome Statute, and is limited only by its Statute and the principles of general

92 D Scheffer, 'The Self-Defeating Executive Order Against the International Criminal Court' (*Just Security*, 12 June 2020) <https://www.justsecurity.org/70742/the-self-defeating-executive-order-against-the-international-criminal-court/> accessed 30 April 2023. Noting that he used to 'make this theoretical international law argument [...] on behalf of the US government many years ago [which] [t]oday holds very little credibility'.

93 Decision on the Prosecution's Request for a Ruling on Jurisdiction under Article 19(3) of the Statute, *Situation in the People's Republic of Bangladesh/Republic of the Union of Myanmar*, ICC-RoC46(3)-01/18, PTC I, ICC, 6 September 2018.

94 Judgment in the Jordan Referral re-Al-Bashir Appeal, *Al Bashir*, *Situation in Darfur, Sudan*, ICC-02/05-01/09 OA2, AC, ICC, 6 May 2019.

95 Judgment on the appeal of Mr Abd-Al-Rahman against the Pre-Trial Chamber II's 'Decision on the Defence "Exception d'incompétence" (ICC-02/05-01/20-302)', *Abd-Al-Rahman, Situation in Darfur, Sudan*, ICC-02/05-01/20 OA8, AC, ICC, 1 November 2021.

96 C Stahn, 'Response: The ICC, Pre-Existing Jurisdictional Treaty Regimes, and the Limits of the Nemo Dat Quod Non Habet Doctrine—A Reply to Michael Newton' (2016) 49 *Vanderbilt Journal of Transnational Law* 443, 447, 488.

97 C Eboe-Osuji, 'The Absolute Clarity of International Legal Practice's Rejection of Immunity Before International Criminal Courts' (*Just Security*, 8 December 2022) available at <https://www.justsecurity.org/84416/the-absolute-clarity-of-international-legal-practices-rejection-of-immunity-before-international-criminal-courts/> accessed 30 April 2023; C Kreß, 'Article 98 – Cooperation with respect to waiver of immunity and consent to surrender' in O Triffterer and K Ambos (eds), *The Rome Statute of the International Criminal Court: Article-by-Article Commentary* 4th edn (CH Beck/Hart/Nomos 2022) 2585–2671 (explaining the role of the ICC in enforcing the *ius puniendi* of the international community).

international law.[98] The debate over the fundamental nature of the ICC's jurisdiction is critical, for it has profound implications regarding the territorial and geographic extent of the Statute's scope and on the question of immunities over nationals of non-States Parties. I return to this in the conclusion of this chapter.

### 3.5 *Adding New Crimes to the Rome Statute*

When the Diplomatic Conference ended, Resolution E of the Final Act left open the possibility of inserting treaty crimes into the Statute including terrorism and drug trafficking.[99] Little has been done to advance this proposal since 1998. Conversely, Resolution F charged the Preparatory Commission that would develop the texts needed to bring the Statute into force with developing 'proposals on a provision on aggression'.[100] A working group on aggression was established immediately, which produced a text submitted to the first ICC Review Conference in Kampala, Uganda, in 2010. The Aggression amendments were adopted at Kampala,[101] but with jurisdictional limitations that departed from the unitary treatment of the four ICC core crimes and their adjudication for unlike the other three crimes, where a referral comes from a State or the Prosecutor *proprio motu,* the Court cannot exercise jurisdiction over the crime of aggression over the nationals of non-States Parties.[102] The Ukraine situation – involving aggression by a non-State Party against a State accepting the ICC's jurisdiction – underscores the inappropriateness of those limits, given the inability of the ICC to address the crime of aggression against Ukraine. This has led to calls for an amendment to the Statute undoing the Kampala restrictions on jurisdiction as well as a concerted push for a 'Special Tribunal

98 L N Sadat, 'The Conferred Jurisdiction of the International Criminal Court', Washington University in St. Louis Legal Studies Research Paper No. 23-03-01, 2 March 2023, < https://ssrn.com/abstract=4376240.>.

99 Resolution E, 'Final Act of the UN Diplomatic Conference of Plenipotentiaries on the Establishment of an International Criminal Court' (17 July 1998) UN Doc A/CONF.183/10 <https://legal.un.org/icc/rome/proceedings/E/Rome%20Proceedings_v1_e.pdf> accessed 30 April 2023.

100 Ibid., Resolution F, para. 7.

101 Adoption of Amendments on the Crime of Aggression, Resolution RC/Res.6 (11 June 2010, Kampala, Uganda) available at <https://asp.icc-cpi.int/sites/asp/files/asp_docs/RC2010/AMENDMENTS/CN.651.2010-ENG-CoA.pdf> accessed 30 April 2023. Among other things, the amendments deleted article 5(2) of the Statute and added article 8*bis* (crime of aggression) and 15*bis* and 15*ter* (jurisdiction over the crime of aggression for State referral, *proprio motu* and Security Council, respectively). Jurisdiction over the crime of aggression was activated by the ASP in December 2017, with effect on 17 July 2018. As of this writing, 44 States have ratified the aggression amendments.

102 Rome Statute, Art. 15*bis*(5).

on Aggression' to try Russian, and possibly Belarus, high-ranking officials who planned or carried out the war against Ukraine.[103] The United States and the United Kingdom were the chief proponents of the jurisdictional restrictions on the crime of aggression, meaning that the United States essentially won at Kampala what it had unsuccessfully sought at Rome.

Additional amendments have also been introduced adding specific war crimes to the Rome Statute, and there is currently a sustained campaign promoting the inclusion of ecocide as a 'fifth crime' in the Rome Statute.[104] Given the problematic incorporation of the aggression amendments, however, the addition of new treaty crimes or other offenses, such as ecocide, which are not yet established in customary international law, could further fracture the Court's jurisdictional regime. Instead, as there is a clear desire to enhance the reach and enforcement of ICL generally, it may be that other implementation measures such as the adoption of new treaties (such as the crimes against humanity and mutual legal assistance treaties mentioned previously), national model legislation on ecocide,[105] or the establishment of new courts such as the proposal for an anti-corruption court[106] could be more effective. The growth and continued development of international criminal law outside the Rome Statute was expected and welcomed by the Statute itself. Article 10 provides that '[n]othing in this Part shall be interpreted as limiting or prejudicing in any way existing or developing rules of international law for purposes other than this Statute'.[107]

### 3.6 *Victims and Witnesses*

Finally, in thinking about the assumptions of the past and the Court's future trajectory, the institution was intended to be much more victim-oriented than its predecessors, and that the Trust Fund for Victims could be an important

---

103 J Trahan, 'The Case for Creating a Special Tribunal to Prosecute the Crime of Aggression Against Ukraine (Part III)' (*Just Security*, 26 September 2022) available at <https://www.justsecurity.org/83238/tribunal-crime-of-aggression-part-three/> accessed 30 April 2023.

104 K Mackintosh and L Oldring, 'Watch This Space: Momentum Toward an International Crime of Ecocide' (*Just Security*, 5 December 2022) available at <https://www.justsecurity.org/84367/watch-this-space-momentum-toward-an-international-crime-of-ecocide/> accessed 30 April 2023.

105 D Robinson, 'Ecocide – Puzzles and Possibilities' (2022) 20 *Journal of International Criminal Justice* 313.

106 M L Wolf, R J Goldstone and R I Rotberg (Cambridge: American Academy of Arts and Sciences, 2022) available at <https://www.amacad.org/publication/proposal-international-anti-corruption-court> accessed 30 April 2023.

107 Rome Statute, Art. 10.

innovation of the Rome Statute system. This has turned out to be correct, and, at the same time, difficult to implement. The TFV needs additional resources to be effective; and the victims' rights regime and reparations jurisprudence of the Statute remain a work in progress.[108] That said, both the TFV and the focus on victim participation and reparations have tremendous potential to bring 'justice' in a practical, as opposed to juridical, sense directly into afflicted communities.

## 4 Conclusion

### 4.1 *The Quest for Universality*

Although much more could be said about the ICC of the future, surely the question of universality looms large, as it goes to legitimacy as well as effectiveness and independence. The ICC only works when States support it, and universal ratification therefore remains a critical goal. States Parties provide funding to the Court and have legal obligations to cooperate. There are 123 States Parties and a handful of others that were parties or have accepted jurisdiction under article 12(3). Armenia has recently announced its decision to ratify, and Ukraine is expected to be next. Increasing that number is paramount and it is likely that more small to mid-sized democracies will join so that the final number will at least achieve two-thirds of the General Assembly's membership, or even the number of signatories (139).

But what of the remaining permanent members of the Security Council?[109] It is hard to imagine now, a decade after Judge Kaul's essay, when the situation in Xinjiang has been labeled a genocide against the Uyghurs,[110] that China will join the ICC anytime soon. Will the United States? Perhaps. While the United States has vacillated between constructive engagement and outright hostility over the years, sustained advocacy inside the United States as well as U.S. support for prosecutions resulting from the conflict in Ukraine have dramatically changed U.S. perceptions. Moreover, much of the change is bipartisan, and

108 See, e.g., S Vasiliev, 'Victim Participation Revisited—What the ICC is Learning about Itself' in C Stahn (ed.), *The Law and Practice of the International Criminal Court* (Oxford University Press, 2015).

109 Iran almost always attends the ICC ASP and India is another populous and important State. Discussion of their positions towards the ICC, or of other regions of the world more generally, is beyond the scope of this short contribution.

110 See, e.g., L Maizland, 'China's Repression of Uyghurs in Xinjiang' (*Council on Foreign Relations*, 22 September 2022) available at <https://www.cfr.org/backgrounder/china-xinjiang-uyghurs-muslims-repression-genocide-human-rights> accessed 30 April 2023.

not limited to Democrats. Following Russia's invasion of Ukraine in February 2022, the U.S. Senate adopted Resolution 546 and the House of Representatives adopted Resolution 76 expressing the sense of Congress that it supports ICC investigations and prosecutions of Russian war crimes.[111] More recently, a bipartisan congressional delegation made an historic visit to the Court and were well-received. At the twenty-first session of the ICC ASP in December 2022, U.S. Ambassador-at-Large for Global Criminal Justice, Beth Van Schaack, noted that the United States 'signed the Rome Statute' and can do much 'to advance the work of the Court', the first unqualified acknowledgement of the U.S's status as an ICC signatory State since December 2000.[112]

As the lead plaintiff in one of two lawsuits brought against the Trump administration, alleging that the sanctions imposed on Prosecutor Fatou Bensouda and Phakiso Mochochko was unconstitutional, I am painfully aware of the vitriol and anger directed at the Court in 2020 by the former administration.[113] Bluster and anger may evince weakness, however, as well as strength. A recent survey of U.S. federal case law revealed 91 federal court decisions citing the ICC Statute as authoritative on various issues.[114] Moreover, the Court polls favorably amongst Americans.[115] Depending on the trajectory of the ICC over the next few years, and the internal political situation in the United States, U.S. opposition could certainly soften, and ratification become envisageable by 2042 (it took the United States forty years to ratify the genocide convention).

---

111 R Goodman, 'Top Cover: Congressional Republicans Pave Way for U.S. Policy Shift on Int'l Criminal Court', (*Just Security*, 13 April, 2022) available at <https://www.justsecurity.org/81093/top-cover-congressional-republicans-pave-wave-for-us-policy-shift-on-intl-criminal-court/> accessed 30 April 2023.

112 Statement on Behalf of the United States of America, 21st Session of the Assembly of States Parties to the Rome Statute, December 6, 2022, Remarks by Ambassador-at-Large for Global Criminal Justice Beth Van Schaack (6 December 2022) available at <https://asp.icc-cpi.int/sites/asp/files/2022-12/ASP21.GD_.USA_.06.12.pdf> accessed 30 April 2023.

113 L N Sadat et al. v Donald J Trump, et al., Civil Case No 21-00416, Complaint, 15 January 2021 <https://www.aclu.org/legal-document/sadat-v-trump-complaint-0> accessed 30 April 2023, Stipulation of Dismissal Under Fed. R. Civ. P. 41(a), 24 May 2021 <https://www.aclu.org/legal-document/sadat-v-biden-stipulation-dismissal> accessed 30 April 2023.

114 The research was conducted in October 2022 using the Westlaw database and has not yet been published. L N Sadat, 'Is the International Criminal Court Statute U.S. Law?', Unpublished Draft (forthcoming 2023).

115 A poll conducted for the American Bar Association in 2018 (during the Trump Administration) showed increased knowledge and awareness of the ICC and increased support for U.S. participation. IPSOS, Number of American Who Support the ICC Grows (11 April 2018) available at <https://www.ipsos.com/sites/default/files/ct/news/documents/2018-04/american_bar_association-factum-2018_04_11.pdf> accessed 30 April 2023.

### 4.2 *Selectivity and Double Standards*

There are many concerns at the ICC regarding selectivity and double standards both *within* situation countries and *between* situation countries. Within situations, self-referrals have led to the concern that only rebel leaders will be prosecuted, not government officials, or that the OTP sometimes acts opportunistically simply because it may have the ability to charge a particular accused. Likewise, between situations, the absence of three members of the Security Council from the Court raises questions of double standards given their ability to refer situations for investigation under Article 13(b) of the Statute. This, as well as the conflict with the African Union, the flurry of State support for the Ukraine referral and the establishment of a Special Tribunal on Aggression relating only to Ukraine (contrasted with the lack of international justice for Syria, for example), the dismissal of the British/Iraq inquiry, and the Prosecutor's decision to 'depriortise' crimes in Afghanistan not committed by the Taliban have led to questions about selectivity and double standards at the Court.

The victims in all the situations that are investigated by the Court. The real issue, then, is what to do for the victims *not* receiving justice. There is no easy answer to this dilemma. The ICC is a treaty court, and some situations are beyond its jurisdiction, and unlikely to be referred by the Security Council. Redoubling efforts to achieve universality and supporting the exercise of the Court's jurisdiction 'without fear or favour', are critically important. Yet for the time being, it will be true that the ICC is limited to prosecuting the individuals over whom it can reasonably acquire jurisdiction.

The public and scholars often discuss ICC situations in terms of winners and losers, States either benefiting from ICC attention when other States are not (like Ukraine), or States being targeted by the ICC when other States are not (like the AU complaints). This narrative misses the mark. The International Criminal Court does not target States. It prosecutes individuals. Crimes committed by high-ranking state officials often represent state policy. However, as Justice Jackson himself observed in Courtroom 600, it was not the German people who were indicted at Nuremberg, but the twenty-two men in the dock. It would be helpful to denationalize the way the Court's jurisdiction is critiqued.

### 4.3 *The Danger of Eroding the Nuremberg Paradigm*

There are signs that the understandings of 1998 are being eroded in terms of the equality of defendants before the law, the inapplicability of immunity for the commission of ICC crimes, and the idea that the nationals of non-States Parties cannot be brought before the Court even if they commit crimes on the territory of ICC States Parties. While limited to the States voting 'no' at Rome, these ideas may be spreading. Some have suggested during the debates concerning the establishment of a Special Aggression Tribunal in the Russia/Ukraine situation that high ranking Russian individuals (such as Vladmir Putin) would be immune before the ICC as a non-State Party national, even for crimes ordered against Ukraine and committed on the territory of Ukraine.[116] A recent draft legal opinion submitted to the European Union makes the same assertion.[117] This was not the understanding that informed the negotiation of Article 27 of the Rome Statute, which was premised on customary international law and the practice of the Nuremberg and *ad hoc* international criminal tribunals.[118] To date, *every* international court or tribunal faced with this issue – without exception – has rejected the plea for immunity, including the ICC Appeals Chamber. If States Parties to the Rome Statute wish to change the meaning of Article 27, it is for them to take the difficult political decision to insert immunity for Heads of State and other government officials into the Rome Statute itself. If they do not, the Appeals Chamber decision has, at this point, settled the question of immunities before the Court. Although it involved a Head of State charged in a case involving a Security Council referral, the referral mechanism should not change the operation or application of the Statute itself, to avoid the double standards problem evoked above. As Claus Kreß has noted, 'the Court was not designed as an institution with two fundamentally different faces depending on whether or not the SC triggered the proceedings before it'.[119] Likewise, the 'delegation theory' does not properly describe the exercise of jurisdiction by the Rome Statute. Of course, if States Parties to the Statute wish for the Court *not* to exercise jurisdiction over the nationals of Non-States Parties, they could amend the Statute to so provide. The fact that they have not suggests that they approve the Chamber's decisions on that question *and* do not consider it to be problematic as a matter of international law or policy.[120]

---

116 Dutch Advisory Opinion (n 88). Ironically the U.S. Congress apparently does not believe he is immune from prosecution at the Court. See (n 111) and sources cited.

117 Copy on file with the author.

118 L N Sadat, 'Heads of State and other government officials before the International Criminal Court: the uneasy revolution continues' in M M DeGuzman and V Oosterveld (eds), *The Elgar Companion to the International Criminal Court* (Elgar 2020), 96–127. See also A Skander Galand, 'The Nature of the Rome Statute of the International Criminal court (and its Amended Jurisdictional Scheme)' (2019) 17 *Journal of International Criminal Justice* 933; Kreß (n 97) 2650.

119 Kreß (n 97) 2650.

120 See also A A Haque, 'Head of State Immunity is too Important for the International Court of Justice' (*Just Security*, 24 February 2020) available at <https://www.justsecurity.org/68801/head-of-state-immunity-is-too-important-for-the-international-court-of-justice/> accessed 30 April 2023.

### 4.4 *Final Thoughts*

As a famous American baseball player, Yogi Berra, once noted, 'it's tough to make predictions, especially about the future'. Given current trends, the future of the ICC is assured if the democracies of the world remain strong and committed to the Court. The Court faces a series of serious internal challenges but appears to be addressing them methodically. Court watchers and the blogosphere have been brutal – and sometimes unfair – in their critiques, a phenomenon that is likely to continue. This means that the ICC must develop a robust public outreach and media presence to present its own side of the story. The current, challenging geopolitical environment underscores the continuing and pressing need for the ICC while, simultaneously, stressing it. While China, the Russian Federation and the United States are not parties to the Statute, at this moment only the Russian Federation appears completely disengaged, even hostile. Conversely, the United States is now actively supporting the institution, although is still not ready to ratify the treaty and the Afghanistan and Palestine situations could test its newfound commitment.

By and large, the States Parties to the Rome Statute have not wavered in their belief that justice and accountability are a cornerstone of a more peaceful world, and in their support for the Court. As Portugal observed in the General Debate at the last ICC ASP,

> As the world's permanent international criminal court, the ICC represents a historic achievement of humankind. It plays a central role in the fight against impunity, bringing justice to victims, and in the prevention of the commission of atrocity crimes, contributing, in a very significant way, to the advancement of the rule of law, and stable, peaceful societies.[121]

Some have worried that the Court's performance has been 'lackluster' and that the original assumptions and design may have been flawed.[122] Yet although many assumptions worked less than foreseen, others outperformed expectations, and not all the surprises over the past twenty years have been unpleasant ones. During the next two decades, we can, and should, expect the unexpected. The ICC clearly faces significant challenges, and how it handles the Ukraine situation will be a real test of its impact in the world. It will need to meet the

121 Statement of Portugal, Twenty-first Session of the ICC Assembly of States Parties (December 2022) available at <https://asp.icc-cpi.int/sites/asp/files/2022-12/ASP21.GD_.PRT_.05.12.pdf> accessed 30 April 2023.

122 WA Schabas, 'The dynamics of the Rome Conference' in MM DeGuzman and V Oosterveld (eds), *The Elgar Companion to the International Criminal Court* (Elgar 2020), 3–19.

moment to ensure its successful future. If it fails in Ukraine, it may lose State support. If it succeeds, meaning that it is able to bring cases within a reasonable period and prosecute them to a high degree of professionalism, without neglecting other important situations on its docket, it will have done much to demonstrate the utility of international justice. The sceptics seem to want the ICC to fail. Like Judge Kaul, however, I prefer to remain optimistic that the ICC of the future can and will succeed. For it seems far better to light a candle than curse the darkness

CHAPTER 25

# Reflections on Ecocide as a Fifth Crime under the Rome Statute of the International Criminal Court

*Phoebe Okowa and Olivia Flasch*

## 1 Introduction

Threats to the environment and the concomitant climate crisis it has precipitated remains the defining issue of our generation. Since the Stockholm Conference of 1972, there has been a plethora of initiatives on how best to respond to the environmental challenges faced by the global community.[1] The period after the Stockholm Conference witnessed increased international awareness as to the centrality of environmental values and how best to respond to them. However, much of this occurred in an incremental fashion and not all environmental concerns received uniform attention. Many of the responses have largely been in the form of regulatory standards enforced through national institutions and treaty compliance regimes, and there has been profound scepticism at the efficacy of some of these regimes.

National implementation is constrained in many countries by the lack of appropriate legislation, financial resources, environmentally sound technologies and institutional capacities. Many of the environmental obligations are obligations of conduct, leaving States with a wide margin of discretion on how to implement them. Compliance failures are hardly backed by any hard sanctions. Liability regimes remain the exception, but even when in place, they can be easily circumvented by corporations who buy themselves out of obligations

1 Report of the United Nations Conference on the Human Environment, Stockholm, 5–16 June 1972, UN Doc. A/CONF.48/14/Rev. 1; ECOSOC, The Role of Criminal Law in the Protection of the Environment, 25 July 1994, UN Doc. E/RES/1994/15, Annex: Recommendations Concerning the Role of Criminal Law in Protecting the Environment; F. Mégret, 'The Case for a General International Crime Against the Environment' in S. Jodoin and M-C. Cordonier Segger (eds), *Sustainable Development, International Criminal Justice, and Treaty Implementation* (CUP 2013), pp. 50–70; M. A. Gray, 'The International Crime of Ecocide' (1996) 26(2) *California Western International Law Journal*, 215.

 DOI:10.1163/9789004529939_026

by treating environmental damage as a culturally accepted consequence of industrial capitalism.[2]

Historically, environmental damage has been assessed against the productive value the industry offered to society. Courts tended to demand tangible proof of injury before granting compensation, and only reluctantly imposed conditions on the future operation of even the most egregious offenders.[3] Moreover, environmental regimes were characterised by systemic weaknesses in connection with enforcement; the emphasis was on prevention, with States being given a wide latitude on how to realise the broad objectives of prevention of environmental damage without recourse to coercive measures. Yet in many instances, these non-coercive measures have proved ineffectual, and there is evidence of an increasing recognition that dealing with key perpetrators of systemic environmental damage requires a multiplicity of social and legal interventions.[4] It is also the case that the ubiquitous absence of a coherent regime of enforcement at the international level, although frequently lamented, has not been properly addressed.[5]

The Independent Expert Panel on The Legal Definition of Ecocide (the "Independent Expert Panel") has recently reignited the debate for the inclusion of ecocide as a fifth crime under the Rome Statute.[6] However, the case for

---

2 J. R. Allum, '"An outcrop of Hell": History, Environment, and the Politics of the Trail Smelter Dispute' in R. M. Bratspies and R. A. Miller (eds), *Transboundary Harm in International Law: Lessons from the Trail Smelter Arbitration* (CUP 2009), pp. 13–26; Mégret (n 1), p. 4.

3 See K Mickelson, 'Notes and Comments: Rereading Trail Smelter' (1993) 31 *Canadian Journal of International Law* 219; P. Okowa, 'The Legacy of *Trail Smelter* in the Field in the Field of Transboundary Air Pollution' in Bratspies and Miller (n 2).

4 See generally F. Mégret, 'The Problem of an International Criminal Law of the Environment' (2011) 36 *Columbia J Env. L* 195.

5 See for instance UNEP, 'Observations on the Scope and Application of Universal Jurisdiction to Environmental Protection' available at: <https://www.un.org/en/ga/sixth/75/universal_jurisdiction/unep_e.pdf> last accessed 20 March 2023; UNEP, 'Environmental Rule of Law: First Global Report' (24 January 2019) available at <https://www.unep.org/resources/assessment/environmental-rule-law-first-global-report> last accessed 20 March 2023.

6 Stop Ecocide Foundation, 'Independent Expert Panel for the Legal Definition of Ecocide: Commentary and Core Text' (June 2021), available at <https://static1.squarespace.com/static/5ca2608ab914493c64ef1f6d/t/60d7479cf8e7e5461534dd07/1624721314430/SE+Foundation+Commentary+and+core+text+revised+%281%29.pdf> (last accessed 20 March 2023) ("Independent Expert Panel"). Although ecocide has entered the Lexicon of Academic Literature, its status in general international law is at best *lex ferenda*. See for instance recent statement by the UNEP Executive Director Inger Andersen in which she categorically stated that ecocide "is not a word which the UN has a definition for. It does not exist in our vocabulary", 'UN has no definition for 'ecocide' – UNEP Executive Director (*Interfax Ukraine*, 17 March 2023), available at: <https://en.interfax.com.ua/news/general/898195.html> last accessed 20 March 2023.

a distinct penal regime for environmental damage goes back much further, to the early days of the environmental movement, especially in the period immediately following the Stockholm Declaration on the Human Environment.[7] The Vietnam War, and the extensive, long-term, and unprecedented environmental damage caused by the United States' use of agent orange brought to the fore the acute need for a distinct legal framework for the protection of the environment in situations of armed conflict.[8] The concerns raised in that conflict were given legal imprimatur when the occasion arose to revise the two Protocols to the Geneva Conventions in 1977.[9] There was nothing particularly radical, though, in terms of the consequences contemplated by the inclusion of environmental harm in the two protocols. The general expectation was that the violation of the distinctly environmental provisions would simply be subject to the normal delictual consequences under the law of State responsibility. Crucially, they would provide a basic yardstick for preventative decision-making. Yet, the seeds for a distinct penal regime, to deal with particularly egregious assaults on the environment, had been gaining currency in the academic literature since the early 1970's.[10]

In a highly influential article published in 1973, Richard Falk drew parallels between genocide and ecocide, and while the former was directed at a specific intent to destroy human beings, deliberate and systemic destruction of the environment would equally be stigmatised as a form of ecocide.[11] In his article, Falk, referring to the war in Indochina, exhorted the international community to capitalise on the increased public sensitivity to the importance of environmental values and to "promote the development of the new law that captures the uniqueness of recent developments and anticipates future dangers" noting that "in particular, the search for clear standards of legal prohibition directed

7 R. Falk, 'Environmental Warfare and Ecocide: Facts, Appraisal, and Proposals' (1973) 9(1) *Belgian Review of International Law*, 1.

8 A. H. Westing, 'The Environmental Aftermath of Warfare in Vietnam' (1983) 23(2) *Natural Resources Journal* 365; A. H. Westing, 'Environmental Consequences of the Second Indochina War: A Case Study' (1975) 4(5/6) *AMBIO* 216; A. Kumar Sen, 'Addressing the Harmful Legacy of Agent Orange in Vietnam' (*USIP*, 27 January 2022), available at: <https://www.usip.org/publications/2022/01/addressing-harmful-legacy-agent-orange-vietnam> (last accessed 20 March 2023).

9 See Protocol Additional to the Geneva Conventions of 12 August 1949, and relating to the Protection of Victims of International Armed Conflicts (Protocol I) (adopted 18 June 1977, entered into force 7 December 1978) 1125 UNTS 3.

10 For an account of the early academic literature, See D. Zeirler, *The Invention of Ecocide: Agent Orange, Vietnam, and the Scientists Who Changed the Way We Think About the Environment* (Athens, University of Georgia, 2011).

11 Falk (n 7).

explicitly toward environmental warfare might help shape the future conduct."[12] Falk anticipated a penal regime to supplement the responsibility of States for environmental damage.[13] He was careful, though, to take a restrictive view of ecocide, confining it to direct attacks on the environment and excluding attacks that resulted in incidental environmental damage that may be regarded as a logical consequence of war. Falk's concerns, like much of the subsequent debate in this field, were largely directed at serious environmental damage in war and no consideration as such was given to systemic environmental damage that may be equally pernicious but taking place in situations of peace.

After the initial flurry of interest inspired by the Vietnam conflict, more than a decade passed before there was any serious discussion on the environmental effects of war. The Gulf War of 1991 brought to the fore in a profound and unexpected way the seriousness of environmental damage caused by warfare. International Conferences,[14] United Nations agencies,[15] and the academic literature[16] immediately started treating the issue as one of some urgency, requiring coherent and comprehensive action at the international level. There were even suggestions that a fifth Geneva Convention, specifically dedicated to preventing environmental damage, should be enacted.[17] The debates also

12 Ibid, p. 3.

13 Ibid, p. 2.

14 First International Conference on Addressing Environmental Consequences of War: Legal, Economic, and Scientific Perspectives (Environmental Law Institute, Washington, D.C., 1998); Consultations on the Law Concerning the Protection of the Environment in Times of Armed Conflict (International Council of Environmental Law/IUCN, Munich, 13–15 December 1991); United Nations, 'Report of the Secretary-General on the Protection of the Environment in Times of Armed Conflict' (1993) UN Doc. A/48/269.

15 UNEP/A. S. Timoshenko, 'Conclusions by the Working Group of Experts on Liability and Compensation for Environmental Damage Arising from Military Activities' (1998), UN Doc. UNEP(02)/L693, paras. 39–42.

16 R. J. Grunawalt *et al.* (eds), *Protection of the Environment During Armed Conflict* (Newport, Rhode Island, Naval War College, 1997); S. Freeland, *Addressing the Intentional Destruction of the Environment During Warfare Under the Rome Statute of the International Criminal Court* (Intersentia, United Kingdom, 2015); P. Higgins *et al.*, 'Protecting the Planet: A Proposal for a Law of Ecocide' (2013) 59(3) *Crime Law and Social Change* 251; P. Higgins, *Eradicating Ecocide: Laws and Governance to Prevent the Destruction of Our Planet* (Shepheard-Walwyn Publishers, London, UK, 2010); See P. Higgins, *Earth Is Our Business: Changing the Rules of the Game* (Shepheard-Walwyn Publishers, London, UK 2012).

17 See G. Plant (ed), *Environmental Protection and the Law of War: A "Fifth Geneva" Convention on the Protection of the Environment in Time of Armed Conflict?* (London, Belhaven Press, 1992), 37, 43–61.

revealed significant gaps in the substantive content of responsibility for war-related damage, which had not until now, addressed the question of who should bear responsibility for environmental harm and what form the distribution of burdens and risks should take.[18]

The case for ecocide stems primarily from the recognition that in cases of serious and persistent environmental damage, punitive measures may have a distinct role to play in any enforcement regime. It recognises that liability regimes, such as those used to date, have the potential to incentivise industrial polluters to buy their way out of egregious environmental harm, and something more robust is needed. Moreover, the debate about environmental damage has until now been singularly concerned with damage to the environment in war. Ecocide pushes the boundary of the debate by requiring accountability for serious environmental damage, not just in situations of armed conflict, but also during peacetime.[19] Many wanton and deliberate peacetime activities such as deforestation, extensive habitat destruction, poaching, dumping of hazardous waste, unsustainable patterns of mining, unacceptable levels of carbon dioxide emissions as well as the destruction of carbon sinks and reservoirs have profound negative implications on the environment. It is in this context that ecocide is seen as yet one more tool in the armoury in the quest for both deterrence and effective accountability.

## 2 The Ecocide Debate and the Rome Statute Conference

The case for expanding the jurisdiction of the International Criminal Court ("ICC") jurisdiction to encompass a broader range of offences beyond the atrocity crimes was much discussed during the negotiation of the Rome Statute and formed a central element of the submissions of a number of States, especially those from the Caribbean. For Trinidad and Tobago, the concern was around the threats posed by drug trafficking.[20] For others, it was

18 P. Okowa, 'Environmental Justice in Situations of Armed Conflict' in J. Ebbesson and P. Okowa (eds), *Environmental Law and Justice in Context* (CUP 2009), p. 231.

19 The case for a unified regime has featured prominently in the literature. See for instance, M. A. Drumbl, 'Waging War Against the World: The Need to Move from War Crimes to Environmental Crimes' in J. E. Austin and C. E. Bruch (eds), *The Environmental Consequences of War* (CUP 2000).

20 See the proposal made by Trinidad to the 44th Session of the United Nations General Assembly in Report of the Sixth Committee of the United Nations General Assembly, UN Doc. A/44/770. See also the preambular paragraph of Resolution 44/39: 'International criminal responsibility of individuals and entities engaged in illicit trafficking in narcotic

terrorism.[21] In both instances, the case for expanding the Court's jurisdiction received a cool reception because it was felt that the Court would be largely ill-equipped to rule on activities, the adjudication of which depended to a great extent on the reception of detailed intelligence from within national legal systems. Moreover, there was the understandable reticence that a court with broad jurisdiction over almost everything would be unacceptable to States. In many cases, the flood gates argument reared its head; that the court would be overburdened with routine investigations that are best carried out at the national level.[22]

The case for a separate penal regime received also short shrift because the problems anticipated in a separate penal regime had been exhaustively canvassed by the International Law Commission ("ILC") during its ill-fated consideration of international crimes in the context of its work on State Responsibility.[23] The inclusion of a parallel regime of state criminality was deeply contentious. It derailed the State responsibility project and in the event was excluded from the entire project when the articles were adopted in 2001. Particularly contentious was the lack of consensus on the appropriate form of punishment and how a penal regime would differ from the normal consequences of delictual responsibility. Second there were concerns about the need to balance environmental damage and development priorities. In the debates in the ILC, proponents of the regime had been unable to isolate a distinct set of consequences that applied to a penal regime. It was not clear how the consequences of an international crime would differ from those of

---

drugs across national frontiers and other transnational criminal activities: establishment of an international criminal court', 4 December 1989, UN Doc. A/RES/44/39, co-sponsored by Antigua and Barbuda, Bahamas, Barbados, Belize, Comoros, Costa Rica, Guyana, Jamaica, Libyan Arab Jamahiriya, Papua New Guinea, Saint Kitts and Nevis, Saint Lucia, St Vincent and the Grenadine, Surinam, Trinidad and Tobago and Vanuatu, cited in P. Robinson, 'The Missing Crimes' in A. Cassese, P. Gaeta and J. Jones (eds), *The Rome Statute of the International Criminal Court* (OUP 2002), p. 500.

21 For an account of the Preparatory Committee's consideration of terrorism, see Robinson (n 20), pp. 510–512.

22 UN General Assembly, 'Report of the Preparatory Committee on the Establishment of an International Criminal Court' (Proceedings of the Preparatory Committee during March-April and August 1996), GAOR Supp. No. 22, UN Doc. A/51/22, para. 103.

23 See Draft Article 19(2)(d) in ILC, 'Report of the International Law Commission on the Work of its Twenty-Eighth Session' (3 May – 23 July 1976), UN Doc. A/31/10, Chapter III(B): Draft Articles on State Responsibility, which contemplated a separate regime of penal responsibility 'for the breach by a State of an international obligation so essential for the protection of the international community that its breach is recognized as a crime by that community as a whole'.

an international delict.[24] Some of the suggested consequences of a regime of State responsibility, such as restitution or guarantees of non-repetition, or the duty not to recognise the situation created as legal, did not seem sufficiently serious to warrant categorisation as a new way of dealing with environmental crimes and were in any case normal consequences of breach under the general law of State responsibility.

The ILC had also contemplated including wilful and severe damage to the environment as a crime against the peace, in the context of its work on the Draft Code of Offences against the Peace and Security of Mankind (the "Draft Code").[25] A draft article on this was provisionally adopted by the ILC on first reading and provided that: 'An individual who wilfully causes or orders the causing of widespread, long-term and severe damage to the natural environment, shall, on conviction thereof, be sentenced.'[26] However, there was profound disagreement on whether damage to the environment possessed the requisite the level of heinousness for it to be included in the Draft Code.

Although inclusion of some form of environmental crime appeared in the earliest drafts of the Rome Statute, ecocide, or its equivalents, made a premature exit during the negotiations, and there was no proposal for environmental crimes to be included.[27] This was because it became quite clear in the early negotiating history that the Court's jurisdiction would be confined to core crimes: genocide; war crimes, crimes against humanity and aggression – crimes which had received recognition as particularly heinous in the history of modern international criminal law and which had largely been defined with precision in the jurisprudence of the United Nations *ad hoc* international criminal tribunals for Rwanda and Yugoslavia.[28] However, the jurisdiction of the Court was not set in stone; in fact, the Rome Statute distinctly contemplated both

24 Ibid, p. 117, para 53; ILC, 'Summary Records of the Meetings of the Forty-Eighth Session', 6 May – 26 July 1996), UN Doc. A/CN.4/SER.A/1996, pp. 22–31; 178–80, 182–4; 191–3.

25 ILC, 'Report of International Law Commission on the work of its Forty-Seventh Session', GAOR, Supp. No. 10, UN Doc. A/50/10. In the Sixth Committee of the General Assembly, a number of State representatives expressed reservations at the inclusion of environmental pollution in the category of International crimes. See Oral and written comments by Bulgaria, Byelorussia, China, Federal Republic of Germany, Hungary, Indonesia, Syria, Ukraine, the United Kingdom, the United States and Russia. See UN Doc. A/C.61/SR.26, para. 25, and UN Doc. A/C.6/SR.21, paras. 34–35.

26 Report of the ILC on the work of its Forty-Seventh Session (n 25).

27 Robinson (n 20), pp. 497, 523.

28 See S. Lamb, 'Nullum Crimen, Nulla Poena Sine Lege in International Criminal Law' in Cassese, Gaeta and Jones (n 20), pp. 758–765.

revision and an extension of the applicable law to take into account new legal developments in international law.[29]

The case for ecocide must thus be evaluated against this backdrop. As a matter of strict law, there is nothing to preclude the extension of the Court's jurisdiction to cover the crime of ecocide. However, any extension of jurisdiction would have to contend with the fact that the ICC was strictly intended to respond to anthropocentric harm by human agencies and would be under considerable strain as an institution if asked to respond to pure environmental harm. Current proponents of ecocide would have to show that there has been a remarkable change in the institutional architecture of the ICC, now making it a suitable forum for the prosecution of such crimes. While the Court itself has acknowledged the distinct need for adaptation to meet the growing concerns about ecological harm (those calls including through the Office of the Prosecutor's case selection policy paper which refers to attacks on the environment, among other related topics),[30] it does not yet have the jurisdiction to deal with free-standing environmental crimes.

## 3 The Case for Ecocide: a Quest for Normative Coherence

Widespread, long-term and severe damage to the environment in situations of war is already criminalised under the Geneva Conventions and Article 8 of the ICC Statute.[31] However, even in relation to war, there are several constraints in its application. First, it only applies to environmental destruction in the context of international armed conflicts, while the predominant type of conflict since the Second World War is intra-state. Second, the requirements of "widespread, long-term and severe damage" are onerous. Third, it only criminalises damage that would be clearly excessive in relation to the concrete and direct overall military advantage anticipated. It is thus an exceptional provision that will be inapplicable in many situations and only of marginal relevance to most contemporary conflicts. Even when applicable, the high burden of proof and threshold offer no realistic prospect of a successful prosecution and conviction in almost any cases.

29 See Rome Statute of the International Criminal Court (adopted 17 July 1998, entered into force 1 July 2002) 2187 UNTS 90, arts. 10, 123.

30 ICC OTP, 'Policy Paper on case selection and prioritisation' (15 September 2016).

31 Additional Protocol I (n 9), art. 55; Rome Statute (n 29), art. 8.

Those advocating for a distinct penal regime for ecocide argue that environmental challenge is far too serious and that international lawyers need additional tools in the armoury to meet the challenge of environmental degradation. Substantively, the addition of a crime of harming the environment whether under the name of ecocide or otherwise would allow the court to directly adjudicate environmental harm irrespective of whether it occurred during armed conflict. It has also been suggested that the inclusion of ecocide would send a powerful symbolic message to the international community on its commitment to redressing environmental harm.[32] So ecocide here is intended as a crime that speaks to our time as an additional tool for addressing the worst forms of environmental harm. It is intended to address environmental harms that are clearly excessive when compared to the community benefits anticipated.

Proponents of a distinct regime for ecocide argue that since environmental damage in peacetime is just as pernicious as in situations of armed conflict, a unified criminal regime for environmental damage, whether occurring in peacetime or war, offers the best possible chance of dealing with the most egregious violations of environmental norms. The term "ecocide" is broad enough to encompass both extensive environmental damage taking place during war (as in the case of the use of defoliants, such as Agent Orange, in the Vietnam War, or the deliberate setting on fire of oil wells by the Iraqi army that occurred during the First Gulf War), and any other serious destruction or degradation of natural habitats or ecosystems.

The crime of ecocide as envisioned by the Independent Expert Panel is intended to supplement and amplify the conflict-specific crime in Article 8 of the Rome Statute, and extend it to systemic harm occurring in peacetime. Moreover, the definition of ecocide, stated below,[33] emphasises the central importance of protecting the environment because of its intrinsic value and not just because of the anthropocentric benefits that human beings derive from it. Perhaps the most innovative aspect of the crime of ecocide lies in its treatment of the environment, not just as an adjunct to anthropocentric needs, but as a freestanding right-holder.

---

32 K. Heller, 'Skeptical Thoughts on the Proposed Crime of "Ecocide" (That Isn't)' (*Opinio Juris*, 23 June 2021), available at: <http://opiniojuris.org/2021/06/23/skeptical-thoughts-on-the-proposed-crime-of-ecocide-that-isnt/> last accessed 20 March 2023.

33 See Section 6 below.

## 4 Historical Context of the ICC's Limited Subject Matter Jurisdiction

The 1998 Rome Statute deliberately gave the Court limited subject matter jurisdiction, confined to crimes that were regarded at the time as unquestionably part of customary international law. The list of four is of course well known, encompassing genocide, war crimes, crimes against humanity and aggression – the latter with a suspensory caveat that it would only be part of the Court's jurisdiction after a subsequent review conference had adopted a definition. This happened at the Kampala Conference in 2010, even though as the current Ukraine crisis illustrates, the problems of implementation are still very much alive.

The history of a penal regime for environmental harm in international law is not very encouraging. The draft prepared by the ILC, which formed the backdrop of the preparatory conference at which the Rome Statute was adopted, had given the Court a much wider subject matter jurisdiction which effectively extended to all crimes defined by existing treaties in force. The Draft Code had in Article 26 provided for the crime of ecocide, which would have penalised wilful and severe damage to the environment irrespective of a link to an armed conflict.

The crimes being defined with reference to their definitions in existing treaties would have eliminated extended debates as to whether the crimes so defined were consistent with the principle of legality. It would also have opened the door to criminalising a wider range of conduct, putatively including egregious environmental damage. The resulting narrow subject matter was instead part influenced by a desire to maximise political support for the creation of the Court. Few States would have signed up for a wide subject matter jurisdiction and an ambitious proposal would almost certainly have suffered the same fate as earlier proposals for an international criminal court. As mentioned above, at the Rome Conference, proposals were made for the inclusion of crimes relating to the illicit trafficking of drugs, international terrorism and even mercenarism,[34] but none of these, for various reasons, were ever included.

## 5 Rationale For Ecocide

It is argued that the mere existence of the crime of ecocide, even if very few prosecutions occur, is likely to have a powerful symbolic effect by highlighting

34 Robinson (n 20).

the scale of the ambition of the international community in its commitment to stop environmental degradation.[35] It is argued that the inclusion of ecocide in the Rome Statute will invigorate accountability options and strengthen environmental protection more generally, and that it would have a powerful deterrent effect and act as a catalyst for robust preventive measures.[36]

Moreover, a generally accepted definition of ecocide could have a far-reaching effect beyond the ICC by giving any court or tribunal with jurisdiction over the crime the power to prosecute not just natural persons but corporations as well. This would be a monumental achievement given the limited nature of the ICC's jurisdiction and the fact that its mandate does not extend to corporations. It also means that courts and tribunals with jurisdiction can act as ultimate custodians of the environment even when the resulting harm has not compromised any anthropocentric interests. Supporters of ecocide have made the case for a freestanding Special Environmental Court, with laxed rules on standing, which would have at its core predominantly ecocentric interests. Such a court, it has been suggested can operate in tandem with and complement the ICC's jurisdiction.[37]

## 6 Analysis of the Independent Expert Panel's Legal Definition of Ecocide

The Independent Expert Panel has defined ecocide as "unlawful or wanton acts committed with knowledge that there is a substantial likelihood of severe and either widespread or long-term damage to the environment being caused by those acts".[38] 'Wanton' means "with a reckless disregard for damage, which would be clearly excessive in relation to the social and economic benefits anticipated".[39] The Panel's aim is to incorporate the definition of ecocide within the existing framework of the Rome Statute through an amendment of Article 8.[40] If this definition was to form the basis of a wide-reaching

35 Heller (n 32).

36 See R. Pezzot and J-P. Graf, 'Ecocide-Legal Revolution or Symbolism?' (Völkerrechtsblog, 3 February 2022), available at: <https://voelkerrechtsblog.org/ecocide-legal-revolution-or-symbolism/#:~:text=Furthermore%2C%20the%20innovative%20way%20the,as%20'the%20crime%20of%20crimes.> last accessed 20 March 2023.

37 M. Gillet, *Prosecuting Environmental Harm before the International Criminal Court* (CUP 2022).

38 Independent Expert Panel (n 6).

39 Id.

40 Id.

convention on ecocide, States would have to aim for consistency in relation to the way in which it is adopted and applied in national legal systems. There are many problems in unpacking the requisite *mens rea* and whether the standard of recklessness aligns with the general requirement under the Rome Statute that crimes be committed with knowledge. These concerns have been exhaustively examined elsewhere in the literature and will not be considered here.[41]

Although the ICC is not a court of universal jurisdiction, given that States have to ratify the treaty and accept the Court's jurisdiction, such acceptance, once undertaken, nevertheless gives the Court competence over all crimes under the Statute. In other words, on ratification, all States parties accept the Court's jurisdiction without qualification. Is the Court's jurisdiction over the proposed crime of ecocide going to be general and automatic upon ratification or is it going to be an opt-in provision, assuming that the requisite majorities can be achieved to secure the amendment? Both models raise problems of political acceptability.

Furthermore, the precise relationship between the Rome Statute definition of ecocide and the definition for purposes of domestic law remains an area of contestation. Is the definition of ecocide going to be limited to the Rome Statute, leaving national governments free to adopt narrower or wider definitions? Is it going to cover only actual or anticipated harm? For instance, will it extend to preventative mechanisms such as liability for incitement to ecocide, which would allow law enforcement to take anticipatory action before the actual attack on the natural environment manifested?

In general, the jurisdiction of the Rome Statute is limited by considerations of gravity and seriousness. Yet such a limitation is very difficult to arrive at in relation to environmental activities, given the varied contexts in which harm to the environment can occur and the fact that many of these activities are rarely prohibited under national law. Mathew Gillet has suggested that that the gravity threshold could be maintained by including a leadership clause in the definition of ecocide for the purpose of the Court's jurisdiction. This would exclude low-level persons from criminal liability and concentrate on those in a leadership position to influence key policy. The precise terms of the clause could follow the definition of aggression under the Rome Statute which requires that the crime of aggression be performed "by a person in a position

41 See for instance A. Greene, 'Mens Rea and the Proposed Legal Definition of Ecocide' (Volkerrechtsblog, 7 July 2021), available at: <https://voelkerrechtsblog.org/mens-rea-and-the-proposed-legal-definition-of-ecocide/> last accessed 20 March 2023.

effectively to exercise control over or to direct the political or military action of a State."[42]

Although such a narrow definition may limit the number of persons or instances where ICC involvement is paramount, it does not resolve the problem of a legal definition for purposes of national courts, nor does it resolve the ambiguity that underpins 'leadership'. Moreover, a situation where national courts can prosecute anyone within their jurisdiction whilst international courts have a very limited personal jurisdiction does not bode well for an accountability framework based on complementarity. In other words, how can the ICC putatively exercise oversight over national prosecutions of ecocide when they have jurisdiction over entirely different categories of persons, with different key elements of the offence?

Delineating the jurisdictional reach of the international and national courts is only one if the many problems that the definition gives rise to. First, significant environmental harm is in many situations tolerated and considered to be acceptable because it is an inherent consequence of beneficial economic activities. In fact, there is likely going to be understandable pushback to the inclusion of a crime of ecocide in the Rome Statute, because almost all environmental harm occurs in the context of activities that have some socio-economic benefits.[43] Precisely where the harm becomes *egregious* and *unacceptable* is deeply contested, as the ILC realised in its attempt to create a bespoke regime for State criminal responsibility, a category that included serious damage to the environment.[44] Moreover, there is no consensus as to who is best placed to undertake the balancing exercise.

There are those who argue that the balancing of environmental harm and putative benefits is a political exercise which should not be undertaken by the courts but by primary decision-makers who are democratically accountable for their decisions. That distant courts far removed from the *situs* of the activities are ill-equipped to weigh the competing national values that inform much

42 Article 8*bis* of the Rome Statute provides that for the purpose of this Statute, 'crime of aggression' means the planning, preparation, initiation, or execution, by a person in a position effectively to exercise control over or to direct the political or military action of a state, or of an act of aggression which, by its character, gravity and scale, constitutes a manifest violation of the Charter of the United Nations'. See 'Amendments to the Rome Statute of the International Criminal Court on the Crime of Aggression' (Kampala, 11 June 2010), available at: <https://treaties.un.org/doc/Treaties/2010/06/20100611%2005-56%20PM/CN.651.2010.pdf> last accessed 20 March 2023.

43 R. White, 'Ecocide and the Carbon Crimes of the Powerful' (2018) 37(2) *University of Tasmania Law Review* 95.

44 Article 19 of the Draft Articles on State Responsibility (n 23).

environmental decision-making. That ultimately if the environment is to be protected from, for instance, wanton and serious pollution, this is likely to be achieved through imposition of emission targets and other standards prescribed by regulatory and licencing authorities which remain the most effective approach to dealing with egregious environmental harm.

A second overarching concern is the realisation that the present environmental crisis has largely been the result of deliberate and unsustainable patterns of resource use by States in the Global North. Many developing countries are likely to argue that economic self-determination remains in all circumstances a valid aspiration for which they should not be penalised by an international legal order that has largely shied away from addressing issues relating to historic responsibility for environmental damage. A definition of ecocide such as that adopted by the Independent Expert Panel would both entrench and exacerbate the existing environmental and economic inequalities. Many of the leading historic polluters such as Russia, China, and the United States, remain deeply opposed to the jurisdiction of the ICC and are not parties to the Court's Statute. The Court's fractious relationship with African States is only likely to reach a new low, were it to assume jurisdiction over a crime where African States are likely to be its primary targets.

Moreover, jurisdiction of the Court over ecocide would have to be prospective and not retroactive in keeping with the rule of law standards that the Court must adhere to in any definition or review of offences that come under its jurisdiction. Why should States in the Global South accept the Court's jurisdiction over ecocide in circumstances where those who have contributed the most to the current environmental crisis are essentially unaccountable for their past conduct?

Clearly any crime of ecocide would have to confront issues of historic responsibility for environmental damage, yet as the COP 27 process has illustrated, the issues that arise here are bitterly contested, and it is difficult to see how progress can be realised in other areas without first situating the problem in its historical context.[45]

The limited number of parties to the Malabo Protocol to the African Court of Justice and Human Rights,[46] the provisions of which create two crimes

45 See S. Nason-Case and J. Dehm, 'Redressing Historical Responsibility for the Unjust Precarities of Climate Change in the Present' in B. Mayer and A. Zahar (eds) *Debating Climate Law* (CUP 2021), p. 170.

46 African Union, *Protocol on the Statute of the African Court of Justice and Human Rights*, (1 July 2008), available at: <https://www.refworld.org/docid/4937f0ac2.html> accessed 20 March 2023, arts. 28L and 28L*bis*. See also D. Etone, 'Addressing Environmental Harm in Conflicts within Africa: Scope of International Criminal Law' in R. M. Paulose (ed.),

regarding harm to natural resources, should serve as a cautionary tale that States are particularly reticent to accept a penal regime in relation to the use of natural resources under their jurisdiction and control.

Finally, it is worth bearing in mind that the Court only has jurisdiction over natural persons, yet the worst forms of environmental degradation are carried out by or at the behest of corporations, most of them in the Global North. Why should corporations in developing countries accept to be penalised for trying to replicate the development models that have been the backbone of economic success in the Global North? Since corporations have no foothold in the Rome Statute, is the definition going to be accompanied by an amendment to Article 25 to extend the Court's jurisdiction to corporations?

Equally, the concept of victims in Rule 85 of the ICC's Rules of Procedure and Evidence has been developed and refined in relation to natural persons. It is these recognised victims who have the right to participate in the Court's proceedings and who are entitled to the compensation under the Court's provisions on reparation. An eco-centric concept of victimhood, which recognises protection of the environment as inherently worthy cannot realistically be achieved without a re-orientation of the Court's current anthropocentric focus. Yet that requires a radical overhaul of the Court's institutional architecture and it is difficult to see how that might be achieved in the current political climate.

The Panel's work has proved divisive, having almost an equal number of supporters and detractors.[47] Perhaps the most problematic aspect of the ecocide definition is the failure to identify clear and unequivocal examples of incidents which, on any view, would qualify as ecocide. Three systemic problems merit consideration and are addressed below.

*Green Crimes and International Criminal Law* (Delaware, United States, Vernon Press, 2021); See also C. Jalloh *et al.*, *The African Court of Justice and Human and Peoples Rights in Context: Development and Challenges* (CUP 2019).

47 Heller (n 32); D. Robinson, Ecocide – 'Puzzles and Possibilities' (2022) 20(2) *Journal of International Criminal Justice* 313; M. Karnavas, 'Ecocide: Environmental Crime of Crimes or Ill-Conceived Concept?' (*Opinio Juris*, 29 July 2021) available at: <http://opiniojuris.org/2021/07/29/ecocide-environmental-crime-of-crimes-or-ill-conceived-concept/> accessed 20 March 2023; K. Ambos, 'Protecting the Environment through Criminal Law?' (EJIL Talk!, 29 June 2021) available at: <https://www.ejiltalk.org/protecting-the-environment-through-international-criminal-law/> accessed 20 March 2023.

## 7 Systemic Problems with the Crime of Ecocide

### 7.1 *Rule of Law Concerns and Compatibility with the Principle of Legality*

Ever since the Nuremberg trials, it has been accepted that international criminal law must develop in a manner that respects the core values that underpin the rule of law, in particular the principle of legality. The failure to respect the principle at Nuremberg was the subject of trenchant criticisms,[48] but all subsequent developments since that time have been remarkably consistent in respecting the principle of legality.[49] Thus, for a crime to give rise to individual accountability, it must be defined with precision and specificity. It must be both certain and predictable, and crucially this should rule out a large area of discretion on the part of the decision-maker. Thus, a workable concept of ecocide must be consistent with both the demands of criminal law and environmental law.[50] It must be able to demonstrate with near certainty what a prosecutor has to prove to secure a conviction. Yet this is going to be difficult with ecocide, because there is no developed case law or practice either in domestic or international law that such a crime could build on.

It is worth remembering that although the application of the core crimes remains problematic, the definitions of genocide, war crimes, and crimes against humanity have been undergoing a process of elaboration in national legislation and in the decisions of international courts since 1946. Unlike ecocide, the three crimes also have the benefit of being defined as largely prohibitive duties in existing treaty regimes, especially the 1949 Geneva Conventions and their Protocols, the 1948 Genocide Convention, and the developed of rules in human rights treaties. The case law of the international criminal tribunals for Rwanda and former Yugoslavia have also elaborated the gradations of responsibility, further clarifying the requisite *mens rea* in different situations.

In the environmental context, with the exception perhaps of hazardous waste, and the offences specified under the Convention on International Trade in Endangered Species of Wild Fauna and Flora in relation to particularly endangered species, there are very few prohibited activities. As the definition of ecocide in the Independent Expert Panel's draft shows, any injunction against harm to the environment cannot be absolute but involves a careful

48 See for instance, G. A. Finch, 'The Nuremberg Trial and International Law' (1947) 41 *AJIL* 20.

49 See S. R. Ratner, J. S. Abrams and J. L. Bischoff, *Accountability for Human Rights Atrocities in International Criminal Law* (3rd edn, OUP 2009) pp. 23–25.

50 See Robinson (n 47).

balancing of competing values. Yet as the many critics have pointed out, the balancing inherent in the definition[51] involves a political choice which is best accomplished by a decision-maker who is democratically accountable for their decision. On this view, courts lack the necessary democratic legitimacy to make what are inherently political choices.

Moreover, the need to prevent harm must be weighed against contextual socio-economic benefits of the activity undertaken. Domestic courts have largely steered away from penal regimes for environmental damage and it may well be asked whether the ICC will have manageable standards for assessing the criminality threshold in environmental harm. The ICC's jurisdiction is by its Statute limited by considerations of gravity and seriousness, thus precluding from the Court's jurisdiction crimes that could be characterised as low-level offences or those which on any view do not meet a subjective threshold of seriousness. Will environmental crimes coming within the ambit of ecocide be episodic or routine? Even accepting that a higher threshold is needed for the ICC's jurisdiction it is difficult to see how the Court can avoid being enmeshed in run-of-the-mill cases which run the risk of overwhelming the Court, especially when the possibilities for national prosecution are limited.

There are many other outstanding difficulties with the Independent Expert Panel definition. For instance, who is to assess the gravity threshold and by what standards? The definition is intended to be preventive, and arguably criminal responsibility will be engaged on account of the wilfulness of the conduct even in the absence of harm. This seems eminently sensible, since any resulting harm ought to be prevented in the first place.

But how do you assess the putative gravity of the intended harm if it has not in fact occurred? There is also a disconnect between the definition and its objectives. If the goal is to protect the environment, why should criminal liability be limited to environmental harm that is wanton or unlawful? Why should it not extend to conduct that is negligent?[52]

### 7.2 *Complementarity Problems*

Under the complementarity framework that informs the institutional architecture of the Rome Statute, the ICC jurisdiction is supplementary to that of national systems.[53] The Court, to paraphrase the language of Article 17 of

---

51 See M. Lam Ching Wang, 'Prosecuting Ecocide vis a New International Environmental Criminal Court' (LSE Law Review Blog, 31 January 2022) available at: <https://blog.lselawreview.com/2022/01/prosecuting-ecocide-via-new-international-environmental-criminal-court> last accessed 20 March 2023.

52 Robinson (n 47).

53 S. Nouwen, *Complementarity in the Line of Fire* (CUP 2013).

its Statute, will only have jurisdiction if national systems are either unable or unwilling to act.[54] Yet there is not much guidance in the draft proposals on ecocide or how the default provisions are to be triggered in the absence of developed domestic systems of individual criminal accountability. Of course, it is possible that the adoption of ecocide within the jurisdiction of the Court will have an important consolidating effect on domestic jurisdiction. However, at the moment, domestic law on criminal responsibility is underdeveloped and largely limited to corporations. Can the Court assume jurisdiction in the absence of parallel domestic prosecutions? Will it be overwhelmed? What standards will it apply in assessing the gravity and criminality thresholds? All these questions, which on any view deserve extended scrutiny, have largely been set aside in the push to adopt a legally binding definition of ecocide.[55]

### 7.3 *Concerns about Forum Appropriateness*

Most environmental harm raises public order concerns that require effective regulation within an administrative law framework. Licencing, penalties and verification is the bedrock of an administrative and civil law framework for dealing with beneficial activities, but which also entail a very high degree of risk of catastrophic harm. It is this regulatory framework that is well equipped to respond to competing interests even if ecocide was to be reserved only for the worst polluters.

Any amendment of the Rome Statute will in any case limit its jurisdiction to natural persons who are nationals of States that accept the Court's jurisdiction or commit crimes on the territory of a State Party. The ICC, on the current proposal, is not intended to have jurisdiction over corporations. It would therefore seem to target the wrong culprits. An effective penal regime should be able to target corporations, who may be ordered to make good any harm and pay compensation to victims. There is no doubt that regimes of restitution and rehabilitation are the critical object of any accountability for environmental damage, but the most effective way of realising this is by visiting direct accountability on corporations and not on individuals.

---

54 See Rome Statute, art. 17.

55 See also the Promise Institute for Human Rights (UCLA) Group of Experts, 'Proposed Definition of Ecocide' (9 April 2021) available at <https://ecocidelaw.com/wp-content/uploads/2022/02/Proposed-Definition-of-Ecocide-Promise-Group-April-9-2021-final.pdf> accessed 20 March 2023.

## 8 Conclusions

Is the addition of ecocide a legitimate priority for the Court, or a distraction, at a time when the Court's resources are spread thin in relation to the core crimes? Perhaps the greatest shortcoming of the definition of ecocide by the Independent Expert Panel is the failure to offer a clear and sustained argument why criminalisation offers a superior and more effective solution than the existing alternatives, such as regulation through civil or administrative law frameworks. It also skirts around the difficult questions of *mens rea* or the fact that acceptability to States cannot be achieved without a radical overhaul of how the Court is structured or without addressing the structural inequalities and pre-existing relations of subordination between States.

The suggestion of the Panel and the UCLA is essentially for a ICC-centric solution. This contribution has attempted to highlight some of the problems inherent in an ICC-centric solution, but if, for the reasons outlined, the focus on the ICC is largely misplaced, what are the alternatives to such a solution?

There are those who argue that the most convenient forum for adjudicating ecocide claims, including its penal elements, would be a special environmental court. Matthew Gillet has made a compelling case for such a court.[56] Proponents argue that it would have the requisite expertise to weigh the competing claims of environmental harm and the economic benefits of the activity. It will be uniquely placed to draw on technical expertise necessary to reach complex decisions of causation and likelihood of harm. Moreover, and importantly, its jurisdiction could extend to corporations. However, the record of specialised environmental courts in international law is not impressive, not least because at the international level, environmental disputes are closely related with other questions of general international law, such as whether the complaining party had itself engaged in the very conduct in respect of which it now complains and can be taken as a matter of general international law to have acquiesced in the conduct in question. In 1994, the International Court of Justice established a specialised environmental court, but for the entire period that it was in existence, States showed very little inclination to use it and its mandate was eventually not renewed when the term lapsed. It is also said that such a tribunal will have the competence to award a range of remedies beyond incarceration and fines to a wide range of actors but the nature of these remedies and how they might be enforced, especially against corporations and non-state actors, remain vague and contestable.

---

56 Gillet (n 37).

One possibility is to opt for a very light touch regulatory model accepting that ecocide is unlikely to be the panacea for all environmental ills. This may simply be limited to adopting a treaty definition of ecocide without any prescription on matters of enforcement, leaving these to develop organically through State practice, such as implementation in national courts. Adopting this strategy may not necessarily galvanise domestic action in the short-to medium-term, but the treaty's precedence may be used by advocacy groups as a rallying point for stronger national action. This, however, is a tall order; treaties realistically only act as a catalyst for international action if they are grounded in the jurisprudence of national legal systems, as was the case with genocide, crimes against humanity, and war crimes.

On the contrary, the absence of national law or prosecutions for aggression has in fact proved to be a major stumbling block to its general acceptance at the international level. The resurgence in litigation for climate justice is perhaps a timely reminder that we may not need new laws or new forums of enforcement. Instead, what is required is the clarification and reinforcement of existing principles and institutions for compliance.

CHAPTER 26

# Aggression against Ukraine and an Object Lesson in ICC's Contributions to International Justice

*Chile Eboe-Osuji*

> The official position of an individual has been *consistently* excluded as a possible defence to crimes under international law in the relevant instruments adopted since the Charter of the Nürnberg Tribunal. (1996)
>
> The International Law Commission*

•••

> *It can no longer be doubted* that as a matter of *general customary international law* a head of state will personally be liable to be called to account if there is sufficient evidence that he authorised or perpetrated such serious international crimes. (2004)
>
> Sir ARTHUR WATTS QC, KCMG**

•••

> There is neither state practice nor *opinio juris* that would support the existence of Head of State immunity under customary international law *vis-à-vis* an international court. (2019)
>
> APPEALS CHAMBER, International Criminal Court***

---

* International Law Commission, 'Draft Code of Crimes against the Peace and Security of Mankind with commentaries 1996' (1996) II(2) *Yearbook of the International Law Commission* 27, commentary (4) to draft article 7 (emphasis added).

** A Watts, 'The Legal Position in International Law of Heads of States, Heads of Governments and Foreign Ministers' (1994) 247 *Recueil des cours* 13, 84 (emphasis added).

*** Judgment in the Jordan Referral re-Al-Bashir Appeal, *Al Bashir, Situation in Darfur, Sudan*, ICC-02/05-01/09 OA2, AC, ICC, 6 May 2019, para 113.

 | DOI:10.1163/9789004529939_027

## 1 Introduction

Nothing could conciliate the cruel circumstance that Russia's invasion of Ukraine constitutes to our civilisation at large and to the victims of that invasion in particular. Still, there is something striking about the invasion spanning the 20th anniversary of the activation of the Rome Statute. The two events collide to concentrate the world's collective mind on the gift that the International Criminal Court is to humanity. It is human nature, however, to take gifts for granted sooner or later.

This commentary addresses one way in which it has been an unfortunate mistake in some quarters to take for granted one important contribution that the ICC jurisprudence has made to the development of international law—a development that was not in truth an original idea of the ICC judges.

### 1.1 *A Vignette of Customary International Law*

Many international law scholars share the view that customary international law of the modern era holds no immunity for state officials, including heads of state, accused of international crimes—and that is certainly the case when the forum for the prosecution is an international criminal tribunal. Sir Arthur Watts, one of the most pre-eminent international lawyers and scholars in recent history famously expressed that view (as quoted in the epigram to this commentary).[1] His superior accomplishments include co-editing *Oppenheim's* (with Robert Jennings),[2] a text generally regarded as the most authoritative textbook of international law in the English-speaking world. But he was not alone. Other notable serious scholars who share the same view include John Dugard, Max du Plessis and Guénaël Mettraux;[3] Charles Jalloh;[4] Claus Kreß;[5]

1 Ibid.

2 See Sir R Jennings QC and Sir A Watts QC (eds), *Oppenheim's International Law* 9th edn, Vol. 1 (Peace 1992).

3 See G Mettraux, J Dugard and M du Plessis, 'Heads of State Immunities, International Crimes and President Bashir's Visit to South Africa' (2018) 18 *International Criminal Law Review* 577.

4 See C Jalloh, 'Reflections on the Indictment of Sitting Heads of State and Government and Its Consequences for Peace and Stability and Reconciliation in Africa' (2014) 7 *African Journal of Legal Studies* 43, 56–59. See also C Jalloh, *The Legal Legacy of the Special Court for Sierra Leone* (Cambridge University Press, 2020), 25, 29, 214, 217, 260, 262, 273 and 275.

5 See C Kreß, 'Article 98—Cooperation with respect to waiver of immunity and consent to surrender' in O Triffterer and K Ambos (eds), *The Rome Statute of the International Criminal Court: Article-by-Article Commentary* 4th edn (CH Beck/Hart/Nomos 2022) 2595ff; C Kreß, *Preliminary Observations on the ICC Appeals Chamber's Judgment of 6 May 2019 in the Jordan Referral re Al-Bashir Appeal* (Occasional Paper Series, Torkel Opsahl Academic EPublisher 2019).

Allain Pellet;[6] Leila Sadat;[7] David Scheffer;[8] and, Herman van der Wilt.[9] It is also very important to note that the International Law Commission has expressed the same view—not only by reporting it as far back as 1951 as a *general principle of international law* recognised in the Charter and judgment of the International Military Tribunal at Nuremberg, but also by reiterating in 1996 that "[t]he official position of an individual has been *consistently* excluded as a possible defence to crimes under international law in the relevant instruments adopted since the Charter of the Nürnberg Tribunal."[10]

A proper understanding of how customary international is made—including through *consistent* repetition of a specific legal norm across international law instruments of a certain kind—eminently bears out the position of these scholars.

•••

For purposes of this commentary, it may be helpful to cast the story of immunity from the perspective of accountability for the crime of aggression. In taking that approach, I merely seek to bring accountability for aggression into the long view, looking at immunity. In the light of Russia's invasion of Ukraine, it is a helpful illustration of just one conduct that international law regards as criminal, and the human toll (to which the world bears witness) that explains why. Otherwise, there is no necessary or special linkage between the crime of aggression and immunity that requires their treatment together in every case.

International law rejects wars of aggression as criminal conduct for which the perpetrator must be punished, possibly before an international criminal

6 A Pellet, 'Response to Koh and Buchwald's Article: Don Quixote and Sancho Panza Tilt at Windmills' (2015) 109 *American Journal of International Law* 557, 563–564.

7 See L N Sadat, 'Heads of state and other government officials before the International Criminal Court: the uneasy revolution continues' in M M de Guzman and V Oosterveld (eds), *The Elgar Companion to the International Criminal Court* (Elgar 2020), 96; L N Sadat, 'Why the ICC's Judgment in the al-Bashir Case Wasn't So Surprising' (*Just Security*, 12 July 2019).

8 American Society of International Law, Panel discussion on 'Head of State Immunity' (Annual General Meeting, 25–26 June 2020). Available at <https://youtu.be/znHErfBwhmY> Timestamp 0:07:26–0:15:19, accessed 28 March 2023.

9 H van der Wilt, 'The continuing story of the International Criminal Court and personal immunities' (2015) 22 *ACIL Research Paper* (Amsterdam Law School Research Paper No 2015–48), forthcoming in: Z Burić et al., *Liber Amicorum for Mirjan Damaška* (provisional title, Duncker-Humblodt 2016).

10 International Law Commission, 'Draft Code of Crimes against the Peace and Security of Mankind with commentaries 1996' (1996) II(2) *Yearbook of the International Law Commission* 27, commentary (4) to draft article 7, emphasis added.

tribunal, with no immunity for heads of state accused of that or other international crimes (genocide, crimes against humanity or war crimes). The march of that (r)evolution in international law began and settled respectively with two European wars of domination—World War I and World War II.

The story begins in 1919. British Prime Minister David Lloyd George and French Premier Georges Clemenceau and the governments they led resolved to prosecute the Emperor of Germany and King of Prussia, Kaiser Wilhelm II, before an international criminal tribunal, immediately after World War I. They firmly rejected considerations of immunity specifically raised in his behalf.[11]

11 In a speech he made to the National Council of Evangelical Free Churches, in August 1918, Lloyd George said: 'We have had treaties before; we must now know that we can give them reality.' And he insisted that 'the world has reached that stage of civilization where justice can be enforced against the most powerful nations that trample upon its decrees.' See D L George, 'A Real League of Nations' (Address Delivered in the City Temple, London, to the National Council of Evangelical Free Churches, April 1918–September 1918) (1918) VIII(2) *New York Times Current History* 351. And during a cabinet meeting of 20 November 2018, Lloyd George made clear his desire to see the German Kaiser prosecuted. Concerning the question of the position of international law at the time regarding the prosecution of a sovereign leader, he said, 'With regard to the question of international law, well, we are making international law, and all we can claim is that international law should be based on justice.' See D L George, *The Truth about the Peace Treaties* (Vol I, V Gollancz 1938), 100. In a speech that his Attorney-General, Sir Frederick E Smith KC, made to the UK Committee of Enquiry into Breaches of the Laws of War (the 'Macdonell Committee'), the Attorney-General communicated the determination of the British Government to deter future wars and atrocities committed under their cover. He declared in that regard 'that the most effective deterrent of all is that *for all ages men* who are tempted to follow the wicked and the bloody path which the Governors of the Central Empires have trodden during the last four years, *shall have present before their eyes, not a picture merely of the brilliant and meretricious glamour of military success, but also the recollection that in this great conflict punishment attended upon crime.*' See UK, Committee of Enquiry into Breaches of the Laws of War, First Interim Report presented to Sir Frederick E Smith KC, His Majesty's Attorney-General (13 January 191), 7 (emphasis added). In their eventual report, the Macdonell Committee recommended that the UK Government should work to create an international tribunal which would try the Kaiser. It is a course of action 'which would help to re-establish and strengthen International Law, *and which in the future would be a deterrent and warning to rulers and highly placed officials who meditated or instigated offences against International Law.*' See ibid., 96, emphases added. From the perspective of France, there was an outpouring of public demand to prosecute German soldiers who had laid waste to northern France as German troops retreated. The public demand included the prosecution of the Kaiser as amongst *les coupables*. Against that background, Premier Clemenceau declared before the French Senate, on 17 September 2018, that nothing 'could justify an amnesty for so many crimes.' See J F Willis, *Prologue to Nuremberg: The Politics and Diplomacy of Punishing War Criminals of the First World War* (Greenwood Pub Group 1982), 50–51. On 4 October 2018, the French Government

Woodrow Wilson wavered at first.[12] He had been under the influence of the opposite advice from by his Secretary of State, Robert Lansing, who was adamantly against the prosecution, arguing amongst other things that the Kaiser enjoyed immunity in international law.[13] But, in the face of pointed and unrelenting pressure from Clemenceau and Lloyd George, Wilson caved in eventually and agreed that the Kaiser must be tried before an international tribunal. And he was to enjoy no immunity.[14]

Notably, Wilson personally drafted the initial text[15] of article 227 of the Treaty of Versailles that set off the march of international law against immunity for

---

issued a statement saying, 'Conduct which is equally contrary to international law and the fundamental principles of all human civilization will not go unpunished. ... The authors and directors of these crimes will be held responsible morally, judicially, and financially. They will seek in vain to escape the inexorable expiation which awaits them.' Ibid., 51. Perhaps, Premier Clemenceau's attitude towards the Kaiser's accountability is best summed up in his interventions during a discussion of the heads of government of the Entente Powers in the afternoon of 8 April 1919, in the course of the Paris Peace Conference of 1919. 'The German Emperor must be tried,' he insisted. See P Mantoux, *The Deliberations of the Council of Four (March 24—June 28, 1919)* (Princeton University Press 1992, translation from the 1955 French original), 189. In an expert inquiry that paralleled the Macdonell Committee in the UK, the French Government had also commissioned their own expert study on the subject of '*la responsabilité pénale de l'Empereur Guillaume II*' [the criminal responsibility of Emperor Wilhelm II]. In their findings, the two French law dons—Professor Ferdinand Larnaude (the Dean of the Law Faculty at the University of Paris) and his colleague of the same faculty, Professor Albert Giouffre de LaPradelle—who conducted the study concluded that the Kaiser Wilhelm II must be tried before an international criminal tribunal, where he would not enjoy immunity, under the new order of international law that the conclusion of World War I had ushered in. According to them, 'irremediable blow would be struck against the new International law if the German Emperor enjoyed impunity.' See F Larnaude and A Giouffre de LaPradelle, *Examen de la responsabilité pénale de l'Empereur Guillaume II* (Imprimerie nationale 1918), 17. Throughout the Paris Peace Conference leaders and delegation of France and Great Britain followed the recommendations of the Larnaude-Lapradelle study and the Macdonell Committee reports respectively.

12 See P Mantoux, *The Deliberations of the Council of Four (March 24—June 28, 1919)* (n 11) 110–111, 118–123, 187–190.

13 See ibid., 188. See also Note from Secretary of State Robert Lansing to President Wilson dated 4 April 1919; Paris Peace Conference Doc No 181.1202/7, US National Archives Microfilm Publications, Microcopy No 820, Roll 142, Vol 115, Doc 0539. See also Paris Peace Conference, 'Report of the Commission on the Responsibility of the Authors of the War and on Enforcement of Penalties: Memorandum Presented by the Representatives of the United States' (1920) 14 *American Journal of International Law* 95, 127ff.

14 See W A Schabas, *The Trial of the Kaiser* (Oxford University Press 2018), 180–181.

15 Ibid., 193.

heads of state before international tribunals. The text of the provision appears at this footnote.[16]

Legal scholars often miss the subtle significance not only of Wilson's eventual agreement to the Kaiser's prosecution, but also that Wilson drafting in his own hand the initial text of the provision that enshrined that agreement. Wilson was a trained lawyer and a former university professor, who believed in taking into his own hands, if he must, actions guided by intellectual solutions. He could draft. Notably, Lansing once complained that Wilson wouldn't let him help in drafting the text of the Paris Peace Treaty.[17]

Contrary to the views of those who continue to see Lansing's objection to the Kaiser's prosecution as an enduring dissent of the United States,[18] Wilson's agreement to the prosecution had, in the outcome, the effect of vacating Lansing's earlier adamant objection. And Wilson's scripting of the initial draft of article 227 means at least that the text was adopted with the full agreement

16 Article 227 of the Versailles Treaty said this: The Allied and Associated Powers publicly arraign William II of Hohenzollern, formerly German Emperor, for a supreme offence against international morality and the sanctity of treaties. A special tribunal will be constituted to try the accused, thereby assuring him the guarantees essential to the right of defence. It will be composed of five judges, one appointed by each of the following Powers: namely, the United States of America, Great Britain, France, Italy and Japan. In its decision the tribunal will be guided by the highest motives of international policy, with a view to vindicating the solemn obligations of international undertakings and the validity of international morality. It will be its duty to fix the punishment which it considers should be imposed. The Allied and Associated Powers will address a request to the Government of the Netherlands for the surrender to them of the ex-Emperor in order that he may be put on trial. Treaty of Peace between the Allied and Associated Powers and Germany (signed 28 June 1919, Versailles).

17 R Lansing, *The Peace Negotiations: a Personal Narrative* (Houghton Mifflin Company 1921), 107. See also Robert Lansing, *The Big Four and Others of the Peace Conference* (Hutchinson 1922), 41.

18 See Schabas, *Trial of the Kaiser* (n 14) 119, where Professor Schabas contends that those who cite the importance of article 227 as a precedent in international law tend to ignore 'the importance of the dissenting views and the total neglect of the Report by the real lawmakers, the Council of Four.' With respect, this view cannot hold. This is because the Council of Four did not neglect the Report of the Commission on Responsibilities, the majority of whom (Lansing dissenting) recommended the prosecution of the Kaiser before an international criminal tribunal. See 'Commission on Responsibilities of the Authors of the War and on Enforcement of Penalties' (1920) 14 *American Journal of International Law* 95 (hereafter '14 *AJIL*'), 121–122. It was precisely on the basis of that report that Lloyd George and Clemenceau insisted within the Council of Four that the Kaiser must be tried before an international tribunal. And in the end, Wilson overruled Lansing's dissent on behalf of the United States, when Wilson not agreed to the prosecution but also drafted the text of article 227 of the Versailles Treaty that sought to implement that agreement.

of the US—not in spite of its objection. The failure of the US Senate to ratify the treaty despite Wilson's best efforts had nothing at all to do with the project of prosecuting the Kaiser, but with concerns about what the League of Nations might entail for American foreign policy.[19]

Following his defeat at the end of World War I, the Kaiser went into exile in the Netherlands, during the night of 9 November 1919.[20] Consequently, the Dutch refused to surrender him to the Allies for his trial before an international criminal tribunal, citing a national tradition of hospitality for those who came to them for refuge.[21] So it was that the Dutch Government frustrated the Allied efforts to prosecute the Kaiser.

•••

The Dutch Government enjoys current reputation as a great promoter of international law. Its capital city, The Hague, is held out as the "City of Peace and Justice."[22] These are well-deserved reputations. For that reason, there would be those who would wish the Dutch government to have taken a different decision in 1919 and surrendered the Kaiser for his criminal trial before an international criminal court. That would no doubt have been a resonant event in legal history, heralding a new dawn in international law and international relations.

But, as a matter of international law, the Dutch refusal to surrender the Kaiser to the Entente Powers is a reasonably defensible position. It was correct of the latter to have known not to force the issue. Here is why. The Netherlands was a neutral country during WWI. The rules of international law concerning rights and duties of neutral states reasonably encompassed the right of the Dutch to grant asylum to the Kaiser.[23] The pressure on the Dutch to surrender

19 See L Ambrosius, 'Woodrow Wilson, Alliance and the League of Nations' (2006) 5 *Journal of the Gilded Age and Progressive Era* 139, 151ff.

20 See S Marks, '"My Name is Ozymandias" The Kaiser in Exile' (1983) 16 *Central European History* 122. See also Willis (n 11) 66; Schabas, *Trial of the Kaiser* (n 14) chapter 3.

21 See US Department of State, *Papers Relating to the Foreign Relations of the United States 1919* (Vol II, The Paris Peace Conference, 1919), 76.

22 See the website of The Hague City, 'History of the City of Peace and Justice' (16 March 2017), here <www.denhaag.nl/en/municipality-of-the-hague/international-the-hague/history-of-the-city-of-peace-and-justice.htm> accessed 28 March 2023.

23 It may be noted in this regard that the Institute of International Law adequately captured that norm in their *Oxford Manual* (1880): 'It is universally admitted that a neutral State cannot, without compromising its neutrality, lend aid to either belligerent, or permit them to make use of its territory. On the other hand, considerations of humanity dictate that asylum should not be refused to individuals who take refuge in neutral territory to escape death or captivity. Hence the following provisions, calculated to reconcile the

the Kaiser, came dangerously close to pressuring the Dutch to violate what in present-day terminology would be called the rule of *non-refoulment* in international law of asylum. This is the rule that prevents an asylum state from handing a refugee over to the people he was fleeing from—or sending him back to such a place—where he might suffer harm.[24] It is true that this principle finds its clearest expression in the Refugee Convention of 1950.[25] Though no claim may be confidently made that as of 1919, when the Dutch were resisting the pressure to surrender the Kaiser, the *non-refoulement* principle had attained the 'constant and uniform usage practised by the States in question' standard laid down in *Asylum Case* as the test of customary international law.[26] But, sympathy for that argument in support of a successful bullying of the Dutch into surrendering the Kaiser to the Allies might have registered to modern sensibilities just as strongly as sympathy would embrace the denial of moral guilt for a foul conduct merely because it took place before society had the good sense to abjure it formally.

### 1.2 *Immunity versus Jurisdiction: Different Functions*

More concerning now are certain points of confusion that are discernible in the advice that has been given to present-day Dutch government by the Advisory

opposing interests involved': see the commentary preceding article 79. It may be noted that the authority of the Oxford Manual lies in its value as a distillation of customary international as understood at the time. The manual's authors indicated that value as follows: 'Rash and extreme rules will not, furthermore, be found therein. The Institute has not sought innovations in drawing up the "Manual"; it has contented itself with stating clearly and codifying the accepted ideas of our age so far as this has appeared allowable and practicable.' The Laws of War on Land (adopted by the Institute of International Law on 9 September 1880) (*Oxford Manual*).

24 See UN High Commissioner for Refugees, 'Advisory Opinion on the Extraterritorial Application of *Non-Refoulement* Obligations under the 1951 Convention relating to the Status of Refugees and its 1967 Protocol' (26 January 2007) available here: <www.unhcr.org/4d9486929.pdf> accessed 28 March 2023.

25 See Convention Relating to the Status of Refugees (adopted 28 July 1951, entered into force 22 April 1954) 189 UNTS 137, Article 33: 1. No Contracting State shall expel or return ('*refouler*') a refugee in any manner whatsoever to the frontiers of territories where his life or freedom would be threatened on account of his race, religion, nationality, membership of a particular social group or political opinion. 2. The benefit of the present provision may not, however, be claimed by a refugee whom there are reasonable grounds for regarding as a danger to the security of the country in which he is, or who, having been convicted by a final judgment of a particularly serious crime, constitutes a danger to the community of that country.

26 See the *Asylum Case* (*Colombia/Peru*) [1950] ICJ Rep 266, 276.

Committee on Issues of Public International Law (CAVV)—the think-tank that advises the government nowadays. The advice appears at this footnote.[27]

These points of confusion—perhaps already manifested in formulations that some readers may see as nuances and others as equivocation—will be something of a gremlin that may trouble the decision of policy makers in their turn.

To begin with, it must be hoped, of course, that policy-decision makers are not caught by a caution of self-interest recurring in the text of the CAVV advice of 12 September 2022 to their government. There is the risk that a timorous policy-maker in a hurry may mistake the advice as saying: 'Keep in mind that if you support the denial of immunity to the senior government officials of other states in their own prosecution for international crimes before an international tribunal, you also expose yourself to denial of immunity if you are ever accused of committing international crimes.' Such a mindset would have

27 In the relevant respect, the Advisory Committee on Issues of Public International Law (CAVV) formulated their advice to the Dutch government in the following way: 8. In principle, foreign officials enjoy functional immunity (or immunity *ratione materiae*). This means that they cannot be prosecuted for acts they have performed in an official capacity. This rule also ensures that Dutch officials, even when they are no longer in office, cannot be summoned before a foreign court on account of Dutch policy that is considered harmful or unlawful abroad. In international legal practice, there is no clear-cut answer to the question of whether there is an exception to functional immunity for international crimes, including the crime of aggression. The CAVV takes the view that not recognising functional immunity for international crimes is currently justifiable as either being consistent with international law or contributing to a legal development that already has strong momentum. The CAVV does not see the logic of distinguishing between the crime of aggression and other international crimes.[…] 9. As regards the question of whether a special exception to immunity applies before international tribunals, the CAVV interprets the case law of the International Court of Justice as meaning that an international tribunal that has been established without the involvement of the defendant's home state and lacks a basis under Chapter VII of the UN Charter must respect the personal immunity of heads of state, heads of government and ministers of foreign affairs. 10. If the Netherlands nonetheless wishes to back a legal development under which personal immunities do not apply before (a larger group of) international tribunals, in keeping with the view of the Special Court for Sierra Leone and the International Criminal Court, it will in any event be important to advocate a distinctive and restrictive definition of the term 'international tribunal.' It is important to note, incidentally, that in the event of such a development, officials in the Netherlands, in particular our prime minister and minister of foreign affairs, would also not be granted personal immunity before an international tribunal. See Advisory Committee on Issues of Public International Law, 'Challenges in prosecuting the crime of aggression: jurisdiction and immunities' Advisory report No 40 (12 September 2022) (provisional translation). Available at <www.advisorycommitteeinternationallaw.nl/publications/advisory-reports/2022/09/12/challenges-in-prosecuting-the-crime-of-aggression-jurisdiction-and-immunities> accessed 28 March 2023.

obscured an accurate story of the evolution of international law and its present state on the question. That story will be summarised presently. For now, however, it is enough to recall the words of Justice Robert H Jackson in 1945 at the dawn of a new era of the development of international law:

> It is futile to think, as extreme nationalists do, that we can have an international law that is always working on our side. And it is futile to think that we can have international courts that will always render the decisions we want to promote our interests. We cannot successfully cooperate with the rest of the world in establishing a reign of law unless we are prepared to have that law sometimes operate against what would be our national advantage.[28]

But the more fundamental point concerns a strain of confusion generally encountered in the debate about immunity of heads of state before international criminal tribunals. It has to do with the obvious anxiety about what may qualify as an 'international tribunal' in whose proceedings immunity may not apply. The anxiety is in the order of the question whether a limited number of states could establish a court which could bind a state that is a stranger to the court's founding treaty, by removing 'immunity' which (some claim) international law has preserved for every state in every tribunal (national or international).[29]

Ultimately, the concern is whether such a court of limited membership could exercise *jurisdiction* in relation to a state that is not a party to the court's founding treaty, because of judicial pronouncements to the effect that *immunity* is not recognised in the proceedings of international criminal courts. This anxiety, in my view, results from an avoidable confusion—the conflation of *jurisdiction* with *non-immunity*. These are different jural concepts that require epistemic decoupling: in the sense of understanding what each of them means and does separately, in order to see how they interact when they must. In the outcome, the fact that immunity is not applicable before a particular court does not mean that the court in question has jurisdiction in the particular case.

---

28 R H Jackson, 'The Rule of Law among Nations' (1945) 39 *American Society of International Law Proceedings* 10, 17–18.

29 See, for instance, D Akande, 'International Law Immunities and the International Criminal Court' (2004) 98 *American Journal of International Law* 407, 417; S Nouwen, 'Return to Sender: Let the International Court of Justice Justify or Qualify International-Criminal-Court Exceptionalism Regarding Personal Immunities' (2019) 78 *Cambridge Law Journal* 596, 608; and A Kjeldgaard-Pedersen, 'Is the Quality of the ICC's Legal Reasoning an Obstacle to Its Ability to Deter International Crimes?' (2021) *Journal of International Criminal Justice* 939, 951–952.

It is important to understand that the *jurisdiction* of an international court is not conferred by customary international law. At the international level, things operate differently from the classic common law tradition, where a basic principle operates to the effect that a common law court—as opposed to a national court created by statute—enjoys a general or inherent jurisdiction to do justice if there is no other court that enjoys exclusive jurisdiction on the particular matter.[30] At the international level, there is no equivalent principle. An international tribunal acquires its jurisdiction through a specific instrument. This could be a treaty (like the Rome Statute that established the ICC in 1998) or a constative resolution of an international organisation (such as the UN Security Council resolution 827 (1993) and resolution 955 (1994) that respectively established the International Criminal Tribunals for the former Yugoslavia and for Rwanda). And then, through the usual process of treaty interpretation, a determination is made about whom the treaty binds for purposes of the court's jurisdiction. So, if there is no applicable jurisdiction, then immunity or lack thereof becomes immaterial.

*Immunity*, on the other hand, serves a different function. It does not give jurisdiction. It only operates against any jurisdiction that is available, from a different source. The absence of immunity does not generate a non-existent jurisdiction. Immunity or its absence can come through either customary international law or through an instrument that binds those that are party to it. Even a resolution of the UN Security Council derives its binding effect from the UN Charter that binds the UN member states.

It may be noted that the consistent statement of norm about immunity across a series of international instruments can generate customary law—as is the case with head of state immunity before international courts. So, when a view of customary international law results in the absence of immunity before a certain kind of court, that is all there is to it. There will be no immunity before *that kind of court* in relation to any jurisdiction that it may have. But *a particular court* that belongs to *that kind of court* must still find its jurisdiction somewhere if it is to exercise it. That many scholars who engage in the immunity discourse have failed to appreciate this nuance has resulted in regrettable confusion of thought, mistaken analyses and startling reactions.

A proper understanding of this distinction will remove the perennial worry that a court of limited membership is an "international tribunal" that may

30 See, for instance, *US v Hudson & Goodwin* 11 US 7 Cranch 32 S Ct (1812). See also *Baxter Student Housing Ltd, et al v College Housing Co-operative Ltd, et al* [1976] 2 SCR 475.

exercise jurisdiction over states not party to the court's founding treaty, because of a finding that immunity is not recognised in that court's proceedings.

Indeed, the foregoing explanation of the difference and relationship between immunity and jurisdiction is wholly consistent with the observations of the International Court of Justice, in a litigation concerning the immunity of foreign ministers from the criminal jurisdiction of peer nations. The Court observed, in passing, that: 'an incumbent or former Minister for Foreign Affairs may be subject to criminal proceedings before certain international criminal courts, *where they have jurisdiction*.'[31] [Emphasis added.] The Court cited the International Criminal Tribunal for the former Yugoslavia, the International Criminal Tribunal for Rwanda and the ICC, as examples of international courts that may exercise such jurisdiction without immunity.[32]

•••

In their advice to the Dutch government, the CAVV opined that '[i]n international legal practice, there is no clear-cut answer to the question of whether there is an exception to functional immunity for international crimes, including the crime of aggression.' Here, care must be taken to separate 'international legal practice' from academic opinions—which are rarely unanimous on any subject.

It is true that there is a division of academic opinions on the subject (and more on that below), but it must also be kept in mind that academic opinions on the law do not amount to 'legal practice' as to what the law is. Without a doubt, the robust clash of worthy academic opinions is generally *always* helpful to judges in their own task. It holds the potential to shine the light in all the possible nooks and crevices of a difficult legal question that judges are called upon to settle. It is for that reason that the ICC Appeals Chamber during this author's tenure instituted the standard practice of inviting eminent scholars to intervene in cases raising more than routine legal questions.

Yet, it is a serious mistake to suppose that academic opinions are the pilots that judicial opinions should follow. That mistake has been repeatedly identified and rejected through the ages. 'The authentical interpretation of law is not that of writers,' wrote Hobbes in the *Leviathan*. 'The authority of writers, without the authority of the commonwealth, maketh not their opinions law, be they never so true,' he continued. For good measure, Hobbes did not preclude

31 See *Arrest Warrant of 11 April 2000* (*Democratic Republic of the Congo v Belgium*) (Judgment) [2002] ICJ Rep 3, para. 61.

32 Ibid.

himself from that disability: 'That which I have written in this Treatise, concerning the moral virtues, and of their necessity, for the procuring, and maintaining peace, though it be evident truth, is not therefore presently law.'[33]

Judicial pronouncements have conveyed the same message. 'Writers on international law,' Lord Chief Justice Cockburn observed in *The Franconia* (1876), 'however valuable their labours may be in elucidating and ascertaining the principles and rules of law, cannot make the law.' A similar point was made in *The Paquete Habana* (1900). Mr Justice Gray, writing for the US Supreme Court, stressed how it is that works of scholars assist tribunals. Judges consult academic works, he wrote, 'not for the speculations of their authors concerning what the law *ought to be*, but for trustworthy evidence of what the law *really is*.'[34] [Emphasis added.]

Also writing for the US Supreme Court earlier in *Hilton v Guyot*, Mr Justice Gray had made sure to point out that the Court had 'not thought it important to state the conflicting theories of continental commentators and essayists as to what each may think the law ought to be, but ha[d] referred to their works only for evidence of authoritative declarations, legislative or judicial, of what the law is.'[35] Ultimately, as it was relevantly observed in *Wheaton's International Law*, 'It is not too much to say that the influence of speculative writers in England is comparatively small.'[36]

It must truly be said that the discourse on immunity of heads of state from international criminal jurisdiction has been astonishingly rife with speculative scholarship, in the form of fanciful arguments presented as law.

•••

As 'international legal practice' takes its meaning from what judges and states do in practice—and not from what academics write in their scholarship—it is incorrect to say that there is no 'clear cut' guidance on the question whether there is immunity before *international criminal tribunals* in proceedings involving *international crimes*.

From the perspective of the opinion of international courts, at least six different panels of international courts—at the final levels of adjudication—have pronounced themselves on the matter. And there is no inconsistency at all in their pronouncements.

---

33 T Hobbes, *Leviathan* (J C A Gaskin ed, Oxford University Press 1996) Ch. 26, para. 22.

34 *The Paquete Habana* 175 US 677 S Ct (1900), 700.

35 *Hilton v Guyot* 159 US 113 S Ct (1895), 214–215.

36 C Phillipson, *Wheaton's Elements of International Law* 5th edn (Stevens and Sons 1916) 23.

An early relevant pronouncement was from the Appeals Chamber of the International Criminal Tribunal for the former Yugoslavia in 1995, in the *Tadić* case. Speaking in the context of the need to counter 'stratagems [that] might be used to defeat the very purpose of the creation of an international criminal jurisdiction, to the benefit of the very people whom it has been designed to prosecute,' the Chamber observed that '[i]t would be a travesty of law and a betrayal of the universal need for justice, should the concept of state sovereignty be allowed to be raised successfully against human rights.'[37]

Next, in the *Blaškić* case, the ICTY Appeals Chamber was confronted in 1997 with the question whether the Republic of Croatia and its Defence Minister should be served a subpoena for the production of documentary evidence needed in the prosecution of a case before the tribunal. The Appeals Chamber began by stating what it described as a general rule of immunity for state officials. In that regard, the Chamber dismissed 'the possibility of the International Tribunal *addressing subpoenas to State officials acting in their official capacity*. Such officials are mere instruments of a State and their official action can only be attributed to the State. They cannot be the subject of sanctions or penalties for conduct that is not private but undertaken on behalf of a State. *In other words, State officials cannot suffer the consequences of wrongful acts which are not attributable to them personally but to the State on whose behalf they act: they enjoy so-called "functional immunity"*. This is a well-established rule of customary international law going back to the eighteenth and nineteenth centuries, restated many times since.'[38] That general rule, as the Appeals Chamber stated it, is based on "sovereign equality of States (*par in parem non habet imperium*).'[39]

But, having said that, the Appeals Chamber made sure to recognise the exception to the general rule, according to which immunity is unavailable in relation to international crimes—prosecuted before national and international courts. As the Chamber put it:

> These exceptions arise from the norms of international criminal law prohibiting war crimes, crimes against humanity and genocide. Under these norms, those responsible for such crimes cannot invoke immunity from

37 Decision on the Defence motion for interlocutory appeal on jurisdiction, *Tadić*, IT-94-1-A, AC, ICTY, 2 October 1995, para. 58.

38 Judgement on the Request of the Republic of Croatia for Review of the Decision of Trial Chamber II of 18 July 1997, *Blaškić*, IT-95-14-PT, AC, ICTY, 27 October 1997, para. 38 (emphasis added).

39 Ibid., para. 41.

> national or international jurisdiction even if they perpetrated such crimes while acting in their official capacity. Similarly, other classes of persons (for example, spies, as defined in Article 29 of the Regulations Respecting the Laws and Customs of War on Land, annexed to the Hague Convention IV of 1907), although acting as State organs, may be held personally accountable for their wrongdoing.[40]

Next came the judgment of the ICJ in 2000 in the *Arrest Warrant Case* in 2000, in the pronouncement recalled earlier. There, the ICJ was confronted with the question whether Belgium may prosecute a former foreign minister of the Democratic Republic of the Congo before its courts. On the broader question of justice, some may consider that there was a latent political irony in the case which would have escaped no one. That irony was that the people of the Congo had been victims of notorious brutality—crimes against humanity—generally attributed to King Leopold of Belgium.[41] Some will no doubt see it as consolatory justice (though eminent jurists have questioned its legal correctness)[42] that the ICJ majority held that the foreign minister of the DRC was immune from the national criminal jurisdiction of Belgium, notwithstanding that his arrest warrant was for international crimes. In that connection, the ICJ majority declared that they 'been *unable to deduce* [...] that there exists under customary international law any form of exception to the rule according immunity from criminal jurisdiction and inviolability to incumbent Ministers for Foreign Affairs, where they are suspected of having committed war crimes or crimes against humanity.'[43]

Nevertheless, the majority went on to hold that 'an incumbent or former Minister for Foreign Affairs may be subject to criminal proceedings before certain international criminal courts, where they have jurisdiction.'[44]

Writing extra-judicially, Antonio Cassese was quick to fault the judgment of the ICJ majority in their inability 'to deduce' that customary international law

---

40 Ibid., para. 41.

41 See A Hochschild, *King Leopold's Ghost: A Story of Greed, Terror, and Heroism in Colonial Africa* (Houghton Mifflin 1998).

42 A Pellet, 'Response to Koh and Buchwald's Article: Don Quixote and Sancho Panza Tilt at Windmills' (2015) 109 *American Journal of International Law* 557, 563–564. See also A Cassese, 'When May Senior State Officials Be Tried for International Crimes? Some Comments on the Congo v. Belgium Case' (2002) 13 *European Journal of International Law* 853.

43 *Arrest Warrant of 11 April 2000* (*Democratic Republic of the Congo v Belgium*) (Judgment) [2002] ICJ Rep 3, para. 58 (emphasis added).

44 See ibid., para. 61.

recognised no immunity in foreign *national courts* in relation to international crimes. He supplied some of the modern examples of where immunity was not recognised in foreign national courts in prosecutions of international crimes.[45]

Cassese was a leading authority in international criminal law during his lifetime. He served as president at both the International Criminal Tribunal for the former Yugoslavia and the Special Tribunal for Lebanon. It may be noted that he was the presiding judge in the *Blaškić* judgment where the ICTY Appeals Chamber held that customary international law recognises no immunity for any state official for international crimes—before national and international tribunals.

This author's research supports the proposition that, in addition to the research that Cassese reported, there are further strong and numerous data that favour the proposition that customary international law recognises no immunity for state officials when prosecuted in foreign national courts for international crimes.[46]

---

45 A Cassese, 'When May Senior State Officials Be Tried for International Crimes? Some Comments on the Congo v. Belgium Case' (2002) 13 *European Journal of International Law* 853, 870ff.

46 Some of the data in that regard include but are not limited to: *Lieber Code* (1863) IV and V; for instance, Article 71 provides: 'Whoever intentionally inflicts additional wounds on an enemy already wholly disabled, or kills such an enemy, or who orders or encourages soldiers to do so, shall suffer death, if duly convicted, whether he belongs to the Army of the United States, or is an enemy captured after having committed his misdeed.' See General Orders No. 100, Instructions for the Government of the Armies of the United States in the Field, 24 April 1863 (*Lieber Code*). See also the *Oxford Manual* (1880) (n 23) Article 84: 'If any of the foregoing rules be violated, the offending parties should be punished, after a judicial hearing, by the belligerent in whose hands they are. Therefore [...] Offenders against the laws of war are liable to the punishments specified in the penal law.' See also L Oppenheim, *International Law* 2nd edn, Vol. 2 'War and Neutrality' (Longmans, Green and Company 1912), para. 251. See also *United States v Bopp* 237 F 283 ND Cal (1916). See also Versailles Treaty 1919, Article 228. See also Paris Peace Conference, 'Report of the Commission on the Responsibility of the Authors of the War and on Enforcement of Penalties' (n 13) 121. See also W Hall, *A Treatise on International Law* 8th edn (Pearce Higgins 1924), para 135. See also *Ex Parte Quirin*, 317 US 1 S Ct (1942), 30–31 and 35–36. See Opening Statement of Sir Hartley Shawcross, Attorney-General of UK, International Military Tribunal, Nuremberg, *Trial of the Major War Criminals before the International Military Tribunal, Nuremberg, 14 November 1945–1 October 1946* (Nuremberg, IMT 1947) vol III, 92. See also T Taylor, Final Report to the Secretary of the Army on the Nuernberg War Crimes Trials under Control Council Law No 10 (15 August 1949), 4. See also Article 49 of Geneva Convention (I) for the Amelioration of the Condition of Wounded, Sick and Shipwrecked Members of Armed Forces in the Field (adopted 12 August 1949, entered into force 21 October 1951) 75 UNTS 31; Article 50 of Convention No II for the Amelioration of the Condition of Wounded, Sick and Shipwrecked Members of Armed Forces at Sea;

Be that as it may, there was no inconsistency between the ICJ judgment in the *Arrest Warrant Case* and the ICTY Appeals Chamber's judgment in *Blaškič* in their ruling that customary international law recognises no immunity for state officials before *international tribunals*, in relation to international crimes.

The third time that an international court made the same pronouncement was when the Appeals Chamber of the ICTY do so once again in *Prosecutor v Krstić*, in 2004. On that occasion, the Appeals Chamber was dealing with a defence application for subpoena of witnesses. The Chamber took the opportunity to remove any doubt about what the Appeals Chamber had said earlier in *Blaškić*, underscoring the absence of immunity before *international courts* trying cases of international crimes. In that connection, the Appeals Chamber observed as follows:

> The reasoning of the Appeals Chamber in the *Blaškič* Subpoena Decision is that, as the State official has acted on behalf of the State, only the State can be responsible for the acts of that official, and that, as a corollary, the State may demand for its State officials (where their acts are attributed only to the State) a 'functional immunity from foreign jurisdiction.' Such a rule, the Appeals Chamber states, undoubtedly applies to relations between States *inter se*, but it must be taken into account and has always been respected by, *inter alia*, international courts. All of the authorities which the Appeals Chamber cited in support of the functional immunity upon which it relied relate to an immunity against prosecution. *It may be the case (it is unnecessary to decide here) that, between States, such a functional immunity exists against prosecution for those acts, but it would be incorrect to suggest that such an immunity exists in international criminal courts.* The Charter of the International Military Tribunal in Nuremberg denied such an immunity to 'Heads of State or responsible officials in Government Departments,' as does this Tribunal's Statute.[47]

The next occasion of importance was when the five judges of the Appeals Chamber of the Special Court for Sierra Leone in 2004, in *Prosecutor v Charles Taylor*.[48]

---

Article 129 of Geneva Convention (III) relative to the Treatment of Prisoners of War (adopted 12 August 1949, entered into force 21 October 1950) 75 UNTS 135; Article 146 of Geneva Convention (IV) relative to the Protection of Civilian Persons in Time of War (adopted 12 August 1949, entered into force 21 October 1950) 75 UNTS 287.

47 Decision on Application for Subpoenas, *Krstić*, IT-98-33-A, AC, ICTY, 1 July 2003, para. 26 (emphasis added).

48 Decision on Immunity from Jurisdiction, *Taylor*, SCSL-2003-01-I, AC, SCSL, 31 May 2004.

And the last time was when the five judges of the Appeals Chamber of the ICC pronounced themselves on the question in 2019, in *Prosecutor v Omar Al-Bashir* (*Jordan Referral re Al-Bashir*).[49]

The resulting case law is therefore crystal clear on the question whether there is immunity before an international criminal tribunal in the prosecution of an international crime. On each occasion the question arose, all five panels of judges at the final level of international adjudication (comprising a total of at least 35 judges of international courts) have—without exception—said there is no such immunity. On no occasion has a final-level panel of an international court come to a different conclusion.

• • •

Apart from the case law of international courts, the matter may also be considered from the perspective of the political/legislative acts of states. From the perspective of consistent practice of states as a source of customary international law, there is no better gauge of both the existence of such evidence and of its consistency—in the sense of the standard of 'constant and uniform usage practised by the States in question' laid down in *Asylum Case* as the test of customary international law[50]—than in the data of decisions that states make when assembled together to answer specific questions on a particular matter. Pronouncements and conducts of states acting separately in their own affairs do not readily provide as sharp a view of state practice—given that not all states may have the opportunity, the inclination or the expertise, to express themselves at all on every topic of international law, let alone do so in a manner susceptible of easy alignment from the perspective of uniformity.[51] It is such disparate circumstances of states in their reactions to the same issue that makes their resolutions in their assemblies the best gauge of state practice on a particular point. And it is their consistent statement of the same norm—the 'constant and uniform usage practised by the States in question'—across a series of resolutions or treaties that generates the best view of customary international law on the point in question.[52]

---

49 Judgment in the Jordan Referral re-Al-Bashir Appeal, *Al Bashir, Situation in Darfur, Sudan*, ICC-02/05-01/09 OA2, AC, ICC, 6 May 2019.

50 See the *Asylum Case* (*Colombia/Peru*) (Judgment) [1950] ICJ Rep 266, 276.

51 See M Shaw, *International Law*, 6th edn (Cambridge University Press 2008) 73.

52 See also Shaw, ibid., 82. In this connection, Professors Akande and Tzanakopoulos are quite correct when they observed as follows: 'Given that the ASP resolution is a statement of the parties to the Rome Statute which explicitly purports to give meaning to a provision

From that point of view, the international community has been clear in rejecting immunity for heads of state before international tribunals tasked with trying international crimes ever since 1919 when they gave that indication in article 227 of the Versailles Treaty.

The rejection of head of state immunity thus first signalled in 1919 was realised more completely in 1945, immediately after World War II. As their predecessors-in-office had done in 1919, the heads of government of the Allied Nations (this time including the Soviet Union) declared their resolve to prosecute the German Fuhrer before an international criminal tribunal.[53]

When Hitler frustrated the resolve of the Allies to prosecute him after the war, by committing suicide as the war was ending, the Allies then prosecuted the surviving members of the Third Reich cabinet—including Grand Admiral Karl Dönitz who succeeded Hitler as Germany's Head of State.[54] They were prosecuted pursuant to the Charter of the International Military Tribunal in Nuremberg. It provided in article 7 that the 'official position of defendants, whether as Heads of State or responsible officials in Government Departments, shall not be considered as freeing them from responsibility or mitigating punishment.'

The period after World War II saw the crystallisation of the norm that rejects head of state immunity from accountability for international crimes. This was achieved on behalf of the United Nations through the leading work of the International Law Commission, notably through their formulation of the Nuremberg Principles, the third of which provides as follows: 'The fact that a

---

of the Rome Statute [...], and to set out how that provision applies in a particular circumstance, the resolution is practice of the parties to the Statute regarding the interpretation of that treaty.' D Akande and A Tzanakopoulos, 'Treaty Law and ICC Jurisdiction Over the Crime of Aggression' (2018) 29 *European Journal of International Law* 939, 944.

53 See United States, Department of State, *Bulletin*, vol XII, No 293, 4 February 1945, 154. See also F D Roosevelt, 'Statement Warning Neutral Nations Against Asylum For War Criminals' of 30 July 1943 (*The American Presidency Project*) available at <https://www.presidency.ucsb.edu/documents/statement-warning-neutral-nations-against-asylum-for-war-criminals> accessed 28 March 2023. See also F D Roosevelt, 'Fireside Chat No 23,' Report on the Home Front, Radio Broadcast of 12 October 1942. See *The War Messages of Franklin D Roosevelt—December 8, 1941 to October 12, 1942* (United States of America 1942) 71. See also note of 14 October 1942, communicating the Soviet Union government's endorsement of President Roosevelt's message of accountability delivered on behalf of the Allies. United States, Department of State, 'Report of Robert H Jackson, United States Representative to the International Conference on Military Trials, London 1945' [1947] 16–17.

54 See generally, *Trial of the Major War Criminals before the International Military Tribunal, Nuremberg, 14 November 1945–1 October 1946* (Nuremberg, IMT 1947), especially at 78.

person who committed an act which constitutes a crime under international law acted as Head of State or responsible Government official does not relieve him from responsibility under international law.'[55] That principle was amply reflected in two draft codes that the ILC produced, pursuant to mandates from the UN General Assembly, regarding crimes against the peace and security of mankind, all of which rejected head of state immunity.[56] Later in the 1990s, the UN Security Council, on behalf of the UN, created international criminal tribunals for the former Yugoslavia and for Rwanda, and authorised the creation of a special war crimes court for Sierra Leone. Without exception, all the founding instruments of these tribunals contained provisions that rejected immunity for heads of state.[57] The same rejection of immunity is repeated in the Rome Statute of the International Criminal Court.[58]

It is important to stress that the occurrence of that norm in the Rome Statute is thus not a new idea. It was, at the adoption of the Statute in 1998, an idea that had been repeated in *every* relevant multilateral instrument of international law since 1919. It is precisely the repeat of that norm in successive relevant international instruments that gives the norm its status as a norm of customary international law. After all said and done, it has become *customary* to see that norm expressed in the familiar way in relevant international legal documents.

There is much significance, in this connection, to the observations of the International Law Commission in 1996 that '[t]he official position of an

55 See ILC, 'Principles of International Law Recognized in the Charter of the Nürnberg Tribunal and in the Judgment of the Tribunal' (1950) II *Yearbook of the International Law Commission* para. 97.

56 See the ILC 'Draft Code of Offences against the Peace and Security of Mankind' (1954) II *Yearbook of the International Law Commission*, Article 3; and the 'Draft Code of Crimes against the Peace and Security of Mankind with commentaries 1996' (1996) II(2) *Yearbook of the International Law Commission* 27, Article 7.

57 See the Statute of the International Criminal Tribunal for the Former Yugoslavia, UNSC Res 827 (25 May 1993) UN Doc S/RES/827, Annex, article 7(2); the Statute of the International Criminal Tribunal for Rwanda UNSC Res 955 (8 November 1944) UN Doc S/RES/955, Annex, Article 6(2); and the Statute of the Special Court for Sierra Leone, UNSC Res 1315 (14 August 2000) UN Doc S/Res/1315, Article 6(2).

58 In that regard, Article 27 of the Rome Statute provides as follows: 1. This Statute shall apply equally to all persons without any distinction based on official capacity. In particular, official capacity as a Head of State or Government, a member of a Government or parliament, an elected representative or a government official shall in no case exempt a person from criminal responsibility under this Statute, nor shall it, in and of itself, constitute a ground for reduction of sentence. 2. Immunities or special procedural rules which may attach to the official capacity of a person, whether under national or international law, shall not bar the Court from exercising its jurisdiction over such a person.

individual has been *consistently* excluded as a possible defence to crimes under international law in the relevant instruments adopted since the Charter of the Nürnberg Tribunal, including the Charter of the Tokyo Tribunal (art 6), Control Council Law No 10 (art 4) and, more recently, the statute of the International Tribunal for the Former Yugoslavia (art 7) and the statute of the International Tribunal for Rwanda (art 6). The absence of such a defence was also recognized by the Commission in the Nürnberg Principles (Principle III) and the 1954 draft Code (art 3).'[59] On any reasonable view, what the ILC correctly observed in 1996 as *consistent* exclusion of immunity is the very definition of customary international law.

### 1.3 *The Academic Objectors*

But some scholars have chosen to ignore the legal significance of the developments summarised above. They insist that customary international law recognises immunity for heads of state even in the proceedings of an international criminal court. Notable amongst the latter school are Dapo Akande,[60] Sarah Nouwen[61] and Astrid Kjeldgaard-Pedersen.[62] Indeed, 'willful' is the most charitable characterisation that restraint would allow for this kind of scholarship.

This commentary focuses mostly on Professor Akande's scholarship. This is because his scholarship is representative of that school, and he has enjoyed a long reputation as its front man.[63] Indeed, to anyone familiar with the field, his is the go-to scholarship that seeks to preserve immunity for heads of state accused of international crimes—even before international courts. In fairness to him—and fairness can also be a double-edged sword in certain circumstances such as the present—he argues the point the strongest in the

59 ILC Draft Code of Crimes against the Peace and Security of Mankind (n 56) commentary (4) to draft article 7, emphasis added.

60 See Akande, 'International Law Immunities and the International Criminal Court' (n 29); see also D Akande, 'The Immunity of Heads of States of Nonparties in the Early Years of the ICC' (2018) 112 *AJIL Unbound* 172; see also D Akande, 'ICC Appeals Chamber Holds that Heads of State Have No Immunity Under Customary International Law Before International Tribunals' (*EJIL:Talk!*, 6 May 2019) available at <https://www.ejiltalk.org/icc-appeals-chamber-holds-that-heads-of-state-have-no-immunity-under-customary-international-law-before-international-tribunals/> accessed 29 March 2023.

61 See Nouwen (n 29).

62 See Kjeldgaard-Pedersen (n 29).

63 In homage to Akande's leading role in that school of thought, one scholar described him as 'as a leading academic expert on question of immunities before the ICC': see Kjeldgaard-Pedersen, ibid., 953. Another scholar indicated that a certain theory of is known within academic circles as 'the Akande route': see Nouwen (n 29) 603.

protection of nationals of states *who have not consented to the jurisdiction* of the international court in question. This, he insists, is because customary international law has preserved that immunity even in the proceedings of international criminal courts.

In a conference in 2016, long before Russia's invasion of Ukraine, he argued as follows:

> I … take the view that under customary international law, there *is* immunity for heads of states before international tribunals, if that state is not a party to that treaty. And I think that that's important because otherwise what we would be saying is that two states, three states, four states can set up an 'international' tribunal to prosecute the head of state of another country.[64]

'I don't believe in regime change by force,' he insisted, stressing his earlier point. 'I don't believe in regime change by international tribunals either. Because that's in effect what we are talking about. To the extent that we take the view that there's no immunity before international tribunals which are created by states, then all we are saying is that two states, three states, fifteen states can set up an "international" tribunal to remove in effect the head of state of another state. I don't think that's conducive to good international relations.'[65]

For those reasons, he repeatedly reproached the Appeals Chamber of the Special Court for Sierra Leone as having delivered a 'flawed'[66] judgment, when they held that the SCSL had jurisdiction to try Charles Taylor and that he had no immunity before that court, because 'the principle seems now established that the sovereign equality of states does not prevent a Head of State from being prosecuted before an international criminal tribunal or court.'[67]

In 2019, the ICC Appeals Chamber decided in *Jordan Referral re Al-Bashir* that 'there is neither State practice nor *opinio juris* that would support the

64 D Akande, oral remarks (Wayamo Foundation Conference, 24–26 March 2016, Panel VII: Immunity of Heads of State under International Law) available at: <https://youtu.be/A_O1Yzvhcpo> at counter 1:15:34 to 1:16.28, accessed 29 March 2023.

65 Ibid.

66 See D Akande, 'ICC Issues Detailed Decision on Bashir's Immunity (… At long Last …) But Gets the Law Wrong' (*EJIL:Talk!*, 15 December 2011). Available here: < https://www.ejiltalk.org/icc-issues-detailed-decision-on-bashir%E2%80%99s-immunity-at-long-last-but-gets-the-law-wrong/> accessed 29 March 2020. See also, Akande, 'The Immunity of Heads of States of Non-parties in the Early Years of the ICC' (n 60) 174.

67 See Decision on Immunity from Jurisdiction, *Taylor*, SCSL-2003-01-I, AC, SCSL, 31 May 2004, para. 52.

existence of Head of State immunity under customary international law *vis-à-vis* an international court.'[68] In that regard, the ICC Appeals Chamber cited with full approval the earlier judgment of the SCSL Appeals Chamber in the case of *Charles Taylor*. [For those who may not know it, though now in academia, this author was the presiding judge in the *Al-Bashir* appeal.]

In effect, all ten judges of the appellate chambers of two international tribunals that have considered that specific question have, following their research, analyses and reflections, given the same answer. In so doing, they effectively rejected the Akande side of the debate and accepted the position of the scholars who say, as Mettraux, Dugard and Du Plessis did in their 2018 piece:

> The era of absolute immunities for heads of States and other State officials suspected of involvement in the commission of international crimes is long gone. Such immunities have been eroded to a point where there is now a customary law exclusion of those as a defence to charges involving international crimes or as an objection to the jurisdiction of a tribunal that is otherwise competent to hear those charges.[69]

On each occasion, Professor Akande promptly rebuked the two Appeals Chamber as rendering 'flawed' judgments. Regarding the ICC Appeals Chamber, it was surprising to read an almost immediate blog post of one page that he delivered only on the basis of the summary of the *Bashir* judgment read out in court, and before anybody else (including himself) had had a chance to read the full judgment comprising more than 400 pages. Perhaps more surprising was his choice of language as the very first person who evidently sought to set the stage for how others should see the judgment. 'Extremely controversial,' he declared, 'stunning,' 'deeply misguided,' 'very dangerous' and 'unwise.'[70] Perhaps, to further underscore the intensity of his feelings against the judgment, he appeared to sympathise with John Bolton—noted for his extreme hatred of the ICC for daring to envisage jurisdiction over US nationals, when the US was a non-party state to the Rome Statute. The haste shown in the blog-post compelled one of its commentators to observe as follows: 'I really thank

68 See Judgment in the Jordan Referral re-Al-Bashir Appeal, *Al Bashir, Situation in Darfur, Sudan*, ICC-02/05-01/09 OA2, AC, ICC, 6 May 2019, para. 113. See also the Joint Concurring Opinion of Judges Eboe-Osuji, Morrison, Hofmanski and Bossa, para. 70.

69 See Mettraux, Dugard and du Plessis (n 3) 620.

70 See Akande, 'ICC Appeals Chamber Holds that Heads of State Have No Immunity Under Customary International Law Before International' (n 60) [Hereafter 'Akande's *EJIL:Talk!* blog of 6 May 2019'].

the author for this expeditious comment on the ICC ruling today but I think waiting for more details from the full judgement enhanced by various grounds will be a better idea.'[71]

Given the limited time that the commentator had not read the full judgment before writing the blog, it was surprising that the blog post was widely repeated on Twitter by individuals—including scholars—who had obviously not had a chance to read the judgment within the very short period of time between its delivery and all the commotion. Indeed, some scholars have continued to cite the one-page blogpost written in those circumstances—and other blogposts—as authority for serious criticism of the judgment.[72]

It is unfortunate, of course, that such strong words were used by an effective party to the litigation, to criticise a judgment that went against his own interest that was partisan in more ways than one.[73] But they underscored the depth of feelings about reasons for disagreeing with the judgment. Still, the apparent reasons are critical in the general epiphanic theme of the present commentary.

---

71 See the comments of Dr Ayman Salama to Akande's *EJIL:Talk!* blog of 6 May 2019, available at <https://www.ejiltalk.org/icc-appeals-chamber-holds-that-heads-of-state-have-no-immunity-under-customary-international-law-before-international-tribunals/> accessed 29 March 2023.

72 See Kjeldgaard-Pedersen (n 29) 948. See also Nouwen (n 29) 604.

73 In his reaction to the judgment of the ICC Appeals Chamber, Akande was substantially in the position of a lawyer who, upon losing a case he argued, then quickly positioned himself as the chief judge in the court of public opinion, to hear the appeal of the same judgment that ruled against him. As a factual matter, besides being on the opposing side of debate between two opposing schools of legal scholarship on the question of immunity of heads of state, Professor Akande was also a consultant-legal advisor to the African Union behind the scenes, precisely on the very subject matter of the litigation in the *Al-Bashir* case—that being the matter of immunity—which the African Union Commission had been much invested, at the behest of certain African leaders who rejected the very idea of removal of their immunity in criminal proceedings at the ICC. On 4 June 2009, as the African Union was entering a particularly difficult relationship with the ICC because of the ICC Prosecutor's indictment of President Omar Al-Bashir of Sudan, regardless of immunity, the Martin School of Oxford University published the following information under the title, '*Dapo Akande appointed as Consultant by the African Union*' [bold script in the original]: 'Dapo Akande, Co-Director of the Oxford Institute for Ethics, Law and Armed Conflict, (currently on sabbatical at Yale), has been appointed as a Consultant by the African Union (AU). *In June 2009, the AU is holding a Ministerial meeting, partly as a result of a request by the International Criminal Court (ICC) for an arrest warrant for the President of Sudan* and partly because all of the situations currently under investigation by the Court and all of the current prosecutions have arisen from the African continent. *Dapo will assist the AU's Commission in preparing a review of the work of the International Criminal Court, including recommendations on the work of the ICC in relation to Africa.* His most recent article on the ICC 'The Legal Nature of Security Council Referrals to the

As always, Professor Akande's obvious complaint was that the Appeals Chamber's 'reasoning appears to assert that parties to the Rome Statute, have, by creating the Court, taken away the rights of non-party states under international law.' It may be pointed out in passing that the ruling was more nuanced than that.[74]

•••

Three short years after the ICC Appeals Chamber handed down the judgment in *Jordan Referral re Al-Bashir*, President Vladimir Putin ordered Russian soldiers to invade Ukraine. The world was shocked. US President Joe Biden famously called Putin a 'criminal' that needed to be put on trial.[75] In a coordinated move Western nations imposed crippling sanctions of every imaginable kind on Russia and its leaders. And the powerful leaders of many Western nations desired Putin prosecuted for international crimes, especially the crime of aggression that the invasion entailed, with some of them saying so openly.[76]

---

ICC and its Impact on Al Bashir's Immunities' is scheduled for publication in the *Journal of International Criminal Justice*.' (Italic emphasis added). Available at <www.oxfordmartin.ox.ac.uk/news/dapo-african-union/>, accessed on 7 June 2022. On any careful review, the protests of the African Union Commission in relation to the non-recognition of immunity are consistent with Professor Akande's views. It must of course be stressed that Professor Akande's work for the AU as a consultant-legal advisor on the Al-Bashir case would not disqualify him from expressing an academic view (for what it is worth) on the matter. It was only fair to his readers and the discourse in general if he had thenceforth disclosed that association systematically, for the sake of readers of his commentaries who were unaware of that association. That disclosure was seldom made, let alone systematically. There is, of course, no need to belabour the point.

74 See *Jordan Referral re Al-Bashir*, above, Joint Concurring Opinion of Judges Eboe-Osuji, Morrison, Hofmanski and Bossa, paras 446–449. In that section of their joint opinion, four out of the five judges of the Appeals Chamber explained that immunity and jurisdiction are different jural concepts that must be appreciated separately, before seeing how they interact. To say that there is no immunity before the ICC does not mean that the ICC has jurisdiction in a particular case.

75 See J Henley and D Smith, 'Biden calls for Putin to face war crimes trial over civilian killings in Ukraine,' *The Guardian*, 4 April 2022, available at <www.theguardian.com/us-news/2022/apr/04/joe-biden-vladimir-putin-face-war-crimes-trial-ukraine> accessed 29 March 2023. See also 'Biden calls Putin a war criminal' *NPR*, 16 March 2022, available at <www.npr.org/2022/03/16/1087011897/biden-putin-war-criminal> accessed 29 March 2023.

76 See for instance, M Brewster and C Paas-Lang, 'Trudeau says Canada backs Ukraine in seeking justice for Putin's "heinous war crimes"' *CBC*, 8 May 2022: available at <www.cbc.ca/news/politics/trudeau-ukraine-visit-1.6445929> accessed 30 March 2023. See also C Gallardo, 'Boris Johnson: Vladimir Putin guilty of war crimes' *Politico*, 2 March

But, a gap that exists in the Rome Statute ensured that Russian leaders could not be prosecuted before the ICC, though Russian nationals could be prosecuted at the ICC for any other international crime (genocide, crimes against humanity and war crimes) alleged against them as part of their conduct on Ukraine's territory.[77]

So, a need was felt to rally global support to create a special *ad hoc* international tribunal just for the crime of aggression committed against Ukraine. Former UK Prime Ministers Gordon Brown and John Major emerged as the political leaders of that effort.[78] Professor Akande, to his own credit, emerged very early on as one of two primary legal voices in support of the effort.[79]

The trouble, of course, is that the issue of immunity would always confront any effort to prosecute the crime of aggression. After all, in its current formulation, the crime of aggression is necessarily a leadership crime. Immunity and the crime of aggression are on opposite sides of the accountability coin. You can see the one side or the other—not both. Soon enough, Professor Akande was confronted with that dilemma. And his fascinating answer deserves quoting in full:

As a matter of general international law, serving heads of state have immunity, certainly from national criminal jurisdiction. And then there's the question of whether they also have immunity if they are sought to be prosecuted by an international tribunal. There's a range of views on that question. So, on whether or not they have immunity before international tribunals. The International Criminal Court gave a decision a couple of years ago, with respect to the then Sudanese President Omar Al Bashir (who was facing the charge of genocide, by the way, at the International Criminal Court) and the International Criminal Court held that though he was a serving head of state,

---

2022: available at <www.politico.eu/article/boris-johnson-accuse-vladimir-putin-war-crime/> accessed 30 March 2023.

77 That gap occurs in the words of article 15*bis*(5) of the Rome Statute which provides: 'In respect of a State that is not a party to this Statute, the Court shall not exercise its jurisdiction over the crime of aggression when committed by that State's nationals or on its territory.' This provision is unique only to the crime of aggression. There is no equivalent provision in relation to genocide, crimes against humanity or war crimes.

78 See G Brown, 'How we plan to prosecute Putin at the International Criminal Court.' (*The Office of Gordon & Sarah Brown*, 14 April 2022) available here: <https://gordonandsarahbrown.com/2022/04/gordon-brown-today-we-publish-the-text-of-a-criminal-indictment-against-president-putin/> accessed 30 March 2023.

79 See 'A Criminal Tribunal for Aggression Tribunal in Ukraine' (Chatham House webinar, 4 March 2022) available at <www.chathamhouse.org/events/all/research-event/criminal-tribunal-aggression-ukraine> accessed 30 March 2023.

he was not immune [from prosecution] under customary international law, because those were proceedings before an international tribunal. Now, that ruling by the ICC was one which was controversial. But that's what they held. And they relied on an earlier judgment which had been given in a case involving Charles Taylor, who was then the head of state of Liberia who was sought by the Special Court for Sierra Leone, which is also an international tribunal. So that's one view. Not everyone accepts that view.

But actually in this case there's another issue which arises, which is that: this is not just a case—Yes, it would be an international criminal tribunal—but it is not just a case of an international criminal tribunal. This is a case where the Government of Ukraine would be delegating the national jurisdiction that it has to prosecute the crime of aggression that occurs on its territory—and against it—to this international tribunal.

And as a matter of international law, looking it more broadly, Ukraine obviously has the right to self-defence, which it is exercising in the circumstance. It has the right to act in self-help. It can use force—and it is using force—to defend itself. It would seem to me to be far-fetched to say, 'Yes, Ukraine can do that. Yes, it can use force. If necessary even it can use force in its aid, acting in self-defence, on the territory of the aggressor state. If necessary, it can even use force to change the government of the aggressor state. But the one thing that it cannot do is actually prosecute the head of state.' That would seem to me to be quite far-fetched.[80]

Without belabouring a point, it may be said that one of the silver linings in Russia's horrid war of aggression in Ukraine is that it has in more ways than one shocked complacent people—notably policymakers and the scholars who advised them—into their senses. This is both in relation to their previous views on both accountability for the crime of aggression and other international crimes, including on the question of immunity.

In that regard, Professor Akande's scholarship deserves special attention. His latter-day championship of a special international tribunal for the crime of aggression in Ukraine (STAU), for the specific purpose of prosecuting alleged crimes by Russia's President Putin, reveals the original misgivings in his previous scholarship, which found traction amongst some scholars.

There may be another occasion for extended discussion of the extent of the many errors of that scholarship. But as will hopefully become clear in the present commentary, a thumb test of the sum of the weaknesses of that

80 See 'A Criminal Tribunal for Aggression Tribunal in Ukraine' (Chatham House webinar, 4 March 2022) available at <www.chathamhouse.org/events/all/research-event/criminal-tribunal-aggression-ukraine>: Video timestamp: 39:27–42:05, accessed 30 March 2023.

scholarship is that every material legal factor in the war in Ukraine such as now animates Professor Akande (and those who follow his advice) were always discernible in the circumstances of the war in Sierra Leone that occasioned a line of jurisprudence that he had reproached before Russia's invasion of Ukraine. It may be considered that the only material difference is that unlike the war in Sierra Leone (a minor African nation), which was sponsored[81] by President Charles Taylor of Liberia (another minor African nation), the war in Ukraine is widely viewed by Western powers as a war of European domination waged by President Putin, who must be stopped and (many insist) be punished for it.

## 2 Why the War in Ukraine Presents No New Legal Problem in International Law

To err is only human, so too is the prerogative to change our minds. For that reason, legal scholars who once expressed peculiar views should be welcomed back to the prevalent views of international law in relation to both the matter of accountability for the crime of aggression and specifically on the absence of immunity for heads of state accused (especially before international criminal courts) of committing international crimes. All hands need to be on deck in support of justice for humanity—and not the immunity of power from accountability. In the present context, however, the only sensible explanation for the return must be the eventual epiphany inspired by the overwhelming shock and revulsion that Russia's invasion of Ukraine occasioned in the Western world. In reality, the war in Ukraine presented no *different situation* as far as the operative legal factors go.

Notably, Akande's theories of 'delegation' of jurisdiction and 'self-defence' that inspired his turn around were always available to the other scenarios in which he previously sought to constrain the jurisdiction of the ICC in relation to the crime of aggression while expanding the scope of immunity for heads of state charged with international crimes before it.

81 See Judgment, *Taylor*, SCSL-03-01-A, AC, SCSL, 26 September 2013 for instance, paras 131–135, 158–167, 173–176, 185–189, 226, 254, 257, 286, 305, 308, 309, 310, 311, 312–343, findings. Professor Charles Jalloh has also synthesised a very useful legal historiography of the Sierra Leone civil war and the work of the Special Court in relation to it, in his useful book *The Legal Legacy of the Special Court for Sierra Leone* (n 4) 218–222. See also C Jalloh, 'The Law and Politics of the Charles Taylor Case' (2015) 43 *Denver Journal of International Law & Policy* 229.

### 2.1 *Delegation of Jurisdiction*

Professor Akande's first argument in justification of support for the proposed STAU is that it is an international tribunal to which Ukraine would be *delegating* the national jurisdiction that it has to prosecute those who commit the crime of aggression on its territory. We may recall him putting the point as follows:

> But actually in this case there's another issue which arises, which is that: this is not just a case—Yes, it would be an international criminal tribunal—but it is not just a case of an international criminal tribunal. This is a case where the Government of Ukraine would be delegating the national jurisdiction that it has to prosecute the crime of aggression that occurs on its territory—and against it—to this international tribunal.[82]

It is enough to say here that Professor Akande's 'delegation theory'[83] is not ideal, though this is not the place to give it a comprehensive evaluation. But, briefly, the following difficulties may be mentioned. It is a poor explanation for the reality that an international tribunal is allowed to operate in *a jural space* that would ordinarily belong to national jurisdiction. The idea of 'delegation' is not the only one that may sensibly describe that phenomenon. Indeed, of all the possible candidates, 'delegation' is the least suitable concept. As the dictionaries tell us, the idea suggests a *principal and agent* relationship.[84] It can thus lead to a faulty view of a court of law—as is the case in these discourses—on any view in which a court of law is seen as the agent of principals standing behind it. The political infelicities of such a view of an international court—in a world in which some states carry more pull than others—are apparent enough.

As a legal matter, the average lawyer knows of the host of obligations that an agent owes to the principal. It is enough to mention lack of independence as one of them. As precedents of international courts go, the Special Court

82 See 'A Criminal Tribunal for Aggression Tribunal in Ukraine' (Chatham House webinar, 4 March 2022) available at <www.chathamhouse.org/events/all/research-event/criminal-tribunal-aggression-ukraine>: Video timestamp: 39:27–42:05, accessed 30 March 2023.

83 See Akande, 'International Law Immunities and the International Criminal Court' (n 29) 421.

84 Notably, the *Oxford Thesaurus of English* indicates the following as synonyms for 'delegate': 'representative, envoy, emissary, commissioner, agent, deputy, commissary; spokesperson, spokesman, spokeswoman; ambassador, plenipotentiary; messenger, go-between, proxy.'

of Sierra Leone would be a classic court that fits what Professor Akande has in mind as an international court to whom a state has 'delegated' its national jurisdiction. This is because Sierra Leone requested the UN to create the SCSL and the UN agreed.[85] But consider this. Article 8(2) of the Statute of the SCSL gives primacy of jurisdiction to the SCSL. That must be at least awkward to the idea of 'delegation' of jurisdiction to an international court. Similarly, the rule is trite that a delegate can have no greater power than the principal (and this is one of the selling values of the "delegation" theory to Professor Akande's scholarship on immunity). It may be noted that the President of Sierra Leone is protected by a constitutional norm of immunity.[86] [Indeed the constitutions of many nations, with very few exceptions,[87] contain similar immunity for their own presidents.] But, article 6(2) of the SCSL Statute rejects immunity for anyone—including heads of state. Does it mean that the President of Sierra Leone would enjoy immunity before the SCSL, on the theory that the SCSL enjoys *delegated* jurisdiction from Sierra Leone, since a delegate can exercise no greater power than the principal? But, that question resonates beyond the SCSL and Sierra Leone. The question troubles Akande's delegation theory even in relation to the ICC. If the ICC is only the joint and several delegate of each of the Rome Statute states parties, what then does the idea do for all those states whose constitutions, like that of Sierra Leone, preserves immunity for their heads of state? Would this not mean that article 27 of the Rome Statute will only bind the gullible states parties who did not take care to provide for presidential immunity in their national constitutions, while their peer nations have done so? The view is indeed a recipe for mass withdrawal from the Rome Statute, on the parts of those leaders who do not want to subject themselves to accountability by having their countries remain parties to the Rome Statute.

•••

More concerning, perhaps, is that Professor Akande has employed the theory of 'delegation' of jurisdiction as a basis to reproach the denial of immunity to

85 See UNSC Res 1315 (14 August 2000) UN Doc S/Res/1315 [on establishment of a Special Court for Sierra Leone]. See also C Jalloh, 'The Law and Politics of the Charles Taylor Case' (2015) 43 *Denver Journal of International Law & Policy* 229, 246–247.

86 See the Constitution of Sierra Leone (1991), s 48(4).

87 Two notable exceptions are the Constitution of France (1958) [see article 67 read together with article 53-2 as amended] and the Constitution of Kenya (2010) [see s 143(4)]—which recognise no immunity where the President is accused of an international crime pursuant to a treaty to which the country is a party.

officials of states who have not consented to the jurisdiction of the international court. As he was known to argue, customary international law preserves immunity for states in inter-state relations: therefore, states cannot exercise 'through' an international court a jurisdiction that they cannot exercise individually.[88]

It may yet be possible to give the 'delegation theory' a value that is no higher than consent to jurisdiction. But it is implausible to use the theory for the purpose of preserving immunity before an international criminal court. This is not only because of the case law of the International Court of Justice in the *Reparation Case*,[89] to the effect that international organisations are independent of the states that created them; but also because courts of law operate on the fundamental ethos of judicial independence. Notably, the ICJ has correctly claimed that independence for itself, even in circumstances where the United Nations General Assembly has requested an advisory opinion from the ICJ.[90]

But, even on the supposedly salutary side, Professor Akande's strategy of using the 'delegation theory' as a basis of jurisdiction for the proposed STAU presents fundamental contradictions to his previous scholarship. It will be recalled in this connection that he had repeatedly criticised the Appeals Chamber of the Special Court for Sierra Leone for ruling that the SCSL had jurisdiction over Charles Taylor, the President of Liberia, with no immunity recognised for him, for aiding and abetting war crimes and crimes against humanity committed during the war in the neighbouring Sierra Leone, including, notably, sending his soldiers into the territory of Sierra Leone to take part in that war.[91] As his scholarship generally suggested, Professor Akande's objection on those occasions was apparently grounded on the fact that the SCSL was established by agreement between the UN and Sierra Leone, which agreement was neither made pursuant to Chapter VII powers of the UN Security Council nor with Liberia's consent to the SCSL jurisdiction.[92]

From those perspectives, the question becomes this. How then will the proposed STAU be different from the SCSL? In the event that the STAU is created, its

88 See Akande, 'International Law Immunities and the International Criminal Court' (n 29) 417.

89 See *Reparation for injuries suffered in the service of the United Nations* (Advisory Opinion) [1949] ICJ Reports 174, at pp 182–184.

90 See, for instance, *Threat or Use of Nuclear Weapons* (Advisory Opinion) [1996] ICJ Rep 226, 234ff.

91 See for instance, Jalloh, *The Legal Legacy of the Special Court for Sierra Leone* (n 4) 221–222.

92 See Akande, 'ICC Issues Detailed Decision on Bashir's Immunity (… At long Last …) But Gets the Law Wrong' (n 66). See also, Akande, 'The Immunity of Heads of States of Non-parties in the Early Years of the ICC' (n 60) 174.

creation will be neither pursuant to Chapter VII powers of the Security Council (because Russia will veto it) nor with the consent of Russia. As the SCSL was established pursuant to an arrangement that would be accommodated within the same 'delegation' theory that Professor Akande espoused to justify the jurisdiction of the STAU over crimes alledegly committed by the Russian Federation, how then would it be correct to recognise the STAU jurisdiction over alleged crimes committed by a head of state, while denying the SCSL jurisdiction over Charles Taylor?

Surely, Akande's delegation theory would serve a purpose beyond the circumstances of Ukraine—and Sierra Leone. It will serve every other situation in which a state would have consented to the jurisdiction of the ICC to prosecute international crimes allegedly committed on its territory by nationals of another state that is or is not a party to the Rome Statute. For instance, on what acceptable rationale would it suit Ukraine in relation to Russia for purposes of the jurisdiction of the proposed STAU, but not Palestine in relation to Israel or Afghanistan in relation to the US, for purposes of the ICC jurisdiction?

### 2.2 *Self-Defence*

From the perspective of contradictions, Professor Akande's self-defence theory fares no better, as a basis of justification of the STAU jurisdiction—sans immunity—over President Putin. It will be recalled that he put it thus:

> And as a matter of international law, looking it more broadly, Ukraine obviously has the right to self-defence, which it is exercising in the circumstance. It has the right to act in self-help. It can use force—and it is using force—to defend itself. It would seem to me to be far-fetched to say, 'Yes, Ukraine can do that. Yes, it can use force. If necessary even it can use force in its aid, acting in self-defence, on the territory of the aggressor state. If necessary, it can even use force to change the government of the aggressor state. But the one thing that it cannot do is actually prosecute the head of state.' That would seem to me to be quite far-fetched.[93]

Again, how different is that theory in relation to Sierra Leone? Did Sierra Leone not have the same right of self-defence and self-help—and so on—against Charles Taylor's Liberia? It may be noted in this regard that Liberian soldiers

93 See 'A Criminal Tribunal for Aggression Tribunal in Ukraine' (Chatham House webinar, 4 March 2022) available at <www.chathamhouse.org/events/all/research-event/criminal-tribunal-aggression-ukraine>: Video timestamp: 39:27–42:05, accessed 30 March 2023.

were said to have entered the territory of Sierra Leone to fight in the Sierra Leone war.[94] This would fit the definition of the crime of aggression which includes the "sending by or on behalf of a State of armed bands, groups, irregulars or mercenaries, which carry out acts of armed force against another State of such gravity as to amount to the acts listed above, or its substantial involvement therein."[95] Would those same rights not justify the SCSL's exercise of jurisdiction over Charles Taylor (without immunity) no less than it would justify the STAU's exercise of jurisdiction over alleged crimes committed by heads of state (without immunity)?

Perhaps, the broader point concerns Akande's previous objections to 'two states, three states, fifteen states' purporting to create an international court that takes away the immunity of a state that is not a party to the treaty creating that court. In international law, the right of self-defence includes the right of collective self-defence.[96] Two states, three states or fifteen states can agree to a pact of collective self-defence. Surely, if the right of self-defence of one state could validate its jurisdiction to prosecute the head of state of another state, then their right of collective self-defence must accommodate their derivative right to prosecute the head of state of a state not party to the self-defence pact.

## 3 Conclusion

In 2019, three years before the world witnessed an alleged act of aggression in Ukraine, the Appeals Chamber of the ICC held that customary international does not recognise immunity for any head of state accused of committing an international crime. That ruling would serve the purposes of the International Criminal Court, as it would serve those of any other international criminal tribunal, including the proposed international tribunal for the crime of aggression in Ukraine. While many legal scholars applauded the judgment, Professor Akande was the leader amongst the few who 'severely criticized' it.[97] His complaint was that 'the reasoning appeared to assert that parties to the Rome Statute, have, by creating the Court, taken away the rights of non-party states under international law.' Although that was a purposeful attempt to drape the decision with absurdum, that mindset still carried the value of communicating the reprobation of any effort seen as giving to an international tribunal

94 See for instance, Jalloh, *The Legal Legacy of the Special Court for Sierra Leone* (n 4) 221–222.

95 See Article 8(2)(g) of the Rome Statute.

96 See Article 51 of the UN Charter.

97 See Kjeldgaard-Pedersen (n 29) 948.

jurisdiction over the nationals and officials of states who are not parties to the founding instrument of the tribunal in question.

If Professor Akande was correct in that mindset, then he must necessarily be wrong to encourage the creation of an international criminal tribunal for the crime of aggression in Ukraine, to which Russia will be a non-party state.

But, in the world of international law, accountability for genocide, crimes against humanity, war crimes and the crime of aggression (which has 'within it the accumulated evil' of all the rest) is not to be treated as a point that law students debate in a moot court. Scholars cannot hope to extricate themselves readily from avoidable intellectual binds that they had woven for themselves. When implausible scholarship has run its course and is eventually exposed, the sensible thing to do is to admit error. For, to err is human. It is unhelpful to continue to muddy the waters by seeking to generate new theories in hopes of sustaining previous arguments that the limits of which have been made plain by later realities.

International law's proscription of both the crime of aggression and ideas of immunity that would prevent accountability before international criminal courts began with aggressive wars of domination that shocked Europe and the world. So it was with the would be revolutionary effort to create an international tribunal to prosecute Kaiser Wilhelm II of Germany in 1919, recognising no immunity for him. So it was with the actualised prosecution of surviving leaders of Germany's Third Reich in 1945 before the International Military Tribunal in Nuremberg, with no immunity recognised for them. And, so it is now, with the proposal to establish a special international criminal tribunal for the crime of aggression in Ukraine, which would try heads of state by alleged crimes committed, with no immunity recognised.

It was an unfortunate mistake that muddied legal waters, when certain scholars ignored those legal dispensations that existed long before Russia's invasion of Ukraine. But all those scholars who made that mistake are welcome to their own epiphany—as a result of the invasion of Ukraine. We have all had our own at one time or another.

CHAPTER 27

# One Regime to Rule Them All: Harmonizing the Conditions for the Exercise of Jurisdiction over Crimes within the Jurisdiction of the ICC

*Astrid Reisinger Coracini*

## 1 Introduction*

### 1.1 *The Ukraine Momentum of International Criminal Justice*

On 24 February 2022, Russian armed forces launched a full-scale invasion of the territory of Ukraine.[1] This dramatic escalation of the armed conflict, which commenced in 2014, generated an exceptional wave of solidarity and political momentum to ensure accountability for crimes under international law committed in and against Ukraine. At the same time, it accentuated weaknesses in the international criminal justice architecture that must be addressed with a view to strengthening international criminal law in and beyond the situation in Ukraine.

In an unprecedented move, a total of 43 States parties to the Rome Statute of the International Criminal Court (ICCSt/Rome Statute),[2] referred the situation in Ukraine to the International Criminal Court (ICC/the Court).[3] Ukraine is not a State party to the Rome Statute, but it deposited two declarations accepting the Court's jurisdiction in accordance with Art. 12(3) ICCSt in 2014 and 2015

* This chapter is an extended and revised version of an earlier text published online as 'Is Amending the Rome Statute the Panacea Against Perceived Selectivity and Impunity for the Crime of Aggression Committed Against Ukraine?' (*Just Security*, 21 March 2023) <https://www.justsecurity.org/85593/is-amending-the-rome-statute-the-panacea-against-perceived-selectivity-and-impunity-for-the-crime-of-aggression-committed-against-ukraine/> accessed 11 April 2023.

1 The international community reacted promptly and in clear terms under the Uniting for peace mechanism, '[d]eploring in the strongest terms the aggression by the Russian Federation against Ukraine in violation of Article 2(4) of the Charter.'; UNGA Res ES-11/1 (2 March 2022).

2 Rome Statute of the International Criminal Court (signed 17 July 1998, entered into force 1 July 2002) 2187 UNTS 3.

3 Situation in Ukraine, ICC <https://www.icc-cpi.int/situations/ukraine> accessed 11 April 2023.

 | DOI:10.1163/9789004529939_028

respectively.[4] On this basis, former Prosecutor Fatou Bensouda conducted a preliminary examination from 2014 to 2020, concluding that there was a reasonable basis to believe that war crimes and crimes against humanity had been committed in Crimea and Eastern Ukraine.[5] Prompted by the February 2022 invasion, Prosecutor Karim Kahn announced the opening of an investigation on the basis of the findings of the preliminary examination and also encompassing any new alleged crimes falling within the jurisdiction of the Court that are committed by any party to the conflict on any part of the territory of Ukraine.[6] In order to avoid the potentially lengthy procedure of seeking the authorization of the pre-trial chamber to initiate a *proprio motu* investigation (Art. 15(3) ICCSt), the Prosecutor encouraged States parties to refer the situation in Ukraine to the Court.[7] This call was answered promptly, as were pleas for additional funds in order to sustain the investigation.[8] On 17 March 2023, ICC Pre-Trial Chamber II issued the first arrest warrants in the situation in Ukraine against Mr. Vladimir Vladimirovich Putin, President of the Russian Federation, and Ms. Maria Alekseyevna Lvova-Belova, Commissioner for Children's Rights in the Office of

4 With its first declaration adopted in February 2014, Ukraine accepted the jurisdiction of the ICC with respect to acts committed on its territory from 21 November 2013 to 22 February 2014 <https://www.icc-cpi.int/sites/default/files/itemsDocuments/997/declarationRecognitionJuristiction09-04-2014.pdf> accessed 11 April 2023. The second declaration adopted in February 2015 extended this time period to acts committed from 20 February 2014 onwards <https://www.icc-cpi.int/sites/default/files/iccdocs/other/Ukraine_Art_12-3_declaration_08092015.pdf#search=ukraine> accessed 11 April 2023.

5 ICC OTP, 'Report on Preliminary Examination Activities 2020' (14 December 2020), 68ff <https://www.icc-cpi.int/sites/default/files/itemsDocuments/2020-PE/2020-pe-report-eng.pdf> accessed 11 April 2023; 'Statement of the Prosecutor, Fatou Bensouda, on the conclusion of the preliminary examination in the situation in Ukraine', ICC OTP (11 December 2020) <https://www.icc-cpi.int/news/statement-prosecutor-fatou-bensouda-conclusion-preliminary-examination-situation-ukraine> accessed 11 April 2023.

6 'Statement of ICC Prosecutor, Karim A.A. Khan QC, on the Situation in Ukraine: "I have decided to proceed with opening an investigation."', ICC OTP (28 February 2023) <https://www.icc-cpi.int/news/statement-icc-prosecutor-karim-aa-khan-qc-situation-ukraine-i-have-decided-proceed-opening> accessed 11 April 2023.

7 Ibid.

8 These voluntary contributions have generated scepticism. On the one side, because the ICC should be able to count on a sustainable funding model in which voluntary contributions are considered the exception. On the other side because, although such contributions cannot legally be earmarked, some governments have publicly linked their contributions to the Prosecutor's call for funding of the situation in Ukraine, which 'raise[s] concerns about perceptions of politicization in the court's work', M E Vignoli, 'Support Builds for ICC Ukraine Investigation: Governments Should Ensure Similar Support Across the Court's Mandate' (*Human Rights Watch*, 20 March 2023) <https://www.hrw.org/news/2023/03/20/support-builds-icc-ukraine-investigation> accessed 11 April 2023.

the President of the Russian Federation, for the war crimes of unlawful deportation of population (children) and of unlawful transfer of population (children) from occupied areas of Ukraine to the Russian Federation.[9]

This exceptionally swift engagement of the ICC in the situation in Ukraine, a blueprint for the successful deployment of the international justice system, however, cannot cover the massive accountability gap that exists with a view to the crime of aggression.

It comes as no revelation that the conditions for the exercise of jurisdiction over the crime of aggression, adopted at the first Review Conference of the Rome Statute in Kampala in 2010,[10] establish a distinct and severely restricted jurisdictional regime. A jurisdictional regime that a majority of States did not favour, but a jurisdictional regime that was accepted as a compromise solution in order to allow the ICC to exercise its jurisdiction over the crime of aggression at all. Absent a referral of a situation by the United Nations (UN) Security Council, the ICC can exercise its jurisdiction only 'over a crime of aggression arising from an act of aggression committed by a State Party' (Art. 15*bis*(4) ICCSt). In addition, it cannot exercise its jurisdiction 'over the crime of aggression when committed by that State's nationals or on its territory' (Art. 15*bis*(5) ICCSt). As neither the Russian Federation nor Belarus are States parties to the Rome Statute,[11] the ICC is bound to remain inactive with regard to the crime of aggression committed against Ukraine. A most unfortunate position for a permanent international criminal court that has subject matter jurisdiction over the crime of aggression, that has temporal, personal, and territorial jurisdiction over the situation in Ukraine, but which is unable to prosecute the very crime of aggression in this very situation.

In order to fill this accountability gap on the international level,[12] States are currently discussing options for the establishment of an *ad hoc* jurisdiction to

9 Art. 8(2)(a)(vii) and 8(2)(b)(viii) ICCSt; see 'Situation in Ukraine: ICC judges issue arrest warrants against Vladimir Vladimirovich Putin and Maria Alekseyevna Lvova-Belova', ICC Press Release (17 March 2023) <https://www.icc-cpi.int/news/situation-ukraine-icc-judges-issue-arrest-warrants-against-vladimir-vladimirovich-putin-and> accessed 11 April 2023.

10 Review Conference of the Rome Statute, Resolution RC/Res.6 'The crime of aggression' (11 June 2010) RC/11 <https://asp.icc-cpi.int/sites/asp/files/asp_docs/Resolutions/RC-Res.6-ENG.pdf> accessed 11 April 2023.

11 By 'allowing its territory, which it has placed at the disposal of another State, to be used by that other State for perpetrating an act of aggression against a third State', Belarus not only participated in an act of aggression committed by the Russian Federation but committed itself an act of aggression in the sense of Art. 8*bis*(2)(f) ICCSt.

12 On the national level, Ukraine as well as a number of other States have launched investigations of crimes under international law committed in Ukraine within their domestic legal system. Estonia, Latvia, Lithuanian, Polish, Romania, Slovakia, Ukraine, and the ICC office

prosecute the crime of aggression against Ukraine. Models include a Special Tribunal for the Crime of Aggression Committed Against Ukraine (STCoA) established on the basis of a bilateral treaty between the United Nations and Ukraine,[13] an international tribunal established by a multilateral treaty, or an internationalized tribunal or chamber established under Ukrainian national law with international elements.[14] At the same time, calls to remove jurisdictional exceptions from the Rome Statute are getting traction and a number of States have linked their support of an *ad hoc* jurisdiction over the crime of aggression committed against Ukraine with the requirement of amending the jurisdictional regime of the Rome Statute.[15] This coincides with a mandatory

---

of the Prosecutor participate in a Joint Investigation Team under the auspices of Eurojust to cooperate in the prosecution of 'genocide, crimes against humanity, war crimes and related criminal offences' (see Art. 4(1)(j) and Annex I of Eurojust Regulation (EU) 2018/1727 as amended by Regulation (EU) 2022/828). At the same time, a new International Centre for the Prosecution of the Crime of Aggression against Ukraine will collect evidence and facilitate case building with a view to the crime of aggression, 'Start of operations of Core International Crimes Evidence Database and new International Centre for Prosecution of the Crime of Aggression to be based at Agency', Eurojust Press Release (23 February 2023) <https://www.eurojust.europa.eu/news/start-operations-core-international-crimes-evidence-database-and-new-international-centre> accessed 11 April 2023.

13 See e.g. L D Johnson, 'United Nations Response Options to Russia's Aggression: Opportunities and Rabbit Holes' (*Just Security*, 1 March 2022) <https://www.justsecurity.org/80395/united-nations-response-options-to-russias-aggression-opportunities-and-rabbit-holes/> accessed 11 April 2023; Just Security series 'U.N. General Assembly and International Criminal Tribunal for the Crime of Aggression Against Ukraine' <https://www.justsecurity.org/tag/u-n-general-assembly-and-international-criminal-tribunal-for-aggression-against-ukraine/> accessed 11 April 2023.

14 For a comprehensive overview see O Corten and V Koutroulis, 'Tribunal for the crime of aggression against Ukraine – a legal assessment', European Parliament (December 2022) <https://www.europarl.europa.eu/RegData/etudes/IDAN/2022/702574/EXPO_IDA(2022)702574_EN.pdf> accessed 11 April 2023; C McDougall, 'The Imperative of Prosecuting Crimes of Aggression Committed Against Ukraine'(2023) *Journal of Conflict and Security Law* 1.

15 A Baerbock, 'Strengthening International Law in Times of Crisis', speech by the German Federal Foreign Minister in The Hague (16 January 2023) <https://www.auswaertiges-amt.de/en/newsroom/news/strengthening-international-law-in-times-of-crisis/2573492> accessed 28 April 2023; Council of Europe, Parliamentary Assembly, Resolution 2482 (2023), 'Legal and human rights aspects of the Russian Federation's aggression against Ukraine' (26 January 2023) <https://pace.coe.int/en/files/31620/html> accessed 28 April 2023; Joint Statement of Albania, Belgium, Costa Rica, Czech Republic, Estonia, Guatemala, Latvia, Liechtenstein, Lithuania, Luxembourg, Marshall Islands, North-Macedonia and Poland on the accountability for the crime of aggression committed on the territory of Ukraine, Permanent Mission of Estonia to the UN (17 April 2023) <https://un.mfa.ee/joint-statement-on-the-accountability-for-the-crime-of-aggression-committed-on-the-territory-of-ukraine/> accessed 28 April 2023.

review of the Kampala aggression amendments, 'seven years after the beginning of the Court's exercise of jurisdiction'[16] that is upcoming in 2025.

### 1.2 *Amending the Rome Statute Is Not an Alternative but a Cumulative Requirement*

Prosecuting the crime of aggression committed against Ukraine before the ICC, would be the ideal scenario. The Court was established to end impunity for all victims of crimes under international law. It is a permanent institution, at the centre of 'a system of global criminal justice',[17] which was perceived as a tool to end the selective *ad hoc* enforcement of international criminal,[18] partly in the form of victors' justice, partly in the form of international(ized) enforcement mechanisms created for some situations but not for others. Nonetheless, the ICC is based on an international treaty that contains inherent limitations. Unless the Rome Statute is universally ratified, the Court's exercise of jurisdiction cannot but remain selective. Against this background, the creation of an *ad hoc* jurisdiction in order to close existing enforcement gaps of the Rome Statute should not encounter allegations of selective justice. It provides for accountability where the ICC cannot fulfill its objective and thus contributes to the reduction of the selective enforcement of international criminal law in a broader sense.

It is mostly the factor time, which makes it unrealistic to assume that amending the Rome Statute could be a genuine alternative to establishing an *ad hoc* jurisdiction in the situation in Ukraine.[19] The crime of aggression falls within the jurisdiction of the ICC since the adoption of the Rome Statute in 1998 (Art. 5(1)(d) ICCSt). It was included on the basis of a compromise. Although it was listed and recognized as one of 'the most serious crimes of concern to the international community as a whole' (Art. 5(1) ICCSt), the Court was unable to exercise its jurisdiction over the crime of aggression until States adopted a provision 'defining the crime and setting out the conditions under which the Court shall exercise jurisdiction' over it (Art. 5(2) of the 1998 ICCSt).[20] After

---

16 RC/Res.6 (n 10) para. 4.

17 F Bensouda, 'Reflections from the International Criminal Court Prosecutor' (2012) 5 *Case Western Reserve Journal of International Law* 505, 508.

18 T L H McCormack, 'Selective Reaction to Atrocity: War Crimes and the Development of International Criminal Law' (1996) 60 *Albany Law Review* 681.

19 L M Ocampo, 'Ending Selective Justice for the International Crime of Aggression' (*Just Security*, 31 January 2023) <https://www.justsecurity.org/84949/ending-selective-justice-for-the-international-crime-of-aggression/> accessed 11 April 2023.

20 UN, Rome Statute of the International Criminal Court (17 July 1998) UN Doc A/CONF.183/9, as corrected by procès-verbaux, <https://treaties.un.org/doc/Treaties/1998/07/19980717%2006-33%20PM/Ch_XVIII_10p.pdf> accessed 30 April 2023.

twelve years of negotiations, a provision was eventually approved at Kampala, Uganda in 2010, at the first Review Conference of the Rome Statute.[21] Yet, the Court's exercise of jurisdiction over the crime of aggression was further delayed 'subject to a decision to be taken after 1 January 2017' (Arts 15*bis*(3), 15*ter*(3) ICCSt). After continued intense negotiations, the Assembly of States Parties to the Rome Statute decided in December 2017, 'to activate the Court's jurisdiction over the crime of aggression as of 17 July 2018'.[22]

This two-decade timeline offers a glimpse into the legal and political complexities involved in these negotiations.[23] Opening this compound of compromises in order to amend the conditions of the Court's exercise of jurisdiction over the crime of aggression will prove to be no less challenging. Even if a swift agreement on amending the conditions of the Court's exercise of jurisdiction over the crime of aggression were possible, it is doubtful that any amendment would enter into force immediately upon adoption. It would arguably be subject to ratification by States, which again might involve a lengthy process. It is therefore unlikely that the Rome Statute could be successfully amended within a few months or within one session of the Assembly of States Parties. Having an accountability mechanism for the crime of aggression in place, in order to collect and secure evidence as well as to prepare an indictment, on the other hand, is a matter of increasing urgency.[24]

This chapter explores options to unify the Court's jurisdiction over all crimes within its jurisdiction. Section 2 lays the scene and discusses the current jurisdictional regimes of the Rome Statute. The default jurisdictional regime for genocide, crimes against humanity, and war crimes, the jurisdictional regime for the crime of aggression, and the jurisdictional regime for amended crimes. Sections 3 and 4 discuss options to amend and thus align the Statute's jurisdictional regimes and propose concrete language for such amendments. Eventually, Section 5 will examine procedural aspects of amending the Rome Statute, before concluding with a look ahead in Section 6.

21 RC/Res.6 (n 10).

22 Activation of the jurisdiction of the Court over the crime of aggression, ICC-ASP/16/Res.5, 14 December 2017 (Thirteenth Plenary Meeting of the ASP) para. 1.

23 J Sarkin and J Almeida, 'Understanding The Activation Of The Crime Of Aggression At The International Criminal Court: Progress And Pitfalls' (2019) 36 *Wisconsin International Law Journal* 518.

24 It appears that the International Centre for the Prosecution of the Crime of Aggression against Ukraine will have a similar role 'to support and enhance investigations into the crime of aggression by securing key evidence and facilitating case building at the earliest possible stage' (n 12). However, the centre will be part of the support structure of the joint investigation team. As such it will serve the national investigations of the participating States. It will depend on the legal framework of the future *ad hoc* jurisdiction whether it would be able to build its work on findings of a distinct and European institution.

## 2 The Three Jurisdictional Regimes of the Rome Statute

### 2.1 *Default Preconditions for the Exercise of Jurisdiction*

The jurisdiction of the ICC is limited to the 'most serious crimes of concern to the international community as a whole', as listed in Art. 5 ICCSt. By becoming a party to the Statute, a State accepts the inherent or automatic jurisdiction over these crimes (Art. 12(1) ICCSt).[25] The jurisdiction of the ICC is also limited in time, to crimes committed after the entry into force of the Rome Statute (Art. 11 ICCSt).[26] While the Court's subject matter and temporal jurisdiction are clearly defined, the personal[27] and territorial reach of the Court's jurisdiction derive from provisions regulating the exercise of its jurisdiction. Arts 12(2) and 13 ICCSt distinguish two procedural regimes according to the way the jurisdiction of the ICC is triggered. If the Security Council acting under chapter VII of the Charter of the United Nations refers a situation to the Prosecutor, the Court may exercise its jurisdiction without further conditions (Arts 12(2), 13(b) ICCSt). If a State party refers a situation to the Prosecutor or the Prosecutor initiates an investigation *proprio motu*, the Court may exercise its jurisdiction only with respect to crimes committed on the territory or by a national of a State party, or of a State that has accepted the Court's jurisdiction *ad hoc* in accordance with Art. 12(3) ICCSt (Arts 12(2), 13(a) and (c) ICCSt). The alternative application of these two jurisdictional links is a fundamental pillar of the final compromise that enabled the adoption of the Rome Statute in 1998.[28] While the principle of territoriality is universally accepted in criminal law, the Court's exercise of jurisdiction over nationals of non-States parties has remained contested by at least two States since the adoption of the Statute.[29]

---

25 For the drafting history, see e.g. E Wilmshurst, 'Jurisdiction of the Court', in R S Lee (ed.), *The International Criminal Court: The Making of the Rome Statute: Issues, Negotiations and Results* (Brill Nijhoff 1999) 127, 130, 133ff.

26 The entry into force of the Statute on 1 July 2002 is an absolute limitation to the Court's temporal jurisdiction. The Court has no jurisdiction with respect to crimes committed before that date. With regard to States that accept/ratify the Statute after its entry into force, the Court has no jurisdiction over crimes committed before the (subjective) entry into force of the Statute for that State. However, Art. 11(2) ICCSt provides the possibility to retroactively extend the temporal jurisdiction of the Court to the date of the objective entry into force of the Statute on 1 July 2002 by way of a declaration accepting the Court's jurisdiction in accordance with Art. 12(3) ICCSt.

27 Further aspects of personal jurisdiction are regulated e.g. in Arts 26, 27 ICCSt.

28 See generally P Kirsch and J T Holmes, 'The Rome Conference on an International Criminal Court: The Negotiating Process' (1999) 93 *American Journal of International Law* 2, 10–11.

29 Israel, United States of America. For the US position, see e.g. D Scheffer, 'The United States and the International Criminal Court', (1999) 93 *American Journal of International Law* 12,

### 2.2 *Conditions for the Exercise of Jurisdiction over the Crime of Aggression*

The conditions for the exercise of jurisdiction over the crime of aggression are established in Arts 15*bis* and 15*ter* ICCSt. Art. 15*ter* ICCSt deals with the referral of a situation by the Security Council and corresponds to the Court's jurisdictional regime over genocide, crimes against humanity, and war crimes. Art. 15*bis* ICCSt on the other hand, dealing with the referral of a situation by a State party or a *proprio motu* investigation by the Prosecutor, deviates significantly from the Statute's general jurisdictional regime. These deviations serve two objectives. First, they acknowledge the Security Council's primary role for international peace and security in accordance with the United Nations Charter. To this end, Art. 15*bis*(6)–(9) introduce a framework of coordination and safeguards between the ICC and the UNSC. This includes an obligation of the Prosecutor to ascertain whether the UNSC has made a determination that an act of aggression was committed in a relevant situation (para. 6). In case such a determination exists, the Prosecutor may proceed with an investigation (para. 7) without prejudice to the Court's independent determination that an act of aggression was committed (para. 9). A positive determination of an act of aggression by the UNSC thus substitutes the judicial authorization of an investigation with respect to a crime of aggression but is not binding upon the Court. In case the UNSC has not determined that an act of aggression was committed, and fails to do so within six months, the Prosecutor may proceed on the basis of a judicial authorization (para. 8). It is important to note that inactivity of the UNSC will not bar the Court from the exercise of jurisdiction over the crime of aggression; however, judicial control is amplified. Different from the authorization by the pre-trail chamber under Art. 15(3) ICCSt, Art. 15*bis*(8) requires a quorum of the entire pre-trial division.

Second, the conditions introduce elements of State consent that conflict with the Court's default judicial regime. These deviations lie at the heart of the Kampala compromise and guaranteed the full application of Art. 13 ICCSt, the principle application of Art. 12 ICCSt among States parties, and judicial proceedings in case of UNSC inactivity. They compensate States claiming to be in a position that would preclude the Court's exercise of jurisdiction over their

20. Given the US's fundamental opposition to the prosecution of third party nationals before international courts and tribunals, the reaction of US President Biden, welcoming the arrest warrant against the President of the Russian Federation, is of particular relevance; see '"It's justified": Joe Biden welcomes ICC arrest warrant for Vladimir Putin', *The Guardian* (18 March 2023) <https://www.theguardian.com/us-news/2023/mar/18/joe-biden-welcomes-icc-arrest-warrant-vladimir-putin> accessed 30 April 2023.

nationals and territory.[30] Although the Kampala compromise does not necessarily sustain the reasoning underlying these claims, by introducing elements of State consent, it ensures that the States concerned would maintain their claimed position. Against this background, Art. 15*bis*(4) and (5) ICCSt limit the Court's exercise of jurisdiction over the crime of aggression:

The Court may, in accordance with Art. 12, exercise jurisdiction over a crime of aggression, arising from an act of aggression committed by a State Party, unless that State Party has previously declared that it does not accept such jurisdiction by lodging a declaration with the Registrar. The withdrawal of such a declaration may be effected at any time and shall be considered by the State Party within three years. (Para. 4).

In respect of a State that is not a party to this Statute, the Court shall not exercise its jurisdiction over the crime of aggression when committed by that State's nationals or on its territory. (Para. 5).

Paragraph 4 concerns the Court's exercise of jurisdiction over a crime of aggression arising from an act of aggression committed by a State party. It is based on the understanding that the Statute's general jurisdictional regime applies, in principle, to the crime of aggression. This understanding recognizes that (a) the crime of aggression has been listed as a crime within the jurisdiction of the Court since 1998 (Art. 5 ICCSt); that (b) in accordance with Art. 12(1) ICCSt '[a] State which becomes a Party to this Statute thereby accepts the jurisdiction of the Court with respect to the crimes referred to in article 5'; and that (c) Art. 5(2) ICCSt provided States with broad discretion in defining the conditions for the Court's exercise of jurisdiction over the crime of aggression. The Statute's general jurisdictional regime applies to the crime of aggression *in principle*, because paragraph (4) provides States parties with the possibility to opt out.

Para (5) concerns the reach of the Court's jurisdiction over non-State parties. It discards the Court's exercise of jurisdiction, which is based alternatively on the principle of territoriality, or the principle of active nationality (Art. 12 ICCSt), whenever a non-State party is involved.

---

30 This concerns the permanent members of the UNSC who could have otherwise vetoed a referral to the Court or a determination that an act of aggression has occurred. It also concerns States parties that do not ratify/accept the Kampala amendments and would fall beyond the Court's reach, if Art 121(5) ICCSt were applied in full. For more detailed accounts of the Kampala Review Conference see e.g. C Kreß and L von Holtzendorff, 'The Kampala Compromise on the Crime of Aggression' (2010) 8(5) *Journal of International Criminal Justice* 1179; A Reisinger Coracini, 'The International Criminal Court's Exercise of Jurisdiction Over the Crime of Aggression – at Last ... in Reach ... Over Some' (2010) 2(2) *Göttingen Journal of International Law* 745.

TABLE 27.1 Conditions for the exercise of jurisdiction over the crime of aggression under Art. 15*bis* ICCSt (the Kampala compromise)[V]

| **By** / **Against** | **A State party that has accepted the amendments** | **A State party that has not accepted the amendments** | **A State party that has accepted the amendments and declared it does not accept the ICC's jurisdiction** | **A State party that has not accepted the amendments and declared it does not accept the ICC's jurisdiction** | **A non-State party** |
|---|---|---|---|---|---|
| A State party that has accepted the amendments | YES (Art. 15*bis*(4) in accordance with Art. 12(2)) | YES (Art. 15*bis*(4) in accordance with Art. 12(2)) | NO (Art. 15*bis*(4)) | NO (Art. 15*bis*(4)) | NO (Art. 15*bis*(4), *a contrario*) |
| A State party that has not accepted the amendments | YES (Art. 15*bis*(4) in accordance with Art. 12(2)) | NO jurisdictional link under Art. 12(2) in accordance with Art. 121(5) first sentence | NO (Art. 15*bis*(4)) | NO (Art. 15*bis*(4)) | NO (Art. 15*bis*(4), *a contrario*) |
| A State party that has accepted the amendments and declared it does not accept the ICC's jurisdiction | YES (Art. 15*bis*(4) in accordance with Art. 12(2)) | YES (Art. 15*bis*(4) in accordance with Art. 12(2)) | NO (Art. 15*bis*(4)) | NO (Art. 15*bis*(4)) | NO (Art. 15*bis*(4), *a contrario*) |

| By / Against | A State party that has accepted the amendments | A State party that has not accepted the amendments | A State party that has accepted the amendments and declared it does not accept the ICC's jurisdiction | A State party that has not accepted the amendments and declared it does not accept the ICC's jurisdiction | A non-State party |
|---|---|---|---|---|---|
| A State party that has not accepted the amendments and declared it does not accept the ICC's jurisdiction | YES (Art. 15*bis*(4) in accordance with Art. 12(2)) | NO jurisdictional link under Art. 12(2) in accordance with Art. 121(5) first sentence | NO (Art. 15*bis*(4)) | NO (Art. 15*bis*(4)) | NO (Art. 15*bis*(4), *a contrario*) |
| A non-State party | NO (Art. 15*bis*(5)) | NO jurisdictional link under Art. 12(2) in accordance with Art. 121(5) first sentence | NO (Art. 15*bis*(4)) | NO (Art. 15*bis*(4)) | NO (Art. 15*bis*(4), *a contrario*) |

Underlying principles of Table 27.1

[V] Revised version of a chart originally published in Reisinger Coracini (n 30) 782, as presented at the Eighteenth Summer Session of the Salzburg Law School on International Criminal Law, Humanitarian Law and Human Rights Law, August 2016.

1. The inter-state relationship of an act of aggression between a State party and a non-State party in relation to the Court's jurisdiction of a crime of aggression is based on the idea of reciprocity. If the ICC cannot exercise its jurisdiction over a crime of aggression arising from an act of aggression by a non-State party, it shall equally not be able to exercise jurisdiction in cases, in which a non-State party was a victim of an act of aggression committed by a State party. This ratio was implemented in Art. 15*bis*(5).
2. The inter-state relationship of an act of aggression between two or more States parties is based upon the application of Art. 12 ICCSt. By ratifying the Statute, States parties have accepted the Court's jurisdiction over the crime of aggression (Art. 12(1) ICCSt)). At least one State party must provide the ICC with a jurisdictional link (Art. 12(2) ICCSt) by accepting/ratifying the Kampala amendments on the crime of aggression. The opt-out declaration under Art. 15*bis*(4) ICCSt only excludes jurisdiction over a crime of aggression arising from an act of aggression by the declaring State not against it.
3. Art. 15*bis*(4) ICCSt in connection with Art. 12(2) ICCSt precludes application of Art. 12(3) ICCSt.

In the aftermath of Kampala, a few States contested the compromise enshrined in Art. 15*bis*(4) ICCSt.[31] They contended that the Kampala amendments could only enter into force in light of the conditions formulated in Art. 121(5) last sentence ICCSt.[32] Consequently, in respect of a State party that does not ratify/accept the Kampala amendments, and despite Art. 15*bis*(4) ICCSt providing otherwise, the Court would not be able to exercise its jurisdiction over a crime of aggression when committed by that States Party's nationals or on its territory. The 2017 activation decision ended this controversy with a political decision in favour of the minority view, but could not unravel the underlying legal question.[33] The exact contents of Art. 15*bis*(4) ICCSt thus awaits authoritative judgment by the judges of the ICC.[34]

Independent of the interpretation of the Kampala compromise, the jurisdictional regime over the crime of aggression thus recognises an exception concerning non-States parties and an optional exception concerning States parties.

### 2.3 *Jurisdiction over Amended Crimes*

Frequently overlooked, the Rome Statute formulates conditions for the exercise of jurisdiction for crimes introduced or altered by an amendment, which arguably reverse the preconditions defined in Art. 12(2) ICCSt.[35] Art. 121(5) ICCSt last sentence foresees that 'In respect of a State Party which has not accepted the amendment, the Court shall not exercise its jurisdiction regarding a crime

---

31 Report on the facilitation on the activation of the jurisdiction of the International Criminal Court over the crime of aggression, ICC-ASP/16/24, 27 November 2017 (Sixteenth Session of the ASP); see also H Tichy et al., 'Recent Austrian practice in the field of international law: Report for 2017' (2018) 73 *Zeitschrift für öffentliches Recht* 147, 175ff.

32 See below at 2.3. That this provision 'has met with quite some legal criticism' and would be reflected as an opt out under Art. 15*bis*(4) ICCSt is expressly stated in the 2010 Introductory Remarks by the President [of the Kampala Review Conference] (10 June, 11.00 a.m.), printed in: S Barriga, C Kreß (eds), *The Traveaux Préparatoires of the Crime of Aggression* (Cambridge Univeristy Press 2012) document #146, 780.

33 ICC-ASP/16/Res.5 (n 22).

34 Ibid., para 3 reaffirming Arts 40(1) and 119(1) ICCSt on the judicial independence of the judges of the Court; see also D Akande and A Tzanakopoulos, 'Treaty Law and ICC Jurisdiction over the Crime of Aggression' (2018) 20 *European Journal of International Law* 939; J Trahan, 'From Kampala to New York – The Final Negotiations to Activate the Jurisdiction of the International Criminal Court over the Crime of Aggression' (2018) 18 *International Criminal Law Review* 197.

35 For an interpretation contrary to the prevailing opinion see A Pellet, 'Entry into Force and Amendment of the Statute', in A Cassese, P Gaeta J R W D Jones (eds), *The Rome Statute of the International Criminal Court: A Commentary* (Oxford University Press 2002), Vol I, 145, 182; A Reisinger Coracini, '"Amended Most Serious Crimes": A New Category of Core Crimes within the Jurisdiction but out of the Reach of the International Criminal Court?' (2008) 21 *Leiden Journal of International Law* 699, 707ff.

TABLE 27.2 Conditions for the exercise of jurisdiction over the crime of aggression in light of Art. 121(5) last sentence ICCSt (the Kampala compromise compromised)[V]

| **By** / **Against** | **A State party that has accepted the amendments** | **A State party that has not accepted the amendments** | **A State party that has accepted the amendments and declared it does not accept the ICC's jurisdiction** | **A State party that has not accepted the amendments and declared it does not accept the ICC's jurisdiction** | **A non-State party** |
|---|---|---|---|---|---|
| A State party that has accepted the amendments | YES (Art. 15*bis*(4) in accordance with Art. 12(2)) | NO (Art. 121(5) last sentence) | NO (Art. 15*bis*(4)) | NO (Art. 121(5) last sentence) | NO (Art. 15*bis*(4), *a contrario*) |
| A State party that has not accepted the amendments | NO (Art. 121(5) last sentence) | NO (Art. 121(5) last sentence) | NO (Art. 15*bis*(4)) | NO (Art. 121(5) last sentence) | NO (Art. 15*bis*(4), *a contrario*) |
| A State party that has accepted the amendments and declared it does not accept the ICC's jurisdiction | YES (Art. 15*bis*(4) in accordance with Art. 12(2)) | NO (Art. 121(5) last sentence) | NO (Art. 15*bis*(4)) | NO (Art. 121(5) last sentence) | NO (Art. 15*bis*(4), *a contrario*) |

TABLE 27.2 Conditions for the exercise of jurisdiction over the crime of aggression in light of Art. 121 (5) last sentence ICCSt (*cont.*)

| **By / Against** | **A State party that has accepted the amendments** | **A State party that has not accepted the amendments** | **A State party that has accepted the amendments and declared it does not accept the ICC's jurisdiction** | **A State party that has not accepted the amendments and declared it does not accept the ICC's jurisdiction** | **A non-State party** |
|---|---|---|---|---|---|
| A State party that has not accepted the amendments and declared it does not accept the ICC's jurisdiction | NO (Art. 121(5) last sentence) | NO (Art. 121(5) last sentence) | NO (Art. 15*bis*(4)) | NO (Art. 121(5) last sentence) | NO (Art. 15*bis*(4), *a contrario*) |
| A non-State party | NO (Art. 15*bis*(5)) | NO (Art. 121(5) last sentence) | NO (Art. 15*bis*(4)) | NO (Art. 121(5) last sentence) | NO (Art. 15*bis*(4), *a contrario*) |

[v] Chart 2 illustrates the Court's exercise of jurisdiction if the Kampala compromise (Art. 15*bis* ICCSt & entry into force in accordance with Art. 121(5) ICCSt first sentence) were submitted to the conditions for the exercise of jurisdiction of amended crimes under Art. 121(5) second sentence ICCSt.

covered by an amendment when committed by that States Party's nationals or on its territory.' If understood as an exception, the Court's exercise of jurisdiction would be blocked, even if the crime in question were committed on the territory or by a national of another State party that has accepted the amendment covering the crime. Consequently, in a situation where one or more States parties (to the Rome Statute) are involved, the preconditions for the exercise of jurisdiction over an amended crime would require the cumulative acceptance of an amendment by both, the State party on the territory of which the conduct took place as well the State party of the nationality of the accused.

The application of the provision not only to new categories of crimes but also to crimes within existing categories has odd effects. This is illustrated by the following hypothetical. Nationals of a State party commit a specific war crime on the territory of another State party. The crime in question is defined as a war crime in the context of an international armed conflict since the adoption of the Rome Statute, but it was introduced as a war crime in the context of a non-international armed conflict by an amendment. The territorial State party has accepted the amendment covering the crime; the State party of the nationality of the accused has not. The exercise of jurisdiction over the same individual committing the same crime would depend on the classification of the armed conflict. If the accused acted as a State organ, the armed conflict will most likely be international in nature and the ICC could exercise its jurisdiction in accordance with Art. 12(2) ICCSt. If the accused acted in a private capacity, not attributable to the State of nationality, the ICC would be barred from exercising its jurisdiction in accordance with Art. 121(5) ICCSt. The situation is not only absurd, it also undermines the foreseeability of criminal accountability and thus the legitimacy of the Court.

It is important to note that the exception formulated in Art. 121(5) last sentence ICCSt is limited to States parties to the Rome Statute.[36] It is not uncommon that international treaties create favourable conditions for parties. In this sense, the provision was described as an incentive for States to join the Rome Statute.[37] However, establishing an environment of impunity as a favourable

---

36 Given the fact that Art. 121(5) ICCSt does not differentiate between trigger mechanisms, a literal interpretation would demand that the conditions for the exercise of the Court's jurisdiction over amended crimes was not reduced to a State party referral and a *proprio motu* investigation by the Prosecutor, but arguably also extended to Security Council referrals; for details see Reisinger Coracini, '"Amended Most Serious Crimes": A New Category of Core Crimes within the Jurisdiction but out of the Reach of the International Criminal Court?' (n 35).

37 G. Hafner/K. Boon/A. Rübesame/J. Huston, 'A Response to the American View as Presented by Ruth Wedgwood' (1999) 10 *European Journal of International Law*, 108, at 119.

position for States parties to a treaty with the object and purpose to fight impunity remains peculiar, to say the least. As the language of Art. 121(5) ICCSt is clearly directed at States parties, the exercise of jurisdiction over a crime covered by an amendment committed on the territory or by a national of a non-State party remains under the scope of Art. 12(2) ICCSt. Unfortunately, the Assembly of States Parties diluted this unequivocal limitation to States parties. The Resolutions introducing amendments to the Rome Statute include identical paragraphs noting the language of Art. 121(5) ICCSt 'and *confirming* its [the Review Conference's] understanding that in respect to this amendment the same principle that applies in respect of a State Party which has not accepted the amendment applies also in respect of States that are not parties to the Statute.'[38] This practice, initiated as a result of the discussions over non-State party exceptions from the Court's exercise of jurisdiction over the crime of aggression in Kampala, and since then reiterated as agreed language, is counterproductive. The understanding is contrary to the language of the Statute. Placed in the Resolution introducing amendments, which is not subject to ratification and is not circulated by the depositary, the paragraph remains without legal significance. In order not to further convey the impression of potentially undermining the integrity of the Statute, States would be well-advised to stop this practice.

## 3 Substantive Options to Amend the Jurisdictional Regime of the Crime of Aggression

If an amendment were proposed to counter the Court's selective exercise of jurisdiction over the crime of aggression, the question would arise as to how much selectivity of Art. 15*bis* ICCSt should be repealed. There are three fundamental options to adjust the conditions for the exercise of jurisdiction over the crime of aggression in order to eliminate or reduce deviations from the Statute's default jurisdictional regime. First, the amendment could eliminate

38 Amendment to article 8 of the Rome Statute, RC/Res.5, 10 June 2010 (Twelfth Plenary Meeting of the Review Conference), preambular paragraph 2; identical Resolution on amendments to article 8 of the Rome Statute of the International Criminal Court (Weapons which use microbial or other biological agents, or toxins; Weapons the primary effect of which is to injure by fragments undetectable by x-rays in the human body; Blinding laser weapons), ICC-ASP/16/Res.4, 14 December 2017 (Twelfth Plenary Meeting of the ASP); Resolution on amendments to article 8 of the Rome Statute of the International Criminal Court (Intentionally using starvation of civilians), ICC-ASP/18/Res.5, 6 December 2019 (Ninth Plenary Meeting of the ASP).

all jurisdictional exceptions from the Court's exercise of jurisdiction over the crime of aggression (Option 1). Second, the amendment could eliminate exceptions linked to the non-party status of a State (Option 2). Third, the amendment could reduce exceptions linked to the non-party status of a State by aligning the status of a non-State party to that of a Statute party that has not accepted the Kampala amendments (Option 3).[39]

### 3.1 *Art. 15bis Amendment (Option 1): Eliminating All Judicial Exceptions*

Eliminating all judicial exceptions from the Court's exercise of jurisdiction over the crime of aggression would be the most far-reaching change. It would also be the most principled solution, which would unify the Court's exercise of jurisdiction over the four categories of crimes within its jurisdiction.[40]

The object and purpose of the amendment would be to eliminate both, the (optional) exceptions granted to States parties as well as those granted to non-States parties in Art. 15*bis* (4) and (5) ICCSt and to ensure the unrestricted application of Art. 12(2) ICCSt to the crime of aggression. As a consequence, the Court would be able to exercise its jurisdiction over a crime of aggression on the basis of a State party referral or a *proprio motu* investigation if either the territorial State or the State of the nationality of the accused (or both) have accepted the jurisdiction of the Court. In other words, if the crime of aggression is committed on the territory of a State party that has accepted the Art. 15*bis* amendment (option 1), the Court may exercise its jurisdiction independent of whether the State of nationality of the accused is a States party to the Rome Statute, or, if it is a party, independent of whether it has accepted the Kampala amendment (Art. 12(2)(a) ICCSt). Conversely, if a national of a State party that has accepted the Art. 15*bis* amendment (Option 1) commits a crime of aggression on the territory of another State, the Court may exercise its jurisdiction independent of whether that other State is a States party to the Rome Statute, or, if it is a party, independent of the fact whether it has accepted the Kampala amendment (Art. 12(2)(b) ICCSt).

Given the alternative application of the territorial link or the nationality link provided in Art. 12(2) ICCSt, an accepting State party would submit conduct that may be attributable to it (acts of aggression committed by its State organs) to the jurisdiction of the Court. At the same time, it would benefit from the judicial protection of the ICC by ensuring that a crime of aggression

39 For the purpose of this section, it is understood the acceptance/ratification of any three of the Art. 15*bis* amendments presupposes the acceptance/ratification of the Kampala amendments. For details on how to ensure a unified approach, see below Section 5.

40 For new categories of crimes, new and amended crimes see below Section 4.

committed against its sovereignty, territorial integrity or political independence may be investigated and prosecuted.

Technically, this objective can be achieved in two ways. Alternative 1 proposes to delete both Art. 15*bis*(4) and (5) ICCSt. By deleting the *lex specialis* regime, the default regime of Art. 12 would apply automatically.

> Option 1/Alternative 1
> Amendments to article 15*bis* of the Rome Statute
> 1. Article 15*bis* paragraph 4 of the Rome Statute is deleted.
> 2. Article 15*bis* paragraph 5 of the Rome Statute is deleted.

Alternative 2 reaches the same objective but, in order to leave no doubt that past exceptions are revoked, expressly states that the default regime of Art. 12(2) ICCSt applies.

> Option 1/Alternative 2
> Amendments to article 15*bis* of the Rome Statute
> 1. The phrase ', arising from an act of aggression committed by a State Party, unless that State Party has previously declared that it does not accept such jurisdiction by lodging a declaration with the Registrar. The withdrawal of such a declaration may be effected at any time and shall be considered by the State Party within three years' in Article 15*bis* paragraph 4 of the Rome Statute is deleted.
> [Article 15*bis* para 4 reads: 'The Court may, in accordance with article 12, exercise jurisdiction over a crime of aggression.'; more fluently, the text could also read: 'The Court may exercise jurisdiction over a crime of aggression in accordance with article 12.']
> 2. Article 15*bis* paragraph 5 of the Rome Statute is deleted.

Eliminating all judicial exceptions, would require a procedural solution with regard to declarations that have been lodged under Art. 15*bis*(4) ICCSt[41] and declarations that might be lodged until the entry into force of the amendment. According to Art. 15*bis*(4) ICCSt, States that have declared not to accept the jurisdiction of the Court may withdraw their declaration at any time. The

41 Thus far, two States parties have lodged declarations under Art. 15*bis*(4), see Declaration of the Government of Kenya of 30 November 2015 <https://www.icc-cpi.int/sites/default/files/2015_NV_Kenya_Declaration_article15bis-4.pdf> and Declaration of the Government of the Republic of Guatemala of 2 February 2018 <https://www.icc-cpi.int/sites/default/files/20180206142750.pdf> both accessed 11 April 2023.

TABLE 27.3 Amendments to Art. 15*bis* ICCSt; Option 1: Eliminating all judicial exceptions

| By<br>———<br>Against | A State party that has accepted the amendments | A State party that has not accepted the amendments | A non-State party |
|---|---|---|---|
| A State party that has accepted the amendments | YES<br>(Art. 15*bis*(4) in accordance with Art. 12(2)) | YES<br>(Art. 15*bis*(4) in accordance with Art. 12(2)) | YES<br>(Art. 15*bis*(4) in accordance with Art. 12(2)) |
| A State party that has not accepted the amendments | YES<br>(Art. 15*bis*(4) in accordance with Art. 12(2)) | NO<br>jurisdictional link under Art. 12(2) in accordance with Art. 121(5) first sentence | NO<br>jurisdictional link under Art. 12(2) in accordance with Art. 121(5) first sentence |
| A non-State party | YES<br>(Art. 15*bis*(4) in accordance with Art. 12(2)) | NO<br>jurisdictional link under Art. 12(2) in accordance with Art. 121(5) first sentence | NO<br>jurisdictional link under Art. 12(2) |

1. Under Option 1, the categories of 'A State party that has accepted the amendments and declared not to accept the ICC's jurisdiction' and 'A State party that has not accepted the amendments and declared not to accept the ICC's jurisdiction' are obsolete.
2. States parties that have not accepted the amendments and non-States parties are in are in the same position.
3. Art. 12(3) ICCSt applies.

Resolution introducing the Art. 15*bis* (Option 1) amendment should reflect this by reminding, or even obliging, States parties to withdraw any such declaration before the entry into force of the amendment.

By removing the link between the Court's exercise of jurisdiction over a crime of aggression and an act of aggression committed by a State party, the State party restriction introduced into Art. 12(2) ICCSt through Art. 15*bis*(4) ICCSt is equally removed. In other words, a State accepting the Court's jurisdiction *ad hoc* in accordance with Art. 12(3) ICCSt could provide the Court with the necessary jurisdictional link under Art. 12(2) ICCSt also in respect of the crime of aggression.

### 3.2 *Art. 15bis Amendment (Option 2): Eliminating the Non-state Party Exception*

At first glance, it may appear that Art. 15*bis*(4) and (5) ICCSt are clearly separate provisions, with 15*bis*(4) regulating the conditions for the exercise of jurisdiction in relation to acts of aggression allegedly committed by State parties and Art. 15*bis*(5) addressing other situations. However, the structure and points of reference of these two paragraphs differ considerably and this affects their interpretation. Paragraph 4 links the exercise of jurisdiction to the collective act of aggression and must be read in conjunction with Art. 12(2) ICCSt. Paragraph 5 links the exercise of jurisdiction to the individual crime of aggression and substitutes Art. 12(2) ICCSt whenever nationals or the territory of a non-State party are concerned. Given the presence of the collective act as a point of reference in paragraph 4 and its absence in paragraph 5, it appears that the phrase '[t]he Court may, in accordance with Art. 12, exercise jurisdiction over a crime of aggression, arising from an act of aggression committed by a State Party, unless' excludes – *argumentum a contrario* – the Court's exercise of jurisdiction over any act of aggression committed by a non-State party.[42] This would mean that the non-State party exception is embedded in Art. 15*bis* ICCSt on two levels. The individual level, concerning the commission of a *crime* of aggression, and the collective level, concerning the commission of an *act* of aggression underlying a crime of aggression by a State.

This structural inconsistency is rooted in the drafting history of Art. 15*bis* ICCSt. Once it was clear that a jurisdictional regime governed by a monopoly of the UNSC was unacceptable to the vast majority of States, negotiations at the Kampala Review Conference shifted to implementing a consent-based regime that would allow departing from Art. 12 ICCSt.[43] The drafting of exceptions to the Statute's default jurisdictional regime during the final days of the conference was inspired by language derived from Arts 12(2) and 121(5) ICCSt, alluding to the link between a crime of aggression and the status of the territorial State or the State of the nationality of the accused.[44] This reference to the

42 Reisinger Coracini, 'The International Criminal Court's Exercise of Jurisdiction Over the Crime of Aggression – at Last ... in Reach ... Over Some' (n 30) 772.

43 See above, text around n 30.

44 See e.g. Compromise Proposal ABS-Canada, Declaration (Draft of 9 June 2010 16.00), printed in Barriga, Kreß (n 32) document #143. 32) document #143. 33), document #143. Draft Art. 15*bis* para 4*bis* 'The Court may exercise its jurisdiction over the crime of aggression committed by a State Party's national or on its territory in accordance with article 12, unless that State Party has filed a declaration of its non-acceptance of the jurisdiction of the Court under paragraph 4 of this Article.' Draft Art. 15*bis* para 4*cor* 'In respect of a State which is not a party to this Statute, the Court shall not exercise its jurisdiction over the

individual crime of aggression was replace by a reference to the collective act of aggression in the first paper presented by the President of the Conference.[45] While this may have been helpful to highlight the act of aggression underlying a crime of aggression, the specific language was rightfully criticised as too State centric for the purpose of individual criminal responsibility.[46] References to territory and nationality of the accused were thus reintroduced with regard to non-States parties.[47] With regard to States parties, however, crime of aggression language was added while the reference to the State act of aggression remained.[48] Thus, while the *travaux préparatoires* suggest that these different points of reference should not interfere with the clear separation of paragraphs 4 and 5, a literal interpretation leads to a different result. This must be reflected in an amendment that aims at eliminating the non-State party exception.[49]

Abolishing the non-State party exception reduces but does not eliminate all jurisdictional exceptions regarding the crime of aggression. It would establishes an imbalance between non-States parties to the Rome Statute and non-States parties to the amended Rome Statute (States parties that have not accepted/ratified the Art. 15*bis* (Option 2) amendment). While the latter are entitled to an optional opt out from the Court's exercise of jurisdiction over the crime of aggression, the former are not. Such an imbalance is not unknown to the Statute. On the contrary, it reflects the conditions for the exercise of jurisdiction over an amended crime in accordance with Art. 121(5) last sentence ICCSt.[50]

crime of aggression as provided in this article when committed by that State's nationals or on its territory.'

45 2010 President's First Paper, printed in Barriga, Kreß (n 32), document #145. Draft Art. 15*bis* para 1*bis* 'The Court may, in accordance with article 12, exercise jurisdiction with respect to an act of aggression committed by a State Party, unless that State has lodged a declaration of non-acceptance with the Registrar.' Draft Art. 15*bis* para 1*ter* 'The Court may not exercise jurisdiction with respect to an act of aggression committed by a Non-State Party.'

46 Reisinger Coracini, 'The International Criminal Court's Exercise of Jurisdiction Over the Crime of Aggression – at Last … in Reach … Over Some' (n 30) 761.

47 Art. 15*bis* para 1*quater* of the 2010 President's Second Paper, Draft resolution: The crime of aggression, printed in: Barriga, Kreß (n 32) document #147. The language of Art. 15*bis* para 1*quater* is equivalent to Art 15*bis*(5) ICCSt.

48 Art. 15*bis*(1*ter*) ibid. The language of Art. 15*bis* para 1*ter* is equivalent to Art. 15*bis*(4) ICCSt.

49 See also Parliamentarians for Global Action ('PGA'), Model proposal for amendments to the Rome Statute of the ICC – Non Paper, on file with the author; for a summary see 'Proposal to Amend the Rome Statute Kampala Amendment on the Crime of Aggression' (*Parliamentarians for Global Action*, 20 February 2023) <https://www.pgaction.org/news/proposal-to-amend-kampala-amendment-crime-of-aggression.html> accessed 11 April 2023.

50 See above at 2.3.

In order to eliminate the non-State party exception, it is clear that the current language of Art. 15*bis*(5) ICCSt must be deleted. The more complex question is how to deal with the exception embedded in Art. 15*bis*(4) ICCSt.

Alternative 1 alters the text of paragraph 4 with the objective of establishing the Court's jurisdiction over any crime of aggression, whereas the reference to the collective act of aggression by a State-party serves solely as a link for the application of the optional opt out regime. Alternative 2 revives the logic of two separate provisions with regard to acts of aggression committed by a State party and those committed by a non-State party. It leaves paragraph 4 unaltered but replaces paragraph 5 with clear language submitting the Court's jurisdiction over a crime of aggression arising from an act of aggression by a non-State party to the Statute's default jurisdictional regime.

> Option 2/Alternative 1:
> Amendments to Article 15*bis* of the Rome Statute
> 1. The phrase 'arising from an act of aggression committed by a State Party,' in Article 15*bis* paragraph 4 of the Rome Statute is deleted.
> 2. The word 'that' in the phrase 'that State Party' in Article 15*bis* paragraph 4 of the Rome Statute is substituted by the word 'the'.
> 3. After the phrase 'that State Party' in Article 15*bis* paragraph 4 of the Rome Statute, the phrase 'committing the act of aggression' is added. [Article 15*bis* para 4 would then read: 'The Court may, in accordance with article 12, exercise jurisdiction over a crime of aggression, unless *the* State Party *committing the act of aggression* has previously declared that it does not accept such jurisdiction by lodging a declaration with the Registrar. The withdrawal of such a declaration may be effected at any time and shall be considered by the State Party within three years.'
> 4. Article 15*bis* paragraph 5 of the Rome Statute is deleted.

> Option 2/Alternative 2:
> Amendments to article 15*bis* of the Rome Statute
> 1. The contents of Art. 15*bis* paragraph 5 of the Rome Statute is deleted.
> 2. The following text is inserted as Art. 15*bis* paragraph 5: 'The Court may, in accordance with article 12, exercise jurisdiction over a crime of aggression, arising from an act of aggression committed by a non-State Party'

Negotiating option 2 (and option 3 for that matter) will likely spark a discussion as to the interpretation of Art. 15*bis*(4) ICCSt in light of the Kampala

TABLE 27.4 Amendments to Art. 15*bis* ICCSt; Option 2: Eliminating the non-State party exception

| By / Against | A State party that has accepted the amendments | A State party that has not accepted the amendments | A State party that has accepted the amendments and declared it does not accept the ICC's jurisdiction | A State party that has not accepted the amendments and declared it does not accept the ICC's jurisdiction | A non-State party |
|---|---|---|---|---|---|
| A State party that has accepted the amendments | YES (Art. 15*bis*(4) in accordance with Art. 12(2)) | YES (Art. 15*bis*(4) in accordance with Art. 12(2)) | NO (Art. 15*bis*(4)) | NO (Art. 15*bis*(4)) | YES (Art. 15*bis*(4) in accordance with Art. 12(2)) |
| A State party that has not accepted the amendments | YES (Art. 15*bis*(4) in accordance with Art. 12(2)) | NO jurisdictional link under Art. 12(2) in accordance with Art. 121(5) first sentence | NO (Art. 15*bis*(4)) | NO (Art. 15*bis*(4)) | NO jurisdictional link under Art. 12(2) in accordance with Art. 121(5) first sentence |
| A State party that has accepted the amendments and declared it does not accept the ICC's jurisdiction | YES (Art. 15*bis*(4) in accordance with Art. 12(2)) | YES (Art. 15*bis*(4) in accordance with Art. 12(2)) | NO (Art. 15*bis*(4)) | NO (Art. 15*bis*(4)) | YES (Art. 15*bis*(4) in accordance with Art. 12(2)) |

TABLE 27.4 Amendments to Art. 15*bis* ICCSt; Option 2: Eliminating the non-State party exception (*cont.*)

| By / Against | A State party that has accepted the amendments | A State party that has not accepted the amendments | A State party that has accepted the amendments and declared it does not accept the ICC's jurisdiction | A State party that has not accepted the amendments and declared it does not accept the ICC's jurisdiction | A non-State party |
|---|---|---|---|---|---|
| A State party that has not accepted the amendments and declared it does not accept the ICC's jurisdiction | YES (Art. 15*bis*(4) in accordance with Art. 12(2)) | NO jurisdictional link under Art. 12(2) in accordance with Art. 121(5) first sentence | NO (Art. 15*bis*(4)) | NO (Art. 15*bis*(4)) | NO jurisdictional link under Art. 12(2) in accordance with Art. 121(5) first sentence |
| A non-State party | YES (Art. 15*bis*(4) in accordance with Art. 12(2)) | NO jurisdictional link under Art. 12(2) in accordance with Art. 121(5) first sentence | NO (Art. 15*bis*(4)) | NO (Art. 15*bis*(4)) | NO jurisdictional link under Art. 12(2) |

1. The State party exception remains in place.
2. The inter-state relationship of an act of aggression between a State party and a non-State party in relation to the Court's jurisdiction of a crime of aggression is not anymore governed by reciprocity but by Art. 12(2) ICCSt.
3. Art. 15*bis*(4) in connection with Art. 12(2) ICCSt precludes application of Art. 12(3) ICCSt.

compromise and the New York activation decision.[51] Should the opt-out mechanism remain in place, it might be advisable to strengthen and institutionalize a monitoring process to ensure the mandatory re-consideration of a declaration not to accept the Court's jurisdiction over the crime of aggression in accordance with Art. 12 ICCSt within three years of its deposit.

Two recent proposals have suggested the elimination of the non-State party exception in Art. 15*bis* ICCSt. Both proposals focus on closing the accountability gap in the situation in Ukraine; consequently, they concentrate exclusively on enabling the Court to exercise its jurisdiction over acts of aggression committed by a non-State party.[52]

Parliamentarians for Global Action have elaborated a Model proposal for amendments to Art. 15*bis* ICCSt (PGA Model proposal).[53] The draft amendment follows the logic of Option 2/Alternative 1. It deletes paragraph 5 and alters the language of paragraph 4 in order to ensure its application to all crimes of aggression. The technical solution of Option 2/Alternative 1 and the PGA Model proposal are similar, the main difference being that the latter purposefully eliminates every reference to the collective act of aggression.

The proposed amendments read

I) Article 15 *bis*, paragraph 4, is amended as follows:
"The Court may, in accordance with article 12, exercise jurisdiction over a crime of aggression [DELETE, arising from an act of aggression committed by a State Party], unless [DELETE that] [REPLACE WITH a] State Party has previously declared that it does not accept such jurisdiction by lodging a declaration with the Registrar. The withdrawal of such a declaration may be effected at any time and shall be considered by the State Party within three years."

II) Article 15 *bis*, paragraph 5, is DELETED.[54]

Former Prosecutor Luis Moreno Ocampo proposes a more limited amendment. By deleting the five words 'by that State's nationals or' in Art. 15*bis*(5) ICCSt, he claims that a supposedly 'simple revision'[55] could be achieved within

51 See above at 2.2.

52 Insofar as Ocampo claims his proposal would end 'selective justice for the international crime of aggression', it fails to reach the objective. With a focus on closing the accountability gap in the situation in Ukraine, the proposal deals exclusively with acts of aggression committed by a non-State party. It does not address exceptions to the ICC's exercise of jurisdiction over acts of aggression committed by a State party. Ocampo (n 19).

53 PGA Model proposal (n 49).

54 PGA Model proposal (n 49) 4–5; with an explanatory note on at 3.

55 Ocampo (n 19).

'a few months'.[56] The remaining text of Art. 15*bis*(5) ICCSt would then read 'In respect of a State that is not a party to this Statute, the Court shall not exercise its jurisdiction over the crime of aggression when committed on its territory.'

Given that the non-State party exception seems embedded in Art. 15*bis*(4) and (5) ICCSt,[57] it is not abundantly clear whether deleting the proposed five words in Art. 15*bis*(5) would permit the exercise of jurisdiction over a crime of aggression based on an act of aggression by a non-State party. Furthermore, any possible effect of deleting these five words would be limited to acts of aggression by a non-State party against a State party that has accepted the Kampala amendments. The latter point is relevant because only an accepting State party may provide the ICC with the necessary jurisdictional link under Arts 15*bis*(4) and 12(2) ICCSt. The conflict between Azerbaijan and Armenia, as well as a U.S. attack in Iraq that killed a senior Iranian military leader, examples provided by Ocampo, would therefore remain beyond the Court's reach; none of these States are parties to the Rome Statute.[58] Likewise, Ukraine, despite having approved the required constitutional changes to ratify the Rome Statute in 2016 (with effect from 30 June 2019), has not yet become a State party.[59] Without amending the language of Art. 15*bis*(4) ICCSt, which limits the Court's exercise of jurisdiction to crimes of aggression arising from an act of aggression committed by a State party, an *ad hoc* declaration accepting the jurisdiction of the Court in accordance with Art. 12(3) ICCSt cannot substitute the ratification of or accession to the Rome Statute.[60]

Finally, it is questionable whether leaving a reference to the territory of non-State parties in Art. 15*bis*(5) ICCSt would not undermine the desired effect. The crime of aggression is committed in both, the territory of the aggressor State

56 Luis Moreno Ocampo, 'A Pragmatic Legal Approach to End Russia's Aggression' (*Just Security*, 23 February 2023) <https://www.justsecurity.org/85218/a-pragmatic-legal-approach-to-end-russias-aggression/> accessed 11 April 2023.

57 See text around n 49.

58 See <https://treaties.un.org/pages/ViewDetails.aspx?src=TREATY&mtdsg_no=XVIII-10&chapter=18&clang=_en> accessed 11 April 2023.

59 For an overview, see <https://www.pgaction.org/ilhr/rome-statute/ukraine.html> accessed 11 April 2023.

60 Art. 12(2) ICCSt distinguishes States parties and States that have accepted the jurisdiction of the Court in accordance with Art. 12(3). If Art. 15*bis*(4) ICCSt invokes Art. 12(2) only with regard to a State party, it *ipso facto* excludes the application of Art 12(3). If the Court's exercise of jurisdiction were not limited to a crime of aggression arising from an act of aggression committed by a State party (Art. 15*bis*(4) ICCSt), the alternative jurisdictional links required under Art. 12(2) ICCSt could be provided either through acceptance/ratification of the amended Rome Statute or acceptance of the Court's jurisdiction in accordance with Art. 12(3) ICCSt; see Art. 12(2) ICCSt and above at 3.1.

as well as the territory of the victim State. Would there be a jurisdictional link under Art. 12(2) ICCSt for acts committed by nationals of a non-State party on the territory of a non-State party (preparation, planning, and initiation)? Would the jurisdictional link provided for acts committed on the territory of the aggressed State (initiation and waging) suffice to allow for the exercise of jurisdiction over preparatory acts?

### 3.3 *Art. 15*bis *Amendment (Option 3): Aligning the Non-state Party Exception with the State Party Exception*

A third option would be to align the position of non-State parties with the status of State parties that have not accepted the aggression amendments. Such an amendment would unify but not eliminate the regime of exceptions from the Court's jurisdiction over the crime of aggression. It would bring non-States parties within the default assumption of the Court's exercise of jurisdiction in accordance with Art. 12(2) ICCSt, while at the same time granting them the option to opt-out of the Court's jurisdictional reach.

Being treated the same as a State party that does not accept the aggression amendments, a non-State party would benefit from the ICC's judicial protection should it become the object of an act of aggression committed by a State party that has accepted the Art. 15*bis* amendment (Option 3). In the reverse scenario, the political cost to elude the Court's exercise of jurisdiction when committing an act of aggression would rise. Under the Kampala amendments, the Court is categorically barred from exercising its jurisdiction over a crime of aggression arising from an act of aggression committed by a non-State party. Under the State party regime, the non-State party would in principle fall within the Court's exercise of jurisdiction in accordance with Art. 12(2) ICCSt and would need to actively opt out.[61]

For those enforcing the Statute, one regime of exceptions to the Court's exercise of jurisdiction over the crime of aggression might be convenient. But in the end, the unification does little to tighten the Court's jurisdictional regime. One may therefore wonder whether the effort would justify the result. Even more so, as opening the State party regime would most probably re-activate the debate around the contents of Art. 15*bis*(4) ICCSt as well as on whether Art. 12(3) ICCSt should apply to the crime of aggression. Finally, Option 3 may raise more complex questions regarding the adoption of the amendment. If the optional declaration of non-acceptance is regarded as a right granted to

61 See above at 2.2.

third States, non-States parties to the Rome Statute must either consent or join a consensus (Arts 34, 36 VCLT).

Option 3
Amendments to article 15*bis* of the Rome Statute

1. The word 'Party' in Article 15*bis* paragraph 4 of the Rome Statute is deleted three times.
   [Article 15*bis* para 4 would then read: 'The Court may, in accordance with article 12, exercise jurisdiction over a crime of aggression arising from an act of aggression committed by a State, unless that State has previously declared that it does not accept such jurisdiction by lodging a declaration with the Registrar. The withdrawal of such a declaration may be effected at any time and shall be considered by the State within three years.']
2. Article 15*bis* paragraph 5 of the Rome Statute is deleted.

## 4 Eliminating the Source of Future Selective Exercise of Jurisdiction

The objective of the amendment to Art. 121(5) ICCSt is to secure one uniform jurisdictional regime for all categories of crimes within the jurisdiction of the Court as well as for all crimes, independent of when they were introduced. In order to achieve this objective, the root cause of deviations from Art. 12(2) ICCSt in respect of amended crimes in Art. 121(5) last sentence ICCSt must be deleted.

Establishing a separate jurisdictional regime for future crimes that undermines one of the major compromises achieved at the Rome Conference, the Court's automatic jurisdiction over most serious crimes of concern to the international community as a whole was an anomaly that is hardly justifiable in a Statute that aims at fighting impunity for such crimes. The existence of exceptions from the Court's jurisdictional reach as well as discussions on creating or maintaining exceptions undermines the legitimacy of the international justice system.

The clause is also unsound with a few to the subject matter jurisdiction of the Court. Only the most serious crimes of concern to the international community as a whole fall within the jurisdiction of the ICC. Arguably, these are crimes under customary international law. The Rome Statute does not create these crimes but merely brings them within an international enforcement system. From a legal but also from a policy point of view, this narrow understanding of the Court's subject matter jurisdiction should prevail. The customary

TABLE 27.5 Amendments to Art. 15*bis* ICCSt; Option 3: Aligning the non-State party exception with the State party exception

| **By / Against** | **A State party that has accepted the amendments** | **A State party that has not accepted the amendments** | **A State party that has accepted the amendments and declared it does not accept the ICC's jurisdiction** | **A State (party or non-Party) that has not accepted the amendments and declared it does not accept the ICC's jurisdiction** |
|---|---|---|---|---|
| A State party that has accepted the amendments | YES (Art. 15*bis*(4) in accordance with Art. 12(2)) | YES (Art. 15*bis*(4) in accordance with Art. 12(2)) | NO (Art. 15*bis*(4)) | NO (Art. 15*bis*(4)) |
| A State party that has not accepted the amendments | YES (Art. 15*bis*(4) in accordance with Art. 12(2)) | NO jurisdictional link under Art. 12(2) in accordance with Art. 121(5) first sentence | NO (Art. 15*bis*(4)) | NO (Art. 15*bis*(4)) |
| A State party that has accepted the amendments and declared it does not accept the ICC's jurisdiction | YES (Art. 15*bis*(4) in accordance with Art. 12(2)) | YES (Art. 15*bis*(4) in accordance with Art. 12(2)) | NO (Art. 15*bis*(4)) | NO (Art. 15*bis*(4)) |

TABLE 27.5 Amendments to Art. 15*bis* ICCSt; Option 3: Aligning the non-State party exception with the State party exception (*cont.*)

| By / Against | A State party that has accepted the amendments | A State party that has not accepted the amendments | A State party that has accepted the amendments and declared it does not accept the ICC's jurisdiction | A State (party or non-Party) that has not accepted the amendments and declared it does not accept the ICC's jurisdiction |
|---|---|---|---|---|
| A State (party or non-Party) that has not accepted the amendments and declared it does not accept the ICC's jurisdiction | YES (Art. 15*bis*(4) in accordance with Art. 12(2)) | NO jurisdictional link under Art. 12(2) (in accordance with Art. 121(5) first sentence) | NO (Art. 15*bis*(4)) | NO (Art. 15*bis*(4)) |

1. Non-States parties are in the same position as States parties (with the exception that only States parties of a treaty can accept/ratify a treaty amendment).
2. States parties as well as non-State parties may lodge a declaration not to accept the jurisdiction of the Court in accordance with the amended Art. 15*bis*(4) ICCSt.
3. As the amended Art. 15*bis*(4) ICCSt refers to 'States' instead of 'States Parties', Art. 12(3) ICCSt applies.

nature of these crimes renders arguments based on consent over the exercise of jurisdiction of such a crime obsolete.[62] Furthermore, for those States which understood Art. 121(5) last sentence ICCSt as a safeguard against the Court's jurisdiction over the crime of aggression, its purpose has elapsed.[63]

> Amendment to article 121(5) of the Rome Statute
>
> 1. The last sentence of Art. 121(5) ICCSt reading 'In respect of a State Party which has not accepted the amendment, the Court shall not exercise its jurisdiction regarding a crime covered by an amendment when committed by that States Party's nationals or on its territory.' is deleted.

## 5 Amendment Procedure

Amendments to the Rome Statute must be adopted by at a meeting of the Assembly of States Parties or at a Review Conference by consensus or by a two-thirds majority of States Parties (Art. 121(3) ICCSt). Adoption is followed by acceptance/ratification of the adopted amendment and its entry into force.[64]

Apart from exclusively institutional amendments (Art. 122 ICCSt), the Rome Statute distinguishes between two entry into force mechanisms. Amendments to Arts 5, 6, 7, 8, and 8*bis* of the Statute enter into force 'for those States Parties which have accepted the amendment one year after the deposit of their instruments of ratification or acceptance' (Art. 121(5) ICCSt). All other amendments enter into force 'for all States Parties one year after instruments of ratification or acceptance have been deposited with the Secretary-General of the United Nations by seven-eighths of them.'

The Statute does not provide a definite answer as to which amendment regime would apply to an amendment of the conditions for the exercise of

62 Reisinger Coracini, '"Amended Most Serious Crimes": A New Category of Core Crimes within the Jurisdiction but out of the Reach of the International Criminal Court?' (n 35) 699ff.

63 Ibid., 716, fn 116; for a detailed account see R S Clark, 'The Crime of Aggression and the International Criminal Court' in J Doria, H-P Gasser and M C Bassiouni (eds), *The Legal Regime of the International Criminal Court: Essays in Honor of Professor Igor Pavlovich Blishchenko* (Brill Nijhoff 2009) 661, 672ff.

64 It appears that Ocampo considers the adoption of an amendment by a two-thirds majority of the assembly (a conference) of States parties sufficient for its application. But this approach would be inconsistent with the amendment mechanisms foreseen in the Rome Statute.

jurisdiction over the crime of aggression. Since Art. 15*bis* is explicitly not listed in Arts 121(5) ICCSt, it seems at first sight that Art. 121(4) ICCSt would necessarily apply. From a temporal point of view, this would substantively delay the practical effect of the amendment, as it would enter into force only if accepted by seven-eighths of States parties (that would be 108 of currently 123 States parties). Yet, it would benefit from the highest possible support of States parties, and it would be applicable to all States parties (unless they use the option of withdrawing from the Statute with immediate effect, Art. 121(6) ICCSt). In order to avoid this delay, the PGA Model Proposal envisions a decision of the Assembly of States Parties in accordance with Art. 58(1)(b) of the Vienna Convention of the Law of Treaties (VCLT) suspending the provisions of Art. 121(4) ICCSt for the amendment of Art. 15*bis* ICCSt. According to another view, the Rome Statute lacks a procedure to amend an amendment, so that an '*inter se* regime' that is not explicitly regulated in the Rome Statute, must be developed.[65] It suggests applying the entry into force quorum of States prescribed in Art. 121(4) ICCSt, but only to the group of those States parties that have ratified or accepted the aggression amendments.[66]

A literal interpretation of Art. 121(5) ICCSt thus excludes its application to amendments of Art. 15*bis* ICCSt. On the other hand, Art. 15*bis* ICCSt was introduced on the basis of Art. 121(5) ICCSt and it might be argued that any future amendment to this provision must follow the same procedure. This may be the case, although the *ratio* for this decision is obsolete. Art. 15*bis* ICCSt was introduced together with the definition of aggression in Art. 8*bis* ICCSt. At the time, it was convincingly argued that the substantive and procedural provisions on the crime of aggression were intrinsically linked and therefore required the application of one uniform amendment regime. Although a new amendment only concerns procedural provisions, it has also been argued that 'the telos of the holistic approach' chosen in Kampala could be transferred to the revision of the jurisdictional regime.[67]

Art. 121(5) ICCSt foresees a subjective entry into force for each accepting/ratifying State party, which raises a number of questions. Would one ratification

65 F Abken and P Rob, 'Amending the Amendment: In Search of an Adequate Procedure for a Revision of the Jurisdictional Regime for the Crime of Aggression in the Rome Statute' (*EJIL:Talk!*, 13 January 2023) <https://www.ejiltalk.org/amending-the-amendment-in-search-of-an-adequate-procedure-for-a-revision-of-the-jurisdictional-regime-for-the-crime-of-aggression-in-the-rome-statute/> accessed 11 April 2023.

66 That would be 39 of currently 44 States parties <https://treaties.un.org/pages/ViewDetails.aspx?src=TREATY&mtdsg_no=XVIII-10-b&chapter=18&clang=_en> accessed 11 April 2023.

67 Abken and Rob (n 65).

suffice to have an objective effect vis-à-vis a non-State party or a non-accepting State party? With regard to the situation in Ukraine, must this one ratification be by (a future State-party) Ukraine? Or would the ratification of Ukraine, be required in any case, independent of the number of ratifications? The Kampala amendments introduced a minimum requirement of 30 ratifications. However, this provision did not alter the entry into force regime of the first sentence of Art. 121(5) ICCSt. It served as a precondition for the exercise of jurisdiction, which meanwhile has been fulfilled.

Currently, two versions of the Rome Statute are in force with a view to the crime of aggression. First, the 1998 Rome Statute among States parties who have not accepted the Kampala amendments and in the relation between States parties that have accepted the Kampala amendments and those that have not (see Art. 40(3) VCLT on amendments of multilateral treaties). Second, a version of the (amended) Rome Statute among States parties that have accepted the amendments. If Art. 121(5) applied to an amendment of Art 15*bis* ICCSt, three versions of the Rome Statute would then exist in parallel until all States parties that have ratified the Kampala amendments ratify the new amendment. In order to avoid the pitfall of creating further sub-regimes, Abken and Rob[68] argue for the suspension of the individual entry into force of the amendment for States parties that have accepted the Kampala amendments until all 'Kampala States' will have ratified the new amendment. Legal precautions would also need to be taken to assure that a State party that has not yet accepted the Kampala amendments or a new State party would not be able to ratify the Kampala amendments without the new aggression amendment.

Amendments to the Court's jurisdictional regimes must also be scrutinized against the rules governing treaties creating or modifying rights or obligations of third States (Arts 34 *et seq* VCLT). It is unconvincing that impunity for perpetrators of crimes under international law should be a right of their State of nationality or the territorial State.[69] Accordingly, amendments to Arts 15*bis*(5) and 121(5) last sentence ICCSt would not revoke or modify rights or obligations of third States (Art. 37 VCLT). However, providing third States the option to declare not to accept the Court's jurisdiction (Art. 15*bis* amendment (option 3)) may well be interpreted as creating a right for a third State. In that case,

68 Ibid.

69 A Reisinger Coracini, 'The Kampala Amendments on the Crime of Aggression Before Activation: Evaluating the Legal Framework of a Political Compromise (Part 2)' (*Opinio Juris*, 2 October 2017), <https://opiniojuris.org/2017/10/02/the-kampala-amendments-on-the-crime-of-aggression-before-activation-evaluating-the-legal-framework-of-a-political-compromise-part-2/> accessed 11 April 2023.

non-States parties would either need to consent to the amendment or, under a presumption of consent, not indicate the contrary (Arts 34, 36 VCLT). The same logic would apply to deleting the State-party exception in 15*bis* amendment (option 1). This amendment could be understood as revoking a right previously granted to a third State (that is a State party that does not accept the Kampala amendments). To revoke or modify such a right would require the consent of the third State (Art. 37 VCLT). This is as long as a right has indeed arisen under Art. 15*bis* ICCSt, which might be questioned if the conditions for the exercise of jurisdiction under Art. 121(5) ICCSt are understood as reversing the contents of Art. 15*bis*(4) ICCSt.[70]

## 6 The Way Forward

Ukraine is a paradigmatic test case of a crime of aggression committed after the activation of the ICC's jurisdiction, which has spotlighted existing gaps in the Court's exercise of jurisdiction. Judicial exceptions, perceived as selective justice, ultimately undermine the credibility and legitimacy of the Court. This can only be countered by amending the conditions for the ICC's exercise of jurisdiction. While several options are convievable to reduce exceptions to the jurisdictional regime over the crime of aggression, the most principled and convincing solution would be to eliminate all jurisdictional exceptions and thus create one regime for all crimes within the jurisdiction of the Court. Next to amending Art. 15*bis* ICCSt, such a uniform jurisdictional regime would eventually also require amendment of Art. 121(5) ICCSt.

The adoption of amendments will spark complex legal questions, which are prone to be discussed alongside or as a pretext for sensitive political questions. Finding common ground will require a thorough discussion among all States parties. Although desirable, this will not be achievable within a few months or within one session of the Assembly of States Parties. Yet, it is paramount to start this conversation promptly. Not only to enable the Court as soon as possible to enforce the crime of aggression in comparable future situations, but also to start preparations for the mandatory review of the amendments on the crime of aggression seven years after the beginning of the Court's exercise of jurisdiction, in 2025.

As it is unpredictable when an amendment of Art. 15*bis* ICCSt will be adopted or enter into force, States parties should not withhold ratifying the Kampala

70 See above, chart 2.

amendments. Their voice as Kampala States will carry particular weight in the amendment process. Undoubtedly, this would also apply to Ukraine as the latest State party to the (amended) Rome Statute.[71] One would also expect that States that support an *ad hoc* jurisdiction for aggression committed against Ukraine would provide their unequivocal support when the principles that they endorse for the situation in Ukraine would be acknowledged in the Rome Statute. The same is true with regard to States that oppose the establishment of an *ad hoc* jurisdiction in the situation in Ukraine for reasons of situational selectivity. Achieving a uniform jurisdictional regime for all crimes within the jurisdiction of the ICC is ultimately a question of political will. The drafting process will allow States to take a clear position on a principled system of international criminal justice.

In the meantime, accountability for the crime of aggression against Ukraine should not be delayed. An *ad hoc* jurisdiction, such as a STCoA, could fill the current enforcement gap of the Rome Statute with regard to the situation in Ukraine and thereby reduce the selective enforcement of international criminal law in the broader sense. The answer to past inaction in the face of aggression cannot be continued inaction. It must be judicial relief for the ongoing aggression and a concerted effort to limit or possibly even eliminate elements of selectivity in the enforcement of international law against future aggression.

---

71 See also G Mamedov, 'Anniversary of aggression: how to punish top leadership of the Russian Federation?', *Ukrainska Pravda* (24 February 2023) <https://www.pravda.com.ua/eng/columns/2023/02/24/7390901/> accessed 11 April 2023.

CHAPTER 28

# Re-imagining the ICC in a Multipolar World

*Carsten Stahn*

## 1 Introduction*

Is the Court adequately equipped to address major challenges of our time? How can we re-imagine an ICC for the future? What macro-changes are necessary to enable the Court to respond better to critiques? These questions are typically sidelined in the daily business of diplomacy and the routine of Court operations. However, they ought be brought to the forefront in the third decade of the ICC[1]

In this closing chapter, I will use the opportunity to propose a few ideas to re-imagine the ICC and think ahead. They are written in the spirit of a 'realistic utopia', as Antonio Cassese put in a different context,[2] namely aimed at broadening perspectives, while envisaging possible reform or course corrections. I will start with some observations on the changing geopolitical context, before formulating a few propositions on ways to re-imagine the ICC beyond the recommendations made in the Independent Expert Review.[3] They relate inter alia to (i) a polycentric vision of international criminal justice, (ii) a focus

---

* This contribution is based on a presentation given at the 2022 Annual Forum of Nuremberg Principles Academy, focused on the 20th anniversary of the Court's operation.

1 On proposals to re-think the ICC, see also Parliamentarians for Global Action, *Modernising the International Criminal Court: Crimes against the Environment, Trafficking in Human Beings, Hybrid Justice and Corporate Accountability* (New York: Parliamentarians for Global Action, 2022), at <https://www.pgaction.org/pdf/2022/report-expanding-the-jurisdiction-of-the-icc.pdf>; M De Hoon, 'The Future of the International Criminal Court' (2017) 17 *International Criminal Law Review* 591; T Buchwald, 'The Path Forward for the International Criminal Court: Questions Searching for Answers' (2020) 52 *Case Western Reserve Journal of International Law* 417; D Guilfoyle, 'Lacking Conviction: Is the International Criminal Court Broken? An Organisational Failure Analysis' (2019) 20 *Melbourne Journal of International Law* 401; J Fraser and McGonigle Leyh (eds.), *Intersections of Law and Culture at the International Criminal Court* (Cheltenham: Edward Elgar 2020).

2 A Cassese (ed.), *Realizing Utopia: The Future of International Law* (Oxford: Oxford University Press, 2012).

3 ICC, Independent Expert Review of the International Criminal Court and the Rome Statute System, Final Report, 30 September 2020, at https://asp.icc-cpi.int/sites/asp/files/asp_docs/ASP19/IER-Final-Report-ENG.pdf.

 | DOI:10.1163/9789004529939_029

on structures of criminality, rather than symptoms, (iii) better engagement with existing hegemonies and claims to universality, (iv) the improvement of resilience and conflict resolution strategies, and (v) greater attention to coherence, fairness and the peripheries of cases.[4]

## 2 Changing Geo-political Context

It is hard to deny that the environment in which the ICC operates has changed fundamentally since 2002. The creation of the Court was strongly associated with ideas of political liberalism, protection of individuals against abuse of power and a more human-centric international order.[5] Some states, like the US, viewed the Court essentially as a security Court, i.e. an institution in the service of international peace and security.[6] However, the Rome Statute embraced a broader vision, when it referred of the 'common bonds' and 'shared heritage' of all peoples'[7] in which it is embedded, its contribution to 'peace, security and well-being of the world'[8] and the idea to guarantee 'lasting respect' for international justice.[9] The underlying cosmopolitan aspiration is perhaps most clearly reflected in the 1995 *Tadić* Interlocutory Appeal Decision, which stated that a 'State-sovereignty-oriented approach has been gradually supplanted by a human-being-oriented approach'[10] and that 'borders should not be considered as a shield against the reach of the law and as a protection for those who trample underfoot the most elementary rights of humanity'.[11] In 1998, UN Secretary-General described it as a 'gift of hope to future generations,

4 I do not engage in-depth with ecocide or aggression here, since they are treated in the chapters by Okowa and Flasch and Reisinger Coracini.

5 See D Robinson, 'A Cosmopolitan Liberal Account of International Criminal Law' (2013) 26 LJIL 127; P Hayden, 'Cosmopolitanism and the Need for Transnational Criminal Justice: The Case of the International Criminal Court' (2004) 104 *Theoria: A Journal of Social and Political Theory* 69; J Biedendorf, *Cosmopolitanism and the Development of the International Criminal Court* (Vancouver: Fairleigh Dickinson University Press, 2019).

6 See generally F Mégret, 'International Criminal Justice as a Peace Project' (2018) 29 EJIL 835.

7 Rome Statute of the International Criminal Court, preamble, para. 1.

8 Ibid., para. 3.

9 Ibid., para. 11.

10 ICTY, *Prosecutor v. Tadić*, Decision on the Defence Motion for Interlocutory Appeal on Jurisdiction, IT-94-1, 2 October 1995, para. 97.

11 Ibid., para. 58.

and a giant step forward in the march towards universal human rights and the rule of law'.[12]

Over the past two decades, these lofty ambitions have been tempered by a greater sense of realism and modesty.[13] The traditional claim of the 1990s that international criminal justice is a tool for the enforcement of human rights[14] rings somewhat hollow.[15] It has become apparent that criminal investigation and prosecution, and the focus on individual criminal responsibility, does not necessarily address the structural causes of human rights violations.[16] There is greater awareness of some of the critical side effects of the international criminal justice project, including its selectivity, its role in ordering, classifying or marginalizing forms of harms and violations,[17] its attention economy[18] or some of the stereotypes ('the global victim', the defendant as pariah)[19] it produces in responding to atrocity crime.[20] In some cases, the very exercise of international criminal justice poses its own human rights dilemmas or might entail human rights violations. For instance, the ICC has struggled to justify a basis for continuing detention of defendants, who satisfy the conditions for

---

12 'Secretary-General says establishment of International Criminal Court is a gift of hope to future generations', UN, Press Release (20 July 1998) SG/SM/6643.

13 See C Stahn, *A Critical Introduction to International Criminal Law* (Cambridge: Cambridge University Press, 2019) 412. For a critique of expectations, see also R Pangalangan, 'The International Criminal Court and the Burdens of Non-Traditional Expectations' (2019) 55 *Gonzaga Law Review* 237, 241 ('While the ICC deals with mass atrocity crimes, it is first and foremost a court of law. It is not designed to meet non-traditional demands, e.g., to root out the communal origins of the evils committed, the societal scale of the harms caused, and the collective remedies required to make the victims whole again').

14 M Cherif Bassiouni, 'Enforcing Human Rights through International Criminal Law and through an International Criminal Tribunal' (1994) 26 *Studies in Transnational Legal Policy* 347.

15 On anti-impunity discourse, see K Engle, 'Anti-Impunity and the Turn to Criminal Law in Human Rights' (2014) 100 *Cornell Law Review* 1069.

16 K Clarke, *Fictions of Justice: The International Criminal Court and the Challenge of Legal Pluralism in Sub-Saharan Africa* (Cambridge; Cambridge University Press, 2009).

17 For a critique of 'penal humanitarianism', see K Lohne, 'Penal Humanitarianism Beyond the Nation State: An Analysis of International Criminal Justice' (2018) 24 *Theoretical Criminology* 145.

18 C Schwöbel-Patel, *Marketing Global Justice* (Cambridge; Cambridge University Press, 2021).

19 M Mutua, 'Savages, Victims, and Saviors: The Metaphor of Human Rights' (2001) 42 *Harvard International Law Journal* 201; T Madlingozi, 'On Transitional Justice Entrepreneurs and the Production of Victims' (2010) 2 *Journal of Human Rights Practice* 208; S Stolk, 'A Sophisticated Beast? On the Construction of an "Ideal" Perpetrator in the Opening Statements of International Criminal Trials' (2018) 29 EJIL 677.

20 K Heller, F Mégret, S Nouwen, J Ohlin, and D Robinson, *The Oxford Handbook of International Criminal Law* (Oxford: Oxford University Press, 2020).

interim release,[21] or for the detention of witnesses, who came to testify in proceedings, but filed asylum claims.[22]

Some of the foundations on which the idea of the Court has been built are under attack. The commitment to multilateralism, on which the Statute is premised, cannot be taken for granted. Globally, there a rise in autocratic regimes.[23] Democratic rule and judicial independence cannot be taken for granted, even in established democratic systems, and human rights defenders are under threat. This development has repercussions for the functioning of international criminal justice. How should a justice system, whose success depends on independent judiciaries, respect of group and individual rights, or the ability to speak truth to power, engage with or seek buy-in from illiberal systems? The rise of nationalist discourses, and the focus on national interests and spheres of influence, polarize attitudes towards the ICC. The Court itself becomes more vulnerable to external manipulation, populism or instrumentalization. It can easily be used as an extension of warfare or political conflict through other means ('lawfare').[24] The limits of the ICC become more apparent. In autocratic contexts, domestic judiciaries or civil society are no longer predictable compliance partners. Treaty amendments remain on hold, since they become dominated by different political agendas. The stalemate in relation to the aggression amendments is a compelling example.[25]

21 See generally M Van Regemorter, *The International Criminal Court and the Right to Interim Release* (Brussels: Bruylant, 2017).

22 On the dilemma of the three detained witnesses from the DRC, see R Pulvirenti, 'Undesirable and unreturnable individuals: Rethinking the International Criminal Court's human rights obligations towards detained witnesses', (2022) 34 LJIL 433.

23 According to the 2023 Democracy Index, 'more than a third of the world's population is subject to authoritarian rule, while only 6.4% enjoy full democracy'. See S Saptparna Nath, 'Democracy Index 2023: Understanding the Global Scenarios', 25 February 2023, at https://thegeopolitics.com/democracy-index-2023-understanding-the-global-scenarios/.

24 K Fisher, 'International Criminal "Lawfare" and its Potential Effects on Post-Conflict Positive Peace' (2019) 19 *International Criminal Law Review* 724.

25 In 2023, 45 states have become parties to the Amendments on the crime of aggression to the Rome Statute of the International Criminal Court. Calls to amend the Kampala amendments have received limited support. See J Trahan, 'The Need to Reexamine the Crime of Aggression's Jurisdictional Regime', *Just Security*, 4 April 2022, https://www.justsecurity.org/80951/the-need-to-reexamine-the-crime-of-aggressions-jurisdictional-regime/; A Reisinger Coracini, 'Is Amending the Rome Statute the Panacea Against Perceived Selectivity and Impunity for the Crime of Aggression Committed Against Ukraine?' *Just Security*, 21 March 2023, at https://www.justsecurity.org/85593/is-amending-the-rome-statute-the-panacea-against-perceived-selectivity-and-impunity-for-the-crime-of-aggression-committed-against-ukraine/.

The Court itself struggles with hegemonic critiques.[26] Its establishment was initially a victory of smaller states and civil society. It portrays itself an impartial and objective agent. But it continues to reflect double standards and produces inequalities or neo-colonial analogies.[27] It has been experienced as a 'white, Western and male' institution[28] in some parts of the world. The situations and cases, which are part of the docket of the Court, send messages about the forms of violence, which qualify as 'most serious crimes', and the perpetrators and victims who are behind them. The ICC's first cases have focused predominantly on 'Black criminality'. As Rachel López has argued, a picture of the list of defendants tried and prosecuted over the first two decades might easily suggest to the world that the gravest crimes have been committed on the continent by Africans. Seen in isolation, these cases have portrayed sexual and gender-based crimes, illicit recruitment of child soldiers, or election violence as African forms of violence.[29] This contributes to a racialized vision of international criminal justice.[30] The gradual decline of legitimacy, and shrinking support from the Global South, is one of the greatest challenges to the Court's credibility and future practice.

The paradigm of victor's justice emerged in new forms.[31] In the context of self-referrals, the ICC has been perceived as a convenient tool for governments to get rid of their political enemies, including members of a former regime or

26 F Jeßberger, L Steinl, and K Mehta (eds.), *International criminal law – a counter-hegemonic project?* (The Hague, T.M.C Asser Press, 2023); X Reynolds, 'The Dark Corners of the World: TWAIL and International Criminal Justice' (2016) 14 JICJ 959; O Okafor and U Ngwaba, 'The International Criminal Court as a "Transitional Justice" Mechanism in Africa: Some Critical Reflections' (2015) *International Journal of Transitional Justice* 90.

27 K Clarke, *Affective Justice: The International Criminal Court and the Pan-Africanist Pushback* (Durham, NC: Duke University Press, 2019).

28 R López, 'Black Guilt, White Guilt at the International Criminal Court', SSRN Paper, 4 October 2022, http://dx.doi.org/10.2139/ssrn.4237581. On race and international criminal law more broadly, see C Lingaas, *The Concept of Race in International Criminal Law* (London: Routledge, 2019).

29 K Clarke, 'Affective Justice: The Racialized Imaginaries of International Justice' (2019) 42 *Political and Legal Anthropology Review* 244 R; C DeFalco and F Mégret, 'The invisibility of race at the ICC: lessons from the US criminal justice system' (2019) 7 *London Review of International Law* 55.

30 K Clarke, 'Negotiating Racial Injustice: How International Criminal Law Helps Entrench Structural Inequality', *Just Security*, 24 July 2020, at https://www.justsecurity.org/71614/negotiating-racial-injustice-how-international-criminal-law-helps-entrench-structural-inequality/.

31 On new paradigms of victor's justice, see also V Peskin, 'Beyond Victor's Justice? The Challenge of Prosecuting the Winners at the International Criminal Tribunals for the Former Yugoslavia and Rwanda' (2005) 4 *Journal of Human Rights* 213.

non-state actors, such as armed groups.[32] The strict reading of the same person, same conduct test in complementarity assessments, according to which domestic proceedings must substantially 'mirror' crimes and incidents of the ICC case, has been as criticized as an emulation of colonial logics ('civilizing mission'). Domestic legal systems need to replicate the model of the ICC, in order to be given an opportunity to investigate and prosecute cases.[33]

The debate on aggression in relation to Ukraine has openly revealed some of the ongoing double standards.[34] Justice Jackson pledged in his Closing Statement of the Nuremberg Trial, that 'we are not prepared to lay down a rule of criminal conduct against others which we would not be willing to have invoked against us'.[35] However, more than seven decades later, major powers continue to work hard to protect their nationals from future prosecution of the crime of aggression under the Rome Statute. They remain reluctant to amend the limited ICC jurisdiction over the crime of aggression, and prefer of the option of a limited hybrid tribunal over a more international one, because they fear that any international precedent in relation to investigation and prosecution of Russian aggression might turn against them in the future.[36] The engagement for accountability remains partial and limited to specific incidents, where it suits their interests. This hypocrisy reinforces the perception of the ICC as hegemonic institution. It has raised suspicion in the eyes of those, who seek accountability for aggression beyond the Russian case, and creates bizarre alliances. It makes it easier for Russia to replicate certain Western narratives, such US contestations of ICC authority, in order to challenge the Court's jurisdiction or refuse to cooperate.[37] As Astrid Reisinger Coracini has argued, the existing imbalance requires a greater alignment of the ICC regime

32 S Nouwen and W Werner, 'Doing Justice to the Political. The International Criminal Court in Uganda and Sudan' (2010) 21 EJIL 941.

33 C Nielsen, 'From Nuremberg to The Hague: The Civilizing Mission of International Criminal Law' (2008) 14 *Auckland University Law Review* 81; C Stahn, 'Justice civilisatrice? The ICC, post-colonial theory, and faces of "the local"' in C De Vos, S Kendall, and C Stahn (eds.), *Contested Justice* (Cambridge: Cambridge University Press, 2015) 46.

34 K Ambos, 'Ukraine and the Double Standards of the West' (2022) 20 JICJ 875.

35 Report of Robert Jackson, United States Representative to the International Conference on Military Trials, London, 1945 (Washington: US Department of State, 1949) 330.

36 J Trahan, 'Don't be Fooled By U.S. Smoke and Mirrors on the Crime of Aggression' *Just Security*, 14 April 2023, at https://www.justsecurity.org/85986/dont-be-fooled-by-u-s-smoke-and-mirrors-on-the-crime-of-aggression/.

37 See Y Vindman, 'It's Time for the United States to Join the ICC', *Foreign Policy*, 11 April 2023 ('American choices made in the coming months and years will either further erode the international system or accelerate Russia's status a global pariah').

over aggression to other crimes, in order to address dilemmas of selective justice regarding aggression more credibly in the future.[38]

The unprecedented seconding of Western staff to the OTP in the situation in Ukraine is a double-edged sword. It enhances the means of the Court in the short term but also causes vigilance in the non-Western world. It is ultimately a short-cut to the resolution of the structural problems of funding, which contribute to the Court's own selectivity.[39] It may be perceived as a false signal that states can influence or 'purchase' services of the Court through voluntary contributions, even if contributions are not earmarked for a particular situation.[40] Both, the collective referral and the financial contributions, create a greater need for the Court, in particular the OTP, to be seen to responding to the Ukraine situation. The speed and scope of response in relation to the Ukraine situation carry a bittersweet undertone: They also illustrate the comparative slowness or unwillingness to act in other contexts.

The Court is both a culprit, and a victim of its own entanglements. It is essential to address these dilemmas on the way forward. As Darryl Robinson has shown, some tensions cannot be solved – they present 'inescapable dyads'.[41] The Court as judicial actor faces limits. It is ill-equipped to transform the hegemonies or power asymmetries that continue to haunt it through judicial means and policies alone. However, it can confront its own weaknesses better. It is important to counter perceptions of bias, confront hegemony and post-colonial continuities, and adjust the Rome system of justice to the realities of a multi-polar world. In the following, I will present some ideas how to address these challenges.

## 3 Polycentric Justice: Not All Roads Lead to Rome

My first proposition relates to the role of Court in the international justice architecture. For many decades, cosmopolitan ideas have focused in the idea that the ICC would be at the centre of international criminal justice. This idea

38 See the chapter by Reisinger Coracini in this volume.

39 See also the chapter by Ford in this volume.

40 C Anselm Odinkalu and S Nakandha, 'Putin Arrest Warrant: International Law and Perceptions of Double Standards' *Opinio Juris*, 27 March 2023, at http://opiniojuris.org/2023/03/27/putin-arrest-warrant-international-law-and-perceptions-of-double-standards/.

41 D Robinson, 'Inescapable Dyads: Why the International Criminal Court Cannot Win' (2015) 28 LJIL 323. See also the chapter by Robinson in this volume.

continues to be repeated in official discourses. It is vividly illustrated by the debate whether there is a space for hybrid tribunals in situations where the Court is active.[42] I would argue that there greater merit in openly recognizing the value of a pluralist system, and refining in it, rather than portraying the Court as centre, and everything around it as periphery.[43]

Empirical research suggests that the Court's treaty-based foundation, its roots in civil society and its symbolic value, count among its greatest strengths.[44] The mere existence of the Court, and its imagined role, strengthen the commitment of domestic societies to prevent and prosecute international crimes, sometimes in unexpected ways, or keep atrocity situations on the radar, that might go lost. However, if one thing is clear after more than two decades of operation, it is the insight that the Court is not an all-encompassing response.

The ICC continues to be the projection of unrealistic expectations from many sides. The OTP is perceived as a global conscience of the world. The ICC has often more power as a symbol or an imagined accountability avenue, than in real life. The idea of ICC engagement in a situation often serves as a carrot and inspiration for accountability strategies of human rights bodies and NGOs.[45] It is the imagined target audience and goal of justice lobbying. The Court sometimes buys into this logic, based on its universal vocation or its struggle over resources. Alternative paths are viewed as second best options. The debate over the establishment of a hybrid/internationalized tribunal in relation to Ukraine shows that discourse easily becomes defensive or dominated by a fight over resources. The time has come to be more imaginative.

It is evident that even in the best possible scenario, ICC investigations and prosecutions cover only a handful of cases and a selected number of crimes. This is a fact and inherent in the ICC design. It will not change in the immediate future. This does not mean that we should discard the ICC, based on its selectivity, but rather invest in institutional creativity and imagination to support polycentricity.

---

42 L Moreno Ocampo, 'A Pragmatic Legal Approach to End Russia's Aggression' *Just Security*, 23 February 2023, at https://www.justsecurity.org/85218/a-pragmatic-legal-approach-to-end-russias-aggression/.

43 See generally S Caserta, 'Western Centrism, Contemporary International Law, and International Courts' (2021) 34 LJIL 321. For a critique of the ICC's centralizing features, see also Stahn, 'Justice civilisatrice' (n 33), 61–64.

44 S Muhammad, B Holá, A Dirkzwager. 'Reimagining the ICC: Exploring Practitioners' Perspectives on the Effectiveness of the International Criminal Court' (2021) 21 *International Criminal Law Review* 126, 149–150.

45 K Lohne, *Advocates of Humanity: Human Rights NGOs and International Criminal Justice* (Oxford: Oxford University Press 2019).

The idea of polycentricity flows from the Greek terms polús ('many') and kentrikós ('center').[46] It implies that a system is not monocentric, but can have different centres. It suggests that the value of international criminal justice derives from the interplay of different justice models and institutions, and its decentralized nature, rather than its projected focus on the ICC as ideal. Or in other words: Not all roads need to lead to Rome.

The first 20 years of operation have shown that is need for accountability avenues in addition to ICC and domestic justice, such as hybrid or regional courts and transitional justice mechanisms. One merit of African critiques is that they have drawn attention to valid alternative ways of addressing accountability. The *Habré* trial has illustrated some of the potentialities of the exercise of universal jurisdiction in hybrid formats.[47] The Protocol on Amendments to the Protocol on the Statute of the African Court of Justice (Malabo Protocol)[48] embraces a more comprehensive vision of the nexus between atrocity crime and transnational crimes and the potential option of regional criminal courts.[49] It is 'part of a long history of attempts by African states to create counter-narratives in opposition to imperial forces'.[50] The Special Court in the Central African Republic shows that ICC justice may work in parallel with regionally supported accountability forums.[51] This is partly novel ground. It goes beyond the narrow complementarity model of the ICC Statute which remains centred on the interplay and ICC jurisdictions. It requires new avenues of mapping relations, based on the virtue of legal pluralism. The polycentric justice model challenges the idea that justice institutions need to model themselves after the ICC, which has caused discomfort and fear of neo-colonial analogies. It means that complementarity should not be understand as a form of emancipatory

---

46 On polycentric governance, see K Carlisle and R Gruby, 'Polycentric Systems of Governance: A Theoretical Model for the Commons' (2019) 47 *Policy Studies Journal* 927.

47 S Weill, K Thuy Seelinger, and K Bree Carlson (eds.), *The President on Trial: Prosecuting Hissène Habré* (Oxford: Oxford University Press, 2020), T B Bouwknegt, 'Beyond "African Solutions to African Problems" at the Extraordinary African Chambers and "Distant Justice" at the International Criminal Court' (2019) 17 JICJ 981.

48 The Protocol was adopted on 27 June 2014 at the 23rd Annual Session of the Assembly of Heads of State and Government of the AU in Malabo, Equatorial Guinea. It was signed by AU members, but has failed to attract the required number of 15 ratifications to enter into force.

49 M Sirleaf, 'The African Justice Cascade and the Malabo Protocol' (2017) 11 *International Journal of Transitional Justice* 71.

50 K. Clarke, 'New frontiers in international human rights: Actionable nonactionables and the (non)performance of perpetual becoming' (2022) 21 *Journal of Human Rights* 141, 153.

51 P Labuda, 'The Special Criminal Court in the Central African Republic: Failure or Vindication of Complementarity?' (2017) 15 JICJ 175.

interaction, with the ICC as role model, but rather as a form of cooperative justice, which respects the need for legitimate difference, contextual adjustments, and greater regional input.

The merit of the Rome Statute system does not lie in the fact that the ICC is a superior justice model, or at the top of the accountability chain. In the first two decades, the Court had to establish trust in its functioning and demonstrate that it is able to run fair and effective investigations and trials. However, on the long term, its strength lies also in its ability to enable networks of justice, contribute to multi-faceted justice, and encourage and support other justice venues. This requires partly different strategies, which go beyond ICC-centricity: More investment in regional connections, agreements to establish a division of labor with other entities, and strengthening multilateral cooperation.[52] The OTP has started to work towards this direction through multinational investigative structures in the context of Ukraine[53] and the conclusion of complementarity agreements to foster domestic investigations or prosecutions (e.g. Guinea)[54] or monitor accountability beyond the closure of ICC preliminary examination (e.g., Colombia).[55] In 2022, the Court envisaged the establishment of its first regional office in Japan.[56] However, these are only first modest steps.

Complementarity approaches need to be revisited more fundamentally. The strict application of the 'same person, same conduct' test,[57] and the mirror image and semantics associated with it, have opened the ICC to critique.[58] They have moved complementarity closer to primacy of ICC jurisdiction. For

52 On the UN War Crimes Commission as precedent, see C Stahn, 'Complementarity and Cooperative Justice Ahead of Their Time? The United Nations War Crimes Commission, Fact-Finding and Evidence' (2014) 25 *Criminal Law Forum* 223.

53 ICC, 'Statement by ICC Prosecutor, Karim A.A. Khan QC: Office of the Prosecutor joins national authorities in Joint Investigation Team on international crimes committed in Ukraine', 25 April 2022.

54 ICC, 'Statement by ICC Prosecutor Karim A.A. Khan KC regarding the opening of the trial related to events of 28 September 2009 in Guinea, signature of Agreement with Transitional Government on complementarity and closure of the Preliminary Examination', 29 September 2022. See also the chapter by Pillai, in this volume.

55 ICC, 'ICC Prosecutor, Mr Karim A. A. Khan QC, concludes the preliminary examination of the Situation in Colombia with a Cooperation Agreement with the Government charting the next stage in support of domestic efforts to advance transitional justice', 28 October 2021.

56 See J Horiuchi, 'ICC head keen to set up court's first regional office in Japan', *Japan Times*, 21 October 2022.

57 R Rastan, 'What is 'Substantially the Same Conduct'? Unpacking the ICC's 'First Limb' Complementarity Jurisprudence' (2017) 15 JICJ 1.

58 KJ Heller, 'Radical Complementarity' (2016) 14 JICJ 637.

instance, the Libyan cases have shown that it is very difficult for countries in transition from armed conflict to peace to challenge admissibility. The requirement to replicate ICC cases under the 'substantially the same conduct' test establishes a very high burden in practices, since domestic justice investigations have to constantly catch up to ICC investigations and replicate their focus. It feeds into old colonial tropes about 'countries being unable to govern themselves'.[59] It has led to situations, where domestic courts and the ICC have chased after the same cases, worked in parallel, or mirrored each other's weaknesses, rather than complementing each other in a productive way.[60] These frictions may be addressed through a more contextual application of complementarity, greater deference to national jurisdictions, the provision of larger time windows for genuine justice processes in transitional contexts, or even the application of 'reverse cooperation', i.e. the assistance and cooperation from the Court to domestic jurisdiction under Art. 93 (10) of the ICC Statute.[61]

The Court requires better structures to apply and monitor complementarity agreements. Existing agreements have produced mixed effects. The Colombian agreement provided a politically convenient strategy to end the preliminary examination, but has been criticized for decreasing the leverage and support for the Special Jurisdiction for Peace in Colombian politics.[62] In Guinea, the agreement created buy-in and support for domestic investigations in trials. In Venezuela, the agreement have been used by domestic political elites to delay ICC intervention or fuel misunderstandings. For instance, Venezuelan Attorney General Tarek William Saab, falsely presented it as a measure through

59 K Clarke, 'Negotiating Racial Injustice: How International Criminal Law Helps Entrench Structural Inequality', *Just Security*, 24 July 2020, at https://www.justsecurity.org/71614/negotiating-racial-injustice-how-international-criminal-law-helps-entrench-structural-inequality/.

60 See M Wierda, *The Local Impact of the International Criminal Court* (Cambridge; Cambridge University Press, 2023).

61 F Gioia, 'Complementarity and reverse cooperation', in C Stahn and M El Zeidy (eds.), *The International Criminal Court and Complementarity From Theory to Practice* (Cambridge; Cambridge University Press, 2011) 807.

62 On 27 April 2022, the International Federation for Human Rights and the Corporación Colectivo de Abogados José Alvear Restrepo requested the Pre-Trial Chamber to review and 'reverse' the Prosecutor's decision to close the preliminary examination in the situation of Colombia pursuant to article 53(3)(b) of the Statute. The Chamber found that it 'does not have the power to review the Prosecutor's decision to close the preliminary examination in the situation of Colombia', since the 'situation in Colombia was neither referred to the Prosecutor by a State Party nor the Security Council'. See PTC I, 'Decision on the 'Request for review of the Prosecutor's decision of 28 October 2021 to close the preliminary examination of the situation in Colombia' and related requests', ICC-RoC46(3)-01/22, 22 July 2022, para. 7.

the which the ICC has 'ceded' the investigation 'to Venezuela'.[63] It is important to understand better under what circumstances 'contracted complementarity' creates greater leverage for accountability,[64] and in what circumstances it may actually contribute accountability gaps (e.g. through delay, inaction, political games). If it is applied inconsistently across situations, it may increase the appearance of double standards. In a similar vein, collaborative investigative structures, such as those applied in relation to Ukraine, need to be extended beyond the European context. Otherwise, they may reinforce ideas of Western exceptionalism.

Moreover, the ICC may need to develop a 'complementarity' strategy in relation to regional or hybrid institutions.[65] This relationship is not directly addressed by Article 17. It needs to be organized along different terms than the *ne bis in idem* rule, which simply applies the 'first-come, first-serve' rule or the 'unable or unwilling' test under Art. 17 test, which gives the ICC a *droit de regard* over domestic jurisdictions. It requires coordination and collaboration (e.g., through MOUs) or the specification of feasible division of labor, in order to avoid duplication of justice efforts and detrimental impacts on witnesses, victims or defendants.

Rupert Skilbeck, Director of Redress, has suggested an even broader structural innovation. He has argued that states should create 'a permanent structure to provide long-term (e.g. 10–15 years) support for national trials of international crimes, providing help with issues such as legal reform, judicial sensitisation, investigations, experts, fundraising, outreach, and reparations'.[66] Such a proposal could be carried under the auspices of the ASP. It would alleviate the burden of the Court in relation to 'positive complementarity', which continues to be viewed with suspicion by those states, who fear that it might turn the ICC into a development agency.

63 TeleSUR News, 'Venezuela and the ICC Sign an Agreement of Understanding', 3 November 2021, at https://www.telesurenglish.net/news/Venezuela-and-the-ICC-Sign-an-Agreement-of-Understanding-20211103-0019.html.

64 G Dancy and F Montal, 'Unintended Positive Complementarity: Why International Criminal Court Investigations May Increase Domestic Human Rights Prosecutions' (2017) 111 AJIL 689.

65 M Jackson, 'Regional Complementarity: The Rome Statute and Public International Law' (2016) 14 JICJ 1061.

66 BIICL, 'Reimagining International criminal tribunals and the International Criminal Court' (Rupert Skilbeck), 3 December 2020, at https://www.biicl.org/reimagining/38/reimagining-international-criminal-tribunals-and-the-international-criminal-court-thursday-3rd-december?cookiesset=1&ts=1680697712.

A key transformation of the past decade is the diversification and multiplication of forms of evidence. Hardly any crime goes unnoticed in the age of social media, investigative journalism, satellite imagery, geolocation and documentation of crimes by NGOs and members of civil society.[67] The question is less whether there is evidence, but rather who gathers, owns or controls it. This poses novel challenges for the treatment and protection of evidence. It is clearly visible that evidence is a form of power. The multiplication of actors chasing after some of the same types of material and information makes it necessary to coordinate access, protect evidence or create a more common system of evidence-management.[68] One way is the recognition of evidence as a common public good. It is a missing piece in the international criminal justice architecture. Atrocity crimes are regarded as crimes affecting the international community or as wrongs breaching a social contract between individuals. According to modern accounts, concepts of universal jurisdiction are grounded in the right of victims of access to justice.[69] Building on this line of thought, one could argue that certain types of evidence qualify as a form of patrimony of humanity.[70] This recognition would recognize the international nature of evidence, based on its value for independent and impartial investigations and prosecutions and victims of atrocity crimes. It would extend protection beyond the confines of domestic law or existing cooperation and assistance treaties. It would require actors to handle evidence in responsible manner, namely in a way which causes no harm or contamination or enables it to be shared with others. It might challenge the digital information monopoly by corporations.

## 4 Targeting Structures of Criminality, Rather Than Chasing Symptoms

A second proposition relates to selection and charging strategy and the framing of ICC engagement in ICC situations more broadly. Situation selection is the symbolic capital of the Court. At present, the Court is involved in many contexts. Choices are often dictated by opportunity or convenience. The OTP has developed nuanced policies on selection of situations and cases.[71] They

---

67 See also the chapters by Khan and Koenig and Freeman in this volume.

68 See also the chapter by Braga da Silva in this volume.

69 D Hovell, 'The Authority of Universal Jurisdiction' (2018) 29 EJIL 427.

70 See C Stahn, 'United in Diversity: International Criminal Justice and the Invisible Community of Courts', Courts Invisible Community' TOAEP Policy Brief No. 131 (2022), 2.

71 ICC OTP, 'Policy paper on case selection and prioritization', 15 September 2016.

are based on legal parameters, such as jurisdiction, admissibility, the nature, scale or impact of crimes, discretionary elements and practical considerations, such as the availability of evidence. However, one recurring critique is that ICC engagement fails to address the underlying drivers of conflict in a given atrocity situation[72] or 'normalises' the forms of violence that go beyond its reach.[73] It is focused on spectacular form of violence or highly visible crimes or types of victimization.[74] It easily neglects slower crimes, structural forms of violence, which perpetuate inequality, such as apartheid, structural racism or socio-economic violations and economic coercion, or less anthropocentric types of harm, such as environmental crimes or resource extraction.[75] For instance, the strong focus and attention to crimes in Ukraine, makes structural violence against non-White victims in other parts of the world less immediate, visible or real.

On the long term, the Court may have greater impact, if it makes a greater effort to confront root causes of violence in accountability strategies, rather than symptoms.

Why? The answer is simple. Both, the visibility of spectacular crimes and the scope of possible accountability mechanisms are likely to increase in the future. This will make it even more necessary for the Court to prove its added value. It raises fundamental questions about the types of criminality that the Court should confront, and the ways how this can be done in the most effective way. It requires a combination of strategies: (i) Making best use of the expressive potential of the Court, including prevention, (ii) focusing on structures, rather than individuals, and (iii) engaging more deeply with the situational context.

In light of its international nature and global visibility, the ICC is particularly well suited to address not only visible and spectacular crimes, but also slower and more neglected types of structural violence. The Court's future relevance and success depends on its ability to determine situational engagement not merely based on gravity grounds (e.g. number of victims, gravity of crimes), but also by reference to expressive rationales and symptomatic types

72 F Mégret, 'The Anti-deterrence Hypothesis: What if International Criminal Justice Encouraged Crime?' (2021) 19 JICJ 859.

73 Balakrishnan Rajagopal, *International Law from Below* (Cambridge: Cambridge University Press, 2003).

74 For a critique, see R DeFalco, *Invisible Atrocities: The Aesthetic Biases of International Criminal Justice* (Cambridge: Cambridge University Press, 2022).

75 See Reynolds (n 26).

of criminality.[76] The virtue of ICC selection policies lies in the fact that it is able to litigate cases, which provide guidance for a multiplicity of cases at the domestic level, and shape accountability practices in areas which are neglected and in need of greater attention.[77] For instance, the Court is particularly well equipped to address certain areas of criminality which are less commonly pursued, such as environmental harm (land-grabbing), business complicity, new technologies, cyberwarfare or forms of slavery. In these areas, one ICC case has the ability to inform many other related cases in other settings.

ICC engagement would further benefit from a greater focus on structures, rather than individuals. Individual criminal responsibility has become the mantra of international criminal justice. It is at the core of the ICC's mandate. It has a dual face: it makes it difficult for perpetrators to hide behind collective structures but it can also marginalize. ICC strategies may be most effective, if they reveal the networks and structures underpinning the commission of crimes. This can be done within the exiting framework of modes of liability under article 25. For instance, company officials could be tried for participation in arms trafficking, environmental degradation or displacement of peoples through resource extraction. However, in terms of system criminality, the ICC Statute is far less developed than other instruments in relation to corporate responsibility. The Special Tribunal for Lebanon has noted that 'in a majority of the legal systems in the world corporations are not immune from accountability merely because they are a legal–and not a natural–person'.[78] For instance, the Protocol on Amendments to the Protocol on the Statute of the African Court of Justice (Malabo Protocol) contains a very modern understanding of corporate responsibility. It links the responsibility of the corporation as legal person not only to attribution of conduct of corporate agents, but also corporate policies and collective decision-making structures.[79] As Elies van Sliedregt has argued, vesting the Court with the 'power to try corporations/

---

76 C Stahn, 'Why a Higher Gravity Threshold May be Part of the Problem Rather than a Solution to the ICC's Dilemmas', *ICC Forum*, The Gravity Question (2021), at https://iccforum.com/gravity#Stahn.

77 C Stahn, *Justice as Message: Expressivist Foundations of International Criminal Justice* (Oxford: Oxford University Press 2020).

78 STL, *Prosecutor v New TV SAL and Al Khayat*, Decision on Interlocutory Appeal Concerning Personal Jurisdiction in Contempt Proceedings, Case No STL-14-05/PT/AP/AR126.1, 2 October 2014, para. 58.

79 See Art. 46 C (2), (4) and (5) of the Malabo Protocol (n 48). See also T Michalakea, 'Article 46C of the Malabo Protocol: A Contextually Tailored Approach to Corporate Criminal Liability and Its Contours' (2018) 7 *International Human Rights Law Review* 225.

legal entities alongside individuals'[80] would enable the ICC to confront the economic structures and corporate cultures behind atrocity crimes more effectively, strengthen its reparative mandate, and counter the perception of double standards in relation to Western criminality.

The ICC could be endowed with the power to exercise jurisdiction over crimes committed by natural and juridical persons, complementary to national criminal jurisdictions.[81] France made such a proposal in the drafting process of the Statute. It suggested to make corporate criminal responsibility dependent on individual criminal responsibility. It provided for the option of corporate responsibility in cases where the crime was committed by a 'natural person acting on behalf of and with the explicit consent' of the juridical person and 'the natural person has been convicted of the crime'.[82] The difficulty to show corporate *mens rea* is not necessarily an obstacle. There are sophisticated legal models to establish corporate knowledge or intent. It can be derived from the liability of corporate agents, attributed through aggregate knowledge of company employees, or be based on corporate policies. For example, the Malabo Protocol states that the *mens rea* of a company can be shown through 'proof that it was the policy of the corporation to do the act which constituted the offence'.[83] The Statute could provide for an alternative set of sanctions against corporations beyond fines or forfeiture, such as measures of surveillance or monitoring. In the alternative, the introduction of civil or administrative responsibility of legal persons could provide a means to enable reparation against legal persons. For instance, it has been suggested to envisage a civil party model, according to which victims could seek reparations from legal persons, in case of a criminal conviction of company officials.[84]

80 BIICL, 'Reimagining International criminal tribunals and the International Criminal Court' (n 66) (Sliedregt). For a discussion, see also C Stahn, 'Liberals vs Romantics: Challenges of an Emerging Corporate International Criminal Law' (2018) 50 *Case Western Reserve Journal of International Law* 91.

81 D Scheffer, 'Corporate Liability under the Rome Statute' (2016) 57 *Harvard International Law Journal Online* 35, J Kyriakakis, 'Corporate Criminal Liability and the ICC Statute: The Comparative Law Challenge' (2009) 56 *Netherlands International Law Review* 333, C Kaeb, 'The Shifting Sands of Corporate Liability Under International Criminal Law' (2016) 49 *George Washington International Law Review* 351.

82 UN Diplomatic Conference of Plenipotentiaries on the Establishment of an International Criminal Court, Summary Records of the Plenary Meetings and of the Meetings of the Committee of the Whole, UN Doc. A/Conf.183/C.1/WGGP/L.5/Rev.2 (Vol. II), (15 June – 17 July 1998), para. 5.

83 Art. 46C (2) of the Malabo Protocol (n 48).

84 For instance, it has been suggested to introduce a civil party model through amendment of Art. 75 (2) of the Statute: 'If the convicted person is a member of a group of persons as provided for in Article 25(3)(c)-(d) or an organization [...], the victims of the crime

One continuing struggle of the ICC is that it continues to be perceived as distant or detached.[85] This challenge goes beyond outreach and communication. Without sustained presence and deeper situational engagement, the ICC stays at the surface of the atrocity contexts. It comes and goes, collects evidence, narratives and stories for investigations and prosecutions, and then disappears from the radar screen and leaves witnesses and victims or intermediaries on their own. At times, ICC justice is perceived as a paternalist form of justice which discards or subordinates traditional justice approaches. It is essential for the Court to improve the ways in which it engages with domestic contexts and cultures. Establishing field offices and meaningful completion strategies is only one part of the equation. Greater attention should be devoted to the situational contexts of ICC action throughout proceedings.

The formality of the law and the technical language of judgments or press releases creates barriers towards those who experience atrocities. The establishment of context through the contextual elements of crimes often paints a fragmented picture. It presents the situational context as a crime scene or lawless zone. There are multiple ways to engage with domestic cultures in a fuller way. For instance, domestic concepts or traditions can be brought in within sentencing or reparation practices. Article 21 (1) (c) of the Statute allows the Court to apply the 'national laws of States that would normally exercise jurisdiction over the crime, provided that those principles are not inconsistent with this Statute and with international law and internationally recognized norms and standards'.[86] This provides an opening to complement ICC sentencing practices by more restorative forms of punishment. ICC reparation policies may be used to stimulate community-based measures and build closer connection to long-term projects, improving economic, cultural and social rights in ICC situations. The gesture in the *Ongwen* trial to read out the names of victims in Court shows some of the creative ways, in which trials can be made more meaningful to affected communities and audiences.

---

may attach civil claims for damages against that organization or group of persons'. See Parliamentarians for Global Action, 'Modernising the International Criminal Court' (n 1), 60.

85 P Clark, *Distant Justice: The Impact of the International Criminal Court on African Politics* (Cambridge: Cambridge University Press, 2018).

86 Article 21 (1) (c) ICC Statute.

## 5 Beyond Lip Service: Confronting Hegemonies, Re-thinking Approaches towards Universality

My third proposition concerns the need to confront hegemonies and dependencies more forcefully and to rethink approaches towards universality.

The Court has both, hegemonic and counter-hegemonic features.[87] It has been perceived as a partly hegemonic institution from a Global South perspective, based on its dependence on the Security Council, its jurisdictional and temporal limitations, preventing it from addressing past or ongoing harms caused by Western powers against peoples under colonial domination, and its struggle to mitigate the gap between formal equality and material inequality. As Kamari Clarke has noted, 'colonialism and neocolonialism' continue to underpin 'the nature of privilege, power, and violence' which are behind crimes in ICC situation countries today.[88] The ICC's marginal attention to these issues maintains the inequalities of world order.

Not all of these tensions can be addressed through law and legal reform. However, a few measures may serve to make the ICC less vulnerable to critique. The first one is a more open countering of hegemonic structures in the ICC system, both externally and internally.

The role of the Security Council is one of the institutional facets, where risks of double standards are most apparent. The relationship was initially seen a means to give the ICC greater reach in terms of jurisdiction and cooperation. However, over time, the institutional bond has turned into a problem for the Court. It became an incarnation of 'sovereign inequality', due to inclusion of problematic exemptions of jurisdiction in the language of Security Council resolutions 1593 (2005) and 1970 (2011), the shifting of costs of referrals to the ICC budget, or attempts to use the Council's deferral powers under Article 16 to shield acting heads of states from prosecution, without sufficient articulation of an underlying peace and justice dilemma.[89] The lack of a referral in relation to Syria, and the conflicts of interest arising in relation to Russian crimes committed in Ukraine, have underscored the frictions. These dilemmas are unlikely to go away and may even increase in a multi-polar world. It is this timely to think about alternatives.

87 Jeßberger, Steinl, and Mehta, *International criminal law – a counter-hegemonic project?* (n 26).

88 Clarke (n 30).

89 R Cryer, 'Sudan, Resolution 1593, and International Criminal Justice' (2006) 19 LJIL 195.

One possible avenue to confront existing impasses and inequalities is to enhance the powers of the General Assembly.[90] Such a step would challenge existing hegemonic power structures. The idea is not entirely novel. It was already contemplated in the ILC discussions on the creation of the ICC[91] and supported by several states from the Global South in the negotiation of the Rome Statute.[92] This option would require an amendment of the ICC Statute. However, it is not precluded by UN law. As rightly noted by Fergal Gaynor, the 'non-availability of Chapter VII-type enforcement action' is not 'a legal or practical barrier to the inclusion of a referral function for the General Assembly in the ICC Statute'.[93] For instance, the General Assembly could rely on its powers under the Uniting for Peace Resolution (Res. 377)[94] to make a referral to the ICC. Such a referral could activate ICC jurisdiction over crimes under the ICC Statute, which also have a firm basis under customary international law. It might even extend ICC jurisdiction to non-states parties if the resolution is read as an instrument through which supporting states delegate their universal jurisdiction in relation to a specific situation to the Court. Such an approach has inter alia been suggested by the UN Commission of Inquiry on Human Rights in the Democratic People's Republic of Korea in 2014. The Commission argued that 'the General Assembly could rely on its residual powers recognized inter alia in the "Uniting for Peace" resolution and the combined sovereign powers of all individual Member States to try perpetrators of crimes against humanity on the basis of the principle of universal jurisdiction'.[95] A GA referral would not in itself create binding obligations of states to cooperate with the Court. But the ICC could invoke the general duty of states to cooperate

---

90 See C Stahn, 'From Uniting for Peace to Uniting for Justice?: Reflections on the Power of the UN General Assembly to Create Criminal Tribunals or Make Referrals to the ICC' (2023) 55 *Case Western Reserve Journal of International Law* 251–286.

91 Report of the International Law Commission on the Work of Its Forty-sixth Session, 49 U.N. GAOR Supp. 10, at 44, U.N. Doc. A/49/10 (1994), reprinted in [1994] 2 *Yearbook International Law Commission*, U.N. Doc. A/CN.4/SER.A/1994/Add.l (Part 2), 44.

92 S Darcy, 'Aggression by P5 Security Council Members: Time for ICC Referrals by the General Assembly' *Just Security*, 16 March 2022, at https://www.justsecurity.org/80686/aggression-by-p5-security-council-members-time-for-icc-referrals-by-the-general-assembly/.

93 F Gaynor, 'General Assembly Referral to the International Criminal Court' in A Heinze and V Dittrich (eds.), *The Past, Present, and Future of the International Criminal Court* (Brussels: Torkel Opsahl Academic EPublisher, 2021) 325, 353.

94 See GA Res. 377 (V) A, 'Uniting for Peace', 3 November 1950.

95 Human Rights Council, Report of the Detailed Findings of the Commission of Inquiry on Human Rights in the Democratic People's Republic of Korea, UN Doc. A/HRC/25/CRP.1, 7 February 2014, para. 1201.

in relation to the prevention and punishment of atrocity crimes, in order to encourage compliance.

Another priority is the targeting of hegemonies within and around the institution.[96] Morten Bergsmo has called for a 'responsible unmasking of power-wielders'.[97] He has argued that the 'invisible college of the professional community of international lawyers' wields 'as much power' over the ICC 'after it was established as informal social networks'.[98] The Independent Expert Review has stressed the close interrelation between workplace misconduct, bullying and harassment structural issues, such as gender imbalance or falsely understood privileges and hierarchies. It found that the 'culture of the Court's workplace' is 'adversarial and implicitly discriminatory against women'.[99] It recognized that 'predatory behavior in the workplace' has an origin in the 'culture of an organisation'.[100] Angela Mundukuti has referred to the ICC's 'Boys Club' problem.[101] It is linked to gender imbalances, and the weight and influence of men over 'the substantive work of the Court and how it is organised', as well as 'recruitment, placements and other staffing decisions'.[102] Such imbalances entrench 'hegemonic ideas' related to 'privilege'.[103] They need to be proactively addressed.

A related problem is the approach towards universality. The notion is all too often used as an empty buzzword. It should not be understood solely in terms of geographical reach or representation, but in a broader normative sense, embracing a commitment to greater inclusiveness in legal reasoning, the approach towards sources, voice, language and tone. The Court should make greater effort to reflect a diversity of legal system in its analysis. Its comparative analysis often remains confined to a few selected legal systems or regional institutions (e.g., IACtHR, ECtHR). As Mohamed Badar has observed,

---

96 M Bergsmo and V Dittrich (eds.), *Integrity in International Justice* (Brussels: Torkel Opsahl Academic EPublisher, 2020).

97 M Bergsmo, 'Unmasking Power in International Criminal Justice: Invisible College v. Visible Colleagues', in M Bergsmo, M Klamberg, K Lohne and C B. Mahony (eds.), *Power in International Criminal Justice* (Brussels; Torkel Opsahl Academic EPublisher, 2020) 1, 46.

98 Id., 5.

99 Independent Expert Review (n 3), para. 209.

100 Ibid., para. 209.

101 A Mudukuti, 'The International Criminal Court's "Boys Club" Problem' (*Opinio Juris*, 7 October 2021) at https://opiniojuris.org/2021/10/07/symposium-on-gender-representation-the-international-criminal-courts-boys-club-problem/. See also her chapter in this volume.

102 Independent Expert Review (n 3), para. 205.

103 A Mudukuti, 'Gender Imbalance at the ICC: The Continued Hegemonic Entrenchment of Male Privilege in International Criminal Law', in Jeßberger, Steinl, and Mehta, *International criminal law – a counter-hegemonic project?* (n 26), 265.

the Court, has thus far failed to carry out a 'deep analysis of Islamic principles of criminal law, despite establishing its jurisdiction over situations in States whose national laws have been enacted on the basis of Islamic Law'.[104] This omission feeds into the critiques of those who seek to portray the ICC as a Western-centric institution.

It is important to broaden the scope of inquiry, in order to provide 'inter-civilisational' perspectives[105] on the foundations of the law underpinning ICC norms and procedures. For instance, it would be helpful to explain the shared foundations of the Statute more fully, when addressing controversial points of law, rather than simply rehearsing case-law or referring to the customary law nature of the Statute, in order to assert authority.[106] Investing in both, the quality and transparency of legal reasoning is essential, in order to translate the commitment to universality more credibly in adjudication.[107] As Ronald Dworkin has shown, adjudication is not a self-centric exercise, but a conversation with invisible others.[108] It requires the willingness to read, listen and engage with alterity as part of the process. It is this openness, inclusiveness and transparency, which may lead to greater universal acceptance of the Court.

One key issue in relation to universality is the question whether the Court's authority is based on delegated jurisdiction or the *jus puniendi* idea, i.e. namely a right to punish based on a responsibility of individuals towards the society of world citizens (*ubi societas ibi ius puniendi*).[109] The ICC has not answered this ontological question in a conclusive way. It is fundamental for the understanding of the nature of the Court and crucial aspects of jurisdiction, immunity

104 M Badar, 'The International Criminal Court, Islamic Legal Tradition, and the Arab World: Quo Vadis?', *ICC Forum*, Legal Traditions Question (2022), at https://iccforum.com/legal-traditions#Badar.

105 See O Yasuaki, 'Toward an intercivilizational approach to human rights' (1997) 7 *Asian Yearbook of International Law* 21.

106 In the *Al-Rahman* case, the Appeals Chamber held in rather sweeping terms: 'In principle, the Appeals Chamber considers that the crimes under the Statute were intended to be generally representative of the state of customary international law when the Statute was drafted'. See ICC, *Prosecutor v Al-Rahman*, 'Judgment on the appeal of Mr Abd-Al-Rahman against the Pre-Trial Chamber II's "Decision on the Defence Exception d'incompétence" (ICC-02/05-01/20-302)', ICC-02/05-01/20 OA8, 1 November 2021, para. 89.

107 See also ICJ, *Application of the Convention on the Prevention and Punishment of the Crime of Genocide* (*The Gambia v. Myanmar*), Judgment of 22 July 2022, Declaration of Judge Ad Hoc Kress, para. 1.

108 R Dworkin, *Law's Empire* (Cambridge, Mass.: Harvard University Press, 1986) 229.

109 C Kress, 'Art. 98', in K Ambos (ed.), *Rome Statute of the International Criminal Court* (München: C.H. Beck, 2022) 2585, 2650. See also F Mégret, 'The International Criminal Court: Between International Ius Puniendi and State Delegation' (2019) 23 *Max Planck Yearbook of United Nations Law* 161, 220.

or cooperation. It came up in the dispute over the scope of ICC jurisdiction in relation to Palestine and the relevance of the Oslo Accords[110] or the understanding of the ICC jurisprudence in relation to head of state immunity. For instance, in the Malawi decision, the Pre-Trial Chamber argued that

> when cooperating with the ICC and therefore acting on its behalf, States Parties are instruments for the enforcement of the jus puniendi of the international community whose exercise has been entrusted to this court when States have failed to prosecute those responsible for the crimes within its jurisdiction.[111]

At present, elements of both approaches can be traced in jurisprudence. The controversy bears synergies with the Faustian dilemma: 'Two souls, alas, are dwelling in my breast'. It involves a choice between a more state-centric and a more humanity-based vision of the Court's jurisdiction. For example, according to the *jus puniendi* model, an act of accession to the Statute merely activates the power of the ICC to exercise a jurisdiction grounded in international law. A clearer commitment to the *jus puniendi* idea is not precluded by the limited jurisdictional titles of the ICC under Article 12 (territory, nationality). The concept is rather grounded in the international nature of atrocity crimes and an 'antecedent international criminalization',[112] which precedes the ICC. According to this understanding, accession of States to the ICC is 'declarative', rather than a 'constitutive act', which recognizes the applicability 'of a body of international repressive norms that exists separately of that recognition and might even apply to them irrespective of it'.[113]

Certain elements of the Rome Statute can be understood as an expression of the *jus puniendi* idea. The preamble recognizes the *erga onmes* nature of international obligations. It reaffirms that is the 'duty of *every State* to exercise its criminal jurisdiction'.[114] It recalls the communitarian foundations of

110 C Stahn, 'The ICC, Pre-Existing Jurisdictional Treaty Regimes, and the Limits of the Nemo Dat Quod Non Habet Doctrine' (2016) 49 *Vanderbilt Journal of Transnational Law* 443, 446–448.

111 PTC I, *Prosecutor v. Al Bashir*, 'Decision Pursuant to Article 87(7) of the Rome Statute on the Failure by the Republic of Malawi to Comply with the Cooperation Requests Issued by the Court with Respect to the Arrest and Surrender of Omar Hassan Ahmad Al Bashir', ICC-02/05-01/09-139, 12 December 2011, para. 46.

112 Mégret, 'The International Criminal Court: Between International Ius Puniendi and State Delegation' (n 109) 172.

113 Id., 172.

114 ICC Statute, Preamble, para. 6.

the international criminal justice project when it states that 'the most serious crimes of concern to the international community as a whole must not go unpunished and that their effective prosecution must be ensured by [...] enhancing international cooperation'.[115] The premise that the justification of the ICC is not solely based on a voluntarist reading of international law, but grounded in broader ideals of human dignity, can be derived from Art. 21 (3), which states that the 'application and interpretation of law' of the Statute 'must be consistent with internationally recognized human rights'.[116] Leila Sadat has used the term 'conferred jurisdiction' to express this.[117]

Of course, the *jus puniendi* concept also carries certain problems. For example, it remains blurry what crimes are covered by it and who is entitled to speak on behalf of the 'international community'. As critical scholarship has brought out, punishment is not necessarily a virtue in itself, but may create its own fallacies. However, rightly understood and cautiously applied, the concept would provide an opportunity to develop the universal foundations of the Court. It would provide a more modern grounding to the nature of the Court, recognizing that jurisdiction is not only a 'state right', but also an 'obligation owed to individuals'[118] and related to 'an individual's right of access to justice'.[119] It explains why initiation of cases, duties of cooperation or challenges to immunity are no longer solely determined by state interests. It might enable the Court to confront some of the existing inequalities and hegemonies of the international legal order more forcefully in the future.

## 6 Towards a More Resilient Court: Navigating Politics, Strengthening Resilience

The current geopolitical environment, and the attacks on the independence or personnel of the Court make it necessary to reflect how the Court can be made more resilient towards external political pressure, friend/enemy' divides and backlash.

115 Ibid., para. 4.

116 Art. 21 (3) ICC Statute.

117 See the chapter by Sadat in this volume, and id., 'The Conferred Jurisdiction of the International Criminal Court', Washington University in St. Louis Legal Studies Research Paper No. 23-03-01, 2 March 2023, at https://ssrn.com/abstract=4376240.

118 A Mills, 'Rethinking Jurisdiction in International Law' (2014) 84 *British Yearbook of International Law* 187, 229.

119 Hovell (n 69) 453.

In the past decades, many international judicial institutions, such as the ECtHR, the IACtHR or the African Court on Human and People's Rights[120] have faced open confrontations, based on pushback and backlash by individual members in response to certain doctrines or decisions, which have been perceived as an infringement on domestic authority.[121] For instance, the Committee of Ministers of the Council of Europe has encouraged the ECtHR since 2012 to give greater prominence to the principle of subsidiarity and the margin of appreciation,[122] partly in result to decisions on prisoner voting rights.[123] In 2019, Argentina, Brazil, Chile, Colombia and Paraguay challenged the conventionality doctrine of the IACtHR in a joint statement, by which they requested the Court to interpret human rights standards and other rules of international law more restrictively.[124] Tanzania withdrew its declaration accepting the right to individual petition to the African Court, following a sequence of decisions condemning due process shortcomings in criminal proceedings and Tanzania's mandatory imposition of the death penalty for murder convictions.[125] The ICC has faced its own institutional crisis with the

120 J T Gathii (ed.), *The Performance of Africa's International Courts* (Oxford: Oxford University Press, 2020).

121 M Rask Madsen, P Cebulak, and M Wiebusch, 'Backlash against international courts: explaining the forms and patterns of resistance to international courts' (2018) 14 *International Journal of Law in Context* 197.

122 High Level Conference on the Future of the European Court of Human Rights, Brighton Declaration, 20 April 2012, para. 12, Council of Europe, Protocol No. 14 to the Convention for the Protection of Human Rights and Fundamental Freedoms, amending the control system of the Convention, Strasbourg, 13 May 2004, Council of Europe Treaty Series No. 194, Protocol No. 15 amending the Convention on the Protection of Human Rights and Fundamental Freedoms, 24 June 2013, Council of Europe Treaty Series No. 213.

123 ECtHR, Grand Chamber, *Hirst v. UK*, Appl. No.74024/01, 6 October 2005, (2006) 45 ILM 467.

124 Argentina, Brazil, Chile, Colombia and Paraguay filed the joint communication on 11 April 2019 to the Inter-American Commission on Human Rights. It called for a strengthening of the subsidiarity principle and the margin the appreciation doctrine. For a discussion, see X Soley and S Steininger, 'Parting Ways or Lashing Back? Withdrawals, Backlash and the Inter-American Court of Human Rights' (2018) 14 *International Journal of Law in Context* 237; P Baldini Miranda da Cruz, 'Trackers and Trailblazers: Dynamic Interactions and Institutional Design in the Inter-American Court of Human Rights' (2020) 11 *Journal of International Dispute Settlement* 69.

125 Republic of Tanzania, Notice of Withdrawal of the Declaration Made under Article 34 (6) of the Protocol of the African Charter on the Establishment of an African Court on Human and Peoples' Rights, 14 November 2019, at https://www.african-court.org/wpafc/wp-content/uploads/2020/10/Withdrawal-Tanzania_E.pdf.

controversy over head of State immunity and the open non-compliance with requests for arrest and surrender.[126]

Courts are ill-equipped to respond to such contestations of authority through judicial rulings alone. Judgments are deemed to speak for themselves. Judges are not meant to engage in public discussions on the merits of their own decisions. For instance, the ICC was highly criticized when it published an anonymous Q&A in the aftermath of the Jordan Referral appeal judgment of 6 May 2019.[127] The document was prepared for 'purposes of public information'.[128] However, it analyzed not only the judgment itself, but the public reactions to it on Twitter or on blogs, and the question whether the 'African Union should refer the issue of Head of State Immunity to the ICJ'.[129] It criticized the critical reception of the decision in public commentary. It stated that in the social media age, 'lawyers engaging in public commentary should exercise particular caution and remain mindful of the cardinal principles that guide the conduct of lawyers, including that of honesty, integrity and fairness'.[130] This comment sent the unfortunate message that 'negative critique' of the Court is unwelcome and that experts and scholars 'should tailor their criticism in a way that it is not perceived as undermining the moral claims of the ICC'.[131]

The ICC thus clearly needs better structures to respond to contestation, critique and attack. One element is a better strategy to address mis-and disinformation. Communication is essential in a 'post-truth' environment, in which reality and fiction are increasingly difficult to distinguish and where 'fake news' or images used to discredit or subvert the authority of judicial institutions.[132] For instance, the Council of Europe, established a Committee of Experts on

126 Some scholars have recommended advisory proceedings before the ICJ to clarify the status of personal immunities in relation to international crimes. See D Tladi, 'Sudan Agrees to Send Al Bashir to the ICC: What Now for the Law?' (*Opinio Juris*, 12 February 2020) http://opiniojuris.org/2020/02/12/sudan-agrees-to-send-al-bashir-to-the-icc-what-now-for-the-law/, S Nouwen, 'Return to Sender' (2019) 78 *Cambridge Law Journal* 596.

127 ICC, 'Q & A regarding Appeals Chamber's 6 May 2019 Judgment in the Jordan Referral Re Al Bashir Appeal', May 2019, ICC-PIOS-Q&A-SUD-02-01/19_Eng, at https://www.icc-cpi.int/sites/default/files/itemsDocuments/190515-al-bashir-qa-eng.pdf.

128 Ibid.

129 Ibid.

130 Ibid.

131 D Jacobs and J Powderly, 'On the impact of online commentary in international criminal law: A vain pursuit of a Socratic ideal?' (2019) 32 LJIL 615, 623.

132 B Kotecha and D J Birkett, 'International Criminal Justice in an 'Age of Misinformation': Guest Editors' Introduction' (2022) 20 JICJ 1; J Anderson and B Duerr, 'In a Storm of Lies and Half-truths: The Role of Media Professionals in Spreading and Combatting Misinformation about the International Criminal Court' (2022) 20 JICJ 191.

the integrity of online information. It is charged with the task of proving guidance on ways to counter 'the spread of online mis-and disinformation through fact-checking and platform design solutions in a human rights compliant manner'.[133] The ICC might benefit from a disinformation task-force, in order to be able to respond to misrepresentations, fake news or fabricated evidence.

It is also necessary to re-think how public information, outreach and legacy can be used more effectively as 'engagement' strategies.[134] Communication is 'both a condition and a constituent of justice'.[135] It should not be treated as an auxiliary activity, but is part and parcel of the core mandate. Existing communicative strategies of international courts are often geared towards global audiences[136] or framed as didactic lessons, rather than dialogical processes. This creates risks of disengagement or 'cognitive dissonance'. Communication strategies should not be confined to one-sided messaging, 'stating truths', or summary of policies and decisions, but aimed at permitting discursive engagement. It requires mutual engagement and listening, including openness to engage with 'ideas one finds most difficult and unpalatable to hear' (radical listening'),[137] rather than a 'marketing' of ideas through outreach or social media. For instance, telling stories of trials through the voice of different agents, witness testimony or key moments in proceedings, may provide a more immediate, authentic and holistic account than technical summaries or outreach presentations.

Media strategies may require re-thinking. Media engagement is essential to set ICC action in context or engage with misrepresentation. In each case, it is a fine line to determine to what extent international courts and tribunals should become engaged in shaping discourses (e.g., countering denial of crimes) or leave intervention to civil society or other organizations.[138] Media

---

133 Council of Europe, 'The Committee of Experts on the integrity of online information (MSI-INF) holds its first meeting', 16 March 2022, at https://www.coe.int/en/web/freedom-expression/-/the-committee-of-experts-on-the-integrity-of-online-information-msi-inf-holds-its-first-meeting.

134 M Karwande, 'Implementing an Engagement Model: Outreach at the Special Court for Sierra Leone' in C Ramirez-Barat, *Transitional Justice, Culture, and Society Beyond Outreach* (New York: Social Science Research Council 2014) 49.

135 K Bruhn Jensen, *A theory of communication and justice* (London: Routledge 2020) 21.

136 Schwöbel-Patel (n 18); M Glasius, 'It Sends a Message': Liberian Opinion Leaders' Responses to the Trial of Charles Taylor'(2015) 13 JICJ 419.

137 L Heldke, 'The Radical Potential of Listening: A Preliminary Exploration' (2007) 5 *Radical Philosophy Today* 25, 29.

138 Institute for Integrated Transitions, 'Changing the Narrative: The Role of Communications in Transitional Justice', Policy Paper 2020, at https://ifit-transitions.org/wp-content/uploads/2021/03/Changing-the-Narrative-The-Role-of-Communications-in-Transitional-Justice.pdf.

discourses are highly mediated, governed by global information politics and national news channels, or dominated by some of their own hierarchies and inequalities. This makes it necessary to diversify. Often those most affected by crimes face most challenges to gain access to reliable information. In a multipolar world, ICC media strategies might require a more proactive engagement with journalists/media from the Global South, in order to mitigate risks of polarization.

Finally, there is a need to improve the political structures which may enable the Court to navigate the difficult politics of international criminal justice. As Salvatore Zappalà has argued, the 'Court needs a political arm which, without interfering, can handle political issues'.[139] ICC representatives are constrained by Court policies and judicial agendas in their external relations. As political body, the ASP is better equipped to assume such a role. It has exercised this function in some instances. In 2020, it has issued a statement which condemned the US sanctions against ICC officials of the ICC.[140] In 2023, it has expressed its 'unwavering support for the International Criminal Court' following Russian threats against the ICC after the issuance of arrest warrants.[141] However, it has mostly acted in a reactive way and in an *ad hoc* fashion. It should be more pro-active, determined and envisage a greater structural role for diplomacy and dispute resolution. Such a support structure is essential in an age where the Court confronts protracted political conflicts or the role of major powers, including officials of permanent members of the Security Council.

Through its political leverage, the ASP can play a much more active role as mediator and broker. This role is key in several areas, such as cooperation, engagement with non-state parties, or navigation of peace and justice dilemmas. For instance, the ASP could use its diplomatic channels more effectively to encourage cooperation with the Court, beyond its formal role under Art. 87 (7) after a judicial finding on non-compliance. The experience of South Africa in relation to the arrest of Al Bashir has shown that the dilemmas start much earlier and that the consultation mechanism under Article 97 to solve problems arising in the execution of requests for arrest and surrender[142] may

139 BIICL, 'Reimagining International criminal tribunals and the International Criminal Court' (n 66) (Salvatore Zappalà).

140 Statement of the International Criminal Court on recent measures announced by the US, 11 June 2020, https://www.icc-cpi.int/news/statement-international-criminal-court-recent-measures-announced-us.

141 'The Presidency of the Assembly of States Parties to the Rome Statute reaffirms its unwavering support for the International Criminal Court', ICC Press Release (22 March 2023) ICC-ASP-20230322-PR1711.

142 Art 97 (c) of the Statute includes conflict with pre-existing obligations under Art. 98.

not always work effectively.[143] The arrest of Vladimir Putin or other high-level Russian officials is likely to pose similar, if not greater challenges.[144] The ICC may not always be able to count on support by domestic judicial authorities to support arrest, as in the case of South Africa, where the Supreme Court of Appeal of South Africa held the South Africa's failure to arrest Al Bashir was unlawful.[145] There may thus be a need for additional diplomatic structures to mediate conflicting positions. The role of ASP may be used more actively to foster a positive and constructive relationship between States Parties and the Court.

As former ICTY and ICTR judge Bakhtiyar Tuzmukhamedov has noted, engagement with 'disengaging states' or non-state parties is another weakness of the ICC system.[146] Although the Court may have bonds with experts, members of the academic community, or civil society, there is limited scope for diplomatic engagement, beyond formal legal channels or treaty negotiations. The examples of Israel or Russia have shown that non-states parties may adopt the strategy of not formally engaging with the Court in legal terms, since they fear that such interaction might recognize the legal impact of Court decisions on their action. In such contexts, it is necessary to entertain political communication, in addition to legal engagement. United States Ambassador David Scheffer has proposed the creation of a 'Select Committee of ICC State Party Representatives' to serve as 'diplomatic arm of the Assembly of States Parties'.[147] It would serve 'critical function' of facilitating relations and building dialogue or communications 'directly with non-party States' or 'break-away States Parties'.[148]

---

143 ICC, 'Registry Report on the consultations undertaken under Article 97 of the Rome Statute by the Republic of South Africa and the departure of Omar Al Bashir from South Africa on 15 June 2015', ICC-02/05-01/09-243, 17 June 2015. South Africa initiated the establishment of a Working Group of the ASP on the implementation of Article 97.

144 H Woolaver, 'South Africa and the ICC Arrest Warrant for Vladimir Putin: Déjà Vu All Over Again?', EJIL Talk, 5 April 2023, at https://www.ejiltalk.org/south-africa-and-the-icc-arrest-warrant-for-vladimir-putin-deja-vu-all-over-again/.

145 Supreme Court of Appeal of South Africa, *Minister of Justice and Constitutional Development and Others v. The Southern Africa Litigation Centre and Others*, Case No. 867/15), 15 March 2016, (2016) ZASCA 17. See G Mettraux, J Dugard and M du Plessis, 'Heads of State Immunities, International Crimes and President Bashir's Visit to South Africa' (2018) 18 *International Criminal Law Review* 577.

146 B Tuzmukhamedov, 'Russia and the International Criminal Court: From Uncertain Engagement to Positive Disengagement' in Heinze and V Dittrich, *The Past, Present, and Future of the International Criminal Court* (n 93), 733, 734.

147 D Scheffer, 'Create a Select Committee of ICC State Party Representatives', *ICC Forum*, Anniversary Question (2018), at https://iccforum.com/anniversary#Scheffer.

148 Ibid.

Finally, the ASP could take on an important role in navigating justice and peace dilemmas.[149] Instances, such as the Dayton peace agreement or the Juba peace talks show that duties of arrest may conflict with the need for ongoing peace negotiations. The International Crisis Group has highlighted this dilemma in relation to the war in Ukraine. It has stated

> [P]rosecuting Russian leaders for the crime of aggression could complicate any future potential diplomacy on the conflict itself ... If and when such negotiations get under way, Russia will almost certainly ask for discharge from criminal liability as part of any settlement. It is unclear how Western nations would meet this request if prosecution is proceeding in an international court.[150]

The ASP needs to contemplate bespoke solutions to address such tensions. There are limited ways to navigate this tension, once an arrest warrant is in the world. Art. 16 of the ICC Statute was created to address such scenarios. It seeks to accommodate this conflict through the possibility of Security Council deferrals. However, this option may be barred, due to incompatible positions within the Council.[151] The possibilities to rely on prosecutorial discretion to mediate conflicts are constrained. The OTP has taken the position that peace and security considerations themselves do not necessarily justify deference under the 'interests of justice' clause. It noted that 'the broader matter of international peace and security is not the responsibility of the Prosecutor; it falls within the mandate of other institutions'.[152] This limits the leeway to rely on Art. 53 to facilitate peace talks. Coordination of peace and justice

---

149 P Hayner, *The Peacemaker's Paradox* (New York: Routledge 2018).

150 International Crisis Group, 'A New Court to Prosecute Russia's Illegal War?', 29 March 2023, at https://www.crisisgroup.org/global-ukraine/new-court-prosecute-russias-illegal-war.

151 See R Hamilton, 'The ICC Goes Straight to the Top: Arrest Warrant Issued for Putin', *Just Security*, 17 March 2023, at https://www.justsecurity.org/85529/the-icc-goes-straight-to-the-top-arrest-warrant-issued-for-putin/ ('It seems equally possible though for Russia, which refuses to recognize the ICC, to decide that pursuing such a resolution would give the ICC undue recognition. If Russia takes this view then even an effort by other members of the UN Security Council to pursue an Article 16 strategy could be thwarted by a Russian veto').

152 OTP, Paper on the Interests of Justice, September 2007, 9, and 8 ('The concept of the interests of justice established in the Statute, while necessarily broader than criminal justice in a narrow sense, must be interpreted in accordance with the objects and purposes of the Statute. Hence, it should not be conceived of so broadly as to embrace all issues related to peace and security').

through sequencing[153] or prosecutorial discretion over the timing of investigations and prosecution is no longer entirely in the hands of the Prosecutor. Any withdrawal of a warrant of arrest that has been issued would require judicial approval by the issuing Chamber. It is bound by the criteria of Art. 58. In such circumstances, the ASP could play a mediating role, for instance by facilitating a political space in which peace negotiations can take place, without undermining the judicial authority of the Court.

As I have argued elsewhere, it would be feasible to envisage the creation of a targeted and sustainable co-ordination structure beyond the Bureau, potentially composed of state representatives from capitals, experts and stakeholders involved in transitional justice or rule of law to facilitate cooperation even beyond existing channels (Art. 87, Art. 97), enable better communications between the Court and non-States Parties or mediate peace and justice conflicts through diplomatic means.[154]

## 7 Not a Conclusion: Coherence, Fairness and the Peripheries of Cases

My last position relates to improvement of coherence, fairness and the peripheries of cases. The ICC judicial system is rather de-centralized and pluralist in terms of judicial organization. There is no binding ruling of precedent. Chambers 'may' apply principles and rules identified in 'previous decisions', but are not bound by them beyond the immediate case that is litigated.[155] Dissenting opinions have become part and parcel of adjudication in pre-trial, trial and appeal. This flexible system has enabled a rich and diverse jurisprudence on many foundational questions. It has served to identify good practices through trial and error.[156] This is an asset in an emerging institution. However, with the passage of time, it becomes essential to move from procedural experimentation to a more coherent jurisprudential system.

The Court has developed a large body of procedural and substantive jurisprudence. Moving forward, the Court should pay greater attention to

153 L Vinjamuri, 'The ICC and the Politics of Peace and Justice' in C Stahn (ed.), *The Law and Practice of the ICC* (Oxford: Oxford University Press, 2015) 13.

154 C Stahn, 'Revitalizing Complementarity a Decade after the Stocktaking Exercise', TOAEP Policy Brief No. 115 (2020), 4.

155 See Art. 21 (2) of the ICC Statute.

156 M Jarle Christensen and N M. Orina, 'The International Criminal Court as a Law Laboratory: Professional Battles of Control and the "Control of the Crime" Theory' (2022) 20 JICJ 699.

coherence within its adjudicative practice and the transparency of reasoning. Foresight and predictability of decision-making are in the interests of legal certainty, fairness and equality before the law. Nothing precludes a deviation from previous practice or the Chamber's Practice Manual,[157] which is a non-binding internal document. However, Chamber should be transparent in their reasoning and provide substantive reasons when they depart from key elements of Appeal Chamber decisions or established lines of jurisprudence.

The treatment of issues, such as victims' rights, the role of witnesses or the admissibility of evidence, has varied considerably among Chambers. The legal regime is constantly litigated anew. This *status quo* impedes legal certainty, creates duplications and may negatively impact the rights of the Defence.[158] As the Independent Expert Review has suggested, it would helpful to introduce an alert system, mandating a Chamber to provide notice, before departing from fundamental lines of jurisprudence, in order to enable parties and participants to prepare adequately.[159] Judges should also invest more into the quality of the deliberative process and a collegial judicial culture, which permits informed and respectful exchange of legal views and efforts to come to common decision.[160] The ICC might benefit from lessons from the ICJ, where the quality of jurisprudence and argument is secured through an intensive deliberative process. As a matter of principle, draft dissenting and majority opinions should be exchanged in advance of the final decision, in order to enable mutual engagement among conflicting positions.[161] A first step is the adoption of 'Principles and procedures in relation to the issuance of dissenting and separate Opinions' in the 7th edition of the Chamber's Practice Manual (July 2023). It specifies expressly that such opinions 'should always be written using respectful language and in a spirit of collegiality' and enable the majority and minority to 'respond to each other's drafts and amend their own findings or reasoning'.[162]

Fairness dilemmas at the peripheries of cases deserve greater attention. The existing system has loopholes. Both, interim release and the release of persons, are part of the 'Achilles verse' of international criminal justice. The ICC cannot

157 ICC, Chambers Practice Manual, 24 November 2022.

158 See also the chapter by Naouri and Jacobs in this volume.

159 Independent Expert Review (n 3), Recommendation 218.

160 Ibid., Recommendation 221.

161 Ibid., Recommendation 223.

162 ICC, Chambers Practice Manual (7th ed., July 2023), adopted following the judicial retreat of 2023. See generally K Wigard, 'Matter of Opinion: Assessing the Role of Individual Judicial Opinions at the International Criminal Court' (2023) 23 *International Criminal Law Review* 387–415.

compel states to accept released or acquitted persons.[163] The dependency on the political will of states creates human rights dilemmas for both the ICC and defendants. For instance, is it legitimate for an institution like the ICC to reject requests for interim release, even if the necessity of detention can no longer shown, simply because no state is willing to accept the defendant?[164] What does this say about the protection of the fundamental human rights to liberty and freedom of movement in the Rome system of justice? The existing cooperation system is as patchy and fragile in relation to the 'right to liberty' as it is in relation to arrest. At present, only a marginal number of countries have concluded an agreements on Interim Release and Release of Persons with the ICC.[165] How long can a person still be detained who has been acquitted or benefits from time served?[166] The ASP should take action to facilitate the establishment of a better system for the release of defendants, including more agreements on the relocation and resettlement of persons acquitted or having served their sentence.[167] As rightly stressed in academic commentary, states 'cannot demand a functioning system of international criminal justice' without 'accepting the burden of maintaining and upholding such system'.[168]

Last but not least, the system for the enforcement of sentences is in need of re-thinking. Here again the conditions of enforcement depend largely on the

---

163 See also the chapter by Lewis in this volume.

164 Rule 119 (3) of the Rules of Procedure and Evidence obliges the Court to seek, inter alia the views of the relevant States before imposing or amending any conditions restricting liberty'. In *Bemba*, the Appeals Chamber decided that the 'Pre-Trial Chamber [had] erred in granting conditional release without specifying the appropriate conditions that make conditional release feasible, identifying the State to which Mr Bemba would be released and whether that State would be able to enforce the conditions imposed by the Court'. See ICC, *Prosecutor v. Bemba*, 'Judgment on the appeal of the Prosecutor against Pre-Trial Chamber II's "Decision on the Interim Release of Jean-Pierre Bemba Gombo"', ICC-01/05-01/08-631-Red, 2 December 2009, para. 109. See also *Prosecutor v. Maxime Jeoffroy Eli Mokom Gawaka*, 'Public redacted version of Decision on interim release', ICC-01/14-01/22-173-Red, 8 March 2023. On ICC practice on interim release, see A Dumbryte, 'The roads to freedom: Interim release in the practice of the ICC' in Stahn, *The Law and Practice of the ICC* (n 153) 1063.

165 See ICC, Framework agreement between The Argentine Republic and the International Criminal Court on the release of persons, ICC-PRES/26-02-18, 28 February 2018.

166 The return of ICTR defendants has posed significant challenges. See B S Lyons, 'The Treatment of the ICTR Acquitted: The "Achilles Heel" of International Criminal Justice' (2020) 2 *International Review of Contemporary Law* 43.

167 C Lecolle, 'Relocation Issues of Released and Acquitted at International Criminal Courts and Tribunals: A Defence Perspective' (2023) JICJ, https://doi.org/10.1093/jicj/mqad012.

168 F Pues, 'Cooperation Cherry-Picking at the ICC: On the Lack of State Parties' Cooperation Concerning the Interim Release of Maxime Mokom', *Völkerrechtsblog*, 21 March 2023, doi: 10.17176/20230321-185033-0.

legal regime of the state willing to execute the sentence. This creates large discrepancies among convicted persons. There is no 'international penal detention mechanism'.[169] ICC sentencing remains heavily dictated by imprisonment as main form of punishment. It is in practice largely a retributive system, i.e. a 'penal colony'. Little energy has been spent to think about the role of more restorative forms of punishment, alternative sentences or rehabilitative measures for victim/perpetrators. Sentencing decisions remain largely disconnected from the regime of enforcement of sentences, which is governed by agreement with states and ICC supervision. In some cases, re-socialization of perpetrators or creative forms of criminal sanction, such as community-service or detention in open custody, would deserve more attention.

As Beatriz E. Mayans-Hermida and Barbora Holá have argued, international criminal justice might benefit from a more communicative and 'reconstructive' type of punishment, which is focused on communication with the defendant, rather than alienation, the recognition of offenders and victims, and backward-and forward-looking rationales of criminal sanction.[170] It might better combine retributive-expressive ideas of censure and rationales of positive general prevention (e.g., restoration of confidence in the law, recognition of victims) with the 'resocialisation' of perpetrators and restorative elements (repairing harm, (re)constructing relationships).[171] A possible way to address dilemmas might be the adoption of guidelines regarding the enforcement of sentences, including better explanation of the choice of the enforcement jurisdiction, penitentiary rules, conditions imposed, and rehabilitative sentencing, as well as a better monitoring system.

Even so many years later, and three decades into the ICC, Jackson's words still resonate, and remain as timely for the future today, as they were at Nuremberg:

> We must never forget that the record on which we judge these defendants today is the record on which history will judge us tomorrow.[172]

---

169 R Mulgrew, *Towards the Development of the International Penal System* (Cambridge: Cambridge University Press, 2013).

170 B E Mayans-Hermida and B Holá, 'Punishing Atrocity Crimes in Transitional Contexts: Advancing Discussions on Adequacy of Alternative Criminal Sanctions Using the Case of Colombia' (2023) 43 *Oxford Journal of Legal Studies* 1, 12–13.

171 Id. 17.

172 R Jackson, 'Opening Address for the United States', Office of the United States Chief Counsel for Prosecution of Axis Criminality, *Nazi Conspiracy & Aggression*, Vol. I, Chapter VII (Washington: United States Government Printing Office, 1946) 116.

# Index

www.ingramcontent.com/pod-product-compliance
Lightning Source LLC
Chambersburg PA
CBHW031318230926
51848CB00001B/5
*9789004529922*